CONSTITUTIONAL LAW

FIFTH EDITION

Other Books in the *Essentials of Canadian Law* Series

- International Trade Law
- Family Law
- Copyright Law
- The Law of Sentencing
- Administrative Law
- Securities Law
- Computer Law 2/e
- International Human Rights Law
- Franchise Law
- Legal Ethics and Professional Responsibility 2/e
- Refugee Law
- National Security Law: Canadian Practice in International Perspective
- Public International Law 2/e
- Individual Employment Law 2/e
- The Law of Partnerships and Corporations 3/e
- Civil Litigation
- Detention and Arrest
- Religious Institutions and the Law in Canada 3/e
- Canadian Telecommunications Law
- Intellectual Property Law 2/e
- Animals and the Law
- Income Tax Law 2/e
- Fundamental Justice
- Mergers, Acquisitions, and Other Changes of Corporate Control 2/e
- Personal Property Security Law 2/e
- The Law of Contracts 2/e
- Youth Criminal Justice Law 3/e
- Bank and Customer Law in Canada 2/e
- The Law of Equitable Remedies 2/e
- Environmental Law 4/e
- Pension Law 2/e
- International and Transnational Criminal Law 2/e
- Remedies: The Law of Damages 3/e
- Freedom of Conscience and Religion
- The Law of Trusts 3/e
- The Law of Evidence 7/e
- Ethics and Criminal Law 2/e
- Insurance Law 2/e
- Immigration Law 2/e
- Criminal Law 6/e
- The Law of Torts 5/e
- Bankruptcy and Insolvency Law 2/e
- Legal Research and Writing 4/e
- Criminal Procedure 3/e
- Canadian Maritime Law 2/e
- Public Lands and Resources in Canada
- Conflict of Laws 2/e
- Statutory Interpretation 3/e
- The Charter of Rights and Freedoms 6/e
- Land-Use Planning

ESSENTIALS OF
CANADIAN LAW

CONSTITUTIONAL LAW

FIFTH EDITION

PATRICK J. MONAHAN

BYRON SHAW

PADRAIC RYAN

IRWIN LAW

Constitutional Law, Fifth Edition

Published in 2017 by

Irwin Law Inc.
14 Duncan Street
Suite 206
Toronto, ON
M5H 3G8

www.irwinlaw.com

ISBN: 978-1-55221-440-4
e-book ISBN: 978-1-55221-441-1

Library and Archives Canada Cataloguing in Publication

Monahan, Patrick, author
Constitutional law / Patrick J. Monahan, Byron Shaw, Padraic Ryan.—Fifth edition.

(Essentials of Canadian law)
Includes the text of the Constitution Act, 1867 (the British North America Act, 1867) and the Constitution Act, 1982.
Includes bibliographical references and index.
Issued in print and electronic formats.
ISBN 978-1-55221-440-4 (softcover).—ISBN 978-1-55221-441-1 (PDF)

1. Constitutional law—Canada. 2. Constitutional history—Canada. I. Shaw, Byron, author II. Ryan, Padraic, author III. Canada. Constitution Act, 1982. IV. Canada. Constitution Act, 1867. V. Title. VI. Series: Essentials of Canadian law

KE4219.M66 2017 342.71 C2016-907851-5
KF4482.M66 2017 C2016-907852-3

Canada

Ontario
Ontario Media Development Corporation
Société de développement de l'industrie des médias de l'Ontario

Printed and bound in Canada.

1 2 3 4 5 21 20 19 18 17

SUMMARY TABLE OF CONTENTS

DETAILED TABLE OF CONTENTS

FOREWORD
TO THE FIRST EDITION

Within any society committed to the principle of the rule of law, an understanding of the country's basic constitutional framework is important. But such an understanding is particularly necessary in Canada, given our continuing debate over the future of the country and its constitution. It is for that reason that I am very pleased that Patrick Monahan has written this lucid and readable text describing Canada's constitution. Professor Monahan's book will be particularly useful for law students, since it sets out in a very clear and logical fashion the history and evolution of our constitution. But I fully expect that this book will also be of value to lawyers and to constitutional specialists, since it includes a detailed and careful consideration of many of the contested legal issues that are now or will soon be before the courts. Not only does Professor Monahan provide a fair and balanced account of the current state of the law but he attempts to clarify areas where the law may be ambiguous. He also offers his views as to the direction in which the constitution can be expected to evolve in the future.

Professor Monahan has already established himself as one of the country's leading constitutional scholars. This book will confirm that reputation, and I am confident that it will prove to be essential reading for students, lawyers, and laypersons with an interest in Canada's constitutional affairs. I am pleased to commend it.

The Right Honourable Brian Dickson
Chief Justice of Canada (retired)

PREFACE

The fifth edition represents a significant update to the fourth edition, published four years ago. During this period, the Supreme Court of Canada has continued to develop the jurisprudence in all areas of constitutional law, particularly the *Canadian Charter of Rights and Freedoms*, as well as the law of federalism and Indigenous rights. All significant developments as of 1 June 2016 have been incorporated into this edition.

We have appended the complete text of the Canadian Constitution, including explanatory footnotes as consolidated by the federal Department of Justice. We expect that this will continue to serve as a useful reference tool for lawyers and students.

As with earlier editions of this book, our aim is to provide lawyers, academics, and law students with a general introduction to, and overview of, the basic elements of the Canadian Constitution. We have also attempted to discuss issues in sufficient detail such that the book will be of value to lawyers who encounter constitutional issues in their daily practice.

The views expressed in this text are solely the personal opinions of the authors and do not reflect the position of the Ministry of the Attorney General or McCarthy Tétrault LLP.

Patrick J. Monahan
Byron Shaw
Padraic Ryan
January 2017

PART ONE

INTRODUCTION

CHAPTER 1

AN INTRODUCTION TO THE STUDY OF THE CANADIAN CONSTITUTION

A. THE CONSTITUTION DEFINED

A country's constitution is the set of fundamental principles that describe the organizational framework of the state and the nature, scope, and limitations on the exercise of state authority. A constitution may be described as a body of rules about law making: it represents a primary set of rules that defines how the ordinary rules or laws in a society are to be made or changed. A constitution defines the relationship among different kinds of laws by establishing their relative priority and clarifying how conflicts are resolved. In addition, a constitution describes how the primary or constitutional rules themselves can be created or changed.

Defined in this generic way, it can be said that all nation states have constitutions, since all countries have certain organizing principles or rules for the exercise of state authority. However, one important distinguishing feature among constitutions of different countries is the extent to which they attempt to place limits on the exercise of legislative or law-making authority.

A constitution does not have to impose any substantive limits on the legislative power of state institutions. The doctrine of parliamentary supremacy, which lies at the heart of the U.K. constitutional tradition, states that Parliament can make or unmake any law on any subject. Thus, the only historical limit on U.K. legislative authority is the inability of

Parliament to bind its successors; that is, one Parliament cannot prevent a later Parliament from amending an existing law.[1]

The alternative approach—one that has become increasingly popular around the world in the past fifty years—is to entrench certain substantive limits on the manner in which state power can be exercised. When rules are "constitutionally entrenched," they are set out in a fundamental constitutional document that takes precedence over all other laws. Furthermore, constitutionally entrenched rules cannot be amended through the ordinary process of law making.

An entrenched constitution places limits on the laws enacted by the legislature. An entrenched constitution permits individuals to challenge government decisions not merely on grounds that they exceed the authority set out in state law, but also because the law itself is invalid because it violates the provisions of the entrenched constitution. In societies with an entrenched constitution, the constitution functions as a kind of "supreme law" against which ordinary legislation can and must be measured.

B. CANADA'S ENTRENCHED CONSTITUTION

1) Written Provisions

The Canadian constitution includes a core set of documents and provisions that are constitutionally entrenched. These core documents include the *Constitution Act, 1867* (formerly known as the *British North America Act, 1867*)[2] and the *Canadian Charter of Rights and Freedoms*. They are identified in the *Constitution Act, 1982*, section 52(1), which states that the provisions falling within this definition are the "supreme law of Canada" and that any inconsistent law is of no force or effect.[3]

The central focus of the study of constitutional law in Canada is the meaning and significance of the provisions that have been consti-

---

1 The *Human Rights Act 1998* (U.K.), 1998, c. 42, permits U.K. courts to declare that legislation adopted by the British Parliament at Westminster is "incompatible" with certain provisions of the European Convention on Human Rights; however, where such a declaration is made, the legislation continues in force until amended.

2 The *British North America Act, 1867* (U.K.), 30 & 31 Vict., c. 3, was renamed the *Constitution Act, 1867* in the constitutional amendments that were enacted in 1982. The Act is referred to as the *Constitution Act, 1867* or, for historical references, the *BNA Act*.

3 The *Constitution Act, 1982*, was enacted by the *Canada Act 1982* (U.K.), 1982, c. 11, Sched. B.

tutionally entrenched in section 52 of the *Constitution Act, 1982*. Since any law that is inconsistent with a constitutionally entrenched provision is invalid, any action or decision taken by state officials in reliance on an unconstitutional law is invalid, because these actions will have been taken without legal authority. The study of constitutional law in Canada therefore focuses largely on the validity of laws and government action based on the authority defined by section 52 of the *Constitution Act, 1982*. Any state decision or action, in order to be legally valid, must be consistent with the provisions that have been constitutionally entrenched in section 52. This does not mean that the particular decision or action must itself be specifically referred to in section 52, but it does require that the legal basis for the decision—most often a statute—must be consistent with these entrenched provisions. The section 52 provisions constitute the set of primary rules that are used to measure the validity of what could be called "secondary rules"—statutes enacted by Parliament or the provincial legislatures and government decisions taken on the basis of those statutory provisions.

Section 52(2) of the *Constitution Act, 1982* states that the "Constitution of Canada" or the "supreme law of Canada" includes the following:

- the *Constitution Act, 1867* (originally the *BNA Act*)—a U.K. statute that established the Dominion of Canada out of three colonies in British North America. The *BNA Act* defined Canada as a federal state, creating four original provinces (Ontario, Quebec, Nova Scotia, and New Brunswick), and set out the respective legislative powers of Parliament and the provincial legislatures. It also provided a mechanism for the admission of new provinces to the Dominion. Although the *Constitution Act, 1867* has been amended (mostly by the U.K. Parliament) more than twenty times since its original enactment, the basic structure established in 1867 remains largely intact and continues to define the basic framework for Canada's political institutions;
- the *Canada Act 1982*—a short four-section U.K. statute that enacted the *Constitution Act, 1982* and abolished the authority of the Westminster Parliament to legislate for Canada in the future. Until 1982, the U.K. Parliament had retained the formal legal authority to amend the *BNA Act*. Since the early twentieth century, however, Britain had exercised this power only at the request of Canadian political authorities, in recognition of Canada's political independence from Great Britain. It was for this reason that the enactment of the *Canada Act* itself required the enactment of a statute by the U.K. Parliament, at the request of the Canadian government. The termination of Westminster's legal authority over Canada in April of 1982 is commonly referred to as the "patriation" of the Canadian constitution;

- the *Constitution Act, 1982*—a U.K. statute that was enacted through the *Canada Act 1982*. The *Constitution Act, 1982* includes the *Charter*, guarantees for Indigenous rights, and a constitutional amendment procedure that permits Canada's political institutions to amend any part of the country's constitution if certain conditions have been met. The *Constitution Act, 1982* also provides for the supremacy of Canada's written or entrenched constitution;
- various statutes or regulations of constitutional significance that were enacted between 1867 and 1982, all of which are specifically enumerated in a schedule to the *Constitution Act, 1982*. These enactments mainly consist of amendments to the *BNA Act*, statutes or orders in council admitting various provinces or territories to Canada between 1870 and 1949,[4] and the *Statute of Westminster, 1931*;[5] and
- all amendments to the statutes or regulations otherwise included in the section 52 definition of the Constitution of Canada. Since 1982, there have been eleven amendments enacted utilizing the amendment procedures set out in the *Constitution Act, 1982*. Most of these amendments have been to constitutional provisions that establish special constitutional rules for particular provinces, such as those providing for language rights or denominational education rights in individual provinces.

2) Canada's Unwritten Constitution

Despite the number and significance of the documents making up Canada's written constitution,[6] section 52(2) does not include many enactments, rules, or principles that define or limit the manner in which state power is exercised in Canada. This is because the 1982 constitutional changes—just like the *BNA Act*—did not purport to comprehensively define the powers of the Canadian state. For example, the documents

---

4 Under s. 146 of the *Constitution Act, 1867*, the colonies of Newfoundland, Prince Edward Island, and British Columbia as well as Rupert's Land and the North-West Territory could be admitted to Canada through orders in council enacted by the British government, on the request of the Canadian Parliament. See Chapter 5, section B(1).

5 (U.K.), 22 & 23 Geo. V, c. 4. This British statute confirmed Canada's legal independence from Great Britain, but provided that only Westminster could enact amendments to the *BNA Act*. See Chapter 5, Section C.

6 Note that the "written constitution" or the "Constitution of Canada" refers only to those enactments that fall within the s. 52(2) definition in the *Constitution Act, 1982*. The "unwritten constitution" refers to enactments or legal rules—even though such enactments or rules may exist in written form—that are not included within the s. 52(2) definition.

included in section 52 do not create or define the office of the prime minister of Canada, who is the single most powerful public official in the country. The section 52 definition also does not include any documents prior to Confederation, such as the *Royal Proclamation, 1763*, the *Quebec Act, 1774*, the *Constitutional Act, 1791*, or the *Union Act, 1840*. Certain key statutes of an "organic" nature[7]—such as the *Supreme Court Act*, the *Canadian Bill of Rights*, the *Canada Elections Act*, the *Financial Administration Act*, the *Indian Act*, the *Citizenship Act*, and various statutes establishing the constitutions of certain provinces are also not referred to. Neither are treaties or agreements between the Crown and Indigenous peoples. There are also many common law principles of constitutional significance that have been developed by the courts in both England and Canada, particularly those dealing with the powers of the Crown and Parliament, which are not included in section 52. Finally, section 52 makes no reference to constitutional conventions, which are rules of political behaviour that are regarded by political actors as binding but are not enforced directly by the courts.[8] Some of the most important rules of political behaviour exist as constitutional conventions.[9] For example, under the *Constitution Act, 1867* the governor general is given the absolute authority to approve or disapprove, on behalf of the monarch, any law passed by the two Houses of Parliament. In strict law, therefore, the governor general has unlimited legal authority to veto any bill passed by Parliament. However, this power is limited by a constitutional convention requiring the governor general to approve all bills that have been duly passed by the two Houses of Parliament.

Accordingly, the documents referenced in section 52 of the *Constitution Act, 1982* do not give a complete picture of how state power is actually exercised in Canada. In 1978, the federal government tabled constitutional amendments setting out such a comprehensive codification of the authority of state officials, but the proposals were never

---

7 R. MacGregor Dawson defined an "organic" statute as a law dealing with fundamental principles of a constitutional nature, such as the organization of state institutions. See R.M. Dawson, *The Government of Canada*, 5th ed., ed. by N. Ward (Toronto: University of Toronto Press, 1970) at 63–64.

8 The term "constitutional convention" in this book refers to political rules that evolve in an informal manner. This usage should not be confused with a constitutional convention used in the sense of a meeting of public officials for the purpose of designing a new constitution. The latter usage of the term "constitutional convention" is sometimes also referred to as a "constitutional assembly."

9 Constitutional conventions usually arise in circumstances where some official or institution is granted a very broad discretion. A constitutional convention will limit the manner in which this discretion can be exercised by specifying the circumstances or the factors that must be taken into account by the official or institution that has been granted the authority in question.

enacted. It is possible that some of these "unwritten" elements of the Canadian constitutional order might eventually be included in the section 52 definition through a process of judicial interpretation.[10] The Supreme Court of Canada has concluded that section 52 is non-exhaustive. Accordingly, it may be argued that section 52 encompasses constitutional documents or principles not specifically enumerated.

For instance, the Supreme Court of Canada has found that certain parliamentary privileges not specifically referred to in section 52 fall within the prescribed definition.[11] In the *Reference Re Provincial Court Judges*,[12] a majority of the Supreme Court held that the Canadian constitution includes an unwritten principle of judicial independence, and that attempts by a number of provinces to reduce the salaries of provincially appointed judges were unconstitutional since they did not respect this unwritten principle. In the landmark 1998 decision, *Reference Re Secession of Quebec*,[13] the Supreme Court unanimously held that the Canadian Constitution included the unwritten principles of federalism, democracy, constitutionalism and the rule of law, and protection for minority rights. The Court stated that this list of constitutional principles was by no means exhaustive. More significantly, the Court indicated that these unwritten principles could be used to fill in the gaps in the entrenched or written constitution, and used either to uphold the validity of legislation or to declare legislation to be invalid. Subsequently, the Court clarified that a number of the unwritten constitutional principles (particularly democracy and constitutionalism) strongly favour upholding the validity of legislation that conforms to the express terms of the Constitution. The Court cautioned that "in a constitutional democracy such as ours, protection from legislation that some may view as unjust or unfair properly lies not in the amorphous underlying principles of our Constitution, but in its text and the ballot box."[14]

Accordingly, although section 52 is non-exhaustive, courts are reticent to add legal rules or principles to the provisions that section 52 expressly identifies as being part of the supreme law of Canada. First,

---

10 We describe these constitutional documents or rules as "unwritten" even though some of them—such as the organic statutes, or the enactments prior to 1867—exist in written form. They are "unwritten" in the sense that they are not contained in the set of core documents identified in s. 52(2) of the *Constitution Act, 1982*, as part of the "supreme law of Canada" and subject to a special amending procedure.

11 *New Brunswick Broadcasting Co. v. N.S. (Speaker of the House of Assembly)*, [1993] 1 S.C.R. 319.

12 [1997] 3 S.C.R. 3.

13 [1998] 2 S.C.R. 217 [*Secession Reference*].

14 *British Columbia v. Imperial Tobacco Ltd.*, [2005] 2 S.C.R. 473 at para. 66. See also *Babcock v. Canada (A.G.)*, [2002] 3 S.C.R. 3.

certain elements of Canada's unwritten constitution—such as constitutional conventions—are principles that are not intended to be legally enforced by the courts. The sanction for breach of these constitutional conventions is political rather than legal. Given the fact that constitutional conventions are legally unenforceable, it would be inappropriate to include them within a category of documents or rules that is intended to be enforced by the courts as part of the supreme law of Canada.

Second, some laws or rules are not intended to take priority over other laws. Inclusion within the section 52 definition would therefore be inappropriate. Some of the organic statutes noted earlier, while important, have never been regarded as being capable of overriding other inconsistent laws. Similarly, common law principles are always subject to modification by Parliament or the provincial legislatures through ordinary legislation. The courts have taken the sensible and restrained position that the legal rules created by judges—rules of common law—must give way to laws enacted by elected representatives. Therefore, the courts should be very cautious in including principles derived entirely from common law sources within the section 52 definition.

Third, it may be inappropriate to include certain laws or rules within the section 52 definition because of the special amending procedures for constitutionally entrenched provisions. Consider, as an illustration, treaties or land claim agreements between the Crown and Indigenous peoples. These documents are constitutionally "recognized and affirmed" in section 35 of the *Constitution Act, 1982* and cannot be changed without the consent of Indigenous peoples. Further, the courts have held that Indigenous rights falling within section 35 may, in certain circumstances, take precedence over conflicting federal or provincial laws. Including treaties or land claim agreements within the section 52 definition would mean that they could be amended only if a certain number of provincial legislatures consented, because the amending procedure requires provincial involvement for most categories of amendments. Most of these treaties and agreements were negotiated between Indigenous peoples and representatives of the Crown, and it has always been assumed that they could be amended without the agreement of the provinces.

Therefore, there are many important legal documents, rules, and principles that are not (and should not be) included within the definition of the Constitution of Canada in section 52. Although these elements of the constitution are not enumerated in section 52, they nonetheless define and limit state power in Canada.[15]

15 These "unwritten elements" are listed in Table 6.2 in Chapter 6.

C. KEY CHARACTERISTICS OF THE CANADIAN CONSTITUTION

1) Canada Is a Federal State

Canada has a federal constitution. In a federal system, sovereignty is divided between two orders of government, with each level of government being restricted to the areas of jurisdiction assigned to it, and neither being able to control or direct the activities of the other.[16] Further, in a federal system, the distribution of powers between the national and local governments is exhaustive, in the sense that there are no fields of jurisdiction that are not distributed to either the federal or the local level of government. Federalism requires an independent judiciary to police the distribution of powers and to ensure that neither level of government exceeds the powers allocated to it under the constitution.

The federal system of government can be distinguished from both a unitary and confederal system. In a unitary state, such as France, undivided sovereignty is conferred on the national government. Although local governments might be established within a unitary system, they are creatures or delegates of the national government, which defines their powers. Only the national government is a constitutionally recognized order of government. In a confederation, by contrast, ultimate sovereignty is retained by the member states, which delegate powers or jurisdiction to a central decision-making authority. The central decision-making authority has the power to make decisions, but it cannot enforce those decisions directly. Instead, enforcement depends on the willingness of the member states to comply voluntarily. The European Community (now Union) in the 1970s and 1980s was an example of a confederal system, although reforms have since strengthened the central institutions and moved the Union in the direction of a federal system.

In Canada, the *Constitution Act, 1867* centralized powers in the national government to such a degree that certain commentators described the original constitution as "quasi-federal."[17] For example, the federal government was given the power to disallow or annul any provincial law within two years of its enactment. The federal government was also given the power to appoint the lieutenant governors of the provinces, and the provincial lieutenant governor could "reserve" any

---

16 "By the federal principle we mean the method of dividing powers so that the general and regional governments are each, within a sphere, co-ordinate and independent": K.C. Wheare, *Federal Government*, 4th ed. (London: Oxford University Press, 1963) at 10.

17 *Ibid.* at 19.

bill passed by the legislature for the approval of the federal government; if there was no approval within two years of the bill's enactment, the bill would have no force or effect. The federal government was also given the power to pass "remedial laws" in the field of education to protect religious minorities from provincial legislation that might interfere with their rights. The federal government had a status akin to a constitutional "police officer," assuming a supervisory role in relation to the provinces, similar to that of Great Britain in relation to the federal government itself.

As discussed in Chapters 4 and 7, Canadian federalism has evolved in a manner quite different from that envisaged by the drafters of the *Constitution Act, 1867*. Most of the centralizing features of the Act, such as the powers of reservation and disallowance, have fallen into disuse. While these powers remain part of the written constitution, there is an overwhelming consensus that their use under any circumstances would be inappropriate and potentially inconsistent with the unwritten principles that underpin the Canadian constitutional order.[18] As a practical matter, therefore, these powers can no longer be exercised. Moreover, the courts have interpreted the distribution of powers between the federal and provincial governments so as to favour the expansion of provincial jurisdiction and to limit federal jurisdiction. Canada today is generally regarded as having one of the more decentralized systems of federalism in the world. Ironically, the U.S., which by its constitution has a relatively decentralized federal system, is much more centralized than Canada. This contrast emphasizes the fact that the formal terms of a country's constitution do not necessarily determine its constitutional development.

2) Canada Is a Constitutional Monarchy

Constitutional theory traditionally distinguishes between a monarchical and a republican system of government. Under a monarchical system, supreme power resides in the Crown. Under a republican system, supreme power resides in the people, who govern through elected representatives. Canada, like the U.K., is a hereditary monarchy, with the

---

18 In *Secession Reference*, above note 13 at para. 55, the Supreme Court of Canada stated that "although the federal power of disallowance was included in the *Constitution Act, 1867*," the written provisions of the Constitution did not provide the "entire picture." According to the Court, the "underlying principle of federalism triumphed early" and scholars have since contended "that the federal power of disallowance has been abandoned."

monarch inheriting the office of head of state.[19] The U.S. is a republic, with an elected president serving as head of state.

Although the monarch—at present, a queen—is Canada's formal head of state, all her powers and responsibilities with respect to Canada have been transferred to the governor general, the queen's personal representative in Canada.[20] The queen, therefore, does not take any active role in the day-to-day administration of Canadian affairs. She does, however, appoint the governor general on the advice of the Canadian prime minister. The governor general has the same constitutional role in Canada as the queen has in the United Kingdom: that is, the governor general has extensive legal powers under the Canadian constitution derived from both statute and common law. For a bill to be passed by the Senate and House of Commons to become law, it must be signed by the governor general. The governor general also appoints the prime minister and members of the Cabinet, senators, superior court judges, and the lieutenant governors of the provinces. However, under the doctrine of responsible government, all the powers of the governor general are to be exercised on the basis of the advice and consent of the prime minister and the Cabinet. Further, the prime minister and the Cabinet members are entitled to hold office and act as the government only as long as they enjoy the confidence of the elected House of Commons.

The doctrine of responsible government removes most of the discretionary power of the governor general since, on the vast majority of matters calling for his or her decision or action, the governor general is bound to follow the advice of elected ministers. There are certain residual powers possessed by the governor general that permit him to exercise some measure of personal discretion, rather than simply following the advice of the prime minister. These residual powers, however, are exercisable only in certain exceptional or unusual circumstances, as discussed in Chapter 3. As a practical matter, therefore, neither the queen nor the governor general governs the country personally on a day-to-day basis. Instead, government is carried on in the name of the queen by accountable officials. Thus, references to "the Crown" or to "the government" do not refer to the sovereign or to the governor gen-

---

19 Section 9 of the *Constitution Act, 1867* states that "[t]he Executive Government and Authority of and over Canada is hereby declared to continue and be vested in the Queen."

20 This transferral is accomplished through letters patent issued by the Crown, constituting the office of governor general. The current version of the letters patent was issued in 1947: see *Letters Patent Constituting the Office of Governor General of Canada* (Imperial Order in Council, proclaimed in force 1 October 1947).

eral personally but to the institutions and officials who act collectively on the queen's behalf and in her name.

It is because of the doctrine of responsible government that Canada is able to function as a modern democracy while retaining a hereditary monarch as its head of state. Since the powers of the Crown are strictly regulated and controlled by the conventions of responsible government, it would be misleading to draw too sharp a contrast between the monarchical form of government as it exists in practice in Canada and the republican form of government in the U.S. In both countries, the state is subject to the control and direction of elected officials who are accountable to the people.[21]

As we have noted, the principles of responsible government are not part of the formal written constitution, the "supreme law of Canada." Instead, the principles of responsible government are constitutional conventions or rules of political behaviour that are not legally enforceable. Their continued acceptance and effectiveness depend on the willingness of the governor general and the members of the government to abide by them, as well as on the insistence of the Canadian public that they do so. Yet the fact that the conventions of the constitution are not legally enforceable is not a cause for concern, since the principles of responsible government are firmly embedded in Canada's political culture.

The decisions of the governor general to prorogue Parliament in 2008 and 2009 provide a modern context in which to examine the office of the governor general and the doctrine of responsible government in Canada. We review the debate over the constitutionality and the wisdom of these decisions in Chapter 3. In addition, we review other eventualities in which doubts about the responsibilities of the governor general could arise, and suggest how these situations could be resolved in accordance with established constitutional principles.

3) The Canadian Constitution Guarantees Individual and Group Rights

The drafters of the *BNA Act* were generally opposed to the notion that the constitution should contain explicit guarantees for individual rights. They opted instead for a constitution "similar in Principle to

---

21 Of course, there are numerous significant differences between the Canadian and the American constitutions. The point made here is simply that both constitutions are grounded in a democratic tradition in which those who exercise political power are ultimately accountable to the electorate.

that of the United Kingdom."[22] This meant that, as long as Parliament or the legislatures stayed within the limits of their jurisdiction as set out in the *BNA Act*, their laws could not be declared invalid on the ground that they infringed the rights of individuals.[23] In this sense, the British doctrine of parliamentary supremacy was a key operative principle of the Canadian constitution, modified only by the necessity to take account of the fact that legislative jurisdiction was divided between two orders of government.

However, even the *BNA Act* included certain guarantees designed to protect minority rights. For example, a province could not pass laws prejudicially affecting certain educational rights of religious minorities (section 93), and the use of the English and French languages was guaranteed in Parliament and the Quebec legislature as well as in certain courts (section 133). Moreover, the adoption of a federal structure was itself motivated by the desire to grant the French-Canadian minority access to and control over provincial political institutions through which they could preserve and promote their culture.

Furthermore, the process of judicial interpretation of the constitution in early federalism cases resulted in the protection of individual rights in certain circumstances. For example, in a series of cases beginning in the 1930s, the Supreme Court struck down certain Alberta and Quebec laws limiting freedom of expression on the grounds that the particular laws at issue were beyond the jurisdiction of the provinces.[24] However, the protection of individual rights through the division of powers jurisprudence was confined to a few relatively isolated instances. Furthermore, these exceptional cases seemed to suggest that only the provinces could be precluded from passing such laws and that Parliament's authority in this regard was unlimited.

The *Canadian Bill of Rights*[25] was the first major step toward the recognition and protection of individual rights in Canada. Following his election as prime minister in 1957, John Diefenbaker tried to persuade the provinces to amend the *BNA Act* so as to provide constitutional protection for individual rights. When the provinces refused to support the amendment, Diefenbaker opted instead to protect individual rights

22 See the preamble to the *BNA Act*.

23 In the *BNA Act*, there were a limited number of exceptions to this generalization: for example, neither level of government could impose tariffs or customs duties on goods crossing provincial borders (s. 121). See also the discussion below regarding ss. 93 and 133.

24 See, for example, *Reference Re Alberta Legislation*, [1938] S.C.R. 100, which struck down a provincial law requiring newspapers to grant a right of reply to the government following publication of an article criticizing government policy.

25 S.C. 1960, c. 44.

through a federal statute. However, the *Bill of Rights* had significant limitations. Because it was only an ordinary federal statute, it applied only to federal laws. Moreover, the courts interpreted the bill very narrowly. Apart from the *Drybones*[26] case in 1970, the Court systematically refused to invalidate any federal law on the ground that it offended the guarantees in the bill.

This situation changed dramatically in 1982 with the enactment of the *Charter*.[27] The drafters of the *Charter* profited from the experience with the interpretation of the *Canadian Bill of Rights* and avoided language that courts had previously relied on to narrow or limit the rights set out in the bill. The courts also indicated that they did not regard the jurisprudence developed under the *Canadian Bill of Rights* as binding in their interpretation of the *Charter*.[28] In general, the courts have interpreted the guarantees in the *Charter* in a comparatively robust and activist fashion when compared to the *Canadian Bill of Rights*.

The rights of the Indigenous peoples of Canada were also constitutionally recognized in 1982. Section 35 of the *Constitution Act, 1982* provides that "the existing aboriginal and treaty rights of the aboriginal peoples of Canada are hereby recognized and affirmed." The courts have interpreted these guarantees as protecting all Indigenous rights that were "existing" in 1982, and have further held that the fiduciary obligation of the Crown toward the Indigenous peoples of Canada has been constitutionally entrenched.[29] Any infringement or limitation of constitutionally protected Indigenous rights requires the government to satisfy a rigorous standard of justification, failing which the infringement will be declared to be unconstitutional.[30]

The enactment of the *Constitution Act, 1982* has profoundly altered the role of the courts and the relationship between the judiciary to the legislature and executive branches of government. Before its enactment, federalism was the main focus of constitutional judicial review. The question for the courts was generally whether the "correct" level of government had acted, *not* whether any level of government could act. The 1982 amendments require the courts to determine the validity of legislation and government action pursuant to constitutional rules binding on both levels of government. The amendments have thereby significantly increased the role of the judiciary and the ability of litigants to

---

26 *R. v. Drybones* (1969), [1970] S.C.R. 282, which ruled that a section of the *Indian Act* was invalid.

27 *Constitution Act, 1982*, Part II.

28 See Chapter 13, section A.

29 See Chapter 15, Section C(1)(a).

30 See, for example, *R. v. Sparrow*, [1990] 1 S.C.R. 1075.

challenge governmental decision making. While certain sections of the *Charter* are subject to a legislative "override" (as provided for in section 33), the override power is politically costly and has been infrequently used. Thus, both the scope and the nature of judicial review have been significantly increased by the 1982 constitutional changes.

4) Political Power Is Concentrated Rather Than Separated

Certain constitutions, most notably the U.S. constitution, firmly embrace the doctrine of the separation of powers. Under this doctrine, there is a strict separation among the executive, legislative, and judicial branches of government, with no single branch being permitted to encroach on the powers or jurisdiction of the others. Thus in the U.S., the president (the head of the executive branch, responsible for enforcing and administering laws) cannot be a member of the legislative branch or Congress. Moreover, the president may not be in a position to control Congress, since a majority of its members may be from a party different from that of the president. The U.S. constitution starts from the premise that concentrating political power in particular institutions or individuals is dangerous, since those who are granted such powers are likely to abuse them at the expense of individual liberty. The American solution is to divide the state into mutually exclusive branches so as to preclude a concentration of power and the resulting abuse that will presumably transpire. The consequence is that no single party or institution is permitted to achieve its objectives without enlisting the voluntary cooperation of others. The U.S. system operates such that in any political battle, opponents of a particular course of action are often able to marshal significant institutional support for their opposition. These checks and balances sometimes make it difficult for a president to implement the political program that led to his or her election. They reflect the American suspicion and mistrust of state power, and the preference for limiting government in order to protect individual liberty.

The separation of powers between the legislative and executive branches has never been a dominant feature of the Canadian or U.K. constitutions. Indeed, far from dividing power, the Canadian and British approach is to concentrate political power in the hands of the executive. This concentration of power is achieved through the doctrine of responsible government, under which both the legislative and the executive branch are subject to the control of the prime minister. The prime minister controls the executive, since the governor general (the formal head of the executive branch of government) must exercise all of his/her powers on the basis of the prime minister's advice. At the same time, the prime minister controls Parliament—the legislative branch—since the governor general is obliged to appoint as prime minister the leader of the party controlling the greatest number of seats in the elected House of Commons. Thus, a Canadian prime minister with a majority in the House of Commons has far greater scope to implement his or her political program than the American president. In fact, this concentration of political power in the hands of a single officeholder has led to a variety of proposals for parliamentary reform, many of them aimed at giving greater autonomy and independence to individual members of Parliament.

While the Canadian and British constitutions do not seek to divide executive and legislative powers, they do recognize the independence of the judiciary as an important constitutional principle. The *BNA Act* included a number of important guarantees of judicial independence, including the fact that superior court judges were removable from office only if both the Senate and the House of Commons passed resolutions calling for their removal.[31] The *Charter* guarantees anyone charged with an offence with the right to be tried by an "independent and impartial tribunal," which has been interpreted to require a degree of independence from the executive branch of government. The courts have also ruled that the other branches of government cannot remove the core jurisdiction of superior courts and transfer it to other institutions or tribunals. Thus, Canada has embraced a limited version of the doctrine of the separation of powers, at least in respect of the independence of the judiciary from the legislature and the executive.

5) The Canadian Constitution Has Become Somewhat Less Flexible since 1982

All constitutions strive to strike a balance between the values of stability and flexibility. Constitutions are designed to provide a stable set of fundamental rules that will endure over time. These fundamental rules provide the framework within which ordinary political debates occur, and are not themselves open to constant debate and revision. Stability is desirable, since it channels political debate and lends a measure of predictability to political life. It also limits the extent to which political majorities can use the power of the state to oppress minorities or to interfere with fundamental democratic and political rights. This is why

31 No superior court judge has ever been removed from office under this procedure, although a judge did resign in 1967 and another in 1996, when it appeared that resolutions calling for their removal were likely to be passed.

constitutions usually provide a special amending procedure calling for a high level of societal consensus.[32]

While constitutional stability is desirable, flexibility is equally important. The constitution should not imprison the state in a legal straitjacket, preventing it from responding effectively to changing social and economic circumstances. A constitution must be capable of evolution and change if it is to remain relevant and effective.

Different countries strike different balances between stability and flexibility. The U.S., for example, is usually cited as an illustration of a country with a relatively inflexible constitution. Strict limits are placed on the powers of the Congress and the states, and those limits can only be modified through an amending formula that requires a high level of societal consensus.[33] The U.K., in contrast, is usually regarded as a country that has opted for a flexible constitution. As discussed above, parliamentary supremacy is a key part of the U.K. constitutional tradition. The doctrine of parliamentary supremacy provides that there are no absolute or immutable limits on legislative power. In the words of the noted nineteenth-century constitutional authority, A.V. Dicey, the doctrine of parliamentary supremacy states that parliament can "make or unmake any law whatever."[34] A country that chooses not to place limits on the jurisdiction of its legislative institutions assumes that political leaders will act in a responsible and self-restrained fashion, and that it is therefore unnecessary to attempt to set up legally enforceable limits on the kinds of laws that can be enacted. It also assumes that public opinion and a tradition of respect for human rights may be more effective tools for protecting freedom than judges and courts.

Canada falls somewhere between the U.S. and the traditional U.K. examples in terms of the flexibility of its constitution. Following the British example, the drafters of the *BNA Act* saw it as unnecessary and undesirable to give the courts a mandate to protect the rights of min-

---

32 In fact, in some countries, such as Germany or India, certain fundamental aspects of the constitution are said to be unamendable, immune even from the constitutional amendment procedure. But the far more common approach—and the one adopted in Canada—is to permit any aspect of a country's constitution to be amended as long as a specified procedure is followed.

33 Constitutional amendments in the U.S. must be ratified by Congress and by the legislatures of three-quarters of the states.

34 A.V. Dicey, *Introduction to the Study of the Law of the Constitution*, 10th ed. (London: Macmillan, 1959) at 40. As noted earlier, however, with the enactment of the *Human Rights Act 1998* (U.K.), c. 42, Britain has taken an important step in the American direction, by granting courts the power to declare statutes to be "incompatible" with guarantees in the European Convention on Human Rights.

orities from parliamentary encroachment.[35] The *BNA Act* also did not spell out many important aspects of the operation of government. For example, as noted above, there is no definition of the office of prime minister, who is — through the conventions relating to responsible government — the single most powerful state official in Canada. Moreover, the *BNA Act* was not subject to any special amending procedure since, as a statute of the U.K. Parliament, it could be amended through the enactment of ordinary legislation at Westminster.

On the whole, therefore, the constitutional framework established in 1867 was highly flexible and subject to continuing adjustment and change. Like the British model on which it was based, it was premised on the notion that political leaders could be trusted to exercise power in a restrained and responsible fashion.

The 1982 constitutional changes reduced the flexibility of the Canadian constitution. The amendments imposed significant new limits on the authority of both Parliament and the provincial legislatures through the incorporation of the *Charter* as well as guarantees for Indigenous rights. The 1982 constitution also abolished the authority of the U.K. Parliament to amend any of the written constitutional documents, opting instead for a Canadian amending formula that has proven very difficult to operate. Indeed, based on the experience with the *Meech Lake Accord* and the *Charlottetown Accord*, discussed in Chapter 6, some experts believe that the Canadian constitution is virtually unamendable in certain important respects. The effect of these changes has been to move Canada more in the direction of an American-style constitution, where governmental power tends to be regarded with suspicion rather than trust, and where government action is subject to a greater degree of scrutiny by the courts.

Notwithstanding these changes, it would be incorrect to suggest that Canada's constitution has become inflexible or incapable of significant change as a result of the amendments enacted in 1982. It is true that formal amendment of the terms of the "written" constitution appears to be rather difficult — although there have been a number of formal amendments enacted since 1982.[36] But the fact that formal constitutional amendment may be difficult ignores the point that significant constitutional change can occur in a number of other less formal, but equally effective ways.

First, as we have already seen, many of the legal rules or documents that regulate the manner in which state power is exercised in

---

35 For exceptions to this generalization, see the discussion around note 23.

36 See Table 6.1 in Chapter 6.

Canada are not included within the definition of the Constitution of Canada in section 52. These "unwritten" elements are therefore not subject to the constitutional amending formula and can be amended through other means, including the enactment of ordinary legislation by Parliament or the provincial legislatures. In the case of constitutional conventions, they can be altered simply by changes in political practices and expectations. Even those documents that are included in the section 52 definition of the written constitution can be modified in informal and indirect ways, such as through political agreements or practices or through judicial interpretation. A good illustration of the magnitude of the changes that are possible is the manner in which the division of powers between Parliament and the provinces has evolved.

Since 1867, there have been relatively few changes to the formal terms of sections 91 and 92 of the *Constitution Act, 1867*—the sections defining the jurisdictions of the federal and provincial orders of government. Yet, despite the paucity of formal amendments, the relative powers of the two levels of government have evolved very dramatically since 1867. In part, these changes have been the result of judicial interpretation, which has tended to interpret provincial powers broadly and federal powers narrowly. But political practice has been an important source of constitutional change as well. Federal and provincial governments have undertaken initiatives and entered into agreements that have tended to blur the distinctions between their respective jurisdictions, and to favour shared or overlapping responsibilities as opposed to exclusive jurisdiction. For example, the federal government has entered into a variety of agreements under which it agrees to provide funding for various social programs falling within provincial jurisdiction and delivered by the provinces. These programs (sometimes called shared-cost programs) were created following court decisions in the 1930s which held that the federal government could not establish such programs itself.[37] These court decisions created serious practical difficulty, since many provinces did not have adequate funds to establish such programs on their own. The creation of shared-cost programs through political agreement enabled both levels of government to overcome this difficulty without amending the formal constitution. With the federal government providing the funding and establishing certain minimum or common conditions, a national system of social programs was established.

While the 1982 constitutional changes may have made formal amendments to the constitution more difficult, they have not eliminat-

---

37 See the discussion in Chapter 7, Section C(4).

ed or restricted these informal avenues of constitutional change. This point is significant, since informal avenues for change—rather than formal constitutional amendment—have proven to be far more important in Canada's constitutional evolution in the past and are likely to continue to do so in the future. In overall terms, therefore, the Canadian constitution remains relatively flexible and capable of adjustment to meet the changing needs and circumstances of Canadian society.

D. JUDICIAL REVIEW

When an individual seeks to challenge the validity of government action before the courts, that person is usually described as an applicant for judicial review. The individual argues that there was no legal authority for the decision or action and that it was therefore unlawful. However, there are two different kinds of arguments that the individual might make to reach this conclusion.

The first is to claim that the decision or action was unauthorized because it failed to comply with the terms or requirements of the law under which the government was acting. The principle of the rule of law requires that all government decisions be authorized by law—either statute law or common law—in order to be valid. For example, suppose that a statute provides that a police officer can search private premises after obtaining a search warrant from a judge. Suppose, further, that the police searched certain premises without obtaining a warrant. The owner of the premises could challenge the decision on the basis that the police failed to obtain a warrant, as required by the statute. The search was outside of the authority of the statute and therefore unlawful, and the officials who carried it out committed a trespass on private property. This kind of argument is non-constitutional in the sense that it does not seek to challenge the constitutional validity of a statute or other legal rule. Rather, the argument is focused on the terms of the law itself and the applicant claims that the government action exceeded the authority conferred. This kind of legal challenge, which does not raise a constitutional issue, might be termed ordinary or non-constitutional judicial review.

Suppose, however, that the example was slightly different and that the police had complied in all respects with the requirements of the statute, including the obtaining of a warrant. The owner of the premises might still be able to challenge the legality of the search through "constitutional" judicial review. In this kind of challenge, the owner would argue that the statute that authorized the search was itself invalid because it was inconsistent with a provision that was constitutionally entrenched in section 52 of the *Constitution Act, 1982*. For example, a statute authorizing searches could be challenged on the basis that it is inconsistent with section 8 of the *Charter*, which protects individuals from unreasonable search and seizure. The owner is now making a constitutional argument since he or she is claiming that, even if the actions of the police were authorized by the statute, the statute authorizing the search is invalid. If the argument is accepted, the police would be in no better position than in the earlier version of our scenario; although they may have complied with the statute, if the statute itself is invalid, anything done pursuant to its terms is unauthorized and therefore unlawful. Government decisions taken without legal authority violate the principle of the rule of law and are for this reason unlawful.

Both of these kinds of judicial review proceedings are constitutionally protected. Individuals are guaranteed access to the courts for purposes of ensuring that officials act within the limits of the authority that has been conferred on them, as well as to ensure that their authority is consistent with the entrenched constitution. The courts have ruled that statutes that purport to prohibit individuals from testing the legal validity of government actions, either through ordinary judicial review or constitutional judicial review, are themselves unconstitutional. Moreover, it is possible to combine both these kinds of argument in a single judicial review proceeding, and individuals who challenge government decisions often make both these kinds of arguments simultaneously.

Although judicial review is not the primary focus of this book,[38] to the extent that we do examine this topic, we will focus on constitutional judicial review. That is, this book will explore the extent to which individuals can challenge laws, statutes, or government actions on the basis that they are inconsistent with the entrenched constitution.[39]

38 The book also explores certain "unwritten" elements of the constitution, on which no claim of constitutional invalidity can generally be made. Further, we do not limit the discussion to an examination of judicial review proceedings (i.e., matters that have been or might be brought before a court).

39 Ordinary judicial review, which is concerned with the principles whereby the courts determine whether officials have acted within the authority conferred on them by law, is explored in another book in this series on administrative law.

E. THE PLAN OF THE BOOK

As the title suggests, this book provides an overview of the rules and principles that define and structure the exercise of state power in Canada. Part Two of the book begins in Chapter 2 with a description of the manner in which Canada's political institutions evolved before the enactment of the *BNA Act* (now known as the *Constitution Act, 1867*). This chapter describes how rules of British law became incorporated in the law of the British North American colonies. It also describes how institutions of representative government, as well as the constitutional conventions relating to responsible government, developed in British North America in the late seventeenth and early eighteenth centuries. The chapter also describes the events leading up to the enactment of the *BNA Act*.

Chapter 3 examines the executive and legislative institutions that were continued or established by the *Constitution Act, 1867*. We describe the power and role of the Crown and the process whereby the prime minister and the Cabinet are appointed to office. The principles of responsible government are examined in detail, particularly the extent to which the governor general continues to possess any "reserve" power to act other than on the advice of the prime minister. We discuss the governor general's decisions to prorogue Parliament following the development of a coalition government in 2008 and 2009. Furthermore, the legislative process by which bills are introduced, debated, and passed by Parliament or the provincial legislatures is also described and analyzed.

Chapter 4 describes the provisions in the *Constitution Act, 1867* dealing with federalism and the judiciary. The division of powers between the federal and provincial orders of government is described, with particular emphasis on the degree to which the drafters of the Act attempted to centralize powers in the hands of the federal Parliament. An overview of the structure of the courts in Canada is provided, and the constitutional guarantees of judicial independence and tenure in sections 96 to 100 are reviewed. The significance and implications of the principle of the rule of law, recognized in the preamble to the 1982 constitution, are also discussed.

Part Three of the book describes the history of and the contemporary rules for constitutional change in Canada. Chapter 5 examines the evolution of the *BNA Act* between 1867 and 1982. We examine the manner in which the Act was amended, and how Canada gradually achieved political and legal independence from Great Britain. We also examine the repeated attempts to "patriate" the Canadian constitution so as to provide a domestic amending formula, and how these attempts failed to meet with success over a period of fifty years. The process ultimately leading to the agreement between the federal government and nine provinces in November 1981, followed by the "patriation" of the constitution in April 1982, is outlined and discussed.

Chapter 6 describes the process of constitutional amendment since 1982. The amending formula established in Part V of the *Constitution Act, 1982* is carefully analyzed. The subsequent efforts to use the 1982 formula in both the Meech Lake and Charlottetown rounds of constitutional negotiations are also described. Finally, the 1995 Quebec referendum on sovereignty and its aftermath, including the Supreme Court of Canada's 1998 decision in the *Reference Re Secession of Quebec*, are examined.

Part Four of the book considers the manner in which the courts have interpreted the federal-provincial division of powers as set out in sections 91 and 92 of the *Constitution Act, 1867*. In Chapter 7, we focus on the division of powers jurisprudence of the Judicial Committee of the Privy Council, which served as Canada's final court of appeal until 1949. The Privy Council's underlying theory was that the categories in sections 91 and 92 were "watertight compartments" that did not overlap. Furthermore, the Privy Council narrowed the most important federal powers — the peace, order, and good government (POGG) power and the power to regulate trade and commerce — so that they did not include matters that were regarded as falling within provincial authority under section 92. The Privy Council simultaneously adopted an extremely expansive view of the provincial power over "property and civil rights," concluding that it granted the provinces exclusive authority to regulate "legal rights" in a province. The result was that the two most important federal powers were rendered virtually nugatory, since they could not be used to legislate in relation to "legal rights in a province."

The formalistic doctrine developed by the Privy Council exacerbated the fiscal and constitutional crisis facing the Canadian state by the 1930s. The most direct cause of the crisis was the Depression, which devastated market economies around the world in 1929. In Canada, the crisis was particularly acute because the provinces, which had been allocated the lion's share of constitutional jurisdiction by the Privy Council, lacked the financial resources to respond effectively to this economic devastation. Conversely, while the federal government was in a position to lead the effort to rebuild the economy, it was prevented from doing so by the Privy Council, which decided that Ottawa lacked the necessary constitutional authority. The challenge facing all governments following the end of the Second World War was to find a way out of the constitutional straitjacket that had been created by the Privy Council. Rather than attempt to rewrite or amend the constitution, governments chose to avoid or even ignore it. The federal government used the power of the purse—the so-called spending power—to overcome the artificial constitutional constraints that had been imposed by the Privy Council. By offering financial inducements to the provinces and the private sector, the federal government was able to assume an effective presence in a wide variety of social and economic policy fields, including hospitals, health care, social welfare programs, and post-secondary education. The provinces also began expanding their activities into areas that had previously been regarded as the preserve of Ottawa or the private sector, as they attempted to boost economic development through government intervention and economic management. The end result of this process, which unfolded over a period of the three decades following the end of the Second World War, was that overlapping and shared jurisdiction between the federal and provincial governments increasingly became the norm in Canadian federalism. The challenge during this period for each level of government was to coordinate and manage joint responses to shared problems, rather than to defend against encroachments by the other level of government.

This fundamental evolution in the nature of Canadian federalism provides the backdrop for the remainder of the analysis in this section of the book, which examines the federalism jurisprudence of the Supreme Court of Canada since it became the final court of appeal for Canada in 1949. Chapter 8 examines POGG, Chapter 9 the federal trade and commerce power, Chapter 10 the provincial power over property and civil rights in the province, Chapter 11 the federal power to enact criminal law, and Chapter 12 the federal and provincial jurisdiction in the field of transportation. In certain of these areas, the Supreme Court has expanded the constitutional authority of Parliament in modest but significant respects. At the same time, the Supreme Court has continued to interpret provincial powers broadly, particularly the power to enact laws in relation to property and civil rights. In essence, the Supreme Court has generally been faithful to the framework developed by the Privy Council and has not engaged in a wholesale revision to the basic division of powers established prior to 1949.

Part Five provides an overview of two key changes to Canada's constitution that were introduced in 1982: the *Charter*, as well as new protections for Indigenous rights. These chapters explain how these developments fit within the overall framework of Canada's constitution. Chapter 13 reviews the debates surrounding the enactment of the *Charter* in the early 1980s, highlighting the concerns that were raised over the expanded powers of the judiciary. With the benefit of hindsight, it is clear that the enactment of the *Charter* represents one of the most significant political developments in Canada in the twentieth century. The courts now routinely review a wide variety of legislative enactments which, prior to April 1982, would have been regarded as wholly outside the province of the judiciary. In Chapters 14 and 15, we then review the manner in which the courts have interpreted the rights set out in the *Charter*. While the Supreme Court of Canada's interpretation of the *Charter* has certainly not been free of criticism, on balance it has been a significant success. The Court has given real meaning and substance to the *Charter*, such that any government contemplating legislation limiting individual rights must carefully consider whether such limits are consistent with the fundamental rights and freedoms the *Charter* guarantees. For the most part, the courts have generally avoided usurping or eliminating the primary role of politicians in shaping Canada's political choices. Moreover, even when statutes have been struck down, the democratic process is arguably enhanced since governments are forced to more carefully tailor their proposals rather than abandon them altogether. In short, a strong case can be made that the enactment of the *Charter* has reinforced and enhanced democratic values and the democratic process in Canada.

Chapter 16 considers the position of Indigenous peoples in the Canadian constitutional order as a result of the historic constitutional recognition of Indigenous and Treaty rights in section 35 of the *Constitution Act, 1982*. The constitutional status and rights of the Indigenous peoples of Canada were fundamentally altered by the enactment of section 35, under which Indigenous rights are no longer subject to the doctrine of parliamentary sovereignty. Section 35 does not, however, provide absolute protection for Indigenous rights from the application of inconsistent federal or provincial laws. Instead, as described in this chapter, the Supreme Court has developed a framework for the interpretation of section 35 that requires a careful balancing of interests between Indigenous rights and the continuing role of Parliament and the provincial legislatures to advance the collective interests of society as a whole. We also describe the extent to which Indigenous rights of self-government may have been constitutionally protected through the enactment of section 35.

Part Six examines the prospects for constitutional change in the years ahead. Whether a future Quebec government will undertake a third sovereignty referendum is unclear. However, the decision of the Supreme Court in the *Secession Reference*,[40] as well as the enactment of

---

40 Above note 13.

the *Clarity Act* in 2000,[41] suggest that federalists may be equipped with the legal and political tools needed to deal more effectively with an unexpected threat of secession. At the same time, the *Secession Reference* decision has altered the dynamic of any future referendum campaign in ways that are not entirely favourable to the federalist option. The nature of these elements, and their implications for a potential third referendum on sovereignty, are identified and discussed.

FURTHER READINGS

BEATTY, D.M., *Constitutional Law in Theory and Practice* (Toronto: University of Toronto Press, 1995) c. 1

BEAUDOIN, G. A., with P. Thibeault, *La Constitution du Canada: Institutions, partage des pouvoirs, droits et libertés*, 3d ed. (Montreal: Wilson & Lafleur, 2004) c. 1

BRUN, H., & G. Tremblay, *Droit Constitutionnel*, 6th ed. (Cowansville, QC: Éditions Yvon Blais, 2014)

DAWSON, R.M., *The Government of Canada*, 6th ed., ed. by N. Ward (Toronto: University of Toronto Press, 1987)

HOGG, P.W., *Constitutional Law of Canada*, loose-leaf (Toronto: Carswell, 2007) c. 1

MALLORY, J.R., *The Structure of Canadian Government*, 2d ed. (Toronto: Gage, 1984) c. 1

SMILEY, D.V., *The Federal Condition in Canada* (Toronto: McGraw-Hill Ryerson, 1987) cc. 1 and 2

WHITTINGTON, M.S., & R.J. Van Loon, *Canadian Government and Politics: Institutions and Processes* (Toronto: McGraw-Hill Ryerson, 1996) c. 5

---

41 *An Act to give effect to the requirement for clarity as set out in the opinion of the Supreme Court of Canada in the Quebec Secession Reference*, S.C. 2000, c. 26.

PART TWO

THE FRAMEWORK AND INSTITUTIONS OF GOVERNMENT

CHAPTER 2

CANADA'S CONSTITUTIONAL DEVELOPMENT BEFORE 1867

A. REPRESENTATIVE AND RESPONSIBLE GOVERNMENT

The Constitution Act, 1867[1] did not attempt to describe comprehensively the institutions of government or their manner of operation. Instead, certain public institutions or practices that had become firmly established in the law of the British North American colonies were simply continued by the 1867 Act. These established institutions or practices in many cases were not explicitly referenced. The only oblique reference to this constitutional continuity was the phrase in the preamble to the Act stating that Canada was to have a "Constitution similar in Principle to that of the United Kingdom." To understand what was contemplated by this reference, it is necessary to examine the manner in which governmental institutions had evolved in both Great Britain and British North America by the middle of the nineteenth century.

It is beyond the scope of this book to describe fully the constitutional or political history of the British North American colonies. Rather, our focus is on two constitutional developments in the late eighteenth and early nineteenth centuries that are key to understanding the manner in which the constitutional arrangements in 1867 were intended to operate. The first is the development of representative government and the second is the development of responsible government.

1 (U.K.), 30 & 31 Vict., c. 3, preamble.

Representative government refers to the requirement that laws can only be made by a legislature that is elected by the people, as opposed to the Crown legislating through the royal prerogative. Responsible government refers to the requirement that the powers of the Crown can be exercised only in accordance with the advice or instructions of political leaders who control a majority of votes in the legislature. Both of these constitutional developments had become incorporated into the legal structure of the British North American colonies by 1867, and the drafters of the 1867 Act simply assumed that they would continue in place following Confederation.

B. REPRESENTATIVE GOVERNMENT

1) Indigenous Government

Before the arrival of Europeans in North America, Indigenous peoples had developed representative political institutions and a body of customary law. These Indigenous forms of government and laws survived European settlement in North America. It is arguable that section 35 of the *Constitution Act, 1982*, which "recognized and affirmed" Aboriginal and Treaty rights, gave some constitutional recognition to them.[2] The interaction between Indigenous forms of government and those of European settlers is a complex topic addressed in Part Five. The focus of this chapter is on the manner in which representative political institutions were imported to North America as part of the colonial law established under British authority.

2) French Civil Law

The earliest permanent European settlement in what is now Canada was established by the French. Following the British conquest in 1759, certain aspects of the legal system of the former colony of New France were retained and incorporated into the legal framework of the colony of Quebec. In particular, although British law governed the relations between the state and individuals, the French civil law was retained in respect of the legal rules governing the relations among private individuals in contract, property, and civil wrongs. This distinctive legal framework continues in place today, with the civil law rules in Quebec being defined in the Quebec *Civil Code*, which traces its origins to the

2 This argument and other issues with respect to Indigenous rights are considered in Chapter 15.

Napoleonic Code adopted in France in 1804. In contrast, the civil law in the other nine provinces is governed by common law decisions of the courts and by various statutes defining the civil rights of private citizens. In this sense, as noted in more detail elsewhere in this book, the Canadian legal system incorporates elements of both the British and the French legal traditions.

3) The Supremacy of Parliament in English Law

In England, the *Bill of Rights* of 1688 had confirmed the supremacy of Parliament over the monarch. Before this time, the sovereign had claimed the right to govern through the exercise of the royal prerogative.[3] The *Bill of Rights* stated that the monarch could not, through the exercise of the prerogative, suspend or dispense with statutes enacted by Parliament. It also stated that taxation could only be imposed through a statute rather than by the sovereign through the power of the prerogative. Further, the monarch's prerogative powers could be limited through the enactment of a statute. The *Bill of Rights* reinforced the famous decision of Lord Coke in the *Proclamations Case*,[4] where Coke had held that the monarch had no power to amend statutes or to alter the common law through the exercise of the prerogative.

Thus, by the end of the seventeenth century, it was clearly established in England that the exercise of the royal prerogative was subject to statute, and that the enactment of legislation or the imposition of taxes required an Act of Parliament. There had developed a right to representative political institutions, in the sense that laws could only be made by an elected Parliament rather than by the monarch exercising the royal prerogative.

4) Representative Political Institutions in the Colonies

The right to representative political institutions did not exist in all British colonies. British common law drew a distinction between colonies regarded as having been acquired by peaceful settlement as opposed to by conquest. In the case of colonies acquired by peaceful settlement, the colonists were deemed to have imported British common law principles with them. These common law principles included the same right to representative political institutions as were enjoyed by British subjects in England. This meant that settlers in a settled colony had a

3 The prerogative is the inherent power of the sovereign to govern dating to the Middle Ages. It is discussed more fully in Chapter 3, Section D(3).

4 (1611), 12 Co. Rep. 74, 77 E.R. 1352.

right to have local colonial laws enacted through an elected assembly, rather than by an appointed governor. Further, taxation could only be imposed through statute—enacted either by a local colonial legislature or by the British Parliament—rather than through the exercise of the royal prerogative.

In colonies conquered by military warfare, the law of the conquered colony remained in force until altered by the appropriate British authorities.[5] There was no automatic right to representative political institutions in a conquered colony and the colony could be governed by the Crown directly, or by a colonial governor as the Crown's representative, without any legislative assembly. Taxes, for example, could be imposed on a conquered colony either by the British government or by the local colonial governor without any need for popular ratification or approval by an assembly. However, according to the principle laid down in *Campbell v. Hall*,[6] if the Crown had granted, or promised to grant, a representative legislative assembly to a conquered colony, it could no longer alter the ordinary law of the colony by order in council. Changes in the law of such a colony required a statute enacted either by the British Parliament or by a representative legislative assembly of the colony.

British law regarded Nova Scotia, New Brunswick, Prince Edward Island, and Newfoundland as "settled colonies," ignoring the fact that large Indigenous populations were present before contact with Europeans. The first legislative assembly in what became Canada was established in Nova Scotia in 1758.[7] Assemblies were established in Prince Edward Island in 1773, in New Brunswick when it was separated from Nova Scotia in 1784, and in Newfoundland in 1832.

5) The *Royal Proclamation of 1763*

The colonies that later became the provinces of Ontario and Quebec, in contrast to those in Atlantic Canada, were regarded for purposes of British law as conquered colonies. They had no automatic right to representative political institutions and could have been governed by the Crown directly. Following the defeat of the French and the establishment of British sovereignty over Quebec in 1760, local governmental powers were exercised by the governor and an appointed Council from

---

5 This rule was subject to the recognition of the ultimate sovereignty of the British Crown over the colony in question.

6 (1774), 1 Cowp. 204, 98 E.R. 1045 (K.B.).

7 It was not the first assembly in a British colony in North America. In 1619, an assembly had been established in Virginia and, the following year, assemblies were summoned in Bermuda and at Plymouth.

which Roman Catholics were excluded. However, in the *Royal Proclamation of 1763*,[8] issued by King George III through the exercise of the royal prerogative, the Crown stated that a legislative assembly would be summoned by the governor "so soon as the State and Circumstances of the said Colonies will admit thereof." The *Royal Proclamation* also stated that English law would replace the pre-existing French civil law and protected certain rights of Indigenous peoples.

Despite the promise of the *Royal Proclamation*, a legislative assembly was not established in the decade immediately following 1763. The British governors, James Murray and Guy Carleton, believed that the "state and circumstances" of the colony were not yet right for a legislative assembly. There were only some 600 English-speaking Americans who had recently come to Quebec, while the French population numbered approximately 65,000. If a representative legislative assembly were established, it would be dominated by representatives of the French-Canadian community; yet the alternative—establishing an assembly elected only by the minuscule minority of English-speaking settlers—seemed wholly impractical.[9] Accordingly, local government remained in the hands of the governor and a twelve-member appointed Council from which Roman Catholics were excluded. Both Murray and Carleton advised the British government that establishing a legislative assembly was ill-advised until such time as immigration from Britain boosted the numbers of English-speaking subjects in the colony.

6) The *Quebec Act, 1774*

The imperial authorities accepted the advice of Murray and Carleton and decided to continue to govern Quebec through a governor and an appointed Council. However, the promise of a legislative assembly that had been made in the *Royal Proclamation* could not be revoked by the Crown unilaterally, given the principle recognized in *Campbell v. Hall*. It would be necessary for the British Parliament to enact a statute repealing that portion of the *Royal Proclamation* that had promised a Legislative Assembly, and then to confer law-making powers on the governor.

This change occurred when the British Parliament enacted the *Quebec Act, 1774*.[10] This was the first occasion on which Britain had set out the form of civil government for a colony in a statute, as opposed to through a Royal Proclamation or order in council. The *Quebec Act, 1774* stated

8 R.S.C. 1985, App. II, No. 1.

9 See G.F.G. Stanley, *A Short History of the Canadian Constitution* (Toronto: Ryerson Press, 1969) at 27.

10 (U.K.), 14 Geo. III, c. 83.

that the provisions in the *Royal Proclamation* with respect to the civil government of the colony "have been found, upon Experience, to be inapplicable to the State and Circumstances of the said Province." The Act stated that it was "inexpedient" to establish a legislative assembly at that time, as had been promised in the *Royal Proclamation*. Instead, a legislative council consisting of between seventeen and twenty-three persons would be appointed by the British Crown. This legislative council, with the consent of the governor, was granted power to make ordinances for the "Peace, Welfare, and good Government" of the colony. The powers conferred on the council were, however, rather limited. The council had no power to levy general taxes,[11] and any ordinance passed by the council had to be forwarded to the British Crown, who could disallow it within two years. Ordinances of the council were also subject to legislation enacted in Britain by the British Parliament.

In addition to these provisions for civil government, the *Quebec Act, 1774* expanded the western limits of the colony so that it included the southern portion of what is now Ontario, upstate New York, and Ohio. These areas had been within the territory of New France before the conquest but, under the *Royal Proclamation*, had become separated from Quebec and established as a separate Indigenous territory. The French-Canadian customary civil law,[12] which had been swept away by the *Royal Proclamation*, was reinstituted for the purposes of private law matters (including the system of landholding, marriage, inheritance, and trade and commerce), while the criminal law of England was to govern in criminal matters.[13]

These provisions outraged the American colonies to the south and were one of the contributing factors to the American War of Independence. The extension of Quebec's boundaries meant that the northern American colonies would be deprived of the opportunity to acquire territory lying immediately to their west. The retention of the French

---

11 There was a provision permitting taxes to be levied within towns or districts for the purpose of maintaining roads or public buildings within those specific areas.

12 The law that had been received into New France before the conquest was the Custom of Paris, a law that was civilian in nature but essentially customary. There was at this time no comprehensive statute or restatement of the civil law. The French Civil, or Napoleonic, Code dates from 1804, several decades after the *Quebec Act, 1774*.

13 The *Quebec Act, 1774* stated that "in all Matters of Controversy, relative to Property and Civil Rights, Resort shall be had to the Laws of Canada." The phrase "Property and Civil Rights" was subsequently used in s. 92(13) of the *Constitution Act, 1867*. The courts gave that provision a wide interpretation, relying in part on the fact that the *Quebec Act, 1774* had used the same language in order to refer to the entire body of civil law matters.

customary law for civil law matters was also controversial, since any American settlers who moved westward would find themselves subject to a legal regime they regarded as wholly foreign, particularly with respect to land tenure.

The *Quebec Act, 1774* made no direct reference to language. However, unlike the *Royal Proclamation*, which had reflected a philosophy of assimilation, the *Quebec Act, 1774* reflected a desire to seek an accommodation with the French-Canadian population of the colony. We have already noted that the *Quebec Act, 1774* reinstated the French customary law as the civil law for the colony. It also expressly recognized the right of individuals to freedom of religion, guaranteed the Roman Catholic Church its "accustomed Dues and Rights, with respect to such Persons only as shall profess the said Religion," and provided for a special oath for Roman Catholics so they could accept seats on the legislative council. (This provision reversed the policy of the *Royal Proclamation*, which had excluded Roman Catholics from seats on the Council.) Further, any ordinance enacted by the legislative council that touched on religion or religious freedom had to be approved by the sovereign in England before it could come into force, thus limiting the power of the legislative council or the governor to tamper with the rights of either Roman Catholics or Protestants. The *Quebec Act, 1774* signalled a British policy of tolerance and religious freedom and was regarded by the French-Canadian community as a source of important constitutional protections.[14]

7) The *Constitutional Act, 1791*

Despite the fact that local British merchants had been key proponents of the form of civil government established by the *Quebec Act, 1774*, the attempt to govern Quebec through an unelected governor and Council became increasingly controversial and problematic among English-speaking settlers in the colony. This dissatisfaction with the *Quebec Act, 1774* became particularly acute in the 1780s following the American War of Independence, when approximately 45,000 Loyalists from the American colonies moved to the western part of the colony of Quebec around Lake Ontario and Lake Erie.[15] The Loyalists had

14 The protections were constitutional in the sense that they were embodied in a statute of the British Parliament, which took priority over any local laws and which could only be amended by the British Parliament itself.

15 Even greater numbers of Loyalists settled in that part of Nova Scotia that later became New Brunswick, leading to the creation of the new colony of New Brunswick in 1784.

been accustomed to government through an elected legislative assembly, and regarded the form of government provided under the *Quebec Act, 1774*—with ordinances being enacted by a governor and an unelected legislative council—as archaic and undemocratic. The Loyalists pressed for the immediate establishment of representative government in the colony. These new settlers were also strongly opposed to the use of the French civil law, particularly for land tenure, and sought the right to have land tenure governed by English common law rather than the French seigneurial system. The British response to these pressures for reform was not long in coming.

The British Parliament enacted the *Constitutional Act, 1791*,[16] which divided Quebec into two colonies, Upper and Lower Canada. In each colony, legislative power would be vested in a lieutenant governor, an appointed Legislative Council (made up of a sufficient number of "discreet and proper Persons" whose members would be summoned by the lieutenant governor to hold office for life), and an elected legislative assembly. To become law, a bill would require the approval of the legislative assembly and the legislative council, as well as the approval of the governor. The jurisdiction of the council and assembly was defined in terms similar to those employed in the *Quebec Act, 1774* . . . to enact laws for the "Peace, Welfare, and good Government" of each province, provided that any such laws could not be "repugnant" to the *Constitutional Act, 1791* itself. The provisions from the *Quebec Act, 1774* permitting the British Crown to disallow local laws were carried forward into the *Constitutional Act, 1791*. The Act also provided that the governor could refuse to consent to laws enacted by the Assembly and the Council, or could reserve any laws for the consideration of the Crown. In the latter case, the laws would not come into force unless they were approved by the British Crown within two years.[17]

The Act also contemplated the appointment of an executive council to advise the governor in the exercise of his powers. There was no requirement, however, that the members of the executive council be chosen from members of the assembly, or that they be otherwise ac-

---

16 (U.K.), 31 Geo. III, c. 31.

17 See arts. XX to XXII of the *Quebec Act, 1774*. These provisions formed the model or template for ss. 55 to 57 of the *Constitution Act, 1867*. The *Constitutional Act, 1791* also provided that legislation that dealt with certain sensitive matters, including rights of religious worship or the establishment of reserves for the Protestant clergy, had to be laid before Parliament in Great Britain before they could become law, and that the king would be obliged to refuse consent to the bill if either the House of Commons or the House of Lords so instructed. See art. XLII.

countable to the assembly. The governor and the executive council in each province were also constituted as a court of appeal and a court of civil jurisdiction. The structure of government as it existed in Upper and Lower Canada in 1791 is depicted in Figure 2.1.

Figure 2.1 Government in Canada, 1791

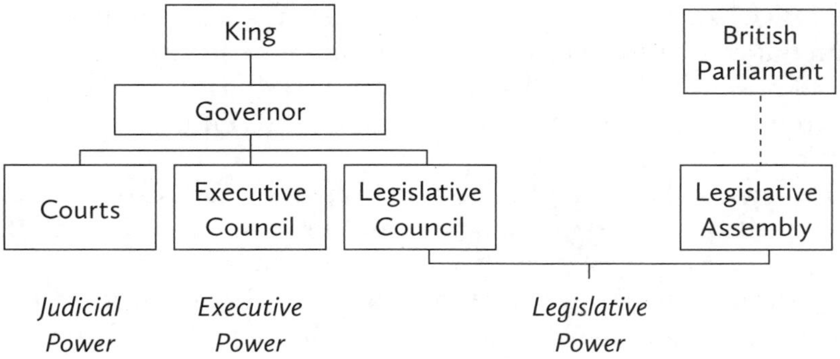

Two general observations are in order about this structure. First, the creation of two separate colonies permitted the retention of the French civil law for Lower Canada, with the English common law in Upper Canada, and gave French Canadians control through their numerical superiority in the population of the Legislative Assembly in Lower Canada. The government was thus "representative" in the sense that the enactment of legislation now required a bill approved by the Legislative Assembly. This was an important new protection for French Canadians since the local majority could use their numbers in the Legislative Assembly to block legislative changes contrary to their interests. At the same time, government in 1791 was by no means democratic or under the real control of the majority. The governor had significant powers to block initiatives of the assembly, either through refusing consent to legislation or "reserving" it for consideration of the imperial authorities. In exercising the considerable powers of that office, the governor was free to act on personal initiative or on instructions issued by the imperial authorities. The governor was also to be advised by an Executive Council, but the members of this council were not subject to the control or scrutiny of the Legislative Assembly, and the governor was free to appoint whomever he pleased to the Executive Council. Further, the governor was not obliged to follow the advice of those he appointed to the Executive Council, although he would certainly look to them for guidance on questions of policy.

The governor in Lower Canada tended to appoint to the Executive Council large numbers of English-speaking and Protestant merchants from Montreal, who came to be known as the "Château Clique." Members of the council used their office to advance their own positions and interests through the control of the government and the dispensation of patronage. Moreover, although the governor and the council could not impose taxation without the approval of the assembly, the executive derived substantial revenues from Crown lands as well as from certain duties that had been authorized under the British statute, the *Quebec Revenue Act, 1774*. This meant that it was possible for the executive to hold out against the assembly and carry on the government without the latter's cooperation.

The tension between the executive and the Legislative Assembly reflected the underlying religious and linguistic cleavages in the colony, since the Legislative Assembly was dominated by the rural French-speaking majority of the province. Every election between 1815 and 1837 was won by a nationalist group led by Louis-Joseph Papineau, who campaigned on a platform of granting the assembly complete powers over public revenue. The struggle between the assembly and the executive culminated in the armed rebellion led by Papineau in 1837, which led to the temporary suspension of the constitution and the vesting of governmental powers in the governor and his council. While Upper Canada did not have the same religious and linguistic cleavages as were present in Lower Canada, a similar tension between the executive and the assembly developed in the 1830s, culminating in the abortive rebellion led by William Lyon Mackenzie in 1837.

The second general observation about the structure of government established in 1791 was that it assumed the continued pre-eminent authority of the British Crown and Parliament. The lieutenant governors were to act on instructions from the British Crown, and laws enacted by the British Parliament took precedence over those enacted locally. In fact, the continued authority of the British Crown was one of the arguments used to oppose reformers who campaigned in favour of "responsible government"—the requirement that the lieutenant governor follow the advice of persons who were accountable to the Legislative Assembly. Since the lieutenant governor had to act on instructions received from England, it was said that he could not also be bound to follow the advice of any group that was accountable to the local Legislative Assembly. According to this line of argument, the lieutenant governor had to have but a single master, and therefore there was no room in the equation for binding the executive to follow the wishes of the Legislative Assembly.

C. RESPONSIBLE GOVERNMENT

1) Lord Durham's Report

Dissatisfaction with the lack of accountability of the executive to the elected Assembly led to abortive rebellions in both Upper and Lower Canada in 1837.[18] The British authorities were sufficiently concerned over the rebellions that they appointed John George Lambton, the Earl of Durham, as the governor general of the British North American colonies with a mandate to recommend political changes that would respond to and remedy the underlying causes of unrest. Durham's report, delivered in 1839, was one of the most significant and controversial documents in British colonial history.[19] He concluded that the colonial governments had become increasingly confused and incompetent. The local governors were the central figures in colonial government, but Durham reported that they tended to refer too many matters to London, which had little knowledge of or interest in Canadian affairs. Similar confusion prevailed with respect to the local Executive Council, since its members did not have clearly demarcated lines of responsibility but, instead, served as a single group of collective advisers who each took an equal part in all governmental matters. The Executive Councils also served as the court of appeal for each colony, even though, as Durham pointed out, its members did not necessarily have any legal training or qualification. Finally, the executive was in no way responsible to the elected Legislative Assemblies, which meant that the government often failed to meet the most elementary political needs of the community.

Durham proposed a sweeping set of reforms, the chief among them being the implementation of responsible government. There are essentially two elements to the principle of responsible government. The first is that the Executive Council (the body responsible for advising the governor) must be composed of persons who command the confidence of the Legislative Assembly and who must resign if they lose that confidence. The second element is that governors are bound to follow

---

18 Of the two rebellions, the one led by Papineau in Lower Canada was far more serious since it enjoyed greater support in the local population. Papineau's rebellion reflected widespread dissatisfaction among the French-Canadian community with British policy, which ensured the domination of English landowners in the rural countryside, where most of the French Canadians lived. Papineau did not have the support of the Roman Catholic Church, however, and the rebellion was defeated by the regular army.

19 Lord Durham, *Report on the Affairs of British North America*, vol. 2, Sir C.P. Lucas, ed. (Oxford: Clarendon Press, 1912).

the advice of the members of the Executive Council in executing their duties and responsibilities.

Durham believed that acceptance of the principle of responsible government would resolve most of the difficulties faced by the colonies. He proposed a division between matters of local concern, in which the principle of responsible government would operate, and matters of imperial concern, in which the governor would act as an agent of the British government to ensure that the local political authorities did nothing to compromise British interests. Durham identified the areas of continuing British interest as being limited to constitutional matters, foreign affairs, external trade, and management of public lands. In all other matters, the implementation of the principle of responsible government would mean that the governor would be bound to act on the advice of persons who commanded the confidence of the Legislative Assembly. This arrangement would have the effect of granting internal self-rule to the colony, since the Legislative Assembly would be in a position to control the policies of the government in matters of strictly local concern.

The second major recommendation of Lord Durham was the union of Upper and Lower Canada into a single province.[20] In a famous passage, Durham reported that the conflict between French- and English-speaking colonists was such that he had found "two nations warring in the bosom of a single state." Durham stated that this "deadly animosity that now separates the inhabitants of Lower Canada into the hostile divisions of French and English" could only be overcome by forcing the assimilation of French Canadians into an English-speaking mainstream.[21] He saw the union of Lower and Upper Canada as a means to bring about this integration and assimilation. Durham also raised the possibility of an even wider union involving all the British North American colonies, which would thereby further submerge the French-Canadian presence within a wider political union. However, he regarded the idea as impractical at the time.

---

20 The idea of the union of the two provinces was not a novel idea. In 1822, a bill had been introduced in the British Parliament providing for the union of Upper and Lower Canada into a single province. However, the bill was not enacted after it aroused strong opposition among the French-Canadian population in Lower Canada.

21 Lord Durham's Report, above note 19 at 16.

2) The *Union Act, 1840*

Many of Durham's recommendations were accepted and acted upon in the *Union Act, 1840*,[22] which was passed by the British Parliament. This Act united Upper and Lower Canada into a single province called Canada, with a governor, a Legislative Council appointed for life by the governor, and an elected Legislative Assembly with forty-two members from each of Canada East and Canada West.[23] English was made the sole official language of both the Legislative Council and Assembly, reflecting Durham's hope and expectation that the new political structure would lead to the assimilation of the French-speaking community. The Legislative Assembly was given power to make laws for the "Peace, Welfare and good Government of the Province of Canada," provided that any such laws were not repugnant to the *Union Act, 1840* itself or to any other British law "which does or shall, by express Enactment or by necessary Intendment, extend to the Provinces."

This provision clarified the relationship between British law and colonial law. Before this time, it was unclear whether a local colonial legislature could enact laws that were inconsistent with British statutes on the same subject—even though those statutes were not expressly applicable to the colony—as well as whether the colonial legislature could amend English common law in its local application. The *Union Act, 1840* resolved these doubts in favour of the colonial legislatures. It made clear that only those British statutes that were intended to apply to the colony . . . as opposed to British statutes on the same subject matter . . . would take priority over colonial statutes and confirmed the jurisdiction of the local legislature to amend the common law of England.[24]

Other innovations of the *Union Act, 1840* included the creation of a Consolidated Revenue (CR) Fund, and the surrender by the Crown of all of its independent revenue from Crown lands and other sources of income into the CR Fund. In return, the Act guaranteed payment of necessary moneys from the CR Fund to carry on the operation of the executive branch, including salaries for the governor, the civil servants, and the judiciary, and for the expenses of various governmental offices. All bills providing for expenditures from the CR Fund had to originate in the Legislative Assembly (as opposed to the Legislative Council),

---

22 (U.K.), 3 & 4 Vict., c. 35.

23 At the time, this distribution of seats favoured Canada West, since it had a smaller population; within a few years, however, the population of Canada West had outstripped that of Canada East and calls began for representation by population.

24 This approach to the relationship between colonial legislation and British law was later applied to all Britain's colonies in the *Colonial Laws Validity Act, 1865*.

and could only be introduced in the Assembly if accompanied by a recommendation from the governor. This important innovation had been recommended by Lord Durham and was carried forward into section 54 of the *Constitution Act, 1867*; it remains in effect today, and it represents one of the means whereby the executive maintains its control over the legislative process.[25]

While Durham's report had provided the blueprint for much of the *Union Act, 1840*, his proposal to implement responsible government for the colony was not accepted. The Act itself made no reference to the principle of responsible government. This omission was not surprising in itself. As Durham had pointed out, responsible government could have been implemented simply by modifying the imperial instructions to require that local governors appoint to the Executive Council persons who enjoyed the confidence of the Legislative Assembly. However, the Colonial Office was not entirely persuaded of the merits of responsible government for the colony. For example, the colonial secretary, Lord John Russell, believed that responsible government would have placed the governor in an impossible position between the British and local authorities.

The first governor of the united colony, Lord Sydenham, implemented certain reforms that moved the colony in the direction of responsible government without fully embracing the principle. Sydenham committed himself to selecting the members of the Executive Council from among the members of the Legislative Assembly. This was a positive change, since the members of the government were now required to answer for government policy in the assembly. Sydenham also made the members of the Executive Council responsible for the running and conduct of different departments of government, thereby increasing the accountability of individual ministers and of the government as a whole. But Sydenham did not agree that the members of the Executive Council could hold office only if they enjoyed the confidence of the Legislative Assembly. He also attempted to act as his own prime minister and endeavoured to build up his own political party through selection of ministers from the assembly. This approach was inherently problematic, since it inserted the governor into the fray of partisan politics and made it difficult for him to maintain the independence and neutrality that had come to be expected of the office. Sydenham also

25 Numerous other aspects of the *Union Act, 1840* were simply a continuation of provisions that had been in place in the previous constitutional arrangements of 1791 and 1774. Thus, the provisions for "reservation" of bills by the governor for the consideration of the British authorities and the power of the British Crown to disallow colonial statutes were carried forward in identical terms in the 1840 Act.

excluded French-speaking ministers from his first Council, reflecting the philosophy of assimilation underlying the *Union Act, 1840* and formed an Executive Council made up exclusively of English-speaking ministers. The attempt to exclude French Canadians from effective participation in government was doomed to fail, given the large numbers of French-Canadian representatives in the Legislative Assembly, and the hastened calls for responsible government.

In early 1842, Sydenham was succeeded as governor by Sir Charles Bagot, who reversed his predecessor's policy of excluding French-Canadians from the Executive Council. His new ministry was headed by two proponents of responsible government, Robert Baldwin and Louis Lafontaine. The appointment of this new ministry represented *de facto* acceptance of the principle that the Executive Council had to enjoy the confidence of the Legislative Assembly. But the principle had not yet been officially recognized, and there were continuing conflicts between the governor and the Executive Council between 1842–47, particularly over the right of the governor to dispense patronage appointments without the approval of the council.

The ultimate acceptance of the principle of responsible government was precipitated by the British election of 1846, which resulted in a change of government and the appointment of Earl Grey to the Colonial Office. Grey instructed newly appointed governors in both Nova Scotia and Canada to accept the principle that decisions in matters of strictly local interest should be made on the basis of advice from persons who enjoyed the confidence of the assembly. The first test of the new policy came in Nova Scotia in January 1848 when, following a general election, the assembly passed a motion of non-confidence in the government. The members of the Executive Council resigned immediately and the governor called on J.B. Uniacke, the leader of the largest group in the assembly, to form a government. In March 1848, the Legislative Assembly in the province of Canada voted non-confidence in the government, prompting the resignation of the Executive Council and its replacement with a group who enjoyed the confidence of the assembly. The principle was accepted almost simultaneously in New Brunswick and, within three years, in Prince Edward Island. Newfoundland achieved responsible government in 1855.

As noted above, the principle of responsible government is not merely concerned with who is to be appointed to the Executive Council but requires, in addition, that governors exercise all of their powers based on the advice and consent of the Executive Council. This second aspect of the principle of responsible government was recognized in 1849 when Lord Elgin, the governor of the province of Canada, gave his assent to a bill compensating Canadians who had suffered injury or damage during the rebellion of 1837, even though Elgin was personally opposed to the measure. Elgin was pelted with rocks and debris by crowds protesting the bill, and the parliamentary buildings in Montreal were burned to the ground by the protestors, an indication of the passions aroused by the bill. The giving of assent in these circumstances was a reflection of the fact that the governor felt bound to exercise discretionary powers based on the advice received from the premier and the members of the Executive Council, regardless of his personal views of the merits of the issue.

Significantly, this momentous political change did not require or receive any formal legal recognition. The provisions of the *Union Act, 1840* referring to the Executive Council were not amended in any way,[26] and the governor's formal legal power to exercise personal choice in appointments to the Council remained unimpaired as a matter of strict law. What had changed, however, was that a constitutional convention respecting the powers of the governor had emerged. Key to the existence of the constitutional convention was the belief of the governor and all political leaders that the powers of the governor were to be exercised on the advice of an Executive Council, the members of which could hold office only as long as they enjoyed the confidence of the Legislative Assembly.

3) From Responsible Government to Cabinet Government

Although the events of 1848–49 had confirmed the acceptance of the principles of responsible government, the move to Cabinet government—in which the governor withdraws from the meetings of the Executive Council—had not yet emerged. The governors in the early 1850s continued to preside personally over the Executive Council. It was not until the mid-decade that the governor withdrew from regular participation in the deliberations of the council, leaving the prime minister to preside. While the governor reserved the right to go into council to discuss measures and to approve them in formal council, the practice developed of the council meeting separately and simply transmitting its decisions to the governor for his separate approval. Meetings of the Executive Council in the absence of the governor came to be known as the council "in committee" or "the Cabinet." Once the decisions of "the

---

26 In fact, the Executive Council is only mentioned in passing in a very limited number of provisions of the *Union Act, 1840* and nowhere are its powers even defined or enumerated. The 1840 Act simply assumed the continued existence of an Executive Council, without any need to specify its precise role of jurisdiction.

Cabinet" had been given formal approval by the governor, they became formal actions of "the Governor in Council." The *de facto* separation of Cabinet from the governor shifted power in favour of the prime minister and further reinforced the convention that the governor was to act on the instructions of his elected ministers. From this point onward, governors in British North America did not participate in Cabinet discussions leading to the formulation of government policy.

Before 1848, there had been loose alliances in the colonial legislatures based on particular issues. However, the acceptance of Cabinet government was a catalyst for the creation of more organized political parties, since control of the legislature now carried with it control of the government. Although party organization and discipline remained weak by modern standards, the dominant group in the Legislative Assembly of Canada tended to be an alliance of English-speaking conservatives in Canada West and the *Bleus* of Canada East. The Liberal-Conservative Party, as this alliance was known, advocated policies of conciliating racial and religious differences and emphasizing economic growth and development. John A. Macdonald and George-Étienne Cartier accepted the principle of duality, the notion that government had to enjoy the support of a majority in both Canada East and Canada West to be effective and legitimate. Thus, all their governments had two first ministers, and certain key portfolios, such as attorney general, had dual office holders. Alternatively, the practice developed of having a portfolio alternate between a minister from Canada East and from Canada West. Duality also led to the acceptance of the principle of "double majority," whereby legislation would be enacted only if it received the support of the overall majority in the entire Legislative Assembly, as well as separate majorities in Canada East and Canada West. The attempt to impose English as the official language of the legislature also failed and, in 1848, the British Parliament amended the *Union Act, 1840* so as to give French a limited status as an official language. Thereafter, all business of the assembly was carried on in two official languages.

The acceptance of the principle of duality was an attempt to ensure that neither of the two main linguistic groups in the colony could govern without the consent of the other. But the double-majority principle meant that it was extremely difficult for any government to remain in office, since no single group could maintain a majority in both sections of the province of Canada. Between 1841 and 1867, there were no fewer than eighteen different governments in office.[27] In an effort to make

27 R.M. Dawson, *The Government of Canada*, 6th ed., ed. by N. Ward (Toronto: University of Toronto Press, 1987) at 281.

government more effective, the size of this assembly was increased to 130 members in 1853—although both Canada East and Canada West retained equal representation—and a majority of members of the Legislative Council was elected beginning in 1856.[28] But as these changes failed to break the political stalemate, calls for wider reforms persisted, setting the stage for the momentous political changes that were agreed on and implemented in the mid-1860s.

D. THE CONSTITUTIONAL NEGOTIATIONS OF 1864–67

Political instability and deadlock in the province of Canada in the early 1860s had convinced political leaders that fundamental structural reform was necessary if government were to become effective and workable. At the same time, the political leadership in the colonies of Nova Scotia, New Brunswick, and Prince Edward Island had been debating the merits of a union of their three colonies. In the spring of 1864, the legislatures of the three maritime colonies had each passed resolutions appointing five delegates to meet in Charlottetown in September 1864. This conference was to decide on the feasibility of a legislative union with a single government and legislature for the three maritime colonies.

In June 1864, the government of the province of Canada, led by Macdonald and Étienne-Paschal Taché, was defeated in the Legislative Assembly. Rather than force an election, the members of the opposition, led by George Brown, proposed formation of a coalition government with the express purpose of seeking a more general union with the other British North American colonies. The coalition government was agreed to and the Canadians secured an invitation to the Charlottetown Conference. Over the summer of 1864, an eight-member Cabinet formulated a proposal for a federal union of British North America. The key feature of the scheme was a federal division of powers that reversed the American system, with the general or residual power residing with

28 This latter change was promoted by conservative elements who believed that electing members of the Legislative Council would increase its political legitimacy and thereby achieve greater protection for the wealthy and propertied minority in the province. The election of forty-eight members of the Legislative Council did infuse new energy into the Council and it took a greater interest in legislation, including money bills and taxation. The government remained responsible to the Legislative Assembly rather than to the Legislative Council, however, and it remained unclear as to whether the parliamentary system of responsible government was compatible with two elected legislative chambers.

the national government, and the provinces or local governments having enumerated powers. This plan was presented to the Charlottetown conference by the eight-member Canadian delegation in early September. After five days of meetings, the maritime delegates agreed to set aside the proposal for a maritime legislative union and to pursue the Canadian proposal for a federal union of British North America. The delegates agreed to meet again in Quebec in early October to work out the details of such a union and to invite delegates from Newfoundland to participate.

The Quebec conference that began on 10 October 1864 produced the blueprint for the *BNA Act*, which is now the *Constitution Act, 1867*. Seventy-two detailed resolutions, which were agreed on by the thirty-three delegates to the two-week conference, dealt with all aspects of the constitution of the new federation that was to be formed from Canada East and Canada West, Nova Scotia, New Brunswick, and Prince Edward Island.[29] Provision was also made for the admission of Newfoundland, the North-Western Territory, British Columbia, and Vancouver. Executive authority for the new federation would continue to reside in the British Crown and the Crown's representative in Canada, the governor general. The British government's power to "disallow" colonial statutes, which had been included in the *Constitutional Act, 1791*, and the *Union Act, 1840*, was to be continued in the new Canadian state. So, too, was the governor general's power to "reserve" a bill for consideration by the British government. A "General Parliament" for Canada was to be established with authority to enact laws for "the peace, welfare and good government of the Federated Provinces." The General Parliament was to be composed of an elected House of Commons, with representation according to population, and an appointed Senate, with equal representation from Quebec, Ontario and the three Maritime provinces. A detailed list of thirty-seven specific subject matters that were especially assigned to the General Parliament was also included, most of which were later included in section 91 of the *BNA Act*. Included in the list of enumerated federal powers were most of the important functions of government at the time, including the regulation of trade and commerce, the raising of money by any mode or system of taxation, defence, criminal law, currency and banking, shipping, and interprovincial works such as canals and railways.

---

29 The conference was attended by two delegates from Newfoundland, seven from New Brunswick, five from Nova Scotia, seven from Prince Edward Island, and twelve from the province of Canada. See "Quebec Resolutions" in G.P. Browne, *Documents on the Confederation of British North America* (Toronto: McClelland & Stewart, 1969) at 153–65.

The *Quebec Resolutions* also included a list of enumerated provincial powers that were more narrowly framed than those assigned to the General Parliament. For example, the provincial taxation power was limited to direct taxation, and provinces could not levy customs and excise duties, which at the time constituted over 80 percent of the colonies' revenues. The provinces were granted power to enact laws in relation to "Property and Civil Rights," with a proviso that this provincial power did not include "those portions thereof [relating to property and civil rights] assigned to the General Parliament."[30] Other centralizing features of the *Quebec Resolutions* included granting the federal government the power to appoint the lieutenant governors of the provinces as well as the judges of the provincial superior courts. The federal government was also given the same powers of reservation and disallowance in relation to provincial laws as the British government in relation to Canadian statutes.

In contrast to the drafting of the *BNA Act*, the *Quebec Resolutions* did not describe either the federal or the provincial lists of enumerated powers as being "exclusive." However, the *Quebec Resolutions* stated that where the powers of the General Parliament overlapped with those of the provinces, the laws enacted by Parliament "shall control and supersede those made by the Local Legislature, and the latter shall be void so far as they are repugnant to, or inconsistent with, the former."[31]

Although the *Quebec Resolutions* stated that "the sanction of the Imperial and Local Parliaments shall be sought for the Union of the Provinces," the only colonial legislature that approved the Resolutions was the Legislative Assembly of the province of Canada.[32] The proposals were debated in the Canadian legislature in February and March 1865 and supported by a margin of ninety-one to thirty-three. However, support was much stronger among the English-speaking members from Canada West; only a bare majority of the French-speaking members from Canada East were in favour. Elsewhere, the *Quebec Resolutions* generated considerable political opposition. The assemblies in Prince Edward Island and Newfoundland decided in the spring of 1865 not to proceed with plans to join the wider federation. In New Brunswick, a general election was held and Premier Samuel Tilley, who had supported the *Quebec Resolutions*, was soundly defeated by anti-confederate politicians. The next year, the lieutenant governor forced another election, which the pro-confederate forces managed to win narrowly.

30 "Quebec Resolutions," *ibid*. While this proviso did appear in the *London Resolutions* of 1866, it did not survive into the *BNA Act* itself.

31 *Ibid*.

32 *Ibid*.

In Nova Scotia, where the proposals were even more controversial, the *Quebec Resolutions* were never voted on directly by either the Nova Scotia assembly or the electorate. Instead, in early 1866, Premier Charles Tupper managed to secure legislative support for a vaguely worded resolution sending delegates to a meeting with the imperial authorities to discuss a broader political union.

In December 1866, sixteen political leaders from Canada East and Canada West, Nova Scotia, and New Brunswick[33] met at the Westminster Palace Hotel in London to hammer out the final details of the new British North American union. Sixty-nine resolutions were agreed on by the delegates, reflecting very limited and minor changes from the scheme that had been settled at Quebec in October 1864. The *London Resolutions* of 1866 were to form the instructions to the parliamentary drafters of the bill that would formally create the new federation of Canada.[34] In January 1867, the Canadian leaders met with the colonial secretary, Lord Carnarvon, and his officials to review a draft version of the *BNA Act*. The bill was introduced at Westminster in February 1867, attracting relatively little attention. It received third reading in the House of Commons in early March and royal assent on 29 March 1867. Proclaimed into law as of 1 July 1867, the Dominion of Canada had come into existence.

FURTHER READINGS

Brown, G.P., *Documents on the Confederation of British North America* (Toronto: McClelland & Stewart, 1969)

Dawson, R.M., *The Government of Canada*, 6th ed., N. Ward, ed. (Toronto: University of Toronto Press, 1987)

Moore, C., *1867: How the Fathers Made a Deal* (Toronto: McClelland & Stewart, 1998)

Russell, P.H., *Constitutional Odyssey: Can Canadians Become a Sovereign People?* (Toronto: University of Toronto Press, 1992) c. 3

Stanley, G.F.G., *A Short History of the Canadian Constitution* (Toronto: Ryerson Press, 1969)

33 There were five delegates from New Brunswick, five from Nova Scotia, and six from the province of Canada in attendance at the London Conference.

34 "London Resolutions" in Browne, above note 29 at 217–28.

CHAPTER 3

THE *CONSTITUTION ACT, 1867*: EXECUTIVE AND LEGISLATIVE POWER

A. INTRODUCTION

The *Constitution Act, 1867*[1] continues to provide the basic framework within which government in Canada operates today. It establishes the basic machinery of government, defining how laws are made, administered, and enforced through the executive, legislative, and judicial organs of the state. It also establishes Canada as a federal state, with jurisdiction divided between the federal and the provincial orders of government. Although the Act was renamed from the *British North America Act, 1867* to the *Constitution Act, 1867* in 1982, relatively few substantive changes to its provisions were enacted at that time. Therefore, a statute that was enacted in 1867 remains the foundation on which the remainder of the Canadian constitution is constructed. Of course, the Act has evolved since the date of its original enactment. This evolution has occurred only in part through formal amendment of its terms.[2] One important source of informal change has been the interpretation and ap-

1 (U.K.), 30 & 31 Vict., c. 3. As discussed in Chapter 1, the *Constitution Act, 1867* was originally enacted by the British Parliament as the *British North America Act, 1867* and was renamed in 1982.

2 The manner in which the Act has been amended subsequent to 1867 is considered in more detail in Chapters 5 and 6.

plication of the Act by both the Judicial Committee of the Privy Council and the Supreme Court of Canada. As shown in later chapters, the judiciary has played a significant role in shaping the relationship between the federal and the provincial governments, through its interpretation of sections 91 to 95 of the 1867 Act. It is impossible to understand the meaning and significance of the *Constitution Act, 1867* without consulting the thousands of judicial decisions by various levels of courts that have interpreted its provisions over the years.

The manner in which the *Constitution Act, 1867* has evolved since its enactment is explored in more detail later in this book. However, the analysis in this chapter and in Chapter 4 is intended to provide a modern as opposed to a historical perspective. The objective is to provide the reader with an introductory understanding of how the Act structures the contemporary functioning of the Canadian state. This chapter focuses on executive and legislative power as defined in the *Constitution Act, 1867*. The overview of the Act is completed in Chapter 4 with a description of the Act's provisions dealing with judicial power and the federal structure.

B. THE *CONSTITUTION ACT, 1867* IS ENTRENCHED

The *Constitution Act, 1867* is included within the definition of the Constitution of Canada set out in section 52 of the *Constitution Act, 1982*. The inclusion of the *Constitution Act, 1867* in this definition has two important consequences, as discussed in Chapter 1. First, any laws that are inconsistent with its provisions, including all amendments since 1867, will be of no force and effect. The *Constitution Act, 1867* is part of the "supreme law of Canada." Second, the Act is subject to a special amending procedure: it can only be amended using the amending procedures set out in the Constitution of Canada. The nature of that amending procedure will be considered in more detail in Chapter 6. Generally, since 1982, amendments to the *Constitution Act, 1867* have required the agreement of the federal Senate, the House of Commons, and a certain number of the provinces. Before April 1982, the Act was amendable by the British Parliament at Westminster, but this British authority was terminated through the *Canada Act 1982*, the U.K. statute that abolished Britain's authority to enact law for Canada.

C. A CONSTITUTION "SIMILAR IN PRINCIPLE"

It is customary for legislation to include a preamble, in which certain background facts or circumstances are recited or noted.[3] The first recital of the preamble to the *Constitution Act, 1867* states that the provinces of Canada, Nova Scotia, and New Brunswick "have expressed their Desire to be federally united into One Dominion under the Crown of the United Kingdom . . . with a Constitution similar in Principle to that of the United Kingdom." Three fundamental aspects of the Canadian constitutional order are highlighted by this recital. First, Canada is a federal as opposed to a legislative union; that is, jurisdiction is divided between the federal government and the provincial orders of government, each order having constitutional recognition and significance. Second, Canada is "one Dominion under the Crown of the United Kingdom." That is, Canada is a constitutional monarchy, as opposed to a republic, and the Crown is the formal head of state. Third, Canada has a constitution "similar in Principle" to that of the United Kingdom. The precise meaning of this phrase is far from clear, particularly because the British constitution is largely unwritten. The preambular reference to the British constitution must mean, at the very least, that the Canadian constitution is itself partly unwritten. The drafters of the *Constitution Act, 1867* signalled that it would be impossible to understand the actual workings of the institutions of the Canadian state simply by reading the terms of the Act itself.

One obvious example of the unwritten character of the Canadian constitution is the principle of responsible government, which, as discussed in Chapters 1 and 2, requires that the powers of the Crown be exercised on the advice of persons who enjoy the confidence of the elected chamber in the legislature. The principle of responsible government was not explicitly referred to anywhere in the *Constitution Act, 1867*. But responsible government had been accepted by both British and colonial politicians for approximately twenty years prior to Confederation, and

---

3 A preamble is not part of the main body of a statute and thus not binding in strict law. Section 52(2) of the *Constitution Act, 1982* (enacted as the *Canada Act 1982* (U.K.), 1982, c. 11, Sched. B.) states that any law that is inconsistent with the "provisions" of the Constitution of Canada is of no force and effect. One might have assumed that the preamble to the *Constitution Act, 1867* is not a "provision" of the constitution and that, therefore, ordinary laws cannot be held to be of no force and effect if they are in conflict with the preamble. However, the Supreme Court of Canada has held that the preamble to the *Constitution Act, 1867* had the effect of importing certain "unwritten constitutional principles" into the Canadian constitution, as defined in s. 52(2) of the *Constitution Act, 1982*.

the "similar in Principle" wording of the preamble reflected the understanding that this constitutional convention would continue after 1867.

D. EXECUTIVE POWER IN THE *CONSTITUTION ACT, 1867*

1) The Queen and the Governor General

Under a constitution, the executive is generally responsible for implementing and administering laws, maintaining public order, conducting military operations, directing foreign policy, and managing state property. Many constitutions also grant the head of the executive branch the right to approve laws that have been drafted by the legislature.

Part II of the *Constitution Act, 1867* defines the nature of executive power in Canada. Section 9 states that executive power over Canada "is hereby declared to continue and be vested in the Queen." The drafters of the Act simply assumed that the queen would remain Canada's head of state, given Canada's continued colonial relationship with Britain at that time.

In the early twenty-first century, how is the queen's position as head of state compatible with Canada's status as an independent country? The answer to this question lies in the fact that the queen's role in Canadian affairs today is entirely ceremonial and symbolic. Most of the queen's legal powers in relation to Canada have been delegated to the governor general, pursuant to letters patent issued by the Crown in 1947.[4] The main legal function still performed by the queen in relation to Canada at the present time is the appointment of a governor general.[5] But this appointment is always made on the advice of the Canadian prime minister, in accordance with the principles of responsible government. The queen herself does not exercise any independent role or discretion in the appointment of a governor general, or in any other aspect of Canadian affairs.

---

4 See *Letters Patent Constituting the Office of Governor General of Canada* (Imperial Order in Council, proclaimed in force 1 October 1947) [*Letters Patent*].

5 The queen also has the power to appoint an additional four or eight senators, on the recommendation of the governor general, pursuant to s. 26 of the 1867 Act. This provision was originally inserted in the *BNA Act* to provide the government, which effectively controls the appointment of additional senators through the conventions of responsible government, with a mechanism to break any deadlock between the House of Commons and the Senate. This power has only been utilized on one occasion, when Prime Minister Mulroney initiated the appointment of additional senators in 1990 to ensure that the Senate would approve legislation imposing a goods and services tax.

Section 10 of the *Constitution Act, 1867* states that, where provisions of the Act refer to the office of the governor general, the reference is intended to apply to the chief executive office or the administrator who is, from time to time, "carrying on the Government of Canada on behalf and in the Name of the Queen." As with section 9, section 10 does not define or create an office or power. Instead, it is merely a provision that defines the manner in which the term "governor general" is to be interpreted elsewhere in the Act. The office of governor general for Canada was actually constituted under letters patent issued by the Crown under the royal prerogative to the first governor general, Viscount Monk, in 1867. The queen normally appoints a governor general for a term of five years, although appointments have on occasion been extended to seven years. In the event of death, incapacity, or removal of the governor general, the chief justice of the Supreme Court of Canada acts as the administrator and may carry out all the duties of the office. Since 1952, with the appointment of Vincent Massey, all governors general have been Canadian. It has also become customary to alternate the position between English- and French-speaking Canadians. The first woman to be appointed governor general was Jeanne Sauvé in 1984.

2) The Crown

As discussed above, section 10 of the *Constitution Act, 1867* refers to the government being carried out "on behalf and in the Name of the Queen." This section acknowledges that the queen is not expected to govern personally. Rather, government is to be carried on by others who act in her name and with her authority. Although section 10 refers only to the governor general, it is obvious that the governor general is not the only individual who acts on behalf of and in the name of the queen. The prime minister and the ministers of the Cabinet, although not named anywhere in the *Constitution Act, 1867*, also take their actions and decisions in the name of the queen. So do all the members, branches, or organs of the executive, which include government departments, the civil service, the armed forces, and the police. When lawyers refer to "the Crown," they refer in a collective sense to all these persons who act on behalf of the queen and in her name. The Crown is generally seen as synonymous with "the government" or "the executive," and each organ of government is regarded, in law, as being part of one indivisible Crown.[6] It is customary to refer to "the sovereign" in matters concern-

6 See P.W. Hogg, P.J. Monahan, & W.K. Wright, *Liability of the Crown*, 4th ed. (Toronto: Carswell, 2011) at s. 1.4.

ing the personal conduct or affairs of the monarch, and to "the Crown" as the collective entity that in law stands for the government.

3) The Powers of the Crown

The *Constitution Act, 1867* does not purport to provide an exhaustive enumeration of the powers of the queen or the governor general. Nor are the powers of the Crown exhaustively catalogued in any other statute or legal enactment. Therefore, it is difficult to offer a precise definition of the exact nature and scope of the powers of the Crown. However, it is widely accepted that the powers of the Crown are derived from two sources, statute and common law.

Statutory powers of the Crown are those defined or created by an Act of Parliament. In the Canadian context, the most obvious example of a statute conferring powers on the Crown is the *Constitution Act, 1867*, which confers sweeping powers on the governor general. These powers include the right to appoint senators, superior court judges, and the lieutenant governors of the provinces (sections 24, 96, and 58); the power to summon and dissolve the House of Commons (sections 38 and 50); the exclusive right to recommend money bills (section 54); and the right to assent to legislation, to refuse assent, or to reserve a bill for consideration of the Queen-in-Council in Britain (sections 55–57). Aside from the *Constitution Act, 1867*—which, as a constitutional statute, can be regarded as falling within a special category—it is commonplace for ordinary statutes to delegate powers to the "Governor General in Council." The Governor General in Council is the governor general acting with the advice of the Queen's Privy Council, which effectively means the Cabinet. Such grants of delegated authority are so common that today the vast majority of powers of the Crown are derived from statute.

The Crown also derives powers from the common law. The common law powers of the Crown, also known as the prerogative, are based on the inherent powers of the monarch dating back to the Middle Ages. At that time, the sovereign claimed absolute power to govern without resort to Parliament, including the power to enact laws and to enforce them. Gradually, however, these prerogative powers were narrowed and limited. For example, it was authoritatively established by the time of the *Bill of Rights* of 1688 that the king could not enact laws, create offences, or raise taxes through the exercise of the prerogative. Only a statute enacted by Parliament could effect such changes in law. The courts have also declared on various occasions that the sovereign cannot interfere with an individual's legal rights, such as rights of contract and property, through the exercise of the prerogative.

The Crown prerogative is subject to statute. If a statute narrows or eliminates a prerogative power, the limitations are binding on the Crown. A.V. Dicey described the prerogative as "the residue of discretionary or arbitrary authority, which at any given time is legally left in the hands of the Crown."[7] He used the term "residue" because Parliament can take away any prerogative and has frequently done so. For example, at common law, the Crown was immune from being sued in tort. This immunity has been abolished by Parliament and the provincial legislatures.[8]

Although the prerogative powers of the Crown have been vastly narrowed over time, they remain significant and real. The main areas in which the Crown prerogative has survived and remains relevant today include the following:[9]

- *Powers relating to the legislature*: The Crown summons, prorogues, and dissolves Parliament pursuant to the prerogative, these powers having been confirmed in the *Constitution Act, 1867.* The appointment of the prime minister and the Cabinet are also derived from the prerogative.
- *Powers relating to foreign affairs*: The conduct of foreign affairs by government is carried on mainly by reliance on the prerogative, including the making of treaties, appointment of ambassadors, issuing of passports, and declarations of war and peace.
- *Powers relating to the armed forces*: The queen is commander-in-chief of the armed forces both by virtue of the prerogative and through section 15 of the *Constitution Act, 1867.*
- *Appointments and honours*: The sovereign is the "fountain of honour" and may grant honours or awards based on the prerogative.
- *Immunities and privileges*: The Crown enjoys certain privileges and immunities, such as the common law rule that statutes do not bind the Crown except by express statement or necessary implication. Although many of these immunities have been narrowed or eliminated by statute, a number of them continue to exist and their ultimate source is the prerogative power of the Crown.

---

7 A.V. Dicey, *Introduction to the Study of the Law of the Constitution,* 10th ed. (London: Macmillan, 1959) at 424. This statement has been approved by the courts on numerous occasions. See: *Reference as to the Effect of the Exercise of the Royal Prerogative of Mercy Upon Deportation Proceedings*, [1933] S.C.R. 269 at 272.

8 See, for example, the *Crown Liability and Proceedings Act,* R.S.C. 1985, c. C-50.

9 This catalogue is drawn from P. Jackson, ed., *O. Hood Phillips' Constitutional and Administrative Law*, 8th ed. (London: Sweet & Maxwell, 2001) at 312–32.

- *The "emergency" prerogative*: Certain cases have held that the Crown enjoys the right to take actions in an emergency that are necessary in order to defend the sovereignty of the country.[10]

While this catalogue of the prerogative powers of the Crown may at first glance seem impressive, it is important to remember that many of the matters listed above are now regulated by statute. For example, the *National Defence Act*[11] regulates most aspects of the government's powers in relation to the armed forces; the legal immunities and privileges of the Crown are generally defined by statute at both the federal and the provincial level; and the *Emergencies Act*[12] defines the powers of the Crown in times of national emergency. The courts have held that where a prerogative power has been regulated or defined by statute, the statute displaces the prerogative and the Crown must act on the basis of the statutorily defined powers.[13] Therefore, despite the theoretically broad reach of the Crown's prerogative powers, today, the overwhelming majority of powers exercised by government flow from statute rather than the prerogative. Furthermore, it is important to recall that the Crown cannot use the prerogative to change the law, including the common law, to interfere with or alter the legal rights of individuals, or to raise taxes. It is also now well established that exercises of prerogative powers that affect the rights of individuals, such as the issuing of a passport or a grant of the royal prerogative of mercy, are subject to judicial review.[14] When the prerogative is exercised in matters of "high policy," such as a declaration of war or the selection of a prime minister's Cabinet, it remains non-justiciable, at least outside of the *Charter* context.[15]

The most recent version of the letters patent constituting the office of the governor general, issued by the sovereign in 1947, delegated to

---

10 See *Burmah Oil Co. (Burmah Trading) Ltd. v. Lord Advocate* (1964), [1965] A.C. 75 at 99 (H.L.), where the House of Lords held that it was lawful for British forces during the Second World War to destroy certain oil installations to prevent them from falling into the hands of the Japanese. The case also held, however, that the Crown was liable to compensate the owners of the installations for the damage caused. The award of damages by the House of Lords was subsequently reversed by statute: see the *War Damage Act 1965* (U.K.), 1965, c. 18.

11 R.S.C. 1985, c. N–5.

12 R.S.C. 1985 (4th Supp.), c. 22.

13 See *Ross River Dena Council Band v. Canada*, [2002] 2 S.C.R. 816 at para. 54, citing *A.G. v. De Keyser's Royal Hotel Ltd.*, [1920] A.C. 508 (H.L.).

14 *Hinse v. Canada (Attorney General)*, [2015] 2 S.C.R. 261; *Abdelrazik v. Canada (Minister of Foreign Affairs)* (2009), [2010] 1 F.C.R.267.

15 *Black v. Canada (Prime Minister)* (2001), 54 O.R. (3d) 215 (C.A.); *Black v. Advisory Council for the Order of Canada*, 2012 FC 1234; *Operation Dismantle v. The Queen*, [1985] 1 S.C.R. 441; *Guergis v. Novak*, 2013 ONCA 449.

the governor general all of the sovereign's powers in relation to Canada.[16] The governor general of Canada can now legally exercise any of the queen's powers, including her prerogative powers. The only exceptions are the appointment of the governor general, which obviously must still be performed by the queen, and an exceptional power to direct the governor general to appoint additional senators pursuant to section 26 of the *Constitution Act, 1867*. However, as discussed in the next section, the principles of responsible government require that all the powers of the Crown must be exercised on the advice of responsible ministers. Therefore, while extensive formal legal powers are retained by the queen and the governor general, as a practical matter, all of these powers are actually exercised by the prime minister and the Cabinet.

4) The Queen's Privy Council for Canada

There is no mention in the *Constitution Act, 1867* of the prime minister or the Cabinet. Instead, the Act provides for the creation of a body called the Queen's Privy Council for Canada, whose members are appointed by the governor general (section 11). Persons appointed to the Privy Council retain the status of Privy Councillor for life, unless removed by the governor general.

The creation of a council to advise the governor in the exercise of his or her powers was not a novel concept. In England, the Privy Council had emerged as a distinct body in the thirteenth and fourteenth centuries. It was a select group of nobles who acted as the sovereign's advisers. During this early period, the sovereign claimed the right to legislate through his Council, as opposed to being required to summon Parliament and enact a statute. The executive branch in the colonial governments in British North America had been structured on this model, with an appointed Executive Council advising a governor. The Executive Councils functioned as quasi-legislative bodies, as opposed to being mere advisers. Before the grant of a Legislative Assembly, the governors would enact laws or ordinances by summoning the Executive Council and seeking its approval for the proposed enactment.[17] The Queen's Privy Council for Canada was, in effect, the successor to these Executive Councils, which had been in existence since the earliest days of British government in the colonies.

As discussed in Chapter 2, by 1849 in British North America, there was an established constitutional convention that the members of the

16 See *Letters Patent*, above note 4 at art. II.

17 See, for example, the *Quebec Act, 1774* (U.K.), 14 Geo. III, c. 83, art. XII.

Executive Council had to be chosen from persons who enjoyed the confidence of the elected Legislative Assembly. These persons made up the Cabinet, and all executive or governmental powers had to be exercised on their instructions or with their approval, in accordance with the principles of responsible government. The Privy Council created by section 11 of the *Constitution Act, 1867* was not, however, synonymous with the Cabinet.

The origins of the institution of the Cabinet can be traced to political developments in seventeenth- and eighteenth-century England, when the practice developed of withdrawing the discussion and direction of government policy into the hands of the king's "confidential advisers." Not all members of the Privy Council were regarded as having the right to participate in these confidential discussions. The king's confidential advisers eventually came to be known as the Cabinet, based on the French term "*cabinet*," meaning a private room set apart for interviews. The Cabinet was so called because it met in the monarch's private chambers.[18] The business of government ceased to be conducted in the full Privy Council, and appointments to the Privy Council came to be regarded as titular or honorific, conveying no right or responsibility to participate in the affairs of government. By the time of the enactment of the *BNA Act*, the distinction between the Cabinet and the Privy Council was well understood, with the former having eclipsed the latter as the policy-making organ and advisory body of the Crown. However, the Cabinet had no formal legal status or role, and its existence was entirely a product of constitutional convention.

The same approach was taken with the drafting of the *BNA Act*. The Queen's Privy Council for Canada was the body that, in strictly formal terms, was charged with the responsibility for advising the governor general about the exercise of the powers of the Crown. However, it was understood that it would be the Cabinet, rather than the entire Privy Council, that would in fact exercise this policy-making and deliberative role. While all members of the Cabinet are members of the Privy Council, not all members of the Privy Council are members of the Cabinet.[19]

18 See Jackson, above note 9 at 340.

19 During the government of Jean Chrétien from 1993–2003, the new ministerial rank of "secretary of state" was created. Secretaries of state were sworn in as members of the Privy Council but were not automatically entitled to attend Cabinet meetings and did not head ministries of the government. They were therefore sometimes described as "junior ministers." During the government headed by Paul Martin from 2003–2006, junior ministers were styled "ministers of state." When Prime Minister Harper was appointed on 6 February 2006, ministers of state were eliminated in order to create a cabinet of "full equals."

Moreover, the Cabinet is not even mentioned in the *Constitution Act, 1867* and has no formal constitutional status.[20]

The Privy Council continues to exist today. Since appointments to the Privy Council are for life, the Privy Council includes not only current but also all former members of the Cabinet. The Privy Council also includes the chief justice of the Supreme Court, a number of provincial premiers, retired governors general, and many persons who have been made Privy Councillors in recognition of their achievements or contributions to public service. On occasion, the leader of the Opposition in the House of Commons has been appointed to the Privy Council. Appointments to the Privy Council are made by the governor general on the advice of the prime minister. There are more than a hundred members of the Privy Council, and its members represent widely differing political viewpoints and affiliations. Over the past fifty years, the full Privy Council has met only on rare occasions, such as on April 17, 1982, when Queen Elizabeth II signed the *Canada Act 1982* into law. The members of the Privy Council have the right to use the titles "Honourable" and "Privy Councillor" for life, while a prime minister is referred to as "Right Honourable" for life.

While membership in the Queen's Privy Council for Canada is a ceremonial honour, the Council still retains a significant formal legal role in the functioning of government. Section 12 of the *Constitution Act, 1867* states that the powers exercised in the former British colonies by the Governor in Council are to be exercised by the governor general acting "with the Advice or with the Advice and Consent of or in conjunction with the Queen's Privy Council for Canada." Section 13 states that references in the *Constitution Act, 1867* to the Governor General in Council shall be construed as referring to the governor general "acting by and with the Advice of the Queen's Privy Council for Canada." There are a number of significant powers in the *Constitution Act, 1867* that are conferred on the Governor General in Council—as opposed to the governor general alone—including the power to appoint the lieutenant governors of the provinces and the power to "disallow" provincial laws within two years of their enactment.[21] Further, ordinary statutes often confer delegated powers on the Governor in Council and, in strict law,

---

However, Mr. Harper later added ministers of state to his ministry, reviving the practice of appointing junior ministers outside of the Cabinet.

20 A number of statutes, however, do make reference to ministers and even to the prime minister: see, for example, the *Salaries Act*, R.S.C. 1985, c. S-3, s. 4.

21 See the *Constitution Act, 1867*, ss. 58 and 90. See discussion of the disallowance power, below, at Section E(2).

these powers are exercisable by the governor general on the advice of the Queen's Privy Council for Canada.

As a practical matter, however, the legal powers of the Privy Council are exercised by members of the Cabinet, and references to the Governor in Council actually refer to the governor general acting by and with the advice of the Cabinet. The Cabinet is in effect a committee of the Privy Council, made up of those members of the Privy Council who are part of the government and entitled to participate in the formulation of government policy. Decisions of the Governor in Council are taken by members of the Cabinet, acting in their capacity as members of the Privy Council, who sign an order in council and submit it to the governor general for his or her approval.

Since the 1850s, the governor general has not actually attended or participated in meetings of the Cabinet. In this sense, the phrase "Governor in Council," which suggests an actual meeting between the governor general and the Privy Council, is misleading. What actually happens is that the Cabinet—rather than the entire Council—meets and then renders its advice to the governor general. In formal legal terms, therefore, the Cabinet merely renders advice to the governor general. However, under the conventions of responsible government, the governor general is obliged to approve all recommendations of the Cabinet.

5) The Prime Minister and the Formation of the Cabinet

The key actor in the formation of the Cabinet is not the governor general but the prime minister. Like the Cabinet itself, the office of prime minister is not mentioned in the *Constitution Act, 1867* and is solely a creature of convention. The functions of the prime minister include forming a government and choosing and presiding over the Cabinet. The prime minister recommends to the governor general the persons who are to be appointed to or dismissed from the Cabinet, and, under the principle of responsible government, the governor general is obliged to act on the prime minister's advice. The prime minister is also personally responsible for tendering advice to the governor general as to when Parliament should be dissolved for an election, and when an elected Parliament should be summoned into session. The governor general does not have any discretion in the choice of prime minister and is obliged to call on the leader of a party that controls a majority in the House of Commons.

Since members of the Cabinet hold office on the basis of the recommendation of the prime minister, the resignation of the prime minister automatically triggers the resignation of the members of the Cabinet as well. The resignation of an individual Cabinet minister, however, does not affect the status or tenure of any other minister. Technically, a minister who resigns is removed when the prime minister advises the governor general to dismiss the minister from the Cabinet.

Section 11 of the *Constitution Act, 1867* does not impose any restrictions on who is eligible to be appointed to the Privy Council. However, by a firmly established constitutional convention, members of the Cabinet must have seats in either the House of Commons or the Senate.[22] A Cabinet minister and even the prime minister may for a brief period not have a seat in either House, but must obtain one within a reasonable time. For example, in June 1984, John Turner assumed the office of prime minister even though he did not have a seat in the House of Commons; since he was obliged to obtain a seat within a short period of time, either through a by-election or a general election, he called a general election in early July 1984. Although Turner won a seat personally in the general election held in September of that year, his party was defeated by the Progressive Conservative Party under Brian Mulroney. Turner was therefore forced to resign as prime minister and Mulroney was appointed to the position.

On occasion, the leader of the party that wins the most seats in a general election is defeated personally in his or her own riding. In these circumstances, the leader may be sworn in as prime minister, but is required to seek a seat in the House of Commons through a by-election as soon as possible. This is what happened in 1985 in the province of Quebec, when Robert Bourassa was immediately sworn in as premier even though he was defeated in his own riding in the general election. A Liberal member of the National Assembly who occupied a "safe seat" resigned, thereby making way for a by-election, which Bourassa won.[23] In this regard, the position of prime minister, or provincial premier, is different from that of any other Cabinet minister. A Cabinet minister who is defeated in a general election is simply not appointed to Cabinet. This option is not available in the case of the prime minister, since all other members of the Cabinet hold office through him or her. The

22 Although unusual and controversial, it is not unprecedented for the prime minister to appoint ministers to the Senate in order to have them take up major Cabinet portfolios. This was done, for example, in 1979 when Prime Minister Joe Clark appointed Jacques Flynn as Justice Minister and Robert de Cotret as Minister of Industry, Trade and Commerce. In 2006, Prime Minister Stephen Harper appointed Michael Fortier to the Senate to serve as Minister of Public Works. Fortier resigned his seat to seek election to the House of Commons in the fortieth general election, but was defeated.

23 Note that the conventions of responsible government are identical at the provincial and the federal levels.

prime minister is therefore required to obtain a seat in the House of Commons, or the provincial legislature, within a reasonable period of time in order for the entire Cabinet to continue in office.

6) Responsible Government

a) Governor's Duty to Follow Advice

By firmly established constitutional convention, the governor general must act on the advice of a prime minister and Cabinet that has the support of a majority in the House of Commons. The binding nature of this obligation is reflected in the fact that the last occasion on which a governor general refused to follow the advice of the prime minister was in 1926. In this way, the considerable legal powers of the Crown are actually exercised by the prime minister and the Cabinet. The governor general's role in government today is almost entirely ceremonial and symbolic. The governor general is the formal head of the Canadian state, but the prime minister is the chief executive officer of the government.[24] The question arises of whether and in what circumstances a governor general would be entitled to refuse to accept the advice of the prime minister. Certain constitutional scholars have argued that the governor general may possess a "reserve" power, which is defined as the right to take a decision based on his or her own personal discretion, as opposed to on the advice of the prime minister and Cabinet.[25]

b) Appointment of the Prime Minister

One situation that has often been discussed in this regard is the act of appointing a prime minister following an election. Technically, the appointment of the prime minister is the one act of the governor general that is not performed on the basis of advice, since, until a prime minister has been appointed, there is no one to offer advice.[26] However, in the vast majority of cases, the governor general's choice is clear: the leader of the party that controls a majority of seats in the elected House is entitled to be appointed as prime minister. A single party has won a

---

24 Many countries divide the functions of head of state and chief executive of the government. In the United States, however, the president assumes both functions.

25 For a discussion of the conflicting views of the academic commentators, see A. Heard, *Canadian Constitutional Conventions: The Marriage of Law and Politics*, 2d ed. (Don Mills, ON: Oxford University Press, 2014) at 40–47.

26 Scholarly authorities generally agree that the governor general is not bound to follow the advice of a prime minister who has been defeated in an election or in the House of Commons as to who should be selected as his or her successor, although such advice is sometimes sought or offered.

majority of seats in the House of Commons in thirty-one of the forty-two general elections that have been held since Confederation, and the governor general has immediately and automatically called on the leader of the victorious party to form a government.[27]

The only situation in which a governor general might conceivably have to exercise independent judgment in the selection of a prime minister would be in a case where it was not clear which party has the support of a majority in the House of Commons. Even in this situation, however, it is likely that negotiations among the various party leaders would lead to the choice of prime minister being made clear. As one leading commentator has put it, the guiding principle which must govern in such situations is that "there should be political decisions, politically arrived at."[28] An important Canadian precedent in this regard is the political negotiations that followed the 1985 Ontario provincial election in which the governing Conservative Party under Frank Miller won fifty-two seats, compared with forty-eight for the Liberal Party under David Peterson, and twenty-five for the New Democratic Party (NDP) under Bob Rae. The three parties negotiated for a number of weeks, resulting in Peterson and Rae signing an accord, which provided that the NDP would support the Liberals on any vote of confidence on the basis that certain legislative and policy initiatives would be undertaken during the first two years of Peterson's government. Peterson, in turn, promised not to seek a dissolution of the legislature during this two-year period. The signing of the accord clearly established Peterson as having the ability to control a majority in the legislature. Following the defeat of Miller's government on a vote of confidence in the legislature,[29] the lieutenant governor was accordingly obligated to

---

27 When an opposition party has obtained a majority of seats in a general election, the incumbent prime minister is expected to offer his or her resignation immediately. However, when the winning party was formerly in opposition, it is generally not in a position to assume office immediately; therefore, the incumbent remains as prime minister during the transition period, typically one week to three weeks. For example, following the defeat of the government led by Paul Martin on 23 January 2006, Mr. Martin remained in office for approximately two weeks until the new government led by Stephen Harper was sworn in on 6 February 2006.

28 R. Brazier, *Constitutional Practice: The Foundations of British Government*, 3d ed. (Oxford: Oxford University Press, 1999) at 33–37, discussing relevant British precedents.

29 Even though Peterson and Rae signed the accord in early June, Miller did not resign until his government was defeated in the legislature. Based on this precedent, it would appear that, where no single party obtains a majority of seats, an incumbent premier is entitled to meet the legislature and seek the confidence of the House in a timely fashion, even in circumstances where it is very likely

call on Peterson to form a government. The lieutenant governor's obligation in this regard was not dependent on whether Miller concurred in the appointment of Peterson, since Miller had lost the confidence of the Assembly and the lieutenant governor was accordingly no longer bound to follow his advice. In any event, Miller advised the lieutenant governor to call on Peterson, thereby obviating any difficulty that might have arisen.

Some constitutional commentators have suggested that the governor general would be called on to exercise personal discretion in appointing a prime minister if the incumbent were to die or to resign suddenly while in office. This situation arose a few times before 1896, when the governor general was called on to select a replacement prime minister after the death or retirement of the existing office holder.[30] However, there has not been a single instance since 1896 where the resignation of a Canadian prime minister has caused the governor general to exercise discretion in choosing a successor. The death or resignation of a prime minister, while technically resulting in the dismissal of an entire government, has not affected the ability of the existing government party to control a majority in the House. In the event of the sudden resignation of the prime minister, the governing party simply selects a new leader (whether on a permanent or an interim basis),[31] and the governor general is obliged to appoint the person so selected by the party as the prime minister. Therefore, in the contemporary context, even the death or sudden resignation of a prime minister should not give rise to the necessity of the governor general to exercise any independent discretion in the choice of a successor.

---

that the government will be defeated. This conclusion is also supported by the 1923 precedent in Great Britain where Conservative Prime Minister Baldwin remained in office and met the new Parliament, following an election in which no single party secured an absolute majority of seats, but where the opposition parties appeared certain to defeat the government. A motion of non-confidence was passed and Baldwin resigned, whereupon the king called on the leader of the opposition to form a government.

30 For a discussion, see P.W. Hogg, *Constitutional Law of Canada*, loose-leaf (Toronto: Carswell, 2007) at 9.7(b). See also A.M. Dodek, "Rediscovering Constitutional Law: Succession upon the Death of the Prime Minister" (2000) 49 U.N.B.L.J. 33.

31 Note that the constitutions of the established political parties all provide a mechanism for the appointment of an interim leader in the event of the untimely death or sudden resignation of the incumbent leader. See, for example, the *Conservative Party of Canada Constitution*, as amended on March 19, 2005, ss. 10.7–10.8; and the *Constitution of the Liberal Party of Canada*, as adopted and amended by the 2006 Biennial Convention and further amended at the Biennial Convention in 2009, s. 54.

As a practical matter, it is difficult to conceive of circumstances in which the governor general would be obliged to exercise independent discretion in the selection of a prime minister. In most cases, the electorate will have made the Crown's choice clear through the election of a majority government. In minority government situations, it can be expected that the political leaders will have bargained among themselves to establish which party is in a position to control a majority in the House. In the unlikely event that such political bargaining does not produce a clear result, the appropriate course would be for the governor general to meet separately with the leaders of each party in the order of their seat strengths in the House of Commons, to ascertain which of them is in the best position to form a government with a reasonable prospect of maintaining an administration in office.[32]

c) Defeat of a Government

Once a prime minister has been appointed, the governor general must follow his or her advice as long as the government enjoys the confidence of the House of Commons. This necessarily implies that the obligation to follow advice persists only as long as the government enjoys the confidence of the House. If a prime minister refused to resign or to seek a dissolution of the House after a defeat on a motion of confidence, the governor general would be entitled to call on someone else to form a government or to dissolve the House on his or her own motion. Conversely, if the prime minister sought to force an election after a defeat in the House, the governor general would not necessarily be obliged to follow the advice. If it was clear that there was another leader that could command a majority in the House, the governor general would be entitled to call on that person to form a government. It is also generally thought that, if a government continues in office as a minority administration after an inconclusive general election obtained by its prime minister and is subsequently defeated in the House of Commons, such a prime minister is not entitled to a second dissolution and must resign.[33]

In December 1979, after the defeat of Prime Minister Joe Clark's minority government on a budget measure, Governor General Ed

32 See Brazier, above note 28 at 41–44.

33 *Ibid.* at 47. Brazier describes the request for a second dissolution as improper on grounds that it is "an attempt to get a recount of the electorate's first decision." On the other hand, when a prime minister who has not previously obtained a dissolution is defeated in the House of Commons and requests a dissolution for the first time, the request would generally be granted unless it were clear that there was another political leader in a position to command a stable majority in the House of Commons.

Schreyer made Clark wait two hours before agreeing to his request for a dissolution. Schreyer's action has been justified by some commentators on the basis that the governor general had to consider whether an opposition leader was able to form a government.[34] However, it is unclear why Schreyer did not agree to Clark's request for a dissolution immediately. The party standings were such that the largest opposition party, the Liberals, were clearly not able to control a majority in the House.[35] Nor did Schreyer use the two-hour period to consult with the leader of the opposition, Pierre Trudeau, about his willingness or ability to form a government. Given these circumstances, the only constitutionally appropriate option open to the governor general was to grant Clark's request for a dissolution and a general election, despite the fact that the previous general election had been held just six months earlier, in May 1979.[36]

In May 2005, the notion of what constitutes an issue of confidence became a matter of controversy. The House of Commons passed a motion requesting a standing committee to amend its report to call for the government to resign.[37] The explicit language of the motion, which passed by three votes, prompted some observers to claim that it was a vote of non-confidence.[38] However, rather than resign or call an election immediately, Prime Minister Paul Martin argued that the matter was merely procedural and that the government would not resign pending a formal vote of confidence to be held the following week. Although the opposition parties repeatedly collaborated to control Parliament by forcing early adjournments in the interim, Martin refused to step down. On an ensuing vote to pass the budget, nine days after the ori-

---

34 See R.J. Jackson and D. Jackson, *Politics in Canada: Culture, Institutions, Behaviour and Public Policy*, 2d ed. (Scarborough: Prentice Hall Canada, 1990) at 196.

35 The Progressive Conservatives held 136 seats in a 282-seat House, with the Liberals holding 114, the NDP 26, and other parties 6.

36 Note that the previous dissolution had been requested by Pierre Trudeau, rather than Joe Clark and, therefore, Clark's request for a dissolution in December 1979 was his first. Even if Clark had been requesting a second dissolution, it is arguable that it would have been appropriate for the governor general to grant the request, given the fact that the opposition liberals under Trudeau were not in a position to control a majority in the House, making another election unavoidable.

37 More precisely, the motion recommended that a report of the Standing Committee on Public Accounts be "recommitted to the [Committee] with instruction that it amend the same so as to recommend that the government resign because of its failure to address the deficiencies in governance of the public service addressed in the report."

38 See A. Heard, "The Confidence Convention and the May 2005 Vote on the Public Accounts Committee Report," online: www.sfu.ca/~aheard/conventions.html.

ginal motion, the government prevailed by one vote,[39] having persuaded one member of the opposition Conservatives to cross the floor with the offer of a Cabinet position. Despite some outcry from commentators,[40] it appears from these events that when the House's confidence in the government is called into question, the government will have the opportunity to hold a clear confidence vote in a timely fashion.

After the defeat of a government on a clearly worded motion of confidence in the House, the existing government must resign, or Parliament must be dissolved, and an election called. Where an election is called, the current government continues to hold office during the campaign, even though it has lost the confidence of the House. However, a government that continues to hold office after a defeat in the House is generally regarded as having a caretaker role only and is precluded from undertaking any significant policy initiatives or making patronage appointments.[41] Some commentators have even suggested that this caretaker role is imposed on all governments during an election campaign, even when the incumbent government has not been defeated in the House. It has been argued that governments, for this reason, usually make final political appointments before the calling of an election, on the assumption that such appointments ought not to be made once the actual campaign has commenced.[42]

---

39 The Speaker of the House voted in support of the government when the House deadlocked at 153–153.

40 See, for example, M. Bliss, "Canada's House of Ill Repute" *National Post* (14 May 2004) A1, where he describes Martin's behaviour as "thumbing his nose at the conventions of responsible government."

41 In 1896, following its defeat in a general election, the incumbent Conservative government attempted to make a number of appointments to the Senate and the judiciary before the swearing in of the new government under Wilfrid Laurier. The governor general refused to make the appointments on the basis that the government no longer enjoyed the confidence of the House. The governor general's refusal was undoubtedly correct, even though the new Parliament had not yet met after the election and, therefore, technically, the government had not been defeated in the House. This precedent would presumably apply in cases where a government had been defeated in the House before the commencement of an election campaign.

42 It is clearly established that governments which have been defeated in the House should not make major political appointments once an election is underway. For example, following the defeat of the Liberal government led by Paul Martin on a confidence motion in late November 2005, the government announced that it would not fill a Supreme Court of Canada vacancy created by the retirement of Justice Jack Major until after the election. (The Liberals were defeated in the election and the Conservatives formed the government, and subsequently appointed Justice Marshall Rothstein to fill the vacancy.) In contrast, Justice Russell Brown was appointed by Conservative Prime Min-

This issue arose during the 1993 federal election campaign when the Progressive Conservative government under Prime Minister Kim Campbell signed contracts providing for the redevelopment of Pearson International Airport in Toronto by a private consortium. Some commentators argued that such significant contracts should not have been entered into by a government in the middle of an election, even though the Conservatives continued to hold a majority in the House of Commons at the time of dissolution.[43] On the other hand, on the same day that the government signed the Toronto airport contracts, it also entered into a multi-million–dollar contract providing for the construction of the fixed-link Confederation Bridge between Prince Edward Island and New Brunswick. There was never any suggestion that the signing of this contract was inappropriate, even though it was entered into during an election campaign.

The view of the Privy Council Office, which heads the federal public service, is that the caretaker convention applies regardless of whether dissolution is because of the loss of confidence vote, by request of the prime minister, or by operation of a fixed election date statute. This view is made public in its *Guidelines on the Conduct of Ministers, Ministers of State, Exempt Staff and Public Servants During an Election*. These guidelines were themselves subject to some controversy during the 2015 general election because of a pre-campaign revision that referred to the "compelling reasons" for a government to continue time-sensitive international treaty negotiations during the caretaker period.[44] This foreshadowing was followed by Canada's signing of the Trans-Pacific Partnership trade deal during the campaign. Consistent with the guidelines, the more difficult to reverse step of ratification of

---

ister Stephen Harper immediately before the dissolution for the 2015 general election campaign. Also relevant is the fact that in June 1984, the government of John Turner made a large number of patronage appointments just before calling an election, the assumption being that it would be inappropriate to make the appointments once the campaign was underway. These appointments proved politically controversial during the campaign, however, leading to the well-known confrontation between Turner and Mulroney during the televised leaders' debate, in which Turner claimed that he had had "no choice" other than to make the appointments.

43 The views of the constitutional commentators were explored in hearings held by a Senate committee on legislation tabled by the government that cancelled the contracts. See, for example, *Proceedings of the Standing Senate Committee on Legal and Constitutional Affairs* (4 July 1994) No. 10.

44 Privy Council Office, "Guidelines on Conduct of Ministers, Ministers of State, Exempt Staff and Public Servants During an Election" (August 2015), online: www.pco-bcp.gc.ca/index.asp?lang=eng&page=convention&doc=convention-eng.htm.

the treaty was left for the future.[45] It would appear that the convention is therefore applicable even in the context of a voluntary dissolution.

d) The King–Byng Incident

Are there any conceivable circumstances in which the governor general is entitled to refuse to follow the advice of a prime minister who still enjoys the confidence of the House? The so-called King–Byng incident in 1926 is sometimes cited as an instance where the prime minister's advice was refused, although the propriety of the refusal remains controversial to this day. In 1925, the government of Prime Minister Mackenzie King had remained in office, even though it had won fewer seats than the Conservatives under Arthur Meighen in that year's general election. The following year, it became clear that King's government would be defeated on a confidence motion. Before the confidence vote, King requested the governor general, Lord Byng, to dissolve Parliament and call an election. Byng refused, instead calling on Meighen to form a government. This response sparked an outcry, with many commentators condemning Byng's actions as an arbitrary intrusion of monarchical power into the democratic process.[46] Meighen's government was defeated in the House shortly thereafter, and King won the subsequent election, primarily due to a campaign against the "undemocratic" actions of the governor general.[47]

However, Lord Byng's decision did not violate the rule that the governor general must follow the advice of a prime minister who enjoys the confidence of the House. At the time that King sought dissolution from Byng, it was clear that the government was about to be defeated in the House. As a practical matter, King had already ceased to enjoy the

45 Foreign Affairs, Trade and Development Canada, News Release, "Canada Concludes Free Trade Agreement with Trans-Pacific Partners" (5 October 2015), online: Foreign Affairs, Trade and Development Canada www.sice.oas.org/TPD/TPP/Negotiations/TTP_Negotiations_concluded_e.pdf.

46 For a discussion, see R. Graham, ed., *The King–Byng Affair 1926: A Question of Responsible Government* (Toronto: Copp Clark, 1967); E.A. Forsey, *The Royal Power of Dissolution of Parliament in the British Commonwealth* (Toronto: Oxford University Press, 1943).

47 Meighen's ability to form a government was hampered by the legal requirement in force at the time that all ministers who headed departments had to vacate their seats and seek re-election in a by-election. Meighen tried to get around this requirement by forming a "temporary ministry" of ministers without portfolios, thereby avoiding the necessity for them to resign and seek re-election. However, Meighen's gambit led to a motion of non-confidence, which passed by one vote, forcing the resignation of his government and an election. The requirement that ministers who assume portfolios must resign and seek re-election was abolished in 1931.

confidence of the House. As discussed above, a prime minister who has been defeated in the House on a confidence vote is not entitled to require the governor general to accept his or her advice. A prime minister should not be allowed to circumvent this rule by submitting a request to the governor general just before a confidence vote and then crying foul in the event that the request is refused. It is also significant that King was requesting a dissolution for a second time, having requested the dissolution that led to the 1925 general election. As suggested above, it is generally the case that a prime minister who has already received one dissolution is not entitled to receive a second dissolution on his or her defeat in the House—essentially King's position in June 1926.

Of course, it should not be supposed that Lord Byng had a free hand in determining whether to call an election, as opposed to asking an opposition leader to form a government. The governor general's role is limited to determining whether there is an individual who is in a position to control a majority in the House of Commons. If there is an individual in such a position, in our view, the governor general is obliged to call on that person to attempt to form a government.

e) Prorogation

The governor general has the power to prorogue Parliament, which ends the parliamentary session. Any legislation that has not completed the legislative process automatically dies, and all parliamentary committee activity ceases. In order for bills to become law in a new session, they must be reintroduced or reinstated, and committees must be formally revived.

In most cases, prorogation is routine and uncontroversial. Where the prime minister enjoys the confidence of the House, the governor general must accept a request to prorogue Parliament. Prorogation has been described by one commentator as "part of the normal conduct of parliamentary business."[48] In the course of Canadian history, no governor general has ever refused the prime minister's advice to prorogue Parliament. However, as the prorogation of December 2008 illustrates, there may be situations in which it is unclear whether the government enjoys the confidence of the House. In this situation, the governor general has a discretion over whether to accede to the prime minister's request. As suggested above, this discretion should be exercised in a manner that promotes resolution of the confidence issue among democratically accountable representatives and that minimizes

48 See Hogg, above note 30 at s. 9.7(d.1).

the degree of involvement of the governor general in political decision making.

On 14 October 2008, Prime Minister Stephen Harper was re-elected with a minority government. Parliament was called into session on 18 November 2008. The Speech from the Throne was delivered on 19 November and was approved on 27 November. However, on that same day, Finance Minister Jim Flaherty delivered a fiscal and economic update, which was controversial for at least two reasons. First, it lacked fiscal stimulus measures to stimulate economic growth in a period of economic recession, something that the opposition parties had advocated. Second, the update contained a proposal to eliminate existing subsidies to political parties based on the number of votes received in the most recent general election.[49] On 1 December 2008, the leaders of the three opposition parties (the Liberals, NDP, and Bloc Québécois) announced that they had lost confidence in the Harper government and that they would introduce a non-confidence motion the following week, on an upcoming opposition day. The leaders of the Liberal and NDP parties also announced that they had reached an agreement on the terms for forming a coalition government to be led by then Liberal leader Stéphane Dion. The Liberal/NDP coalition would continue in effect until 30 June 2011, and BQ leader Gilles Duceppe promised to refrain from voting no-confidence in the coalition government before 30 June 2010.

On 4 December 2008, faced with an imminent non-confidence motion, Prime Minister Harper asked the governor general to prorogue Parliament until 26 January 2009. He also indicated that the government would introduce a new budget on 27 January, which would be a matter of confidence. That December day, Governor General Michaëlle Jean met with Harper for more than two hours at Rideau Hall and she also met separately with her legal adviser, constitutional scholar Professor Peter Hogg. Following the meeting, Harper announced that the governor general had accepted his advice and that Parliament was prorogued until 26 January 2009.

Given the time it took for the governor general to reach her decision, and the fact that she consulted with her own legal adviser, it is apparent that she believed that she had an independent discretion over whether to accept Harper's advice. Although some scholars have

---

49 This proposal was withdrawn prior to the announcement of the opposition coalition on 1 December 2009, but was part of the impetus for the formation of the coalition of opposition leaders.

offered only tentative views,[50] most agree that the governor general did have a discretion.[51] As discussed above, the governor general is not obliged to follow the advice of a prime minister who is about to lose a vote of non-confidence. Otherwise, the prime minister could simply evade confidence motions by advising the governor general to prorogue Parliament continuously, for a period of up to one year.[52] Furthermore, the proposition that the governor general had a discretion over whether to prorogue Parliament is consistent with the King–Byng precedent reviewed above. Although in that case the governor general's decision to call on Arthur Meighen to form a government was controversial, it is generally agreed that Lord Byng had the right to independently assess the prime minister's request to dissolve Parliament given the imminent defeat of the government.[53] As of 4 December 2008, the opposition coalition was about to introduce a non-confidence motion that would have passed just four days later. Governor General Michaëlle Jean was therefore entitled to make an independent assessment of whether to prorogue Parliament.

The more controversial question is whether the governor general exercised her discretion correctly. In hindsight, prorogation appears to have been a wise decision. By the time Parliament reconvened on 26 January 2009, Dion had been replaced by Michael Ignatieff. On 27 January, the Conservative government introduced a new budget as promised, containing measures to stimulate the economy. The following day, Mr. Ignatieff announced that the Liberals would support the

---

50 J. Leclair & J-F. Gaudreault-Desbiens, "Of Representation, Democracy and Legal Principles: Thinking about the *Impensé*" in P. Russell & L. Sossin, *Parliamentary Democracy in Crisis* (Toronto: University of Toronto Press, 2009) at 105–20.

51 See P.W. Hogg, "Prorogation and the Power of the Governor General" (2009) 27 N.J.C.L. 193 at 199; C.E.S. Franks, "To Prorogue or Not to Prorogue: Did the Governor General Make the Right Decision?" in Russell & Sossin, *ibid.* at 33 and 46; A. Heard, "The Governor General's Suspension of Parliament: Duty Done or a Perilous Precedent?" in Russell & Sossin, *ibid.* at 55; L. Weinrib, "Prime Minister Harper's Parliamentary 'Time Out': A Constitutional Revolution in the Making?" in Russell & Sossin, *ibid.* at 65–66; B. Slattery, "Why the Governor General Matters" in Russell & Sossin, *ibid.* at 89; D.R. Cameron, "Ultimately, the System Worked" in Russell & Sossin, *ibid.* at 191. See also: A.M. Dodek, "Judicial Independence as a Public Policy Instrument" CLPE Research Paper No. 10/2009 at 27, available online: http://ssrn.com/abstract=1338285, accessed 11 April 2016.

52 Under s. 5 of the *Constitution Act, 1982* there must be a session of Parliament at least once every twelve months.

53 See Hogg, "Prorogation and the Power of the Governor General," above note 51 at 198; Franks, above note 51 at 36.

budget, and the coalition formally disbanded. However, the wisdom of the governor general's decision must be examined based on the circumstances that existed at the time, and without the benefit of hindsight. The course of events could not have been predicted (at least not perfectly) by the governor general on 4 December 2008.

In our view, the governor general's decision to prorogue Parliament was appropriate based on the circumstances at the time. By 4 December 2008, Mr. Harper had already declared that he did not recognize the coalition government as legitimate. It is almost certain that he would not have stepped aside willingly to allow Mr. Dion to form a government and that he would have requested dissolution and a general election. The governor general would then have been faced with two choices: dissolve Parliament and call an election or appoint Mr. Dion as prime minister and ask him to form a government. However, Prime Minister Harper had just sought a dissolution three months previously and had been re-elected with a minority government. As discussed above, a prime minister is not generally entitled to seek successive dissolutions within such a short period. Certainly, putting the country through another election would have been "unthinkable."[54] Appointing Mr. Dion would also have been highly problematic. It is fair to say that as of 4 December 2008, the stability of the coalition was uncertain. Mr. Dion was only an interim leader of the Liberal Party and the coalition was formed at least in part in response to outrage over funding policies for political parties that had since been abandoned. Moreover, the Liberal party had never formed an alliance with the NDP in periods of minority government and the BQ had committed only to refrain from voting no-confidence in the coalition for a defined period.[55]

On the other hand, the request to prorogue Parliament was time-limited and tied to a promise by the Harper government to introduce a new budget that would test the confidence of the government. Granting the request only sacrificed seven days of scheduled sitting time, since the House had already been scheduled to adjourn between 12 December 2008 and 26 January 2009 for the holidays. Furthermore, the Harper government had promised to and did consult widely with the opposition in the interim on stimulus measures that had been omitted from the economic update—one of the stated reasons for the formation of the opposition coalition in the first place. Finally, prorogation would provide time for the viability of the opposition coalition to be tested, and for it to either strengthen (as it may have) or fracture (as it did). In

54 See Hogg, above note 30 at s. 9.7(d.1).

55 See Hogg, *ibid.*; and Hogg, "Prorogation and the Power of the Governor General," above note 51 at 199–201.

our view, therefore, the decision to grant the prime minister's request to prorogue Parliament in December 2008 was the preferable course. It enabled the issue of confidence to be resolved principally among the political actors themselves.[56]

On 30 December 2009, Prime Minister Harper advised the governor general to prorogue Parliament yet again, this time until 3 March 2010. The governor general accepted the advice, putting an end to the parliamentary session that had commenced less than a year earlier. The request for prorogation came after the Conservative government had refused to provide certain documents to a parliamentary committee inquiring into the handover of prisoners in Afghanistan. The prorogation was seen by critics to be motivated by a desire to put an end to the committee's work.[57] Furthermore, at the time of the request, there were still thirty-six government bills in Parliament, including measures that formed a key part of the government's legislative objectives. Prime Minister Harper was highly criticized for the decision and there were numerous public protests opposing prorogation across the country and internationally. However, it is noteworthy that the criticism mainly focused on the prime minister. Whatever the merits of his advice to prorogue, it seems clear that the governor general had no choice but to accept it. Unlike in 2008, the prime minister enjoyed the confidence of the House and there was no scheduled vote of non-confidence.[58]

Harper's use of the prorogation power has led to various calls for reform from academics and politicians alike. A modest reform, for example, would subject the prorogation power to a super-majority vote in the House of Commons.[59] However, the *Constitution Act, 1982* requires that an amendment in relation to "the office of the Queen [or] the Governor General" be subject to the unanimous consent of the provinces. Similarly, in the *Senate Reference*, the Supreme Court interpreted the constitutional amendment procedure as requiring that changes to Can-

---

56 It is true that the governor general's decision to prorogue Parliament did affect political outcomes. Had Mr. Dion been appointed, for instance, it may well be that the coalition government would have strengthened. However, refusing the prime minister's request to prorogue—and either granting yet another request to dissolve Parliament or directly appointing a new coalition government—would have involved the governor general far more directly in political decision making.

57 See, for example, "Harper Goes Prorogue" *The Economist* (7 January 2010).

58 See Hogg, "Prorogation and the Power of the Governor General," above note 51 at 22.

59 P. Aucoin, M.D. Jarvis, & L. Turnbull, *Democratizing the Constitution: Reforming Responsible Government* (Toronto: Emond Montgomery, 2011) at 224.

ada's "constitutional architecture" be subject to provincial agreement.[60] Therefore, prorogation may be another example of how Canada's very high threshold for constitutional amendments has calcified our government structure.

f) Refusal to Accept Unconstitutional Advice?

It has been suggested that it may be appropriate for a governor general to refuse to follow the advice of a prime minister if the government were pursuing illegal or unconstitutional actions, even though the prime minister enjoyed the confidence of the House. In 1982, for example, Governor General Schreyer revealed that he might have considered forcing an election over the government's proposals to patriate the constitution without the consent of the provinces. Schreyer indicated that, if Prime Minister Trudeau had been unable to secure the consent of the provinces and had insisted on proceeding unilaterally with a request for amendment by the Westminster Parliament, "the only way out . . . would have been to cause an election to be held and the Canadian people asked to decide."[61] In our view, such action by Schreyer would have been clearly inappropriate.

The governor general was proposing to dismiss a government that had been elected with a strong majority less than two years previously on grounds that the government appeared to be violating a constitutional convention relating to provincial consent. Yet the government's constitutional proposals had been approved by large majorities in both the Senate and the House of Commons. Nor was there any question of the government's actions being illegal, since the Supreme Court had ruled in September 1981 that unilateral patriation by the British Parliament at the request of the Canadian Parliament would have been constitutionally valid.[62] The government's request might have been in breach of a constitutional convention—assuming that the provinces had failed to come to an agreement with the federal government at the November 1981 conference—but conventions are rules of political conduct and are binding only in the political sphere. Moreover, the governor general would have been acting entirely on his own initiative, as opposed to responding to a request from the prime minister. In addition, the governor general's consent was not legally required for the amendment, since the patriation request took the form of a resolution passed by the House of Commons and the Senate, as opposed to a statute or an order in council. Furthermore, there is no Canadian precedent for a governor

---

60 *Reference re Senate Reform*, [2014] 1 S.C.R. 704 at para. 60 [*Senate Reference*].

61 See Heard, above note 51 at 33.

62 These events are discussed in more detail in Chapter 5.

general dismissing a government for breach of a constitutional convention. Accordingly, the governor general was proposing to insert himself into the middle of an inherently political dispute. This intrusion would have politicized the office and made him the object of partisan attack by the prime minister and other political leaders. In our view, the governor general would have clearly overstepped his role had he purported to insert himself in this manner.

Even in situations where the government is proposing to take actions that are unconstitutional or illegal, which was not the case in the patriation amendments, it is difficult to see how the governor general should or could take an independent and active role. The judiciary is the appropriate institution to deal with illegal or unconstitutional actions by government, not the governor general. Although judges are not elected, under the Canadian constitution, they are charged with the responsibility to rule on the constitutionality of government action, for good reason. Judges have the necessary skills, expertise, and experience to rule on questions of constitutional validity. Governors general, in contrast, are not equipped to determine the constitutional validity of government actions, and their judgments in this regard would rightly be criticized as political rather than legal.[63] Therefore, if a governor general or a lieutenant governor were to insert him or herself into such a process, attention would be deflected away from the government's allegedly improper activities and focused instead on the improper intervention of the governor. As a general rule, the governor general should continue to act on the advice of the prime minister, assuming that he or she continues to enjoy the confidence of the House and should leave issues of legality or constitutionality to be adjudicated before the courts.

There may be one exception to this rule arising where a government persists with a course of action that has been declared unconstitutional or illegal by the courts. In the event that the government sought the governor general's participation in a decision that had previously been declared unconstitutional, it may be appropriate for the governor general to refuse to participate. Such a scenario may seem wholly unrealistic, since governments in Canada typically comply with declarations or rulings by the courts. However, in the fall of 1996, the Quebec government declared that it did not recognize the jurisdiction of Canadian courts to pass judgment on the validity of its own unilateral declaration of independence after a referendum on sovereignty. The Quebec govern-

63 See the convincing argument to this effect in H.V. Evatt, *The King and His Dominion Governors*, 2d ed. (Melbourne: Cheshire, 1967) cc. 19 & 20. See also Hogg, above note 30 at 9.7(a).

ment indicated that it would carry on with its course of conduct and ignore any court rulings that declared its conduct illegal. In this kind of exceptional situation—in which a government would be attempting to overthrow the existing constitution and the rule of law—the provincial lieutenant governor could not be expected to participate in the illegality. This exception is narrowly framed, arising from a deliberate refusal by government to abide by the rule of law and an attempt to enlist the lieutenant governor's participation in lawless conduct. It would not authorize the lieutenant governor to go further and undertake initiatives of his or her own, such as dissolving the legislature and calling an election. Undertaking such an initiative on his or her own accord would undoubtedly make the lieutenant governor the central figure in the political controversy, thereby shifting the attention from the substantive issue.

It is interesting to note in this regard that a former lieutenant governor of Quebec, Jean-Louis Roux, suggested at the time of his appointment in 1996 that he might be called on to exercise his powers to defend the validity of the Canadian constitution in the event that the Quebec government attempted to secede from Canada illegally.[64] The analysis offered here suggests that, while the lieutenant governor may indeed have a role to play in this situation, it is a limited and subsidiary one. Lieutenant governors and governors general should always be guided by the principle that their very broad legal powers must be exercised in accordance with the instructions of democratically accountable office holders and the rulings of the courts. Even in crisis or exceptional situations where the legitimacy of the constitution itself is called into question, appointed lieutenant governors or governors general are ill equipped to play a leading role in defending basic constitutional values. Moreover, there will almost always be other institutions or officials who can more legitimately and effectively take the lead in upholding the rule of law and the validity of the constitution. Losing sight of this reality would only compound and deepen a crisis, rather than resolve it.

7) Lieutenant Governors of the Provinces

The obligations of a governor general and of lieutenant governors of the provinces have been referred to in identical terms. A lieutenant governor plays the same role on the provincial level as the governor general does on the federal level. Thus, despite the fact that the lieuten-

64 Roux was forced to resign in the fall of 1996 when it was revealed that he had worn a swastika on his sleeve on at least one occasion during the 1940s.

ant governor is appointed by the federal Cabinet,[65] he or she acts on the advice and instructions of the provincial Executive Council or Cabinet. In the 1892 *Maritime Bank* case,[66] the Privy Council held that the lieutenant governors of the provinces were the direct representatives of the Crown in each province, as opposed to being mere delegates of the federal government. Accordingly, the lieutenant governors possessed all the prerogative powers of the Crown, including the Crown's prerogative to claim priority over other creditors of a debtor.

The lieutenant governor's role was not always conceived of in these terms. In the early decades of confederation, the federal government tended to regard the lieutenant governor as a federal officer who represented federal or national interests in provincial affairs. Section 90 of the *Constitution Act, 1867* granted the lieutenant governor the right to reserve bills for the approval of the Governor in Council,[67] and this power was exercised on seventy occasions in the late nineteenth and early twentieth centuries.[68] However, the power to reserve a bill has been exercised only once since 1937 and, on that occasion, Prime Minister John Diefenbaker disapproved of the lieutenant governor's actions.[69] Today, by firmly established constitutional convention, the lieutenant governor is required to act on the advice of the provincial premier or first minister. Accordingly, the power to reserve a bill for the approval of the federal Cabinet can no longer be used.[70]

Once appointed, the lieutenant governor is required to act on the advice of the provincial premier. However, the premier has no role in

---

65 Section 58 of the *Constitution Act, 1867* provides that the lieutenant governors of the provinces are appointed by the Governor in Council, which means the federal Cabinet.

66 *Maritime Bank (Liquidators of) v. N.B. (Receiver General)*, [1892] A.C. 437 [*Maritime Bank*].

67 This was the equivalent on the provincial level of the power of the governor general to reserve federal bills for the approval of the Queen-in-Council in Britain.

68 See R.I. Cheffins & P.A. Johnson, *The Revised Canadian Constitution: Politics as Law* (Toronto: McGraw-Hill Ryerson, 1986) at 84.

69 The incident in question occurred in 1961 when the lieutenant governor of Saskatchewan reserved a bill that had been passed by the Legislative Assembly. The federal government immediately passed an order in council approving the bill and criticized the lieutenant governor for acting without consulting the prime minister.

70 For the same reason, the lieutenant governor cannot exercise any independent judgment in determining whether to assent to legislation. Since Confederation, a lieutenant governor has refused assent in twenty-eight cases but on only one occasion (in 1945) was this done without the prior approval or advice of the premier: see Cheffins & Johnson, above note 68 at 84–85.

the selection of a lieutenant governor and the decision is made by the prime minister of Canada. In 1996, following the resignation of Jean-Louis Roux as lieutenant governor of Quebec, Premier Lucien Bouchard argued that, if the post of lieutenant governor were retained, the National Assembly should have the right to select Roux's successor.[71] Although the governor general would retain the formal legal power to make the actual appointment, Bouchard proposed that the governor general would appoint whomever was selected by a vote of the National Assembly, rather than act on the advice of the prime minister of Canada and the federal Cabinet. This procedure would bear some similarity to the process for appointment of the governor general, in which the queen acts on the advice of the Canadian, as opposed to the British, prime minister. However, Bouchard was proposing the innovation of having the entire National Assembly vote on the appointment, rather than simply the premier and Cabinet.

Although the federal government refused to accede to Bouchard's request, it is important to observe that the change he proposed would have required a constitutional amendment approved by the House of Commons and the Senate and all ten provinces.[72] Section 58 of the *Constitution Act, 1867* specifically states that the lieutenant governor is to be appointed by the Governor General in Council. The requirement that the governor general act on the advice of the federal Cabinet is thus a legal requirement set out in the written constitution. If section 58 had conferred the appointment power on the governor general alone, the requirement to seek the advice of the Privy Council would have been a matter of constitutional convention rather than strict law; in these circumstances, it is arguable that Bouchard's proposed change would have required only a change in a constitutional convention rather than a formal constitutional amendment.

---

71 Premier Bouchard tabled a motion in the Quebec National Assembly calling for the abolition of the office of lieutenant governor on grounds that the post was "outdated and archaic [and] a colonial relic" (Motion proposant que l'Assemblée réclame que le fédéral nomme à titre de lieutenant-gouverneur la personne qu'elle aura désignée, *Débats de l'Assemblée Nationale*, 20 November 1996). However, recognizing that abolishing the office of lieutenant governor would require a constitutional amendment, Bouchard proposed the interim step of changing the process for appointment.

72 Constitutional amendments in relation to the office of the governor general or the lieutenant governor require unanimous consent under s. 41(a) of the *Constitution Act, 1982*. Since Bouchard's proposed change would have necessitated an amendment to s. 58 of the *Constitution Act, 1867*, it would have fallen under s. 41(a) of the *Constitution Act, 1982*.

E. LEGISLATIVE POWER

1) Legislative Power in Canada

The legislative function is the power to enact general rules that determine the structure and authority of the state, as well as the rights and obligations of individuals, both in relation to the state and as among one another. Since the *Bill of Rights* of 1688, English law has recognized that the exercise of legislative power requires a statute enacted by Parliament, and that the sovereign cannot legislate through the exercise of the royal prerogative. As discussed in Chapter 2, this same requirement was incorporated into the law of the British North American colonies with the establishment of legislative assemblies in each colony.

This principle was carried forward into the *Constitution Act, 1867*. The power to enact laws for Canada in areas of federal jurisdiction is vested in the Parliament of Canada, which is defined as consisting of the appointed Senate, the elected House of Commons, and the queen (section 17). In order to enact a law, a bill must be approved by both the House of Commons and the Senate, and be signed by the queen or her representative, the governor general. Within each province, laws in relation to areas of provincial jurisdiction may be enacted by the elected Legislative Assembly of the province and approved by the lieutenant governor. Although five provinces at one time had appointed upper chambers akin to the federal Senate, they have all been abolished.

The British Parliament no longer has any authority to legislate for Canada. The *Canada Act 1982* provides that no Act of the Parliament of the United Kingdom enacted after 17 April 1982 shall extend to Canada as part of its law.[73] Therefore, only Canadian political authorities and institutions have the power to enact laws for Canada.

2) Approval of the Governor General and the Lieutenant Governor

As a matter of strict law, neither the governor general nor the lieutenant governor is required to approve a bill that has been passed by the Senate and the House of Commons or by a provincial legislature. Section 55 of the *Constitution Act, 1867* states that the governor general shall declare "either that he assents . . . [to a bill] in the Queen's Name, or that he withholds the Queen's Assent, or that he reserves the Bill for the Signifi-

73 See Chapter 5, Section D.

cation of the Queen's Pleasure."[74] The same provisions are made applicable to the lieutenant governors and permit the reservation of provincial bills for the approval of the Governor in Council (section 90). However, under the principles of responsible government, all of the Crown's powers must be exercised on the advice of the elected prime minister and his or her Cabinet. Therefore, any bill that is approved by the elected legislative chamber must automatically be signed into law by the governor general. As for the power of the British government to disallow Canadian laws, an Imperial Conference in 1930 stated that the powers of reservation and disallowance of Canadian laws could no longer be used because they were inconsistent with Canadian sovereignty.[75] Thus, while they have not been formally repealed,[76] as a practical matter the sections of the *Constitution Act, 1867* dealing with reservation and disallowance of Canadian laws by British authorities are now moribund.[77]

---

74 As noted in Chapter 2, bills that were reserved under s. 55 did not become law unless they were approved by the British government within two years (s. 57). The British government was also given the power to disallow within two years any bill that had been signed into law by the governor general (s. 56).

75 In fact, the power of reservation was last used in 1878, when the instructions of the governor general from Britain were modified so as to eliminate the power. The power of disallowance was used on only one occasion, in 1873.

76 Section 4 of the *Statute of Westminster, 1931* (U.K.), 22 & 23 Geo. V, c. 4 required that the British Parliament obtain Canadian consent before enacting laws for Canada but did not deal with the power of disallowance exercised by the British government. Similarly, the *Canada Act 1982* (U.K.), 1982, c. 11, terminated the authority of the Westminster Parliament to enact law for Canada but did not refer to the powers of reservation and disallowance in the *Constitution Act, 1867*.

77 Although the lieutenant governor's power to reserve a bill for the approval of the federal Cabinet was last used in 1961, it too is now a dead letter because it has been expressly disavowed by a Canadian prime minister and its use would be inconsistent with the independent status of the provinces. See the discussion in Section D, above in this chapter. As for the federal power to disallow provincial laws, the Supreme Court has suggested that the power has been abandoned: see *Reference Re Secession of Quebec*, [1998] 2 S.C.R. 217 at para. 55. However, no Canadian prime minister has ever expressly renounced the power of disallowance and in 1975, Prime Minister Pierre Trudeau suggested that disallowance might be appropriate in a case where a provincial law "cuts directly across the operation of federal law or creates serious disorder particularly beyond the borders of the province" (Prime Minister Trudeau, in a letter dated 18 July 1975, quoted in J.R. Hurley, *Amending Canada's Constitution: History, Processes, Problems and Prospects* [Ottawa: Supply and Services Canada, 1996] at 15–16).

3) Parliamentary Supremacy and the Rule of Law

The principle of parliamentary supremacy, as developed in Great Britain, means that there are no legal limitations on the legislative competence of Parliament. A.V. Dicey, writing in the late nineteenth century, described the legislative supremacy of Parliament as "the right to make or unmake any law whatever; and, further, that no person or body is recognized by the law of England as having a right to override or set aside the legislation of Parliament."[78] According to Dicey's formulation, courts must always give effect to the laws enacted by Parliament, no matter how unwise or unjust they might appear.

Although the preamble to the *Constitution Act, 1867* states that Canada was to have a constitution similar in principle to that of the United Kingdom, the principle of parliamentary supremacy was modified in its application to Canada. The jurisdiction of both the Parliament of Canada and the provincial legislatures is defined and limited by the *Constitution Act, 1867*. The most obvious example of these limits are those associated with federalism — the power to enact laws is divided between Parliament and the provincial legislatures. The courts have always assumed that they have been entrusted with the function of deciding whether acts of Parliament or the legislatures fall within the limited jurisdictions specified in sections 91 and 92 of the *Constitution Act, 1867*. This judicial review function has been expressly confirmed in section 52 of the *Constitution Act, 1982*, which provides that any law that is inconsistent with the provisions of the Constitution of Canada is of no force and effect.

Prior to April 1982, the courts held that the doctrine of parliamentary supremacy applied in Canada, subject to the division of powers under sections 91 and 92 of the 1867 Act. For example, in the 1883 *Hodge* case,[79] the Privy Council stated that the provincial legislatures had authority

> as plenary and as ample within the limits prescribed by sect. 92 as the Imperial Parliament in the plenitude of its power possessed and could bestow. Within these limits of subjects and area the local legislature is supreme, and has the same authority as the Imperial Parliament.[80]

---

78 Dicey, above note 7 at 40.

79 *Hodge v. R.*, [1883] 9 App. Cas. 117 (P.C.).

80 *Ibid.* at 132. For a similar statement with respect to the authority of the federal Parliament, see *British Coal Corp. v. R.*, [1935] A.C. 500 at 519–20 (P.C.).

In other words, as long as Parliament or the legislatures remained within the limits defined by sections 91 and 92 of the *Constitution Act, 1867*, they had the same supreme power possessed by the British Parliament. It was also sometimes said that the distribution of powers between Parliament and the provinces was exhaustive in the sense that the federal Parliament and the provincial legislatures possessed, among them, a totality of legislative power.

The constitutional changes in 1982 considerably modified the principle of parliamentary supremacy in Canada. The *Canadian Charter of Rights and Freedoms* requires the courts to strike down legislation on the basis that it infringes certain guaranteed rights. Furthermore, section 35 of the *Constitution Act, 1982* provides that the Aboriginal and Treaty rights of Aboriginal peoples of Canada are recognized and affirmed. In light of these constitutional changes, it can no longer be said that the jurisdiction of Parliament or the legislatures is supreme. All laws, regardless of subject matter, are subject to review on the basis that they offend fundamental rights of individuals or groups under the *Charter*, or Indigenous rights under the 1982 Act. Nor can it be said that the jurisdiction of Parliament and the provinces is exhaustive, since there are now many kinds of laws that cannot be enacted by either order of government. In this sense, the principle of constitutionalism and the rule of law—which requires that all actions of the state be authorized by law and consistent with constitutional requirements—has significantly narrowed the principle of parliamentary supremacy in Canada.

4) The Senate

a) The Senate and the House of Commons Are Co-equal in Law

The Senate was the successor to the Legislative Councils that had been established in the British colonies at the time of granting of elected Legislative Assemblies. Its members are appointed until the age of seventy-five by the governor general.[81] In most cases, the legal powers and status of the Senate equal those of the House of Commons, despite the fact that Senators are appointed. In order for a bill to become law, it must be passed in identical terms by both the Senate and the House, and neither chamber has the power to override the veto of the other.[82] Most bills can be introduced in either chamber, although virtually all

---

81 Originally, members of the Senate were appointed for life; a constitutional amendment in 1965 provided that senators were to retire at the age of seventy-five. The Senate is also called the Upper House or Upper Chamber.

82 However, in the case of constitutional amendments, the Senate can be overridden by the House if the Senate does not approve an amendment

government bills are introduced in the House of Commons.[83] As a practical matter, however, the Senate, which is an appointed body, lacks the legitimacy of the elected House of Commons. Therefore, for most of the twentieth century, the Senate tended to automatically approve bills that had been passed by the House of Commons. This tendency toward acquiescence has been reinforced by the fact that the prime minister controls the appointment of senators. Therefore, the party that controls the House of Commons has most often controlled a majority in the Senate.

b) Functions of the Senate

The drafters of the *BNA Act* intended the Senate to serve two main functions. First, the Senate was designed to represent regional interests. This is why the allocation of seats was on a regional basis, as opposed to representation by relative population: the maritime, Ontario, and Quebec regions were given equal representation in the original Senate.[84] Second, the Senate was intended to perform a role similar to that of the House of Lords in England, namely, to provide a "sober second thought" and technical review of legislation approved by the House of Commons. (Moreover, the Senate also protected propertied interests, since senators were required to be at least thirty years of age and to own property valued at a minimum of $4000 in the province they represented.[85])

---

within 180 days of its approval in the House, and the House repossesses the amendment in its original form after the expiry of the 180-day period.

83 Bills imposing taxes or providing for the expenditure of money cannot be introduced in the Senate. However, such bills must still be approved by the Senate to become law.

84 The Senate originally consisted of 72 members appointed for life by the governor general, with each of the three initial regions—Quebec, Ontario, and the two Maritime provinces (Nova Scotia and New Brunswick)—being equally represented by 24 members. Today there are four divisions in the Senate—the fourth consisting of the provinces of Manitoba, Saskatchewan, Alberta, and British Columbia—represented by 24 senators each. Newfoundland and Labrador, which is not included in the maritime division, has 6 senators, and the three northern territories each have 1 senator, for a total of 105 members.

85 See s. 23(1) of the *Constitution Act, 1867*. There were additional requirements for senators from Quebec. Each Quebec senator was appointed from one of the twenty-four electoral divisions that had been represented in the Legislature Council of Canada East. Moreover, senators were required to have their "Real Property Qualification" in the electoral division for which they were appointed (ss. 22 and 23(6)). These requirements had the effect of guaranteeing that senators from Quebec would include representatives of both the French- and English-Canadian communities. There were comparable requirements for the Quebec electoral districts in the House of Commons, but these requirements

Overall, the Senate has failed to fulfil these original hopes and expectations. This is mainly because it is inconsistent with democratic principles for an appointed institution to override the wishes of the elected House of Commons. The Senate's lack of legitimacy has been reinforced by the fact that appointments have tended to be used as a vehicle for the prime minister to reward supporters of the government party. Governments have also tended to appoint senators at the end of their political careers. For these reasons, the Senate has not been regarded as having a legitimate role to play in the public policy process. Other institutions, particularly the provincial governments, have come to be seen as more effective representatives of regional interests.[86]

For a short period in the 1980s, however, the Senate asserted a more independent and meaningful role. The election of the Mulroney Progressive Conservative government in 1984, after years of Liberal rule, meant that the government no longer controlled a majority in the Senate. In 1988, Liberal senators announced that they would not approve the legislation implementing the Canada–U.S. Free Trade Agreement until the issue had been submitted to the Canadian people in an election. The government was unable to secure passage of the legislation until it was returned to office after the election held in November 1988. After the election, the Liberal senators threatened to veto legislation enacting the Goods and Services Tax. The threat forced the prime minister to resort to a little-known provision permitting the appointment of up to eight additional senators.[87] This provision, which had never been used before, enabled the prime minister to add sufficient senators to secure passage of the law.[88] However, the Senate subsequently defeated

---

were abolished by the Quebec National Assembly in 1970. See s. 80 of the *Constitution Act, 1867* and the *Act respecting electoral districts*, S.Q. 1970, c. 7.

86 The historian Christopher Moore argues that the drafters of the *Constitution Act, 1867* never intended the Senate to be a functioning check on the Lower House, and planned to use it for the patronage appointments that are now seen as a design flaw; see Christopher Moore, *Three Weeks in Quebec City: The Meeting That Made Canada* (Toronto: Allan Lane, 2015). It is notable that the delegates at the constitutional conferences included sitting members of the upper legislative chambers of the colonial governments.

87 Section 26 of the *Constitution Act, 1867* permits the governor general to appoint either four or eight additional senators. This section also states that the queen is to direct the governor general to make the appointment, although the queen's direction is made on the recommendation of the governor general. This rather circuitous legal route is simplified by the reality that all powers of the queen and governor general are exercised on the instructions of the prime minister.

88 The federal government had made three previous attempts to add additional senators pursuant to s. 26, the most recent occurring in 1912 in connection with Senate obstruction of a naval bill that was supported by the government.

amendments to the *Criminal Code* limiting access to abortions and also turned down legislation restructuring the Canada Council.

In the early 1990s, the Liberals were forced to taste some of their own Senate medicine. The Conservatives maintained control of a majority in the Senate for close to three years after the October 1993 election of Jean Chrétien as prime minister. The Conservatives used their majority to force extensive public hearings on government legislation limiting compensation for the cancellation of contracts for the redevelopment of Pearson International Airport in Toronto. The bill was eventually defeated in the Senate even though, by the time of the final vote, the Liberals had a bare majority in the Upper House.[89] In 1996, the Senate also attempted to amend a constitutional amendment on denominational schools in Newfoundland, which had previously been approved by both the House of Commons and the Newfoundland House of Assembly. Because the Senate can only delay constitutional amendments, however, the House of Commons subsequently voted to override the Senate, and the amendment was proclaimed into law.

The Senate has been justified in acting independently on these types of issues on the basis that it was protecting the constitutional rights of individuals and minority groups. In the debate over the Pearson Airport legislation, for example, the Conservative senators emphasized that their concern was not with the policy of the government to the effect that certain contracts should be cancelled, but rather with the right of the developers to seek redress through the courts for the contract cancellation. A Senate committee held extensive hearings on the issue of whether access to the courts was constitutionally guaranteed. A majority of the scholars consulted concluded that such access was implicit in a constitution founded on the rule of law.[90] In the Newfoundland schools amendment, the senators objected to the proposal on the grounds that it altered constitutionally protected rights of the

---

However, on each occasion, the British government refused the request. Such a refusal would no longer be appropriate, given the fact that the queen today exercises all her powers in relation to Canada strictly on the basis of advice received from her Canadian ministers rather than the British government. For a description of the circumstances surrounding the previous attempts to invoke s. 26, see J.R. Mallory, *The Structure of Canadian Government*, 2d ed. (Toronto: Gage, 1984) at 249–50.

89 The defeat was the result of a Liberal senator unexpectedly voting with the Conservatives against the bill.

90 The rule of law is recognized in the preamble to the *Constitution Act, 1982*. These arguments have been extensively analyzed elsewhere: see P.J. Monahan, "Is the Pearson Airport Legislation Unconstitutional? The Rule of Law as a Limit on Contract Repudiation by Government" (1995) 33 Osgoode Hall L.J. 411.

Roman Catholic minority without their consent.[91] These precedents suggest that the Senate may be attempting to define a role for itself as a legitimate protector of the constitutional rights of individuals or minorities.[92]

There have been numerous calls for Senate reform over the decades. During the debates preceding patriation, for instance, the Canada West Foundation in Calgary published a report describing a model of a "Triple E" Senate; that is, elected (a single transferable vote system in each province), equal (equal numbers of senators in each province), and effective (primacy of the House of Commons for the adoption of bills, Senate veto on constitutional amendments, certain appointments and certain exceptional Crown powers). These concepts were featured during the debates over constitutional amendments at Meech Lake and Charlottetown.

In 2013, the government of Conservative prime minister Stephen Harper, which had a long-held platform of Senate reform and had previously introduced several bills to that effect, sought the Supreme Court's opinion on the applicability of the constitutional amending formula to a variety of potential reforms.[93] The result is that it is now clear that many of the Senate's features cannot be modified without substantial or unanimous provincial consent. This was not a surprise, as the text of the *Constitution Act, 1982* mentions amendments to the "powers of the Senate and the method of selecting senators" as being subject to the general (7/50) formula.[94]

In particular, the Court opined that the Senate cannot be abolished without unanimous consent and that the implementation of consultative elections or senatorial term limits requires provincial agreement under the 7/50 formula. The only available unilateral federal change identified

91 Although the amendment had been approved in a province-wide referendum by a 55-percent majority, analysis of the voting results suggested that a majority of Roman Catholics who cast ballots had probably opposed the measure. Note also that a different constitutional amendment was subsequently approved by an unequivocal majority in a provincial referendum and enacted in 1998. See the discussion in Chapter 6 at note 22.

92 It should be noted, however, that the Senate has also taken an independent stand on bills where no constitutional issues arose. In early 1997, for example, the Senate threatened to veto legislation providing for new child support requirements on divorce (Bill C-41, *An Act to amend the Divorce Act, the Family Orders and Agreements Enforcement Assistance Act, the Garnishment, Attachment and Pension Diversion Act and the Canada Shipping Act*, 2d Sess., 35th Parl., 1996). However, the government eventually agreed to make certain compromises and the bill was enacted.

93 *Senate Reference*, above note 60.

94 Section 42(1)(b).

by the Court was the repeal of the property qualification, other than in Quebec.[95] Therefore, formal constitutional amendment to the structure of the Senate would be extremely unlikely to achieve. However, this does not appear to have stood in the way of non-binding modifications to the practice of Senate appointments, as in January 2016 the Trudeau government announced the establishment of an Independent Advisory Board for Senate Appointments, which has a mandate to recommend non-partisan appointments to the prime minister.[96]

5) The House of Commons

The House of Commons is elected in general elections that must be held at least once every five years.[97] It originally consisted of 181 members, but that number has been gradually increased to the current total of 308. The drafters of the *Constitution Act, 1867* believed that the allocation of seats in the House of Commons should be based on the principle of representation by population. This principle is reflected in section 51 of the *Constitution Act, 1867*, which provides that the number of members of the House of Commons and the representation of the provinces shall be adjusted in accordance with the results of each decennial census. However, over the years, the principle of representation by population has been seriously compromised. Various "floors" or guarantees of representation for the smaller provinces have been built into the formula for calculating seats. In 1915, for example, each province was guaranteed that its number of members of the House of Commons would never fall below its number of senators.[98] As a result, Prince Edward Island has a minimum of four and New Brunswick of ten members of the House of Commons, even though their relative

95 The property qualification for Quebec is subject to the bilateral amending formula due to the fact that senators represent particular districts from Quebec and must hold property in their district in particular (s. 23(6), *Constitution Act, 1867*).

96 Government of Canada, *Independent Advisory Board for Senate Appointments*, online: www.canada.ca/en/campaign/independent-advisory-board-for-senate-appointments.html.

97 See ss. 37 and 50 of the *Constitution Act, 1867* and section 4 of the *Constitution Act, 1982*.

98 See s. 51A of the *Constitution Act, 1867*, added to the Act in 1915 by the *Constitution Act, 1915* (U.K.), 5 & 6 Geo. V, c. 45. The current version of s. 51 of the *Constitution Act, 1867* (as enacted by the *Representation Act, 1985*, S.C. 1986, c. 8, Part I) guarantees a province that its representation will not fall below the level it attained in 1976. This guarantee compounds the deviation from the principle of representation by population.

share of the national population would not justify this representation. These guarantees for the smaller provinces, combined with limits on the overall size of the House, mean that more populous provinces such as Ontario and British Columbia are significantly under-represented. In the Parliament elected in January 2006, for example, Ontario had approximately eleven fewer seats in the House of Commons than it would have been entitled to if seats were allocated strictly on the basis of relative provincial shares of the national population.[99] These deviations from the principle of representation by population have been possible since section 51 of the *Constitution Act, 1867*, which sets out the provincial distribution of seats, can be altered by ordinary legislation enacted by the federal Parliament.[100] Section 3 of the *Charter* enshrines the right to vote, which has been interpreted to protect a degree of proportionality between ridings within provinces, but cannot be used to strike down other parts of the constitution.[101]

The *Fair Representation Act* of 2011 was an amendment pursuant to section 44 of Part V, and one that moved the House's representation much closer to proportionality.[102] It sets a general rule of one seat for every 111,166 people in Canada (to be adjusted based on future censuses), but also maintains the minimum floor of seats for those provinces that would otherwise fall below their floor based on population. Notably, the formula tops up any previously *over*-represented provinces who are rendered under-represented by the application of the floor rules, namely Quebec, but fails to do so for provinces that were previously *under*-represented and continue to be so disadvantaged. Regardless, even this watered down formula yielded many new MPs for the growing populations of Alberta, Ontario, and British Columbia in a larger House, with 338 MPs returned in the 2015 general election. A larger

---

99 Ontario, with 106 seats, would be entitled to approximately 117 seats in a 308-seat house if seats were allocated purely in accordance with representation by population. Similarly, B.C. is under-represented by 4 seats (36 instead of 40) and Alberta is under-represented by 2 seats (28 instead of 30).

100 Before 1982, Parliament could amend s. 51 pursuant to the power of amendment set out in s. 91(1) of the *Constitution Act, 1867*, which was enacted in 1949 by the *British North America (No. 2) Act, 1949* (U.K.), 13 Geo. VI, c. 81. Although s. 91(1) was repealed in 1982, s. 44 of the *Constitution Act, 1982* preserved Parliament's power to amend s. 51 through ordinary legislation, subject to certain guarantees of representation described in ss. 41 & 42. Amendments made under s. 44 must still be consistent with the "principle of proportionate representation of the provinces in the House of Commons," which is subject to the general amending formula in s. 42.

101 *Reference Re Provincial Electoral Boundaries (Sask)*, [1991] 2 S.C.R. 158.

102 *Fair Representation Act*, S.C. 2011 c. 26.

House minimizes the distortionary effect of the floor rules, as the floor is based on an absolute number of members, not a proportion.

The proceedings of the House of Commons are presided over by the Speaker, who is elected by members of the House.[103] Before 1986, the Speaker was nominated by the prime minister and was usually appointed without opposition. Since that time, however, the Speaker has been elected by secret ballot, with balloting continuing until one MP has a majority of all the votes cast. This process has given the office of the Speaker greater independence from the prime minister and the government, and greater legitimacy as an arbiter of the affairs of the House. Despite the fact that the balloting is secret, in cases where the government has a majority, the Speaker will almost invariably be chosen from among the ranks of the government party. However, in a minority situation, members of the government party have on occasion been prepared to support an opposition member as Speaker, presumably on the basis that this eliminates one opposition vote in any matter of confidence.[104] Peter Milliken, a Liberal MP, served as the Speaker of the House from 2001 to 2011 and on 12 October 2009 became the longest-serving Speaker in Canadian history.

6) Parliamentary Privilege

The courts have held that the Senate and the House of Commons and the members thereof possess powers and privileges necessary to their capacity to function.[105] Parliamentary privilege has been defined as the "sum of the privileges, immunities and powers enjoyed by the Senate, the House of Commons and provincial legislative assemblies, and by each member individually, without which they could not discharge

---

103 See s. 44 of the *Constitution Act, 1867*.

104 For example, following the January 2006 election, 124 Conservatives, 103 Liberals, 51 Bloc Québécois, and 29 New Democrats were elected. Liberal MP David Emerson crossed the floor to sit as a Conservative, bringing the Conservatives to 125 seats and reducing the Liberals to 102. Liberal Peter Milliken was then re-elected as Speaker, reducing the Liberal caucus to 101, and making it potentially possible for the Conservative government to survive a vote of confidence with the support of the NDP. Similarly, after the election of a minority government in May 1979, Prime Minister Clark asked Liberal James Jerome, who had been the Speaker in the previous Parliament, to carry on in the post. However, there does not appear to be any instance in which a prime minister with a majority in the House has gone outside the ranks of his or her own party to nominate a Speaker.

105 *New Brunswick Broadcasting Co. v. Nova Scotia (Speaker of the House of Assembly)*, [1993] 1 S.C.R. 319 at 342 [*New Brunswick Broadcasting*].

their functions."[106] In essence, it is a form of immunity that allows legislators to do their "legislative work" free from interference by the Crown or the scrutiny of the courts.[107] The doctrine developed in the United Kingdom out of a long history of conflict among Parliament, the Crown, and the judiciary. Prior to 1640, the Crown and the courts routinely interfered in parliamentary affairs. For instance, in 1629, Charles I arranged for Sir Jon Eliot and two other Members of Parliament to be charged for sedition for words spoken in the House of Commons. Gradually, areas of privilege developed through statute and the common law to prevent such intrusions. For instance, the *Bill of Rights* of 1688 provided that "the freedom of Speech and Debates or Proceedings in Parliament ought not to be impeached or questioned in any Court or Place out of Parliament." In an early nineteenth-century decision, the English Court of Queen's Bench ruled that "[w]hat is said or done within the walls of Parliament cannot be inquired into in a court of law."[108]

Section 18 of the *Constitution Act, 1867* contemplates the incorporation of parliamentary privileges developed in the United Kingdom into Canada. It provides that the "privileges, immunities and powers" of Parliament shall be defined by Acts of Parliament, but may not exceed the privileges enjoyed by the U.K. House of Commons as of 1867. Section 4 of the *Parliament of Canada Act*[109] (an ordinary federal statute) confers on the Senate and the House of Commons the full extent of privileges permitted under section 18 of the 1867 Act. However, the statute does not define or categorize privileges, but merely incorporates by reference whatever privileges were "held, enjoyed and exercised" by the U.K. House of Commons in 1867. Therefore, the existence and scope of parliamentary privilege must be ascertained by reference to the law and customs of the U.K. House of Commons, including both the statute and common law.[110]

---

106 *Canada (House of Commons) v. Vaid*, [2005] 1 S.C.R. 667 at para. 29 [*Vaid*], citing A. Fraser, W.F. Dawson & J.A. Holtby, *Beauchesne's Rules & Forms of the House of Commons of Canada with Annotations, Comments and Precedents*, 6th ed. (Toronto: Carswell, 1989) at 11; *New Brunswick Broadcasting*, above note 105 at 380.

107 *Vaid*, above note 106, citing J.P.J. Maingot, *Parliamentary Privilege in Canada*, 2d ed. (Montreal: McGill-Queen's University Press, 1997) at 12; *New Brunswick Broadcasting*, above note 105 at 341; *Fielding v. Thomas*, [1896] A.C. 600 at 610–11 (P.C.) [*Fielding*]; *Kielley v. Carson* (1842), 4 Moo. P.C. 63, 13 E.R. 225 at 235–36.

108 *Stockdale v. Hansard* (1839), 9 Ad. & E. 1 at 48, 112 E.R. 1112.

109 R.S.C. 1985, c. P-1.

110 *Vaid,* above note 106 at para. 36.

The Supreme Court of Canada has held that parliamentary privileges have a special constitutional status. As discussed in Chapter 1 of this book, section 52(2) of the *Constitution Act, 1982* provides that the Constitution of Canada "includes" certain written constitutional documents, including the *Constitution Act, 1867* and the *Charter of Rights and Freedoms*. In *New Brunswick Broadcasting*,[111] a majority of the Supreme Court held that the use of the word "includes" means that the definition is non-exhaustive and that the doctrine of parliamentary privilege forms part of the Constitution of Canada. The reason offered by the Court was that the preamble to the *Constitution Act, 1867* provides that Canada is to have "a constitution similar in principle to that of the United Kingdom." While the court acknowledged that "we do not share the turbulent history of the United Kingdom with respect to the relationships between the different branches of government," it held that there was "no question that the maintenance of the independence" of legislative bodies from the judicial and executive branches of government was essential to our constitutional order. Therefore, parliamentary privileges formed part of the Constitution of Canada.[112] As discussed further in Chapters 5 and 6, the Court's reasoning in this regard is open to serious criticism and is difficult to reconcile with the text of the *Constitution Act, 1982*.[113]

---

111 Above note 105.

112 *Ibid.* at 354, Lamer C.J.

113 Although s. 52(1) is non-exhaustive, it refers exclusively to written instruments, and may therefore be taken to exclude unwritten constitutional principles by implication. Moreover, as Sopinka J., dissenting, held in *New Brunswick Broadcasting*, *ibid.* at 346, the preambular reference to a constitution "similar in principle" to the U.K. is a poor basis on which to add new elements to the Constitution of Canada. For one thing, it is not a "provision" of the *Constitution Act, 1867*. Moreover, by adding parliamentary privileges, including those at the provincial level, to the "constitution of Canada," the majority reasoning would tend to suggest that provincial legislatures cannot alter parliamentary privileges by ordinary statute. As a matter of principle, this is inconsistent with the principle of parliamentary supremacy and is incongruent with the very purpose of parliamentary privilege, which is to protect the independence of the legislative bodies from interference by the Crown and the courts. In addition, s. 18 of the *Constitution Act, 1867* expressly enables Parliament to define the scope and extent of parliamentary privileges at the federal level, subject only to the limitation that they cannot exceed those enjoyed by the U.K. House of Commons in 1867. (However, it may be that parliamentary privileges at both the federal and provincial levels can enjoy constitutional status and be amended by federal and provincial statute. Sections 44 to 45 of the *Constitution Act, 1982* provide that Parliament and the provincial legislatures may amend the constitution of Canada and the constitution of the provinces by ordinary statute: see *Fielding*, above note 107 and Hogg, above note 30 at 1.7.)

Furthermore, the Supreme Court of Canada has held that inherent parliamentary privileges are not subject to the *Charter*. In *New Brunswick Broadcasting*, a majority of the Court held that the Nova Scotia legislature was entitled to ban the televising of its proceedings pursuant to the privilege to exclude "strangers" from the House of Commons, which was said to be "inherent" in the creation of provincial legislatures under the constitution. Since the *Charter* did not apply to parliamentary privileges, the Court held that it did not consider whether the ban on televising legislative proceedings violated the right to freedom of speech under section 2(b) of the *Charter*. In a later case, the Court stated that parliamentary privileges at the federal level also enjoy constitutional status and suggested that they are not subject to the *Charter* either.[114] This reasoning is also suspect. As discussed above, ordinarily, all powers of government must be measured against the rights and freedoms guaranteed in the *Charter*. It is not clear why parliamentary privileges should be exempt from this rule.[115] Furthermore, by virtue of the *Parliament of Canada Act*, the "main body" of privileges enjoyed by the federal Parliament are "legislative privileges."[116] Normally, all government statutes are subject to the *Charter*. Therefore, the laws of Parliament in relation to parliamentary privilege should be subject to *Charter* review.[117] Strangely, however, the Supreme Court has held that "parliamentary privilege enjoys the *same* constitutional weight and status as the *Charter* itself."[118]

The courts do have an important role to play in defining the scope of parliamentary privileges. In particular, courts will assess whether a certain category of privilege is necessary for the proper functioning of the legislative body in a contemporary context; moreover, "necessity" is to be read broadly, as encompassing the "necessary sphere of matters without which the dignity and efficiency of the House cannot be upheld."[119] However, proof of necessity is required only to establish the existence and scope of a category of privilege. These include freedom of speech in Parliament; control over debates and proceedings in Parliament, including day-to-day procedure in the House; the power to exclude strangers from parliamentary proceedings; and the disciplinary authority over members and non-members who interfere with

114 *Vaid*, above note 106 at para. 33.
115 See the discussion in Hogg, above note 30 at 1.7.
116 *Vaid*, above note 106 at para. 36.
117 *New Brunswick Broadcasting*, above note 105 at 364, Lamer C.J.
118 *Vaid*, above note 106 at paras. 34–35, rejecting the reasoning of Lamer C.J. in *New Brunswick Broadcasting*, above note 105.
119 *New Brunswick Broadcasting*, *ibid.* at 383; *Vaid*, above note 106 at para. 29.

the discharge of parliamentary duties, including the power to sanction members for contempt.[120] These examples are not exhaustive. A Member of Parliament or a provincial legislature may claim a new class of privilege by demonstrating that the sphere of activity in question is closely and directly connected with the fulfilment by the assembly or its members of their functions as a legislative body.[121]

Questions have been raised as to whether parliamentary privileges may override the terms of an inconsistent statute. For example, it has been suggested that the power of a committee of the House of Commons to order the production of documents prevails over the contrary provisions of a statute.[122] However, as noted above, Parliament has the authority to define (and therefore to limit) the scope of parliamentary privileges through statute.[123] Where Parliament chooses to limit the privileges and immunities of the House or of its committees through statute, any such limitation must be binding on the House of Commons, its committees, and members. This follows from the basic constitutional distinction between Parliament (comprised of the Senate, the House of Commons, and the queen) and any one of the Houses of Parliament. If Parliament as a whole has chosen to define privileges and immunities in a particular manner through statute, it cannot be that one of the two houses, much less a committee or individual member thereof, can unilaterally ignore or override such requirements.

---

120 *Vaid*, *ibid.*; New *Brunswick Broadcasting*, above note 105 at 342. The contempt power is a broad power that is difficult to define. Generally, it preserves the ability of the House to sanction members for interference with its proceedings. Contempts may vary in their gravity, ranging from breach of decorum to grave attacks on the authority of Parliament. See A. O'Brien & M. Bosc, eds., *House of Commons Procedure and Practice*, 2d ed. (Ottawa: House of Commons, 2009) c. 3.

121 *Vaid*, above note 106 at paras. 44 and 46.

122 See, for example, the legal opinion of the Law Clerk and Parliamentary Counsel of the House of Commons provided on 18 June 2009 to the Standing Committee on Public Accounts, in Report of the Standing Committee on Public Accounts, "The Power of Committees to Order the Production of Documents and Records," 2d Sess., 40th Parl., December 2009 at 4, online: www.parl.gc.ca/HousePublications/Publication.aspx?DocId=4262218&Language=E&Mode=1&Parl=40&Ses=2, where it is stated: "In summary, constitutional law has priority over statute law, that is, the provisions of a statute, such as the *Privacy Act*, are to be read in a manner that is consistent with the constitutional laws of Canada . . . . Accordingly, there can be no doubt that, as a matter of law, the power of a House committee to order the production of documents prevails over the seemingly contrary provisions of a statute, including the *Privacy Act*."

123 See *Constitution Act, 1867*, s. 18.

7) The Legislative Process

When Parliament is summoned by the governor general after an election, the first order of business—following the election of the Speaker of the House of Commons—is the reading of the Speech from the Throne. Members of the House of Commons, senators, Supreme Court judges, and invited guests gather in the Senate to hear the governor general read the speech. The speech is drafted by the prime minister and his senior advisers. It outlines the government's proposed legislative agenda for the session of Parliament. Following the reading, members of the House return to the House of Commons, where the government immediately introduces a bill—symbolizing the House of Commons' prerogative to discuss any business it sees fit before considering the Speech from the Throne. The Speech from the Throne is then followed by a debate, which lasts up to six days.

The first stage in the enactment of legislation is the introduction of a bill into either the House of Commons or the Senate.[124] Bills are of two kinds, private or public. A private bill alters the law only in respect of an individual or a legal entity, such as a corporation. Private bills are often first introduced in the Senate, where they are debated and refined before being considered by the House of Commons. Public bills, in contrast, are intended to alter the law applicable to the public generally.

Public bills can themselves be subdivided into two categories: government and private members' bills. Private members' bills are public bills[125] introduced by MPs who are not members of the government (including backbench MPs from the government party who are not ministers or parliamentary assistants to ministers). Because the government controls the agenda in the House of Commons, private members' bills are rarely debated or voted on unless the government itself decides to adopt and sponsor a particular private member's initiative. However, rule changes adopted in 2003 have guaranteed that a limited number of private members' bills or motions will be debated and brought to a vote each session, and this has increased the likelihood that private members' bills will be enacted.[126]

---

124 This is subject to the requirement that money bills can only be introduced into the House of Commons: *Constitution Act, 1867*, s. 53.

125 They are public bills in the sense that they are intended to alter the general law, as opposed to private bills which, as discussed, alter the law in relation to a particular person only.

126 Under the 2003 rule changes, a lottery is held by the Speaker to determine the ranking of MPs for Private Members Business. A high ranking in the lottery guarantees the member the right to introduce a bill that is votable in the House during the current Parliament's lifespan. The introduction of these rules,

Government bills, as the name implies, are public bills introduced by a minister in the House of Commons. A government bill has been approved by the Cabinet and represents government policy, and the expectation is that all members of the government party in the Commons will support it. A government bill is preceded by a notice of motion tabled at least forty-eight hours before the introduction of the bill, specifying the title of the bill and providing a short explanation of its provisions. The vast majority of the time of the House of Commons is taken up with the consideration of government bills, which can themselves be divided into money and non-money bills. Money bills deal with the financing of government: they authorize the raising of money through taxation or its expenditure by the government.[127] Money bills can only be introduced into the House of Commons by a minister of the government. They must also be recommended by the governor general.[128]

Bills are voted on, or "read," three times in each of the House of Commons and the Senate. First reading occurs when the sponsor of a bill moves "that this bill be read a first time and be printed." A motion for first reading is non-debatable and non-amendable and is usually approved as a matter of routine. Second reading is a motion to approve the principle of the bill and to refer it to a committee for detailed examination. No amendments are permitted at this stage, although there is usually an extensive debate on the merits of the legislation. After second reading, the bill is considered by a committee, which may propose amendments and report the bill back to the full House or Senate. At the report stage, amendments agreed to by the committee are considered, and any member of the House may propose amendments to the bill. Finally, the bill is voted on at third reading. Once a bill has been given three readings in one House, it goes to the other House, where the process of three readings begins all over again.

Bills that have been passed by both the Senate and the House of Commons are then presented for approval, or royal assent, to the gov-

---

coupled with the fact that recent elections have returned minority governments, has significantly increased the likelihood that private members' bills can become law. For example, over the twenty-year period from 1983 to 2003, just thirty-seven private members' bills received royal assent, and most of them dealt with obscure or innocuous items; in the first eight months following the adoption of the 2003 rule changes, seven private members' bills received royal assent, including several substantive and controversial ones such as former NDP MP Svend Robinson's bill adding "sexual orientation" to the hate propaganda section of the *Criminal Code*.

127 Taxation measures are called "ways-and-means" measures, while expenditures measures are called "supply."

128 These requirements are mandated by ss. 53 & 54 of the *Constitution Act, 1867*.

ernor general. Royal assent is given by the governor general in the Senate chamber before members of both houses, at which point the bill becomes an Act or statute of Parliament. A statute does not necessarily have the force of law on the giving of royal assent. Where the statute is silent as to the date of its legal effectiveness, the Act comes into force once royal assent has been given.[129] Sometimes, however, a statute will provide that it does not come into force until some future date, either a date specified in the statute itself or a date to be fixed by proclamation.[130] Accordingly, where a statute comes into force by proclamation, it does not take legal effect until an order in council is issued by the federal Cabinet proclaiming the Act into force.

Only statutes or Acts of Parliament—or regulations enacted pursuant to such statutes, usually by the Governor in Council—have the force of law. Other actions, decisions, or instruments of the House of Commons or the Senate will generally not be given any legal effect by the courts. This includes resolutions or motions that may be approved by the Senate or the House of Commons. For example, resolutions may be approved to express the views of the members of one or both houses on a particular subject, or to call on the government or some other entity to take action to redress some political problem or situation. Despite the fact that such resolutions may be voted on and approved by one or both houses, they will not have the force of law. Thus, after the 1995 Quebec referendum, the House of Commons adopted a resolution recognizing that Quebec constitutes a "distinct society" within Canada. However, this resolution is not legally binding and is merely the expression of the political will of the members of the House.

This is not to say that a resolution or motion might not lead to a change in the law through the enactment of legislation. For example, the enactment of the *Canada Act 1982* and the *Constitution Act, 1982* by the Westminster Parliament was preceded by resolutions passed by the Senate and the House of Commons. These resolutions requested the queen to lay before Parliament at Westminster the bills that eventually were enacted as part of the Canadian constitution. But the resolutions themselves did not have any legal effect. Nor was the queen required, as a matter of strict law, to comply with the request of the Senate and House

129 Section 5(2) of the *Interpretation Act*, R.S.C. 1985, c. I-21 provides that if "no date of commencement is provided for in an Act, the date of commencement of that Act is the date of assent to the Act." Similar provisions exist in statutes enacted at the provincial level.

130 A proclamation is an order in council issued by the Governor in Council.

of Commons. Only the actual statutes enacted by the Westminster Parliament had the legal effect of amending the Canadian constitution.

8) Proroguing and Dissolving Parliament

The parliamentary calendar is divided into sessions, with each session commencing with a reading of a Speech from the Throne. There is no fixed length of time for a session; it may be as short as a few months, or continue for two or three years. In recent years, sessions have been quite short, owing to successive minority governments and the successive prorogations of Parliament discussed above. For example, the first session of the fortieth Canadian Parliament commenced on 18 November 2008 and lasted until Parliament was prorogued on 4 December 2008. The second session began on 26 January 2009 and lasted until prorogation on 30 December 2009. The third session lasted just under a year, from 3 March 2010 until the passing of the non-confidence vote following a parliamentary committee finding that the conservative government was in contempt of Parliament.

It is up to the government to determine how long a particular parliamentary session will continue. As discussed above, a session is brought to a close when the governor general prorogues Parliament. Any legislation that has not completed the legislative process in both the Senate and the House of Commons automatically dies when Parliament is prorogued. Thus, the government usually waits until most of its important pieces of legislation have been passed before instructing the governor general to prorogue Parliament. Prorogation is followed by the governor general summoning MPs and senators to a new session and the reading of a new Speech from the Throne.

The dissolution of Parliament is a proclamation by the governor general bringing the Parliament itself to a close and ordering a general election for the House of Commons. The House of Commons must be dissolved within five years of the return of the writs from the previous general election.[131] The writs from a general election are usually returned within a few weeks of a general election, so a government that wished to extend its mandate to the absolute limit could wait slightly more than five years before calling another election. However, over the past several decades, governments have tended to call elections approximately every four years. After the election, the governor general selects the leader of the majority party to form a government, and the parliamentary cycle begins again.

---

131 See s. 50 of the *Constitution Act, 1867* and s. 4(1) of the *Constitution Act, 1982*.

F. NO SEPARATION OF POWERS BETWEEN THE EXECUTIVE AND THE LEGISLATURE

The doctrine of the "separation of powers" was developed in the seventeenth and eighteenth centuries by the English philosopher John Locke and by the French jurist Charles-Louis Montesquieu. Both Locke and Montesquieu believed that there should be a clear separation among the executive, legislative, and judicial branches of government. They reasoned that such separation was necessary to prevent tyranny. As Locke stated: "[i]t may be too great a temptation to humane frailty, apt to grasp at Power, for the same Persons who have the power of making laws, to have also in their hands the power to execute them."[132] The principle of the separation of powers is expressed most clearly in the U.S. constitution. There is a clear separation between the executive and the legislative branches, with neither the president nor members of the Cabinet permitted to sit or vote in Congress. Nor does the president have the power to direct the affairs of Congress or to compel it to adopt legislation. The U.S. constitution also incorporates a complicated series of checks and balances that prevents either the executive or the legislature from dominating the other branch. For example, the president has the power to veto legislation, but this veto may itself be overridden by a two-thirds vote in each House of Congress. Treaties may be negotiated by the president but must be approved by a two-thirds majority in the Senate. Many of the president's appointments to key office, including the Supreme Court, are subject to confirmation by Congress.[133]

There is no such separation of legislative and executive functions in the Canadian context. The key members of the executive, the prime minister and the Cabinet, must hold seats in Parliament. The government also has the power to control and direct the affairs of the House of Commons. In part, this control is derived from the fact that, in accordance with the principles of responsible government, the government controls a majority of seats in the House of Commons. It can therefore be assured that most of its legislative proposals will be adopted by the House and the Senate. The government's control over the House is reinforced through its ability to set the House agenda and to determine which matters will be debated and voted on. The vast majority of the

---

132 J. Locke, *Second Treatise of Civil Government*, c. 12, para. 143, quoted in M.J.C. Vile, *Constitutionalism and the Separation of Powers* (Oxford: Clarendon Press, 1967) at 62.

133 Under the U.S. constitution, the judicial branch is also separate and independent from both the executive and the legislature. This aspect of the doctrine of separation of powers is discussed in Chapter 4.

House's time is devoted to "government orders"—that is, the consideration of government legislation or other business. Although a limited amount of time is set aside for the consideration of private members' business as well as for what are termed "opposition days,"[134] the government can usually prevent measures or proposals that it opposes from coming to a vote, particularly where it has a majority.[135]

Thus, far from separating the executive and legislative functions, the parliamentary system concentrates executive and legislative powers in the hands of the executive. In fact, the nineteenth-century constitutional theorist Walter Bagehot described the "efficient secret [of the British constitution as the] close union, the nearly complete fusion, of the executive and legislative powers."[136] While some commentators have criticized Bagehot's use of the term "fusion," there can be no doubt that the parliamentary system is characterized by the concentration of power rather than its dispersal or separation, as is the case in the American system. The Anglo-Canadian approach has both advantages and disadvantages. While the concentration of power in the hands of the executive means that a government is more likely to be able to implement its electoral program, critics of the parliamentary system argue that there are insufficient checks on the power of the government and no way of forcing it to account for its actions other than during relatively infrequent election campaigns.

G. EXECUTIVE AND LEGISLATIVE POWER AT THE PROVINCIAL LEVEL

Part V of the *Constitution Act, 1867*, entitled "Provincial Constitutions," sets out the framework for executive and legislative power in the provinces. In each province, there is to be an officer known as the lieutenant governor, who is to be appointed by the Governor General in Council for a five-year term.[137] The salary of the lieutenant governor is to

134 A total of twenty days, spread over three supply periods, are allotted to the opposition. On these days, opposition motions take precedence over government business, and speeches are limited to twenty minutes. However, the scheduling of these days remains within the control of the government.

135 Note, however, the 2003 rule changes, described at note 126 above, that make it somewhat easier for private members' bills to come to a vote.

136 W. Bagehot, *The English Constitution* (London: C.A. Watts, 1964; repr. 1867 ed.) at 65.

137 Sections 58 & 59 of the *Constitution Act, 1867*. As discussed above, the lieutenant governor is the representative of the Crown in the province and exercises all the

be fixed and provided by federal law,[138] thereby giving the lieutenant governor a measure of independence from the provincial legislature and government. The 1867 Act also provides for the establishment or continuation of Executive Councils in each province, appointed by the lieutenant governor from "such Persons as the Lieutenant Governor from Time to Time thinks fit."[139] Of course, the principles of responsible government require the lieutenant governor to choose the members of the Executive Council in accordance with the advice of a first minister who enjoys the confidence of the Legislative Assembly, and to exercise all the Crown's powers in accordance with the advice of the Executive Council so appointed.

Legislative power in each province is exercised by an elected Legislative Assembly. Bills become law when they receive three readings in the Legislative Assembly, in a process similar to that described in relation to the federal Parliament, and are approved by the lieutenant governor. At one time, Manitoba, New Brunswick, Prince Edward Island, Quebec, and Nova Scotia had appointed Legislative Councils (the provincial equivalent of the federal Senate), which also had to approve bills before their submission to the lieutenant governor for assent. These Legislative Councils were subsequently abolished by provincial legislation, with Quebec being the final province to abolish its Legislative Council in 1968.

FURTHER READINGS

BRAZIER, R., *Constitutional Practice: The Foundations of British Government*, 3d ed. (Oxford: Oxford University Press, 1999)

DAWSON, R.M., *The Government of Canada*, 6th ed., ed by N. Ward (Toronto: University of Toronto Press, 1987) cc. 9 and 11

FORSEY, E.A., *The Royal Power of Dissolution of Parliament in the British Commonwealth* (Toronto: Oxford University Press, 1943)

---

powers of the Crown in Right of the province. This role was not specified in the *Constitution Act, 1867*, although the Act did refer to the lieutenant governor as the chief executive officer of the province (s. 62). However, subsequent judicial interpretation of the Act held that the lieutenant governor was the queen's representative, as opposed to being the delegate or representative of the federal government. See *Maritime Bank*, above note 60.

138 Section 60 of the *Constitution Act, 1867.*

139 *Ibid.* s. 63, which describes the Executive Council of Ontario and Quebec.

HEARD, A., *Canadian Constitutional Conventions: The Marriage of Law and Politics* (Toronto: Oxford University Press, 1991)

HOGG, P.W., *Constitutional Law of Canada*, loose-leaf (Toronto: Carswell, 2007), c. 1

———, "Prorogation and the Power of the Governor General" (2009) 27 N.J.C.L. 193

———, P.J. MONAHAN, & W.K. WRIGHT, *Liability of the Crown*, 4th ed. (Toronto: Carswell, 2011)

JACKSON, P., & PATRICIA LEOPOLD, eds., *O. Hood Phillips' Constitutional and Administrative Law*, 8th ed. (London: Sweet & Maxwell, 2001)

MAINGOT, J.P., *Parliamentary Privilege in Canada*, 2d ed. (Montreal: McGill-Queen's University Press, 1997)

MALLORY, J.R., *The Structure of Canadian Government* (Toronto: Gage, 1984) cc. 2, 3, and 7

MCCAY, W.R., ed., *Erskine May's Treatise on the Law, Privileges, Proceedings and Usage of Parliament*, 23d ed. (London: LexisNexis UK, 2004)

O'BRIEN, A., & M. BOSC, eds., *House of Commons Procedure and Practice*, 2d ed. (Ottawa: House of Commons, 2009) c. 3

RUSSELL, P., & L. SOSSIN, *Parliamentary Democracy in Crisis* (Toronto: University of Toronto Press, 2009)

WADE, E.C.S., *Constitutional and Administrative Law*, 13th ed. (New York: Longman, 2003)

WHITTINGTON, M.S., & R.J. VAN LOON, *Canadian Government and Politics: Institutions and Processes* (Toronto: McGraw-Hill Ryerson, 1996) cc. 18–20

CHAPTER 4

THE CONSTITUTION ACT, 1867: FEDERALISM AND JUDICIAL POWER

A. FEDERALISM DEFINED

K.C. Wheare put forward the classic definition of the federal principle: a "method of dividing powers so that the general and regional governments are each within a sphere co-ordinate and independent."[1] Wheare's definition provides that under a federal system, the general and regional governments each has an autonomous sphere of power that can be exercised independently of the other. Further, the powers of the central government are exercised directly in relation to individual citizens, rather than indirectly through the states or provinces. A similar definition of federalism was offered by A.V. Dicey, who identified the three leading characteristics of a "completely developed federalism" as including: (1) the distribution of powers among governmental bodies, each with limited and coordinate powers; (2) the supremacy of the constitution; and (3) the authority of the courts as the interpreters of the constitution.[2]

Although Wheare's definition has been criticized by some commentators as being unduly legalistic[3] and as placing undue stress on

1 K.C. Wheare, *Federal Government*, 4th ed. (London: Oxford University Press, 1963) at 11.

2 A.V. Dicey, *Introduction to the Study of the Law of the Constitution*, 10th ed. (London: Macmillan, 1959) at 140.

3 See, for example, P.T. King, *Federalism and Federation* (Baltimore: Johns Hopkins University Press, 1982) at 77.

the separateness of the central and regional authorities,[4] it provides a basis for distinguishing federal from other forms of government and remains widely accepted. Donald Smiley, building on Wheare's formulation, offered the following three-part working definition of a federal state,[5] which we adopt for purposes of this book:

1) legislative powers are distributed between a central and a regional government;
2) the powers of the central and regional governments are not subject to change by the other level of government; and
3) individual citizens are subject to laws enacted by both the central and the regional governments.

This formulation clearly distinguishes federal systems from unitary or confederal systems of government. In a unitary state, ultimate political authority resides in the central or national government. The central government may establish regional or local governments, but local government powers are not constitutionally entrenched and are subject to unilateral change by the central government. France and New Zealand are examples of unitary states.

In confederations, on the other hand, ultimate political authority resides in the states or regional governments, and the central government acts as their delegate. In this model, the central government may not even have the power to enact laws directly affecting individual citizens. For example, the Articles of Confederation adopted by the American colonies in 1777 did not grant the national government any free-standing power of taxation. Instead, the national government's sole source of funds was grants received from the state governments. Only the states had the power to levy taxes directly on the population.[6]

---

4 See A.H. Birch, *Federalism, Finance and Social Legislation* (Oxford: Clarendon Press, 1955) at 306.

5 See D.V. Smiley, *The Federal Condition in Canada* (Toronto: McGraw-Hill Ryerson, 1987) at 2.

6 A consensus emerged among the states after the conclusion of the American War of Independence in the 1780s that the national government's powers needed to be strengthened. This led to the Constitutional Convention of 1787 and the adoption of the final form of the American constitution, which granted the national government significant new powers such as the right to levy taxes and to regulate interstate and foreign commerce. The U.S. thus transformed what had been a confederacy into the first example of a truly federal form of government.

B. CANADA AS A FEDERAL STATE

The preamble to the *Constitution Act, 1867*[7] states that the provinces have "expressed their Desire to be federally united into One Dominion." However, despite this stated desire, the terms of the *Constitution Act, 1867* did not establish Canada as a true federal union. In a number of important respects, the provinces were subordinated to the federal government. In fact, the relationship between Ottawa and the provinces, at least in 1867, has been described by one leading expert as a colonial one, in which Canada was to be governed from Ottawa similar to a unitary state.[8] According to Wheare, Canada was, in law, a quasi-federal state.[9]

Although there were many centralizing features of the *Constitution Act, 1867*,[10] two features were particularly significant: the powers of reservation and disallowance. Under the *Constitution Act, 1867*, the federal government could appoint the lieutenant governors of the provinces and instruct them to withhold consent to provincial bills or to reserve them for the consideration of the federal government.[11] Furthermore, the federal government had the power to disallow or nullify any Act passed by the provincial legislature within two years of its enactment.[12] Moreover, in one particularly important area of legislation, education, the federal Parliament was not limited to disallowing provincial laws but could actually enact remedial legislation of its own to override a valid provincial law or a decision taken by a provincial authority pursuant to a valid provincial law.[13]

The federal disallowance power was used extensively in the late nineteenth century, both in cases of allegedly unconstitutional statutes and in relation to provincial laws that were regarded by Parliament

---

7 (U.K.), 30 & 31 Vict., c. 3.

8 See the discussion in J.R. Mallory, *The Structure of Canadian Government*, 2d ed. (Toronto: Gage, 1984) at 367–70.

9 Wheare, above note 1 at 18–20.

10 For a discussion of other centralizing features, including the federal power to appoint judges of the provincial superior courts and the federal power to "declare" works and undertakings to be subject to exclusive federal jurisdiction, see P.W. Hogg, *Constitutional Law of Canada*, loose-leaf, 5th ed. (Toronto: Carswell, 2009) at 5.3(a).

11 See the *Constitution Act, 1867*, ss. 55–57, 58, and 90.

12 See *ibid.*, ss. 55–57 and 90.

13 See *ibid.*, ss. 93(3)–(4). This power could be exercised to override any decisions of provincial authorities which, in the opinion of the federal government, affected guaranteed rights of religious minorities in relation to denominational schools.

as unjust or unwise.[14] However, the disallowance power has not been used for more than seventy years.[15] Where the federal government disputes the constitutional validity of a particular provincial statute, it now proceeds through the courts rather than resorting to the power of disallowance.[16] Similarly, the power of the lieutenant governor to reserve bills for the consideration of the federal government has not been used since 1961.[17] Although the powers of reservation and disallowance have never been repealed and remain part of the formal Canadian constitution, they are now regarded as moribund on the basis that they are inconsistent with the principle of federalism. Today there is a firm constitutional convention that the powers of reservation and disallowance cannot be used under any circumstances.[18] In fact, in *Reference Re Secession of Quebec*,[19] the Supreme Court of Canada noted that many constitutional scholars have contended that the federal disallowance

---

14 During the period 1867–96, 66 provincial statutes were disallowed. Disallowance was used in cases where a provincial law was "contrary to 'sound principles of legislation.'" It was used, in other words, as a means to keep "the provincial legislatures in order and . . . as a check on unjust and oppressive legislation." See R.M. Dawson, *The Government of Canada*, 6th ed., ed by N. Ward (Toronto: University of Toronto Press, 1987) at 225. In the period following 1896, strong provincial objections to the disallowance power led to a significant reduction in its use by the federal government.

15 The most recent use of the disallowance power was in relation to the 1943 Alberta statute *An Act to Prohibit the Sale of Lands to any Enemy Aliens and Hutterites for the Duration of the War*, Alberta 6 Geo. VI, c. 16. See D.M. Jackson, *The Crown and Canadian Federalism* (Toronto: Dundurn Press, 2013) at 117.

16 As noted above, the federal use of the disallowance power in the nineteenth century was not limited to cases where the federal government believed a provincial statute to be unconstitutional, but extended to provincial bills that the federal government regarded as "discriminatory or unjust." Given that the federal government no longer invokes the disallowance power in cases of alleged unconstitutionality, *a fortiori*, it would never seek to disallow a provincial law on the basis that it represented bad or unwise policy.

17 In 1961, the power of reservation was used by the lieutenant governor of Saskatchewan, who reserved a bill that gave the provincial government the power to alter certain mining contracts. The lieutenant governor had taken this action on his own initiative, contrary to the policy of the federal government dating to 1882 requiring the power of reservation to be exercised only on the instructions of the federal government.

18 The same could be said of the federal power to enact remedial education laws. The last occasion on which the federal government contemplated using this power was 1896. Today, disputes over provincial laws dealing with education and religious minorities are resolved through the courts rather than through an appeal to the federal Cabinet to enact remedial laws.

19 [1998] 2 S.C.R. 217 [*Secession Reference*].

power has been abandoned in the context of discussing the unwritten constitutional principle of federalism.

The *Constitution Act, 1867* contained other centralizing features, which tended to subordinate the provinces to the federal government. As with the powers of reservation and disallowance, in many cases these federal powers have now fallen into disuse or have been abandoned.[20] In other cases, the courts have interpreted the centralizing constitutional provisions so as to restrict the ability of the federal government to interfere with the autonomy and independence of the provinces.[21]

Today there can be no doubt that both in law and in practice, the provinces are independent of the federal government; in fact, Canada is widely regarded as having one of the most decentralized federal systems in the world. The provinces in Canada enjoy much more power than the states in the United States, despite the fact that under the terms of the U.S. constitution of 1787, state power is described in much more expansive terms than in Canada. It is clear, therefore, that Canada is a federal state.

C. FEDERAL DISTRIBUTION OF LEGISLATIVE POWERS

1) Division of Powers in Sections 91–93

Part VI of the *Constitution Act, 1867*, made up of sections 91 to 95, distributes legislative powers between the Parliament of Canada and the legislatures of the provinces. Sections 91 to 93 confer what are described in the Act as "exclusive" powers on Parliament and the provincial legislatures.

Section 91, under the heading "Powers of Parliament," defines the legislative powers of the Parliament of Canada. There are two distinct parts to section 91. The first part—sometimes called the "opening words" or the "peace, order, and good government" (POGG) clause—states that Parliament may make laws "for the Peace, Order, and good Government of Canada, in relation to all Matters not coming within the Classes

---

20 See, for example, the federal power to enact remedial education laws set out in the *Constitution Act, 1867*, as discussed above.

21 The most obvious example is the interpretation of the division of powers in the *Constitution Act, 1867*, ss. 91 & 92, discussed below. The courts have generally given a narrow interpretation to federal powers and an expansive interpretation to provincial powers. These principles are discussed below and in more detail in Chapter 7.

of Subjects by this Act assigned exclusively to the Legislatures of the Provinces." The phrase "peace, order, and good government" is similar to terminology that had been used in the *Union Act, 1840* and the *Constitutional Act, 1791* and was intended to signify a general grant of law-making power.[22] However, describing this clause as a "peace, order, and good government" clause is somewhat misleading. In fact, the key words in the clause are those that follow it: the authority of Parliament is limited to the enactment of laws in relation to matters not coming within the provincial classes of subjects set out in section 92. In this sense, the clause might more accurately be described as a "not coming within" clause.[23] It confers a residual power on Parliament, consisting of the residue of legislative power that is left over after taking into account the classes of subjects over which "exclusive jurisdiction" has been allocated to the provinces. The drafters of the *Constitution Act, 1867* believed that conferring this residual power on the federal Parliament would lead to a strong national government and would avoid the mistake that had been made in the United States, where residual power was conferred on the states. In fact, during the confederation debates, John A. Macdonald boasted that the general government would be the dominant government because "we have expressly declared that all subjects of general interest not distinctly conferred upon the local governments and local legislatures shall be conferred upon the General Government and Legislature—We have thus avoided that great source of weakness which has been the source of the disruption of the United States."[24]

The second part of section 91 consists of thirty specific classes of subjects over which "exclusive Legislative Authority" is assigned to the

22 For example, the *Union Act, 1840* (U.K.), 3 & 4 Vict., c. 35, had conferred power onto the legislature of Canada to make laws for the "Peace, Welfare, and good Government of the Province of Canada."

23 This point is made convincingly by K. Lysyk in "Constitutional Reform and the Introductory Clause of Section 91: Residual and Emergency Law-Making Power" (1979) 57 Can. Bar Rev. 531. Although the clause might more properly be described as a "not coming within" clause, the general practice used in this book is to describe the opening words as the "POGG" power.

24 *Confederation Debates*, 6 February 1865, quoted in Smiley, above note 5 at 36–37. Of course, Macdonald's predicted result implicitly assumed that the enumerated powers of the provinces would be interpreted narrowly; if the enumerated powers are interpreted broadly, the residue is correspondingly reduced. The latter is what occurred in both the United States and Canada in the twentieth century, with the courts in both countries interpreting the enumerated powers broadly, leaving relatively little room for the residual power (which, in the U.S., is conferred on the states).

Parliament of Canada.[25] Section 91 states that the list of Parliament's exclusive powers is included "for greater Certainty, but not so as to restrict the Generality of the foregoing Terms of this Section." Following the enumeration of these thirty classes of subjects, section 91 states that matters coming within any of these classes "shall be deemed not to come within" the class of matters of a local or private nature assigned to the provinces.

Section 92, under the heading "Exclusive Powers of the Provincial Legislatures," provides that the provincial legislatures may "exclusively make Laws in relation to Matters coming within the Classes of Subjects next hereinafter enumerated." A list of sixteen classes of subjects is set out. Many of the enumerated classes in section 92 are framed in very narrow and specific terms and have proven to be of limited significance in terms of the development of provincial jurisdiction. However, one of the classes in section 92, "Property and Civil Rights in the Province," has been particularly significant. Since virtually all provincial laws regulate "rights" in some way, almost all provincial laws could be said to be within the scope of section 92(13). The courts have interpreted section 92(13) extremely broadly. In fact, section 92(13), as interpreted by the courts, is so sweeping that there are usually only two ways in which a provincial law regulating rights can be found to be unconstitutional. The first possibility is if the provincial legislation deals directly with a particular matter that falls squarely within one of the classes of subject enumerated in section 91. The second possibility is that the provincial law deals directly with rights of individuals or entities outside the province such that the provincial law is not restricted to matters "within the province."[26]

Section 92A, which was added in 1982, confers exclusive legislative authority on the provinces to enact certain laws dealing with non-renewable natural resources, forestry resources, and electrical energy within a province. The provinces are also granted non-exclusive or concurrent power to enact laws dealing with the export from a province to another part of Canada of these resources, and to impose indirect taxes on such resources.[27] Section 93 grants the provinces exclusive power to

---

25 Section 91 of the *Constitution Act, 1867* originally consisted of twenty-nine classes of subjects. Between 1867 and 1982, two additional classes of subjects were added through constitutional amendments (*Constitution Act, 1982* (enacted as *Canada Act 1982* (U.K.), 1982, c. 11, Sched. B.)); in 1982, one of those additional classes was repealed, leaving an existing total of thirty federal classes.

26 This notion of extraterritoriality is discussed in further detail in Chapter 10, Section C.

27 Section 92A of the *Constitution Act, 1867* was added by the *Constitution Act, 1982* in response to provincial complaints about a number of Supreme Court deci-

enact laws in relation to education, subject to the condition that these laws cannot prejudicially affect any rights or privileges enjoyed by religious minorities in respect of denominational schools at the time of Confederation.[28] There was also a right to appeal to the federal Cabinet from any provincial law or decision affecting the rights or privileges of a denominational minority and, in such cases, the federal Parliament could enact a remedial law implementing or giving effect to the federal Cabinet's decision.[29]

2) Overlap of Federal and Provincial Powers

The lists of powers enumerated in sections 91 and 92 are each described as "exclusive." The difficulty with this description is that the powers of the federal Parliament overlap with those of the provinces. For example, the "Regulation of Trade and Commerce," which is an enumerated federal power, will inevitably involve the regulation of rights—particularly rights of contract or property—and, in this sense, appears to overlap with "Property and Civil Rights." How, then, can each of these powers be exclusive?[30]

The courts have struggled to give effect to the use of the term "exclusive" in sections 91 and 92 by interpreting the federal heads of power so as to exclude the provincial heads of power, and *vice versa*. This process of "mutual modification" proceeds by "cutting out of whatever may be the larger, the more general, the wider, the vaguer enumeration of one section, so much as is comprised in some narrower, more definite, more precise enumeration in the other section."[31] For example, the federal power over "Bills of Exchange and Promissory Notes," which is precise and narrow, has been excised from the more general provincial

sions in the late 1970s that limited provincial powers to enact laws dealing with the natural resource sector. It is discussed in more detail in Chapter 10.

28 Similar guarantees for denominational schools were entrenched in Manitoba, Alberta, Saskatchewan, and Newfoundland when these provinces joined Confederation.

29 As noted above, this power has never been used and a constitutional convention has developed to the effect that the exercise of this power would be inappropriate.

30 The use of the adjective "exclusive" in ss. 91 & 92 of the *Constitution Act, 1867* was a departure from the approach taken in the *London Resolutions* of 1866, which simply provided that both Parliament and the legislatures had "power to make laws respecting the following subjects": see *Westminster Palace Hotel (London) Resolutions on Federation*, December 4, 1866, reprt. in W.P.M. Kennedy, *Statutes, Treaties and Documents of the Canadian Constitution 1713–1929*, 2d ed. (London: Oxford University Press, 1930) at 611 [*London Resolutions*].

31 See Edward Blake in argument before the Privy Council in *Canadian Pacific Railway v. Notre Dame de Bonsecours (Parish)*, [1899] A.C. 367 (P.C.) [*Bonsecours*].

power over property and civil rights. Certain cases have even gone so far as to describe the federal and provincial classes of subjects as constituting "watertight compartments" that do not in any way overlap with one another.[32] However, as discussed below and in more detail in Chapter 7, the courts have also developed a number of doctrines that permit considerable overlap between federal and provincial laws.[33] Today, in most areas of legislative policy, there is a significant regulatory presence of both the federal and the provincial levels of government. In fact, one survey of federal and provincial legislation and regulation found that the only exclusive federal areas[34] were military defence, veterans' affairs, the postal service, and monetary policy; in all other areas of federal law and regulation, the provinces had enacted laws or regulations dealing with the same subjects or issues. Conversely, the only exclusive provincial areas were municipal institutions, elementary and secondary education, and some areas of law related to property and other non-criminal matters.[35] In this sense, it is misleading to conceive of the federal and provincial classes of subjects as being mutually exclusive watertight compartments.

3) General Federal Legislative Power: POGG

As noted, the POGG power is residual or secondary to the provincial list of powers. That is, POGG grants the federal Parliament power to enact laws only in relation to matters that have not been assigned to the provinces. What about the relationship between POGG and the enumerated classes of subjects in section 91 over which Parliament is granted exclusive authority? The text of section 91 states that the enumerated classes of subjects are included merely "for greater Certainty, but not so as to restrict the Generality" of the POGG power. This terminology has led some constitutional commentators to argue that the POGG clause represents the true grant of federal power, and that the enumerated

---

32 Lord Atkin in *Can. (A.G.) v. Ont. (A.G.)*, [1937] A.C. 326 at 354 (P.C.) stated: "While the ship of state now sails on larger ventures and into foreign waters she still retains the watertight compartments which are an essential part of her original structure."

33 The most important of these doctrines is the "double aspect" doctrine, under which different aspects of a single matter may be subject to both federal and provincial regulation.

34 Namely, areas in which the federal government was active and the provinces were not.

35 G. Stevenson, "Federalism and Intergovernmental Relations" in M.S. Whittington and G. Williams, eds., *Canadian Politics in the 21st Century* (Scarborough: Nelson, 2000) at 88.

classes of subjects are merely instances of the more general power of Parliament to legislate in relation to the peace, order, and good government of Canada.[36] However, as discussed in Chapters 7 and 8, the courts have taken precisely the opposite view. Section 91 has been interpreted as having two distinct components: the enumerated classes of subjects and the POGG power. Furthermore, as discussed above, POGG is a "residual" power and its application has been limited to situations in which a matter does not fall within any of the enumerated federal powers in section 91 or the enumerated provincial powers in section 92.

Some critics believe that this "two compartment" view of section 91 has stripped the opening words (or POGG clause) of its true meaning and led to the undue weakening of federal authority.[37] This is because virtually no field of jurisdiction can be found that is not covered by one or more enumerated heads of power in sections 91 or 92. Thus, while the enumerated heads of federal authority were preceded by the express proviso that they were not to limit the generality of the POGG power, this is precisely what occurred. R. MacGregor Dawson has concluded that "the enumerated part became of greater consequence in interpretations than the general grant it illustrated 'for greater certainty.'"[38]

We consider the judicial interpretation of section 91 in more detail later in this book. However, it should be noted here that, in our view, the significance attached by critics to the relationship between the POGG power and the enumerated classes of section 91 seems overstated. Despite the literal wording of section 91, it seems difficult to accept that the enumerated classes in section 91 are merely illustrations of the POGG power. The enumerated heads of federal power overlap with and thereby derogate from the enumerated provincial heads of power in section 92, particularly the sweeping provincial power over "Property and Civil Rights." For instance, many of the enumerated classes in section 91, such as "Trade and Commerce," "Banking," "Bills of Exchange and Promissory Notes," "Interest," "Legal Tender," "Bankruptcy and Insolvency," "Patents,"

---

36 Former Chief Justice Laskin, in his academic writings before his appointment to the bench, was the most articulate and vigorous exponent of this "one compartment view" of s. 91 in the *Constitution Act, 1867*. See, in particular, B. Laskin, "Peace, Order and Good Government Re-examined" (1947) 25 Can. Bar Rev. 1054.

37 See, in particular, the famous *O'Connor Report: Report to the Honourable Speaker of the Senate of Canada by the Parliamentary Counsel of the Senate Relating to the Enactment of the British North America Act, 1867* (Ottawa: King's Printer, 1939). The description of this view as a "two compartment" interpretation of s. 91 is derived from G.P. Browne, *The Judicial Committee and the British North America Act* (Toronto: University of Toronto Press, 1967), whose book is a sustained critique of the *O'Connor Report*.

38 See Dawson, above note 14 at 310.

and "Copyrights" may have been interpreted as falling within the provincial head of power over "Property and Civil Rights," had they not been expressly included in section 91. In fact, the potential overlap between the enumerated classes in section 91 and property and civil rights in section 92 was foreseen by the drafters of the *Constitution Act, 1867.* The *London Resolutions* of 1866 stated that the provincial legislatures would be granted the power to enact laws over property and civil rights "excepting portions thereof assigned to the General Parliament."[39] In the final version of the *Constitution Act, 1867*, this proviso carving out of property and civil rights the "portions thereof assigned to the General Parliament" was deleted. However, in its place, the drafters described the powers of Parliament in relation to the enumerated classes in section 91 as being "exclusive."[40] Federal power in relation to the enumerated classes was also described as operating "notwithstanding anything in this Act." In other words, in the case of overlap between the classes of subjects in sections 91 and 92, the federal list was intended take priority. This is a clear indication that the enumeration in section 91 is not mere surplus but significantly defines the scope of federal legislative authority.

Furthermore, in considering the POGG power, it is the interpretation of *provincial* powers in section 92—and not the relationship between POGG and the enumerated classes in section 91—that is critical. Even if the enumerated classes in section 91 are mere illustrations of POGG, the POGG power is subordinate to the classes of subjects in section 92. As discussed above, the POGG power is confined to matters "not coming within" section 92. Thus, if section 92 is interpreted in a broad and expansive manner, the scope of POGG must inevitably be reduced.

4) Enumerated Powers in Sections 91 and 92

a) Federal Enumerated Powers

There is clear historical evidence that certain of the Fathers of Confederation intended to draft the enumerated powers in sections 91 and 92 so as to create a strong central government. Sir John A. Macdonald proudly declared in the confederation debates that: "We have given the General Legislature all the great subjects of legislation." This centralization resulted, in Macdonald's view, from the fact that "all subjects of general interest not distinctly conferred upon the local governments and local legislatures shall be conferred upon the General Government

39 The *London Resolutions*, above note 30.

40 The *London Resolutions* had not described either the federal or the provincial classes of subjects as exclusive (see the discussion above at note 30).

and Legislature."[41] What were these "great subjects" of legislation? One of the principal motivations behind political union in British North America had been the desire to create a political unit that was sufficiently large and stable to permit westward expansion and the creation of a transcontinental economy. Westward expansion required the financing and construction of expensive transportation links, particularly railways. Rail and canal projects had nearly bankrupted a number of the former colonies, and it was clear that the significant new infrastructure construction that would be required for expansion could simply not be financed by the colonies separately. Therefore, the *Constitution Act, 1867* was carefully designed to ensure that the federal government would have all the tools necessary to undertake westward expansion, including the financing and construction of necessary transportation infrastructure.

The first four enumerated classes of federal authority in section 91 are particularly significant in this regard. They grant Parliament exclusive power to enact laws dealing with: "Public Debt and Property" (section 91(1)); "[t]he borrowing of Money on the Public Credit" (section 91(4)); the raising of money "by any Mode or System of Taxation" (section 91(3)); and "[t]he Regulation of Trade and Commerce" (section 91(2)). The exclusive power to enact laws dealing with the public debt of Canada would guarantee existing creditors that they would be repaid and encourage others to lend the money required for new infrastructure construction. The unlimited power of taxation would ensure that the central government would have the capacity to raise sufficient revenues to service such borrowing. Finally, the broad trade and commerce power was a signal that the economic ground rules in the new country would be set by the national government, ensuring that the provinces would not be able to erect barriers to interprovincial trade. Business would therefore invest in the new country secure in the knowledge that it will be able to exploit the opportunities for growth and expansion that a transcontinental economy would provide.[42]

These broad economic powers in the first four subsections of section 91 were reinforced and strengthened by a variety of other grants of power to the federal Parliament. Ownership of existing canals and rail-

---

41 *Confederation Debates* (6 February 1865), quoted in Smiley, above note 5 at 36–37.

42 The language of s. 91(2) was deliberately broader than the comparable clause in the U.S. constitution, which limited Congress's power to the regulation of "Commerce . . . among the several States" (U.S. Const. art.1, § 8, cl. 3). Ironically, however, the American courts' interpretation of congressional power to regulate commerce has been much more expansive than that of the Privy Council and Canadian courts in relation to Parliament's power under s. 91(2).

ways was transferred to the federal government,[43] and exclusive legislative jurisdiction over such "Works and Undertakings" was granted to the federal Parliament.[44] The federal government specifically committed itself to the commencement of the construction of the Intercolonial Railway, linking the Maritime provinces with the port of Montreal.[45] It was also granted exclusive powers in relation to any other matters that might impair the creditworthiness of the state or private enterprise, or which might affect the stability of the economy. These powers included exclusive jurisdiction over currency and coinage (section 91(14)); banking, bank incorporation, and the issue of paper money (section 91(15)); bills of exchange and promissory notes (section 91(18)); interest (section 91(19)); legal tender (section 91(20)); and bankruptcy and insolvency (section 91(21)).

What emerges clearly from this catalogue of federal powers is that Parliament was granted sweeping powers to regulate the economic affairs of the new nation. The federal power over "Trade and Commerce" in section 91(2) represented the most general expression of this intention. This general power was reinforced by specific grants of power in order to ensure that any matters that might impact on the financial structure or integrity of the new country or on the transportation or trade links that would be needed to ensure its viability, would be reserved to Parliament alone.

b) Provincial Enumerated Powers

The provinces were granted certain powers that might affect economic and financial matters, but these powers were framed much more narrowly than those assigned to the federal Parliament. The provincial taxing power, for example, is subject to three limits: (1) it must be "Direct Taxation";[46] (2) it must be "within the Province"; and (3) it must be

---

43 See s. 108 and the Third Schedule of the *Constitution Act, 1867*.

44 See ss. 91(29) and 92(10)(a) of the *Constitution Act, 1867*.

45 See s. 145 of the *Constitution Act, 1867*. Halifax merchants had pressed for the Intercolonial on the basis that it would provide them with access to markets in central Canada. But the Intercolonial would also provide exporters in Montreal with an ice-free port in winter.

46 The distinction between direct and indirect taxation is notoriously ambiguous and elusive. The courts defined a direct tax based on the analysis of J.S. Mill in *Principles of Political Economy*, ed by J. Riley (Oxford: Oxford University Press, 1994): "A direct tax is one which is demanded from the very persons who it is intended or desired should pay it. Indirect taxes are those demanded from one person in the expectation and intention that he shall indemnify himself at the expense of another" (*Bank of Toronto v. Lambe* (1887), 12 App. Cas. 575 (P.C.)). But this definition has proven itself very difficult to apply in practice since, as a prac-

"in order to the raising of a Revenue for Provincial Purposes." Of these limits, the first was clearly the most significant at the time of Confederation. Approximately 80 percent of government revenues in 1867 were derived from customs and excise duties, which were classified as indirect taxes. Yet, since the provinces were prohibited from levying indirect taxes, these revenues were reserved to the federal government.[47] Direct taxes such as corporate and personal income tax—the most important source of revenues for all governments in Canada today—were unknown in 1867. Grants from the federal government, rather than revenues from direct taxes, were the most important source of provincial revenues immediately after Confederation. For example, the early budgets of the province of Ontario in the late 1860s reveal that over 55 percent of provincial revenue was derived from federal government grants.[48] While these grants were constitutionally guaranteed and could not be reduced unilaterally by the federal government,[49] they could not be increased without an amendment to the *BNA Act*. In this way, the provinces were deprived of the ability to raise sufficient revenues to fund their operation and were fiscally dependent on the federal government.

Not only were the provinces constrained in their ability to raise revenue, but they were also given a limited scope of regulatory power in comparison with the broad powers granted to the federal Parliament. In contrast to the expansive and open-ended language employed in section 91, virtually all the classes of subjects allocated to the provinces were subject to qualifiers or limitations. Many of the provincial powers were limited to matters "in the province" (for example, property and civil rights "in the Province" or the administration of justice "in the Province"). Other provincial heads of power were limited to laws with

---

tical matter, taxes are generally passed to others, as, for example, in the case of a business that passes on "direct" taxes in the form of higher prices to consumers.

47 The exception to this generalization was royalties from Crown lands and property, which were reserved to the provinces even though they were an indirect form of taxation. See s. 109 of the *Constitution Act, 1867*.

48 For example, in 1869 total revenues for Ontario were estimated to be approximately $2,465,000; approximately $1.4 million (or about 56 percent) was received in the form of various grants or subsidies from the federal government. The next largest source of revenue was receipts from Crown lands, estimated at approximately $500,000: see *Speech of the Hon. E.B. Wood Delivered on the 15th of December 1868 in the Legislative Assembly of Ontario* (Toronto: Hunter, Rose and Co., 1869) App. F at 58–59.

49 See s. 18 of the *Constitution Act, 1867*. This section was repealed in 1950 by the *Statute Law Revision Act, 1950* (U.K.), 14 Geo. VI, c. 6, when a new system of federal grants made the original section obsolete.

"provincial objects" (for example, the incorporation of companies "with Provincial Objects" or the imposition of licence fees for the raising of revenues for "Provincial, Local, or Municipal purposes"). It is true that the wording of section 92(13) "Property and Civil Rights in the Province" was potentially very broad. But it must be remembered that all the provincial powers in section 92 were assumed by the drafters of the *Constitution Act, 1867* to be subject to the exclusive powers of Parliament. Any overlap in sections 91 and 92 would be resolved in favour of the exclusive regulatory power of Parliament, owing to the "notwithstanding anything in this Act" language employed in relation to the enumerated federal powers in section 91 and the POGG power. Moreover, the federal powers of reservation and disallowance were also intended to serve as a check on provincial legislation that might interfere with the economic interests of the country. These federal powers were used in the early years following Confederation to overturn provincial laws that interfered with rights of property or contract.[50]

c) Judicial Interpretation: Role Reversal

Ironically, the judicial interpretation of sections 91 and 92 has tended to stand the two sections on their heads. The enumerated provincial powers have been interpreted far more broadly than the powers assigned to the federal Parliament. The courts have employed two main interpretive devices to arrive at this result. First, the provincial power over property and civil rights in section 92(13) has been interpreted very broadly so as to potentially cover rights of any kind in the province. Second, the courts have narrowed the scope of any federal power that might potentially overlap with section 92(13) in the name of ensuring that the federal and provincial powers remain "exclusive."

The diminution of federal authority has emerged most clearly in relation to the federal power over "Trade and Commerce." On its face, the "Regulation of Trade and Commerce" is just as broad and potentially all-encompassing as "Property and Civil Rights." The courts, particularly the Judicial Committee of the Privy Council in the early decades of the twentieth century, concluded that anything that involved "Property and Civil Rights in the Province" must necessarily be excluded from the federal power over "Regulation of Trade and Commerce." However, since "Property and Civil Rights" was such an all-encompassing subject, the "Regulation of Trade and Commerce" was reduced to virtual insignificance.

---

50 See J.R. Mallory, *Social Credit and the Federal Power in Canada* (Toronto: University of Toronto Press, 1954) c. 2.

This approach to the interpretation of the federal and provincial heads of power is plainly inconsistent with the wording of section 91 and the intentions of the drafters of the *Constitution Act, 1867*. As discussed above, the enumerated federal powers in section 91 are described as granting Parliament exclusive power "notwithstanding anything in this Act." This wording suggests that in cases where the federal enumerated classes in section 91 overlap with the provincial enumerated classes in section 92, preference should be given to the federal powers. In other words, the overlap between sections 91(2) and 92(13) should have led to the narrowing of the provincial power over property and civil rights rather than the narrowing of the federal power over trade and commerce. By taking precisely the opposite approach, the courts have ignored the original intention of the drafters to ensure that the national government would have exclusive responsibility for shaping national economic policy. As discussed in more detail in later chapters, in some cases, this has led to fragmented and divided economic policy, with the provinces assuming an increasingly important role at the expense of the national government. Although the Supreme Court of Canada has resuscitated the scope of the trade and commerce power somewhat in recent years, the scope of the power is a mere shadow of what the drafters of the *Constitution Act, 1867* envisaged.

5) Concurrent Powers

While the vast majority of legislative powers in the *Constitution Act, 1867* were described as exclusive, section 95 granted Parliament and the provincial legislatures concurrent power over agriculture and immigration. Section 95 also provided that, in the event of a conflict between a federal and a provincial law, the federal law would be paramount. In other words, any provisions of a provincial law that were inconsistent with a federal law dealing with the same matter would be suspended.

Under section 94, Parliament was granted the power to enact laws providing for the uniformity of laws dealing with property and civil rights in Ontario, New Brunswick, and Nova Scotia. However, a federal law in relation to property and civil rights could only take effect in provinces that had adopted and enacted the federal law. Quebec was excluded from section 94, providing additional constitutional protection for French civil law. Whereas other provincial legislatures could agree through the enactment of an ordinary statute to cede jurisdiction over property and civil rights to Parliament, the Quebec legislature was incapable of agreeing to such a transfer of jurisdiction. Section 94 has never been used and, as a practical matter, is now spent, since it is inconceivable that any province would consent to a federal law in relation to property and civil rights in the province. The fact that the framers contemplated uniform private law in Canada outside of Quebec is another example of planned centralization which never came to be, and is in fact quite at odds with contemporary notions of Canadian federalism.[51]

In 1951, section 94A was added to the *Constitution Act, 1867*, granting Parliament concurrent power to enact laws in relation to old-age pensions.[52] However, any federal legislation enacted pursuant to this section is subject to provincial laws, which will take precedence in case of conflict. Thus, the general rule that favours federal paramountcy in cases of conflict between federal and provincial legislation is reversed in the case of section 94A. This formula, which has been termed "concurrency with provincial paramountcy" (CPP), has been proposed as a means of meeting demands for greater provincial autonomy, particularly those of Quebec.[53] However, this approach is controversial, since it could lead to significant variation in laws applicable to areas that are now subject to exclusive federal regulation. Neither the federal government nor the provinces has endorsed the CPP approach outside of section 94A, and it was not incorporated in either the *Meech Lake* or the *Charlottetown Accords* discussed in later chapters.[54]

6) Judicial Characterization of Laws in Federalism Cases

a) The Pith and Substance Doctrine

In order to determine whether particular laws enacted by Parliament or the provincial legislatures are valid, the courts have applied what has been termed the "pith and substance" doctrine. The doctrine has

---

51 See, for example, *Reference re Securities Act*, [2011] 3 S.C.R. 837 for a spirited defence of non-harmonized private law.

52 The section was amended in 1964 to grant Parliament power to enact laws dealing with supplementary benefits. See the *British North America Act, 1951* (U.K.), 14 & 15 Geo. VI, c. 31 and the *Constitution Act 1964* (U.K.), 1964, c. 73. The provinces already possessed legislative jurisdiction in relation to these matters by virtue of s. 92(13), Property and Civil Rights in the Province.

53 See, in particular, D. Milne, "Equality or Asymmetry: Why Choose?" in R.L. Watts and D.M. Brown, eds., *Options for a New Canada* (Toronto: University of Toronto Press, 1991) at 285.

54 There is one exception. In the *Charlottetown Accord*, provincial laws dealing with certain aspects of the election of senators to a reformed Senate would have taken priority over inconsistent federal laws on the same subject. But the accord generally took the approach that any powers granted to one province should be granted to all equally.

two steps.[55] Step one requires the court to determine the "pith and substance" of the law. Step two involves a determination of how the law fits within the heads of power set out in the *Constitution Act, 1867*.

In step one, the court attempts to determine the "pith and substance" of the law. The term "pith and substance" has been variously described as the "matter" of the legislation,[56] its "true meaning or essential character, its core";[57] its "most important feature" or its "dominant" or "leading" characteristic.[58] The court determines the pith and substance of the law by examining both the purpose of the law and its effects. The purpose of legislation may be revealed by reference to a purpose clause in the statute itself, or through consideration of extrinsic material such as debates in Parliament or the relevant legislature, testimony before Standing Committees, government reports, and similar material.[59] Courts also often look to the problems the legislation was meant to address—the so-called mischief approach—to determine its purpose.

Courts will generally consider the legal effects of the law, considering how it will actually operate, in order to assist in determining its purpose. However, this does not involve the courts attempting to determine whether the law will actually achieve its purposes, since the question of the efficacy of the law is a matter for Parliament rather than the courts.[60] Rather, the courts look to the manner in which the law will

---

55 See, generally, *Reference Re Firearms Act*, [2000] 1 S.C.R. 783 at paras. 15–16 [*Firearms Reference*]. See also: *Reference re Employment Insurance Act (Can.), ss. 22 and 23*, [2005] 2 S.C.R. 669 [*Reference Re Employment Insurance Act*]; *Kitkatla Band v. British Columbia (Minister of Small Business, Tourism & Culture)*, [2002] 2 S.C.R. 146 [*Kitkatla*]; and *Quebec (Attorney General) v. Lacombe*, [2010] 2 S.C.R. 453 [*Lacombe*].

56 *Firearms Reference*, above note 55 at para. 16; *Lacombe*, above note 55 at para. 19.

57 *Firearms Reference*, above note 55.

58 *Kitkatla*, above note 55 at para. 52; *R. v. Swain*, [1991] 1 S.C.R. 933 at 998.

59 While at one time the courts considered such extrinsic material to be inadmissible, it is now well accepted that the legislative history, Parliamentary debates, and similar material might be considered in order to ascertain the purpose of the legislation, provided that it is relevant and reliable and is not assigned undue weight. See *Global Securities Corp. v. British Columbia (Securities Commission)*, [2000] 1 S.C.R. 494 at para. 25. Courts can sometimes note that such extrinsic material is not admissible in order to interpret or apply a particular provision in a statute. See, for instance, *R. v. Morgentaler*, [1993] 3 S.C.R. 463.

60 This point was emphasized in *Firearms Reference*, above note 55, where the Supreme Court noted that the attorney general of Alberta had challenged a law in part on the basis that it would not achieve its purpose. For example, Alberta had argued that the legislation, which required the registration of guns, would be ineffective in combating crime since criminals would simply refuse to register their guns. The Supreme Court ruled, at para. 18, that these concerns were

actually operate in order to determine "how the law sets out to achieve its purpose in order to better understand its 'total meaning'."[61] Where the effects of the law seem to diverge from its ostensible or stated purposes, this may suggest that the law is in fact being enacted for a reason other than the stated purpose. In short, the pith and substance doctrine is primarily concerned with the purpose or aim of the law. Consideration of the law's effects is subsidiary in the sense that it is undertaken in order to more clearly understand the underlying purpose.

In the second step of the analysis, the court matches the legislation as characterized in step one to the appropriate category of legislative power. Courts describe this process as a determination of what head of power the particular statute is "in relation to." If a statute is in relation to a head of power that is within the jurisdiction of the enacting legislature, it is valid; otherwise, it is invalid and will be of no force and effect. Of course, many laws may be in relation to more than one head of power. In determining whether a law is valid, courts distinguish between the pith and substance of the law and its "incidental effects." The fact that the law may have an effect on another head of power outside the jurisdiction of the enacting legislature is irrelevant for constitutional purposes. As long as the law, in pith and substance, falls within a head of power assigned to the enacting legislature, it will be upheld.[62]

As suggested above, the two steps of the analysis, although analytically distinct, overlap in practice. Furthermore, the pith and substance analysis is highly discretionary and requires the courts to exercise a significant degree of judgment, particularly at the second stage. The reasoning in the *Firearms Reference* case illustrates this point. The federal *Firearms Act* required all owners of firearms to obtain licences and to register their guns. The federal government argued that the legislation was valid criminal legislation, which is a matter allocated to Parliament under section 91(27) of the *Constitution Act, 1867*. However, a number of provincial governments, most notably Alberta, argued that

---

properly directed to Parliament and not the courts because "within its constitutional sphere, Parliament is the judge of whether a measure is likely to achieve its intended purposes; efficaciousness is not relevant to the Court's division of powers analysis."

61 *Ibid.*

62 See *Lacombe*, above note 55, where the Supreme Court described the incidental effects doctrine at para. 36 in the following terms: "[t]he incidental effects rule . . . applies when a provision, in pith and substance, lies within the competence of the enacting body but touches on a subject assigned to the other level of government. It holds that such a provision will not be invalid merely because it has an incidental effect on a legislative competence that falls beyond the jurisdiction of its enacting body."

the legislation lacked the trappings of a traditional criminal law, since it was aimed at regulating the possession of firearms, which are lawful items of personal property. The provinces argued that criminal legislation generally prohibits dangerous acts rather than regulating possession of lawful property.

The Supreme Court unanimously rejected Alberta's argument and upheld the legislation as valid criminal law.[63] In the first step of the pith and substance analysis, the Court looked to speeches by the minister and the mischief the law was intended to address. The Court found that Parliament had enacted the registration scheme to control the misuse of firearms and the threat posed by guns on public safety. In light of this public safety purpose, the Court turned to the second step of the pith and substance analysis. Acknowledging that this process was "not an exact science," the Court recognized that legislation enacted by one level of government will often impact on matters within the jurisdiction of the other. In this case, the law had features which indicated that it might potentially fit either within criminal law—a matter of federal jurisdiction—or property and civil rights—a matter of provincial jurisdiction. However, giving primacy to considerations of purpose, the Court found that the objective of protecting public safety had traditionally been recognized as a valid criminal law purpose. The fact that the legislation might affect property and civil rights (i.e., the property rights of gun owners) was merely incidental to the achievement of this purpose as opposed to its main aim. The Court also found that the federal registration scheme was distinguishable from other forms of provincial regulation requiring registration of property such as land or automobiles, since firearms were inherently dangerous whereas other forms of provincially regulated property are not.

The Court in the *Firearms Reference* acknowledged that the process of constitutional adjudication in division of powers cases requires courts to exercise a significant degree of judgment. The Court stated that in difficult cases that lie on the margins between federal and provincial jurisdiction, the courts must seek to maintain an "appropriate balance . . . between the federal and provincial heads of power."[64] In striking this balance, the courts will be guided by what the late Professor William Lederman referred to as a conception of federalism. In difficult and contested cases involving novel legislation, the overarching question is whether the law is the kind of law that should be enact-

63 The legislation had been referred to the Alberta Court of Appeal, which had upheld the legislation by a narrow three to two margin; on appeal to the Supreme Court, the appeal was unanimously dismissed in an opinion rendered by "The Court."

64 *Firearms Reference*, above note 55 at para. 48.

ed at the federal or the provincial level.[65] In answering that question, courts will typically look to the kinds of statutes that have traditionally been enacted at the federal and provincial level and measure the new enactment by analogy to what has been accepted in the past. While discretionary, these judgments are necessary and unavoidable in a federal system where legislative power is divided between the federal and provincial orders of government.[66]

As suggested above, the pith and substance doctrine tends to result in the enactment of overlapping federal and provincial legislation. The doctrine permits both levels of government to enact legislation with similar effects, as long as the purposes being pursued are distinct. For example, Parliament might enact a law regulating pollution of lakes or streams on the basis of its power over fisheries (section 91(12)), Indian lands (section 91(24)), or interprovincial pollution (under the POGG power), while a province may enact a similar law on the basis of its powers over property and civil rights (section 92(13)). Provided that the courts are able to characterize the laws as having distinct purposes, and provided that each law has a purpose that is in relation to a legislative power conferred on the enacting legislature, both laws will be upheld.[67]

In cases where Parliament and the provinces have enacted virtually identical laws for similar purposes, the courts have on some occasions upheld both laws on the basis that the subject matter had a "double aspect." For example, courts have held that laws granting a civil remedy for insider trading have both a "corporate law aspect"—permitting federal legislation on the basis of the federal power to incorporate companies—and a "securities law aspect"—permitting identical provincial legislation on the basis of the provincial power over property and civil rights.[68] In the past, the double aspect doctrine has been applied relatively infrequently, and the Supreme Court has cautioned that it should only be invoked in "clear cases where the multiplicity of aspects is real and not merely nominal."[69] Otherwise, the exclusive fields of

---

65 See W.R. Lederman, *Continuing Canadian Constitutional Dilemmas* (Toronto: Butterworths, 1981) at 241.

66 For a discussion, see P.J. Monahan, "At Doctrine's Twilight: The Structure of Canadian Federalism" (1984) 34 U.T.L.J. 47; K.E. Swinton, *The Supreme Court and Canadian Federalism* (Toronto: Carswell, 1990) c. 5.

67 As the Supreme Court noted in the *Reference Re Employment Insurance Act*, above note 55 at para. 8: "The power of one level of government to legislate in relation to one aspect of a matter takes nothing away from the power of the other level to control another aspect within its own jurisdiction."

68 *Multiple Access Ltd. v. McCutcheon*, [1982] 2 S.C.R. 161 [*Multiple Access*].

69 *Bell Canada v. Quebec (Commission de la santé et de la sécurité du travail)*, [1988] 1 S.C.R. 749 at 766, Beetz J. [*Bell 1988*].

federal and provincial jurisdiction in sections 91 and 92 of the *Constitution Act, 1867* would be converted into a single, more or less concurrent, field of legislative power exercised jointly by both levels of government. However, in recent decades, the Supreme Court has emphasized that the "dominant tide" of constitutional jurisprudence is to allow a degree of overlap between federal and provincial powers and to uphold laws that may incidentally affect matters outside the jurisdiction of the enacting legislature.[70]

b) The Ancillary Powers Doctrine

Historically, federalism cases had been decided exclusively by reference to the pith and substance doctrine outlined above. However, in *General Motors v. City National Leasing*,[71] the Supreme Court of Canada suggested that a somewhat different methodology should be applied, at least in cases where a constitutional challenge is brought against a particular provision in a statute as opposed to the statute as a whole. Chief Justice Dickson proposed a three-step process that involves a consideration of: (1) the impugned provision to ascertain whether it intrudes on the jurisdiction of the other level of government (i.e., the government that did not enact the measure in question); (2) whether the impugned provision is contained within a valid regulatory scheme; (3) the fit between the impugned provision and the valid regulatory scheme. The point of the analysis was that, even where a particular provision of a law intruded on the jurisdiction of another level of government, it may still be upheld if it can be characterized as being ancillary or necessarily incidental to an otherwise valid regulatory scheme.[72]

The focus of this necessarily incidental doctrine is on the second and third stages, namely, the consideration of the fit between the impugned provision and a valid regulatory scheme. According to Dickson C.J.: "in most cases like the present . . . it will be concluded that the impugned provision can be characterized, *prima facie*, as intruding to some extent on [the other jurisdiction's] powers: the question is to what

70 *O.P.S.E.U. v. Ontario (Attorney General)*, [1987] 2 S.C.R. 2 at 17; *General Motors of Canada Ltd. v. City National Leasing*, [1989] 1 S.C.R. 641 at 669 [*General Motors*]; *Canadian Western Bank v. Alberta*, 2007 SCC 22 at paras. 36–37 [*Canadian Western Bank*]; *British Columbia (Attorney General) v. Lafarge Canada Inc.*, 2007 SCC 23 at para. 4 [*Lafarge*].

71 Above note 70.

72 Note that, although the *General Motors* case concerned federal legislation, the Supreme Court has held that the same three-stage methodology can also be applied in relation to provincial laws. See *Global Securities v. B.C. (Securities Commission)*, [2000] 1 S.C.R. 494 at para. 19 and *Lacombe*, above note 55.

extent."[73] Dickson C.J. held that, depending on the extent of intrusion into the jurisdiction of the other level of government, the degree of fit required between the impugned provision and the regulatory scheme will vary. In cases where the intrusion is minimal, it may be sufficient for the impugned provision to be "functionally related" to the regulatory scheme. If the intrusion is more significant, the test for validity will be stricter and the enacting government will be required to demonstrate that the provision in question is necessarily incidental or truly necessary to the regulatory scheme as a whole.[74]

Although this methodology is different from the classic pith and substance doctrine,[75] the application of the ancillary powers doctrine may in some cases lead to the same result. In both instances, the court is required to consider the impugned measure in its larger regulatory context, which will generally lead to similar outcomes. For example, in *Reference Re GST*,[76] Lamer C.J., for a majority of the Court, upheld impugned provisions in federal legislation imposing a goods and services tax on the ground that they were necessarily incidental to the overall tax scheme. La Forest J., in a concurring judgment, reached the same result on the basis that the legislation as a whole was clearly valid under the pith and substance doctrine, and therefore any incidental effects on matters of provincial jurisdiction were constitutionally irrelevant.[77]

---

73 *General Motors*, above note 70 at 667.

74 See, for example, *Kirkbi AG v. Ritvik Holdings Inc.*, [2005] 3 S.C.R. 302, where the Supreme Court found that s. 7(b) of the federal *Trademarks Act*, which created a civil cause of action that essentially codified the common law tort of passing off, involved a minimal intrusion into provincial jurisdiction. Therefore, it was sufficient that the provision be functionally related to the federal statute of which it was a part, and the Supreme Court of Canada upheld the provision on this basis. See also *Lacombe*, above note 55.

75 In *Lacombe*, *ibid.* at para. 36, the Supreme Court explained the distinction between the two doctrines as follows: "[t]he ancillary powers doctrine is not to be confused with the incidental effects rule. The ancillary powers doctrine applies where . . . a provision is, in pith and substance, outside the competence of its enacting body. The potentially invalid provision will be saved where it is an important part of a broader legislative scheme that is within the competence of the enacting body. The incidental effects rule, by contrast, applies when a provision, in pith and substance, lies within the competence of the enacting body but touches on a subject assigned to the other level of government. It holds that such a provision will not be invalid merely because it has an incidental effect on a legislative competence that falls beyond the jurisdiction of its enacting body. Mere incidental effects will not warrant the invocation of ancillary powers."

76 [1992] 2 S.C.R. 445.

77 See, however, *Lacombe*, above note 55, in which a majority of the Court held that a municipal by-law prohibiting the construction of aerodromes on a lake throughout a municipality's territory was an invalid attempt to regulate aero-

c) Interjurisdictional Immunity

As we have seen, under the pith and substance doctrine, incidental effects of a law are constitutionally irrelevant. Legislation may be upheld even if it touches on matters that, viewed in isolation, might be outside the legislative jurisdiction of the enacting legislature. The courts have also developed a doctrine of interjurisdictional immunity, which provides that certain entities may be immune from the *application* of valid laws. Although the law remains valid and generally applicable, the law is "read down" by the court such that a particular person or entity is exempt or immune from the law's application.

The principle underlying the doctrine of interjurisdictional immunity is that there is a "core" or a "basic, minimum and unassailable content" of legislative powers that cannot be encroached upon by laws enacted by the other level of government.[78] In this way, the doctrine of interjurisdictional immunity is an exception to the pith and substance doctrine. As Binnie J. explained in *Lafarge*, interjurisdictional immunity is an exception to the ordinary rule "under which legislation whose pith and substance falls within the jurisdiction of the legislature that enacted it may . . . affect matters beyond the legislature's jurisdiction without necessarily being unconstitutional."[79] (Although the immunity doctrine has been said to be reciprocal in theory, it has only ever been applied to protect federal persons or entities from provincial encroachment. While there is judicial dicta[80] and academic commentary[81]

---

nautics (a federal matter). The by-law was not saved by the ancillary powers doctrine. Although the by-law was generally valid legislation in relation to land use planning, the majority held that the general ban on aerodromes was not rationally or functionally connected to the by-law.

78 *Bell 1988*, above note 69 at 839.

79 *Lafarge*, above note 70 at para. 41.

80 *Caron v. The King*, [1924] A.C. 999 at 1006 (P.C.); *City of Medicine Hat v. A.G. Can.* (1985), 18 D.L.R. (4th) 428 (Alta C.A.). In *Canadian Western Bank*, above note 70, at para. 35, the Supreme Court stated that the doctrine is reciprocal in theory, but recognized that "the jurisprudential application of the doctrine has produced somewhat 'asymmetrical' results." The court cited examples of instances in which the doctrine was used to "read down" federal statutes. However, strictly speaking, none of the cases concerned the doctrine of interjurisdictional immunity. Rather, the cases involved a determination of the constitutional *validity* of federal statutes, rather than their application to provincial entities. See: *Attorney General of Canada v. Law Society of British Columbia*, [1982] 2 S.C.R. 307, *Dominion Stores Ltd. v. The Queen*, [1980] 1 S.C.R. 844, and *Labatt Breweries of Canada Ltd. v. Attorney General of Canada* (1979), [1980] 1 S.C.R. 914.

81 See R.M. Elliot, "Interjurisdictional Immunity after *Canadian Western Bank* and *LaFarge Canada Inc.*: The Supreme Court Muddies the Doctrinal Waters—Again" (2008) 43 Sup. Ct. L. Rev. (2d) 433 at 468–69; Hogg, above note 10 at 15.8(f).

suggesting that the doctrine may be applied in favour of either the federal or provincial orders of government, the Supreme Court declined to do so in 2011 when British Columbia argued that the *Controlled Drugs and Substances Act* intruded on provincial jurisdiction over health.)[82]

The scope of the doctrine of interjurisdictional immunity has been a continuing source of controversy. The doctrine initially developed in cases concerning federally incorporated companies. For example, in *John Deere Plow Co. v. Wharton*,[83] the Privy Council held that it was not open to the provinces under their authority to regulate companies to require a federally incorporated company to obtain a licence as a condition of carrying on business. This would prevent the federal company from exercising the powers with which it was endowed by federal authority.

The immunity doctrine was later extended to federally regulated "Works and Undertakings." Section 92(10) of the *Constitution Act, 1867* provides that the provinces may legislate in relation to "Local Works and Undertakings" other than those listed in certain classes, which are reserved to Parliament. The enumerated classes include: (1) steamlines, railways, canals, telegraphs, and other works and undertakings connecting the province with another province or extending beyond the limits of the province; (2) lines of steamships between the province and a British or foreign country and; (3) works situated within the province that have been declared by Parliament to be for the general advantage of Canada or two or more provinces.[84] In *Ontario (A.G.) v. Winner*,[85] the Privy Council held that an interprovincial bus line was immune from New Brunswick legislation that prohibited the company from dropping off or picking up passengers in the ravines of New Brunswick. Lord Porter held that application of the legislation would result in the bus line being "sterilized in all its functions and activities" and impair "its

---

82 *Canada (Attorney General) v. PHS Community Services*, [2011] 3 S.C.R. 134 at paras. 57–70.

83 [1915] A.C. 330 (P.C.). See also: *Great West Saddlery v. The King*, [1921] 2 A.C. 91 (P.C.); *Manitoba (Attorney General) v. Canada (Attorney General)*, [1929] A.C. 260 (P.C.); *Lymburn v. Mayland*, [1932] A.C. 318 (P.C.); *Canadian Indemnity Co. v. British Columbia (Attorney General)*, [1977] 2 S.C.R. 504; *Re Upper Churchill Water Rights*, [1984] 1 S.C.R. 297.

84 The words "Works and Undertakings" are to be read disjunctively. A "Work" is a physical thing, such as a railway, canal, or telegraph line. An "Undertaking" is not a physical thing, but an arrangement under which a physical thing is used. For instance, the company in the *Winner* case, below note 85, operated an interprovincial transportation undertaking, transporting passengers in and out of New Brunswick.

85 [1954] 4 D.L.R. 657 (P.C.) [*Winner*].

status and essential capacities . . . in a substantial degree."[86] Similarly, in *Campbell-Bennett v. Comstock Midwestern*,[87] the Supreme Court of Canada held that provincial legislation providing for liens against real property was inapplicable to an interprovincial oil pipeline undertaking. The Court noted that allowing a lien attachment to the assets of the pipeline would allow the sale of parts of the pipeline to realize the lien claim and lead to the dismemberment of the undertaking.

The language of "impairment" or "sterilization" was relaxed in later cases so as to expand the doctrine of interjurisdictional immunity and enlarge the scope of protection for federal works and undertakings from the application of provincial laws. In the *Bell 1966* case,[88] the Supreme Court held that a federally regulated entity would be exempt from the application of a provincial law that "affects" its vital and essential elements or a "vital part" of its "management and operation."[89] Bell Canada, an interprovincial phone company, was held to be immune from a provincial minimum wage law, even though there was no federal minimum wage law in place. In a trilogy of cases decided in 1988,[90] the Supreme Court applied the *Bell 1966* test and held that provincial legislation regulating labour relations, working conditions, and occupational health and safety all affect vital aspects of federally regulated undertakings.

However, the scope of the doctrine of interjurisdictional immunity was significantly narrowed by the Supreme Court in subsequent years. First, in *Irwin Toy v. Quebec*,[91] the Court held that a Quebec law prohibiting advertising directed at children was applicable to a federal broadcasting undertaking, even though advertising was acknowledged to be a vital and essential part of its operation. According to the Court, the provincial law had only an indirect effect on the undertaking, since it applied to advertisers rather than the media and therefore did not *directly* affect the undertaking. Similarly, in *R. v. Canadian Pacific Ltd.*,[92] the Supreme Court upheld the application of section 13(1)(a) of the Ontario *Environmental Protection Act* to Canadian Pacific, a federally regulated undertaking. CP had burned dead grass on its right of way in order to fulfil requirements under the federal *Railway Act* that it keep

86 *Ibid.* at 676.

87 [1954] S.C.R. 207.

88 *Québec (Commission du Salaire Minimum) v. Bell Telephone Co. of Canada*, [1966] S.C.R. 767 [*Bell 1966*].

89 *Ibid.* at 772.

90 *Bell 1988*, above note 69; *Canadian National Railway Co. v. Courtois*, [1988] 1 S.C.R. 868; *Alltrans Express v. British Columbia (Workers'/Workmen's Compensation Board)*, [1988] 1 S.C.R. 897.

91 [1989] 1 S.C.R. 927.

92 (1993), 13 O.R. (3d) 389 (C.A.), aff'd [1995] 2 S.C.R. 1028 [*Canadian Pacific*].

its right of way free from dead grass and other combustible matter. The Supreme Court dismissed CP's appeal from this decision in a judgment consisting of a single paragraph, stating that it regarded the case as falling squarely within the principles in the *Bonsecours* case.[93] In *Bonsecours*, the Privy Council held that provincial law could be applied so as to require CP Rail to keep a ditch along its right of way free of rubbish or other obstructions. Significantly, the activity in *Canadian Pacific* fell squarely within CP's mandate as a federal undertaking. Indeed, the company was under a statutory obligation under federal law to keep its right of way clear of combustible matter, and the controlled burn was undertaken in order to fulfil that obligation. Moreover, the activity in question took place on CP's own right of way, rather than on a public road or thoroughfare. However, the Supreme Court nonetheless found it straightforward and obvious that CP's activities were subject to provincial environmental regulation.

In *Canadian Western Bank*[94] and *Lafarge*,[95] the Supreme Court held that the doctrine of interjurisdictional immunity should be narrowly confined. The Court overruled the more lenient version of the test for impairment put forward in the *Bell 1988* line of cases and reverted to the language of impairment used in the early federal company cases. According to the Supreme Court, in order for the doctrine to apply, the provincial law must *impair*—as opposed to merely affect—a vital and essential part of the federal work or undertaking. Furthermore, the terms "vital and essential" are critical; the activity in question must be "absolutely dispensable or necessary" to the federal entity in order for it to be immune. In *Canadian Western Bank*, the Court held that federal banking undertakings were not immune from provisions of the Alberta *Insurance Act*, which regulated the sale of insurance in the province. The Court held that the provincial statute did not impair the vital and essential functions of banks, since the promotion of authorized insurance did not form part of the essential functions of banking. In *Lafarge*, the Court held that the doctrine of interjurisdictional immunity did not exempt a federal port authority constituted under the *Canada Marine Act* from obtaining a development permit as required by a municipal zoning and development by-law in the city of Vancouver. The Court stated that "federal ownership of land does not create an enclave from which all provincial laws are excluded."[96]

---

93 Above note 31.
94 Above note 70.
95 *Ibid*.
96 *Lafarge*, above note 70 at para. 55.

In *Canadian Western Bank* and *Lafarge*, the Supreme Court identified certain perceived deficiencies with the doctrine of interjurisdictional immunity that led the Court to confine its scope, including: (1) its centralizing tendency, which was said to be inconsistent with the "dominant tide" of constitutional interpretation; (2) the inherent uncertainty associated with attempts to identify "core" or "unassailable" aspects of heads of legislative power; and (3) the possibility that the doctrine will give rise to regulatory vacuums in which there is no legislation that applies to the entity sought to be exempt (as in the *Bell 1966* minimum wage case). Furthermore, the Court observed that the doctrine often overlapped with the doctrine of paramountcy and held that interjurisdictional immunity should only be invoked after the paramountcy doctrine had been applied.[97] In a more recent decision, the Court has also cast doubt on the validity of those past interjurisdictional immunity cases where the provincial law only met the past standard of "affecting" the core of the federal head of power.[98]

As a result of the Supreme Court's decisions in *Canadian Western Bank* and *LaFarge*, it would appear that the doctrine of interjurisdictional immunity will be difficult to successfully invoke and that federal entities will ordinarily be subject to provincial laws provided that they are not in conflict with federal laws dealing with the same subject matter.

d) Paramountcy

The courts have developed the doctrine of federal paramountcy to deal with the situation in which federal and provincial laws conflict. In the case of conflicting federal and provincial laws dealing with the same matter, the paramountcy doctrine provides that the federal law prevails. The provincial law is rendered *inoperative* to the extent (and only

97 This aspect of the Court's ruling does not make logical sense. As discussed above, the doctrine of interjurisdictional immunity provides that a law is to be interpreted so as not to apply to the extrajurisdictional entity. The doctrine of paramountcy provides that in the case of conflict between federal and provincial laws, the federal law is paramount and the provincial law is *inoperative* to the extent of the inconsistency. As a matter of logic, interjurisdictional immunity should be applied before paramountcy, since paramountcy can only be invoked if there are two valid and conflicting laws. In other words, there can be no conflict if the law is "read down" through the doctrine of interjurisdictional immunity not to apply to the federal entity in question. See the dissenting judgment of Bastarache J. in *Canadian Western Bank*, above note 70 at paras. 113–14; Elliot, above note 81 at 495–96 and Hogg, above note 10 at note 124a.

98 *Marine Services International Ltd. v. Ryan Estate*, [2013] 3 S.C.R. 53 at para. 64.

to the extent) that it is inconsistent with the federal law.[99] The rule of federal paramountcy is a judge-made rule of interpretation and was not formally identified in or required by the terms of the *Constitution Act, 1867*.[100]

It is now settled that there are two types of conflict that may engage the doctrine of paramountcy. First, there may be "operational conflict," in the sense that it is impossible for a citizen to simultaneously comply with valid provincial and federal laws. Second, the application of the provincial law may frustrate the purpose of a federal enactment.

An operational conflict occurs where there is an express contradiction between the two laws, such that compliance with one law necessarily involves a breach of the other. As Dickson J. stated in *Multiple Access*, conflict occurs "where one enactment says 'yes' and the other says 'no'; 'the same citizens are being told to do inconsistent things'; compliance with one is defiance of the other."[101] The Court in *Multiple Access* held that federal and provincial laws regulating insider trading did not conflict since it was possible to comply with both laws simultaneously.

Early cases assumed that the doctrine of paramountcy was limited to cases of true operational conflict. Therefore, even though a federal and provincial law might be pursuing conflicting purposes, both laws would be upheld if it were possible for private citizens to comply with each — for example, where the laws were permissive only and did not impose mandatory duties.[102] More recently, the Supreme Court has held that a conflict will also occur where the provincial law frustrates the purpose of the federal enactment.

---

99 It should be noted that the provincial statute is not rendered invalid or *ultra vires* by virtue of the conflict with the federal statute. Thus, in the event that the federal statute is amended or repealed such that the conflict between the two statutes disappears, the provincial statute becomes operative and can be applied in accordance with its terms.

100 Section 95 of the *Constitution Act, 1867* provided for concurrent federal and provincial jurisdiction in respect of agriculture and immigration. However, there was no general requirement that federal laws would take precedence over conflicting provincial laws. Since 1867, two constitutional amendments have dealt with the issue of paramountcy in specific contexts. In one case, a rule of provincial paramountcy was adopted: see s. 94A, enacted in 1951 and 1964 by the *BNA Act, 1951* (U.K.) and the *Constitution Act 1964* (U.K.), above note 52, dealing with old-age pensions; in the other, a rule of federal paramountcy was preferred: see s. 92A(3), enacted by the *Constitution Act, 1982*, permitting the provinces to enact legislation regarding the export of natural resources.

101 Above note 68 at 190–91.

102 See, for example, *Ross v. Registrar of Motor Vehicles*, [1975] 1 S.C.R. 5; *Robinson v. Countrywide Factors*, [1977] 2 S.C.R. 753; *Clarke v. Clarke*, [1990] 2 S.C.R. 795.

For example, in *M & D Farm Ltd. v. Manitoba Agricultural Credit Corp.*,[103] a federal statute provided for a stay of legal proceedings against farmers who were in financial difficulty. Following the issuance of a stay under the federal statute in favour of a particular farmer, a creditor commenced proceedings under a provincial statute for enforcement of its rights under a mortgage granted to the farmer. The creditor argued that there was no express contradiction between the federal and provincial statutes, since it had refrained from obtaining any remedy against the farmer until after the expiry of the stay period under the federal statute. Therefore, from the perspective of the farmer and creditor, compliance with both statutes was possible and the provincial statute should remain. However, the Supreme Court held that there was an express contradiction between the statutes. Binnie J. reasoned that the existence of this contradiction emerged when the laws were viewed as directives to the courts, since the federal statute prohibits the commencement of proceedings while the provincial statute permits such proceedings. Therefore, the provincial statute was rendered inoperative and the proceedings that had been commenced under it were a nullity. The approach to paramountcy in *M & D Farm*, in which statutes are recast as directives to the judiciary, broadens the circumstances in which courts might find an express contradiction between federal and provincial laws and thus hold provincial statutes to be inoperative.

The emphasis on purposes was reaffirmed in *Law Society of British Columbia v. Mangat*.[104] In *Mangat*, a provincial statute required representatives appearing before the provincial Immigration and Refugee Board to be licensed as lawyers under the *Legal Profession Act*. The federal *Immigration Act* provided that non-lawyers could represent refugees before the Board. Although it was possible to comply with the requirements of each law—by being a registered lawyer—the provincial legislation was held to be in conflict with the purpose of federal legislation. Requiring only registered lawyers to appear before the Board would frustrate the federal goal of an expedited and inexpensive process in which non-lawyers could act as representatives. Therefore, the provincial law was ruled inoperative.

Similarly, in *Rothmans, Benson & Hedges v. Saskatchewan*,[105] the Supreme Court considered an apparent conflict between the federal *Tobacco Act*, which allowed retailers to display tobacco products and accessories, and Saskatchewan's *Tobacco Control Act*, which banned all advertising, display, and promotion of tobacco products in any premises

103 [1999] 2 S.C.R. 961 [*M & D Farm*].
104 [2001] 3 S.C.R. 113 [*Mangat*].
105 [2005] 1 S.C.R. 188.

in which persons under the age of eighteen are permitted. The Court held that the relevant provision in the federal statute was merely intended to narrow a more general prohibition on the promotion of tobacco products elsewhere in the statute, and was not intended to grant a positive entitlement to display tobacco products. Therefore, enforcing the prohibition on the display of tobacco products in the provincial statute did not frustrate the legislative purposes underlying the federal statute. As it was possible for retailers to comply with both the federal and provincial statutes (by complying with the stricter provincial statute) and as there was no conflict in the underlying legislative purposes, there was no conflict between the statutes and the provincial statute was operative.

In the *Lafarge* case discussed above, the Supreme Court considered both the operational conflict test and the purposes test again. Lafarge wanted to build a ship offloading/concrete batching facility on waterfront lands owned by the Vancouver Port Authority (the "VPA"), a federal undertaking constituted under the *Canada Marine Act*. The City of Vancouver and the VPA approved the project, but a citizens group opposed it, and brought an application to enjoin the project from going ahead in the absence of a building permit from the city. The relevant zoning by-law imposed a 30-foot height restriction on buildings, which could be increased only at the discretion of the city. The Court held that there was an operational conflict between the federal *Canada Marine Act*—which governed dedicated land within the port area for uses related to shipping—and the city zoning by-law, pursuant to the reasoning in *M & D Farm*. If the citizens group had succeeded in persuading the city to enjoin the Lafarge project from going ahead without a permit, a judge could not have simultaneously given effect to the federal law (which would have led to a dismissal of the application) and the municipal law (which would have led to the granting of an injunction). Furthermore, the Court held that the application of the municipal law would frustrate the purpose of the federal *Canada Marine Act* by depriving the VPA of its authority to develop a project pursuant to the power to regulate federal real property set aside for the purposes of navigation and shipping.

The proper scope of the two branches of the paramouncty doctrine was debated extensively in a 2016 trilogy of cases.[106] In *Moloney*, the Court was called on to consider the interplay between provincial traffic

---

106 *Alberta (Attorney General) v. Moloney*, [2015] 3 S.C.R. 327 [*Moloney*]; *407 ETR Concession Co. v Canada (Superintendant of Bankruptcy)*, [2015] 3 S.C.R. 397; *Saskatchewan (Attorney General) v. Lemare Lake Logging Ltd.*, [2015] 3 S.C.R. 419.

safety legislation and the federal *Bankruptcy and Insolvency Act*.[107] Mr. Moloney caused a car accident while he was uninsured. The province of Alberta compensated a person who was injured in the accident and sought to recover the amount of the compensation it paid from Mr. Moloney pursuant to Alberta's *Traffic Safety Act*.[108] The Alberta government suspended his licence pursuant to a provision of the *TSA*, which allows the province to suspend an individual's driver's licence until the amount of the compensation owed to the injured party has been paid. Mr. Moloney made an assignment in bankruptcy under the federal *BIA* and was discharged from bankruptcy pursuant to the Act. The *BIA* provides that upon discharge, the debtor is released from all debts that are claims provable in bankruptcy. Mr. Moloney challenged the suspension of his licence, arguing that the *BIA* discharge provisions were paramount and that the *TSA* provisions were therefore inoperative.

The Court was unanimous that the federal legislation was paramount. All members of the Court agreed that there was purpose conflict. A central purpose of the *BIA* discharge provisions is the financial rehabilitation of the debtor through a "fresh start." The *TSA* provisions frustrated that purpose by allowing the province to withhold the debtor's driver's licence unless and until its claim for unpaid compensation had been reimbursed.[109] The majority held that there was an operational conflict; yet, the minority held that there was a purpose conflict only. According to the majority, the "test for operational conflict cannot be limited to asking whether the respondent can comply with both laws by renouncing the protection afforded to him or her under the federal law or the privilege he or she is otherwise entitled to under the provincial law." In analyzing the operational conflict, the majority found it significant that the province was "compelling payment of a provable claim that has been released, which is in direction contradiction" with the *BIA* debt discharge provisions.[110] By contrast, the minority held that operational conflict is limited to situations where there is true incompatibility "on the face of the provisions themselves."[111] According to the minority, the debtor could simply choose not to drive, which would prevent the province from enforcing its claim. Alternatively, the debtor could voluntarily pay the discharged debt, in which case the province would have nothing to enforce. In either case, the minority

107 R.S.C. 1985, c. B-3, s. 243 [*BIA*].

108 R.S.A. 2000, c. T-6 [*TSA*].

109 *Moloney*, above note 106 at paras. 77–83.

110 *Ibid*. at para. 60.

111 *Ibid*. at para. 108.

concluded that the bankrupt is still "discharged" within the meaning of the *BIA*.[112]

The Court's split in *Moloney* illustrates that application of the operational conflict test is not always straightforward. Although there is agreement on the articulation of the test—impossibility of dual compliance—the majority endorses a broader interpretation of the test, while the minority would limit the test to a very literal analysis based on the wording of the federal and provincial laws alone. The close split in the *Moloney* trilogy may open the door to further debate on the scope of the two branches of the paramountcy doctrine in the future.

D. JUDICIAL POWER IN THE CANADIAN CONSTITUTION

1) The Structure of the Courts

a) The Supreme Court of Canada

i) *History*

The Supreme Court of Canada is the highest court in Canada. It has final jurisdiction over all matters of Canadian law, including matters falling under both federal and provincial jurisdiction. It has the right to hear appeals from provincial courts established and maintained by the provinces as well as from federal courts established and maintained by Parliament.

There is no mention of the Supreme Court of Canada in the *Constitution Act, 1867*. At the time of Confederation, the system of courts that had existed in each of the former colonies was continued by virtue of section 129 of the *Constitution Act, 1867*. Responsibility for the organization and maintenance of these local courts was allocated to the provincial governments pursuant to section 92(14). Appeals from these section 92(14) courts could be taken to the Judicial Committee of the Privy Council (JCPC) in England.[113]

112 *Ibid*. at para. 97.

113 Virtually all appeals to the JCPC were heard by the twelve permanent members of the House of Lords, the predecessor to the Supreme Court of the United Kingdom. The JCPC, chiefly composed of members of the Supreme Court who are cross-appointed, still hears appeals from several Commonwealth realms. Judges from the jurisdictions from which appeals are taken to the JCPC are also appointed from time to time as members of the Board. These appointments are made by the Queen on advice of the British Cabinet.

Although the Supreme Court of Canada did not exist in 1867, its eventual creation was contemplated by section 101 of the *Constitution Act, 1867*, which granted Parliament legislative authority to provide for the creation of a "General Court of Appeal for Canada." Pursuant to this authority, Parliament enacted the *Supreme Court Act* in 1875, creating the Supreme Court of Canada. At that time, the Supreme Court was not Canada's ultimate legal authority, since appeals could still be taken from the Supreme Court to the JCPC.[114] However, Privy Council appeals in civil cases were abolished in 1949 pursuant to an ordinary federal statute[115] and, since that time, the Supreme Court has served as the final court of appeal in all matters of Canadian law.

ii) Appointment Process

The *Supreme Court Act*[116] provides that the members of the Court are to be appointed by the federal Governor in Council, or Cabinet. There are currently nine judges of the Court, and the *Supreme Court Act* provides that three of them must be appointed from the province of Quebec. There is no other legal requirement respecting regional composition, although the practice has generally been to appoint three judges from Ontario, two from the four western provinces, and one from Atlantic Canada. In order to be eligible for appointment to the Supreme Court, individuals must be judges of a superior court of a province or the Federal Court of Canada, or be lawyers who have been members of the bar of a province for at least ten years. The general practice has been to appoint Supreme Court judges from the ranks of sitting judges, although occasionally the government appoints a practising lawyer directly to the Supreme Court.[117]

There is no requirement of consultation with the provinces, or for approval by Parliament, before an appointment by Cabinet to the Court. The minister of justice has consulted widely with the legal community regarding the suitability of candidates for appointment to the Court, but the nature of this advice, as well as the process leading to the ultim-

114 In fact, appeals could also be taken directly from the provincial courts to the JCPC, bypassing the Supreme Court of Canada altogether.

115 Appeals to the Privy Council in criminal matters had been abolished by federal statute in 1888 but, in 1926, the Privy Council held this statute to be invalid on grounds that it conflicted with two imperial statutes. The *Statute of Westminster, 1931* (U.K.), 22 & 23 Geo. V, c. 4, conferred power on Canada to amend imperial statutes, and criminal appeals were once again abolished. In 1935, the Privy Council held that the abolition of criminal appeals was valid.

116 R.S.C. 1985, c. S-26.

117 For example, Justice Ian Binnie was appointed directly from practice. Justice Binnie replaced Justice John Sopinka, who was also appointed directly from practice.

ate appointment by the government, has traditionally remained confidential. The confidential nature of the process has been justified on the basis that potential judicial candidates would not allow their names to be considered if the process were public. However, the secretive nature of the appointment process has been a target of frequent criticism and, in recent years, a number of proposals have called for greater provincial and public input.[118]

Since 2004, in response to these criticisms, there have been significant changes to the appointment process for Supreme Court justices, although the ultimate constitutional responsibility of the Governor in Council to make appointments remains and these modified procedures have not themselves been consistently used.[119] In August 2004, following the appointment of Justices Abella and Charron to the Supreme Court, Minister of Justice Irwin Cotler appeared before the House of Commons Standing Committee on Justice to explain and justify the appointments. In 2005, with the vacancy created by the retirement of Justice Major, the minister established a nine-member advisory committee to review candidates under consideration for the replacement appointment. This advisory committee, made up of MPs from each major political party, representatives of the Canadian Judicial Council, the provincial attorneys general, the provincial law societies, and two lay members, was provided with a list of five to eight candidates by the minister of justice. The committee reduced the list to a short-list of three candidates through a process of documentary review and consultation with third parties (but no personal interviews with the candidates). Before the government could act on the advisory committee's recommendations and select the preferred candidate, the government was defeated and an election was called.

Following the election of the Harper government in January 2006, the new minister of justice, Vic Toews, announced that the government would select from the short-list of three candidates already provided by the advisory committee. The minister also announced that the nominee would be required to appear before an *ad hoc* committee of members of the House of Commons to answer questions. The government would then take into account the results of this structured interview in determining whether to proceed with the appointment. Justice Marshall

---

118 For example, both the *Meech Lake* and *Charlottetown Accords* would have provided for appointment of Supreme Court judges from lists of names provided by the provinces.

119 In fact, as we argue in Chapter 6, Section E, it would be necessary to enact a constitutional amendment under Part V of the *Constitution Act, 1982* in order to alter the responsibility of the Governor in Council for Supreme Court appointments.

Rothstein of the Federal Court of Appeal was announced as the nominee and, on 27 February 2006, appeared before the *ad hoc* committee in a televised hearing. The hearing was moderated by Professor Peter Hogg, who cautioned the committee to avoid attempting to determine how Justice Rothstein might decide future cases, or to pose personal questions that intruded on his privacy. Although considerable doubt had been expressed about the appropriateness of a public hearing process, the restrained nature of the questioning in this first experiment seems to have allayed many of these concerns.[120]

Justice Michel Bastarache retired from the Supreme Court in 2008. It was anticipated that his successor would be chosen after a short-list of three names had been generated by a selection panel composed of five Members of Parliament (two from the government and one from each of the three opposition parties). The person chosen by the prime minister would then be questioned before a parliamentary committee. However, on 5 September 2008, Prime Minister Harper and Justice Minister Rob Nicholson announced that Justice Thomas Cromwell (then a judge of the Nova Scotia Court of Appeal) would be appointed to the Supreme Court. Although Prime Minister Harper indicated that Justice Cromwell would be questioned by an *ad hoc* all-party committee of the House of Commons, Parliament was dissolved and an election called almost immediately after the announcement. Prime Minister Harper was re-elected with a minority government but Parliament was prorogued on 4 December 2008 following the threat of the no-confidence motion by the opposition coalition.[121] During the period of prorogation, Prime Minister Harper announced that Justice Cromwell would be appointed without appearing before a parliamentary committee.[122]

Justices Moldaver and Karakatsanis (formerly of the Ontario Court of Appeal) were appointed to the Supreme Court of Canada in 2011, following the retirement of Justices Binnie and Charron. Justices Moldaver and Karakatsanis were selected from a short-list of six candidates prepared by a selection panel that included Members of Parliament from each party, with government members holding that majority. After their appointments were announced on 17 October 2011, Justices

120 For a discussion of the various concerns raised about the hearings process, see P. Monahan, "A Very Judicious Process: Requiring Supreme Court Nominees to Appear before a Parliamentary Committee Shines a Much Needed Spotlight" *Globe and Mail* (22 February 2006) A21.

121 See the discussion in Chapter 3, Section 6(e).

122 See P. Hogg, "Special Series on the Federal Dimensions of Reforming the Supreme Court of Canada: Appointment of Thomas A. Cromwell to the Supreme Court of Canada" (Kingston, ON: Institute of Intergovernmental Relations School of Policy Studies, Queen's University, 2009).

Moldaver and Karakatsanis appeared before an *ad hoc* committee of Parliament for questioning on 19 October 2011. The questioning process was again moderated by Professor Peter Hogg.[123]

A similar procedure was used for the appointment of Justice Richard Wagner in 2012. In 2013, it was again used for the purported appointment of Justice Marc Nadon. As discussed in Chapter 6, that appointment was ultimately set aside by the Supreme Court as invalid under the *Supreme Court Act*. In the wake of the failed appointment, Prime Minister Harper simply announced the subsequent three appointments by press release.[124]

Therefore, the state of parliamentary input in the Supreme Court selection process is in a state of some flux. In our view, Canada will likely ultimately adopt a consistent practice of involvement of the opposition parties in the selection process and the questioning before Parliament of newly appointed Supreme Court judges. In 2015, Prime Minister Trudeau's mandate letter to the Attorney General tasked her with engaging all parties in the House of Commons "to ensure that the process of appointing Supreme Court Justices is transparent, inclusive and accountable to Canadians," and noted that appointees should be functionally bilingual.[125]

iii) Caseload

In terms of the Court's caseload, until 1975, most of the appeals heard by the Supreme Court were as of right.[126] However, amendments to the *Supreme Court Act* enacted in 1975 abolished most appeals as of right and required the vast majority of litigants to obtain leave—that is, permission of the Court—to have their appeal heard.[127] Today, very few appeals are brought to the Supreme Court as of right.[128] The test that is

123 Transcripts of appointment proceedings can be found on the Department of Justice Website, online: www.justice.gc.ca/eng/news-nouv/ja-nj.asp?tid=4.

124 Justice Suzanne Côté and Justice Clément Gascon in 2014 and Justice Russell Brown in 2015.

125 Office of the Prime Minister, "Minister of Justice and Attorney General of Canada Mandate Letter," online: http://pm.gc.ca/eng/minister-justice-and-attorney-general-canada-mandate-letter.

126 For example, before 1975 in any civil case in which the amount in controversy exceeded $10,000, the case could be appealed all the way to the Supreme Court of Canada.

127 The provincial courts and the Federal Court of Appeal also have the power to grant leave to the Supreme Court: *Supreme Court Act*, R.S.C. 1985, c. S-26, ss. 37 and 37.1. However, this power is exercised very sparingly.

128 The most significant numbers of appeals as of right are those in criminal cases where there is a dissenting opinion on a question of law in the court of appeal. In 1997, Parliament amended the *Criminal Code* to narrow slightly the automat-

generally applied by the Supreme Court is whether a case raises a question of public importance sufficient to warrant a decision.[129] It is relatively difficult to obtain leave to appeal from the Supreme Court: the Court generally grants leave in only 10 to 13 percent of the approximately 525 applications it receives each year.[130] Although they receive the most attention in public and media discussions,[131] constitutional cases have made up less than one-fifth of the Court's workload in recent years.[132] The single largest category of cases before the Supreme Court in recent years is non-constitutional criminal law matters.[133]

In addition to hearing appeals from provincial courts or the Federal Court of Appeal, the Supreme Court also provides advisory opinions on questions referred to it by the federal government. These advisory opinions or references are not strictly binding in law but have always been treated as binding by the federal and provincial governments. References to the Supreme Court may raise questions respecting the laws or powers of either the federal Parliament or the provinces.[134] Only the federal government, however, may refer questions directly to the Supreme Court.[135] Since the first reference in 1892, the federal government has made eighty-one references to the Supreme Court. It has also

ic right of appeal to the Supreme Court in criminal cases. Previously, there had been an appeal as of right where a court of appeal had reversed an acquittal at a criminal trial, even if there was no dissenting opinion in the court of appeal. The *Criminal Code* amendment now requires a dissent on a question of law in the court of appeal for an appeal as of right, even if the court of appeal reversed an acquittal: see s. 691(2) of the *Criminal Code*, enacted by S.C. 1997, c. 18. This has reduced appeals as of right by one-half.

129 See *Supreme Court Act*, s. 40(1).

130 See Supreme Court of Canada, *Statistics 2005 to 2015* (Ottawa: Supreme Court of Canada, 2016), online: www.scc-csc.ca/case-dossier/stat/index-eng.aspx?res.

131 One analysis of media coverage of the Supreme Court found that *Charter* cases accounted for almost three-quarters of CBC coverage and over half of CTV coverage of the Supreme Court in 1995. In fact, in 1995, only four decisions of the Supreme Court received any substantive coverage, three of which were *Charter* cases: see L. Miljan & A. Allen, "Courts and the Media: Providing a Climate for Social Change" (1996) 9:9 On Balance 1 at 3–4.

132 For example, in 2010, only about 9 percent of the cases heard by the Supreme Court raised non-criminal *Charter* issues; a further 11 percent of cases included *Charter* criminal issues.

133 See P.J. Monahan, "The Supreme Court of Canada in the 21st Century" (2000) 80 Can. Bar Rev. 374.

134 See, for example, the reference to the Supreme Court consisting of three questions relating to the power of Quebec to secede from Canada: *Secession Reference*, above note 19.

135 The provinces have each enacted legislation enabling the provincial government to refer questions to their respective courts of appeal, and there is an automatic

heard many appeals of those advisory opinions issued by provincial courts of appeal, for which appeals are available by right.[136]

The *Supreme Court Act* is not explicitly identified as part of the definition of the Constitution of Canada pursuant to section 52 of the *Constitution Act, 1982*. However, the Supreme Court has interpreted references to the Court in Part V of the 1982 Act, which sets out the formula for amendments to the constitution, as meaning that changes to the composition of the Court are subject to the unanimous consent of the federal government and the provinces, while other "essential features" are subject to the 7/50 formula.[137] There is, therefore, no doubt that the Court is now part of the architecture of the Constitution of Canada.

b) Superior and Provincial Courts

Before Confederation, in each of the British North American colonies, there had been three levels of courts. The highest level consisted of a "superior court" with jurisdiction throughout the province unlimited by subject matter. The superior court consisted of a trial division and an appellate division.[138] Below the superior court in all provinces except Canada East were county or district courts, with jurisdiction limited by subject matter and also by territory to a local county or district. Below the county or district courts were "inferior courts" staffed by magistrates with jurisdiction over minor criminal or civil matters. These courts were all continued after Confederation by virtue of section 129 of the *Constitution Act, 1867*, and responsibility for their organization and maintenance was granted to the provinces under section 92(14).

Pursuant to section 92(14), the provinces have passed laws reorganizing their courts.[139] However, the power to appoint the judges of the superior, district, and county courts was granted to the governor general (effectively the federal Cabinet) pursuant to section 96 of the *Constitution Act, 1867*.[140] There is no requirement of consultation with or

---

right of appeal in such matters to the Supreme Court. See, for example, *Courts of Justice Act*, R.S.O. 1990, c. C.43, s. 8.

136 *Supreme Court Act*, s. 36.

137 *Reference re Supreme Court Act, ss. 5 and 6*, [2014] 1 S.C.R. 433.

138 In the late eighteenth century, the members of the various colonial courts of appeal had also been members of the Executive Council. However, by the 1840s, legislation had been passed that prohibited members of a colonial court of appeal or superior court from sitting as a member of the Executive Council.

139 For example, all provinces have now abolished the county or district courts and provide for a single s. 96 court.

140 The power to appoint judges of the "inferior courts" was granted to the provinces under s. 92(14) of the *Constitution Act, 1867*.

approval by the provinces.[141] This appointing power is significant, since the provincial courts are courts of general jurisdiction with authority over the interpretation and application of all provincial laws.[142] Thus, the federal government is given the power to select the judges who have ultimate authority over the manner in which provincial laws are applied. This system is different from the approach taken in many federal states, where the provinces or states are granted the power to appoint judges charged with the responsibility of interpreting local laws.[143]

c) Federal Courts

Section 101 of the *Constitution Act, 1867* also granted Parliament power to establish additional courts for the "better Administration of the Laws of Canada." Parliament established the Exchequer Court of Canada pursuant to this power in 1875. Its jurisdiction covered suits against the Crown in right of Canada, as well as suits in relation to patents, copyright, and admiralty law. It also eventually acquired jurisdiction in tax and citizenship matters and in relation to certain offences under the *Combines Investigation Act*. However, the vast majority of litigation involving matters falling under federal legislative jurisdiction remained with the provincial courts maintained by the provinces under section 92(14).

The Exchequer Court was abolished and replaced by the Federal Court of Canada in 1971. The Federal Court's jurisdiction is substantially larger than that of the Exchequer Court. The Federal Court has been given the power to review decisions of officials or tribunals exercising powers delegated by federal statutes. The Federal Court also has concurrent jurisdiction, along with the provincial superior courts, over proceedings against the Crown in right of Canada.[144] Until 2003, the Federal Court of Canada consisted of two divisions: an Appeal and a Trial Division. With amendments to the *Federal Courts Act*, which came into force on 2 July 2003, these divisions became two separate courts: the Federal Court of Appeal and the Federal Court. Judges of these two courts, who are appointed by the federal Cabinet, are required to

141 However, the federal appointing power is limited by ss. 97 & 98 of the *Constitution Act, 1867*, which require that these federally appointed judges must have been members of the bar of their respective province for at least ten years.

142 Provincial superior courts also have jurisdiction over the application of many federal laws, but some matters of federal law are subject to the exclusive jurisdiction of the Federal Court of Canada.

143 For example, in both the United States and Australia, the judges of the state courts are appointed by the states rather than the national government.

144 Before the 1990 amendments to the *Federal Courst Act*, R.S.C. 1985, c. F-7, the Federal Court had exclusive jurisdiction in such matters.

reside in the National Capital Region, although the vast majority of these courts' hearings occur in other major cities across the country.

The Supreme Court of Canada has held that section 101 of the *Constitution Act, 1867* limits the ability of Parliament to confer jurisdiction on the Federal Court. The reference to "laws of Canada" in section 101 means that only matters governed by an "applicable and existing federal law, whether under statute or regulation or common law,"[145] can be heard in the Federal Court. Thus, an action for breach of contract was held to be beyond the jurisdiction of the Federal Court—despite the fact that the subject matter was within federal legislative jurisdiction—since the matter was governed by the contract law of the particular province.[146] In order for a matter to be subject to Federal Court jurisdiction, there must be an existing federal statute regulating the matter, or it must be subject to "federal common law."[147] The fact that Parliament might possess legislative jurisdiction over a particular matter is not sufficient to vest jurisdiction over that matter in the Federal Court.

The Court has also held that the Constitution Acts are not "laws of Canada" within the meaning of section 101, since they were not enacted by Parliament.[148] This means that it is beyond the competence of Parliament to exclude the jurisdiction of the provincial superior courts to review the constitutional validity of federal laws.[149] Where a constitutional challenge is brought against a federal law, concurrent jurisdiction over the matter will be vested in both the provincial superior courts and the Federal Court.

2) The Independence of the Judiciary and the Rule of Law

It is sometimes said that the doctrine of the "separation of powers"—under which there is a strict separation between the executive, the

---

145 *Quebec North Shore Paper Co. v. Canadian Pacific Ltd.*, [1977] 2 S.C.R. 1054 at 1065–66.

146 *Ibid.*

147 Although a number of cases have referred to the existence of a "federal common law," the precise content of federal common law is not entirely clear. The Supreme Court in *Roberts v. Canada*, [1989] 1 S.C.R. 322, has held that the law of Indigenous title is federal common law for the purposes of s. 101 of the *Constitution Act, 1867*. Other cases have suggested that it is common law which is beyond the capacity of the provinces to change: see *Associated Metals & Minerals Corp. v. "Evie W." (The)* (1977), [1978] 2 F.C. 710 (C.A.). The Supreme Court has also held that the common law rules respecting the Crown's position as a litigant is federal common law.

148 See *Northern Telecom Canada Ltd. v. C.W.O.C.*, [1983] 1 S.C.R. 733 at 745.

149 *Canada (A.G.) v. Law Society of British Columbia*, [1982] 2 S.C.R. 307.

legislature, and the judiciary—is not recognized in the Canadian constitution. This is true in the sense that Canadian constitutional law does not separate executive from legislative functions. Indeed, as discussed in Chapter 3, the principles of responsible government led to the concentration of both executive and legislative powers in the hands of the executive. However, Canadian law does recognize a separation between the executive and legislature on the one hand and the judiciary on the other. The judiciary has constitutional status as a separate and independent branch of government. The constitutional status and independence of the judicial branch is protected by particular provisions of the constitution, particularly sections 96 to 100 of the *Constitution Act, 1867*, which guarantee judicial tenure and salaries. However, these guarantees are reflective of a more general constitutional principle—the principle of judicial independence. An independent judiciary is necessary in any society committed to the rule of law. The rule of law requires, among other things, that government must be conducted according to law, including the law of the constitution. Particularly because the government will often be a party to litigation, it has long been recognized that judges can only uphold the rule of law if they are independent of the government and other agencies of the state. Only an independent judiciary can render decisions that might be unfavourable to a sitting government or that might limit the powers of the state. Therefore, the independence of the judiciary is essential to the effective performance of the judicial function and the maintenance of the rule of law.

The principle of judicial independence has two aspects:[150] first, that judges be autonomous and independent of the other branches of government, particularly of the executive; and second, that judges be immune from the normal legal consequences of their actions taken while performing their judicial functions. The first of these principles was secured in England in the *Act of Settlement* of 1700, which provided that judges would hold office *quamdiu se bene gesserint* ("during good behaviour") and that their salaries would be "ascertained and established." This latter guarantee was subsequently interpreted to mean that judicial salaries could not be reduced once a judge had assumed office, on the theory that the state should not be able to exert indirect influence on the judiciary by threatening to reduce their salaries. The *Act of Settlement* also established that judges could be removed only on a

150 See W.R. Lederman, "The Independence of the Judiciary" (1956) 34 Can. Bar Rev. 769.

motion passed by both the House of Commons and the House of Lords, rather than simply through an order or decision of the government.

3) Sections 96 to 100 of the *Constitution Act, 1867*

These guarantees of judicial tenure were incorporated into sections 96 to 100 of the *Constitution Act, 1867*. Section 99 provides that judges of the superior courts of the provinces shall hold office "during good behaviour, but shall be removable by the Governor General on Address of the Senate and House of Commons." Under the federal *Judges Act*, complaints brought against judges are referred to the Canadian Judicial Council, which is composed of the chief justice of Canada and the chief justices of all of the superior courts. The Judicial Council must investigate and report on the complaint before any action can be taken to remove a judge. No superior court judge has ever been removed pursuant to section 99, although on three occasions, judges resigned when it appeared that resolutions seeking their dismissal were likely to be passed by the Senate and the House of Commons.[151]

Judicial salaries are constitutionally protected under section 100 of the *Constitution Act, 1867*, which provides that the salaries of judges of the superior, district, and county courts of the provinces shall be "fixed and provided by the Parliament of Canada." This requirement means that judges' salaries must be set by federal statute, as opposed to a mere regulation or other legal instrument. Judges of the provincial superior, district, and county courts are thereby insulated from the provincial governments, since the provinces have no role in the payment of their salaries. The use of the phrase "fixed and provided" in section 100 has also been interpreted so as to incorporate the British rule that the salaries of sitting judges cannot be lowered once they have been appointed

---

151 In 1967, Mr. Justice Leo Landreville of the Ontario Supreme Court resigned after a royal commission had recommended his removal for certain of his activities before his appointment to the bench. A motion calling for his dismissal had been introduced in the Senate when Justice Landreville resigned. In late 1996, Mr. Justice Bienvenue of the cour supérieure de Québec resigned after a Canadian Judicial Council investigation and report into certain derogatory statements he had made about women and Jews during the course of a court proceeding. The government had indicated that it was prepared to proceed with a motion calling for his removal, but no such motion had actually been introduced at the time of his resignation. In 2009, Ontario Superior Court Justice Paul Cosgrove resigned after the Canadian Judicial Council recommended his removal to the federal justice minister. Justice Cosgrove was found to have engaged in improper conduct during a criminal trial in which he was perceived to have been aligned with defence counsel.

to office.[152] It is unclear whether the guarantee in section 100 would prevent the government from reducing salaries of federally appointed judges as part of a non-discriminatory, across-the-board reduction in public service salaries.[153]

The second aspect of the principle of judicial independence is that judges are immune from legal liability for actions taken while performing their judicial duties. This immunity is part of the common law, which states that a judge is immune from liability in tort for any act done within his/her jurisdiction.[154] The Crown was also immune at common law from suits in respect of anything done by judges in the performance of their duties, and this common law immunity has been specifically preserved through statute.[155]

In *Reference Re Remuneration of Judges*,[156] the Supreme Court held that the unwritten principle of judicial independence had been incorporated into the Constitution of Canada through the preamble to the *Constitution Act, 1867*. Since judicial independence is an unwritten constitutional norm, the express provisions of the *Constitution Act, 1867* protecting judicial independence are not exhaustive. Rather, the specific provisions are mere illustrations of the broader principle. As such, guarantees of judicial independence relating to security of tenure, financial security, and administrative independence apply to both federally and provincially appointed judges.[157]

---

152 See Mallory, above note 8 at 321–22.

153 In 1932, when the federal government reduced civil service salaries by 10 percent, it imposed a special income tax of 10 percent on judicial salaries. The application of this special tax, as opposed to directly reducing judicial salaries, was seen by the government as achieving the desired savings without running afoul of s. 100 of the *Constitution Act, 1867*. It is arguable, however, that a special income tax singling out judges for more onerous treatment is itself a violation of s. 100. See Mallory, *ibid.* at 322. The ability of the provincial governments to reduce the salaries of provincial court judges has been the subject of litigation that has reached the Supreme Court: see the discussion in the next section of this chapter.

154 See P.W. Hogg, P.J. Monahan, & W.K. Wright, *Liability of the Crown*, 4th ed. (Toronto: Carswell, 2011) at 283.

155 This immunity has been preserved in statutes that have made the Crown generally liable in tort for actions of Crown servants. See, for example, *Proceedings Against the Crown Act*, R.S.O. 1990, c. P.7, s. 5(6).

156 [1997] 3 S.C.R. 3 [*Judges' Remuneration Reference*].

157 The specific issue in the *Judges' Remuneration Reference* was whether legislation in a number of provinces reducing the compensation of provincial court judges as part of wider government restraint measures was constitutionally valid. Lamer C.J. concluded for a majority of the Supreme Court that provinces are under a constitutional obligation to establish judicial compensation commissions and,

The express guarantees of judicial tenure and independence in sections 96 to 100 of the *Constitution Act, 1867* are limited to particular courts. For example, the section 99 guarantee against removal except through a parliamentary address applies only to superior courts, while the section 100 guarantee regarding salaries applies somewhat more broadly to superior, district, and county courts in the provinces.[158] However, there is no mention in either section 99 or 100 of the judges of the Supreme Court, the Federal Court, or other provincial courts appointed by the provinces pursuant to section 92(14). The *Judges' Remuneration Reference* effectively decided that some form of protection respecting these matters is constitutionally required in respect of all members of the judiciary, although the Supreme Court noted that the guarantees for provincial court judges need not necessarily be identical to those applicable to superior courts. It would also appear that some form of institutional independence is required in the case of deputy judges of the Small Claims Court,[159] justices of the peace,[160] and case management masters.[161] The *Judges' Remuneration Reference* led to continued disputes and litigation over judicial salaries between governments and the judiciary, and in late 2005 the Supreme Court dealt with a series of disputes arising from four different provinces. Subsequently, the Supreme Court clarified that recommendations of salary review commissions are advisory rather than binding, and that the government could depart from these advisory committee recommendations if justified with "rational" reasons; this low threshold should be relatively easy to meet and should—at least in theory—reduce litigation over judicial salaries in the future.[162]

In addition to judicial independence, section 96 has been interpreted to guarantee access to the superior courts. The Court has stated that the principle of the rule of law guarantees individuals a right of access to courts as "one of the foundational pillars protecting the

---

further, in the absence of recourse to such commissions, any change to or freeze in the remuneration of provincial court judges is unlawful.

158 Note, however, that the practical significance of the distinction between these different s. 96 courts has now disappeared, since all provinces have amalgamated the county and district courts into the provincial superior court. This case held that a government could reject the recommendations of an advisory commission as long as it had "rational" reasons for doing so.

159 *Ontario Deputy Judges Association v. Ontario (A.G.)* (2006), 80 O.R. (3d) 481 (C.A.).

160 *Ontario Federation of Justices of the Peace Associations v. Ont. (A.G.)* (1999), 43 O.R. (3d) 541 (Div. Ct.).

161 *Masters' Association of Ontario v. Ontario*, 2011 ONCA 243.

162 *Provincial Court Judges' Association (New Brunswick) v. New Brunswick (Minister of Justice)*, [2005] 2 S.C.R. 286.

rights and freedoms of our citizens."[163] One example of how such access was unconstitutionally obstructed was the imposition of prohibitively high hearing fees in the British Columbia Supreme Court. A majority of the Supreme Court of Canada held that such fees violated section 96 by denying people the right to have their disputes resolved in superior courts, and noted the connection of the judicial function, the rule of law, and access to justice.[164]

4) Judicial Review Constitutionally Guaranteed

Judicial review is the process whereby the courts determine whether the exercise of public power is in accordance with the law. Where public bodies exceed the powers conferred on them, the decisions are said to be invalid or *ultra vires* and will be declared invalid by the courts. As discussed in Chapter 1, two distinct kinds of arguments might be raised by a person seeking to challenge government action. First, it may be argued that the statute purporting to authorize the public body's actions is inconsistent with a provision of the Constitution of Canada. Second, assuming the relevant statute is constitutionally valid, it may be argued that the public body exceeded the powers conferred on it by statute. If a public authority exceeds the limits of its powers, depending on the circumstances, the claimant may be entitled to compensation or other relief.[165]

The courts have determined that both of these kinds of judicial review proceedings are constitutionally guaranteed. Before Confederation, the courts had exercised a constitutional judicial review function. Local colonial legislatures were not permitted to exceed the limited powers that had been conferred on them by enabling British statutes.[166]

---

163 *British Columbia Government Employees' Union v. British Columbia (Attorney General)*, [1988] 2 S.C.R. 214 at 230 [*B.C.G.E.U.*].

164 *Trial Lawyers Association of British Columbia v. British Columbia (Attorney General)*, 2014 SCC 59.

165 See *Roncarelli v. Duplessis* (1958), [1959] S.C.R. 121.

166 For example, *The Union Act, 1840* (U.K.), 3 & 4 Vict., c. 35, art. III, had stated that the Legislature of Canada could enact laws that were not "repugnant to this Act, or to such Parts of [the *Constitutional Act, 1791* (U.K.), 31 Geo. III, c. 21] . . . as are not hereby repealed, or to any Act of [the U.K.] Parliament made or to be made . . . which does or shall, by express Enactment or by necessary Intendment, extend to the Provinces of Upper and Lower Canada." The same formula was reproduced in *The Colonial Laws Validity Act, 1865* (U.K.), 28 & 29 Vict., c. 63, which provided for the paramountcy of British statutes that were intended—either expressly or through necessary implication—to apply to a colony. This formula provided for a measure of local or colonial autonomy, since the colonial legislature could enact laws that were inconsistent with the

This judicial review function was continued after Confederation by virtue of section 129 of the *Constitution Act, 1867*. The courts have also held that attempts by the legislature to limit the ability of courts to review statutes or actions of public bodies to ensure consistency with the constitution are unconstitutional. For example, in *Amax Potash Ltd. v. Saskatchewan*,[167] the Supreme Court struck down a Saskatchewan statute that attempted to bar recovery of taxes that had been levied pursuant to an unconstitutional statute. The Court held that, in a federal state, the "bounds of sovereignty are defined and supremacy circumscribed."[168] While courts could not question the wisdom of enactments, they did have a responsibility to ensure that the limits imposed by the constitution were observed: "it is the high duty of this Court to insure that the Legislatures do not transgress the limits of their constitutional mandate and engage in the illegal exercise of power."[169] The Court held that any attempt by the legislature to prevent access to the courts for purposes of determining the constitutional validity of a statute would be an invalid infringement of this judicial role. The attempt by Saskatchewan to limit recovery of illegally levied taxes was an attempt to do indirectly what could not be done directly, and was also invalid.

The guarantee of access to the courts for purposes of testing the constitutional validity of statutes or the actions of public bodies was confirmed and reinforced by the *Constitution Act, 1982*. The preamble to the 1982 Act refers to the constitutional status of the rule of law. Furthermore, the Supreme Court has confirmed that the rule of law is a foundational principle of the Canadian constitutional order.[170] The maintenance of the rule of law would be impossible if unconstitutional actions by legislatures or government could not be challenged in the courts. The Supreme Court has held that guarantees of access to the courts for the determination of individuals' legal rights is one aspect of the principle of the rule of law.[171] Accordingly, it is the responsibility of the courts to make findings of consistency and/or inconsistency with the constitution and any attempt by the legislatures or by government to prevent the courts from fulfilling this function would be invalid.

---

common law or with British statutes that were not intended to apply to the colony in question.

167 (1976), [1977] 2 S.C.R. 576.

168 *Ibid.* at 590.

169 *Ibid.* See also *Reference Re B.C. Motor Vehicle Act*, [1985] 2 S.C.R. 486 at para. 14.

170 *Secession Reference*, above note 19; *Reference re Manitoba Language Rights*, [1985] 1 S.C.R. 721 [*Manitoba Language Rights*]; *British Columbia v. Imperial Tobacco Canada Ltd.*, [2005] 2 S.C.R. 473 [*Imperial Tobacco*].

171 *B.C.G.E.U.*, above note 163.

Judicial review is also constitutionally guaranteed in cases where it is alleged that a person has exceeded the limits of a delegated power. This kind of claim does not raise a constitutional issue; the claim is simply that the legal limits established by a statute have been exceeded. It has become increasingly common in recent decades for legislatures to attempt to limit the ability of courts to review decisions of tribunals or other persons exercising powers under statute through what are known as "privative clauses." In *Crevier v. Quebec (A.G.)*,[172] the Supreme Court held that privative clauses could not prevent superior courts from reviewing a provincially appointed tribunal's decisions so as to ensure that the tribunal stayed within the limits of its jurisdiction as defined by statute. Laskin C.J. held that to permit a provincially appointed tribunal to determine the limits of its own jurisdiction would be to turn that tribunal into a section 96 court: "I can think of nothing that is more the hallmark of a superior court than the vesting of power in a provincial statutory tribunal to determine the limits of its jurisdiction without appeal or other review."[173] Since judges of section 96 courts must be appointed by the governor general, privative clauses purporting to totally oust judicial review are inconsistent with section 96 and are invalid.

Some commentators have suggested that the reasoning in *Crevier* does not apply to privative clauses protecting federal tribunals or courts. This conclusion is said to follow from the fact that section 96 of the *Constitution Act, 1867* prevents the provinces from appointing section 96 court judges but grants such power to the governor general. Provided that members of federal tribunals—it is claimed—are appointed by the governor general, thereby complying with section 96, there should be no objection to a privative clause in a federal statute ousting judicial review, even on jurisdictional grounds.[174] The difficulty with this conclusion, however, is that it fails to consider whether privative clauses ousting judicial review on jurisdictional grounds are consistent with the principle of the rule of law. The Supreme Court has held that the rule of law requires that "the law . . . [be] supreme over officials of the government as well as private individuals, and thereby preclusive of the influence of arbitrary power."[175] It could be argued

172 [1981] 2 S.C.R. 220.

173 *Ibid.* at 237.

174 This is the conclusion drawn by Hogg, above note 10 at s. 7.3(f). See also *Pringle v. Fraser*, [1972] S.C.R. 821, upholding a federal privative clause precluding review on jurisdictional grounds of the decisions of the federal Immigration Appeal Board.

175 *Manitoba Language Rights*, above note 170 at 748.

that any attempt to totally oust judicial review would represent a denial of the supremacy of law, since it would prevent the courts from ensuring that those exercising delegated power remained within the legal limits prescribed by the legislature. Since the rule of law binds Parliament in the same way as the provincial legislatures, the limits on privative clauses established in *Crevier* must apply equally to federal and provincial administrative tribunals.[176]

The decision in *Crevier* provoked a good deal of academic criticism;[177] however, there has been no real attempt or effort by governments to overturn its result. In fact, a proposed amendment to section 96 put forward by the federal government in 1983 specifically preserved the ability of superior courts to review decisions of administrative tribunals on jurisdictional grounds.[178] Moreover, in the *Charlottetown Accord* negotiations in 1992, which featured a vast array of constitutional concerns and grievances, there was no mention of amending section 96.[179] It would seem, then, that the rule established by *Crevier* has not proven to be a significant impediment to the practical operation and effectiveness of provincial administrative tribunals.[180]

5) Section 96 and Administrative Tribunals

The Supreme Court of Canada has also interpreted section 96 of the *Constitution Act, 1867* as limiting the extent to which adjudicative functions can be conferred on provincially appointed administrative tribu-

176 This conclusion that the requirements of s. 96 apply to Parliament as well as the provinces was confirmed by the Supreme Court in *MacMillan Bloedel v. Simpson*, [1995] 4 S.C.R. 725, applying s. 96 to the federal *Young Offenders Act*.

177 See, for example, D. Mullan, "The Uncertain Constitutional Position of Canada's Administrative Tribunals" (1982) 14 Ottawa L. Rev. 239; H.W. Arthurs, "Protection against Judicial Review" (1983) 43 R. du B. 277.

178 The proposed amendment was designed to reverse the decision in the line of cases culminating in *Reference Re Residential Tenancies Act of Ontario*, [1981] 1 S.C.R. 714 [*Residential Tenancies Reference*], holding that the provinces could not confer s. 96 powers on administrative tribunals. However, the amendment also provided that any decision of a tribunal would be subject to review by a superior court on grounds of jurisdiction. For text of the proposed amendment, see P. Macklem *et al.*, *Canadian Constitutional Law*, vol. 1 (Toronto: Emond Montgomery, 1994) at 451.

179 For a review and analysis of the many issues that were included in the negotiations, see K. McRoberts & P.J. Monahan, eds., *The Charlottetown Accord, the Referendum, and the Future of Canada* (Toronto: University of Toronto Press, 1993).

180 In *Dunsmuir v. New Brunswick*, [2008] 1 SCR 190 at para. 31, the Supreme Court reaffirmed the "inherent power of superior courts to review administrative action and ensure that it does not exceed its jurisdiction", which "stems from the judicature provisions in ss. 96 to 101."

nals. The courts have held that it is appropriate to confer adjudicative functions on administrative tribunals where the function is ancillary to the tribunals' administrative or policy-making function. However, section 96 will be violated where the adjudicative function is the sole or central function of the tribunal, and where the power sought to be conferred broadly conforms to a function or power that was exercised by superior courts at the time of Confederation. In the *Residential Tenancies* case,[181] the Supreme Court held that certain powers of a rent tribunal to make orders evicting tenants or requiring landlords or tenants to comply with the rent control legislation broadly conformed to powers exercised by superior courts in the province at the time of Confederation; moreover, since these powers were not ancillary to the tribunal's policy-making role, they could not be saved by the institutional setting in which they were to be exercised.

The *Residential Tenancies* doctrine has been criticized on the basis that it is both unduly vague and arbitrary. One aspect of the test that is particularly problematic is the question of whether the particular adjudicative function in question conforms to a power that was exercised by superior courts in a province at the time of Confederation. This requirement leads to inconsistent results. In a subsequent case from Quebec, the Supreme Court found that landlord–tenant disputes were resolved by both superior and inferior courts at the time of Confederation. This finding led the Court to conclude that powers that were broadly similar to those struck down in *Residential Tenancies* had been validly conferred on a Quebec administrative tribunal.[182] More recently, the Supreme Court has also ruled that Nova Scotia legislation conferring powers on provincial civil servants to investigate, mediate, and adjudicate disputes between landlords and residential tenants was unconstitutional, because superior courts in that province had exclusive jurisdiction over tenancy disputes at the time of Confederation.[183]

Although these results appear anomalous, the fact remains that only a small fraction of the hundreds of administrative tribunals operating at present in the various provinces have had their powers subject to challenge on the basis of section 96. Even after the *Residential Tenancies* decision in 1981, the provinces continued throughout the 1980s to create a wide variety of new tribunals with extensive powers.[184] A

181 *Reference Re Amendments to the Residential Tenancies Act (N.S.)*, [1996] 1 S.C.R. 186 [*Residential Tenancies*].

182 *Quebec (A.G.) v. Grondin*, [1983] 2 S.C.R. 364.

183 *Residential Tenancies*, above note 181.

184 For a review of these developments, see Ontario, Management Board of Cabinet, *Directions: Review of Ontario's Regulatory Agencies* [*Macauley Report*] (Toronto:

variety of reviews of the operations and effectiveness of provincial tribunals has been carried out, and none has identified section 96 as a significant impediment to the ability of provincial governments to implement policy goals through the establishment of expert administrative tribunals in place of the courts.[185] Nor did the provinces put forward any proposals to amend section 96 in the comprehensive negotiations that led up to the *Charlottetown Accord* in 1992. Thus, despite the difficulties with certain aspects of the Court's jurisprudence surrounding section 96, the doctrine does not appear to have significantly impaired the ability of the provinces to create tribunals and endow them with effective powers.

6) The Rule of Law and Crown Immunity

Although the Courts have interpreted section 96 of the *Constitution Act, 1867* as constitutionally entrenching the right to judicial review, it has always been assumed that there are no constitutional restrictions on statutes immunizing the Crown from liability for interfering with private rights. The starting point for this analysis is the basic proposition that the Crown is generally liable, either through the common law or statute, for interference with private rights that would amount to a tort or a breach of contract.[186] However, it has also always been assumed that Parliament and the provincial legislatures can limit or eliminate this potential liability through the enactment of a statute. Although the courts will tend to interpret such statutory immunity clauses narrowly, effect will be given to legislative attempts to immunize the Crown for otherwise actionable conduct. For example, in *Churchill Falls (Labrador) Corp. v. Newfoundland (A.G.)*,[187] Newfoundland enacted legislation purporting to cancel a contract for the supply of hydroelectric power to Hydro-Quebec. The Supreme Court ultimately decided that the statute was *ultra vires* on other grounds but simply assumed that a provin-

---

Queen's Printer, 1989), which found that there were over 500 tribunals operating in the province in the late 1980s.

185 For example, the *Macauley Report*, *ibid.*, did not recommend any change to s. 96 of the *Constitution Act, 1867*.

186 The Crown was liable as a matter of common law for breach of contract. While, at common law, the Crown was not liable in tort, statutory reforms in all Canadian jurisdictions now make the Crown vicariously liable for torts committed by its servants or agents, and directly liable for certain kinds of tortious conduct: see, for example, the *Crown Liability and Proceedings Act*, R.S.C. 1985, c. C-50.

187 [1984] 1 S.C.R. 297.

cial legislature could validly expropriate contractual rights within the province.[188]

Since the enactment of the *Constitution Act, 1982*, however, the Supreme Court has placed increased emphasis on the principle of the rule of law, which was identified in the *Secession Reference* as one of the four key principles of the Constitution of Canada. What use constitutional litigants may make of this principle, however, is not clear. Although the Court has stated that the rule of law constitutes an "implied limitation" on the legislative jurisdiction of Parliament and the provincial legislatures, it has gone on to expressly rule that unwritten principles, including the rule of law, do not provide an independent basis for striking down legislation.[189]

E. DIVISION OF REVENUES, ASSETS, AND DEBTS IN 1867

In addition to the division of powers between Parliament and the provinces, another key feature of the *Constitution Act, 1867* is the division of debts, assets, and sources of revenue between Canada and the provinces. Before Confederation, a number of the colonies in British North America had accumulated large debt loads to finance the construction of public works such as railways and canals. One advantage of Confederation was that the larger political unit would be in a better position to service this existing debt load and to finance additional railway construction needed for westward expansion. These matters were dealt with in Part VIII of the *Constitution Act, 1867* comprising sections 102 to 126.

Part VIII of the *Constitution Act, 1867* establishes Consolidated Revenue Funds for Canada and each of the provinces, and provides that all revenues under the control of either Parliament or the provinces shall automatically accrue to the appropriate Consolidated Revenue Fund.[190] No moneys can be appropriated from the Consolidated Revenue Fund without statutory authority.[191] These constitutional requirements were by no means novel, since the *Bill of Rights* in England in 1688 had

188 *Ibid.* at 327, McIntyre J.

189 *Imperial Tobacco*, above note 170.

190 See ss. 102 and 126 of the *Constitution Act, 1867*. Note that s. 102 provides that all revenues of the former colonies were to accrue to the Consolidated Revenue Fund of Canada unless specifically allocated to the provinces.

191 *Ibid.*, s. 106. This constitutional requirement is reinforced by statute: see the *Financial Administration Act*, R.S.C. 1985, c. F-11, s. 40.

provided that all expenditures of public funds must be authorized by statute. However, they also constitutionally entrenched the principle that had been recognized in British North America in the 1830s that the Crown was not entitled to any sources of revenue independent of the Consolidated Revenue Fund (as discussed in Chapter 2, section C(2)). Because all revenues accruing to the Crown from its property or any other revenue source must automatically accrue to the Consolidated Revenue Fund, the Crown is forced to go to Parliament to obtain moneys necessary to fund the operation of government. The underlying purpose was to buttress the constitutional conventions associated with responsible government, since the government would not be able to carry on its operations without maintaining the confidence of the House of Commons.[192]

Part VIII also divided the assets and debts of the former British colonies between Canada and the provinces. All provincial debts in 1867 were to be assumed by Canada,[193] and Canada received title to the public works that had occasioned these large debts, particularly canals and railways.[194] All other Crown property not specifically transferred to Canada was to remain in the hands of the provincial governments.[195] The provinces were also entitled to the revenue derived from this property. In 1867, however, the revenue from Crown property was relatively modest. Moreover, the provincial taxation power was limited to direct taxation, which accounted for a small proportion of government revenue. The provinces therefore had to rely on annual subsidies from the federal government to fund their basic operations. The federal taxation power was legally unlimited, defined in section 91(3) as the right to raise money by "any Mode or System of Taxation." The right

192 This same purpose was reflected in s. 53 of the *Constitution Act, 1867*, which required that all money bills originate in the House of Commons.

193 See s. 111 of the *Constitution Act, 1867*. The Act established a formula whereby those provinces with a proportionately smaller debt at Confederation were entitled to payments from Canada, while provinces with a proportionately larger debt would have interest on this "excess debt" deducted from the annual subsidies that would otherwise be payable to them by the federal government under s. 118. In the first few years of Confederation, the federal government did deduct interest on the "excess debt" of Ontario and Quebec. However, in 1873 it was agreed that this "excess debt" would be eliminated and no further deductions on account of interest would be made: see 36 Vict. c. 30. In 1884 the amounts that had previously been deducted as interest were refunded through increases in the annual subsidies payable to Ontario and Quebec: see 47 Vict. c. 4.

194 See s. 108 of the *Constitution Act, 1867* and the Third Schedules. The public works in question included canals, public harbours, lighthouses and piers, steamboats, railways, public buildings, and military lands.

195 See ss. 109 and 117 of the *Constitution Act, 1867*.

of the provinces to receive an annual subsidy from the federal government—equal to $0.80 per person, based on the 1861 census—was constitutionally entrenched in section 118. In the years immediately following Confederation, federal subsidies made up close to 60 percent of total provincial revenue, reflecting their financial dependency on the national government at this time.

By the early twentieth century, the provinces had begun to develop new sources of revenue, and federal subsidies made up only one-quarter of provincial revenues. However, disputes over the fairness of these subsidies were a continuing source of federal–provincial and inter-provincial conflict. Many of the poorer provinces argued that their subsidies should be increased to compensate them for the adverse effects of previous federal policies, such as the high tariffs associated with Macdonald's National Policy. In 1907, the formula for calculating the provincial subsidies in section 118 was amended by Great Britain at the request of the Canadian Parliament, but British Columbia objected to the new subsidy formula. In the 1920s and 1930s, a number of royal commissions were appointed to examine the issues and to recommend adjustments to ensure that all provinces share "proportionately with the other provinces of Canada in the economic advantages accruing from Confederation."[196] It was not until after the Second World War that the original federal subsidies were scrapped in favour of a new system of fiscal transfers from the federal government, which were designed to equalize the revenue-raising capacities of provinces.[197] This new approach to federal–provincial revenue-sharing has now received constitutional recognition in section 36 of the *Constitution Act, 1982*, which, among other things, commits the federal government and Parliament to the principle that equalization payments should be made to the provinces to ensure that they have "sufficient revenues to provide reasonably comparable levels of public services at reasonably comparable levels of taxation."

The decision to vest ownership over most Crown property in the provincial Crown does not appear to have been particularly controversial among the drafters of the *Constitution Act, 1867*.[198] However, this

---

196 Mallory, above note 8 at 404–5, citing Canada, *Report of the Royal Commission on Dominion-Provincial Relations* (Ottawa: King's Printer, 1940) [*Rowell-Sirois Commission Report*].

197 The *Rowell-Sirois Commission Report*, *ibid.*, in 1940 had recommended that the ramshackle system of federal subsidies be scrapped and replaced by a new system of fiscal transfers.

198 This approach to the division of Crown property was reflected in the *Quebec Resolutions* of 1864 and carried forward into the *London Resolutions* of 1866

decision had far-reaching consequences and proved a source of considerable federal–provincial controversy in the twentieth century. One such major issue was sparked by the federal government's reserving to itself the ownership of Crown lands when the prairie provinces of Alberta and Saskatchewan were created. This differential treatment, designed to ensure that the development of the west remained under the control of the federal government, was a sore point with these provinces, which regarded themselves as being relegated to second-class status. This situation was finally rectified in 1930 when the *Natural Resources Agreements* transferred to the prairie provinces the same kinds of assets held by the other provinces.[199]

While the drafters of the *Constitution Act, 1867* hoped that "we shall find in our territorial domain . . . additional sources of revenue far beyond the requirement of the public service,"[200] few could have foreseen the huge growth in revenue from Crown lands and property and the increasingly important role that natural resources would play in provincial economic development in the twentieth century. Particularly after the discovery of oil and gas in western Canada in the middle of the last century, the uneven distribution of revenue from natural resources contributed to significant disparities in the revenue-raising capacities of the various provinces. This disparity became a major source of conflict between the federal government and the resource-rich provinces beginning in the 1970s, with the federal government attempting to appropriate and redistribute some of this revenue through the federal taxing power. The provinces, meanwhile, attempted to use their control over natural resources as a means to diversify their provincial economies by, for example, requiring that resources be processed locally before being exported. These conflicts culminated in a number of high-profile court cases during the 1970s, which imposed significant restrictions on the ability of the provinces to tax natural resource revenue or to control the development of resources so as to promote local economic development.[201]

(both reprinted in Kennedy, above note 30 at 541 and 611, respectively) and the *Constitution Act, 1867*.

199 These Agreements are included within the definition of the Constitution of Canada in s. 52 of the *Constitution Act, 1982*, and are therefore constitutionally entrenched.

200 A. Galt in the Confederation Debates, as quoted in G.V. La Forest, *Natural Resources and Public Property under the Canadian Constitution* (Toronto: University of Toronto Press, 1969) at 14.

201 See, for example, *Canadian Industrial Gas & Oil Ltd. v. Saskatchewan* (1977), [1978] 2 S.C.R. 545, striking down Saskatchewan tax and royalty scheme on oil produced in the province.

These court cases, in turn, led to the enactment of section 92A of the *Constitution Act, 1867*, as part of the constitutional package in 1982. This amendment reinforced the provincial power to control and manage natural resources in each province and also gave the provinces the power to raise revenues "by any Mode or System of Taxation" in respect of certain kinds of natural resources in the province.

FURTHER READINGS

BRUN, H., & G. TREMBLAY, *Droit Constitutionnel*, 6th ed. (Cowansville, QC: Yvon Blais, 2014) c. 6

DAWSON, R.M., *The Government of Canada*, 6th ed., ed by N. Ward (Toronto: University of Toronto Press, 1987)

ELLIOT, R.M., "Interjurisdictional Immunity after *Canadian Western Bank* and *LaFarge Canada Inc.*: The Supreme Court Muddies the Doctrinal Waters—Again" (2008) 43 Sup. Ct. L. Rev. (2d) 433

HOGG, P.W., *Constitutional Law of Canada*, loose-leaf (Toronto: Carswell, 2007) cc. 15–16

———, & R. GODIL, "Narrowing Interjurisdictional Immunity" (2008) 42 Sup. Ct. L. Rev. (2d) 623

KING, P.T., *Federalism and Federation* (Baltimore: Johns Hopkins University Press, 1982)

LASKIN, B., "Peace, Order and Good Government Re-examined" (1947) 25 Can. Bar Rev. 1054

———, "Occupying the Field: Paramountcy in Penal Legislation" (1963) 41 Can. Bar Rev. 234

LEDERMAN, W.R., "The Independence of the Judiciary" (1956) 34 Can. Bar Rev. 769

———, "The Concurrent Operation of Federal and Provincial Laws in Canada" (1963) 9 McGill L.J. 185

MALLORY, J.R., *Social Credit and the Federal Power in Canada* (Toronto: University of Toronto Press, 1954) c. 2

———, *The Structure of Canadian Government* (Toronto: Gage, 1984) c. 9

RUSSELL, P.H., *The Judiciary in Canada: The Third Branch of Government* (Toronto: McGraw-Hill Ryerson, 1987)

SMILEY, D.V., *The Federal Condition in Canada* (Toronto: McGraw-Hill Ryerson, 1987)

STEVENSON, G., "Federalism and Intergovernmental Relations" in M.G. Whittington & G. Williams, eds., *Canadian Politics in the 1990s*, 4th ed. (Scarborough, ON: Nelson, 1995)

WATTS, R.L., *Comparing Federal Systems in the 1990s*, 3d ed. (Kingston, ON: Institute of Intergovernmental Relations, Queen's University, 2008)

WEILER, P.C., "The Supreme Court and the Law of Canadian Federalism" (1973) 23 U.T.L.J. 307

WHEARE, K.C., *Federal Government*, 4th ed. (London: Oxford University Press, 1963)

PART THREE

CONSTITUTIONAL CHANGE

CHAPTER 5

CONSTITUTIONAL AMENDMENT, 1867–1982

A. AMENDMENT OF THE *BRITISH NORTH AMERICA ACT, 1867*, BY THE BRITISH PARLIAMENT

The *British North America Act, 1867*,[1] did not contain a general amending procedure. However, as an ordinary U.K. statute, the *BNA Act* could be amended by the British Parliament, just as the previous "constitutional" statutes applicable to British North America had been repealed or amended by Westminster.[2] However, unlike the constitutional arrangements established by Westminster for Australia and South Africa a generation later, the *BNA Act* did not provide any mechanism for Canada to amend the statute without the intervention of Britain. Between 1867 and 1982 the British Parliament amended the *BNA Act* twenty-one times.[3] In addition, the British Parliament enacted a number of other

1 The *British North America Act, 1867* (now the *Constitution Act, 1867* (U.K.), 30 & 31 Vict., c. 3).

2 Namely, the *Quebec Act, 1774* (U.K.), 14 Geo III, c. 83, the *Constitutional Act, 1791* (U.K.), 31 Geo. III, c. 31, and the *Union Act, 1840* (U.K.), 3 & 4 Vict., c. 35, discussed in Chapter 2.

3 The amendments until 1965 are described in G. Favreau, *The Amendment of the Constitution of Canada* (Ottawa: Queen's Printer, 1965). In addition to amendments by Westminster to the Act itself, the British government admitted new provinces to Canada through the enactment of orders in council. See the discussion below at Section B(1).

statutes of a constitutional nature that applied to Canada, such as the *Statute of Westminster, 1931*.[4]

Until 1982, the formal legal power of the British Parliament to amend the *BNA Act* was unlimited. However, each amendment to the *BNA Act* was preceded by a prior request from Canada. As explained below, by the late nineteenth century, a constitutional convention had developed such that Britain would not enact laws applicable to Canada except on the request and with the consent of Canada. This convention was given the force of law in section 4 of the *Statute of Westminster, 1931*, which provided that no future British statute would apply to Canada unless it expressly declared that Canada had requested and consented to its enactment.[5] However, section 4 did not apply to the amendment of the *BNA Act* itself. Consequently, until 1982, limitations on the legal power of the Westminster Parliament to amend the *BNA Act* continued to be based entirely on constitutional convention.

B. POWERS OF AMENDMENT IN THE *BNA ACT*

Although the *BNA Act* did not contain a general amending procedure, the Act did include a number of limited powers of amendment. Some of these amending powers were included in the original enactment in 1867; others were added later. The three bodies empowered to amend the *BNA Act* were the British Cabinet, the Parliament of Canada, and the legislatures of the provinces.

1) Amendments by the British Cabinet: Admission of New Provinces

In 1867, Canada included only a small portion of the lands that now make up the country. The original *BNA Act* divided Canada into the four provinces of Ontario, Quebec, Nova Scotia, and New Brunswick.[6] In addition, the 1867 boundaries of Ontario and Quebec comprised

4 (U.K.), 22 & 23 Geo. V, c. 4.

5 Section 7 of the *Statute of Westminster, 1931* stated that it did not apply to the amendment of the *BNA Act*. Of course, the residual legal power of the U.K. Parliament to enact any law for Canada, including amendments to the *BNA Act*, was abolished by the *Canada Act 1982* (U.K.), 1982, c. 11. See discussion in this chapter below at Section D.

6 See s. 5 of the *Constitution Act, 1867*. New Brunswick and Nova Scotia retained their pre-Confederation boundaries, while the province of Canada was divided into the provinces of Ontario and Quebec.

less than half of the lands now included within those provinces.[7] Yet, while Canadian territory in 1867 was extremely limited, the drafters of the *BNA Act* envisaged that the boundaries of the federal state would be extended to the north, east, and west, so that all the British colonies and territories in British North America would eventually form part of the Dominion. Section 146 of the *BNA Act* explicitly contemplated this possibility and set out a procedure whereby the colonies of Newfoundland, Prince Edward Island, and British Columbia, as well as Rupert's Land and the North-Western Territory, could be admitted to Canada. Section 146 granted the British Cabinet the power to approve the admission of the three colonies through an order in council, provided that the Canadian Parliament and the legislature of the particular colony concerned had approved the terms of admission.[8] The admission of Rupert's Land and the North-Western Territory required a British order in council and the approval of the Canadian Parliament. An order in council approved pursuant to section 146 was to have effect as if enacted as part of the *BNA Act* itself.

Pursuant to the authority set out in section 146, the British Cabinet approved orders in council admitting Rupert's Land and the North-Western Territory in 1870, British Columbia in 1871, Prince Edward Island in 1873, and all remaining British possessions and territories in North America and the adjacent islands, except the colony of Newfoundland, in 1880.[9] All these orders are included within the

---

7 The northern boundaries of Ontario and Quebec in 1867 were not clearly delineated, since the dividing line between Canadian territory and the territory owned by the Hudson's Bay Company (Rupert's Land) had not been settled. In 1867, however, a large portion of what is today included within the territory of Ontario and Quebec was part of Rupert's Land. The boundaries of Ontario and Quebec were subsequently settled through statutes enacted by Westminster in 1889 and Canada in 1898. See the *Canada (Ontario Boundary) Act, 1889* (U.K.), 52 & 53 Vict., c. 28, and *An Act respecting the north-western, northern and north-eastern boundaries of the province of Quebec*, S.C. 1898, c. 3.

8 Section 146 of the *Constitution Act, 1867* provided that the admission of the colonies was to be "on such Terms and Conditions in each Case as are in the Addresses [from Canada and the relevant colony] expressed and as the Queen thinks fit to approve." The approval was to be expressed by Parliament, rather than the government of Canada. This provision foreshadowed the requirement that emerged in relation to amendments to the *BNA Act* itself, where a constitutional convention developed such that a parliamentary resolution (as opposed to a mere order in council) was required before an amendment by Westminster.

9 The territories were admitted, respectively, by: *Rupert's Land and North-Western Territory Order* (23 June 1870) (item 3 of the Schedule to the *Constitution Act, 1982*); *British Columbia Terms of Union* (16 May 1871) (item 4 of the Schedule to the *Constitution Act, 1982*); *Prince Edward Island Terms of Union* (26 June 1873)

definition of the Constitution of Canada in section 52 of the *Constitution Act, 1982*.[10]

2) Amendments by the Canadian Parliament

a) Creation of New Provinces

While section 146 of the *BNA Act* set out a procedure whereby various colonies and territories could be admitted to Canada, it did not specify the manner in which additional provinces could be created out of the territories admitted or the procedure for establishing or altering the boundaries between any provinces that might be created. Nor did section 146 state who would be responsible for establishing a form of civil government in any new province or territory. The federal government initially took the position that it had the legislative authority to create new provinces and provide for civil government in areas admitted to Canada pursuant to its residual power to enact laws in relation to classes of subjects not expressly allocated to the provinces. For instance, in 1869, when it became apparent that Rupert's Land would be admitted to Canada, the Canadian Parliament enacted a statute providing for a temporary form of civil government for the North-Western Territory that became effective once the British order in council approving the admission came into force.[11] In 1870, the Canadian Parliament passed a second statute creating the province of Manitoba.[12]

At the same time, it was argued that the power to establish provinces and provincial governments was not provided for in the *BNA Act* and therefore remained within the exclusive jurisdiction of the Westminster Parliament. In order to resolve these doubts, the British Parliament enacted the *British North America Act, 1871* (now the *Constitution Act, 1871*), which retroactively confirmed the validity of the 1869 federal statute that established Rupert's Land and the *Manitoba Act, 1870*.[13] The *Constitution Act, 1871* also granted the federal Parliament the power to: create new provinces out of lands that were part of Canada but not within any province, and to provide for the constitution and administration of any such province (section 2); alter the boundaries of any

(Item 6 of the Schedule to the *Constitution Act, 1982*); and *Adjacent Territories Order* (31 July 1880) (item 8 of the Schedule to the *Constitution Act, 1982*).

10 Schedule B to the *Canada Act 1982* (U.K.), 1982, c. 11.

11 *An Act for the temporary government of Rupert's Land and the North-Western Territory when united with Canada*, S.C. 1869, c. 3.

12 *Manitoba Act, 1870*, S.C. 1870, c. 3. The province was to be created as of the admission of Rupert's Land. The *Manitoba Act* received Royal Assent on 12 May 1870. Rupert's Land was admitted to Canada on 23 June 1870.

13 *Constitution Act, 1871* (U.K.), 34 & 35 Vict., c. 28.

province with the consent of the legislature of the province affected (section 3);[14] and provide for civil government in any territory not forming part of a province (section 4). Pursuant to this authority, the Canadian Parliament clarified and extended the boundaries of Quebec (in 1898 and 1912), Ontario (in 1912), and Manitoba (in 1881, 1912, and 1930) by adding to each province adjacent territory that had previously been within the original North-Western Territory. Canada also created the provinces of Alberta and Saskatchewan in 1905 pursuant to section 2 of the *Constitution Act, 1871*. In 1898, Parliament created the Yukon Territory as a separate territory with its own form of government.

The *Constitution Act, 1982* now requires the consent of at least seven provinces with 50 percent of the total population of the ten provinces and the consent of Parliament, in order to create new provinces or to extend provincial boundaries.[15] However, the *Constitution Act, 1871* continues to govern the process for establishing civil government in territories that are not included within any province. Thus, Parliament has passed statutes implementing land claim and self-government agreements negotiated with Indigenous peoples in the Yukon, and enacted legislation creating the territory of Nunavut.[16] These changes were implemented by ordinary federal statute pursuant to section 4 of the *Constitution Act, 1871* and did not require the consent of any of the provinces.

b) Changes to the Senate and the House of Commons

The *Constitution Act, 1867* provided that Parliament could make certain changes to the composition and operation of the Senate and House of Commons. However, the authority of Parliament in this regard was limited to what might be termed "housekeeping" matters. For example, section 52 of the *Constitution Act, 1867* granted Parliament the power to increase the number of members of the House of Commons, provided that the principle of proportionate representation "is not thereby disturbed."[17] Other provisions in the *Constitution Act, 1867* that provided for subsequent adjustments by Parliament included: the establishment or alteration of electoral districts for Parliament (section 40); the manner and time for adjusting provincial representation in the House of

14 While the determination of the boundaries of a new province was made by Parliament alone, once a province had been created, its boundaries could not be altered without its consent.

15 Sections 42(e)–(f) of the *Constitution Act, 1982*.

16 See the *Yukon First Nations Land Claims Settlement Act*, S.C. 1994, c. 34, the *Yukon First Nations Self-Government Act*, S.C. 1994, c. 35, the *Nunavut Act*, S.C. 1993, c. 28, and *Constitution Act (Nunavut), 1999*, S.C. 1998, c. 15.

17 See the discussion on proportionate representation in Chapter 3.

Commons in accordance with the results of the most recent decennial census and pursuant to the rules set out in section 51; federal electoral laws (section 41); the number of senators required for a quorum in the Senate (section 35); and the privileges and immunities of members of Parliament (section 18). Furthermore, the Parliament of Canada did not possess the authority to amend the terms of the *BNA Act* itself. Consequently, on any matter of significance regarding federal institutions, the intervention of the Westminster Parliament was required.

c) Section 91(1) Power of Amendment

The Imperial Conference of 1926 recognized that Canada, Australia, Eire, New Zealand, and South Africa were independent of Great Britain.[18] After the Imperial Conference, the federal government and the provinces began to negotiate a "domestic" formula for amending the *BNA Act*.[19] The provinces and the federal government failed to agree on a new amending formula at dominion–provincial conferences held in 1927, 1931, and 1935–36. However, they had reached general agreement on three categories of amendments to the *BNA Act*: (1) amendments that concerned the federal government alone and that could be enacted through an ordinary Act of Parliament; (2) amendments that concerned the provinces alone and that could be enacted by the provinces concerned; and (3) amendments concerning the federal government and some or all the provinces, which required joint action of the federal government and some or all the provinces. The precise dividing line between these three categories and the level of provincial consent required for amendments falling into the third category remained unsettled.[20]

The original *BNA Act* had granted the provinces the right to amend provisions respecting the "Constitution of the Province," provided that such amendments did not affect the office of the lieutenant govern-

---

18 This "Balfour Declaration" described the relationship between Great Britain and these self-governing members of the Commonwealth: "They are autonomous Communities within the British Empire, equal in status, in no way subordinate one to another in any aspect of their domestic or external affairs, . . . associated as members of the British Commonwealth of Nations" (see R.M. Dawson, *The Government of Canada*, 6th ed., ed by N. Ward (Toronto: University of Toronto Press, 1987) at 291).

19 By a "domestic" formula, we refer to a procedure whereby the *Constitution Act, 1867* could be amended by Canadian political authorities, without the intervention or participation of Westminster.

20 See Favreau, above note 3 at 17–25; J.R. Hurley, *Amending Canada's Constitution: History, Processes, Problems and Prospects* (Ottawa: Supply and Services Canada, 1996) c. 2.

or.[21] However, apart from the ability to make the narrow housekeeping changes noted earlier, there was no comparable provision granting an amending power to the federal Parliament. In 1949, the federal government asked the British Parliament to amend the *BNA Act* so as to grant the Parliament of Canada the power to amend the Constitution of Canada in relation to matters of exclusive concern to the federal government. Westminster agreed to the request. Section 91(1) to the *BNA Act* empowered Parliament to amend the Constitution of Canada except for matters falling into certain specified classes. The most significant of the exceptions to the new federal amending power were amendments relating to provincial legislative powers or to other rights and privileges of the provinces.[22]

The federal government did not obtain the consent of the provinces for the addition of section 91(1). The federal position was that provincial consent was unnecessary because the new amending power was of concern to the federal government alone and could not be used to affect provincial powers. The provinces rejected this justification and claimed that section 91(1) could nonetheless operate to permit the federal government to enact amendments that would indirectly affect provincial interests in the federation. Prime Minister Louis St. Laurent ignored these provincial objections, and Westminster enacted the amendment in the precise terms requested by Ottawa.

Parliament subsequently relied on section 91(1) to amend section 51 of the *BNA Act* to revise the formula for distributing seats in the House of Commons in 1952 and again in 1974.[23] Parliament also used section 91(1) to impose a compulsory retirement age of seventy-five for senators,[24] and to adjust the representation of the Northwest Territories and the Yukon in the Senate and the House of Commons.[25] There do

---

21 Section 92(1) of the *BNA Act*, discussed below.

22 Other matters excepted from the amending power in s. 91(1) of the *BNA Act* were minority education rights; provisions respecting the use of the English or the French language; and the requirements that there shall be a session of the Parliament of Canada at least once a year and that no House of Commons shall continue for more than five years.

23 See *British North America Act, 1952*, S.C. 1952, c. 15; *Constitution Act, 1974*, S.C. 1974–75–76, c. 13.

24 See *Constitution Act, 1965*, S.C. 1965, c. 4.

25 See *Constitution Act (No. 1), 1975*, S.C. 1974–75–76, c. 28 (increasing the representation of the Northwest Territories in the House of Commons from one to two members); *Constitution Act (No. 2), 1975*, S.C. 1974–75–76, c. 53 (providing that the Yukon and the Northwest Territories shall each have one senator).

not appear to have been any objections by the provinces to any of these federal statutes.[26]

In 1978, the federal government under Prime Minister Trudeau proposed to replace the existing Senate with a new House of the Federation, half of whose members would be appointed by the House of Commons and the other half by the provincial legislatures. The federal government initially took the position that this amendment could be enacted pursuant to section 91(1) through an ordinary federal statute. However, after the provinces objected, it referred the issue to the Supreme Court for a definitive ruling. In 1980, the Court released its judgment, which surprised many commentators.[27] The Court gave a narrow reading to section 91(1) and held that it did not authorize abolition or alteration of the Senate.[28] Although the Court acknowledged that section 91(1) permitted some changes to be made to the Senate by Parliament alone, it ruled that it was not open to Parliament to make alterations that would affect the "essential characteristics" of the Senate. The Court identified these essential characteristics as being the representation of regional and provincial interests in the federal legislative process, and acting as a chamber of "sober second thought" for measures approved by the House of Commons. The effect of the Supreme Court's decision was that section 91(1) would not authorize any changes to the *BNA Act* that were "of interest to the provinces," and that the intervention of Westminster would have to be obtained for any significant changes. This decision provided further impetus for the provinces and the federal government to come to an agreement on a domestic amending formula for the *BNA Act*.

In 1982, section 91(1) was repealed and section 44 of the *Constitution Act, 1982* was enacted in its place. Section 44 provides that the Parliament of Canada may exclusively make laws amending the Constitution of Canada "in relation to the executive government of Canada or the Senate and House of Commons." However, this power is subject to a number of important exceptions set out in sections 41 and 42 that limit the scope of section 44. As discussed in Chapter 6, the amending powers of Parliament under section 44 of the *Constitution Act, 1982* are similar to those that existed previously under section 91(1).

---

26 The Supreme Court in *Reference Re Legislative Authority of Parliament of Canada*, [1980] 1 S.C.R. 54 [*Reference Re Senate*] described these amendments as dealing with "housekeeping matters," suggesting that they were squarely within the amending power of Parliament pursuant to the *Constitution Act, 1867*.

27 See, for example, P.W. Hogg, "Comment" (1980) 58 Can. Bar Rev. 631.

28 *Reference Re Senate*, above note 26.

3) Provincial Power to Amend "the Constitution of the Province"

Section 92(1) of the *BNA Act* granted the provinces the power to amend "the Constitution of the Province, except as regards the Office of Lieutenant Governor." Part V of the *BNA Act*, entitled "Provincial Constitutions," had provided for executive and legislative institutions in the four original provinces. Similar provisions were included in respect of the other provinces at the time of their creation or entry into confederation. Section 92(1) indicated that these provisions were subject to alteration by the provinces through ordinary statute, at least to the extent that any changes did not alter the office of the lieutenant governor.

The provinces have used section 92(1) to implement a number of significant changes to their legislative and executive institutions. For example, five provinces have used the section 92(1) power to abolish the appointed Legislative Councils that were in existence at the time of their creation or entry into confederation.[29] Section 92(1) has also been used to alter the privileges or immunities of members of a Legislative Assembly[30] and to extend the term of a Legislative Assembly beyond the customary five years.[31]

Section 92(1) was repealed in 1982. The right of the provinces to enact amendments to the "constitution of the province" was carried forward into section 45 of the *Constitution Act, 1982*. This provision is considered in greater detail in Chapter 6.

4) Constitutional Conventions Limiting Westminster's Authority

The amending powers conferred on the British Cabinet, the Canadian Parliament, and the provincial legislatures were all quite limited in scope. Apart from these limited categories of amendments, all other changes to the *BNA Act* required a statute enacted by the Westminster Parliament. This requirement was not particularly controversial in 1867. However, as Canada gradually acquired the status of a sovereign

---

29 The five provinces were Prince Edward Island, New Brunswick, Nova Scotia, Manitoba, and Quebec. In the *Senate Reference*, *ibid.*, the federal government relied on the fact that these provinces had abolished their Legislative Councils to justify a similar unilateral power in Parliament to abolish or alter the composition of the Senate. The Supreme Court rejected the federal government's argument on this point.

30 *Fielding v. Thomas*, [1896] A.C. 600 (P.C.).

31 *R. v. Clark*, [1943] O.R. 501 (C.A.).

and independent state, the need for British legislation to alter the country's constitutional arrangements became increasingly anachronistic.

The British Parliament retained the formal legal authority to amend the *BNA Act* until 1982. However, by the early twentieth century, two important constitutional conventions had developed. These conventions limited the circumstances in which the amending power could be exercised by the Westminster Parliament and ensured that political control over the amendment process would be exercised in Ottawa rather than London.

The first constitutional convention required that Britain could amend the *BNA Act* only on the request of Canadian political authorities. Arguably, this constitutional convention had begun to crystallize at the time of Confederation. For instance, the *Union Act, 1840* had been enacted by Britain on the advice of Lord Durham, rather than the local Canadian political authorities. With the acceptance of the principle of responsible government in British North America in the late 1840s, however, Westminster began a practice of enacting "constitutional" amendments[32] in response to requests from the colonial political leadership. In 1848, the French language was given status as an official language in the Canadian legislature and, in 1856, it was provided that future members of the Legislative Council would be elected. Both changes were made by Westminster at the request of the colonial leaders. This practice was reinforced by the enactment of the *BNA Act* itself, which was drafted to give effect to the Quebec and London Resolutions, which had been agreed to by delegates from Canada, Nova Scotia, and New Brunswick.[33]

After Confederation, each amendment to the *BNA Act* was preceded by a prior request from Canada. Moreover, in each instance in which Canada requested an amendment, Westminster enacted the legislation in the same terms requested by Canada.[34] Thus, by early in the twentieth century, a constitutional convention had begun to emerge such

---

32 In this context, a constitutional amendment is an amendment to the British statute constituting a colony and its form of civil government, such as the *Union Act, 1840.*

33 The only significant change to the *BNA Act* inserted at the request of the British authorities was s. 26, which provided for the appointment of four or eight additional senators. (See Chapter 3, note 5.)

34 In addition to the *Constitution Act, 1871*, Westminster enacted amendments in 1875 (amending s. 18 of the *BNA Act*); 1886 (authorizing Parliament to provide for parliamentary representation of the territories); 1893 (repealing some obsolete provisions); and 1895 (confirming procedure for appointing a deputy Speaker in the Senate).

that Britain would amend the *BNA Act* only on the request of Canada.[35] This constitutional convention was reflected by and reinforced in a declaration issued by the British prime minister and the prime ministers of the dominions at the Imperial Conference in 1930, which stated that "no law hereafter made by the Parliament of the United Kingdom shall extend to any dominion otherwise than at the request and with the consent of that dominion."[36]

The second constitutional convention that emerged in the late nineteenth and early twentieth centuries required that a resolution embodying the terms of a Canadian request be approved by Parliament before it was forwarded to Westminster. The requirement of a parliamentary resolution, as opposed to a request from the government alone, was a matter of controversy in relation to the enactment of the *Constitution Act, 1871*. The government had originally requested an amendment from Westminster without submitting the matter to Parliament. When the opposition condemned the government for failing to seek parliamentary approval, the government agreed that such matters should be referred to Parliament. The House of Commons unanimously adopted a resolution stating that "no changes in the provisions of the *British North America Act* [would] be sought by the Executive Government without the previous assent of the Parliament of this Dominion."[37] With only one exception, parliamentary resolutions in all subsequent cases were obtained before the requests for amendments were forwarded to Britain.[38] Thus, by the early twentieth century, a firm constitutional convention had emerged such that the sanction of Parliament was required for a request to the British Parliament for an amendment to the *BNA Act*.[39]

---

35 See Favreau, above note 3 at 15.

36 *Ibid.*

37 *Ibid.* at 11.

38 The one exception was the amendment of 1895 (*Canadian Speaker (Appointment of Deputy) Act, 1895* (U.K.), 59 Vict., c. 3), which confirmed a Canadian statute that had provided for the appointment of a deputy Speaker of the Senate during the illness or absence of the Speaker. Although a parliamentary resolution was not obtained in this case, the amendment merely confirmed the terms of the statute that had been previously enacted by the Canadian Parliament; moreover, the preamble to the British statute recited the fact that Canada had previously passed the statute in question, and that the purpose of the amendment was to remove doubts that had arisen as to the validity of the Canadian enactment.

39 Favreau, above note 3 at 15.

C. THE SEARCH FOR A DOMESTIC AMENDING FORMULA

1) Early Federal Predominance

Before the First World War, the development of a domestic constitutional amending formula was not regarded as a significant political issue. Canadian political leaders appeared content to leave the power to amend the *BNA Act* in the hands of Westminster, particularly since there were few amendments requested during this period and none of the amendments involved major changes to the federation. Nor was the issue of provincial involvement in the amending process a particularly controversial issue. The only occasion on which the federal government consulted with the provinces on a constitutional change during the first fifty years of confederation was in 1907, when Ottawa sought an amendment establishing a new scale of financial subsidies to the provinces in place of those set out in section 118 of the *BNA Act*. Eight of the nine provinces consented to the amendment, but British Columbia remained opposed. The British government made minor changes in the text of the draft bill, and the amendment was enacted over British Columbia's objections.

Most of the amendments enacted during the first fifty years of confederation did not have a direct impact on the provinces. However, the amendment of 1915 redefined the senatorial divisions of Canada to take into account the provinces of Manitoba, Saskatchewan, Alberta, and British Columbia. As the Supreme Court noted in its judgment many years later in the *Upper House Reference*, the provincial distribution of seats in the Senate has a clear impact on provincial and regional interests.[40] However, the 1915 amendment was passed without consultation with the provinces and without provincial government representations concerning its enactment.

In short, during this early period, there was no constitutional convention requiring the consultation or consent of the provinces before a constitutional amendment, even when the amendment had a direct impact on provincial or regional interests.

2) A Convention Requiring Provincial Consent Emerges

After the end of the First World War, domestic constitutional amendment became a significant political issue. However, before the authority

40 *Senate Reference*, above note 26.

of Westminster over the *BNA Act* could be terminated, it would be necessary to arrive at a consensus as to the respective roles of the federal and the provincial governments in future amendments. The need for federal–provincial agreement on a domestic amending formula acquired some urgency after the issuance of the Balfour Declaration in 1926, which recognized the political independence of the self-governing dominions. The British government agreed to enact a statute granting the dominions the right to amend imperial statutes applicable to the former colonies. At dominion–provincial conferences in 1927 and 1931, the federal government and the provinces were unable to come to an agreement on the appropriate domestic procedure for amending the *BNA Act*. Therefore, when the British Parliament enacted the *Statute of Westminster, 1931*, granting the Canadian Parliament and the provincial legislatures the power to amend or repeal imperial statutes applying to Canada, a section was added stating that nothing in the statute applied to the amendment of the *BNA Act*.[41] The practical effect of this "carve out" was to retain the legal authority of Westminster over the *BNA Act*.

The search for a domestic amending formula continued at federal–provincial conferences and meetings in 1935–36, 1950, 1960–61, and 1964. The broad outlines of a consensus on an appropriate amending formula gradually began to emerge at these meetings. In particular, there was general agreement that constitutional changes affecting the rights or powers of the provinces required their consent. It was also clear that for certain fundamental matters, the consent of all the provinces should be required, while for other matters touching on provincial interests the consent of some but not all provinces should be sufficient. The precise dividing line between amendments requiring provincial unanimity and amendments requiring something less than unanimity remained uncertain. In addition, the precise scope of federal power to amend the constitution was a controversial issue. The provinces continued to argue that section 91(1) was too broadly framed, and that amendments falling into this category needed to be defined more narrowly.

In the meantime, the *BNA Act* was amended nine times between 1931 and the mid-1960s. In three of those instances (1940, 1951, 1964), the amendments directly affected provincial powers by adding to the legislative authority of the Parliament of Canada.[42] On each of these occa-

41 The *Statute of Westminster, 1931*, above note 4, s. 7. This section was added at the request of the Canadian Parliament, and its text had been agreed to by all the provinces at a conference held in April 1931.

42 In 1940, the federal Parliament acquired exclusive authority to enact laws in relation to unemployment insurance; in 1951, Parliament was granted concurrent powers with the provinces to make laws in relation to old-age pensions; and in

sions, unanimous provincial consent for the amendment was obtained. On other occasions, however, the federal government failed to obtain provincial consent before obtaining an amendment that affected provincial interests. As discussed above, in 1949, section 91(1) was added to the *BNA Act*, granting the federal Parliament the power to enact constitutional amendments, without provincial consent. Nor was the consent of the other provinces obtained in 1949 for the constitutional amendment admitting Newfoundland to confederation.[43] The provinces also objected to the fact that their consent was not obtained before the constitutional amendments in 1943 and 1946.[44]

By the 1960s, therefore, a constitutional convention had begun to emerge such that any amendment directly affecting the legislative powers of the provinces would be sought from Westminster only after the consent of the provinces had been obtained. This convention was reflected in the fact that the amendments which had altered provincial legislative powers had all been approved by the provinces before the submission of the parliamentary request to the British government. However, as the federal government concluded in a 1965 white paper, the "nature and degree of provincial participation in the amending process . . . have not lent themselves to easy definition."[45]

3) Constitutional Negotiations in the 1960s and 1970s

During the 1960s and early 1970s, the federal and provincial governments came very close to achieving unanimous agreement on a new amending formula on two separate occasions. In October 1964, the "Fulton–Favreau amending formula" was unanimously accepted at a

---

1964 Parliament acquired concurrent power to provide for supplementary benefits to old-age pensions. Also significant was the fact that the 1930 amendment extending the western provinces' rights over natural resources was unanimously agreed to by all provinces affected.

43 The admission of Newfoundland could have been achieved through s. 146 of the *BNA Act*, which required the consent of the Canadian Parliament and Newfoundland only. However, rather than proceed under s. 146, which required only an order in council of the British government, a statute was passed by Westminster confirming the *Terms of Union* that had been agreed to by Newfoundland and Canada.

44 The 1943 amendment (*British North America Act, 1943* (U.K.), 6 & 7 Geo. VI, c. 30) postponed the redistribution of seats in the House of Commons, while the 1946 amendment (*British North America Act, 1946* (U.K.), 9 & 10 Geo. VI, c. 63) readjusted the formula for representation in the House of Commons in s. 51 of the *BNA Act*.

45 See Favreau, above note 3 at 15.

first ministers conference.[46] This formula provided that the unanimous consent of the federal Parliament and all provincial legislatures would be required to make any changes in the division of powers between the federal government and the provinces. However, Quebec premier Jean Lesage subsequently withdrew his government's support for the proposal, arguing that the unanimity requirement would block Quebec from obtaining the additional legislative powers it sought from Ottawa. The federal government decided not to proceed with the amendment in the absence of Quebec's support.

At a conference in Victoria in June 1971, the first ministers reached unanimous agreement on the *Canadian Constitutional Charter, 1971*, which subsequently came to be known as the *Victoria Charter*.[47] The general amending formula in the *Victoria Charter* required the consent of the federal Parliament and the provinces of Ontario and Quebec, as well as a majority of both the western provinces and the Atlantic provinces. The *Victoria Charter* would also have added constitutional protection for fundamental political rights and language rights. Furthermore, it would have entrenched the Supreme Court of Canada in the constitution and provided for provincial participation in the selection of Supreme Court judges.[48] However, the *Victoria Charter* prompted protest in Quebec. Premier Robert Bourassa was criticized for having failed to obtain any additional legislative powers for his province. Furthermore, critics in Quebec opposed the addition of section 94A to the *BNA Act*, which would have granted the federal Parliament a new legislative power in relation to "family, youth and occupational training allowances."[49] Even members of Bourassa's own Cabinet were opposed to the *Victoria Charter* and, within days of returning to Quebec City from the

---

46 E.D. Fulton and Guy Favreau had been the federal justice ministers and chairs, respectively, of the meetings of attorneys general held in 1960 and 1964 at which the formula had been drafted.

47 Reported in A. Bayefsky, ed., *Canada's Constitution Act 1982 & Amendments: A Documentary History*, vol. 1 (Toronto: McGraw-Hill Ryerson, 1989) at 214.

48 Under the *Victoria Charter*, if the federal and a provincial attorney general could not agree on an appointee to the Supreme Court of Canada, the provincial attorney general had the right to have the appointment made by a "nominating council" (which, at the option of the provincial minister, could be composed of the attorney general of Canada and the attorneys general of the provinces); the nominating council would select the appointee from a list of at least three names submitted by the attorney general of Canada.

49 The new federal legislative power was concurrent with provincial power over the same matter, and provincial laws would have been paramount in the event of a conflict between legislation enacted by Parliament and a provincial legislature.

meeting in Victoria, Bourassa announced that he was withdrawing his support for the agreement.

Quebec was not the only province where the *Victoria Charter* proved controversial. Within months of the agreement being negotiated, elections in Saskatchewan and Alberta resulted in new governments that opposed the new amending formula. The main objection in the west was that the *Victoria Charter* provided vetoes to Quebec and Ontario but not to any other province. Newly elected Alberta premier Peter Lougheed announced that the veto proposal was fundamentally unacceptable and would have created two classes of provinces.[50]

Given the widespread provincial opposition to the *Victoria Charter*, the federal government decided not to proceed and the issue of constitutional reform faded from the public agenda for the next five years. However, in November of 1976, the election of the separatist Parti Québécois government under the leadership of René Lévesque thrust the issue of constitutional reform back onto centre stage. In 1978, the federal government under Prime Minister Trudeau proposed legislation that would have comprehensively rewritten the Canadian constitution. The federal government acknowledged that much of what it proposed, including a new amending formula and the codification of the powers of the Crown, would have required the approval of the Westminster Parliament. However, Ottawa maintained that significant parts of the proposed reform package—including the replacement of the Senate with a new House of the Federation—could be implemented through ordinary federal legislation enacted pursuant to section 91(1). In late 1979, the Supreme Court ruled against the federal government in the *Upper House Reference* and concluded that the proposed changes to the Senate could only be accomplished through an amendment to the *BNA Act* enacted by Westminster.[51] This decision effectively scuttled the federal initiative because, by the time the Court ruling was handed down, the Trudeau Liberal government had been defeated in the May 1979 election and replaced by a government led by Progressive Conservative Joe Clark. Clark had already indicated that he did not intend to proceed with the previous government's constitutional proposals.

---

50 See P. Lougheed, "The *Charlottetown Accord*: A Canadian Compromise" in K. McRoberts & P.J. Monahan, eds., *The Charlottetown Accord, the Referendum, and the Future of Canada* (Toronto: University of Toronto Press, 1993) at 171–72.

51 *Senate Reference*, above note 26.

4) The Patriation Round

The Lévesque government elected in 1976 had promised to hold a referendum in Quebec on sovereignty-association during its term in office. It was not until May 1980 that Quebec held a referendum to seek a mandate to negotiate sovereignty-association with Canada.[52] Approximately 60 percent of Quebeckers who cast ballots voted against the proposed negotiations. During the referendum campaign, Trudeau, who had been re-elected as prime minister in the federal general election held in February 1980, had promised certain unspecified changes in the Canadian constitution in return for a "No" vote. He immediately instructed his justice minister, Jean Chrétien, to commence negotiations with the provinces aimed at achieving a consensus on a package of amendments. Chrétien and Saskatchewan attorney general Roy Romanow co-chaired a committee of ministers that met over the summer of 1980, culminating in a first ministers conference in September of that year. Although there was substantial agreement on a number of items at the conference, significant points of disagreement remained, particularly on the issues of the entrenchment of a charter of rights and a new amending formula.

Trudeau had previously indicated that he intended to proceed without the provinces if the September conference failed to achieve a consensus. A leaked memo authored by senior federal official Michael Kirby describing plans to "go over the heads of the premiers" in the event of a deadlock had soured the atmosphere at the conference and was widely seen as having contributed to its failure. In early October 1980, Trudeau tabled a resolution in Parliament proposing a series of far-reaching changes to the existing constitution. There were three main elements to the Trudeau package: "patriation" of the constitution — the termination of the authority of Britain to amend the *BNA Act*; enactment of a charter of rights and freedoms that would be binding on both the federal and the provincial governments; and a new amending formula based on the *Victoria Charter*. The parliamentary resolution asked the queen to table a bill incorporating these changes before the Westminster Parliament, which would enact them into law.

Only Ontario and New Brunswick supported the federal initiative. The remaining "gang of eight" opposed it and launched constitutional challenges against the federal resolution in three provincial Courts

52 Quebec's proposals were detailed in a document published in 1979 entitled *Quebec-Canada: A New Deal* (Quebec: Éditeur officiel, 1979), which argued that Quebec should become sovereign but should maintain a common market and some political institutions linking it with Canada.

of Appeal.[53] The provincial reference cases asked two general types of questions. First, they asked whether the federal initiative violated a constitutional convention that required the federal government to obtain the consent of the provinces before requesting a constitutional amendment from Westminster affecting provincial powers. Second, they asked whether this manner of proceeding was in breach of some legal rule of the Canadian constitution. In early 1981, the Courts of Appeal in Manitoba and Quebec held that the federal initiative was in accordance with the formal terms of the Canadian constitution as well as unwritten constitutional conventions. However, the Newfoundland Court of Appeal ruled that the federal initiative was contrary to constitutional convention and that it violated the legal requirements of the Canadian constitution. With the validity of the federal initiative cast into doubt, the federal government announced that it would not proceed until the Supreme Court had had an opportunity to render a definitive ruling on the matter.

The Supreme Court heard argument in May 1981 and handed down its decision on 28 September 1981. The Court ruled by a seven to two majority that the federal government had the constitutional authority to submit a request for a constitutional amendment without obtaining the consent of the provinces. However, it also ruled, by a six to three majority, that the federal initiative violated a constitutional convention requiring "substantial provincial consent" before an amendment could be sought that directly altered federal-provincial relationships.[54]

By giving something to each side, while denying both a total victory,[55] the Supreme Court set the stage for a new round of constitutional

53 The provinces were forced to proceed in this manner because they do not have the power under the *Supreme Court Act*, R.S.C. 1985, c. S-26, to refer questions directly to the Supreme Court.

54 *Reference Re Amendment of Constitution of Canada (Nos. 1, 2, 3)*, [1981] 1 S.C.R. 753. The ruling that "substantial provincial consent" was required, as opposed to unanimous consent, surprised some observers, given the fact that the precedents of 1930, 1940, 1951, and 1964 seemed to support a convention requiring unanimous consent. However, the Supreme Court relied on the statement in the 1965 white paper, to the effect that the precise degree of provincial consent required had not been clearly defined, in support of its finding that "substantial" consent was all that was necessary.

55 While the federal government immediately proclaimed victory on the basis that the Supreme Court had upheld the initiative as legal, the federal loss on the issue of constitutional convention forced Ottawa back to the bargaining table. At the same time, by ruling that only the substantial consent of the provinces was required, the Court made clear that no one province could block the federal initiative. This decision made it risky for the provinces to hold out for their preferred positions, since by holding out they might find themselves excluded from any bar-

bargaining that produced an agreement between the federal government and nine of the provinces in early November 1981. The key to the November agreement was Trudeau's willingness to accept two key compromises that he had previously resisted. First, he accepted the main elements of an amending formula that had been drafted by the eight provinces that opposed his initiative. This "Vancouver formula" did not give any one province a veto; instead, it required the consent of seven provinces, with 50 percent of the total population of the ten provinces, for most amendments. Up to three provinces could "opt out" of an amendment, so it was unnecessary to provide a veto for any single province.[56] The other key compromise made by Trudeau was his acceptance of the right of provincial legislatures or Parliament to override certain provisions of the charter of rights for a period of up to five years. However, Trudeau insisted that the legislative override would not apply to the guarantees of language rights in the charter, a condition that was accepted by the nine provinces who signed the agreement.

Quebec was the only province that refused to endorse the compromise agreement. In November 1981, Trudeau proposed two changes to the package designed to garner Quebec's approval. However, both the Quebec government and the Liberal opposition led by Claude Ryan voted against the modified federal package in the Quebec National Assembly.[57] Quebec also asked its Court of Appeal to rule on whether proceeding with the constitutional amendments without its consent violated the constitutional convention requiring "substantial provincial consent" that had been recognized by the Supreme Court in its September 1981 ruling. Both the Quebec Court of Appeal and the Supreme Court of Canada found that there was no constitutional convention guaranteeing Quebec a veto. Both courts relied heavily on the fact

---

gain that might be reached by the federal government and the remaining provinces. In effect, then, the Supreme Court decision provided incentives for both sides to compromise, thus laying the foundation for the November agreement.

56 While Trudeau accepted the concept of opting out, he rejected a provincial proposal that an opted-out province would be entitled to compensation from the federal government. Quebec premier Lévesque cited this modification to the Vancouver formula as one of the main reasons for his refusal to endorse the agreement.

57 The two changes were a right to compensation for a province that opted out of a constitutional amendment transferring provincial legislative powers relating to "education or other cultural matters" to the Parliament of Canada; and a provision stating that the minority language education rights guaranteed by s. 23(1)(a) of the *Charter* would not come into force in Quebec until agreed to by the Quebec legislature.

that Lévesque had earlier supported the Vancouver amending formula, which did not guarantee Quebec or any other province a veto.[58]

The November 1981 agreement was also controversial among certain women's organizations and Indigenous groups. Women's organizations were concerned by the fact that equality rights were subject to the override power in the *Charter*, while Indigenous peoples objected to the deletion of a clause that had been included in an earlier federal draft protecting Indigenous and Treaty rights. The federal government and the nine provinces agreed to make changes to accommodate these concerns.[59]

In early December 1981, the amended resolution was approved by the Senate and the House of Commons and forwarded to Britain, where legislation giving effect to the Canadian request was enacted by the U.K. Parliament on 29 March 1982. The *Canada Act 1982* came into force immediately, while the *Constitution Act, 1982*, including the *Canadian Charter of Rights and Freedoms* and the new amending formula, came into force on 17 April 1982, when it was proclaimed as law by the queen in a ceremony held on Parliament Hill in Ottawa.

D. THE *CANADA ACT 1982*

The two main purposes of the *Canada Act 1982* were to terminate the legal authority of the Westminster Parliament to legislate for Canada, and to define the procedure whereby the English and French versions of the *Constitution Act, 1982* could be brought into force. Patriation was accomplished by section 2 of the *Canada Act 1982*, which stated that "[n]o Act of the Parliament of the United Kingdom passed after the *Constitution Act, 1982* comes into force shall extend to Canada as part of its law." At the same time, sections 4 and 7(1) of the *Statute of Westminster, 1931*, which had recognized the continuing authority of Westminster to legislate for Canada, were repealed.[60] Consequently, since 17 April

58 See *Qué. (A.G.) v. Can. (A.G.)*, [1982] 2 S.C.R. 793.

59 Women's concerns were addressed by adding s. 28 to the *Charter*, Part I of the *Constitution Act, 1982*, above note 10, which was thought to exempt gender equality rights from the override power; the clause protecting Indigenous and Treaty rights was reinserted into the agreement, although the protection was limited to "existing" rights. The addition of the word "existing" to s. 35 of the *Constitution Act, 1982* led some Indigenous peoples to oppose the revised agreement when it was forwarded to Britain, but the amendment was enacted despite their objections.

60 This repeal was accomplished through the combined operation of s. 53(1) and the Schedule item 17, col. II of the *Constitution Act, 1982*.

1982, the Westminster Parliament can no longer enact any changes in Canadian law, including changes to the Constitution of Canada.[61]

Although the *Canada Act 1982* terminated the legislative authority of Westminster, it did not affect the position or office of the queen. Those provisions of the *Constitution Act, 1867* recognizing the queen as Canada's head of state were unaffected by the *Canada Act 1982*. The queen's powers and prerogatives in relation to Canada have largely been delegated to the governor general, but she continues to exercise or perform certain limited functions, such as the appointment of the governor general or of additional senators under section 26.

The *Canada Act 1982* also provided that the English and French versions of the *Constitution Act, 1982*, which took the form of Schedules to the *Canada Act 1982*, were to come into force in accordance with their terms. Section 58 of the *Constitution Act, 1982* states that it comes into force when proclaimed by the queen. In this way the proclamation issued by the queen on 17 April 1982 brought the *Charter* and the new amending formula into effect. It also fixed the precise date for the termination of the authority of the British Parliament to legislate for Canada.

Section 3 of the *Canada Act 1982* provides that the English and French versions of the *Constitution Act, 1982* are equally authoritative. This recognition of the equal legal status of both official language versions of the Act was a departure from previous British practice, which had been to enact only English versions of amendments to the *BNA Act*. Sections 55 and 56 of the *Constitution Act, 1982* require that these previous British enactments be translated into French and set out a procedure whereby authoritative French versions can be enacted into law. While official translations of the enactments were tabled in Parliament in 1990 in accordance with section 55, they have not been enacted by Parliament and the provincial legislatures in accordance with sections 55 and 56. Therefore, only the original English versions of the *BNA Act* itself and the amendments enacted by Westminster from 1867 to 1964 have official legal status. Does the fact that many provisions of the Constitution of Canada, including the entire *Constitution Act, 1867*, have not been officially enacted in French affect the legal validity of

61 Hogg argues that this result does not flow from s. 2 of the *Canada Act 1982*, but from the fact of Canada's political independence from Britain, which would lead Canadian courts to ignore the enactments of a foreign legislature. See P.W. Hogg, *Constitutional Law of Canada*, 5th ed., loose-leaf (Toronto: Carswell, 2007) at 3.5. Regardless of the theoretical basis for the conclusion, the practical result is that all future changes in Canadian law must be enacted by Canadian political authorities.

these enactments? In 1996, in response to a challenge by Guy Bertrand to the constitutional validity of a binding Quebec referendum on sovereignty, the attorney general of Quebec argued that the failure to enact official French versions of the Constitution of Canada in accordance with sections 55 and 56 meant that those provisions which had been enacted in English only were invalid.[62] The basis of the argument was that section 55 states that French versions of the various enactments "shall be prepared by the Minister of Justice of Canada as expeditiously as possible and, when any portion thereof sufficient to warrant action being taken has been so prepared, it shall be put forward for enactment." The cour supérieure de Quebec did not make a definitive ruling on the Quebec attorney general's argument; it merely determined that the issues raised by Bertrand should be decided at a trial on the merits. The better view, however, is that the failure to enact official French versions in accordance with section 56 should not lead to the invalidity of such provisions. Otherwise, the entire legislative authority of the Parliament of Canada and of the provincial legislatures would be rendered void, since the *Constitution Act, 1867* (from which these bodies derive their authority), would be invalid. The purpose of sections 55 and 56 was to establish a procedure whereby official French versions of all constitutional enactments could be brought into force, not to create a vacuum of legal and legislative authority. In our view, therefore, section 55 should be read as a "directory" rule only and, even assuming that it has been breached,[63] this should not result in the invalidity of any provisions of the written Constitution of Canada.[64]

---

62 *Bertrand* v. *Quebec* (*A.G.*) (1996), 138 D.L.R. (4th) 481 (Que. Sup. Ct.).

63 As noted above, translations of the various enactments have been tabled in Parliament. To bring these French versions into force, resolutions would be required from the Parliament of Canada and the provincial legislatures. Therefore, it is questionable whether the failure of Parliament to adopt a resolution can be regarded as a breach of s. 55 of the *Constitution Act, 1982*, since a parliamentary resolution would not be sufficient to bring the French versions into force.

64 This conclusion is also supported by s. 53(1) of the *Constitution Act, 1982*, which states that the enactments referred to in the Schedule, most of which have not been enacted in French, "shall continue as law in Canada under the names set out in Column III thereof."

FURTHER READINGS

HURLEY, J.R., *Amending Canada's Constitution: History, Processes, Problems, and Prospects* (Ottawa: Privy Council, 1996)

MILNE, D., *The Canadian Constitution: The Players and the Issues in the Process That Has Led from Patriation to Meech Lake* (Toronto: Lorimer, 1991)

PELLETIER, B., *La modification constitutionnelle au Canada* (Toronto: Carswell, 1996)

ROMANOW, R., J.D. Whyte, & H. Leeson, *Canada—Notwithstanding: The Making of the Constitution, 1976–82* (Toronto: Carswell/Methuen, 1984)

RUSSELL, P.H., *Constitutional Odyssey: Can Canadians Become a Sovereign People?* (Toronto: University of Toronto Press, 1992)

STRAYER, B.L., *Canada's Constitutional Revolution* (Edmonton: University of Alberta Press, 2012)

CHAPTER 6

CONSTITUTIONAL CHANGE SINCE 1982

A. AMENDMENTS TO THE CONSTITUTION OF CANADA

Part V of the *Constitution Act, 1982*,[1] sets out a procedure for amending the Constitution of Canada. As noted in Chapter 1, the term "Constitution of Canada" is defined in section 52 of the *Constitution Act, 1982*. Section 52 also states that any amendments to the Constitution of Canada "shall be made only in accordance with the authority contained in the Constitution of Canada." Section 52 does not expressly state that Part V represents an exhaustive source of authority for amending the Constitution of Canada, but it is not clear that there are any other powers of amendment.[2] In any event, Part V deals comprehensively with all aspects of the amendment of the Constitution of Canada.

---

1 The *Constitution Act, 1982*, being Schedule B to the *Canada Act 1982* (U.K.), 1982, c. 11.

2 Most of the amending powers used before 1982 were repealed or abolished with the enactment of the *Canada Act 1982* and the *Constitution Act, 1982*. The amending power of Westminster, as well as the amending powers in ss. 91(1) and 92(1) of the *Constitution Act, 1867* were repealed in 1982. The only amending power prior to 1982 that continues to exist appears to be the power to create new provinces or to alter provincial boundaries established in the *Constitution Act, 1871* (U.K.), 34 & 35 Vict., c. 28. As discussed later in this chapter, there is some doubt as to whether this amending authority has survived the enactment of Part V.

The definition of the Constitution of Canada set out in section 52(2) includes the *Constitution Act, 1867*, the *Canada Act 1982*, the *Constitution Act, 1982*, any amendments to those Acts and a detailed list of Acts and orders referred to in a schedule. Table 6.1 provides a comprehensive list of such documents.

Table 6.1 Canada's Written Constitution

Category	Document
U.K. statutes	*Constitution [BNA] Act, 1867* Amendments to *Constitution Act, 1867* (1871, 1886, 1907, 1915, 1930, 1940, 1946, 1949, 1960, 1964) *Parliament of Canada Act, 1875* *Canada (Ontario Boundary) Act, 1889* *Statute of Westminster, 1931* *Canada Act, 1982* *Constitution Act, 1982*
U.K. orders in council	1870 Order admitting Rupert's Land to Canada 1871 Order admitting British Columbia to Canada 1873 Order admitting PEI to Canada 1880 Order admitting Arctic Archipelago to Canada
Canadian statutes	*Manitoba Act, 1870* *Alberta Act, 1905* *Saskatchewan Act, 1905* Amendments to *Constitution Act, 1867* (1965, 1974, 1975 (no. 1), 1975 (no. 2))
Constitutional amendments since 1982	*Constitution Amendment Proclamation, 1983* (re: Indigenous rights *Constitution Act, 1985* (Representation), S.C. 1986, c. 8, Part I (re: representation in House of Commons) *Constitution Amendment Proclamation, 1987 (Newfoundland Act)* (re: denominational school rights) *Constitution Amendment Proclamation, 1993* (NB) (re: language rights) *Constitution Amendment Proclamation, 1993* (PE) (re: fixed link) *Constitution Amendment Proclamation, 1997* (NF) (re: denominational school rights) *Constitution Amendment Proclamation, 1997* (QC) (re: denominational school rights) *Constitution Amendment Proclamation, 1998* (NF) (re: denominational school rights) *Constitution Act, 1999 (Nunavut)*, S.C. 1998, c. 15, Part II *Constitution Amendment, 2001* (Newfoundland and Labrador) *Fair Representation Act, 2011*

The enactments falling within this definition represent Canada's "written constitution," in the sense that they are supreme over all other Canadian law and can be amended only by the procedures established by the Constitution of Canada.

There are, however, many statutes and other constitutional rules that are not included in the definition of the Constitution of Canada in section 52(2). These "unentrenched" documents include all the pre-Confederation constitutional documents such as the *Royal Proclamation of 1763*, the *Constitution Act, 1791*, and the *Union Act, 1840* that were reviewed in Chapter 2. Constitutional conventions, ordinary statutes of an organic character, and treaties with Indigenous peoples are likewise not included in the definition of the Constitution of Canada set out in section 52 (see Table 6.2).

Table 6.2 Other Elements of the Constitution of Canada

Category	Elements or Illustrations
Constitutional enactments before 1867	The *Royal Proclamation of 1763* Provincial constitutions of Nova Scotia, Prince Edward Island, New Brunswick, Newfoundland, British Columbia
Constitutional conventions	Principles of responsible government Conventions regulating federal-provincial relations
Judicial decisions	Interpretations of the *Constitution Acts* Common law doctrines defining powers of the Crown, Parliament, or state officials
Organic statutes	*Canada Elections Act* *Financial Administration Act* *Citizenship Act*
Prerogative orders	*Letters Patent* of 1947 constituting the office of the governor general
Indigenous agreements	Treaties 1 to 11 *James Bay and Northern Quebec Agreement Inuvialuit Final Agreements* *Yukon First Nations Final Agreements* *Nisga'a Final Agreement*
Other	Constitutional principles (i.e., federalism, democracy, rule of law, minority rights, independence of judiciary) recognized by courts as constitutionally binding

Since these statutes and rules are not part of the Constitution of Canada, they are not subject to the amending procedures in Part V of the *Constitution Act, 1982*. For example, the conventions of responsible government that define the circumstances in which the powers and prerogatives of the queen and the governor general can be exercised are not part of the Constitution of Canada. Therefore, section 41(a) of Part V—which states that amendments to the Constitution of Canada in relation to the office of the queen or the governor general require the unanimous consent of the provinces and Parliament—does not apply to changes to constitutional conventions.[3]

The definition of the Constitution of Canada in section 52(2) uses the word "includes," which, in contrast to the word "means," is normally regarded as non-exhaustive. Does this mean that the Constitution of Canada could include other matters not identified in the section 52(2) definition that would be subject to the amending procedures in Part V? In *New Brunswick Broadcasting Co. v. Nova Scotia (Speaker of the House of Assembly)*,[4] the Supreme Court of Canada answered this question in the affirmative. The Court held that the unwritten doctrine of parliamentary privilege, including the right to exclude "strangers" from the legislative chamber, was part of the Constitution of Canada. Subsequent decisions have confirmed that unwritten constitutional principles can be incorporated into the section 52 definition of the Constitution of Canada and utilized to invalidate statutes enacted by Parliament or the provincial legislatures.[5]

Professor Hogg has criticized the decision in *New Brunswick Broadcasting*, arguing that it opens the door to further judicial additions to the Constitution of Canada and destroys the certainty apparently afforded by the specific list of enactments set out in section 52. He argues that *New Brunswick Broadcasting* should be read as permitting additions to the definition of the Constitution of Canada only in cases of unwritten doctrines, such as parliamentary privilege, and that the scheduled list of instruments in section 52 should still be treated as exhaustive.[6] In our view, however, the Court was correct in *New Brunswick Broadcasting* to treat the definition of the Constitution of Canada as being non-exhaustive.

---

3 Professor Hogg shares this view: see P.W. Hogg, *Constitutional Law of Canada*, 5th ed., loose-leaf (Toronto: Carswell, 2007) at 4.2(c). For a contrary viewpoint, arguing that all constitutional conventions relating to the Crown have effectively been constitutionalized, see R.I. Cheffins & P.A. Johnson, *The Revised Canadian Constitution: Politics as Law* (Toronto: McGraw-Hill Ryerson, 1986).

4 [1993] 1 S.C.R. 319.

5 See *Reference Re Remuneration of Judges of the Provincial Court of PEI*, [1997] 3 S.C.R. 3 [*Judges' Remuneration Reference*] (holding that the principle of judicial independence has constitutional status); *Reference Re Secession of Quebec*, [1998] 2 S.C.R. 217 [*Secession Reference*] (holding that unwritten principles of federalism, democracy, constitutionalism, and the rule of law, and the protection of minority rights, have constitutional status).

6 See Hogg, above note 3 at 1.4.

First, as noted above, the Court's conclusion on this point is consistent with the established judicial approach to the interpretation of the term "includes."

Second, the approach in *New Brunswick Broadcasting* permits flexibility. It would seem unwise to establish a categorical rule that prevents expanding the items included within the Constitution of Canada. Circumstances may develop in the future that militate in favour of including a statute or rule within the definition of the Constitution of Canada.

Third, the failure to expand the definition may produce anomalous results or render other constitutional provisions ineffective. For example, section 41(d) of Part V provides that unanimous provincial consent is required for amendments in relation to the "composition of the Supreme Court of Canada." The effect of this provision was considered in the *Supreme Court Act Reference*, discussed in more detail below.[7] The *Supreme Court Act*[8] currently provides for a nine-member Court, three members of which must be appointed from the bar of Quebec. However, the *Supreme Court Act* is not listed in the schedule of enactments included with the definition of the Constitution of Canada. Therefore, if the section 52 definition were not treated as exhaustive—at least with respect to enactments—changes to the composition of the Supreme Court would not be amendments to the Constitution of Canada and would fall completely outside Part V. The difficulty with this interpretation is that it renders section 41(d) wholly ineffective. For example, Quebec's guaranteed representation on the Supreme Court could be eliminated without its consent, through an ordinary federal statute. Moreover, the only way that Quebec could obtain constitutional protection against this kind of unilateral federal change in its Supreme Court representation would be to obtain the agreement of all other provinces. Any amendment entrenching the current composition of the Supreme Court in the constitution would clearly be an amendment "in relation to the composition of the Supreme Court of Canada" and therefore be subject to section 41(d). Thus, even if the Senate, the House of Commons, and nine provinces (including Quebec) agreed that Quebec's right to three judges on the Supreme Court should be constitutionally entrenched, the amendment could be blocked by a single province. In the *Supreme Court Act Reference*, therefore, the Court held

7 *Reference re Supreme Court Act, ss. 5 and 6*, [2014] 1 S.C.R. 433 [*Supreme Court Act Reference*].

8 R.S.C. 1985, c. S-26.

that the provisions that codify its composition are part of the Constitution of Canada and subject to the unanimity amending formula.[9]

If the section 52 definition were exhaustive, the result would be doubly anomalous when considered in the context of Part V as a whole. The general amending formula in section 38 protects the "legislative powers, the proprietary rights or any other rights or privileges of the legislature or government of a province" from change, either by requiring provincial consent or by granting a right to "opt out" of an amendment. The underlying purpose of the amending procedure, in other words, is to protect the provinces from having their rights or privileges negatively affected without their consent. This includes provincial interests in the design and operation of key national institutions such as the Senate and the House of Commons. Yet, by treating section 41(d) as ineffective, the provinces would be granted absolutely no protection when it comes to the Supreme Court, a key institution of the federation. In our view, this interpretation is inconsistent with the underlying purpose of Part V.

Although the Constitution of Canada is non-exhaustive, the courts should be very cautious about expanding the scope of section 52(2). As discussed below, significant consequences follow from a decision to include a rule or enactment within the Constitution of Canada.

B. LEGISLATIVE VERSUS EXECUTIVE AMENDMENT

Before 1982, the only legislative bodies involved in the process of securing amendments to the *BNA Act* were the Parliaments of Canada and Westminster. While there was a constitutional convention requiring provincial consent, this consent was provided by provincial governments rather than legislatures. For example, the only provincial legislature that approved the constitutional agreement of 5 November 1981, was Alberta, on 10 November. Later in the month, Prime Minister Trudeau and the premiers agreed to make certain changes in the proposed constitutional reform package designed to win the support of the province of Quebec, as well as organizations representing women and Indigneous peoples. However, these changes were negotiated and agreed to by the respective governments and, aside from the National

9 The Court cited the above passage from the previous edition of this text with approval in the *Supreme Court Act Reference*, above note 7 at paras 98 and 100.

Assembly in Quebec,[10] no provincial legislature voted on the proposed modifications.

Critics of this process argued that it was insufficiently democratic, since it did not provide a guarantee that constitutional amendments would be debated by provincial legislatures. On the other hand, the process prior to the 1982 amendments did provide some opportunity for public debate, since any request for a constitutional amendment required a resolution passed by the Senate and the House of Commons. This process was also extremely flexible and enabled governments to make changes to a proposed amendment while the amendment was proceeding through the legislative approval process. This flexibility was demonstrated by the manner in which governments were able to effect modifications to the constitutional resolution following the original 5 November 1981 constitutional agreement. Since there was only a single legislative resolution embodying the proposed amendment (the joint Senate–House of Commons resolution), it was a straightforward matter to amend the resolution to reflect any modifications that were acceptable to the various governments involved.

The enactment of Part V effected a fundamental shift from executives to legislatures in the constitutional amendment process. Henceforth, provincial approval of constitutional change required legislative resolutions as opposed to agreement by the executive. The significance of this change was not debated extensively at the time, although it was widely accepted as a greater opportunity for public debate and input into the process of constitutional change. Ironically, however, one could argue that the need to have constitutional amendments enacted by provincial legislatures has indirectly reduced the flexibility which governments may require in order to accommodate public concerns in the amendment process. Part V requires each participating legislature to adopt an identically worded constitutional amendment before the amendment can become law. But Part V does not contemplate a mechanism for the debate and accommodation of the concerns identified in the different legislatures. Instead, each legislature considers any proposed constitutional resolution independently of the others. Thus, if one legislature makes changes to a particular amendment after it has been approved by other legislatures, each of the other legislatures must adopt the change that is being proposed, or the amendment cannot proceed. This process, involving as many as eleven different legislatures required to enact an identical resolution, can be contrasted with the process leading to the

10 The Quebec National Assembly voted against the modified package on 1 December 1981, one day before it was approved in the House of Commons.

1982 amendments, where a single resolution could be amended by a government with a majority in the House of Commons.

At the time Part V was enacted in 1982, it was probably assumed that the actions of the different provincial legislatures would be co-ordinated by the process of executive federalism. That is, the provincial and federal governments would arrive at a position that reflected all of the various interests at stake, and a compromise amendment would be enacted in identical form by the different legislatures. This is how constitutional change had always been effected in the past, and it was no doubt assumed that the process would continue, notwithstanding the need to obtain supporting resolutions from the provincial legislatures. In this way, executive federalism would provide the necessary co-ordination and links among the different provincial legislatures to ensure that the amendment process remained effective and workable.

In negotiating the *Meech Lake Accord* in 1986–87, for example, governments resolved their differences and agreed to a compromise package on 30 April 1987.[11] Because all governments assumed that the compromise package would be adopted in precisely the form agreed to by Parliament and all the provincial legislatures, the prime minister and the premiers agreed to the wording of a precise legal text reflecting the terms of the proposed amendment after an all-night negotiating session in early June 1987. The first ministers insisted that the terms of the amendment had to be enacted without any changes since, they argued, the agreement reflected a complicated series of trade-offs and compromises that together formed a "seamless web." The process contemplated was similar to that involved in the negotiation of complex agreements, such as international trade agreements, where each party to the agreement agrees to ratify it as a single package without amendments. If a compromise deal were open to subsequent amendments by individual parties acting independently of the others, any agreement would almost certainly unravel.[12]

As had been the case after the November 1981 constitutional agreement, the *Meech Lake Accord* proved extremely controversial in a num-

---

11 For a discussion of the nature of the compromises that were made by the different governments in the negotiations leading up to the *Meech Lake Accord*, see P.J. Monahan, *Meech Lake: The Inside Story* (Toronto: University of Toronto Press, 1991) c. 4.

12 Before the commencement of negotiations with the U.S. over a free-trade agreement in the late 1980s, for example, Canada insisted that the U.S. Congress agree to a "fast track" procedure for ratification of any agreement. Under this procedure, Congress voted on the Treaty as a single package, without the possibility of proposing amendments.

ber of respects.[13] However, in contrast to 1981, when these concerns could be accommodated through informal negotiations among first ministers, the Meech Lake package required identical legislative resolutions to become law. If each legislature had been free to enact changes to the package, the trade-offs and compromises that had created the package in the first place would have been undermined. This was particularly the case since the amendments demanded in one legislature might well be the opposite of those sought elsewhere.[14] To avoid the piecemeal unravelling of the agreement, all governments insisted that the Meech Lake package had to be enacted "as is" and that any concerns or objections had to be dealt with in subsequent rounds of constitutional negotiations. The insistence by governments that the *Meech Lake Accord* was a "seamless web" itself proved controversial and stimulated opposition. Some opponents suggested that they agreed in principle with the constitutional changes being proposed, but argued that the accord should be defeated because the negotiating process leading up to the accord was undemocratic. Moreover, the fact that the accord had to be debated in each provincial legislature ensured that opponents of the agreement would have ample opportunity to block or delay its passage. The hearings and debates that occurred in the different provinces also created an expectation that changes or modifications would and should be possible. When governments refused to honour those expectations and would not permit even minor changes, the objections to the executive-dominated process were heightened even further.

Thus, the legislative-based process of constitutional amendment established in 1982 was plagued by an inherent contradiction. The requirement to debate and adopt constitutional changes in each legislature stimulated demands and expectations that constitutional agreements negotiated between governments could be changed to accommodate public objections. At the same time, the need for eleven

13 Women's and Indigenous organizations were concerned about various aspects of the accord. There were a variety of other objections as well (see the discussion below at Section L).

14 For example, suppose the Quebec National Assembly had enacted changes to the distinct-society clause, strengthening the clause in a manner that was unacceptable to other provinces or the federal government. This would undoubtedly have been the result if changes had been permitted after the accord had been negotiated, since the hearings that were held on the accord in Quebec in May 1987 indicated that many witnesses felt that the distinct-society clause did not grant Quebec new constitutional powers. A similar unravelling of the accord would have resulted had other provinces been free to unilaterally enact changes to the accord, since those changes would likely have made the amended package unacceptable in Quebec.

identical constitutional resolutions and the absence of any co-ordinating mechanism among the different legislative processes caused governments to insist that no changes could be contemplated until after the original accord was ratified in its existing form. While Part V moved from an amendment process under the exclusive control of governments to one that also involved legislatures, it made the entire process of constitutional reform much more inflexible than it had been before 1982. This inflexibility, in turn, stimulated public opposition to governments negotiating constitutional changes behind closed doors. The result is an amending formula that is extremely difficult to operate, to the point where some commentators argue that it is virtually impossible to enact amendments that require the support of either seven or ten provincial legislatures.[15] Significantly, of the constitutional amendments since 1982, over two-thirds of them have been enacted under the section 43 formula, which requires the support of only the federal houses and the province(s) directly affected by the amendment.[16] Given the difficulty of operating the general amending procedure, it can be expected that governments in the future will seek to make maximum use of the more flexible procedure set out in section 43.[17]

C. THE ROLE OF REFERENDUMS

The original constitutional reform package tabled by Prime Minister Trudeau in the fall of 1980 had provided for the possibility of enacting constitutional amendments through a national referendum. However, most of the provinces were opposed to the referendum option and demanded that Parliament and the provincial legislatures have exclusive control over the constitutional amendment process. In the November 1981 agreement, Trudeau acceded to this demand. The amending procedures

---

15 See P.J. Monahan, "The Sounds of Silence" in K. McRoberts & P.J. Monahan, eds., *The Charlottetown Accord, the Referendum, and the Future of Canada* (Toronto: University of Toronto Press, 1993) at 222–48. See also P.H. Russell, "The End of Mega Constitutional Politics in Canada?" *ibid.* at 211–21.

16 The list of constitutional amendments since 1982 is set out in Table 6.1. Two other amendments were enacted as ordinary statutes of the Parliament of Canada pursuant to s. 44 of the *Constitution Act, 1982*, and did not require any provincial consent. In the result, only the 1983 amendment dealing with Indigenous rights has been enacted pursuant to the s. 38 general amending procedure.

17 However, as discussed below, s. 43 of the *Constitution Act, 1982* applies only in a very limited range of circumstances. For example, s. 43 cannot be used to amend ss. 91 or 92 of the *Constitution Act, 1867*.

set out in the 1982 Act do not provide for a referendum procedure to effect constitutional change.

While Part V does not require a referendum on constitutional change, it does not prohibit such popular consultation either. In 1992, Parliament enacted the *Referendum Act,* which permits, but does not require, the government of Canada to order a referendum on questions relating to the Constitution of Canada.[18] Some provinces have gone even further and enacted legislation requiring a "binding"[19] referendum before the adoption of a constitutional resolution by the legislature.[20] Pursuant to the federal Act, a national referendum was held on the *Charlottetown Accord* in October 1992.[21] Although the results of a referendum held under federal law are not legally binding, as a practical matter, it is very unlikely that any government would be able to ignore the results of a referendum it had ordered. For example, after the *Charlottetown Accord* was defeated in a 1992 referendum, Canadian governments recognized that it could not proceed.[22]

---

18 See the *Referendum Act*, S.C. 1992, c. 30.

19 While the legislation set out in the note following describes referendum results as "binding," an ordinary statute could not prevent the legislature from adopting a constitutional resolution. However, statutes can bind governments and thus the requirement to hold a referendum is presumably binding on the governments of these provinces.

20 Both Alberta and B.C. require a binding referendum before the adoption of a constitutional resolution by the Legislative Assembly. For Alberta, see the *Constitutional Referendum Act*, R.S.A. 2000, c. C-25, ss. 2(1) and 4(1); for B.C., see the *Constitutional Amendment Approval Act*, R.S.B.C. 1996, c. 67, s. 1, and the *Referendum Act*, R.S.B.C. 1996, c. 400, ss. 1, 4, & 5. In Saskatchewan, the government is not required to hold a referendum on a constitutional amendment, but there is a process whereby electors can force a referendum; the results are said to be binding if a 60 percent majority is achieved. See the *Referendum and Plebiscite Act*, S.S. 1990–91, c. R-8.01 as amended by the *Elections Act*, S.S. 1996, c. E-6.01. Other provinces permit the holding of referendums, but do not describe the results as being binding.

21 The federal legislation provided the authority for the referendum in nine provinces and the territories. In the province of Quebec, the referendum was held under the authority of the provincial referendum legislation.

22 This has been reinforced by the results of a series of subsequent provincial referenda. When a proposed constitutional amendment dealing with denominational school rights in Newfoundland was defeated in a referendum in 1995, the government held a second referendum on a revised proposal in 1997. Given the strong support in that referendum for the revised proposal, the government proceeded with the amendment. However, a 2004 referendum in Nova Scotia on Sunday shopping and referenda in British Columbia, Prince Edward Island, and Ontario on electoral reform failed to receive the required level of support, and these proposals were not carried out. In British Columbia, a proposed new electoral system was supported by slightly more than 57 percent of those voting

The referendum requirements at the federal and provincial levels have no official constitutional status and are not a substitute for the constitutional amendment process in Part V. Even if a constitutional amendment has been approved in a referendum, it must be adopted by the appropriate number of legislative bodies. Moreover, since the referendum requirements are contained in ordinary statutes and are not part of the Constitution of Canada, they can theoretically be repealed at any time. Yet, given the widespread opposition among Canadians to closed-door constitutional negotiations, it seems more likely that existing referendum requirements will be strengthened rather than diminished in the future. Moreover, given the precedent established with the *Charlottetown Accord*, it would seem likely that any future constitutional amendment involving significant changes to the Canadian constitution will have to be submitted for approval through a referendum that will be, for all practical intents and purposes, binding.

D. THE GENERAL AMENDING FORMULA: SECTION 38

1) The Scope and Application of Section 38

The marginal note to section 38 of the *Constitution Act, 1982* describes it as the "[g]eneral procedure for amending [the] Constitution of Canada"—a description which suggests that it operates as a kind of residual provision that applies whenever a proposed amendment does not fall into one of the more specific procedures in Part V. The wording of section 38, which states that amendments "may" be made under its authority, reinforces this interpretation. The wording of sections 41, 42, and 43, in contrast, provide that amendments falling into certain classes may be made "only" in accordance with their provisions, while sections 44 and 45 reference the "exclusive" authority of Parliament and the provincial legislatures to enact certain amendments. The inclusion of the words "only" and "exclusively" in the latter sections, coupled with their absence in section 38, suggests that section 38 operates in cases where sections 41 to 45 do not apply. By construing section 38 in this fashion, the result is that no part of the Constitution of Canada is

---

in the 2005 referendum, but failed to meet the required threshold of 60 percent. Given the results, the government elected to stage a second referendum in 2009, but the proposal was rejected by a majority of voters. It is therefore apparent that lack of sufficient support in a referendum makes it politically impossible for governments to proceed with a proposed constitutional change.

unamendable, since any amendment not specifically provided for elsewhere must be possible under the general procedure.[23]

Section 38 requires identical resolutions of the Senate and the House of Commons and the Legislative Assemblies of at least two-thirds of the provinces that have, in the aggregate, at least 50 percent of the total provincial population in the ten provinces.[24] Once the required resolutions are passed, the governor general issues a proclamation bringing the amendment into force. The federal government is to advise the governor general to issue the proclamation immediately on the adoption of the required number of legislative resolutions.[25] Provinces may revoke resolutions supporting an amendment at any time before the issuance of the proclamation. Once the governor general has issued a proclamation, however, the right to revoke provincial consent in respect of that amendment is terminated. A province unhappy with an amendment that has already been proclaimed would have to initiate an entirely new process repealing the original amendment.

The general amending procedure in section 38 is modelled on the "Vancouver formula" proposed by the eight provinces that were opposed to the federal government's patriation proposals before the agreement reached in November 1981, as discussed in Section C(4) in Chapter 5. This so-called "7–50" formula[26] does not permit any single province to veto an amendment that is supported by the required number of provinces, thereby giving effect to the principle of the equality of the provinces. However, because the formula takes into account relative provincial populations, the three provinces with the largest populations (Ontario, Quebec, and British Columbia) have proportionately more weight. For example, the combinations of Ontario and Quebec, as

---

23 In *Secession Reference*, above note 5, the Supreme Court confirmed that all parts of the existing Constitution are subject to amendment, stating at para. 85 that "[i]t lies within the power of the people of Canada, acting through their various governments duly elected and recognized under the Constitution, to effect whatever constitutional arrangements are desired."

24 For purposes of calculating whether this percentage has been achieved, the population of any territories not within a provincial boundary is excluded.

25 Section 48 of the *Constitution Act, 1982*. This requirement eliminates the possibility of the federal government delaying the formal enactment of an amendment that has the required legislative support. Section 39 imposes a one-year waiting period for amendments under s. 38(1).

26 The "7–50" formula is derived from the fact that, at present, the two-thirds requirement in s. 38 of the *Constitution Act, 1982* translates into at least seven provinces. The "50" refers to the population requirement.

well as Ontario and British Columbia,[27] could veto an amendment that was supported by the other eight provinces.[28]

2) Opting Out and Compensation

While the general amending procedure does not provide a veto for any individual province, it does protect provincial interests by providing a right for a dissenting province to "opt out" of an amendment that derogates from its powers. In order for a province to exercise this right of dissent, the provincial legislature must pass a resolution supported by an absolute majority of its members before the issuance of a proclamation by the governor general bringing the amendment into force.[29] The right of dissent applies only in instances where an amendment derogates from provincial powers; an amendment which adds to provincial powers or which has no negative impact on the provinces cannot be the subject of a dissenting resolution.[30] Provinces that have opted out may revoke the dissenting resolution at any time before or after the coming into force of the amendment, at which point the amendment automatically applies to the province in question.[31]

During the 1981 constitutional negotiations, the provinces opposed to the federal proposals had demanded that they receive financial compensation from the federal government in cases where they exercised their right to opt out.[32] They justified the need for compensation on the basis that residents of an opted-out province would be taxed twice: once to finance the federal government program delivered in other provinces—and which was not available in the opted-out

---

27 Ontario and Quebec combined have over 60 percent of the total population of the ten provinces, while Ontario and B.C. combined have over 50 percent.

28 This does not take account of the effect of *An Act respecting constitutional amendments*, S.C. 1996, c. 1 (subsequently referred to as the *Regional Veto Act*), discussed in Section K below. The Act has the effect of granting each of Ontario, Quebec, B.C., and Alberta a veto over certain amendments initiated under s. 38 of the *Constitution Act, 1982*.

29 See s. 38(3) of the *Constitution Act, 1982*. The requirement of an absolute majority ensures that any amending resolution will enjoy government support.

30 This is the effect of the combined operation of ss. 38(2) & (3) of the *Constitution Act, 1982*. In respect of these "non-derogating" amendments, the federal *Regional Veto Act*, above note 28, grants Ontario, Quebec, B.C., and Alberta an effective veto.

31 Section 38(4) of the *Constitution Act, 1982*. The dissenting resolution must be adopted before the proclamation of the amendment in order to be effective.

32 The formula originally proposed in Vancouver by the "gang of eight" provinces had provided that any province opting out of a constitutional amendment transferring jurisdiction to Parliament would receive financial compensation.

province—and a second time to finance the provincial program dealing with the same matter in their own province. Although Trudeau reluctantly accepted the concept of opting out in the November 1981 constitutional agreement, he refused to agree to the provincial demand for a right to compensation. Trudeau's concern was that an open-ended right to compensation would encourage provinces that were otherwise in favour of an amendment to dissent simply in order to receive compensation.[33]

The deletion of the clause providing for financial compensation for opting out provinces in the November 1981 constitutional agreement was one of the principal objections raised by Quebec premier René Lévesque. Later in November, in an attempt to secure Quebec's support, Trudeau agreed to recognize a right to compensation in cases where an amendment transferred legislative powers over "education or other cultural matters" from the provinces to Parliament. The precise scope of the term "cultural matters" is not defined in section 40, where the right to compensation is set out.

The *Meech Lake Accord* would have amended section 40 to provide for a right to compensation for any amendment transferring provincial legislative powers to Parliament, whether or not the amendment involved education or other cultural matters. It is not clear whether this change to section 40 would have had any practical significance. First, because of the potentially open-ended meaning of the term "cultural matters" in section 40, the existing right to compensation would arguably apply in virtually any instance where an amendment appeared particularly significant or controversial. The province of Quebec, for example, would argue that all of its existing legislative powers are necessary to protect and promote the distinctive identity of the province. It could argue that *any* amendment proposing to transfer legislative powers from the provinces to Ottawa would involve "cultural matters," thereby giving rise to a right to compensation under section 40. Second, section 40 is extremely unlikely to be triggered. Section 40 applies only in instances where the provinces agree to transfer provincial legislative powers to Parliament. Although there have been a limited number of

33 As noted below, the debate is largely academic, for the simple reason that the required number of provinces is unlikely to agree to transfer legislative powers to the federal government and the question of compensation is therefore unlikely to arise. Any future amendments to the division of powers are likely to involve transfers from the federal level to the provincial level, in which case there would not be a right to opt out and thus no right to compensation.

such amendments in the past, there have been none since 1964.[34] The focus in past constitutional amendment proposals has been on the extent to which the federal Parliament should transfer its powers to the provinces. For example, both the *Meech Lake* and *Charlottetown Accords* proposed transfers of federal powers to the provinces, but none in the opposite direction. Debates over the extent of the provincial right to compensation under section 40 may thus turn out to be largely academic since the provinces are unlikely to agree to transfer legislative powers to Parliament.

3) Timing and Initiation of Amendments

Under section 39, amendments under section 38 cannot be proclaimed until at least one year has passed from the date of the adoption of the first resolution commencing the amendment process. The purpose of the one-year waiting period is to provide each province with sufficient time to study a proposed amendment before it is required to express its opinion. The one-year waiting period is waived if all the provinces have passed resolutions either assenting to or dissenting from a proposed amendment. The one-year waiting period does not apply to amendments enacted under provisions in Part V other than section 38(1).

Section 39 establishes a three-year time limit for the amendments enacted under section 38(1). This limit operated in the case of the *Meech Lake Accord*, when the required number of provinces failed to adopt resolutions in support of the accord within the three-year time limit.[35] After the three-year period, it is still possible to proceed with a similar or even identical amendment, but all resolutions previously adopted expire and the process must be recommenced with fresh resolutions from Parliament and the provinces.

Resolutions proposing constitutional amendments may be introduced in either the Senate or the House of Commons or any of the provincial legislatures (section 46(1)).[36] This section was a significant

---

34 In 1964, s. 94A of the *Constitution Act, 1867* was broadened (see *Constitution Act 1964* (U.K.), 1964, c. 73) to give Parliament increased powers in relation to old-age pensions and supplementary benefits.

35 By 22 June 1990, three years after the first amending resolution was adopted by Quebec, supporting resolutions had been adopted in eight provinces representing over 90 percent of the total provincial population. However, since certain items in the accord were subject to s. 41 and required unanimous consent, the resolution could not be proclaimed, notwithstanding the fact that the "7–50" requirement in s. 38(1) of the *Constitution Act, 1982* had been satisfied.

36 This option exists with respect to amendments under ss. 38, 41, 42, & 43 of the *Constitution Act, 1982*.

change. Prior to 1981, only the federal Parliament could initiate the procedure for a constitutional amendment.

E. APPLICATION OF GENERAL PROCEDURE IN SPECIAL CASES

Section 42 provides that for amendments falling into six classes,[37] the amendment shall be made "only in accordance with subsection 38(1)." Further, section 42 states that the opting out provisions in section 38 do not apply to amendments enacted under section 42. By implication, this also excludes the possibility of any claim for compensation under section 40, since the dissent right under section 38(3) is a prerequisite to a claim for compensation.

While some of the categories enumerated in section 42 appear relatively straightforward, commentators have raised potential ambiguities in the interpretation of certain provisions. For example, section 42(1)(d) refers to amendments in relation to the "Supreme Court of Canada." Section 42(d) also states that it is subject to section 41(d), which requires unanimous consent for amendments in relation to the "composition of the Supreme Court of Canada." As discussed above, the difficulty with section 42(1)(d), as well as section 41(c), is that the *Supreme Court Act* is not referred to in the schedule of enactments included within the definition of the Constitution of Canada in section 52.

In the *Supreme Court Act Reference*, the Court was called upon to resolve this issue through an unprecedented course of events. In 2013, Prime Minister Stephen Harper announced the appointment of Justice Marc Nadon to the Supreme Court. Justice Nadon would have filled a vacancy on the Court following the retirement of Justice Morris Fish, who had been appointed to the Supreme Court from the Quebec Court of Appeal. Section 5 of the *Supreme Court Act* states "[a]ny person may be appointed a judge who is or has been a judge of a superior court of a province or a barrister or advocate of at least ten years standing at the bar of a province." Section 6 states "[a]t least three of the judges shall be appointed from among the judges of the Court of Appeal or of the Superior Court of the Province of Quebec or from among the advocates of

37 The matters identified in s. 42 are the principle of proportionate representation of the provinces in the House of Commons; the powers of the Senate and the method of selecting senators; the number of members by which a province is entitled to be represented in the Senate and the residence qualifications of senators; subject to s. 41(d), the Supreme Court; the extension of existing provinces into the territories; and the establishment of new provinces.

that Province." Justice Nadon had been a member of the Quebec bar for almost twenty years. In 1993, he was appointed to the Federal Court, Trial Division. He was elevated to the Federal Court of Appeal in 2001.

A 6:1 majority of the Supreme Court concluded that a former member of the Quebec bar who sits on the Federal Court is ineligible for appointment under section 6. According to the majority, persons appointed to the three Quebec seats under section 6 must be current members of the Quebec bar, or judges of the Quebec Court of Appeal or Superior Court of Quebec. Prior to the *Supreme Court Act Reference*, Parliament had introduced legislation amending the *Supreme Court Act* to clarify that a former member of a provincial bar may be appointed to the Court under section 5 and that a former member of the Quebec bar is eligible for appointment under section 6. This required the Court to consider whether the amendments were permissible in light of Part V of the *Constitution Act, 1982*. The majority concluded that they were not, and quashed the appointment of Justice Nadon.

In reaching this conclusion, the Court not only considered the fact that its composition was expressly mentioned in Part V, but went further. The Court declared that it had become constitutionally entrenched *prior to* patriation in 1982 because of its emergence as the final court of appeal and the role it played as constitutional arbiter in division of powers disputes. The *Constitution Act, 1982*, therefore, only "confirmed" its constitutional status. Accordingly, the omission of the *Supreme Court Act* from the schedule of the *Constitution Act, 1982* identifying constitutional documents did not detract from the Court's constitutional status. Instead, sections 4(1), 5, and 6, which define the composition of the Court as made up of nine judges including three from Quebec, were part of the "Constitution of Canada" within the meaning of section 41(d) and subject to the unanimity formula.

As for section 42(1)(d), which applies to amendments to the Supreme Court on matters other than the Court's composition, the Court agreed that this section does not constitutionalize every aspect of the *Supreme Court Act* and the *Rules of the Supreme Court*. The Court agreed with previous commentators, who have observed that the *Supreme Court Act* and the *Rules* contain provisions dealing with minutiae as the colour of memoranda. It cannot have been intended that such rules would be subject to amending procedures in Part V of the *Constitution Act, 1982*.[38] The Court held that only its "essential features" are captured by s. 42(1)(d). These features are subject to the general amending formula

38 See S.A. Scott, "Pussycat, Pussycat or Patriation and the New Constitutional Amendment Processes" (1982) 20 U.W.O. L. Rev. 247 at 272, and P. Monahan & B. Shaw, *Constitutional Law*, 4th ed. (Toronto: Irwin Law, 2013) at 204–5.

in s. 38(1). The Court identified two such features: its jurisdiction as a final court of appeal and its independence. The Court made clear this was not an exhaustive list.[39] While the Court's analysis focused on its judicial role as a final court of appeal, in our view this interpretation of Part V is correct largely due to the underlying provincial interests at stake.[40] In a federation, it is indisputable that the forum that serves as a final arbiter of legal disputes between national and sub-national governments engages the interests of both groups.

Another interpretive difficulty in relation to section 42 arises from the references to amendments creating new provinces or extending the boundaries of existing provinces into the territories (see sections 42(1)(e) and (f)). The *Constitution Act, 1982*, did not repeal the *Constitution Act, 1871*, which provided that Parliament could unilaterally establish new provinces in federal territories and that it could alter provincial boundaries with the consent of only those provinces affected. Professor Hogg has argued that the creation of new provinces or the extension of provinces into the territories could still be accomplished under the rules set out in the *Constitution Act, 1871*, rather than on the basis of the "7–50" formula.[41] The difficulty with this interpretation is that it would render section 42(1)(e) and (f) largely ineffective. Under Hogg's interpretation, the only effect of these provisions is to constitutionally entrench the federal unilateral powers to create new provinces, since any attempt to limit such powers would require the consent of at least seven provinces. Furthermore, Hogg's interpretation ignores the legislative history leading up to the enactment of these provisions. The federal power to extend provincial boundaries had been a long-standing grievance of the Maritime provinces, particularly Nova Scotia. In 1867, the four original provinces were of roughly equal size. However, Ontario and Quebec subsequently had their boundaries extended northward through bilateral agreements with the federal government, without any requirement of the consent of the other provinces. The Maritime provinces complained that these boundary extensions had a dramatic impact on their relative weight in the federation. Section 42(1)(e) was included in the Vancouver formula at the insistence of Nova Scotia to ensure that any

39 *Supreme Court Act Reference*, above note 7 at paras. 88–95.

40 James Ross Hurley, who served as constitutional adviser to the federal government during the relevant period, reports that the intention was to constitutionally protect the Supreme Court from unilateral federal alteration. See J.R. Hurley, *Amending Canada's Constitution: History, Processes, Problems and Prospects* (Ottawa: Supply and Services Canada, 1996) at 72, 76.

41 See Hogg, above note 3 at 4.3(g).

future boundary extensions would require the participation and consent of the provinces.[42]

The reference to "the creation of new provinces" was also included in section 42 at the insistence of the provinces. At an annual premiers conference in 1976, the provinces unanimously agreed that the establishment of new provinces should be governed by the general amending formula and not be subject to the prerogative of Parliament acting alone.[43] The provinces argued that the creation of new provinces had a direct impact on provincial interests in the Senate, the House of Commons, and under the amending formula. Section 42(1)(f) was therefore included in the Vancouver formula drafted by the eight provinces with the purpose of protecting provincial interests by requiring their consent before the creation of any additional provinces.[44]

In short, while the matter is not free of doubt,[45] the better view would appear to be that sections 42(1)(e) and (f) have indirectly amended the *Constitution Act, 1871* by subjecting the creation of new provinces, as well as the extension of provincial boundaries, to the requirements of the "7–50" formula.[46] It is now clear from the *Supreme Court Act Reference* that a statute can have constitutional status even if it is not included in the Schedule to the *Constitution Act, 1982*. The fact that amendments can be enacted under section 42 over the objections of up to three provinces, and with no possibility of opting out, was one of the principal objections of the province of Quebec to the 1982 amending formula. The *Meech Lake Accord* would have incorporated all the items in section 42 into

---

42 See J.P. Meekison, "The Amending Formula" (1983) 8 Queen's L.J. 99 at 117.

43 See *ibid.*, citing the 14 October 1976 letter from Peter Lougheed, as chair of the premiers conference, to Prime Minister Trudeau.

44 *Ibid.*

45 What remains puzzling is the inclusion of the "notwithstanding" clause in s. 42(1)(f) but not s. 42(1)(e) of the *Constitution Act, 1982*. This appears to signal an intention that s. 42(1)(f) overrides any other provision providing for the creation of new provinces, but that s. 42(1)(e) not have the same effect in relation to the extension of existing provinces. Thus, it may be possible to argue that only s. 42(1)(f) has impliedly repealed the provisions of the *Constitution Act, 1871*, and that s. 3 of the *Constitution Act, 1871* remains the operative power for the extension of the boundaries of an existing province.

46 This interpretation is also supported by the fact that, in 1992, the *Charlottetown Accord* proposed to "rescind" the current amending formula provisions dealing with the creation of new provinces and to return to the "pre-1982 provisions allowing the creation of new provinces through an Act of Parliament." The assumption, in other words, was that the current amending formula in Part V required the consent of seven provinces: see Consensus Report on the Constitution, Charlottetown, 28 August 1992, Final Text, App. I, Item 58 (Establishment of New Provinces), reprinted in McRoberts & Monahan, above note 15 at 307.

section 41, thereby giving all provinces a veto over these matters. This change would have given Quebec the protection it was seeking, without violating the principle of the "equality of the provinces." However, it was also one of the main objections raised by critics of the accord, who argued that granting each province a veto would make certain changes—particularly Senate reform or the creation of new provinces in the north—practically impossible.

With the defeat of the *Meech Lake Accord* and the *Charlottetown Accord*, changes in relation to matters in section 42 remain subject to the general amending formula. However, in 1996, the federal Parliament passed legislation providing for a scheme of regional vetoes before the federal government would support an amendment under section 42.[47] This legislation has responded to Quebec's concern about the possibility of an amendment being enacted over its objection, but it has also made the section 42 procedure significantly more difficult to operate.[48]

F. UNANIMITY PROCEDURES

Section 41 sets out five categories of amendments for which the unanimous consent of the two federal houses and the provincial legislatures is required. The first category is amendments in relation to "the office of the Queen, the Governor General and the Lieutenant Governor of a province."[49] A number of provisions of the *Constitution Act, 1867* deal with the monarchy and its representatives in Canada,[50] and changes to these provisions would fall within section 41(a). However, it is noteworthy that

---

47 See the discussion in Section K below of the *Regional Veto Act*, above note 28.

48 According to the *Regional Veto Act*, *ibid.*, Ontario, Quebec, British Columbia, and Alberta, along with at least three other provinces, must support an amendment in order for the proposal to proceed under s. 42 of the *Constitution Act, 1982*. This requirement effectively raises the population threshold that must be met under s. 42 to above 92 percent of the total population of the ten provinces.

49 The remaining categories included in s. 41 of the *Constitution Act, 1982* are: the right of a province to a number of members in the House of Commons not less than the number of senators by which a province is entitled to be represented at the time this Part comes into force; subject to s. 43, the use of the English and the French language; the composition of the Supreme Court; and an amendment to Part V.

50 These provisions include ss. 9–17 of the *Constitution Act, 1982* (defining the executive authority of Canada); s. 17 (defining Parliament as including the queen); ss. 54–57 (providing for certain powers of the governor general in relation to the legislative process); ss. 58–68 (providing for provincial executive power); and s. 90 (providing for the application of certain constitutional provisions in relation to the provinces).

the office of the governor general itself is not created by the *Constitution Act, 1867*. It is established through letters patent issued by the queen pursuant to the prerogative rather than through the Constitution Acts.[51] The letters patent also establish the duties and powers of the office of the governor general, authorizing the governor general "with the advice of Our Privy Council for Canada . . . to exercise all powers and authorities lawfully belonging to Us in respect of Canada."[52]

The letters patent are not listed in the schedule to section 52 of the *Constitution Act, 1982*. It might be argued, therefore, that the letters patent are not included within the definition of the Constitution of Canada and that the office could be abolished or its powers amended through ordinary legislation enacted by Parliament, without having to rely on the amending procedure in section 41(a). However, this would clearly defeat the purpose of section 41(a). In our view, the letters patent must be interpreted as falling within the section 52 definition of the Constitution of Canada and, thus, subject to the requirements of section 41(a), at least to the extent that it creates the office of the governor general and defines the powers of the office.

Some commentators have suggested that the entire system of Cabinet government, including the appointment of the first minister and the Cabinet by the governor general, has now been entrenched in the constitution by virtue of section 41(a).[53] However, there is no reference to the institution of the Cabinet or the office of the first minister in the Constitution of Canada. The powers of the first minister are almost entirely defined through constitutional conventions. These conventions will continue to evolve as political practices and the beliefs of the relevant political actors change to deal with new circumstances. There does not appear to be any principled basis for interpreting section 41(a) as constraining this process of informal and flexible evolution. In short, the better view would seem to be that section 41(a) does not constitutionally entrench the entire system of Cabinet government.

Section 58 of the *Constitution Act, 1867* provides that there be a lieutenant governor for each province appointed by the Governor General in Council. The conventions of responsible government mean that the prime minister of Canada effectively exercises the appointment power. In late 1996, the premier of Quebec, Lucien Bouchard, suggested that future Quebec lieutenant governors should be appointed on the rec-

---

51 See *Letters Patent Constituting the Office of Governor General of Canada* (Imperial Order in Council, proclaimed in force 1 October 1947), art. I, reprinted in R.S.C. 1985, App. II, No. 31.

52 *Ibid*., art. II.

53 See Cheffins & Johnson, above note 3 at 74.

ommendation of the Quebec National Assembly rather than the prime minister. Because such a change would involve an amendment to section 58,[54] it would be subject to the requirements of section 41(a) and require the consent of the Senate and the House of Commons as well as all the provinces.

Secession of a province would also appear to involve an amendment to the office of the lieutenant governor of a province and fall under section 41(a). The office of the lieutenant governor would necessarily be abolished in any province that seceded from Canada.[55] It is clearly not open to any province to unilaterally abolish the office of lieutenant governor. Therefore, inasmuch as the secession of a province would entail the abolition of the office of the lieutenant governor of the province, it would appear to amount to an amendment in relation to the office of the lieutenant governor and fall under section 41(a).[56]

Section 41(c) states that changes to the use of the English or the French language fall under the unanimity procedure "subject to section 43." Section 43 creates special requirements for amendments involving changes to provisions that apply to one or more but not all provinces. Therefore, constitutional provisions that set out generally applicable requirements (i.e., requirements applicable in all provinces) for the use of the English or the French language fall under section 41(c) and can only be changed under the unanimity procedure. However, where an existing constitutional provision sets out requirements for the use of the English or the French language in some but not all provinces,[57] such provision can be changed under section 43 and does not require unanimous provincial consent.

As discussed above, section 41(d) states that changes to the Constitution of Canada in relation to the "composition of the Supreme Court of Canada" can only be made in accordance with the unanimity procedure. For reasons explained earlier in relation to section 42(1)

---

54 Note also the fact that s. 13 of the *Constitution Act, 1867* states that references to the Governor General in Council (the body that appoints the lieutenant governors of the provinces) "shall be construed as referring to the Governor General acting by and with the Advice of the Queen's Privy Council for Canada."

55 The lieutenant governor is an appointee of the government of Canada. Any province achieving political independence from Canada could not permit Canadian officials to continue to exercise authority over Quebec territory.

56 Other commentators have taken a different view, arguing that the secession of a province would not be an amendment in relation to the office of the governor general and would therefore fall under the s. 38 general amending formula. These arguments are reviewed in more detail later in this chapter.

57 See, for example, s. 133 of the *Constitution Act, 1867* and ss. 16(2), 17(2), 18(2), 19(2), and 20(2) of the *Constitution Act, 1982*.

(d), this provision has been interpreted so as to require all provinces to approve changes to the composition of the Supreme Court.

G. THE SPECIAL ARRANGEMENTS PROCEDURE

There are a number of provisions in the Constitution of Canada that set out special arrangements applicable to some but not all provinces.[58] Section 43 provides that amendments in relation to any of these "special arrangement" provisions may be made only where authorized by resolutions of the Senate and the House of Commons and the Legislative Assemblies of each province to which the amendment applies.

One of the purposes of section 43 is to ensure that, where the constitution already contains a special arrangement applicable to certain provinces, such arrangement cannot be changed without the consent of the provinces affected. In this sense, section 43 establishes a necessary condition (although not necessarily a sufficient condition) for the passage of such an amendment, by requiring that such an amendment can be passed "only" if the provinces affected by it have agreed.

A number of difficult interpretive issues arise in relation to section 43.[59] The first is whether it establishes a separate and distinct amending process in its own right, or whether it merely adds additional requirements to the other amending formulas set out in Part V. The wording of sections 46(1) and 47(1) suggests that section 43 does establish a distinct amending process.[60] This interpretation is consistent with historical experience. Since 1982, there have been several amendments enacted pursuant to section 43 and, in each instance, the amendment was adopted by the federal houses and the affected provinces only. In no case was it seen as necessary for any other province to pass a supporting resolution.

The amendments that have thus far been passed pursuant to section 43, however, have not involved matters falling within either section 41 or 42. The question that arises is what amending formula would apply

---

58 See, for example, the provisions referred to in the previous note, as well as ss. 93(2), 94, and 98 of the *Constitution Act, 1867*; s. 26 of the *Constitution Act, 1930* (U.K.), 20 & 21 Geo. V, c. 26; and s. 59 of the *Constitution Act, 1982*.

59 This section is indebted to Scott's admirable analysis of s. 43 of the *Constitution Act, 1982*, which he identifies as the "Rubik's Cube of the 1982 Act." See Scott, "Pussycat," above note 38 at 293.

60 Section 47(1) of the *Constitution Act, 1982* refers to the procedures for amendment "under section 38, 41, 42 or 43."

in cases where an amendment was being made to a "special arrangement" provision of the constitution that *also* fell within section 41 or 42. For example, suppose it were proposed to extend the boundaries of a province into the territories. Would such an amendment fall under section 42(1)(e) and require the consent of seven provinces, or could it be accomplished under section 43 with the consent of only the province affected?[61] In our view, such an amendment would necessarily have to satisfy the requirements of both sections 42(1)(e) and 43. Sections 41 through 43 all state that amendments to certain matters may be made "only" through the procedures they establish. The word "only" suggests that the requirements of these sections are *cumulative* rather than mutually exclusive. Each of sections 41 to 43 establishes necessary (but not sufficient) conditions for the enactment of constitutional amendments falling within one or more of these sections.[62] Thus, in the hypothetical situation outlined above, at least seven provinces would have to consent to the alteration of the provincial territory, and the province whose border was being extended would also have to consent.

Section 43 can only be used for amendments that affect some but not all provinces. It would appear, therefore, that it cannot be used to amend existing constitutional provisions that apply to all provinces. For example, it should not be possible to amend section 92 of the *Constitution Act, 1867* so as to provide additional legislative powers for certain provinces (but not others) using the section 43 procedure. Section 92 is not a provision that applies to "some but not all provinces," and therefore does not fall within the class of provisions that can be changed through section 43.[63] On the other hand, it should be possible to create new or additional "special arrangements" that apply to particular provinces, as long as there is no necessity to amend an existing constitutional provision that applies to all provinces. Thus in 1993, section 16.1 was added to the *Constitution Act, 1982*, providing for

61 The argument in favour of the application of s. 43 of the *Constitution Act, 1982* is based on the fact that the constitutional provisions establishing the boundaries of a province are provisions that apply to "one or more, but not all, provinces."

62 Section 41(c) of the *Constitution Act, 1982* creates an exception to this general rule, since it is expressly made subject to s. 43. Therefore, an amendment in relation to a provision that creates a special arrangement for the use of the English or the French language can be enacted with the consent of only the provinces that will be affected by the amendment.

63 For the same reason, it would not be possible for Quebec to introduce a distinct-society clause, providing that the constitution shall be interpreted in a manner consistent with the recognition of the distinct identity of Quebec through s. 43 of the *Constitution Act, 1982*. Since such an interpretive clause would apply to the entire constitution, it would indirectly amend provisions that apply to all provinces.

equality of status of the English and French linguistic communities in New Brunswick through the section 43 amending procedure.[64]

Section 43 requires only the consent of the province(s) affected by the amendment.[65] For example, suppose it were proposed to amend section 93 of the *Constitution Act, 1867* so as to alter the rights in respect of denominational schools in one province only. Despite the fact that section 93 applies to six provinces, only the consent of the province to be affected by the amendment would be necessary.[66]

H. UNILATERAL FEDERAL PROCEDURE

Section 44 provides that the federal Parliament may enact amendments to the Constitution of Canada in relation to "the executive government of Canada or the Senate and House of Commons." However, the section 44 power is subject to sections 41 and 42, which require the consent of either seven or ten provinces, depending on the subject matter of the amendment. A number of matters in sections 41 and 42 operate so as to constrain the scope of section 44, including the office of the queen and the governor general (section 41(a)); minimum provincial representation in the House of Commons (section 41(b)); the principle of proportionate representation in the House of Commons (section 42(1)(a)); the use of the English or the French language (section 41(c)); the powers of the Senate and the method of selecting senators (section 42(1)(b)); and provincial representation in the Senate and the residence qualifications of senators (section 42(1)(c)). These exceptions deal with aspects of federal legislative and executive institutions that affect provincial interests.

Section 44 was intended to replace section 91(1) of the *Constitution Act, 1867*, which had granted Parliament the power to amend the Constitution of Canada subject to a number of exceptions. Section 91(1) was repealed in 1982 at the time of the enactment of section 44. As noted earlier, in *Upper House Reference*, the Supreme Court construed section 91(1) in a narrow fashion. The Court held that section 91(1) could not be used to alter the "fundamental features, or essential char-

---

64 See *Constitution Amendment Proclamation, 1993 (New Brunswick Act)*, SI/93-54.

65 Section 43 of the *Constitution Act, 1982* requires the consent of the "legislative assembly of each province to which the amendment applies."

66 See *Constitution Amendment, 1997 (Quebec)*, SI/ 97-141 (amending s. 93 by providing that paras. (1)–(4) do not apply to the province of Quebec). The Quebec Court of Appeal upheld the validity of this proclamation in *Potter c. Quebec (P.G.)*, [2001] J.Q. No. 5553.

acteristics, given to the Senate as a means of ensuring regional and provincial representation in the federal legislative process." That Parliament's unilateral power to enact amendments to the Senate is made subject to significant exceptions in sections 41 and 42 suggests that the drafters of the new federal amending power were attempting to codify the Supreme Court's analysis in *Upper House Reference*. Thus, section 42 provides that important matters such as the powers of the Senate, the method of selecting senators, the number of members by which a province is entitled to be represented in the Senate, and the residence qualifications of senators, are all "fundamental" or "essential" matters that require the consent of at least seven provinces representing at least 50 percent of the provincial population.

Since 1982, the section 44 amending power has been utilized in order to enact statutes amending the rules for the decennial redistribution of seats in the House of Commons, and to provide for representation for the new territory of Nunavut in the Senate and House of Commons.[67] The ability of Parliament to use section 44 to enact reforms to the Senate, however, is now quite limited in light of the Supreme Court's holding in the *Senate Reform Reference* in 2014.[68]

In 2014, the government of Prime Minister Stephen Harper, a longstanding advocate of Senate reform, sought an opinion from the Court on the availability of several different types of reforms under section 44. The result was a very limited scope for unilateral federal action, meaning that the Senate will be with us for some time. The only unilateral federal amendment that the Court found permissible under section 44 was the repeal of the requirement that senators hold property. The historical purpose of this requirement was to protect the propertied class against the democratic House of Commons. Changes to the tenure of

67 See the *Constitution Act, 1985 (Representation)*, S.C. 1986, c. 8; and the *Constitution Act, 1999 (Nunavut)*, S.C. 1998, c. 15, Part II. It is also arguable that, as the so-called *Clarity Act* (*An Act to give effect to the requirement for clarity as set out in the opinion of the Supreme Court of Canada in the Quebec Secession Reference*, S.C. 2000, c. 26) imposes limitations on the power of the Government of Canada to negotiate a constitutional amendment providing for the secession of Quebec from Canada, the amending power in s. 44 supported the enactment of the Act. As such, it could be regarded as a law amending the "Constitution of Canada in relation to the executive government of Canada." For a helpful discussion of the scope of s. 44 see: W.J. Newman, "Defining the 'Constitution of Canada' Since 1982: The Scope of the Legislative Powers of Constitutional Amendment under Sections 44 and 45 of the *Constitution Act, 1982*" (2003) 22 Sup. Ct. L. Rev. (2d) 423; and W.J. Newman, "Living with the Amending Procedures: Prospects for Future Constitutional Reform in Canada" (2007) 37 Sup. Ct. L. Rev. (2d) 383.

68 *Reference re Senate Reform*, [2014] 1 S.C.R. 704 [*Senate Reform Reference*].

senators or their election rather than appointment require the use of the general amending formula. Abolition of the Senate is subject to the unanimity formula.

In our view, the *Senate Reform Reference* has created significant uncertainty about the scope of section 42 by treating its text as a non-exhaustive list. Section 44 gives exclusive jurisdiction to the federal Parliament to make amendments "in relation to . . . the Senate," subject only to the exceptions set out in sections 41 and 42. While the "powers of the Senate" and the "method of selecting Senators" are expressly identified in section 42, their tenure is not mentioned. The Court deliberately gave this language a very broad meaning in order to protect provincial interests. However, the provinces already benefit from an amending formula that is one of the most difficult to meet in the world. Given the constitutional gridlock that has plagued Canada since patriation and the arguably declining role of the Senate, judicial interpretation should favour a more narrow reading of sections 41 and 42.

For example, the unilateral formula should be sufficient for Parliament to modify the electoral system used to determine representation in the House of Commons, a change promised by Prime Minister Justin Trudeau in the 2015 election. Subject to the qualification in section 52 of the *Constitution Act, 1867* that the proportionate representation of the provinces in the House not be disturbed, amendments to the *Canada Elections Act* that mandate the use of a ranked ballot or amendments to the *Constitution Act, 1867* allocating seats on the basis of proportional representation are clearly "in relation to the . . . House of Commons" as contemplated by the text of section 44. The *Senate Reform Reference*'s invocation of "constitutional architecture" should not be stretched to the point of requiring provincial consent for every change to a significant federal institution. Although there has been judicial commentary in the *Charter* context that the first-past-the-post electoral system is "one of Canada's core political institutions,"[69] a plain reading of section 44 suggests that Parliament has the ability to modify the electoral system unilaterally.

69 *Figueroa v. Canada (Attorney General)*, [2003] 1 S.C.R. 912 at para. 157, LeBel J. concurring.

I. UNILATERAL PROVINCIAL PROCEDURE

Section 45 permits the provincial legislatures to unilaterally amend the "Constitution of the Province," subject to section 41.[70] The term "Constitution of the Province" is not defined. However, case law dealing with the scope of section 92(1) of the *Constitution Act, 1867,* which section 45 effectively replaced,[71] had defined the term as those matters involving "the operation of an organ of the government of a province."[72] As such, the scope of section 45 should be similar to that of section 44 despite the different wording. Provinces should be able to unilaterally alter their executive or legislative institutions, subject only to the exceptions set out in section 41.

J. SENATE APPROVAL

Although sections 38, 41, 42, and 43 appear to require Senate approval, the Senate has the power only to delay rather than to block amendments enacted under these provisions. Section 47 provides that, if the Senate has failed to approve an amendment under any of these sections within 180 days of the adoption of an authorizing resolution by the House of Commons, the House of Commons may thereafter adopt the resolution a second time. Re-adoption by the House of Commons after this six-month waiting period renders Senate approval unnecessary.

In the fall of 1996, the House of Commons rejected changes that were proposed by the Senate to an amendment to Term 17 of the *Newfoundland Terms of Union* and re-enacted its original resolution.[73] While

---

70 Section 45 of the *Constitution Act, 1982*, unlike s. 44, is not subject to s. 42. However, this difference does not appear to be of any practical significance, since none of the matters in s. 42 would appear to fall within the term "constitution of the province" and thus could not be amended pursuant to s. 45.

71 Section 92(1) of the *Constitution Act, 1867* granted the provinces power to amend the constitution of the province, except as regards the office of the lieutenant governor. Section 92(1) was repealed in 1982.

72 See *O.P.S.E.U. v. Ontario (Attorney General)*, [1987] 2 S.C.R. 2.

73 The House of Commons adopted the original resolution authorizing the amendment on 3 June 1996. When the Senate proposed changes, the House re-adopted the original resolution on 4 December 1996. The Newfoundland House of Assembly had previously passed an identical resolution, and thus the amendment was proclaimed by the governor general. (Note, however, that the following year a further amendment to Term 17 was requested by the Newfoundland government, and this amendment was passed by both the Senate and House of Commons, as well as the Newfoundland House of Assembly.)

the Senate can be overridden with respect to amendments under sections 38, 41, 42, and 43, Senate approval is required for statutes enacted by Parliament alone under section 44.[74] The Supreme Court held in the *Senate Reform Reference* that abolition of the Senate is only available pursuant to the section 41 unanimity formula, given that such an amendment would fundamentally alter the architecture of the Constitution of Canada.[75] Therefore, while any province may veto the Senate's abolition, the Upper House itself lacks such power and can only delay its own demise.

K. REGIONAL VETO LEGISLATION

The operation of the amending procedure has been made significantly more difficult by the enactment in 1996 of the *Regional Veto Act*.[76] This Act prohibits any minister of the Crown from proposing a resolution for a constitutional amendment unless the consent of certain provinces has been obtained. The provinces that must consent are Ontario; Quebec; British Columbia; at least two of the Atlantic provinces that have at least 50 percent of the combined population of the Atlantic provinces; and at least two of the three Prairie provinces that have at least 50 percent of the combined population of the Prairie provinces. Because Alberta currently has over 50 percent of the population of the three Prairie provinces, its consent must be obtained in order to satisfy the latter requirement. The manner in which this provincial consent must be manifested is not specified in the Act. Presumably, however, the requirements of the Act should be read in light of the general procedures for constitutional amendments set out in Part V, which require resolutions of the provincial legislatures.

The *Regional Veto Act* was enacted to fulfil the commitment made by Prime Minister Chrétien during the 1995 Quebec referendum campaign to secure a veto for Quebec over any future constitutional change. The effectiveness of the statute depends on the fact that the approval of the House of Commons is necessary for any constitutional amendment under sections 38 or 42. The statute lends this federal veto to the provinces whose consent is required, thus indirectly securing a veto for

74 This difference applies because s. 44 of the *Constitution Act, 1982* is not listed in s. 47, which establishes the power to override the Senate.

75 *Senate Reform Reference*, above note 68 at para. 110.

76 Above note 28.

those provinces.[77] However, the Act is not an amendment to the Constitution of Canada and, as an ordinary federal statute, is theoretically subject to repeal or amendment by a subsequent Parliament.

Section 1 of the *Regional Veto Act* states that it does not apply to constitutional amendments in cases where a province may exercise a veto under section 41 or 43, or where a province has a right of dissent under section 38(3).[78] Thus, the main effect of the Act will be in relation to amendments under section 38(1) where no right of dissent is permitted. This would include amendments under section 42(1), which mandates recourse to section 38(1), as well as other constitutional amendments where there is no derogation from provincial powers. While such amendments can continue to be enacted with the consent of seven provinces, the effect of the Act is to raise the population requirement from 50 percent to over 92 percent.[79] Furthermore, because certain provinces whose consent is required under the *Regional Veto Act* themselves require a provincial referendum before a constitutional resolution can be approved by the legislature, the federal Act has indirectly made these provincial referendum requirements a condition of federal approval. The cumulative effect of these changes is to make the likelihood of future amendments being enacted under section 38 even more remote. This result is ironic. Federalists in Quebec continue to seek constitutional amendments (such as a recognition of Quebec's distinctiveness) that can only be enacted under section 38. The *Regional Veto Act*, enacted to fulfil a commitment made to Quebec federalists, has made the realization of their aspirations for constitutional reform significantly more difficult.

---

77 The statute does not purport to constrain the ability of the House of Commons itself to adopt a constitutional resolution. (Had it done so, it would arguably have been an amendment to Part V of the *Constitution Act, 1982* and would have had to satisfy s. 41(e).) Rather, it simply prevents a minister of the Crown from introducing a resolution into Parliament unless the required provincial consent has been obtained. However, in any situation where the government controls a majority in the House of Commons, the practical result of binding ministers is that the House will not endorse any resolution that the government opposes.

78 Although the Act does not refer to s. 44 of the *Constitution Act, 1982*, it would appear that there was no intention to constrain the unilateral federal amending power under s. 44 and that such amendments continue to require only an ordinary Act of the federal Parliament.

79 The 92 percent figure is obtained by adding together the present populations of Ontario, Quebec, British Columbia, Alberta, Saskatchewan, New Brunswick, and Newfoundland and Labrador.

L. THE *MEECH LAKE ACCORD*

The failure of the Quebec government to consent to the enactment of the 1982 constitutional changes did not affect the legal validity of the amendments in that province. Nor did the enactment of these changes over the objections of the Quebec government violate any constitutional convention requiring Quebec's consent.[80] Despite the legal effectiveness of the 1982 constitutional package, however, many federalist politicians and opinion leaders, both inside and outside the province of Quebec, argued that it was important eventually to obtain the consent of the Quebec government to the 1982 constitutional reforms.[81] In the 1984 federal election campaign, Brian Mulroney pledged that, if elected prime minister, he would attempt to reach an accommodation with the Quebec government that would enable Quebec to voluntarily accept the 1982 constitution "with honour and enthusiasm."[82] In the 1985 provincial election in Quebec, Robert Bourassa obtained a mandate to undertake negotiations designed to permit Quebec to "sign" the 1982 constitution. Then, in May 1986, the new Quebec minister of intergovernmental affairs, Gil Rémillard, outlined five changes that would have to be made to the Canadian constitution to make it acceptable to the Liberal government in Quebec City: (1) recognition of Quebec as a distinct society; (2) a greater role for Quebec in immigration to the province; (3) a role for Quebec in appointments to the Supreme Court of Canada;

---

80 In late 1981, the Quebec government sought a ruling from its Court of Appeal to the effect that the reduction of its legislative powers without its consent violated the constitutional convention that the Supreme Court had recognized in *Reference Re Amendment of Constitution of Canada (Nos. 1, 2, 3)*, [1981] 1 S.C.R. 753. (As noted in Chapter 5, the Supreme Court had held in September 1981 that there was a constitutional convention that the "substantial consent" of the provinces would be obtained for constitutional changes directly affecting their powers.) In early April 1982, just days before the *Constitution Act, 1982* was scheduled to be proclaimed, the Quebec Court of Appeal rejected the Quebec government's argument and held that there was no convention requiring Quebec's consent. In late 1982, the Supreme Court affirmed this judgment: see *Que. (A.G.) v. Can. (A.G.)*, [1982] 2 S.C.R. 793.

81 For example, the Macdonald Commission, in a comprehensive analysis of the future of the country, concluded in 1985 that it was necessary to seek "a renewed understanding between Quebec and the rest of Canada": see Royal Commission on the Economic Union and Development Prospects for Canada, *Summary of Conclusions and Recommendations* (Ottawa: Supply and Services Canada, 1985) at 53–54.

82 This discussion is based on a recounting of the events in Monahan, above note 11 at 38–136. See also: A. Cohen, *A Deal Undone: The Making and Breaking of the Meech Lake Accord* (Vancouver: Douglas and McIntyre, 1990).

(4) limitations on the ability of the federal government to spend money in areas of exclusive provincial jurisdiction; and (5) a veto for Quebec over future constitutional changes.

In the summer of 1986, the annual premiers conference issued a communiqué stating that the participants' "top constitutional priority is to embark immediately upon a federal–provincial process, using Quebec's five proposals as a basis of discussion, to bring about Quebec's full and active participation in the Canadian federation."[83] Negotiations began in the fall of 1986, and concluded with an agreement in principle between all first ministers after an eleven-hour meeting at Meech Lake, Quebec, on 30 April 1987.

Reflecting Quebec's desire to be recognized as a distinct society, the *Meech Lake Accord* proposed to add a clause to the *Constitution Act, 1867* stating that the Constitution of Canada "shall be interpreted in a manner consistent with . . . the recognition that Quebec constitutes within Canada a distinct society." This distinct-society clause also "affirmed the role" of the Quebec government and legislature to "preserve and promote" this distinct identity. However, the recognition of Quebec's distinct identity was balanced by a recognition that "English-speaking Canadians, concentrated outside Quebec [but also present in Quebec, constitute] a fundamental characteristic of Canada." All legislatures affirmed their role to "preserve" this fundamental characteristic. The distinct-society clause also specified that it did not take away any existing federal or provincial powers.

Quebec's remaining four conditions were generalized so they applied in roughly equal fashion to all the provinces. All provinces were given the right to require the federal government to negotiate an agreement giving provinces a greater role in immigration; any such agreement would then be constitutionally entrenched, in the sense that either party could not change it unilaterally. The federal government would make future appointments to the Supreme Court from lists of names submitted by the provinces. Quebec's right to three judges on the nine-member Court was also constitutionally entrenched. Furthermore, provinces would be permitted to opt out of any new shared-cost program in areas of exclusive provincial jurisdiction and still receive reasonable compensation, providing that they undertook initiatives consistent with the "national objectives." With respect to the amending formula, all provinces would be given a veto over matters identified in section 42 of the *Constitution Act, 1982*, and the right to receive compensation in cases where a prov-

---

83 For the text of both the agreement of 30 April 1987 and the final legal text, see Monahan, above note 11, App. 2 "Meech Lake Communiqué, 30 April 1987" and App. 3 "The 1987 Constitutional Accord."

ince opted out of a constitutional amendment transferring jurisdiction to Parliament would be broadened. The federal government also agreed to appoint senators from lists of names submitted by the provinces, and to discuss Senate reform and "roles and responsibilities in relation to fisheries" at annual constitutional conferences of first ministers.[84]

Because the accord dealt with matters falling under section 41,[85] it required unanimous provincial consent as well as the consent of the Senate and the House of Commons. The accord was also subject to a three-year time limit, since it dealt with matters in section 42 and thereby required resolutions in accordance with sections 38(1) and 39(2). Quebec was the first to ratify the accord on 23 June 1987, which set the three-year time limit in motion.

Initial opinion polls indicated that public support for the accord was high, with those expressing an opinion supporting the accord by a margin of more than three to one.[86] However, public support began to wane as critics attacked a wide variety of the accord's provisions. Former prime minister Trudeau criticized the accord in newspaper articles published in late May, just before the meeting in early June where the legal text of the accord had been settled by the first ministers. Over the summer of 1987, a joint Senate–House of Commons Committee heard from a variety of other groups with serious concerns about the accord. They argued that the distinct-society clause would permit Quebec to undermine the rights of the English-speaking minority in Quebec. Women's organizations feared that the accord would lead to weakened protections for gender equality rights in Quebec. Indigenous peoples objected to the fact that their distinct identity and role in Canada was not recognized and that the accord would make it more difficult to create new provinces in the north by requiring unanimous provincial consent for such a change. Finally, social activists in English-speaking Canada criticized the accord's limitation on the ability of the federal government to create new shared-cost programs in areas of exclusive provincial jurisdiction.

Eight provinces as well as the Senate and the House of Commons eventually ratified the accord, but newly elected governments in Mani-

---

84 These Senate proposals were added as a result of concerns raised by Alberta premier Don Getty that the accord would make Senate reform very difficult, by requiring unanimous provincial consent for future changes to the Senate.

85 The accord would have enacted amendments to the composition of the Supreme Court and the amending formula.

86 A Gallup poll released in mid-June 1987 found that 56 percent of those polled favoured the accord, 16 percent were opposed, and 28 percent had no opinion: see Monahan, above note 11 at 139.

toba, New Brunswick, and Newfoundland[87] refused to proceed with ratification unless changes were made. A week-long meeting in early June 1990 resulted in a unanimous agreement to ratify the accord and to proceed with a host of additional constitutional initiatives in a second round of negotiations. New Brunswick immediately ratified the accord. However, Manitoba MLA Elijah Harper was able to block the accord from being put to a final vote in the Manitoba legislature before the 23 June 1990 deadline. Once it became apparent that Manitoba would not be able to ratify the accord in time, Newfoundland premier Clyde Wells decided not to put the accord to a vote in the Newfoundland House of Assembly. Since the accord had failed to achieve the required approvals by 23 June 1990, all previous resolutions supporting it were rendered ineffective and the accord died.

The failure of the accord provoked a surge of nationalism in Quebec. Opinion polls indicated that two-thirds of Quebec residents then supported sovereignty-association, while a majority was in favour of outright independence. Just days after the death of the accord, a crowd of 200,000 marched in the annual St-Jean Baptiste parade in Montreal chanting nationalist slogans and waving the Quebec flag. Lucien Bouchard, who had resigned as a minister from the government of Brian Mulroney in May 1990, formed a new separatist political party—the Bloc Québécois—and announced that the party would field candidates in all Quebec ridings in the next federal election. Quebec premier Robert Bourassa and Parti Québécois leader Jacques Parizeau agreed to establish a commission, chaired by Michel Bélanger and Jean Campeau, to consider Quebec's constitutional options in light of the failure of Meech. Bourassa also appointed Jean Allaire to head a Quebec Liberal Party committee that would prepare a new constitutional platform for the party.

Outside Quebec, on the other hand, political attitudes toward Quebec's demands began to harden. By early 1990, approximately 60 percent of Canadians were opposed to the accord, with respondents in English-speaking Canada citing the distinct-society clause as being particularly problematic. There was also opposition to the closed-door process for the negotiation and drafting of the accord and demands for greater transparency. In an attempt to respond to this criticism, the federal government established the Citizen's Forum on Canada's Future, chaired by Keith Spicer, to listen to Canadians and to ensure that their concerns were reflected in future constitutional discussions. Spicer claimed to

87 In April 1990, after the election of Clyde Wells as premier, the Newfoundland House of Assembly rescinded the province's prior approval of the accord.

have consulted over 600,000 Canadians mainly outside Quebec and reported in the summer of 1991. However, he did not offer any substantive recommendations on ways to reconcile the growing nationalism in Quebec with the hardened attitudes in the rest of Canada.

M. THE *CHARLOTTETOWN ACCORD*

In the spring of 1991, both the Bélanger-Campeau Commission and the Allaire Committee recommended that Quebec hold a referendum on sovereignty unless significant offers of renewed federalism were forthcoming from the rest of Canada. The Quebec National Assembly passed legislation requiring a referendum on the sovereignty of Quebec by 26 October 1992. This deadline served as the catalyst for a new round of constitutional negotiations, culminating in the *Charlottetown Accord* in the summer of 1992.[88]

The federal government was determined to avoid what it regarded as the two key mistakes that had resulted in the defeat of the *Meech Lake Accord*. First, it described the new process as a Canada Round, designed to deal with the constitutional concerns of all Canadians, in contrast with the Quebec-centred focus of the *Meech Lake Accord*. Second, the federal government committed itself to extensive public consultations before any agreement was signed.

In September 1991, the federal government unveiled an initial package of constitutional proposals and referred the package to a parliamentary committee co-chaired by Senator Gérald Beaudoin[89] and Conservative MP Dorothy Dobbie for public hearings. The federal proposals included all of the elements of the failed *Meech Lake Accord* but went much further and proposed far-reaching changes to matters such as the Senate, the division of powers, the Canadian economic union, and the recognition of Indigneous rights.[90] In early 1992, a series of five publicly televised conferences were held on various aspects of the proposals. The public conferences were attended by politicians, representatives of interest groups, and Canadians chosen at random from newspaper advertisements. This public consultation process culminated in the pub-

88 The discussion in this section is based on Monahan, above note 15. See also the account by P.H. Russell, *Constitutional Odyssey: Can Canadians Become a Sovereign People?* (Toronto: University of Toronto Press, 1992) c. 10.

89 The committee was originally chaired by Senator Claude Castonguay, who resigned and was replaced by Senator Beaudoin.

90 See Canada, *Shaping Canada's Future Together* (Ottawa: Supply and Services Canada, 1991).

lication of the report of the Beaudoin–Dobbie Committee at the end of February 1992, where a significant number of modifications to the original federal proposals were recommended.

At this point, a second intergovernmental phase of the discussions began. In mid-March 1992, the federal government and the provinces agreed to establish a multilateral negotiation process to refine the Beaudoin–Dobbie recommendations. Representatives of the territories and the four national Indigenous organizations were also invited to participate in the negotiations. Quebec, which had been boycotting federal-provincial negotiations since the failure of the *Meech Lake Accord*, declined to participate. This multilateral process, chaired by federal minister for constitutional affairs and former prime minister Joe Clark, met regularly over the next three months. On 7 July 1992, to the surprise of most observers—including Prime Minister Mulroney, who was in Europe attending the annual G7 meeting at the time—the participants unanimously agreed on a comprehensive package of reforms. The key breakthrough leading to the so-called Pearson Accord[91] was Ontario's decision to accede to demands from the western provinces and Newfoundland that a reformed Senate have equal representation from each province. Another important element was an agreement to entrench an inherent right of Indigenous self-government and the recognition of Indigenous governments as a "third order of government" within Canada.

The Pearson Accord effectively forced Quebec back to the bargaining table. A new round of meetings, chaired by Mulroney and attended by Bourassa, led to the signing of the *Charlottetown Accord* by all first ministers, along with territorial and Indigenous leaders, on 28 August 1992. The *Charlottetown Accord* modified the Pearson Accord proposals in a number of important respects: while an equal Senate was retained, its powers in relation to the House of Commons were reduced; the provisions on Indigenous self-government were softened somewhat to deal with Quebec's concerns that no new Indigenous rights to land should be created; and Quebec was guaranteed a minimum of 25 percent of the seats in the House of Commons. It was also agreed that a national referendum would be held on 26 October 1992, to be followed by legislative ratification in accordance with the process mandated by Part V.

Initial public opinion polls indicated that a majority of Canadians supported the accord. However, as with the *Meech Lake Accord*, the critics of the *Charlottetown Accord* soon gathered momentum and the tide

91 So named because it was negotiated at the Lester B. Pearson Building, the headquarters for the Department of Foreign Affairs in Ottawa.

of public opinion turned sharply negative. In Quebec, the accord was denounced because the proposed transfers of legislative jurisdiction were regarded as insufficient; in the west, it was said that the reformed Senate would be too weak to check the House of Commons and that the guarantee of 25 percent of the Commons seats to Quebec was unacceptable; in Indigenous communities, the accord was criticized on the basis that it undermined traditional Treaty rights. On 26 October 1992, 55 percent of the 13.7 million Canadians who cast ballots voted against the accord, with the "No" side gaining majority support in six provinces, the Yukon, and in Indigenous communities. The accord was particularly unpopular in British Columbia, Alberta, and Manitoba, where over 60 percent voted "No."[92] The decisive defeat of the *Charlottetown Accord* brought an immediate halt to any further constitutional discussions. Constitutional reform did not feature in the 1993 federal election campaign, other than in the pledge by Jean Chrétien that he would not reopen constitutional negotiations in the foreseeable future. The consensus view was that Canadians in all regions of the country wanted nothing further to do with constitutional reform.

N. THE 1995 QUEBEC REFERENDUM AND ITS AFTERMATH

In September 1994, the Parti Québécois, led by Jacques Parizeau, defeated the Liberal government of Daniel Johnson, who had succeeded Robert Bourassa when he retired in early 1994. Parizeau had pledged to hold a referendum on sovereignty within a year of being elected. In December 1994, he tabled draft legislation which, if enacted, purported to grant the Quebec National Assembly the power to unilaterally declare Quebec to be a sovereign country. The draft legislation also dealt with a wide variety of contentious matters that would arise on Quebec's accession to sovereignty, including Quebec's territory, currency, borders, treaties, and citizenship.[93]

Polls published in early 1995 indicated that, if a referendum were held on the Quebec government's draft sovereignty legislation, the government's proposals would be defeated by a sixty-to-forty margin. This opposition forced Parizeau to shift his strategy. In June 1995, he signed

---

92 The official voting results are published in McRoberts & Monahan, above note 15, App. 3.

93 See Draft Bill, *An Act respecting the sovereignty of Quebec*, 1st Sess., 35th Leg., Quebec, 1994.

an agreement with Lucien Bouchard, leader of the Bloc Québécois, and Mario Dumont, the leader of a small Quebec nationalist party, in which he pledged that Quebec would make a formal offer of an economic and political partnership with Canada before declaring sovereignty. Then, in early October 1995, Parizeau appointed Bouchard as Quebec's chief negotiator in the proposed talks aimed at achieving a new partnership with Canada. The announcement of Bouchard's appointment triggered a surge in support for the "Yes" side in the final weeks of the campaign. In the final week of the referendum campaign, with the increase in popular support for the "Yes" side, Chrétien had made two solemn pledges to Quebec residents in an effort to shore up federalist support in the province. The first pledge was an endorsement of the constitutional recognition of Quebec as a distinct society. The second was that he would ensure that no future constitutional amendments affecting Quebec's powers would be enacted without Quebec's consent. The result of the referendum on 30 October 1995 was a narrow victory for the "No" side, by a margin of 50.6 to 49.4 percent.

In the days immediately following the referendum, some key provincial premiers indicated that they were unwilling to embark on another round of formal constitutional negotiations. Accordingly, the federal government attempted to honour the prime minister's two referendum campaign pledges without having to resort to the amending formula in Part V. The *Regional Veto Act*, described earlier, was the federal government's attempt to make good on the second pledge. As for the first, on 29 November 1995, Chrétien introduced a resolution[94] into the House of Commons stating that the House recognized "that Quebec is a distinct society within Canada [which] includes its French-speaking majority, unique culture and civil law tradition." The resolution also encouraged "all components of the legislative and executive branches of government to take notice of this recognition and be guided in their conduct accordingly." The federal government suggested that this resolution was an interim measure, and it continued to seek support among the provinces for a constitutional amendment that would entrench the recognition of Quebec's distinctiveness in the Constitution of Canada.

The narrowness of the "No" victory also stimulated the emergence of a so-called Plan B—the idea of preparing contingency plans to deal with the possibility of a third Quebec sovereignty referendum. The proponents of Plan B argued that the refusal of the federal government to discuss how it would respond to a majority "Yes" vote had left the

94 Resolutions, unlike bills, are non-binding declarations of the intention or views of a legislative body on a particular subject. They do not have the force of law.

Parti Québécois with a free hand to define the terms of the debate to its advantage.[95] Plan B advocates urged the federal government to lead attempts to set clear ground rules in advance of a future referendum. Clear referendum ground rules would define the Canadian position on such matters as the wording of the referendum question, the majority required to commence sovereignty negotiations, the rights of Indigenous peoples and minorities within Quebec who wished to remain within Canada, the legality of a unilateral declaration of independence, and the sharing of the debt.

O. THE QUEBEC SECESSION REFERENCE[96]

1) The Reference Questions

The federal government took an important step in the direction of Plan B when, in the fall of 1996, it referred a series of three questions to the Supreme Court on issues relating to Quebec secession. Prior to the reference, a private Quebec citizen, Guy Bertrand, had commenced litigation both before and after the 1995 referendum claiming that the referendum, which sought to confer on the Quebec National Assembly a mandate to unilaterally declare sovereignty from Canada, was unconstitutional and amounted to a breach of his constitutionally protected rights.[97] The Quebec government brought two separate motions to strike out Bertrand's claims on the grounds that the issues raised were political and/or hypothetical and, therefore, beyond the jurisdiction of the courts. The motions were dismissed and, in August 1996, a judge

---

95 See, for example, P.J. Monahan, M. Bryant, & N. Côté, *Coming to Terms with Plan B: Ten Principles Governing Secession* (Toronto: C.D. Howe Institute, 1996); G. Robertson, "Contingency Legislation for a Quebec Referendum" (1996) 4 Canada Watch 93; P.W. Hogg, "The Effect of a Referendum on Quebec Sovereignty" (1996) 4 Canada Watch 89.

96 Above note 5. The decision sparked considerable academic debate and commentary. See, for example, the collection of essays in volume 11 of the *National Journal of Constitutional Law* (November 1999); D. Schneiderman, ed., *The Quebec Decision: Perspectives on the Supreme Court Ruling on Secession* (Toronto: James Lorimer and Co., 1999); W.J. Newman, *The Quebec Secession Reference: The Rule of Law and the Position of the Attorney General of Canada* (Toronto: York University Centre for Public Law and Public Policy, 1999).

97 *Bertrand v. Quebec (Procureur général)* (1995), 127 D.L.R. (4th) 408 (Que. S.C.); *Bertrand v. Quebec (Procureur général) (No. 2)* (1996), 138 D.L.R. (4th) 481 (Que. S.C.) [*Bertrand (No. 2)*].

of the cour supérieure de Quebec referred a number of the issues raised by Bertrand to trial.[98]

The three questions posed by the federal government on the Quebec *Secession Reference* to the Supreme Court were based on the issues identified by the judge in the *Bertrand* case. The first was whether Quebec had the right under the Canadian constitution to declare its sovereignty from Canada unilaterally. The second was whether international law permits Quebec to unilaterally secede from Canada. The third was whether domestic law or international law would prevail in Canada in the event of a conflict between them.

2) Question One: The Canadian Constitution and Secession

The first question turned on whether secession can be achieved through a constitutional amendment enacted pursuant to Part V of the *Constitution Act, 1982*. As explained in Section F, above, secession is legally possible through a constitutional amendment under section 41. Secession engages section 41(a), since an amendment authorizing secession would involve the abolition of the office of the lieutenant governor. Secession would also involve changes to the composition of the Supreme Court (section 41(d)), the use of the English and French language (section 41(c)), and minimum representation in the House of Commons (section 41(b)), all of which would require unanimity.

While the Supreme Court declined to specify which of the amending procedures in Part V would apply, it did confirm that the secession of Quebec would require an amendment to the Constitution of Canada and that such an amendment could not be enacted by the province acting unilaterally.[99] The constitution binds all governments, both federal and provincial, and government action must comply with the law, including the constitution.[100] However, the Supreme Court also stated that, although Quebec did not have the legal right to declare sovereignty unilaterally, the federal government would have a constitutional duty to negotiate secession following a clear majority favouring this option on a clear referendum question. The recognition of this duty to negotiate surprised many observers, since it had not even been raised by the *amicus curiae* appointed by the Court to argue against the position

98 See *Bertrand (No. 2)*, *ibid*.

99 *Secession Reference*, above note 5 at paras. 84–85, 104.

100 *Ibid*. at para. 72. See also *Air Canada v. B.C.*, [1986] 2 S.C.R. 539 at 546.

of the Attorney General of Canada.[101] The key element of the Supreme Court's reasoning in support of this duty to negotiate is the Court's finding that the constitution is based on at least[102] four general principles: federalism, democracy, constitutionalism and the rule of law, and protection of minorities. The Court also held that, while constitutional principles "could not be taken as an invitation to dispense with the written text of the Constitution," it is permissible to have resort to unwritten principles in order to form "the premises of a constitutional argument that culminates in the filling of gaps in the express terms of the constitutional text."[103] The Court relied on the unwritten principles of "democracy" and "federalism" to create a constitutional duty to negotiate secession in the event of a clear majority in favour of that option in a clearly worded referendum.[104] The Court noted that the constitution makes no express reference to the legal effect of a referendum. However, in the Court's view, a referendum may provide a democratic method of ascertaining the views of the electorate on important political questions on a particular occasion.

This approach to the application of unwritten constitutional principles has the potential to significantly expand the nature and scope of constitutional obligations. The constitution provides only a general framework within which the political process is intended to operate. The constitution makes express provision for only a limited number of fundamental issues, leaving the vast majority of matters free to be settled through the ordinary political process. Reliance on unwritten principles may effectively rewrite the text of the constitution.

---

101 The Quebec government refused to participate in the *Secession Reference*, taking the position that the Court had no jurisdiction to determine the legality of unilateral secession. As a result, in July 1997, the Supreme Court appointed Quebec City lawyer André Joli-Coeur as *amicus curiae* to ensure that the Court received arguments on both sides of the reference questions.

102 Note that in the *Secession Reference*, above note 5 at para. 32, the Court states that the principles it identifies are not exhaustive of the principles underlying the constitution.

103 *Ibid.* at para. 53, citing *Judges' Remuneration Reference*, above note 5.

104 Newman, above note 96 at 46, has argued that s. 46 of the *Constitution Act, 1982*, which permits the constitutional amendment process to be initiated at the provincial as well as the national level, provides some textual support for the duty to negotiate secession following a referendum mandate (at 46). However, Dawson points out that s. 46 "is a provision that would appear to be more of a purely technical, procedural one than one that would found such an important concept as the duty to negotiate": see M. Dawson, "Reflections on the Opinion of the Supreme Court of Canada in the *Quebec Secession Reference*" (1999–2000) 11 N.J.C.L. 5 at 32.

The Court's reasoning in the *Secession Reference* should be interpreted as supporting the use of unwritten constitutional principles only where they are necessarily implied by the constitutional text.[105] Implicit principles are those that flow logically or of necessity from the terms of the written constitution. They must be assumed by the existing text to be constitutionally guaranteed and are therefore required in order to give proper effect to the text itself. This necessary implication test explains and rationalizes most of the cases in which the Supreme Court has relied on unwritten constitutional principles in the past and ensures the primacy of the written constitutional text.

In the *Secession Reference*, the Supreme Court stated that the judiciary has no supervisory role over the political aspects of secession negotiations, including the circumstances in which they must be commenced. According to the Court, it is the "obligation of the elected representatives to give concrete form to the discharge of their constitutional obligations which only they and their electors can ultimately assess."[106] However, the Court did make a number of comments as to the circumstances in which negotiations must be undertaken and the nature of those negotiations:

- the duty to negotiate secession is only triggered if a "clear majority" votes in favour of a "clear question on secession" (paras. 87, 88, and 100);
- no single party could dictate either the agenda or the outcome of these negotiations; while negotiators would have to contemplate the possibility of secession, "there would be no absolute legal entitlement to it and no assumption that an agreement reconciling all relevant rights and obligations would actually be reached" (para. 97);
- the parties to the negotiations would include at least the government of Canada and the governments of all the provinces (paras. 88 and 92); it is arguable that representatives of Indigenous peoples in the seceding province would have some role to play in the negotiations (para. 139);[107]

---

105 See P.J. Monahan, "The Legal Framework Governing Secession in Light of the Quebec *Secession Reference*" in P.J. Monahan, Hon. E.A. Cronk, & N. Finkelstein, Program Chairs, *Law Society of Upper Canada Special Lectures 2000: Constitutional and Administrative Law* (Toronto: Irwin Law, 2002).

106 Above note 5 at para. 101.

107 For a discussion of the implications of the *Secession Reference* on the duty to negotiate with Indigenous peoples, see P. Joffe, "Assessing the *Delgamuukw* Principles: National Implications and Potential Effects in Quebec" (2000) 45 McGill L.J. 158.

- negotiations would address "the interests of the federal government, of Quebec and the other provinces, and other participants, as well as the rights of all Canadians both within and outside of Quebec" (para. 92); the issues to be addressed would include the national economy and the national debt, the borders of the seceding province, and rights of linguistic and cultural minorities, including Indigenous peoples (para. 96);
- the actions of all parties must be informed by the constitutional principles of federalism, democracy, constitutionalism and the rule of law, and respect for minority rights; the refusal of a party to conduct negotiations in a manner consistent with constitutional principles and values would seriously put at risk the legitimacy of that party's assertion of rights and could influence the decision of the international community on whether to recognize a sovereign Quebec (paras. 94, 95, and 103).

3) Question Two: Secession under International Law

Question Two asked whether international law, particularly the principle of self-determination of peoples, gave Quebec the right to secede from Canada unilaterally. Although the *amicus* focused his argument primarily on international law, he took a somewhat novel approach on these issues—at least in terms of how the arguments had traditionally been debated within Quebec circles. Quebec sovereigntists had traditionally argued that, although secession may be prohibited under domestic Canadian law, the international law principle of self-determination of peoples justified unilateral secession. The Attorney General of Quebec had raised arguments based on the principle of self-determination in his motions to dismiss the two *Bertrand* proceedings challenging unilateral secession, for example. In the *Secession Reference*, *amicus* M. Joli-Coeur placed almost no emphasis on the right of self-determination of peoples. This was largely because the international law experts he retained conceded that, even if the right of self-determination might give rise to a right of secession, these circumstances clearly did not apply to or exist in the case of Quebec.[108] The *amicus* therefore chose to approach the analysis of Question Two differently.

The *amicus*' argument on Question Two was based on two interrelated propositions. First, although international law did not grant any

108 The experts for the Attorney General of Canada, as well as most of the expert reports from the *amicus*, accepted this view. However, the *amicus* did file a brief by former Quebec Liberal leader Claude Ryan, who maintained that Quebec would have a right to secede based on the principle of self-determination.

positive entitlement to secede from their host states to sub-national units, it did not prohibit attempts at secession. The issuance of a unilateral declaration of independence was therefore not a breach of any rule or principle of international law. Second, the sole legal criterion according to which an attempted secession is judged under international law is its political success or effectiveness. Where a seceding unit is able to establish effective control of its territory and to oust the authority of the host state, the international community will eventually come to recognize the seceding unit as an independent state with full legal personality on the international stage. This latter principle was termed the "effectivity principle," and was the focus of much of the *amicus*' argument, both in the voluminous briefs he filed and in oral argument.

The Court made short work of these arguments. The Court pointed out that, while international law did not contain a specific prohibition of secession, it did accord primacy to the principle of territorial integrity of existing states. International law expects that the right to self-determination will be exercised by peoples within the framework of existing sovereign states and consistently with the maintenance of their territorial integrity. The Court was remarkably frank in making it clear that the limited exceptions to the territorial integrity principle, including the situation of colonial or oppressed peoples or cases where peoples are denied access to government, simply had no application to Quebec. The Court observed that for close to forty of the past fifty years, the prime minister of Canada has been from Quebec, and that the prime minister, the chief justice of the Supreme Court, the chief of staff of the Canadian Armed Forces, and the Canadian ambassador to the United States were all from Quebec at the time. The failure to reach agreement on constitutional amendments following the patriation of the Constitution in 1982, although "a matter of concern," did not place Quebec in a "disadvantaged position within the scope of the international law rule."

As for the so-called effectivity principle, the Court pointed out that unilateral secession might eventually be accorded legal status by Canada and other states, in the sense that, if secession is "successful in the streets, [it] might well lead to the creation of a new state."[109] However, the Court stated that this did not support the "more radical contention that subsequent recognition of a state of affairs brought about by a unilateral declaration of independence could be taken to mean that secession was achieved under colour of a legal right."[110] While a change

109 *Secession Reference*, above note 5 at para. 142.
110 *Ibid*. at para. 144.

in factual circumstances sometimes results in a change in legal status, it is "quite another matter to suggest that a subsequent condonation of an initially illegal act retroactively creates a legal right to engage in the act in the first place."[111] Accordingly, the Court's answer to Question Two was "No."[112] This made it unnecessary for the Court to answer Question Three, which asked whether Canadian domestic law would prevail over inconsistent international law, since both systems of law were consistent with each other on the issues raised.

P. THE *CLARITY ACT*

1) The Terms of the Legislation

Although the Supreme Court decision provided these important clarifications regarding the domestic and international legal framework governing secession, it also made plain that political leaders, and not the courts, have the responsibility to define the concepts of a clear majority and a clear question. In December 1999, the federal government responded to this invitation by introducing the *Clarity Act* into the House of Commons.[113] The legislation, which was enacted into law in June 2000, consists of three sections. Section 1 of the bill deals with the Supreme Court's requirement of a clear question, section 2 with the requirement of a clear majority, and section 3 with certain aspects of the secession negotiations.

With respect to the meaning of a clear question, within thirty days of a provincial government officially releasing a referendum question on secession, the House of Commons would be asked to express its opinion through a resolution as to whether the question is clear. In making that assessment, the House of Commons is instructed to consider "whether the question would result in a clear expression of the will of the population of a province on whether the province should

---

111 *Ibid.* at para. 146.

112 One unusual feature of the judgment is that, unlike its custom in all other previous Reference cases, the Court never clearly set out answers to the questions posed. The answer to Question Two as it is set out in the text is our own interpretation of the Court's answer, which is not expressly stated in the judgment. The Court's departure from previous practice in not directly answering the questions was apparently based on a concern that providing straightforward answers would be "misleading": *ibid.* at para. 31.

113 *Clarity Act*, above note 67.

cease to be a part of Canada and become an independent state."[114] This formulation is almost a direct quotation from the Supreme Court passages on this issue. The federal government is prohibited from entering into negotiations on secession if the House of Commons determines that a referendum question is not clear. The legislation also restricts the exercise of discretion by the House of Commons, by deeming certain questions to be unclear, such as a question that "merely focuses on a mandate to negotiate without soliciting a direct expression of the will of the population of that province on whether the province should cease to be part of Canada" or a question that "envisages other possibilities in addition to the secession of the province from Canada, such as economic or political arrangements with Canada, that obscure a direct expression of the will of the population of that province on whether the province should cease to be part of Canada."[115]

With respect to the requirement of a clear majority, section 2 of the *Clarity Act* requires the House of Commons to express its view, by resolution, on whether there has been a "clear expression of a will by a clear majority of the population of that province that the province cease to be part of Canada." The House is instructed to take a number of factors into account in forming that assessment, including the size of the majority of valid votes cast in favour of the secessionist option and the percentage of eligible voters voting in the referendum. The House is also required to take into account the views of other political actors, in a fashion similar to that outlined in relation to the determination of the clarity of the question. The federal government is prohibited from entering into

---

114 *Ibid*, s. 1(3). The House of Commons is also required to take into account the views of other political actors on the wording of the question, including all parties in the legislative assembly of the province whose government is proposing secession, the governments and legislatures of the other provinces, the Senate, and representatives of the Indigenous peoples of Canada, especially those in the province whose government is proposing the referendum (s. 1(5)).

115 *Ibid*, s. 1(4). There is no doubt that the 1995 referendum question, with its convoluted reference to an offer of partnership "within the scope of the bill respecting the future of Quebec and of the agreement signed on June 12, 1995" was confusing. It is not self-evident, however, that a referendum question that "envisages other possibilities in addition to the secession of the province from Canada, such as economic or political arrangements with Canada," would necessarily obscure the expression of the will of the population of the province on whether it should cease to be part of Canada. However, it is possible to interpret the *Clarity Act* as only deeming questions to be unclear where they refer to continuing economic or political arrangements with Canada in such a way as to obscure the will of the population that it wishes to secede. In this way, the requirements can be interpreted as being consistent with the requirements for clarity established by the Supreme Court.

negotiations on secession unless the House of Commons determines that there has been "a clear expression of a will by a clear majority of the population of that province that the province cease to be a part of Canada" (section 2(4)).

While section 2 of the *Clarity Act* is consistent with the Supreme Court's decision on the notion of a clear majority, it does not clarify the analysis offered by the Court. Section 2 simply refers to certain factors that must be considered by the House of Commons in determining whether the majority is clear. However, it does not specify the nature of the consideration that must be given to these various factors. Arguably, it would have been preferable for the government to enact a threshold that must be achieved in order to trigger secession negotiations. This would promote accountability and transparency, since it would allow citizens and political actors to know the basis on which the government of Canada will exercise its discretion in advance. It would also reduce the possible confusion and disorder that could result in the aftermath of a very close vote on secession.

Finally, section 3 of the Act specifies that secession would require a constitutional amendment, and that the negotiations for such an amendment would involve "at least the governments of all the provinces and the Government of Canada."[116] This reference to the involvement of the provinces can be traced directly to the Supreme Court's decision. Moreover, the use of the term "at least" indicates that other political actors may well have a right to play a direct role in the negotiations which, again, is consistent with the Court's reasoning. Section 3 also indicates certain matters which much be "addressed in negotiations [including] the division of assets and liabilities, any changes to the borders of the province, the rights, interests and territorial claims of the Aboriginal peoples of Canada, and the protection of minority rights." Significantly, while such matters must be "addressed in negotiations," they need not necessarily be addressed in the constitutional amendment itself. This is also in keeping with the Court's decision, which states that there are no predetermined outcomes on any of the matters that would be the subject of negotiations. Thus, while the issue of borders or the territorial claims of Indigenous peoples must be considered, they need not result in actual border changes. All that is required is that both parties be prepared to negotiate such matters in good faith.

---

116 Note the requirement that all the provinces be participants in the negotiations. While the federal government has refused to take a position on whether secession would require an amendment supported by all of the provinces or merely by seven provinces representing 50 percent of the total population of the ten provinces, the Act mandates the involvement of all the provinces in the negotiation process.

2) The Constitutional Validity of the *Clarity Act*

In the debate during the Parliamentary consideration of the *Clarity Act*, certain questions were raised as to its constitutional validity. The legislation can be supported as constitutionally valid on either of two alternative grounds. First, it may be argued that the *Clarity Act* is legislation in relation to the executive government of Canada and the House of Commons and is therefore validly enacted pursuant to Parliament's legislative authority under section 44 of the *Constitution Act, 1982*.[117] Second, it may be argued that the *Clarity Act* is legislation in relation to matters that do not come within any of the classes of subjects assigned to the exclusive jurisdiction of the provinces and is therefore validly enacted pursuant to Parliament's authority to enact laws for the Peace, Order, and Good Government of Canada under section 91 of the *Constitution Act, 1867*.[118]

Once the *vires* of the legislation is properly established, it becomes apparent that there is no intrusion into provincial jurisdiction. As discussed in Chapter 4, it is an elementary principle of constitutional law that actions taken by one government may incidentally affect or impact on the activities of another level of government. Such incidental effects are permitted as long as the pith and substance of the law, or its dominant purpose, is directed at a matter within the enacting body's jurisdiction.

The *Clarity Act* is directed at a matter within federal jurisdiction, namely, the circumstances in which the government of Canada should be permitted to negotiate the secession of a province. It is true that the legislation provides for the House of Commons to make a finding on the clarity of a referendum question to be posed by a provincial govern-

117 The legislation imposes certain legal constraints on the prerogative powers of the executive, namely, the circumstances under which the executive can enter into secession negotiations. Section 44 of the *Constitution Act, 1982* provides express authority for Parliament to enact legislation in relation to the Crown where the legislation is in relation to the constitutional position of the Crown, subject to the matters provided for under ss. 41 & 42. Entering into negotiations on secession does engage the constitutional obligations of the federal Crown (for the reasons outlined in the previous paragraph) and is not a matter provided for under ss. 41 & 42.

118 The Peace, Order, and Good Government (POGG) clause permits Parliament to enact legislation dealing with a national emergency. Moreover, Parliament need not wait until an emergency has actually occurred before legislating, but may take action to prevent an emergency or to establish procedures to deal with it before it actually arises. The attempted secession of a province may constitute a national emergency; thus, Parliament may be authorized under POGG to enact legislation to deal with secession.

ment to the population of a province. But, as the Supreme Court confirmed in the *Secession Reference*, the wording of such a question is a key consideration in determining whether the constitutional obligation to negotiate secession is engaged. The Supreme Court also stated that whether a referendum question is clear is a determination that must be made by political actors, as opposed to the courts. The government of Canada and the House of Commons would certainly be included within the class of political actors required to make such a determination. Nor does the legislation restrict the right or capacity of other political actors, such as the other provinces, from making their own determination as to the clarity of a referendum question. The concern of the statute is merely to establish certain preconditions that must be met before the government of Canada can be permitted to commence secession negotiations or to propose a constitutional amendment providing for secession.

An alternative criticism of the legislation, raised in the debate in the Senate of Canada, is that the statute is invalid since it is inconsistent with the constitutional principle of the indivisibility of Canada.[119] The indivisibility principle is said to be inherent in the preamble of the *Constitution Act, 1867*, which refers to the desire of certain provinces to be "federally united into One Dominion under the Crown . . . with a Constitution similar in principle to that of the United Kingdom." The simple answer to this objection is that Canada is legally divisible rather than indivisible and, therefore, the *Clarity Act* cannot be challenged on the basis that it recognizes the divisibility of Canadian territory.

Prior to 1982, the Westminster Parliament retained unlimited legal authority to amend the *BNA Act*, as was confirmed by the Supreme Court in the *Patriation Reference* in September of 1981.[120] Therefore, between 1867 and 1982, there was no legal or constitutional bar to the divisibility of Canada, since Canada could have been divided by an ordinary statute passed by the Westminster Parliament. The 1982 constitutional amendments were intended to confer complete and entire powers of self-government on Canadian political institutions. For example, it became possible for Canadian political institutions to abolish the institution of the monarchy within domestic Canadian law through

---

119 See in particular the speech of the Honourable Serge Joyal on Second Reading of Bill C-20, *Debates of the Senate*, 36th Parl., 2d Sess., (10 May 2000).

120 See *Re Resolution to Amend the Constitution*, [1981] 1 S.C.R. 753 at 805–7 [*Patriation Reference*] (rejecting the argument that the preamble to the *Constitution Act, 1867* restricted the power of the Canadian Parliament to pass resolutions seeking amendments or the power of the U.K. Parliament to amend the *BNA Act*).

constitutional amendment under section 41(a). There is no class of constitutional change that was withheld or ruled to be off-limits to Canadian political institutions, provided that the procedures identified in the *Constitution Act, 1982* were followed. Canada became fully self-governing in 1982. This includes the power to redefine Canada's territory through a constitutional amendment providing for the secession of a province.

One final matter that merits brief mention is the fact that the *Clarity Act* provides that the House of Commons alone determines whether a referendum question and the result of the referendum is clear. While the House is directed to take account of any formal statements or resolutions of the Senate on these matters, the House is not bound to act in accordance with the views of the Senate. When Bill C-20 reached the Senate, a number of senators expressed the view that the legislation was subject to challenge on the grounds that it was inconsistent with the bicameral nature of the federal Parliament.[121] The better view is that the Act does not offend the bicameral nature of Parliament. The Senate has never had a determining legal role in defining the circumstances in which the executive can commence constitutional negotiations. Therefore, the fact that the *Clarity Act* provides for such a role for the House of Commons but not the Senate does not offend or diminish the traditional prerogatives, powers, or privileges of the Senate. Indeed, the existing constitution provides the Senate with a mere suspensive veto over the enactment of constitutional amendments. To permit the Senate to prohibit the government from entering into constitutional negotiations on secession would grant the Upper House a determining role that was expressly denied of that body when the constitutional amending formula was drafted in 1982.

It would also seem to be entirely appropriate, as a matter of constitutional policy, that the House of Commons play the role assigned to it by the legislation. The House of Commons is the only legislative chamber elected by all Canadians. The government is politically responsible to the House. Assuming that the legislation states clearly the criteria that must be satisfied before secession negotiations can commence, there is much to be gained by providing for an open debate and determination by the elected members of the federal Parliament, rather than by the government alone, on the clarity of the question and the result.

---

121 See, for example, the speech of the Honourable Jerahmiel S. Grafstein on Second Reading of Bill C-20, *Debates of the Senate*, 36th Parl., 2d Sess, (25 May 2000).

FURTHER READINGS

BEAUDOIN, G.A., WITH P. THIBAULT, *La Constitution du Canada: Institutions, partage des pouvoirs, droits et libertés*, 3d ed. (Montreal: Wilson & Lafleur, 2004) c. 6

DAWSON, M., "Reflections on the Opinion of the Supreme Court of Canada in the *Quebec Secession Reference*" (1995) 11 N.J.C.L. 5

FINKELSTEIN, N., et al., "Does Quebec Have a Right to Secede at International Law?" (1995) 74 Can. Bar Rev. 225

HURLEY, J.R., *Amending Canada's Constitution: History, Processes, Problems and Prospects* (Ottawa: Supply and Services Canada, 1996)

MEEKISON, P., "The Amending Formula" (1983) 9 Queen's L.J. 99

MONAHAN, P.J., *Meech Lake: The Inside Story* (Toronto: University of Toronto Press, 1991)

NEWMAN, W.J., "Defining the 'Constitution of Canada' Since 1982: The Scope of the Legislative Powers of Constitutional Amendment under Sections 44 and 45 of the *Constitution Act, 1982*" (2003) 22 Sup. Ct. L. Rev. (2d) 423

———, *The Quebec Secession Reference: The Rule of Law and the Position of the Attorney General of Canada* (Toronto: York University Centre for Public Law and Public Policy, 1999)

PELLETIER, B., *La modification constitutionnelle au Canada* (Toronto: Carswell, 1996)

SCOTT, S.A., "Pussycat, Pussycat or Patriation and the New Constitutional Amendment Processes" (1982) 20 U.W.O. L. Rev. 247

———, "The Canadian Constitutional Amendment Process" (1982) 45 Law & Contemp. Probs. 249

PART FOUR

THE COURTS AND CANADIAN FEDERALISM

CHAPTER 7

THE COURTS AND CANADIAN FEDERALISM: FROM WATERTIGHT COMPARTMENTS TO SHARED RESPONSIBILITY

A. INTRODUCTION

Sir John A. Macdonald believed that the *Constitution Act, 1867*,[1] had been drafted to ensure that "'all conflict of jurisdiction' had been avoided" and that the courts would therefore assume a relatively minor role in the evolution of Canadian federalism.[2] His prediction proved to be wildly inaccurate. First, the language used in the *BNA Act*, although apparently clear to its drafters, turned out to be ambiguous and open-ended in practice. Second, and more significantly, the division of legislative responsibility reflected an era in which government played a modest and limited role. Within a matter of decades, the entire conception of the role of the state in Canada had changed, with governments being called on to intervene in areas of economic regulation and social policy that were simply unknown in 1867. The drafters of the *BNA Act* naturally did not address how these new roles and responsibilities would be shared between different levels of government.

It largely fell to the courts to structure a division of powers for Canada. While the courts rendered their decisions in accordance with the categories of legislative powers set out in sections 91 and 92 of the *BNA Act*, these categories merely provided a framework for decision making.

1 The *Constitution Act, 1867* (formerly, the *British North America Act, 1867* (U.K.), 30 & 31 Vict., c. 3).

2 Quoted in W.P.M. Kennedy, "The Interpretation of the *British North America Act*" (1943) 8 Cambridge L.J. 146 at 151.

Before 1949, the highest court in Canada was the Judicial Committee of the Privy Council (the JCPC or the Board). As Mallory has pointed out, in some respects, the JCPC was an ideal court of constitutional appeal.[3] Made up of British judges who were members of the House of Lords, the JCPC was clearly impartial and disinterested as between the federal and provincial governments in Canada. The Board was also well positioned to defend the liberty of individuals and the rule of law; law lords sitting in distant Whitehall were far removed from short-term political pressures in Canada. Despite these potential advantages, the Privy Council's record in the interpretation of the Canadian constitution is, at best, mixed and highly controversial. The clear intention of the *BNA Act* was to create a centralized federation. However, the JCPC interpreted the Act so as to allocate many of the most important areas of legislative jurisdiction to the provinces. Furthermore, the scheme of federalism created by the JCPC turned out to be unworkable in many respects. The twentieth century witnessed a dramatic expansion in the role of government, with the state assuming responsibilities in social and economic policy that were unheard of in 1867. Yet most of these new responsibilities were regarded by the Privy Council as matters for the exclusive jurisdiction of the provinces, which lacked the necessary financial resources to deal effectively with these new challenges. One of the largest challenges facing both levels of government in Canada since 1945 has been to devise mechanisms that will permit them to escape or to bypass the impractical constitutional framework created by the JCPC.

This chapter begins with an overview of the manner in which the JCPC interpreted the division of legislative powers in sections 91 and 92 of the *BNA Act* until 1949. We also explain how this body of jurisprudence contributed to a fiscal and constitutional crisis that emerged in the 1930s, which forced governments at both the federal and the provincial level to begin to search for new solutions. Finally, we trace the manner in which governments since 1949 have developed cooperative, intergovernmental mechanisms for coordinating shared jurisdiction.

---

3 See the discussion of the role of the JCPC in J.R. Mallory, *The Structure of Canadian Government*, 2d ed. (Toronto: Gage, 1984) at 377–81.

B. THE JCPC'S WATERTIGHT COMPARTMENTS VIEW

The JCPC conceived of its function (at least in its written judgments)[4] as strictly legal and apolitical. The law lords favoured doctrines and concepts that established "bright lines," that is, clear points of demarcation around and between the categories in sections 91 and 92. Such "categorical" reasoning avoided the appearance of judges assessing political considerations of the wisdom of legislation. Indeed, the JCPC reminded its readers on many occasions that it was for the legislature and not the courts to evaluate the wisdom of an enactment. For the JCPC, an open assessment of the relative importance of a particular statute, or of its necessity to the economic and political life of the nation, was anathema to the judicial function. The Board therefore attempted to fashion a series of tests that could be applied without reference to such considerations.

The JCPC proceeded on the assumption that the categories in sections 91 and 92 were mutually exclusive: the Canadian ship of state, in Lord Atkin's celebrated metaphor, retains the "watertight compartments which are an essential part of her original structure."[5] This meant that the categories in sections 91 and 92 should be interpreted so as to avoid, to the greatest extent possible, any overlap between them. The compartmental approach seemed to follow from the fact that the twenty-nine enumerated categories in section 91 and the sixteen enumerated categories in section 92 were each described as conferring "exclusive" legislative jurisdiction. This, in itself, might not have been a fatal interpretive move had it not been for a further doctrinal decision made by the JCPC in the first few years after Confederation.

---

4 A consistent refrain in the Privy Council judgments is that the Board is merely "interpreting" the *BNA Act* and that this function is purely legal rather than political. However, in a remarkable academic article written in 1899, Lord Haldane suggested that the function of an imperial judge "of the very first order" is to act as "a statesman as well as a jurist, to fill in the gaps which Parliament has deliberately left in the skeleton constitutions and laws that it has provided for the British Colonies." According to Lord Haldane, Parliament had taken the view that the constitutions for the colonies must be in large measure "unwritten, elastic, and capable of being silently developed and even altered as the Colony develops and alters." It fell to the judges of the Privy Council to ensure that the colonial constitutions were "altered" in order to fit changing circumstances, a task Lord Haldane described as one of "immense importance and difficulty": see Lord R.B. Haldane, "Lord Watson" (1899) 11 Juridical Rev. 278 at 279.

5 *Can. (A.G.) v. Ont. (A.G.)*, [1937] A.C. 326 at 354.

In what was arguably its single most important interpretive decision in terms of the *BNA Act*, the Board interpreted the terms "Property and Civil Rights" in section 92(13) in their broadest possible sense, as including any and all forms of legal rights possessed by persons within the province. The consequence of this broad interpretation was that the provinces were recognized as having authority to enact laws on virtually any subject, since *all* provincial laws would necessarily deal with civil rights in one form or another. The only real limit on the scope of section 92(13) was territorial: the province could only enact laws in relation to rights "in the Province." But as long as the subject matter of the law was found to be within the province, the legislation would be valid because it would be a law dealing with rights.[6]

If the provinces have exclusive power to enact laws dealing with property and civil rights, then, the JCPC reasoned, it must follow logically that Parliament lacked such power. But how could this be so, when most of the legislative powers of Parliament set out in section 91 would also inevitably affect rights? For example, any law regulating trade and commerce, which is recognized in section 91(2) as an "exclusive" power of Parliament, must surely also be a law in relation to property and civil rights. Similarly, any law enacted in relation to the "Peace, Order, and Good Government" (POGG) of Canada would also inevitably affect legal rights of persons within Canada. It would have been possible to develop doctrines of interpretation that permitted extensive overlap between federal and provincial laws. In some limited circumstances, the JCPC did develop doctrines favouring or permitting concurrency.[7] But the dominant approach adopted by the JCPC was to narrow or limit the categories in section 91—particularly the federal powers over trade and commerce and the POGG power—so they did not overlap with the subjects allocated to the provinces in section 92. In effect, the broader categories in section 91 were construed as being residual, in the sense that they could not encompass matters referred to in section 92.[8] The

---

6 Of course, as discussed previously in Chapter 4, it was also possible that the courts could find a provincial Act invalid on the ground that it was directed toward a matter specifically reserved to Parliament under s. 91. However, as indicated below, the JCPC tended to interpret the federal heads of authority under s. 91 very narrowly.

7 The most important of such doctrines was the "aspect" doctrine, under which federal and provincial laws dealing with a particular matter can both be valid, provided that they deal with different "aspects" of the matter in question: see *Hodge v. R.* (1883), 9 App. Cas. 117 (P.C.), discussed below.

8 The JCPC did not openly acknowledge that it had adopted this approach. In fact, in *Citizens' Insurance Co. v. Parsons* (1881), 7 App. Cas. 96 (P.C.) discussed below, at note 30, the JCPC asserted that the enumerated categories in s. 91

difficulty was that, owing to the virtually unlimited scope that had been given to the provincial power over property and civil rights, the JCPC truncated a number of the most important federal powers.

C. THE JCPC AND POGG

1) A Promising Beginning: The *Russell* Case and the Pith and Substance Doctrine

Given the extremely restrictive approach that the JCPC eventually adopted in relation to federal heads of power, it is somewhat ironic that the initial Canadian cases decided by the Board favoured a broad reading of federal powers. The Privy Council's first opinion on the scope of the POGG power reflects this early but short-lived trend. In the *Russell* case,[9] the issue before the Board was the validity of the *Canada Temperance Act*, a federal statute permitting local areas to prohibit the sale of intoxicating liquor. An individual charged with violating the Act argued that the statute was constitutionally invalid because it dealt with property and civil rights, a matter reserved to the provinces. The Privy Council rejected this argument, noting that the legislation was valid because it dealt with "an evil which is assumed to exist throughout the Dominion." The fact that liquor could be held as property did not prevent Parliament from restricting its use when this was deemed dangerous to public health or safety. According to Sir Montague Smith, Parliament could enact laws under the POGG power that incidentally affected property and civil rights as long as it did so for a valid purpose:

> Few, if any, laws could be made by Parliament for the peace, order and good government of Canada which did not in some incidental way affect property and civil rights; and it could not have been intended, when assuring to the provinces exclusive legislative authority on the subjects of property and civil rights, to exclude the Parliament from the exercise of this general power whenever any such incidental interference would result from it. The true nature and character of the legislation in the particular instance under discussion must

---

took precedence over the subjects in s. 92. At the same time, however, the JCPC narrowed the interpretation of the broader federal powers in s. 91. The effect of this approach was to make the categories in s. 92 dominant and those in s. 91 subsidiary for all practical purposes.

9 *Russell v. R.* (1882), 7 App. Cas. 829 (P.C.).

> always be determined, in order to ascertain the class of subject to which it really belongs.[10]

Thus, according to Montague Smith, in assessing the validity of legislation, it is necessary to determine the statute's "true nature and character." This true nature or character can only be ascertained by considering the underlying purpose or objective of the legislation. Because the object of the *Canada Temperance Act* was to preserve public health and safety, the law was valid, notwithstanding that it might incidentally touch on or deal with matters of property or civil rights. The decision in *Russell* seemed to open the door to considerable jurisdictional overlap between Parliament and the provinces.

Russell was significant because it represented the first attempt to articulate what came to be known as the pith and substance doctrine, discussed in Chapter 4. Under this doctrine, the court determines the pith and substance of a law by ascertaining its main or dominant feature. If a federal law is, in pith and substance, in relation to a federal head of power, then the law may have incidental effects on a provincial head of power without being rendered invalid (and *vice versa*). In other words, the pith and substance doctrine focuses on the purposes of the legislation, rather than its incidental effects.

The pith and substance doctrine opens the door to jurisdictional overlap precisely because it ignores the incidental effects of legislation in determining constitutional validity. In *Russell*, for example, the fact that the federal legislation also affected property rights was constitutionally irrelevant. As Montague Smith noted, if such incidental effects were regarded as the primary focus of the analysis, the federal POGG power would be rendered virtually nugatory since "[f]ew, if any, laws could be made by Parliament for the peace, order and good government of Canada which did not in some incidental way affect property and civil rights."[11] Montague Smith held that it could not have been intended that the POGG power should be stripped of all its significance or effect. The preferred approach was to permit Parliament to legislate on matters of national importance, even though such laws would also inevitably have incidental effects on property rights in the provinces.

2) The *Hodge* Case and the Aspect Doctrine

The *Russell* case did not decide or suggest that Parliament alone could regulate liquor. In fact, a close reading of the judgment indicates that

---

10 *Ibid.* at 839–40.

11 *Ibid.*

the validity of the *Canada Temperance Act* as federal legislation did *not* exclude provincial laws on the same subject. In the 1883 *Hodge* case,[12] the Privy Council upheld an Ontario statute regulating the sale of liquor. According to Sir Barnes Peacock, "subjects which in one aspect and for one purpose fall within sect. 92, may in another aspect and for another purpose fall within sect. 91."[13] Thus, while it was true that Parliament could enact temperance legislation to deal with federal aspects of the problem, the provinces could enact legislation dealing with its local aspects. According to the Board, the provincial legislation in the *Hodge* case was "confined in its operation to municipalities in the province of Ontario, and is entirely local in its character and operation."[14] Moreover, the provincial regulations did not in any way interfere with federal legislation on the same subject. It was therefore valid legislation in relation to the powers conferred on the provinces under sections 92(8), (13), and (16) of the *BNA Act*.

The aspect doctrine, like the related pith and substance doctrine, represents a powerful tool for upholding the validity of legislation passed by both levels of government. The aspect doctrine essentially asks whether Parliament or the provinces have a sufficient interest in a particular social or economic problem such that they should be permitted to regulate it. As the *Russell* and *Hodge* cases demonstrate, it may be possible that *both* the federal *and* the provincial governments have sufficiently important interests at stake for each of them to legislate. Most significant social and economic problems are multifaceted and have both local and national impact. Moreover, by framing the problem in this manner, the judiciary will most likely tend to defer to the judgment of the political branches. The judiciary is ill-suited to make an assessment of whether a particular social or economic problem is one of national as opposed to local significance. The aspect doctrine inexorably pulls the judiciary in the direction of upholding the validity of legislation enacted by both Parliament and the provinces.

The problem with the aspect doctrine, from the perspective of the JCPC, was that it seemed to embroil the judges in political decision making. The aspect doctrine seemed to ask judges to review the conclusions of Parliament and the provincial legislatures as to whether there were sufficiently important national or local aspects to a given social or economic problem. It is hardly surprising that the Privy Council subsequently backed away from its early endorsement of the aspect doctrine, arguing that the principle was to be applied only in the most

12 Above note 7.

13 *Ibid.* at 130.

14 *Ibid.*

exceptional circumstances. In its place, the JCPC developed formalistic, bright-line tests that enabled the judiciary to assess the validity of federal laws through reference to apparently objective legal criteria.

3) POGG as a Residual Power

Lord Watson's judgment in the *Local Prohibition Reference* in 1896[15] was the first watershed in the attempt by the Privy Council to narrow the scope of federal POGG power. Until this point, the precise relationship between POGG and the enumerated heads of power in section 91 had not been clearly settled. On one view, POGG constituted the general grant of power to Parliament, and the enumerated heads were illustrative only. The *Russell* case seemed to support this broad reading of POGG. But a competing, narrower interpretation gave primacy to the enumerated powers in both sections 91 and 92, and relegated POGG to a purely residuary position. On this view, POGG was applicable to matters that did not fall within any of the classes of subjects in sections 91 or 92.

In the *Local Prohibition Reference*, Lord Watson clearly opted for the narrower view, making a clear distinction between POGG and the enumerated categories in section 91. Whereas Parliament's exercise of its enumerated powers could "occasionally and incidentally, involve legislation upon matters which are *prima facie* committed exclusively to the provincial legislatures by s. 92," a different rule had to be applied in the case of POGG. In legislating under POGG, Parliament "has no authority to encroach upon any class of subjects which is exclusively assigned to provincial legislatures by s. 92." Moreover, POGG ought to be "strictly confined to such matters as are unquestionably of Canadian interest and importance, and ought not to trench upon provincial legislation with respect to any of the classes of subjects enumerated in s. 92." Lord Watson acknowledged that it was possible that certain matters "in their origin local and provincial, might attain such dimensions as to affect the body politic of the Dominion," and in such instances Parliament could rely upon POGG. At the same time, he observed that "great caution" must be observed in applying this principle.[16]

The *Local Prohibition Reference* was also significant because it held that the pith and substance and aspect doctrines could not be applied to support legislation enacted under POGG. Although Lord Watson did not make this conclusion explicit, he stated that federal laws enacted under POGG could not "encroach upon" or "incidentally affect" matters under

15 *Ont. (A.G.) v. Can. (A.G.)*, [1896] A.C. 348 (P.C.) [*Local Prohibition Reference*].
16 *Ibid.*

section 92. Only laws enacted under the enumerated classes in section 91 could have incidental effects on matters in section 92. We have already noted that the Privy Council had interpreted the provincial power over property and civil rights in section 92(13) broadly. Given this broad interpretation, virtually any law enacted under POGG would have some incidental effects on matters of property and civil rights in the province. The result was that, after the *Local Prohibition Reference*, there would be very few circumstances in which POGG could be relied upon. Of course, this point had been made by Montague Smith in *Russell*, where he had observed that "it could not have been intended, when assuring to the provinces exclusive legislative authority on the subjects of property and civil rights, to exclude the Parliament from the exercise of this general power."[17] In the *Local Prohibition Reference*, Lord Watson was decidedly lukewarm toward *Russell*, noting that it had "relieved their Lordships from the difficult duty of considering whether the *Canada Temperance Act* of 1886 relates to the peace, order, and good government of Canada" and that *Russell* "must be accepted as an authority to the extent to which it goes."[18]

While the *Local Prohibition Reference* significantly limited the scope of the POGG power, Lord Watson did hold out the possibility of its application in cases that were "unquestionably of Canadian interest and importance." But how was the identification of matters of national importance a workable legal test for a court to apply? Moreover, if Parliament concluded that a matter was unquestionably of Canadian interest and importance, on what basis were the law lords in England to disagree? Thus, even as Lord Watson had reduced POGG to a purely residual power that would almost never come into operation, a test based on the importance of a subject was certain to make the strict constructionists in the Privy Council uncomfortable.

4) POGG as an Emergency Power

In a series of now-infamous cases decided in the 1920s, Lord Haldane picked up where Lord Watson had left off and narrowed the scope of POGG even further.[19] In the *Board of Commerce* case, decided in 1922, Lord Haldane suggested that POGG might come into operation in "special circumstances, such as those of a great war"; however, in normal

17 Above note 9 at 839.

18 *Local Prohibition Reference*, above note 15 at 362.

19 See *Reference Re Board of Commerce Act, 1919 (Can.)*, [1922] 1 A.C. 191 (P.C.) [*Board of Commerce*]; *Toronto Electric Commissioners v. Snider*, [1925] A.C. 396 (P.C.) [*Snider*].

circumstances, the provinces have "quasi-sovereign authority" with respect to "the regulation and restriction of . . . civil rights." He also attempted to restrict the application of the aspect doctrine, noting that "[t]his is a principle which, although recognized in earlier decisions, such as that of *Russell v. The Queen* . . . has always been applied with reluctance, and its recognition as relevant can be justified only after scrutiny sufficient to render it clear that the circumstances are abnormal." Lord Haldane effectively marginalized the aspect doctrine so that, like the POGG power itself, it could not be used to uphold federal legislation in "normal circumstances."[20]

In the *Snider* case, decided in 1925, Lord Haldane developed this emergency theory further, stating that the POGG power might be relied upon in "cases arising out of some extraordinary peril to the national life of Canada, as a whole, such as the cases arising out of a war, where legislation is required of an order that passes beyond the heads of exclusive Provincial competency." Lord Haldane even suggested that the *Russell* case was consistent with his novel theory regarding the scope of the POGG power. The Board in *Russell* must have assumed, he asserted, that "the evil of intemperance at that time amounted in Canada to one so great and so general that at least for the period it was a menace to the national life of Canada so serious and pressing that the National Parliament was called on to intervene to protect the nation from disaster."[21]

Before 1914, the Canadian legal establishment was extremely deferential to the decisions of the JCPC. But the patently unreasonable interpretations of federal powers advanced by Lord Haldane in the 1920s provoked a torrent of criticism from previously deferential Canadian jurists.[22] From the Privy Council's vantage point, however, the emergency interpretation of POGG had at least one attraction. It constituted a clear bright line that made the task of delineating the scope of POGG a relatively straightforward matter. In effect, apart from altogether exceptional circumstances such as war or famine, POGG was a dead letter and could simply be ignored. The division of powers between federal and provincial levels of government could be determined almost entirely through reference to the enumerated heads of power in sections 91 and 92 alone.

The emergency theory of POGG set the stage for a series of important decisions that struck down much of the Canadian "new deal" legis-

---

20 *Board of Commerce*, above note 19 at 200.

21 *Snider*, above note 19 at 412.

22 For example, H.E. Smith, commenting on the *Snider* case, *ibid.*, argued that "I do not think it is going too far to say that this result is the precise opposite of that which our fathers hoped and endeavoured to attain": see "The Residue of Power in Canada" (1926) 4 Can. Bar Rev. 432 at 434.

lation[23] enacted by the Conservative government of R.B. Bennett in 1934–35 in response to the Great Depression. Bennett's government put forward a significant legislative package, including legislation regulating hours of work, providing administrative arrangements for specifying a minimum wage, establishing unemployment insurance for industrial workers, protecting farmers from their creditors, and regulating the marketing of agricultural products.[24] After Bennett's Conservatives were defeated by the Liberals under Mackenzie King in the 1935 general election, King referred the constitutional validity of these statutes to the Supreme Court, which was fairly evenly divided. A number of the statutes were ruled unconstitutional (including *The Natural Products Marketing Act, 1934*); others were upheld (including *The Farmers' Creditors Arrangements Act, 1934*); and the Court divided three to three on the validity of the statutes regulating hours of work and dealing with the minimum wage. On further appeal to the Privy Council, the Board ruled that all of these statutes were unconstitutional. The Board's discussion of the POGG power in each instance was brief and perfunctory. The Privy Council relied on the emergency doctrine propounded by Haldane, and held that the economic crisis posed by the Depression fell far short of the "exceptional conditions" necessary in order to "override the normal distribution of powers."[25] Certain important social and economic circumstances—including the fact that 33 percent of non-agricultural workers were unemployed, that national output had fallen 30 percent, that personal incomes had fallen almost 50 percent, and that prices had fallen 18 percent—were not mentioned in any of the Privy Council's judgments. "It is only necessary," said Lord Atkin in one case, "to call attention to the phrases in the various cases . . . [which] it is to be hoped, form the *locus classicus* of the law on this point, and preclude further disputes."[26]

The Privy Council's new deal decisions exacerbated the fiscal crisis facing the Canadian state in the 1930s. The Depression had caused a steep drop in the revenue base of all governments, but the impact on the provinces and municipalities was particularly severe. In fact, many

23 The "new deal" terminology, although not used by Canadian Prime Minister R.B. Bennett at the time, has since been applied to the package he proposed in 1934, since his reforms were broadly similar to U.S. President Roosevelt's "new deal" legislation.

24 The statutes were, respectively, the *Limitation of Hours of Work Act*, S.C. 1935, c. 63; the *Minimum Wages Act*, S.C. 1935, c. 44; the *Employment and Social Insurance Act*, S.C. 1935, c. 38; the *Farmers' Creditors Arrangements Act, 1934*, S.C. 1934, c. 53; and the *Natural Products Marketing Act, 1934*, S.C. 1934, c. 57.

25 *Can. (A.G.) v. Ont. (A.G.)*, above note 5 at 353 (Lord Atkin).

26 *Ibid*.

municipalities across the country were facing bankruptcy as a result of the collapse in real estate prices and the resulting reduction of the property tax base. Now the Privy Council had decreed that the only level of government with the fiscal resources to mount an effective response was constitutionally barred from intervening directly. The insistence that these matters fell within the exclusive jurisdiction of the provinces placed the entire country in a constitutional straitjacket, since the provinces lacked the fiscal resources needed to take effective action.

It was obvious to all political leaders in Canada that fundamental changes in the fiscal and constitutional framework of the country were required for the Canadian state to respond to the challenges posed by the Depression. In 1938, the federal government initiated discussions with the provinces over a constitutional amendment transferring exclusive jurisdiction over legislation on unemployment insurance from the provinces to Parliament. The provinces unanimously agreed to the transfer (although Quebec had been initially reluctant) and the amendment to the *BNA Act* was enacted by Westminster in 1940.

However, piecemeal reforms were clearly insufficient to deal with the crisis facing the Canadian state. In 1937, the federal government appointed the Rowell-Sirois Commission to undertake "a re-examination of the economic and financial basis of Confederation and of the distribution of legislative powers in the light of the economic and social developments of the last seventy years."[27] Its 1940 report proved highly influential in pointing governments toward a new paradigm for federal–provincial relations, which remains dominant today.

The formalistic and dysfunctional Privy Council decisions on the new deal legislation strengthened the resolve of Canadians who had been pressing for the abolition of civil appeals to the Privy Council. Ironically, just prior to the abolition of appeals in 1949, the Privy Council seemed to develop second thoughts regarding the wisdom of its previous jurisprudence on the POGG power. In the *Ontario (Attorney General) v. Canada Temperance Federation* case,[28] Viscount Simon expressly disapproved of the emergency doctrine. He stated that the "true test" in respect of POGG is whether federal legislation deals with a matter that "goes beyond local or provincial concern or interests and must from its inherent nature be the concern of the Dominion as a whole." Viscount Simon also attempted to revive the application of the aspect doctrine in respect of POGG, noting that federal legislation in

27 Canada, *Report of the Royal Commission on Dominion-Provincial Relations* (Ottawa: King's Printer, 1940) Book 1 at 9.

28 *Ontario (Attorney General) v. Canada Temperance Federation*, [1946] A.C. 193 (P.C.) [*Canada Temperance Federation*].

relation to a matter of inherent national concern could be valid even if "it may in another aspect touch on matters specially reserved to the provincial legislatures."[29] Viscount Simon's national concern doctrine featured prominently in the subsequent jurisprudence of the Supreme Court of Canada after 1949, as discussed in the next chapter. But this doctrine represented a partial retreat only, one that failed to resolve the constitutional imbalance that the restrictive jurisprudence of the previous seventy-five years had created. The remedy was found not in formal constitutional change or in decisions of the courts, but in new intergovernmental arrangements that enabled the federal and provincial governments to achieve joint and coordinated action to deal with multifaceted societal problems.

D. THE JCPC AND TRADE AND COMMERCE

The JCPC's jurisprudence on the scope of the trade and commerce power in section 91(2) followed the same pattern as the POGG jurisprudence. The leading case on section 91(2) was *Citizens' Insurance Co. v. Parsons*,[30] a case involving a challenge to an Ontario statute regulating the terms of insurance policies. Sir Montague Smith, who delivered judgment on behalf of the Board, began by asking whether the Act fell within any of the classes of subjects enumerated in section 92. Citing the historically broad meaning of the words "Property and Civil Rights" in section 92(13), he concluded that this provincial class of subjects must include the regulation of contracts of insurance. But this consideration was not sufficient to dispose of the case because the regulation of contracts could also be characterized as the "Regulation of Trade and Commerce," a class of subjects assigned exclusively to Parliament in section 91(2). Indeed, Sir Montague Smith noted: "The words 'regulation of trade and commerce,' in their unlimited sense are sufficiently wide, if uncontrolled by the context and other parts of the Act, to include every regulation of trade ranging from political arrangements in regard to trade with foreign governments, requiring the sanction of parliament, down to minute rules for regulating particular trades."[31]

The Board held that such a conflict between sections 92(13) and 91(2) could not have been intended; the two sections must therefore be read together in order to avoid any apparent overlap. The result of

29 *Ibid.* at 205.
30 Above note 8.
31 *Ibid.* at 112.

this process of mutual modification was that the words "Regulation of Trade and Commerce" could not be given their full, literal meaning: "Construing therefore the words 'regulation of trade and commerce' by the various aids to their interpretation above suggested, they would include political arrangements in regard to trade requiring the sanction of parliament, regulation of trade in matters of interprovincial concern, and it may be that they would include general regulation of trade affecting the whole dominion."[32]

This passage remains the starting point for the judicial analysis of the federal trade and commerce power. It has been interpreted as establishing two distinct branches. Under the first branch, the dividing line between trade and commerce and property and civil rights is based on a distinction between interprovincial and export trade on the one hand and local trade on the other. The provinces have power to regulate trade within the province, while Parliament has power to regulate trade between provinces or with foreign states. The first branch exemplifies a categorical approach, in which jurisdiction is allocated on the basis of a bright line separating interprovincial from intraprovincial trade.

The second branch—"general regulation of trade affecting the whole dominion"—is less clearly defined. The phrase "trade affecting the whole dominion" seems to invite an assessment of the relative importance of an economic activity to the national economy, as well as whether such activity should be regulated by Parliament as opposed to the provinces. This is an open-textured, functional analysis that is quite different from the analysis mandated by the first branch of the test.

Given the Privy Council's general preference for categorical reasoning as opposed to balancing of interests, it is hardly surprising that it would have preferred the first branch of *Parsons* to the second. Indeed, the Board's discomfort with the second branch is reflected in *Parsons* itself. Montague Smith merely suggested that it "may be" that Parliament possesses a general trade power; his Lordship refrained from expressing an authoritative opinion on the point. In the dozens of cases in which the Privy Council considered the trade and commerce power, it essentially ignored the second branch entirely and analyzed the issues exclusively in terms of the first branch. Moreover, the Privy Council applied the first branch in a highly formalistic and technical manner. The validity of a federal trade statute depended on whether the statute applied directly to transactions, persons, or activities that were located within a single province. If so, the federal statute would automatically be ruled invalid, no matter how close the connection between the

32 *Ibid.* at 113.

transaction, person, or activity regulated and interprovincial or international trade and commerce.

The 1916 decision in *Canada (A.G.) v. Alberta (A.G.)* is a good example of the Privy Council's approach to the trade and commerce power.[33] The case concerned federal authority to regulate the insurance business through a system of licensing. The evidence indicated that the insurance business had expanded enormously in the period following Confederation and, by 1912, it was a nationwide industry generating millions of dollars in revenues. The insurance business had surely become a matter of general concern throughout the country and was therefore a candidate for federal regulation on the basis of the second branch of *Parsons*. Indeed, this was precisely the line of argument adopted in the Supreme Court of Canada. Davies J. noted that "[t]he ramifications of such business extend to every city, town, village and hamlet of the Dominion." As the bankruptcy of one of these nationwide enterprises would be nothing short of national disaster, Davies J. concluded that the national interest demanded recognition of federal authority in this area.[34]

But Lord Haldane in the Privy Council apparently considered the national importance of the insurance industry to be constitutionally irrelevant. For Haldane, the case could be resolved on the simple and straightforward basis that the trade and commerce power does not authorize regulation of a "particular trade in which Canadians would otherwise be free to engage in the provinces."[35] The Act was not restricted to interprovincial contracts of insurance but purported to apply to insurance companies whose business was conducted entirely within particular provinces. Since all local transactions or businesses are subject to exclusive provincial regulation, the federal legislation was *ultra vires*.

The irony of the Privy Council's reasoning in *Alberta (A.G.)* was that the drafters of the *BNA Act* had expressly refused to limit federal power over trade and commerce to matters of interprovincial trade, as had been done in the U.S. constitution. The interpretation of section 91(2) adopted by the Privy Council was therefore precisely the opposite of that intended. Once again, this result stemmed from the Privy Council's preference for a bright-line test that avoided the need to consider the relative importance of a particular trade for the economy as a whole.

33 [1916] 1 A.C. 588 (P.C.) [*Alberta (A.G.)*].

34 *Reference Re Insurance Act 1910 (Canada) ss. 4 & 70* (1913), 48 S.C.R. 260 at 274.

35 *Alberta (A.G.)*, above note 33 at 596.

E. THE WATERTIGHT COMPARTMENTS SPRING LEAKS: THE MODERN ERA

The Supreme Court of Canada's gradual departure from the early decisions of the Privy Council is traced in detail in subsequent chapters. As these chapters make plain, since 1949 the Supreme Court of Canada has followed the broad doctrinal outlines established by the Board. However, the Court has tended to expand the scope of federal legislative jurisdiction in certain limited but significant ways.

The point to be made here is more general. Canadian federalism in the first decade of the twenty-first century is radically different from that in 1949. The largest difference is the obvious growth in the size and scope of government. But a related difference is the fact that both levels of government are active in most of the new social and economic policy fields that have emerged over the past fifty years. In contemporary Canada, the watertight compartments idealized by the Privy Council have been supplanted by shared and divided jurisdiction. Wherever government is active—whether it involves stimulating the economy to overcome shortfalls in aggregate demand, regulating markets to protect consumers, imposing environmental controls, or retraining workers—both levels of government have a legitimate role and a range of policy instruments at their disposal.[36] In fact, one of the largest challenges facing Canadian federalism is how to manage a situation in which the activities of one level of government overlap with those of the other. The question posed in the present chapter is how we arrived at this point. What are the forces that have driven the evolution of Canadian federalism in the direction of shared jurisdiction and functional concurrency?

While there are many factors that have driven this evolution, the judiciary has played a relatively minor and subsidiary role. To be sure, the judiciary has facilitated the growth of shared jurisdiction between governments. In addition to permitting a modest expansion of federal legislative jurisdiction, for example, the Supreme Court has also given greater prominence to certain interpretive doctrines—particularly the pith and substance and the aspect doctrines—that tend to favour overlapping or concurrent jurisdiction. However, the major impetus for

36 See, generally, G. Stevenson, "The Division of Powers in Canada" and J.D. Whyte, "Constitutional Aspects of Economic Development Policy," both in R. Simeon, ed., *Division of Powers and Public Policy* (Toronto: University of Toronto Press, 1985) at 71 and 29, respectively.

the evolution of Canadian federalism has come from other factors and sources.

1) Contemporary Problems Are Untidy and Expensive

Chief among these factors shaping the evolution of Canadian federalism has been a change in the nature of the problems faced by government. Contemporary public policy issues are multifaceted and complex as well as untidy, in the sense that they cannot be dealt with effectively in isolation from other issues. The policies pursued by one level of government have had a significant impact on policies of other levels. This overlap led to a growing recognition that no single level of government can deal comprehensively with the major social and economic problems facing contemporary government. To take one obvious example, the problem of harm to the environment is at one and the same time local, national, and international. Activities that are environmentally harmful on a local or regional level will, if left unchecked, eventually cause harm on a national or even international scale. Therefore, regulating activities that harm the environment cannot be the sole responsibility of a single level of government. Moreover, there is a need to coordinate the activities of the different regulators in the field because the actions (or inactions) of one level of government will necessarily have an impact on the policies of others.

A related factor that has promoted overlapping and functional concurrency is that many of the problems facing government today require the expenditure of large sums of money. Put simply, the modern welfare state is expensive, with total government outlays now equalling approximately 40 percent of the total annual output of the economy. In this context, the ability to raise revenues becomes far more important than whether a matter happens to fall under federal or provincial jurisdiction. This fiscal reality has favoured the expansion of the role of the federal government, since it has the greatest capacity to raise and expend funds. The federal government has used its spending power — the ability to spend money and to attach conditions to the receipt of such money — to intervene in areas that are notionally under the exclusive control of the provinces.[37]

---

37 The courts have confirmed that both Parliament and the provincial legislatures may authorize the expenditure of money in areas outside of their legislative jurisdiction. See *Reference Re Canada Assistance Plan*, [1991] 2 S.C.R. 525; *Lovelace v. Ontario*, [2000] 1 S.C.R. 950.

2) The Declining Importance of the Division of Powers in Sections 91 and 92

Today, the categories in the *Constitution Act, 1867* omit reference to many of the most important functions of modern government. While the *Constitution Act, 1867* sets out an extensive list of powers for each level of government, these lists were drafted at a time when the role of government was much more limited, as discussed above. The lists of powers in the *Constitution Act, 1867* do not reflect the complexity or the expanse of the contemporary roles of government.

An illustration can be found by considering one attempt to rewrite the division of powers in the early 1990s. In 1991, the Constitutional Committee of the Quebec Liberal Party published a report calling for a wholesale devolution of powers from Parliament to the provinces. The Allaire Report (named after its chair, Jean Allaire) set out a list of twenty-two powers, which, according to its authors, should be under the full sovereignty of the province of Quebec. Significantly, over two-thirds of these powers are not listed in the *Constitution Act, 1867*. Of the twenty-two exclusive Quebec powers identified in the report, only municipal affairs, education, natural resources, agriculture, industry and commerce, and public security are even mentioned in the Act. The other sixteen powers, including the environment, regional development, research and development, culture, health, social affairs, and housing, are not referred to explicitly in either section 91 or section 92. They are, instead, categories that reflect our contemporary understanding of what government does, which have no counterpart in the *Constitution Act, 1867*.

How is jurisdiction over these matters allocated between the federal and the provincial governments? The short answer is that, on a *de facto* basis, both levels of government are active in virtually all these areas. The provinces are active in twenty-one of the twenty-two fields of jurisdiction identified by Allaire. In fact, the only area that is not currently under provincial authority—unemployment insurance—would be subject to exclusive provincial jurisdiction but for a constitutional amendment in 1940.[38] The federal government, likewise, has also been active in virtually all the twenty-two policy areas identified in the Allaire Report. In most of these areas—including culture, housing, education, recreation and sports, health, tourism, regional development, and the environment—federal involvement is based on the exercise of the spending power.

38 As noted earlier, unemployment insurance was not mentioned in the *Constitution Act, 1867*, but the Privy Council determined in the 1930s that it fell within provincial responsibility for "Property and Civil Rights."

In this sense, the phrase "division of powers" to describe sections 91 and 92 is somewhat misleading, since the *Constitution Act, 1867* does not formally divide many of the most important functions of modern government. Provincial ministries of health, for example, consume by far the largest proportion of all provincial tax dollars. Yet the division of powers set out in the *Constitution Act, 1867* makes no explicit reference to legislative responsibility for health care.[39] This open-endedness has permitted a high degree of flexibility in the evolution of the division of powers; as new areas of government responsibility emerge, the absence of a specific allocation of responsibility in the field will typically permit intervention by either level of government.[40]

The fact that the categories in the *Constitution Act, 1867* do not mention many of the important contemporary aspects of public policy has permitted a high degree of functional concurrency. In this sense, it is wrong for governments in Canada to complain that they lack "jurisdiction." With relatively few exceptions (i.e., the judicially imposed limitations on federal regulation over the economy), "jurisdiction" as such is not a problem under the Canadian constitution. Either level of government has sufficient constitutional authority to intervene in virtually any policy area that is deemed to be of contemporary significance. The suggestion that the division of powers needs to be comprehensively rewritten in order to "transfer jurisdiction" either to the provinces or to the federal government is simply unfounded. Indeed, it is precisely because of the flexibility inherent in the current division of powers that the country is able to operate under a set of categories drafted nearly 150 years ago. As new social, political, or economic problems have arisen, both levels of government have been able to adapt and respond to new challenges. This is one of the great virtues of the *Constitution Act, 1867* and a key explanation for its durability.

3) A Return to Watertight Compartments?

An emerging critique of this structure is that such a permissive system is inefficient—that it leads to too much overlapping of jurisdiction, too

---

39 Note, however, that s. 92(7) does assign to the provinces exclusive responsibility over "Establishment, Maintenance and Management of Hospitals," which comprise the largest single component of expenditures on health care.

40 For example, the federal Parliament can enact legislation in relation to health matters pursuant to its criminal law power. See *RJR-MacDonald Inc. v. Can. (A.G.)*, [1995] 3 S.C.R. 199, describing "health" as a matter not specifically allocated to either federal or provincial levels of government and therefore permitting both levels to legislate.

much government, and is too costly to the taxpayer. From time to time it has been argued that the Canadian federal system is too expensive and that costs could be reduced by constitutionally limiting the role of the federal government. This could be accomplished by reducing the fields of overlapping jurisdiction and restoring some form of compartmentalization to the formal division of powers, largely by eliminating any federal presence in a wide range of policy areas. In our view, however, such a comprehensive revision to the division of powers is neither necessary nor desirable.

Attempting to restore a set of watertight compartments would inevitably fail, since contemporary problems are inherently multifaceted and demand coordinated action from all levels of government. One need only consider those rare areas where our division of powers has been interpreted to preclude such coordination, such as in the Supreme Court's decision that a national securities regulator is *ultra vires* the federal Parliament, to appreciate the limits of the rigid federalism of the Privy Council.[41] The great virtue of the existing division of powers is its permissive and flexible character. The challenge is to develop institutions and mechanisms that can manage concurrency more effectively rather than to devote efforts to rewriting the categories in the 1867 Act.

FURTHER READINGS

BROWNE, G.P., *The Judicial Committee and the British North America Act* (Toronto: University of Toronto Press, 1967)

CAIRNS, A.C., "The Judicial Committee and Its Critics" (1971) 4 C.J.P.S. 301

LASKIN, B., "Peace, Order, and Good Government Re-examined" (1947) 25 Can. Bar Rev. 1054

STEVENSON, G., "The Division of Powers in Canada: Evolution and Structure", in R. Simeon, ed., *The Division of Powers and Public Policy* (Toronto: University of Toronto Press, 1985)

WHYTE, J.D., "Constitutional Aspects of Economic Development Policy," in R. Simeon, ed., *The Division of Powers and Public Policy* (Toronto: University of Toronto Press, 1985)

41 *Reference re Securities Act*, [2011] 3 S.C.R. 837.

CHAPTER 8

PEACE, ORDER, AND GOOD GOVERNMENT

A. SCOPE OF THE PEACE, ORDER, AND GOOD GOVERNMENT (POGG) POWER

The opening words of section 91 of the *Constitution Act, 1867*,[1] taken literally, appear to represent a very broad grant of legislative authority to the Parliament of Canada. Parliament is authorized to enact laws "for the Peace, Order, and Good Government of Canada, in relation to all Matters not coming within the Classes of Subjects by this Act assigned exclusively to the Legislatures of the Provinces." Similar language had been employed in earlier British statutes establishing colonial governments in British North America to signify a general grant of law-making authority on any matter of public importance.[2] Furthermore, section 91 goes on to provide that the enumerated subjects in section 91 are merely illustrative of the POGG power and should not "restrict the Generality of Peace, Order, and Good Government." However, as noted in Chapter 7, the Judicial Committee of the Privy Council (JCPC) adopted a narrow interpretation of the POGG power, construing it strictly as a residual power that came into operation only with respect to matters not falling within the enumerated subjects in sections 91 or 92. Furthermore, the JCPC

1 The *Constitution Act, 1867* (formerly, the *British North America Act, 1867*) (U.K.), 30 & 31 Vict., c. 3.

2 See, for example, the language employed in the *Constitutional Act, 1791* (U.K.), 31 Geo. III, c. 31, and the *Union Act, 1840* (U.K.), 3 & 4 Vict., c. 35, discussed in Chapter 2.

interpreted the provincial power over property and civil rights in section 92(13) as all-encompassing. Since matters included within section 92 were automatically subtracted from the purely residual POGG power, POGG was rarely invoked as a basis for upholding federal laws by the JCPC. By the 1920s, POGG had been reduced to essentially an emergency power, available only in cases of war or other similar national crises.

The Supreme Court of Canada has broadened the scope of the POGG power somewhat. It is now recognized that there are three distinct branches of the POGG power, which can be relied on to support federal legislation. The first is the emergency power—the category that had been established by the JCPC. The second is the gap or residual branch of POGG—the power to legislate in relation to matters not included within any of the enumerated classes of subjects in sections 91 or 92. The third is the national concern branch—the power to legislate in relation to distinct matters of inherent national concern.

In addition, it is arguable that there is a fourth branch of POGG, which permits Parliament to legislate in relation to matters of interprovincial concern or significance. This branch, although not yet identified as a separate source of authority under POGG, is arguably implicit in decisions of the Supreme Court. As we argue below, the power of Parliament to deal with matters of interprovincial concern or significance under POGG is sufficiently distinct from the first three branches so as to merit recognition as a separate and independent source of federal authority.

B. THE EMERGENCY BRANCH

The leading case on the scope of the emergency branch of POGG is *Reference Re Anti-Inflation Act, 1975 (Canada).*[3] The *Anti-Inflation Reference* arose out of the decision by the federal government in the fall of 1975 to impose a comprehensive program of controls on wages, prices, and profits. The program applied to the federal public sector, to provincial government employees where the province had opted in to the scheme, and to large private-sector firms.[4] If firms or employees fell within the *Anti-Inflation Act*, all of their activities—including transactions or activities occurring entirely within a single province—were sub-

3 [1976] 2 S.C.R. 373 [*Anti-Inflation Reference*].

4 The *Anti-Inflation Act*, S.C. 1974–75–76, c. 75, applied to firms with more than five hundred employees, construction firms with more than twenty employees, and professionals.

ject to the limits established by the legislation. The regulation of such intraprovincial activities or transactions had always been regarded by the courts as falling within exclusive provincial jurisdiction, pursuant to the property and civil rights power in section 92(13). A number of public sector unions launched a constitutional challenge to the legislation on the basis that it regulated matters coming within the exclusive jurisdiction of the provinces. The provinces themselves did not initiate a court challenge, since they all supported the program. To resolve any doubts about the validity of the legislation, the federal government decided in March 1976 to refer the matter to the Supreme Court.

The federal government's main constitutional argument was that inflation was a problem of inherent national concern and, therefore, the legislation could be justified under the national dimensions branch of the POGG power. A majority of the Court rejected this argument, as discussed later in this chapter. However, the Court held by a seven to two majority that the legislation could be supported on the basis of the emergency branch of the POGG power. Laskin C.J., who wrote the leading judgment on this aspect of the case, appeared to assume that the burden was on the parties challenging the legislation to establish that inflation did *not* constitute a national emergency. Moreover, Laskin C.J. indicated that, in order to overturn the legislation, it would be necessary to find that Parliament did not have a "rational basis" for regarding inflation as a national emergency. He also gave little weight to a brief before the Court supported by thirty-nine of the country's leading economists denying the existence of an emergency. Laskin C.J. held that the fact that inflation had exceeded 10 percent in 1974 and 1975 supported the conclusion that Parliament had a rational basis for deciding there was a national emergency. Laskin C.J. also noted that the legislation was temporary—it automatically ceased to have effect after three years unless extended by a Cabinet order approved by the Senate and the House of Commons. This limitation supported the validity of the Act as an emergency measure.

One of the controversial aspects of Laskin C.J.'s decision in *Anti-Inflation Reference* was that Parliament did not appear to rely on the emergency power in enacting the legislation. Speeches made by federal ministers in the House of Commons seemed to indicate that Parliament was enacting the legislation under the national concern branch, rather than on the basis of a national emergency. Beetz J., dissenting, relied on these statements and held that Parliament could not rely on the emergency power unless it clearly declared the existence of an emergency. However, Laskin C.J. pointed to the preamble to the Act, which stated that "the containment and reduction of inflation has become a matter of *serious* national concern" and that "to accomplish such containment and reduction of inflation it is *necessary* to restrain profit margins, prices, dividends and compensation."[5] In Laskin C.J.'s view, it was not necessary for Parliament to use the word "emergency." He acknowledged that the absence of any preamble at all in the legislation would have "weaken[ed] the assertion of crisis conditions," but, in his view, the preamble in the *Anti-Inflation Act* was "sufficiently indicative that Parliament was introducing a far-reaching program prompted by what in its view was a serious national condition."[6]

Some commentators argued that the effect of Laskin C.J.'s judgment in the *Anti-Inflation Reference* is to permit Parliament to invoke the emergency power at will.[7] However, these concerns are arguably overstated. It is true that the Court indicated that it would adopt a deferential attitude in assessing whether a national emergency exists. However, such deference is surely appropriate given the limited ability of the Court to determine the existence of an emergency situation requiring legislative intervention. It is also relevant that in the several decades that have passed since the Court's decision in *Anti-Inflation Reference*, there has not been a single instance in which Parliament's finding of an emergency has been contested before the courts. Clearly, the fears of commentators who believed that the federal Parliament would be able to extend its jurisdiction through questionable and controversial reliance on the emergency power have not been realized.

In 1988, the federal government enacted the *Emergencies Act*[8] in place of the *War Measures Act*. The *Emergencies Act* defines a "national emergency" as an urgent and critical situation of a temporary nature that

(1) seriously endangers the lives, health or safety of Canadians and is of such proportions or nature as to exceed the capacity or authority of a province to deal with it, or
(2) seriously threatens the ability of the Government of Canada to preserve the sovereignty, security and territorial integrity of Canada.

The Act establishes four different categories of national emergencies[9] and provides in each case that, in order to exercise any of the pow-

5 *Anti-Inflation Reference*, above note 3 at 422, Laskin C.J. [emphasis in original].

6 *Ibid.*

7 See, for example, P. Patenaude, "The *Anti-Inflation* Case: The Shutters Are Closed but the Back Door Is Wide Open" (1977) 15 Osgoode Hall L.J. 397; and C. Tennenhouse, "The Emergency Doctrine and the Anti-Inflation Case: Prying Pandora's Box" (1977) 8 Man L.J. 445.

8 R.S.C. 1985 (4th Supp.), c. 22.

9 The categories of emergencies established under the *Emergencies Act* are public welfare, public order, international, and war.

ers provided for under the Act, the government must first declare the existence of an emergency. Such a declaration may be made where the government believes "on reasonable grounds" that an emergency exists, and the declaration must be laid before Parliament for debate and confirmation. The declaration must also be preceded by prior consultation with the province(s) concerned and, where the direct effects of the emergency are confined to a single province, the provincial Cabinet must agree that it is unable to deal with the situation.

While Parliament's constitutional authority to respond to emergencies cannot be defined by or made to conform to the terms of an ordinary statute, the definitions of emergency in the *Emergencies Act* would be relevant in future constitutional litigation involving the use of the emergency branch of the POGG power. The Act establishes various classes of emergencies and contains relatively specific definitions of each category. These definitions establish boundaries around the types of situations that would justify Parliament in invoking the emergency branch of POGG. In other words, the definitions in the Act would tend to serve as a check on the unbounded or indiscriminate reliance on the emergency branch of POGG. If Parliament enacted "emergency" legislation that could not be justified under any of the defined categories under the *Emergencies Act*, this would be a relevant (though not a conclusive) consideration in a constitutional challenge before the courts. As discussed above, the *Emergencies Act* requires the government to explicitly declare the existence of an emergency before the powers established under the Act can be invoked. This requirement amounts to an acceptance of Beetz J.'s judgment in *Anti-Inflation Reference* that the federal government should only invoke its emergency powers when it expressly and openly declares an emergency. It would seem difficult for the government to support legislation under the emergency branch of POGG in the absence of a declaration as contemplated by the *Emergencies Act*.

One potential situation that might give rise to a declaration of emergency is the attempted secession by a province from Canada. An attempted secession may amount to a "public order emergency," which the *Emergencies Act* defines as "an emergency that arises from threats to the security of Canada and that is so serious as to be a national emergency" (section 16). Where the federal Cabinet has issued a declaration of a public order emergency, it may issue orders in council dealing with a variety of matters, including prohibiting public assemblies that might be reasonably expected to lead to a breach of the peace, prohibiting travel within Canada, and requiring any person to render essential services for dealing with the emergency. But the powers in the Act would not cover the full range of matters that would arise in the event of an attempted secession, and it would undoubtedly be necessary for Parliament to enact additional legislation dealing with a wide variety of other matters. For example, Gordon Robertson has argued for the enactment of "contingency legislation" to deal with issues such as the process for achieving sovereignty, the legal ineffectiveness of a unilateral declaration of independence, and the status of Canadian political institutions in the event of a secession.[10] In 2000, Parliament enacted the *Clarity Act*, which deals with certain of the matters discussed by Robertson.[11] The legislation is sustainable on the basis of the emergency branch of POGG, as discussed in Chapter 6.

The *Anti-Inflation Reference* held that in the context of an emergency, the division of powers between Parliament and the legislatures set out in sections 91 and 92 is effectively suspended for the duration of the emergency. Thus, once the emergency branch of POGG comes into play, Parliament can enact legislation on any of the subjects in sections 91 or 92, as long as it is reasonably necessary to deal with the circumstances of the emergency. It has also been settled that Parliament can enact legislation to pre-empt or avoid an emergency, and does not have to wait until the emergency has actually commenced before taking action. In this sense, contingency legislation of the kind proposed by Robertson and now enacted by Parliament through the *Clarity Act*, can still be sustained on the basis of the emergency branch of POGG.[12]

C. POGG AS A PURELY RESIDUAL POWER

The residual branch of POGG comes into play in relation to matters that fall outside the enumerated classes in section 92 and yet cannot be characterized as falling within any of the enumerated subjects in section 91. Since the distribution of legislative powers between Parliament and the provincial legislatures is exhaustive, matters that do not come within any of the enumerated classes of subjects in sections 91 or 92 must, by definition, fall within the opening words of section 91. For

---

10 See G. Robertson, "Contingency Legislation for a Quebec Referendum" (1996) 4 Canada Watch 93.

11 The "*Clarity Act*" is the short form for *An Act to give effect to the requirement for clarity as set out in the opinion of the Supreme Court of Canada in the Quebec Secession Reference*, S.C. 2000, c. 26, which is discussed in Chapter 6.

12 As discussed in Chapter 6, the *Clarity Act* can also be upheld on the basis that it is legislation in relation to the executive government of Canada and the House of Commons, enacted on the basis of s. 44 of the *Constitution Act, 1982*, being Schedule B to the *Canada Act 1982* (U.K.), 1982, c. 11.

example, all of the legislative powers in section 92 are limited to matters "within the province." This means that provinces do not have any authority to directly regulate matters on lands or waters that fall within Canadian territory and yet are not within the boundaries of a particular province. Therefore, legislation regulating matters within such Canadian territory would necessarily fall within Parliament's jurisdiction. At the same time, there may not be any provision of the constitution explicitly conferring authority on Parliament to legislate in relation to certain Canadian lands or waters. If this is correct, then according to the residuary theory, legislation dealing with these matters must be within Parliament's competence on the basis of POGG. This was precisely the analysis applied by the Supreme Court of Canada in *Reference Re Seabed and Subsoil of Continental Shelf Offshore Newfoundland*,[13] a case concerning whether the seabed off the coast of Newfoundland fell within the province of Newfoundland. Having determined that the seabed was outside the province, the Court disposed of the remaining issues in the case in a single paragraph, noting that legislative jurisdiction over the seabed fell with the Parliament's POGG power "in its residual capacity."

A similar analysis was employed by the Supreme Court in *Jones v. New Brunswick (A.G.)*.[14] The Court upheld the federal *Official Languages Act*, which dealt with the status of the English and the French languages in Parliament and in executive institutions. The regulation of the use and status of the English and the French languages within federal institutions could not fall within provincial jurisdiction, since the provinces cannot regulate the manner in which Parliament or the federal executive conducts its affairs. However, there was nothing in the enumerated subjects in section 91 that expressly conferred such legislative authority on Parliament. Therefore, the Court concluded that the power to enact legislation establishing official languages within federal institutions must be allocated to Parliament through the operation of POGG.

The residual branch of POGG may also be engaged in cases concerning matters addressed in an incomplete fashion in either the federal or the provincial lists of powers. For example, section 92(11) grants the provincial legislatures power to enact laws in relation to the incorporation of companies "with provincial objects." Because section 92(11) is framed in this manner, the incorporation of companies with objects extending beyond a province must necessarily be within Parliament's

13 [1984] 1 S.C.R. 86.
14 [1975] 2 S.C.R. 182.

jurisdiction. However, there is no reference to a federal power to enact company legislation. The courts filled this gap in the distribution of powers by holding that Parliament has the authority to enact company legislation pursuant to the residuary branch of the POGG power.[15]

In general, however, the residuary branch of POGG has rarely been relied upon as the exclusive basis for upholding federal statutes. The courts have construed the provincial power over property and civil rights very broadly. This broad scope of section 92(13) means that there are very few cases in which a matter will fall within federal jurisdiction under the residuary branch of POGG. In the vast majority of cases, sustaining federal authority over a matter—whether on the basis of POGG or of the enumerated heads of section 91—will require that the competing provincial claim based on property or civil rights must be superseded. Since the purely residual branch of POGG cannot achieve this result, it will be engaged only rarely.

D. THE NATIONAL CONCERN BRANCH

1) Introduction

As noted in Chapter 7, in the 1920s, the Privy Council under Lord Haldane had characterized POGG as an emergency power that was applicable only in response to exceptional national crises such as war. However, in the *Canada Temperance Federation* case in 1946, the Privy Council expressly rejected Lord Haldane's narrow emergency theory of POGG and held that POGG authorized Parliament to deal with matters of inherent national concern:

> [T]he true test must be found in the real subject matter of the legislation: if it is such that it goes beyond local or provincial concern or interests and must from its inherent nature be the concern of the Dominion as a whole . . . [as, for example, in the *Aeronautics* case

---

15 The courts have not always applied the logic of this gap analysis. For example, s. 132 of the *Constitution Act, 1867* grants Parliament the power to implement treaties signed by Britain on behalf of Canada. Section 132 does not deal with the implementation of treaties signed by Canada on its own behalf. In the *Labour Conventions* case (*Can. (A.G.) v. Ont. (A.G.)*, [1937] A.C. 326 (P.C.)), discussed in Chapter 9, Sections D(2) & (3), the courts refused to hold that this gap in the distribution of powers meant that the power to implement Canadian treaties fell within POGG; instead, the Privy Council held that the power to implement such treaties was divided between Parliament and the provinces, depending on the subject matter of the Treaty.

> and the *Radio* case], then it will fall within the competence of the Dominion Parliament as a matter affecting the peace, order and good government of Canada, though it may in another aspect touch on matters specially reserved to the provincial legislatures.[16]

The *Canada Temperance Federation* case provides that matters which must "from . . . [their] inherent nature be the concern of the Dominion as a whole" fall under the federal Parliament's POGG power. But what criteria or indicia are used to identify inherently national matters? Cases in the following decades applied the national concern doctrine without clearly setting out the applicable criteria.

In *Johannesson v. West St. Paul (Rural Municipality)*,[17] the Supreme Court of Canada determined that the regulation of aeronautics was a matter of inherent national concern. In reaching this conclusion, the Court noted the tremendous growth in interprovincial and international air travel since the end of the First World War. The Court also noted that the extension of air links between the settled parts of the country and the north was essential to the opening up of the country and the development of the resources of the nation. According to Locke J., "[i]t requires merely a statement of these well recognized facts to demonstrate that the field of aeronautics is one which concerns the country as a whole. It is an activity which . . . must from its inherent nature be a concern of the Dominion as a whole."[18] While these observations were certainly correct, the Court—as well as the Privy Council before it—had on many previous occasions rejected arguments in favour of federal jurisdiction based on the national importance of an activity or industry. The Court in *Johannesson* made no attempt to reconcile the decision with the earlier jurisprudence.

Nor was the scope of the national concern doctrine clarified in subsequent cases. The Court did not apply the national concern doctrine again until 1966, in *Munro v. Canada (National Capital Commission)*.[19] *Munro* concerned the validity of the *National Capital Act*, federal legislation that created a National Capital Commission with zoning and expropriation powers in the Ottawa–Hull region. Zoning and expropriation powers are traditionally regarded as matters falling within provincial jurisdiction over property and civil rights. It was argued that the federal legislation was *ultra vires*, since it purported to confer these powers on a federal agency. The Supreme Court rejected this

16 *Ont. (A.G.). v. Canada Temperance Federation*, [1946] A.C. 193 at 205 (P.C.) [*Canada Temperance Federation*].

17 [1952] 1 S.C.R. 292 [*Johannesson*].

18 *Ibid.* at 326–27.

19 [1966] S.C.R. 663 [*Munro*].

argument and upheld the Act, placing particular emphasis on the purposes underlying the creation of the national capital region. According to section 10 of the *National Capital Act*, the purpose of the National Capital Commission was to ensure that the "nature and character of the seat of the Government of Canada may be in accordance with its national significance." The Court asked whether this was a matter that could possibly fall under provincial jurisdiction under section 92 of the *Constitution Act, 1867*. The answer, according to the Court, was virtually self-evident: only the national government could possibly undertake responsibility for ensuring that the capital region was developed "in accordance with its national significance." The provinces, either individually or collectively, could not undertake this national responsibility, since provinces are necessarily limited to provincial concerns and interests. "I find it difficult," held Cartwright J., "to suggest a subject matter of legislation which more clearly goes beyond local or provincial interests and is the concern of Canada as a whole than the development, conservation and improvement of the National Capital Region in accordance with a coherent plan in order that the nature and character of the seat of the Government of Canada may be in accordance with its national significance."[20]

A similar analysis was applied in *Reference Re Offshore Mineral Rights (British Columbia)*,[21] decided a year later. The case concerned the ownership and control of the minerals in the seabed under Canadian waters off the British Columbia coast. In holding in favour of the federal government, the Supreme Court relied in part on the residuary branch of POGG, emphasizing the fact that the territorial sea fell outside the boundaries of any particular province. Ownership rights must, therefore, be accorded to Canada, which had become a sovereign state under international law in the early twentieth century and succeeded to rights previously held by Britain. However, the Court also relied on the national concern branch of POGG, stating that "[t]he mineral resources of the lands underlying the territorial sea are of concern to Canada as a whole and go beyond local or provincial concern or interests."[22]

The difficulty with these cases was twofold. First, they failed to elaborate the criteria that should be used to identify matters of inherent national concern. Second, the decisions are difficult to reconcile with cases in which matters of significance to the country as a whole had nevertheless been found to be subject to exclusive provincial jurisdiction under the property and civil rights power. As such, the precise

20 *Ibid*. at 671.

21 [1967] S.C.R. 792 [*Offshore Mineral Rights*].

22 *Ibid*. at 817.

scope and significance of the national concern branch remained somewhat uncertain.

2) The Beetz–Lederman Thesis

W.R. Lederman wrote a seminal article that appeared in the *Canadian Bar Review* in 1975.[23] Lederman propounded a theory of the "spirit and philosophy of our Canadian system for the division of legislative powers." This spirit and philosophy, which Lederman traced through numerous court decisions, was based on the idea that governments should be granted jurisdiction over limited and discrete subject areas. In Lederman's view, there was a need "to keep the power-conferring phrases of our federal-provincial division of powers at meaningful levels of specifics and particulars."[24] Overly general or all-encompassing categories were inappropriate as a basis for allocating jurisdiction, since they would grant sweeping powers to a single level of government and could "lead to constitutional chaos or to the end of federalism."[25] Lederman offered a number of examples of the kinds of sweeping categories he regarded as inappropriate as a basis for dividing jurisdiction in a federal state. One such category was culture: Lederman noted that today "everything is cultural," including literature, automobiles, tools, computers, home comforts, lifestyle, and the Boeing 747.[26] If culture were recognized as an area of exclusive jurisdiction of either the provinces or the federal government, it would effectively spell the end of the division of powers. Lederman suggested that all-pervasive categories such as environmental pollution, economic growth, quality of life, language, and culture "cannot be allowed to dominate our distribution-of-powers system from within." Instead, these general categories should be regarded as "outside the system . . . [and] subdivided into appropriate parts so that necessary legislative action can be taken by some combination of both federal and provincial statutes."[27]

Lederman's theory of the spirit and philosophy of Canadian federalism was soon embraced by the Supreme Court. In the *Anti-Inflation Reference*,[28] Beetz J., dissenting, cited Lederman's analysis in holding

23 W.R. Lederman, "Unity and Diversity in Canadian Federalism: Ideals and Methods of Moderation" (1975) 53 Can. Bar Rev. 597.

24 *Ibid.*

25 *Ibid.* at 615.

26 *Ibid.* at 611, quoting from an article by G. Cormier published in *La Presse* (9 November 1973).

27 *Ibid.* at 616.

28 *Anti-Inflation Reference*, above note 3.

that "inflation" was too diffuse a subject matter to serve as a basis for federal legislative jurisdiction. According to Beetz J., the national concern branch of POGG could be invoked only in cases where "a new matter was not an aggregate but had a degree of unity that made it indivisible, an identity which made it distinct from provincial matters and a sufficient consistence to retain the bounds of form."[29] Beetz J. also held that the scale of impact on provincial powers of recognition of a new matter of national concern was relevant; the courts must be careful to preserve the "equilibrium of the Constitution" and would not recognize a subject matter as one of inherent national concern where the effect would be to smother or render nugatory existing and well-established provincial powers.

Although Beetz J. dissented in the result in the *Anti-Inflation Reference*, his reasoning on the national concern branch of POGG was endorsed by a majority of the Court.[30] The Beetz–Lederman analysis has since been accepted and applied by the Supreme Court in a number of subsequent cases, most notably in *R. v. Crown Zellerbach Canada Ltd.*[31]

In *Crown Zellerbach*, the Supreme Court held that marine pollution was a single matter of national concern. Le Dain J., for the majority, set out the following four propositions that were "firmly established" by the earlier cases:

- the national concern doctrine is separate and distinct from the national emergency doctrine of the peace, order, and good government power;
- the national concern doctrine applies both to new matters which did not exist at the time of Confederation as well as to matters which, although originally matters under provincial jurisdiction, have since become matters of national concern;
- to qualify as a matter of national concern, a matter must have "a singleness, distinctiveness and indivisibility that clearly distinguishes it from matters of provincial concern and a scale of impact on provincial jurisdiction that is reconcilable with the fundamental distribution of legislative power under the Constitution"; and

---

29 *Ibid.* at 458.

30 Ritchie J., who wrote for himself and two others, concurred with Beetz J.'s analysis of the national concern branch of POGG, even though Ritchie J. agreed with Laskin C.J. that the legislation before the Court could be upheld on the basis of Parliament's emergency powers.

31 [1988] 1 S.C.R. 401 [*Crown Zellerbach*]. See also: *R. v. Hydro-Québec*, [1997] 3 S.C.R. 213 at para. 154.

- it is relevant to consider what would be the effect on extraprovincial interests of a failure to deal effectively with the control or regulation of the intraprovincial aspects of the matter.

The first of these propositions simply notes the existence of the national concern doctrine as a separate branch of POGG. However, the second, third, and fourth propositions attempt to clarify points that had emerged in previous cases, and each merit a detailed consideration.

3) Newness

Le Dain J.'s second proposition raises the question: is the "newness" of a matter relevant in assessing whether it is of national concern? Earlier cases had suggested that the national concern branch was particularly applicable to new matters which had not been contemplated as the subject of government regulation in 1867. For example, in the *Anti-Inflation Reference*, Beetz J. relied on the fact that inflation was "a very ancient phenomenon" in holding that legislation directed at the control of inflation could not be justified on the basis of the national concern doctrine. In the 1979 *Hauser*[32] case, on the other hand, Pigeon J. held that the federal *Narcotics Control Act* could be upheld on the basis of the national concern branch because it was legislation aimed at a "genuinely new problem which did not exist at the time of Confederation."[33]

Subsequent commentators, including Hogg and Lysyk, have criticized this reasoning. Hogg has argued that "newness is irrelevant and unhelpful in this context."[34] Le Dain J.'s second proposition in *Crown Zellerbach* clearly indicates that the national concern doctrine can apply both to new as well as to old matters. It is therefore clearly established that newness is not a necessary element in order to justify the application of the national concern doctrine.[35]

---

32 *R. v. Hauser*, [1979] 1 S.C.R. 984 [*Hauser*].

33 Note, however, that in *R. v. Malmo-Levine*, [2003] 3 S.C.R. 571 at para. 70 [*Malmo-Levine*], the Supreme Court disagreed with the conclusion in *Hauser* that the *Narcotics Control Act* was justified under a "newness" test. However, it was not necessary for the Court to decide whether the legislation could be justified under the POGG power, since the relevant provision was upheld on the basis of the federal criminal law power.

34 See P.W. Hogg, *Constitutional Law of Canada*, 5th ed., loose-leaf (Toronto: Carswell, 2009) at 17.3(d). See also K. Lysyk, "Constitutional Reform and the Introductory Clause of Section 91: Residual and Emergency Law-Making Authority" (1979) 57 Can. Bar Rev. 531.

35 In *Malmo-Levine*, above note 33, the Court rejected the proposition that the *Narcotics Control Act* could be upheld on the basis of POGG as a "new" matter. However, the Court indicated that this did not foreclose the possibility that the legislation

On the other hand, Le Dain J. does not go so far as to suggest that newness is entirely irrelevant to the scope of the national concern branch of POGG. The dissenting judgment of La Forest J. in *Crown Zellerbach* also seems to hold that the claim for federal authority is stronger in relation to new matters than it is in relation to old or established matters.[36] While it is true in a purely logical sense that newness alone does not make a matter of national concern, newness is related to another consideration that features prominently in the cases. This related consideration is what Beetz J. in the *Anti-Inflation Reference* termed the "scale upon which these new matters enabled Parliament to touch on provincial matters."[37] In purely practical terms, if a subject has only recently emerged into public debate, it is unlikely that the provinces will have a firmly entrenched claim to jurisdiction over it. Thus, placing such a matter under federal authority will not intrude unduly onto areas of established provincial jurisdiction, nor will it upset the existing equilibrium of the constitution. Thus, the courts had little difficulty in placing matters such as radio,[38] aeronautics,[39] and nuclear energy[40] under federal control pursuant to the national concern branch of POGG. In each instance, the novelty of the subject matter ensured that Parliament could occupy the field without unduly interfering with or diminishing the scope of provincial legislative powers. Accordingly, while the national concern branch of POGG applies to both new and old matters, newness is a relevant consideration; federal authority is more likely to be sustained in relation to novel matters where the provinces have not previously had a regulatory presence.

4) Distinctiveness

The third proposition in *Crown Zellerbach* is that a matter must have a "singleness, distinctiveness and indivisibility" that clearly distinguishes it from matters of provincial concern in order to fall under the national concern branch of POGG. This reasoning was applied by the Court in *Friends of the Oldman River Society v. Canada (Minister of Transport)*.[41] In this case, it was argued that the provinces had exclusive jurisdiction over certain aspects of the environment and that a federal environ-

---

could be upheld as a matter of "national concern," and left that issue open (since the legislation was valid as criminal law).

36 *Crown Zellerbach*, above note 31 at 458.

37 *Anti-Inflation Reference*, above note 3 at 458.

38 *Reference Re Regulation & Control of Radio Communication in Canada*, [1932] A.C. 304 (P.C.).

39 See *Johannesson*, above note 17.

40 *Ontario Hydro v. Ont. (Labour Relations Board)*, [1993] 3 S.C.R. 327 [*Ontario Hydro*].

41 [1992] 1 S.C.R. 3.

mental assessment scheme was therefore *ultra vires* or inapplicable to provincial projects. La Forest J. rejected this argument, noting that the environment was an inappropriate basis for dividing legislative jurisdiction. The reason, according to La Forest J., was that the environment was an amorphous and all-encompassing category that lacked the necessary definition to serve as a constitutional category under sections 91 or 92 of the *Constitution Act, 1867*: the environment "could never be treated as a constitutional unit under one order of government in any constitution that claimed to be federal, because no system in which one government was so powerful would be federal."[42] Accordingly, the environment was not an independent matter of legislation under the constitution but was an aggregate of matters. For constitutional purposes, this meant that either level of government could pass laws with environmental purposes or effects. In the result, the Supreme Court upheld the right of the federal government to apply the environmental guidelines to the Oldman River dam project, while recognizing that the project was also subject to provincial regulation.

The Supreme Court has recognized that subjects such as aeronautics, radio, nuclear energy, marine pollution, and the national capital all have the required distinctiveness and indivisibility to satisfy this test. What seems to be required is that federal legislation be aimed at a matter that has defined boundaries, so that recognizing this matter as being subject to POGG will not unduly interfere with or negate existing provincial regulatory powers.

5) The Provincial Inability Test

The fourth proposition established by Le Dain J. has sometimes been described as a "provincial inability test." This label is somewhat misleading, since the test actually focuses on the effects in other provinces of a *failure* by one province—as opposed to the *inability* of that province—to deal effectively with the control or regulation of a matter.

One important question is whether the provincial inability test is a requirement that must be met before the national concern branch can apply, or whether it is merely a *factor* that might be taken into account by the courts in determining the scope of federal authority. Le Dain J. in *Crown Zellerbach* suggested that the provincial inability test is merely "one of the indicia for determining whether a matter has that character of singleness or indivisibility required to bring it within the

---

42 *Ibid.* at 63–64, quoting D. Gibson, "Constitutional Jurisdiction over Environmental Management in Canada" (1973) 23 U.T.L.J. 54 at 85.

national concern doctrine."[43] This would suggest that the provincial inability test is not a necessary condition for the national concern branch of POGG.

This conclusion is supported by earlier cases concerning the national concern branch of POGG. For example, in the *Munro* and *Offshore Minerals* cases, the Court first asked whether the purpose or subject matter of the federal statute fell within the catalogue of provincial powers. In both cases, the Court found that the statutes in question dealt with matters which could not possibly fall under provincial jurisdiction. In *Munro*, this was because the purpose of the legislation was necessarily national in scope; in the *Offshore Mineral Rights* case, the land in question fell outside of provincial boundaries and thus could not be regulated provincially. Having found in both instances that the matters in question fell outside the categories in section 92, the Court analyzed the nature of the matter before it to determine whether it was of national scope or significance. In both instances, the answer to this second question was "yes". In *Munro*, the Court was dealing with the seat of the national government and, in *Offshore Mineral Rights*, with ownership over resources that did not belong to any particular province. The scope led the Court in both cases to conclude that these matters must necessarily fall under the federal POGG power as matters of inherent national concern.

It is important to note that the Court's conclusion in these cases did not depend on any argument about provincial inability or the harm that would flow from a lack of provincial action or cooperation. In *Munro*, the issue was the ability of the federal government to create a National Capital Commission with effective powers; but the justification for creating the commission was not the avoidance of harm that would flow from lack of provincial cooperation. Provincial cooperation, or lack of it, was beside the point. *Only* the national government could ensure the development of the capital region in accordance with its national significance. Therefore, the legislation establishing the commission must necessarily be enacted by the national government. Similarly, in *Offshore Mineral Rights*, there was no question of any harm that might have resulted from the absence of federal regulation. The rationale was simply that the lands in question were beyond provincial boundaries and thus must necessarily fall under federal ownership and control, since these federal powers are designed to promote common values and national identity. In effect, federal legislation deals with Canadians as

---

43 *Crown Zellerbach*, above note 31 at 434.

citizens of the country as a whole, rather than as residents of any particular province.

Some commentators have expressed concerns that the majority decision in *Crown Zellerbach* would lead to undue expansion of federal jurisdiction on the basis of the national concern branch of POGG. In fact, after *Crown Zellerbach*, the Supreme Court has applied the national concern branch of POGG in a very cautious manner. For example, in the *Ontario Hydro* case,[44] the Supreme Court, by a four to three majority, relied on the national concern branch of POGG to uphold exclusive federal jurisdiction over labour relations at Ontario Hydro's nuclear generating stations. Previous lower court decisions had found that the regulation of atomic energy constituted a matter of inherent national concern,[45] and this was accepted by all seven members of the Court in *Ontario Hydro*. However, the Court divided on whether the federal jurisdiction over nuclear energy could justify exclusive federal authority over labour relations at nuclear generating stations. La Forest J., speaking for three of the four members of the majority,[46] noted that the whole purpose of exclusive federal jurisdiction over nuclear energy plants would be frustrated if Parliament could not govern the standards and conditions of employment of individuals who actually operate the plants. He also noted that the courts had earlier determined that the regulation of labour relations was an integral part of exclusive federal jurisdiction over interprovincial works and undertakings, pursuant to sections 92(10)(a)–(c) of the *Constitution Act, 1867*. The three Ontario members of the Court dissented from this view,[47] holding that labour relations at nuclear generating plants are not part of a "single matter" of atomic energy. The division of the Court in the apparently straightforward case is indicative of the extremely cautious manner in which the Court has approached the national concern branch of POGG.[48]

---

44 Above note 40.

45 See, for example, *Pronto Uranium Mines Ltd. v. Ontario (Labour Relations Board)*, [1956] O.R. 862 (H.C.J.).

46 *Ontario Hydro*, above note 40. L'Heureux-Dubé and Gonthier JJ. concurred with La Forest J., while Lamer C.J. wrote separate concurring reasons.

47 *Ibid*. Iacobucci J. wrote dissenting reasons with which Sopinka and Cory JJ. concurred.

48 Note that in *R. v. Hydro-Quebec, et al*., [1997] 3 S.C.R. 213, the federal government sought to uphold certain provisions of the *Canadian Environmental Protection Act*, dealing with the regulation of toxic substances on the basis of the national concern branch of POGG. The majority of the Court (La Forest, L'Heureux-Dubé, Gonthier, Cory, and McLachlin JJ.) upheld the provisions on the basis of the criminal law power and did not consider POGG. However, Lamer C.J. and Iacobucci J., with whom Sopinka and Major JJ. concurred, found that the legis-

E. MATTERS OF INTERPROVINCIAL CONCERN OR SIGNIFICANCE

In addition to the three branches of POGG described above, certain Supreme Court cases suggest that there is a fourth ground on which legislation might be upheld under the POGG power. This fourth branch involves the regulation of matters which have interprovincial impact or effects and which cannot be regulated on the basis of any of the enumerated powers in section 91 of the *Constitution Act, 1867*. One example of such a matter is polluting activity taking place in one province, which has effects in other provinces. In *Crown Zellerbach*, Le Dain J. simply noted in passing that it was conceded that Parliament would have authority to regulate polluting activity having extraprovincial effects. But Le Dain J. did not elaborate on the precise basis for Parliament's legislative authority in this regard. The dissenting judgment of La Forest J., however, dealt with this point in more detail. La Forest J. noted that the federal POGG power, combined with the criminal law power, gave Parliament "very wide scope to control ocean pollution." La Forest J. suggested that the POGG power gave Parliament the authority to control pollution with extraprovincial effects, and this would include the power to regulate activity causing such pollution at its source:

> The power above described [POGG] can be complemented by provisions made pursuant to the criminal law power. . . . While it would not be proper for me to enter into the validity of the provisions of the *Clean Air Act* . . . which were upheld in *Re Canada Metal Co. and the Queen*, . . . those provisions do indicate that a combination of the general federal legislative power and the criminal power could go a long way towards prohibiting the pollution of internal waters as well as those in territorial waters and the high seas.[49]

---

lation could not be justified on the basis of the criminal law power. They went on to find that the environmental provisions at issue lacked the singleness and distinctiveness necessary to be supportable under the national concern branch of POGG; they also held that the provisions did not satisfy the provincial inability test, since the provinces could have enacted similar regulations on a local basis. Indeed, the legislation itself contained an equivalency provision, pursuant to which federal regulation would not apply in any province where equivalent provincial regulations had been enacted. The dissenting judgment of Lamer C.J. and Iacobucci J. cited this provision as evidence of the fact that the provinces were fully capable of dealing with the environmental problems that had led to the enactment of the federal legislation and regulations.

49 *Crown Zellerbach*, above note 31 at 447. The provisions of the *Clean Air Act* referred to by La Forest J. in this passage establish emissions standards in respect

La Forest J. then stated that "the potential breadth of federal power to control pollution by use of its general power is so great" that the challenge for the courts may be the development of strategies to "confine its ambit." La Forest J. stated:

> It must be remembered that the peace, order and good government clause may comprise not only prohibitions, like criminal law, but regulation. Regulation to control pollution, which is incidentally only part of the even larger global problem of managing the environment, could arguably include not only emission standards but the control of the substances used in manufacture, as well as the techniques of production generally, in so far as these may have an impact on pollution.[50]

Precisely because the federal general power to control pollution was potentially so broad, La Forest J. was unwilling to uphold the impugned section of the *Ocean Dumping Control Act* at issue in *Crown Zellerbach*. The section prohibited the depositing of any substance in waters, without regard to whether the substances actually had a polluting effect.

These passages must be read alongside the conclusion that "pollution" was too broad a matter to constitute a distinct matter of national concern. Thus, Parliament cannot claim to regulate pollution that causes effects outside the province on the basis of the national concern branch of POGG. Nor do the emergency or gap branches assist Parliament's claim to regulate such polluting activity. As to the emergency branch, the *Clean Air Act* provisions referred to by La Forest J. were permanent rather than temporary legislation and thus could not be justified on the basis of the emergency power. Nor is there any gap in the division of powers in relation to pollution, since the provinces are perfectly capable of regulating all polluting activity within the province, regardless of whether the effects of such pollution are limited to that province alone. It must be, therefore, that Parliament's power to regulate polluting activity having extraprovincial effects flows from a separate and independent branch of the POGG power.

This interpretation of the POGG power is supported by La Forest J.'s comments in two other cases. The first of these cases is *Morguard Investments Ltd. v. De Savoye*,[51] a case dealing with recognition and enforce-

---

of emissions that would, *inter alia*, constitute a "significant danger to the health of persons." These provisions have now been incorporated in the *Canadian Environmental Protection Act*, R.S.C. 1985 (4th Supp.), c. 16.

50 *Crown Zellerbach*, above note 49 at 447–48.

51 [1990] 3 S.C.R. 1077 [*Morguard*]. For a helpful discussion of the constitutional implications of this case, see J. Walker, "Interprovincial Sovereign Immunity

ment of interprovincial judgments. La Forest J. noted that Canadian courts had traditionally treated judgments rendered in other provinces as "foreign judgments." In order for a judgment against a defendant in a "foreign" province to be recognized and enforceable, the defendant had to be present in the province where the judgment was rendered or engage in acts that amounted to submission or "attornment" to the jurisdiction. But La Forest J. argued that it was wrong to treat other provinces within Canada as if they were foreign states. According to La Forest J., treating sister provinces as foreign states flies "in the face of the obvious intention of the Constitution to create a single country."[52] La Forest J. went on to state that, in his view, a regime of mutual recognition of judgments by provincial courts across the country "is inherent in a federation." He also pointed out that the "integrating character of our constitutional arrangements" may have important implications for the division of legislative authority between Parliament and the provincial legislatures:

> The integrating character of our constitutional arrangements as they apply to interprovincial mobility is such that some writers have suggested that a "full faith and credit" clause must be read into the Constitution *and that the federal Parliament is, under the "Peace, Order and Good Government" clause, empowered to legislate respecting the recognition and enforcement of judgments throughout Canada* . . . . The present case was not, however, argued on that basis, and I need not go that far. For present purposes, it is sufficient to say that, in my view, the application of the underlying principles of comity and private international law must be adapted to the situations where they are applied, and that in a federation this implies a fuller and more generous acceptance of the judgments of the courts of other constituent units of the federation. [Emphasis added.][53]

Revisited" (1997) 35 Osgoode Hall L.J. 379. See also: Elizabeth Edinger, "The Constitutionalization of the Conflict of Laws" (1995) 25 Can. Bus. L.J. 38. In *Club Resorts Ltd. v. Van Breda*, [2012] 1 S.C.R. 572, the Supreme Court revisited the test to be applied to determine whether the Superior Courts have jurisdiction over a particular dispute. Le Bel J., writing for a unanimous Court, held that the "real and substantial connection test" established in *Morguard* had both a constitutional element and a private law element (para. 23). The constitutional test of a "real and substantial connection . . . places limits on the reach of the jurisdiction of a province's courts and on the application of provincial laws to interprovincial or international situations." However, "it does not establish the actual content of rules and principles of private international law, nor does it require that those rules and principles be uniform" (para. 23).

52 *Morguard*, above note 51 at 1079.

53 *Ibid*. at 1100–101.

Since *Morguard* involved common law rules respecting recognition of judgments, it was not necessary for La Forest J. to determine the implications of his analysis for the division of legislative powers between Parliament and the provinces. Nevertheless, he strongly hints (in the italicized portion of the above passage) that the federal Parliament has the legislative authority under POGG to provide for the terms on which the judgments of one court should be recognized in another. This was a remarkable suggestion, since it had always been assumed that recognition of foreign judgments by provincial superior courts fell under the exclusive jurisdiction of the provinces.[54] Moreover, it is difficult to see how recognition of judgments of one provincial court by the courts of other provinces could be said to be a distinct matter of inherent national concern. Judgments involve a huge range of subject matters, many of which are *prima facie* matters of provincial jurisdiction.

In the subsequent case of *Hunt v. T & N plc*,[55] La Forest J. elaborated on the analysis presented in *Morguard*. In *Hunt*, the Court was called on to consider the constitutional validity of a provincial "blocking" statute, the Quebec *Business Concerns Records Act*. This legislation prohibited the removal from the province of documents relating to any business concern in Quebec pursuant to orders by a judicial authority outside the province. La Forest J. stated that the "integrating character of our constitutional arrangements" has a significance that extends beyond the narrow issue considered in *Morguard*—namely, the recognition by courts of extraprovincial judgments.[56] These are "constitutional imperatives" that have significance for the division of powers, both in terms of imposing limits on the jurisdiction of the provinces as well as conferring legislative authority on Parliament. In terms of provincial jurisdiction, the provinces cannot override what La Forest J. termed "the minimum standards of order and fairness addressed in *Morguard*."[57] He held that the Quebec legislation could not apply to prevent a British Columbia court from obtaining records necessary to the effective conduct of litigation in British Columbia.

In terms of federal jurisdiction, La Forest J. expanded on his earlier comment in *Morguard* that the imperatives of the Canadian economic union confer authority on Parliament to enact legislation for the purpose of protecting and maintaining the union:

54 There are provincial statutes addressing the circumstances in which extraprovincial judgments may be recognized and enforced: see, for example, *Reciprocal Enforcement of Judgments Act*, R.S.O. 1990, c. R.5.

55 [1993] 4 S.C.R. 289 [*Hunt*].

56 *Ibid.* at para. 56.

57 *Ibid.*

> I noted in *Morguard* . . . that a number of commentators had suggested that the federal Parliament had power to legislate respecting the recognition and enforcement of judgments, and in my view that suggestion is well founded. This issue is ultimately related to the rights of the citizen, trade and commerce and other federal legislative powers, including that encompassed in the peace, order and good government clause. But subject to these overriding powers, I see no reason why the provinces should not be able to legislate in the area, subject, however, to the principles in *Morguard* and to the demands of territoriality as expounded in the cases, most recently in *Reference Re Upper Churchill Water Rights Reversion Act*.[58]

La Forest J. effectively suggested that Parliament may, pursuant to the POGG power, enact legislation providing for the free movement of persons or for the enhancement of the economic union. Yet the subject of economic integration and interprovincial mobility is extremely broad and all-encompassing, such that legislation on this topic could not possibly satisfy the test for a distinct matter for purposes of the national concern branch of POGG. Moreover, in the passage quoted above, La Forest J. stated that both the federal government and the provinces could enact legislation dealing with such matters. This is also a departure from the jurisprudence under the national concern branch; provinces cannot legislate so as to affect vital aspects of matters of inherent national concern (such as aeronautics or radio).

Morguard and *Hunt* can therefore be interpreted as providing support for a fourth, independent source of federal authority under POGG. This fourth branch would permit Parliament to legislate in relation to matters of interprovincial concern, impact, or significance. Under the fourth branch of POGG, Parliament would have the ability to enact legislation directed at persons, transactions, or activities within particular provinces, as long as it does so in order to remedy the interprovincial impacts or effects of such matters. Examples of the kinds of laws that may be authorized by this branch include laws regulating polluting activity within one province where the pollution has effects extending beyond that particular province; laws providing for the recognition in one province of judgments issued by the courts of other provinces; and laws aimed at enhancing or protecting interprovincial mobility or the free movement of persons, capital, and goods across the Canadian economic union. It is not necessary that the legislation under the fourth branch of POGG be directed at a distinct subject matter, as that term has been defined under the national concern branch. Rather, what is

58 *Ibid.* at para. 60.

required is that the legislation be directed at the regulation of a matter that has interprovincial significance or effects extending beyond one province. Further, recognition of the validity of federal legislation under this fourth branch does not prevent the provinces from enacting laws on the same subject, provided that such provincial laws are aimed at a provincial aspect of the matter in question.

FURTHER READINGS

Beaudoin, G.A., with P. Thibault, *La Constitution du Canada: institutions, partage des pouvoirs, Charte canadienne des droits et libertés*, 3d ed. (Montreal: Wilson & Lafleur, 2004) c. 8

Brun, H., & G. Tremblay, *Droit Constitutionnel*, 6th ed. (Montreal: Éditions Yvon Blais, 2014)

Hogg, P.W., *Constitutional Law of Canada*, 5th ed., loose-leaf (Toronto: Carswell, 2007) c. 17

Leclair, J. "The Elusive Quest for the Quintessential 'National Interest'" (2005) 38 U.B.C. L. Rev. 355

Lederman, W.R., "Unity and Diversity in Canadian Federalism: Ideals and Methods of Moderation" (1975) 53 Can. Bar Rev. 597

Lyon, N., "The *Anti-Inflation Act Reference*: Two Models of Canadian Federalism" (1977) 9 Ottawa L. Rev. 176

Lysyk, K., "Constitutional Reform and the Introductory Clause of Section 91: Residual and Emergency Law-Making Power" (1979) 57 Can. Bar Rev. 531

CHAPTER 9

TRADE AND COMMERCE

A. INTRODUCTION

As discussed in Chapter 7, the decision of the Privy Council in *Citizens' Insurance Co. v. Parsons*[1] is the starting point for the federal trade and commerce power under section 91(2) of the *Constitution Act, 1867*.[2] In *Parsons*, the Privy Council held that there were two branches of the trade and commerce power: (1) the regulation of interprovincial and international trade; and (2) "general regulation of trade affecting the whole dominion." In neither of these categories, however, could the federal power over trade and commerce extend to the regulation of the contracts of a particular trade or business within a province.

As previously discussed, the Privy Council severely restricted the scope of the second branch of the trade and commerce power. Early cases held that the trade and commerce power was effectively limited to the regulation of goods, persons, or activities crossing provincial borders. This chapter examines the extent to which the Supreme Court has departed from the Privy Council's restrictive approach and broadened the ambit of the trade and commerce power, particularly in relation to the second branch of *Parsons*.

1 (1881), 7 App. Cas. 96 (P.C.) [*Parsons*].
2 The *Constitution Act, 1867* (formerly the *British North America Act, 1867*) (U.K.), 30 & 31 Vict., c. 3.

B. INTERNATIONAL AND INTERPROVINCIAL TRADE

1) The Scope of Federal and Provincial Authority

A key distinction in the trade and commerce jurisprudence is between "interprovincial and international trade" on the one hand and "local trade" on the other. Parliament has exclusive legislative authority to regulate international and interprovincial trade—the regulation of goods, persons, capital, or services crossing provincial or Canadian borders for a commercial purpose. Provincial jurisdiction is limited to the regulation of trade within a province. The text of section 92 of the *Constitution Act, 1867* limits the provinces to the regulation of transactions, activities, or persons "in the province." Provincial power over local trade is derived from section 92(13) "Property and Civil Rights in the Province" and section 92(16), "Matters of a merely local or private Nature in the Province." Accordingly, the provinces have no jurisdiction to regulate transactions, activities, or persons entering or leaving the province.[3]

Parliament has exercised its authority to regulate imports, exports, and interprovincial trade in a wide variety of contexts for various policy objectives.[4] Few doubts have ever been raised about the constitutional validity of these enactments. However, doubts have been raised about Parliament's ability to regulate local or intraprovincial trade.

In the *Margarine Reference*,[5] for example, the Supreme Court of Canada considered the validity of federal legislation banning the manufacture, importation, or sale of oleomargarine. It was conceded that oleomargarine was substantially as nutritious and fit for human consumption as butter. According to the Supreme Court, the purpose of the legislation was "to give trade protection to the dairy industry in

---

3 See *Ont. (A.G.) v. Can. (A.G.)*, [1896] A.C. 348 (P.C.), holding that the provinces have no power to prohibit the importation of intoxicating liquor into the province. Importation of liquor is regulated by Parliament under the *Importation of Intoxicating Liquors Act*, R.S.C. 1985, c. I-3. See also: *Canadian Industrial Gas & Oil Ltd. v. Saskatchewan* (1977), [1978] 2 S.C.R. 545.

4 See, for example, *Energy Efficiency Act*, S.C. 1992, c. 36, s. 4 (prohibiting interprovincial transportation or importation of energy-using products unless product complies with applicable standard); *Meat Inspection Act*, R.S.C. 1985 (1st Supp.), c. 25, ss. 6–9 (prohibiting export, import, and interprovincial transportation of meat products that do not comply with applicable standards); and *Motor Vehicle Safety Act*, S.C. 1993, c. 16, ss. 4 & 5 (prohibiting importation and interprovincial shipment of motor vehicles unless applicable standards are met).

5 *Reference Re Validity of s. 5(a) of Dairy Industry Act (Canada)*, [1949] S.C.R. 1 [*Margarine Reference*].

the production and sale of butter as against substitutes"[6] and "to benefit one group of persons as against competitors in business in which, in the absence of the legislation, the latter would be free to engage in the provinces."[7]

The legislation considered in the *Margarine Reference* did not merely ban the importation of oleomargarine; it also prohibited its local manufacture and sale. The Supreme Court held that the federal prohibition on manufacture and sale was invalid, since it amounted to regulation of property and civil rights in the province. However, the Court stated that the legislation would have been upheld if it had been restricted to a prohibition on importation:

> There is next the prohibition of importation of these substances . . . . Such scope of action is clearly necessary to the nation's jurisdiction over trade with other states. Only Parliament can deal with foreign commerce; provincial power cannot in any mode, aspect, or degree govern it: and it would be anomalous that the jurisdiction to which regulation is committed, which alone can act, and which in this segment of trade is in substance sovereign, should be powerless to employ such an ordinary measure of control.[8]

In the result, the Court upheld the portion of the legislation banning importation on the basis that it could be severed from the invalid attempt to regulate local manufacture or sale.

The Supreme Court drew a similar distinction between interprovincial and international trade on the one hand and intraprovincial trade on the other in *R. v. Dominion Stores Ltd.*[9] The case concerned the constitutionality of Part I of the *Canada Agricultural Products Standards Act*, which established and regulated the use of grade names for various classes of agricultural products. Part I of the Act applied to the local sale and possession of agricultural products. Part II of the Act compelled the use of the same grade names in the export and interprovincial movement of agricultural products. Part I was held to be unconstitutional in its application to intraprovincial trade. However, the validity of Part II was both conceded by the party challenging the legislation and assumed by the Court.[10] While Parliament could not

---

6 *Ibid.* at 27–28.

7 *Ibid.* at 50.

8 *Ibid.* at 52–53.

9 [1980] 1 S.C.R. 844 [*Dominion Stores*].

10 *Ibid.* at 849, Laskin C.J. Although Laskin C.J., dissenting, would have upheld Part I, he observed that the validity of Part II of the Act had been conceded by the appellant. This observation was not questioned by the majority.

regulate grade names for agricultural products traded locally, it could apply precisely the same regulations to products traded interprovincially or internationally.

Similarly, in *Labatt Breweries*,[11] the Court struck down section 6 of the federal *Food and Drugs Act* on the basis that it applied to the manufacture and sale of light beer within a province. The Court suggested that the legislation would have been valid if it had been limited to the regulation of interprovincial or international trade.[12] Parliament subsequently amended section 6 of the Act so as to restrict its mandatory application to importation or interprovincial movement of food articles.[13] There has been no suggestion that the amended legislation would be open to constitutional challenge. Indeed, any such a challenge would fail, since the amended statute conforms to the criteria identified by the Court as necessary to support federal trade legislation.

2) Ability to Regulate Local Trade as an Incident of International or Interprovincial Trade

Early attempts to support federal legislation that incidentally impacted on local trade were rejected by the Privy Council. For example, in the 1937 case of *British Columbia (A.G.) v. Canada (A.G.)*,[14] the Privy Council held that a federal statute regulating trade in natural products was invalid—even though the natural products were almost entirely exported—because the legislation directly regulated certain transactions that could be completed within a single province.

The Supreme Court of Canada has departed from the Privy Council's restrictive approach and permitted federal attempts to regulate local trade in several important ways. First, the Supreme Court has upheld federal legislation providing for voluntary regulation of local trade with mandatory federal standards. Second, the Supreme Court has upheld federal legislation that is part of a cooperative and comprehensive federal–provincial marketing scheme. Third, some cases may be interpreted to suggest that Parliament may enact legislation that incidentally

---

11 *Labatt Breweries of Canada Ltd. v. Can. (A.G.)*, [1980] 1 S.C.R. 914 [*Labatt Breweries*].

12 Estey J., for the majority, stated: "Nowhere are the impugned statutory regulations or provisions concerned with the control or regulation of the extraprovincial distribution of these products or their movement through any channels of trade. On the contrary, their main purpose is the regulation of the brewing process itself by means of a 'legal recipe.'" See *Labatt Breweries*, *ibid.* at 943.

13 See *An Act to amend the Food and Drugs Act*, R.S.C. 1985 (3rd Supp.), c. 27, s. 1.

14 [1937] A.C. 377 (P.C.).

regulates local trade where the legislation is necessary to a scheme for the regulation of interprovincial or international trade.

a) Voluntary Restrictions on Local Trade

One approach employed by Parliament to address the limitation on its trade power is to apply mandatory restrictions on interprovincial or international trade and voluntary restrictions on local trade. For example, under the *Motor Vehicle Safety Act*,[15] Parliament creates a national safety mark and prescribes standards that must be met before the mark can be affixed to a motor vehicle. It is mandatory to affix the mark to vehicles that move across provincial borders and, thus, mandatory for all such vehicles to comply with the applicable product standard. Local manufacturers have the option of affixing the safety mark for vehicles sold within the province of production. However, in the event that a manufacturer chooses to affix the mark to a vehicle, the vehicle must comply with the standards applicable to that mark. The legislation has been upheld on the ground that Parliament may establish national trademarks and regulate their use.[16] Thus, Parliament can regulate the use of a national safety mark even by manufacturers engaged in the local production and sale of a product.

Although the standards in the *Motor Vehicle Safety Act* are ostensibly voluntary in relation to vehicles sold within a province, in practical terms they are mandatory for all vehicles. The vast majority of vehicles manufactured in Canada cross either a provincial or an international border. Moreover, it is impossible to separate vehicles traded locally from vehicles traded interprovincially or internationally at the point of production. In practice, all vehicles are produced to meet a common North American standard, and vehicles intended for local trade are indistinguishable from those intended for export. Therefore, the manufacturer voluntarily affixes the mark to all the vehicles produced, regardless of their ultimate point of sale. In short, the practical effect of the federal scheme is to require that all motor vehicles produced in Canada meet federally prescribed standards.

The courts have imposed some limitations on the ability of Parliament to regulate local production through use of voluntary schemes,

---

15 *Motor Vehicle Safety Act*, above note 4.

16 Parliament's power to establish national trademarks and regulate their use has been upheld under the second branch of *Parsons*, above note 1. See *Ont. (A.G.) v. Can. (A.G.)*, [1937] A.C. 405 (P.C.) [*Canada Standard*] and *Kirkbi AG v. Ritvik Holdings Inc.*, [2005] S.C.R. 302 at para. 18 [*Kirkbi*]. See also the discussion of the second branch of the trade and commerce power at Section C, below in this chapter.

however. In *Labatt Breweries*,[17] the Supreme Court struck down regulations enacted under the federal *Food and Drugs Act* that established compositional standards for light beer. Producers that labelled, packaged, or sold a product as light beer were required to comply with federal standards. The federal government argued that the regulations should be upheld on the basis that they established voluntary labelling regulations, detailing the standards that must be met if specific designations were used on food labels.[18] The federal government argued that such a voluntary labelling scheme could be justified under Parliament's trade powers.

This reasoning was accepted by Pigeon J. in dissent. However, Estey J., for the majority, held that the federal legislation was invalid. According to Estey J., the regulations specified standards for products using such common names as "beer" or "light beer." As a practical matter, producers of beer or light beer must use these terms in marketing their product, since that is how they are known in the marketplace. Estey J. concluded that the federal government could not "arrogate" common names and prescribe standards for their use through the use of the federal trademark power.[19]

In *Dominion Stores*,[20] the Supreme Court further restricted Parliament's power to establish voluntary product standards for local trade. The *Canada Agricultural Products Standards Act* established mandatory standards for certain agricultural products traded interprovincially, and voluntary standards for products traded locally.[21] Dominion Stores was charged with selling apples under the federal grade name "Canada Extra Fancy" without complying with the standards applicable for that grade. It was ultimately acquitted on the basis that the federal

---

17 Above note 11.

18 In addition, the federal government sought to justify the regulations under the peace, order, and good government power as well as the criminal law power. Both of these justifications were rejected by the majority of the Supreme Court. The discussion in the text is limited to the Court's analysis of the trade and commerce power. Chapter 11 discusses the Supreme Court's reasoning on the criminal law power.

19 "[T]he arrogation here by Parliament of words from the language as 'common names' to be used on a mandatory basis by anyone selling a malted liquor of any of the prescribed standards, creates no trade mark rights and obligations": *Labatt Breweries*, above note 11 at 946.

20 Above note 9.

21 The scheme was structured in precisely the same fashion as the *Motor Vehicle Safety Act*, with certain "grade names" being established for products, and standards prescribed for any products that used those names. Use of the grade names was mandatory for products traded interprovincially but optional for products traded locally.

regulations were inapplicable to local trade in apples. Estey J., for the majority, found it significant that provincial legislation required the use of identical grade names for locally traded products. In effect, a producer was required to comply with the federal standard, since it was compulsory to use the prescribed name regardless of whether the apples were intended for local sale or for export. While a local apple trader could be charged for breach of the provincial statute, the trader could not be charged for failing to comply with the federal statute unless the apples in question had been traded interprovincially.

With respect, Estey J.'s reasoning in *Dominion Stores* is inconsistent with constitutional principles and other decisions of the Court. As a matter of constitutional principle, the validity of federal legislation should not depend on the enactment of a related provincial law. If Parliament can regulate the voluntary use of names in local trade, federal regulation should not be rendered *ultra vires* by a provincial enactment requiring the use of the same name. Similarly, the repeal of a valid provincial law should not affect the validity of federal legislation.

As a matter of authority, the decision is difficult, if not impossible, to reconcile with other decisions of the Court. In the 1937 *Canada Standard*[22] case, the Privy Council upheld a federal statute that established a national "Canada Standard" mark for various products. If the mark was used, the producer had to comply with prescribed federal standards. In *Dominion Stores*, Laskin C.J., for the minority, found the *Canada Standard* case indistinguishable and would have upheld the federal enactment. However, Estey J., for the majority, distinguished the *Canada Standard* case on the basis that the *Canada Agricultural Products Standards Act* did not create a mark that was vested in the Crown. As James MacPherson (now a judge of the Ontario Court of Appeal) has observed, "it is doubtful that the vesting of a property right in the federal Crown was crucial to the constitutional validity of the scheme [in the *Canada Standard* case]" and it is "difficult to see the relevance of Estey J.'s distinction."[23]

Dominion Stores has been described as a weak precedent.[24] Indeed, Estey J. himself observed that "[i]t may well be that the state of the interpretation of the *British North America Act*, which I have summarized at the outset . . . is not now a correct description of the federal power

22 Above note 16.

23 J.C. MacPherson, "Economic Regulation and the British North America Act: Labatt Breweries and Other Constitutional Imbroglios" (1980) 5 Can. Bus. L.J. 172 at 178.

24 See P.W. Hogg, *Constitutional Law of Canada*, 5th ed., loose-leaf (Toronto: Carswell, 2007) at 20.2(b).

under s. 91(2)."[25] In any event, Estey J.'s reasoning would seem to be limited to situations in which an otherwise voluntary federal regulation of local trade is made mandatory through the application of overlapping provincial legislation. Such overlapping provincial legislation is in many cases unnecessary since, as a practical matter, a manufacturer will not want to separate goods produced for a local provincial market from goods intended for export. Segmenting products in this manner is extremely costly and usually serves no business purpose. Therefore, manufacturers will tend to prefer to comply with a single national standard. In this sense, the federal power to set mandatory standards for interprovincial trade and voluntary standards for local trade will often be sufficient to establish an effective national scheme of product standards.[26]

b) Cooperative Marketing Schemes

The Supreme Court has upheld federal legislation that regulates local trade where the federal legislation is part of a comprehensive and cooperative federal–provincial marketing scheme. In *Reference re Agricultural Products Marketing Act, 1970 (Canada)*,[27] the Court upheld a complex scheme of interlocking federal and provincial legislation establishing a national egg marketing agency with power to set production and marketing quotas and to impose levies on producers. The scheme was designed to share the interprovincial and export market for eggs by allocating quotas to each province and each egg producer. While the federal legislation was primarily concerned with interprovincial and international trade in eggs, it fastened certain obligations on local egg producers. For example, the federal legislation authorized the imposition of levies on all egg producers, even if their entire product was sold within the province of production. The federal regulation of local trade was reinforced by provincial legislation, which mirrored the requirements of the federal law.

As discussed above, in *Dominion Stores*, the existence of overlapping provincial legislation was found to be fatal to the constitutional validity of the federal legislation. However, in the *Egg Reference*, the Court came to precisely the opposite conclusion. Far from undermining the validity of the federal legislation, the existence of the provincial statutes was

---

25 *Dominion Stores*, above note 9 at 866.

26 However, the use of voluntary schemes will probably not be effective where Parliament is attempting to control the quantity of a product or its price. In such instances, local producers have a clear incentive to produce in excess of the prescribed quantities or below prescribed prices.

27 [1978] 2 S.C.R. 1198 [*Egg Reference*].

an important factor in persuading the Court to uphold the legislation. Pigeon J., who wrote the majority judgment, noted that the federal–provincial marketing scheme was the product of a sincere cooperative effort between all governments and that "it would really be unfortunate if this was all brought to nought."[28] As mentioned above, the existence of a provincial law should, strictly speaking, be irrelevant to the constitutional validity of a federal law. Pigeon J.'s forthright acknowledgement in *Reference re Agricultural Products Marketing Act* makes clear that the Court was persuaded to uphold the federal legislation—despite its effects on local trade—because of the degree of cooperation between the federal government and the provinces.

The Supreme Court came to a similar conclusion in *Fédération des producteurs de volailles du Québec v. Pelland* in 2005.[29] The Court upheld provincial regulation setting chicken-production quotas that applied to both intraprovincial and interprovincial trade. Again, the Court commented favourably on the existence of a comprehensive and cooperative federal–provincial marketing scheme. Although the case concerned the validity of provincial quotas, the decision implicitly approved of the result in the *Egg Reference* and suggested that federal production quotas that applied to both interprovincial and intraprovincial trading would have been upheld.

c) Regulation of Local Trade Necessary to an Effective Interprovincial or International Scheme

It may be argued that Parliament should have the ability to regulate local trade that is inextricably bound up with a regulatory scheme whose primary purpose, or pith and substance, is the regulation of interprovincial and international trade.[30] However, the Privy Council was generally unsympathetic to this argument. In a series of cases beginning in the 1930s, the Privy Council ruled that Parliament may not directly apply controls on the production or local marketing of a product even if such local regulation is merely incidental to a scheme aimed at controlling interprovincial or international trade. The result was that the federal power to regulate products traded interprovincially

28 *Ibid.* at 1296.

29 [2005] 1 S.C.R. 292 [*Pelland*].

30 This is the position in the U.S., where Congress has authority to regulate local trade where such regulation is an "appropriate means to the attainment of a legitimate end, the effective execution of the granted power to regulate interstate commerce." See *United States v. Wrightwood Dairy Co.*, 315 U.S. 110 at 119 (1942), upholding the power of Congress to regulate marketing of milk produced and sold intrastate but in competition with milk marketed interstate. (For a discussion of the pith and substance doctrine, see Chapter 4, Section C(6)(a).)

or internationally was rendered nugatory; the inability to control local production or trade effectively precluded the federal government from regulating trade at the interprovincial or international level.

The 1971 *Caloil* case[31] has been cited as an example of an early departure by the Supreme Court from the Privy Council's restrictive approach. Caloil Inc. of Montreal had been importing petroleum from Algeria and Spain and selling its product through gasoline stations in Ontario and Quebec. In 1970, the National Energy Board Regulations were amended to provide that the Board "may issue a licence to import oil for consumption in the area of Canada specified therein, in such quantities, at such times and at such points of entry into Canada as it may consider appropriate." The Board restricted Caloil's importation of gasoline to the Atlantic provinces, Quebec, and a small area in eastern Ontario in an attempt to preserve the key Ontario market for producers in western Canada. Caloil claimed that the amended regulations were invalid because they regulated the local transportation and sale of a product, a matter reserved exclusively to the provinces. Pigeon J., who delivered the main judgment, upheld the restrictions, noting that they were a necessary part of a scheme for the regulation of interprovincial and export trade, "a purpose that is clearly outside provincial jurisdiction and within the exclusive federal field of action."[32] The fact that the regulations might "affect" local transactions in the imported product did not change the fact that they were in "pith and substance" aimed at international trade.

While the regulations in the *Caloil* case were upheld, the decision did not significantly broaden the federal authority over local trade. The regulations were framed in a narrow fashion and applied only to the domestic use of imported oil. An earlier version of the regulation considered in *Caloil* that had purported to control the sale of both imported and domestically produced oil had been struck down by the Exchequer Court on grounds that it amounted to the regulation of local trade.[33] The *Caloil* case established that Parliament may impose controls on the manner in which imported goods may be used once they have entered the country. But *Caloil* is consistent with the proposition that Parliament cannot control domestically produced goods, even where such controls are necessarily incidental to the effective regulation of interprovincial or international trade.

---

31 *Caloil Inc. v. Canada (A.G.) (No. 2)*, [1971] S.C.R. 543 [*Caloil*].

32 *Ibid.* at 550.

33 See *Caloil Inc. v. Can. (A.G.) (No. 1)*, [1970] Ex. C.R. 512. No appeal was taken from this judgment; instead the government amended the regulations so as to restrict their application to imported oil only.

However, two cases from the Supreme Court may be interpreted to suggest that Parliament can regulate purely local transactions where that regulation is necessary to the effective regulation of interprovincial or international trade. In *Global Securities v. British Columbia (Securities Commission)*,[34] the Supreme Court upheld a provision in a British Columbia statute that empowered the B.C. Securities Commission to gather information for securities regulators in other jurisdictions. The Court held that the provision would assist in uncovering misconduct abroad by domestic registrants in the province of British Columbia. As the Court noted, it is well accepted that securities regulation is concerned not only with securities, but also with the people who sell them. The provincial securities commission is therefore legitimately concerned with the honesty and good repute of local registrants. This concern is not limited to activities occurring within the province itself; the fact that a local registrant may have violated the securities laws of another jurisdiction "is clearly relevant to the fitness of that registrant to continue trading in the province."[35] Therefore, the province could carry out its own inquiry with respect to foreign violations, or delegate that task to an agency in another province, since inquiries regarding the extraprovincial activities of a registrant are relevant to the fitness of the registrant to carry on business in the province.[36]

Similarly, in *Committee for the Equal Treatment of Asbestos Minority Shareholders v. Ontario (Securities Commission)*,[37] the Court upheld the jurisdiction of the Ontario Securities Commission to inquire into a

---

34 [2000] 1 S.C.R. 494 [*Global Securities*].

35 *Ibid.* at para. 36. Iacobucci J. also noted a second, related purpose of the impugned provision, namely, to promote cooperation and reciprocal sharing of information amongst different securities regulators. This purpose also was designed to enhance the enforcement of local securities laws.

36 Significantly, Iacobucci J. did not find it necessary to rely on the ancillary doctrine in order to uphold the impugned provision. The ancillary doctrine becomes relevant where one level of government has enacted a provision that intrudes or extends into the jurisdiction of the other. In such a case, even an "intruding" provision can be upheld if it can be shown to be "necessarily incidental" to a general scheme of regulation. Iacobucci J. found that it was not necessary to rely on the ancillary doctrine because the impugned provision did not intrude into federal jurisdiction. (This was because, as explained above, the purpose of the impugned provision in *Global Securities* was not to regulate foreign transactions directly but merely to assist in the enforcement of local securities laws.) However, Iacobucci J. went on to hold that, even if the impugned provision were not in pith and substance provincial, it would have been valid anyway on the basis of the ancillary doctrine, since it was "necessarily incidental" to the provincial scheme of securities regulation.

37 [2001] 2 S.C.R. 132 [*Asbestos Minority*].

transaction that had occurred in the province of Quebec for the purpose of determining whether certain entities should lose trading exemptions under Ontario law. The Court stated that Ontario had a "public interest" jurisdiction that entitled it to inquire into these activities. This public interest jurisdiction included a mandate to protect investors from unfair, improper, or fraudulent practices and to foster fair and efficient capital markets and confidence in capital markets. There was no requirement that the transaction in question have an Ontario "nexus" before this broad-ranging public interest jurisdiction was engaged. The Court also observed that "capital markets and securities transactions are becoming increasingly international" and pointed out that "there are a myriad of overlapping regulatory jurisdictions governing securities transactions."[38] This overlapping jurisdiction supported the need for harmonization and coordination of securities regulation regimes, a goal that was reflected in Ontario's securities legislation.

Although *Global Securities* and *Asbestos Minority* dealt with the reach of provincial regulation, the cases may have implications for the ability of the federal government to regulate local trade. Based on the reasoning in *Global Securities* and *Asbestos Minority*, federal regulation of trade within a province could arguably be upheld on one of two grounds. First, it may be argued that the regulation is in pith and substance related to Parliament's jurisdiction over interprovincial or international trade. For instance, based on the reasoning in *Asbestos Minority*, it could be argued that regulating local trading in securities is necessary to assess the fitness of registrants to engage in interprovincial or international trading and to foster investor confidence in the integrity of Canadian capital markets. As such, the regulation of purely intraprovincial activities would not involve an intrusion into provincial jurisdiction.

Second, the regulation could be upheld on the basis that it was ancillary or necessarily incidental to Parliament's jurisdiction over interprovincial or international trade. In *Global Securities*, Iacobucci J. held that a provincial inquiry into a foreign securities transaction was necessarily incidental to a general provincial scheme of regulation. He held that there was a sufficiently close fit between the impugned provision and the scheme of regulation as to satisfy the most rigorous version of the ancillary doctrine. By parity of reasoning, the regulation of local activities of market participants otherwise engaged in interprovincial and international dealing in securities could be viewed as necessarily incidental to the effective enforcement of a federal regulatory scheme.

38 *Ibid*. at para. 62.

However, as discussed below in Section C(3), the Supreme Court of Canada has held that the day-to-day regulation of securities trading falls within provincial jurisdiction.

C. GENERAL REGULATION OF TRADE AFFECTING THE WHOLE DOMINION

1) Early Cases

In *Parsons*, the Privy Council stated that in addition to the authority over interprovincial and international trade, Parliament might also have jurisdiction over the "general regulation of trade affecting the whole Dominion." In subsequent cases, the Privy Council declined to explain or apply this so-called second branch of the trade and commerce power. Indeed, the law lords analyzed federal and provincial trade jurisdiction almost exclusively in terms of the first branch of *Parsons*. In order for federal trade regulation to be upheld, it was necessary to demonstrate that the law was limited to persons, transactions, or activities crossing provincial borders. The Privy Council largely ignored the possibility that federal regulation directed at local trade might nevertheless be upheld on the basis that it involved the general regulation of trade affecting the whole dominion.

A possible exception was the 1937 *Canada Standard* case discussed above.[39] Although the Privy Council did not expressly refer to the general regulation of trade branch of *Parsons*, it did state that the statute was supportable on the basis of the trade and commerce power. Since the statute applied to goods traded locally as well as interprovincially, the *Canada Standard* case is usually regarded as having been implicitly decided under the second branch of the trade and commerce power.[40]

2) The Revival of the General Trade and Commerce Power: The *General Motors* Test

The first indication of the Supreme Court's revival of the second branch of *Parsons* came in *Reference Re Anti-Inflation Act, 1975 (Canada)*,[41] which was discussed in detail in Chapter 8. In that case, federal legislation establishing a wage-and-price control program was upheld on

39 Above note 16.

40 This constitutional basis for the *Trade-marks Act* has now been made explicit. See *Kirkbi*, above note 16.

41 [1976] 2 S.C.R. 373 [*Anti-Inflation Reference*].

the basis of the peace, order, and good government power. Given the previous jurisprudence on the federal trade and commerce power, the attorney general of Canada did not even argue that the legislation could be upheld under section 91(2). The legislation before the Court in the *Anti-Inflation Reference* was not restricted to interprovincial or international trade and applied directly to firms and persons engaged in local trade. Despite the previous jurisprudence and the lack of argument from the parties, Laskin C.J. suggested that the legislation might have been supportable on the basis of the trade and commerce power. Laskin C.J. pointed to the second branch of *Parsons*, noting that section 91(2) "provides the Parliament of Canada with a foothold in respect of 'the general regulation of trade affecting the whole dominion.'"[42] He stated that the legislation was not directed to any particular trade but, rather, "is directed to suppliers of commodities and services in general and to the public services of governments, and to the relationship of those suppliers and of the public services to those employed by and in them, and to their overall relationship to the public."[43]

Laskin C.J.'s unsolicited *obiter* comments were surprising in light of the moribund status of the second branch of the trade and commerce power at the time. Laskin C.J. seemed to be suggesting that the second branch would support federal legislation that directly regulated local trade, as long as it dealt with "trade in general" as opposed to particular trades or industries.[44] The following year, Laskin C.J. expanded on his comments in *MacDonald v. Vapor Canada Ltd.*[45] At issue in *Vapor* was a federal law providing a civil remedy for any act or business practice "contrary to honest industrial or commercial usage in Canada." The Supreme Court held that the legislation was unconstitutional since it created civil causes of action, which was a matter of property or civil rights in the province. However, Laskin C.J., who wrote the decision of the Court, suggested that the result may have been different if the law had been part of a regulatory scheme administered by a federally appointed agency. The legislation could not be supported on the basis of the trade and commerce power because enforcement was "left to the

42 *Ibid.* at 426.

43 *Ibid.*

44 This interpretation was consistent with the *Canada Standard* case, above note 16, which had involved legislation establishing a trademark that could be applied to a variety of different commodities. But it also went far beyond *Canada Standard*, since that case had involved the voluntary use of a trademark, whereas the anti-inflation legislation applied on a mandatory basis to persons engaged in local trade.

45 [1977] 2 S.C.R. 134 [*Vapor*].

chance of private redress without public monitoring by the continued oversight of a regulatory agency."[46]

Laskin C.J.'s *dicta* were subsequently adopted by Dickson C.J. in an important and comprehensive restatement of the jurisprudence on the second branch of the trade and commerce power. In the 1989 *General Motors* case,[47] Dickson C.J. set out a non-exhaustive five-part test for the general trade power under section 91(2). The first three indicia were derived from Laskin C.J.'s judgment in *Vapor*: (1) the impugned legislation must be part of a regulatory scheme; (2) the scheme must be administered by the continuing oversight of a regulatory agency; and (3) the legislation must be concerned with trade as a whole rather than with a particular industry. To this list, Dickson C.J. added two further indicia: (4) the legislation should be of a nature that the provinces jointly or severally would be constitutionally incapable of enacting; and (5) the failure to include one or more provinces or localities in a legislative scheme would jeopardize the successful operation of the scheme in other parts of the country. Dickson C.J. stated that these indicia would serve to ensure that federal legislation "does not upset the balance of power between federal and provincial governments."[48]

On its face, the five-part test in *General Motors* would seem to represent a high hurdle for the federal government to support legislation under the second branch of the trade and commerce power. However, Dickson C.J. held that it was not necessary for federal legislation to satisfy all five indicia. He described the five indicia as a "preliminary checklist, the presence of which in legislation is an indication of validity under the trade and commerce power." At the same time, he stated that "the presence or absence of any of these five criteria [need not be] necessarily determinative." The overriding consideration is whether "what is being addressed in a federal enactment is genuinely a national economic concern and not just a collection of local ones."[49]

It is important to keep this "overriding consideration" in mind when applying the second branch of the trade and commerce power. In our view, the relevance of the first two indicia is unclear. Whether a particular legislative provision is part of a regulatory scheme (the first indicia) or whether the legislation provides for a regulatory agency

---

46 *Ibid.* at 165.

47 *General Motors of Canada Ltd. v. City National Leasing*, [1989] 1 S.C.R. 641 [*General Motors*]. See also: *Can. (A.G.) v. Canadian National Transportation Ltd.*, [1983] 2 S.C.R. 206 [*Canadian National Transportation*], Dickson C.J., dissenting.

48 *General Motors*, above note 47 at 663.

49 *Ibid.* at 662–63, quoting from *Canadian National Transportation*, above note 47 at 268.

(the second indicia), seem unrelated to the issue of whether the underlying economic problem being addressed is truly national in scope. The first two indicia seem more concerned with the form of federal legislation rather than with the substance of the economic problem being addressed. It may be that they reflect a previous era of an expanding public sector. Indeed, Laskin C.J. wrote his 1977 judgment in *Vapor* at the height of government expansion, and it is understandable that he might regard the establishment of a regulatory agency and the existence of a regulatory scheme as natural and desirable. In the contemporary environment, when governments are contracting and downsizing rather than expanding, it seems anachronistic to make the validity of federal legislation contingent on these formal criteria.

The relative significance of the five indicia in *General Motors* can be discerned from the manner in which they were applied by Dickson C.J. The statute at issue in *General Motors* was the *Combines Investigation Act*.[50] In the past, federal legislation regulating anti-competitive practices had been upheld under Parliament's criminal law power. However, amendments enacted in 1986 had placed a greater emphasis on regulation as opposed to criminal sanctions, and it was therefore necessary to consider whether the legislation could be upheld on the basis of the trade and commerce power. Dickson C.J. concluded that the legislation satisfied all five indicia and was supportable under the second branch of *Parsons*: (1) the Act embodied a "complex scheme of economic regulation," since it contained three elements: an elucidation of prohibited conduct, the creation of an investigatory mechanism, and the establishment of a remedial mechanism; (2) the scheme "operate[d] under the watchful gaze of a regulatory agency . . . the Director of Investigation and Research and . . . the Restrictive Trade Practices Commission";[51] (3) the Act was "quite clearly concerned with the regulation of trade in general, rather than with the regulation of a particular industry or commodity";[52] and (4)–(5) the deleterious effects of anti-competitive practices "transcend provincial boundaries" and ensure that a competitive economy is "not an issue of purely local concern but one of crucial importance for the national economy."[53]

Dickson C.J.'s application of the fourth and fifth indicia is particularly noteworthy. There is an obvious parallel between the fourth and fifth criteria and the "provincial inability" test to determine whether a

---

50 This statute has now been repealed and replaced by the *Competition Act*, R.S.C. 1985, c. C-34.

51 *General Motors*, above note 47 at 677.

52 *Ibid*. at 678.

53 *Ibid*.

matter qualifies as a matter of national concern under the peace, order, and good government (POGG) power. As discussed in Chapter 8, the provincial inability test in the POGG jurisprudence considers "the effect on extra-provincial interests of a provincial failure to deal effectively with the control or regulation of the intra-provincial aspects of the matter."[54] However, in *General Motors*, Dickson C.J. concluded that the federal legislation could not operate effectively if it were restricted to interprovincial and international trade. In coming to this conclusion, he rejected the Quebec attorney general's argument that the provinces were capable of regulating competition within their respective boundaries. Dickson C.J. agreed that the provinces had jurisdiction over anti-competitive practices within the province pursuant to the property and civil rights power. However, in his view, restricting the federal legislation to anti-competitive practices in interprovincial and international trade would render the federal legislation ineffective: "Because regulation of competition is so clearly of national interest and because competition cannot be successfully regulated by federal legislation which is restricted to interprovincial trade, the Quebec argument must fail."[55] Accordingly, the crucial consideration under the fourth and fifth indicia is the effect of Parliament's failure to regulate local aspects of the matter on the entire federal scheme at issue, rather than the ability of the provinces to regulate the same subject matter.

Parliament's power to enact legislation directed at the "general regulation of trade" has been infrequently relied upon over the past decade. One of the few cases to rely upon this constitutional authority is *Kirkbi AG v. Ritvik Holdings Inc.*[56] In *Kirkbi*, the Supreme Court unanimously upheld the constitutional validity of the *Trade-marks Act* on the basis of the "second branch" of the federal trade and commerce power. The decision merely made explicit what had been implicit in the Privy Council's decision in *Canada Standard*.

3) The Securities Reference

The issue of whether Parliament has the ability to regulate securities trading under the second branch of the trade and commerce power has been a source of long-standing debate and controversy. In the 1932 decision of *Lymburn v. Mayland*,[57] the Privy Council held that the provinces have the jurisdiction to regulate intraprovincial trading in se-

54 *R. v. Crown Zellerbach Canada Ltd.*, [1988] 1 S.C.R. 401 at para. 33.
55 *General Motors*, above note 47 at 681.
56 Above note 16.
57 [1932] A.C. 318 [*Lymburn*].

curities pursuant to the property and civil rights power under section 92(13) of the *Constitution Act, 1867*. In *Multiple Access v. McCutcheon*,[58] Dickson J. affirmed *Lymburn*, stating:

> It is well established that the provinces have the power, as a matter of property and civil rights, to regulate the trade in corporate securities in the province, provided the statute does not single out federal companies for special treatment or discriminate against them in any way. . . . Since the decision of the Privy Council in *Lymburn v. Mayland* . . . the provisions of provincial securities acts have been given a wide constitutional recognition.[59]

As discussed above, in *Global Securities*, the Supreme Court upheld a provision of the B.C. *Securities Act* allowing the B.C. Securities Commission to require registered brokers in the province to produce records to assist in the administration of securities laws of another jurisdiction under the property and civil rights power. Iacobucci J., for the Court, stated that the pith and substance of the provision "is the effective regulation of domestic securities, a task that has long been recognized to fall within provincial authority."[60]

As *Global Securities* suggests, each province and territory has comprehensive securities regulation, and provincial securities commissions regulate securities market participants. However, the mere fact that the provinces have enacted securities regulation does not necessarily preclude federal securities regulation.

Since around the time the *Lymburn* case was decided, there have been numerous proposals for federal securities legislation and a national regulator.[61] It has been argued that such proposals can be upheld as constitutionally valid under the second branch of the trade and commerce power. The calls for federal intervention have increased with the

---

58 [1982] 2 S.C.R. 161 [*Multiple Access*].

59 *Ibid.* at 183.

60 *Global Securities*, above note 34 at para. 40.

61 For instance, in 1935, the Royal Commission on Price Spreads recommended the formation of an investment securities board to oversee the issuance of securities by federal companies: see *Report of the Royal Commission on Price Spreads* (Ottawa: King's Printer, 1935). The 1964 Royal Commission on Banking and Finance (commonly referred to as the "Porter Commission") advocated for uniform legislation and administration of the Canadian securities industry: see *Report of the Royal Commission on Banking and Finance* (Ottawa: Queen's Printer, 1964). Three years later, the Ontario Securities Commission put forward a proposal for a single national securities regulator charged with achieving uniformity in the regulation of securities across the country: see Ontario Securities Commission. "CANSEC: Legal and Administrative Concepts" (November 1967), OSCB 61.

pace of technological change and the increasing degree of interprovincial and international integration of securities markets. In 2003, the "Wise Persons' Committee"—a committee established by the federal minister of finance—recommended adoption of comprehensive federal securities legislation and a federal regulator.[62] The 2006 Crawford Panel on a Single Canadian Securities Regulator advocated in favour of a federal statute entitled the *Canadian Securities Act* and the introduction of a Canadian Securities Commission.[63] Following the release of the Crawford Panel's report, an Expert Panel on Securities Regulation (the "Hockin Panel") released a report in 2009 recommending a comprehensive national regime of securities regulation to be brought into force in participating jurisdictions through the (voluntary) repeal of provincial or territorial securities legislation.[64]

In 2009, the federal government prepared draft legislation[65] based on the recommendations of the Hockin Panel. The proposed legislation would have created a single Canadian securities regulator. The stated purpose of the Act was to provide for investor protection, to foster fair, efficient, and competitive capital markets, and to contribute to the integrity and stability of Canada's financial system. The Act included provisions regulating aspects of securities trading that resembled provisions in provincial and territorial securities statutes, including registration requirements for securities dealers, prospectus filing requirements, disclosure requirements, specific duties for market participants, a framework for the regulation of derivatives, civil remedies, and regulatory and criminal offences pertaining to securities. The proposed federal legislation was not mandatory but was permissive; provinces and territories were free to opt in to the federal legislative scheme.

Following provincial references to the Alberta[66] and Quebec[67] Courts of Appeal, both of which ruled the federal statute unconstitutional,[68] the Governor in Council referred the issue of the validity of the proposed legislation to the Supreme Court of Canada. The govern-

---

62 WPC: Committee to review the structure of securities regulation in Canada: *It's Time* (Ottawa: Department of Finance, 2003).

63 Crawford Panel on a Single Canadian Securities Regulator, *Blueprint for a Canadian Securities Commission—Final Paper* (Ottawa: Government of Ontario, 2006).

64 Expert Panel on Securities Regulation, *Creating an Advantage in Global Capital Markets—Final Report and Recommendations* (Ottawa: Department of Finance, 2009).

65 *Proposed Canadian Securities Act*, Order in Council, P.C. 2010-667.

66 *Reference Re Securities Act (Can.)*, 2011 ABCA 77.

67 *Québec (A.G.) v. Canada (A.G.)*, 2011 QCCA 591.

68 Dalphond J.A. dissented at the Quebec Court of Appeal.

ment of Canada, supported by the Attorney General of Ontario and various interveners, argued that the legislation could be sustained as valid federal legislation, relying exclusively on the second trade branch of the trade and commerce power. The Attorney General of Alberta, the Attorney General of Quebec, and other provincial attorneys general and various interveners opposed the Act, arguing that it fell within the property and civil rights power under section 92(13) and matters of a merely local or private nature under section 92(16) of the *Constitution Act, 1867*. In a unanimous decision authored "by the Court," the Supreme Court of Canada held that the proposed legislation was unconstitutional.[69]

The Court held that the second branch of the general trade and commerce power—as opposed to the power to regulate interprovincial and international trade—is seemingly broad. However, it cautioned against an overly expansive interpretation of the second branch, noting that this would "upset the constitutional balance envisaged by ss. 91 and 92 and undermine the federalism principle."[70] According to the Court, the general trade and commerce branch is "necessarily circumscribed."[71] After reviewing *Canadian National Transportation*, *General Motors*, and *Kirkbi*, the Court discerned the following "common theme" in the jurisprudence in the second branch of section 91(2) of the *Constitution Act, 1867*:

> Provided the law is part of a general regulatory scheme aimed at trade and commerce under oversight of a regulatory agency, it will fall under the general federal trade and commerce power if the matter regulated is genuinely national in importance and scope. To be genuinely national in importance and scope, it is not enough that the matter be replicated in all jurisdictions throughout the country. It must, to use the phrase in *General Motors*, be something that the provinces, acting either individually or in concert, could not effectively achieve. To put it another way, the situation must be such that if the federal government were not able to legislate, there would be a constitutional gap. Such a gap is constitutional anathema in a federation.[72]

The Court went on to state that the *General Motors* test does not involve a consideration of "what is optimum as a matter of policy" but rather "what is constitutionally permissible."[73] While the fifth *General*

69 *Reference Re Securities Act*, [2011] 3 S.C.R. 837 [*Securities Reference*].
70 *Ibid*. at para. 70.
71 *Ibid*. at para. 74.
72 *Ibid*. at para. 83.
73 *Ibid*. at para. 90.

Motors factor asks whether the failure of the provinces "to participate in the regulatory scheme would 'jeopardize the successful operation of the scheme in other parts of the country,' . . . the reference to 'successful operation,'" according to the Court, "should not be read as introducing an inquiry into what would be the best resolution in terms of policy."[74] In other words, the relative efficacy of federal versus provincial legislation is an irrelevant consideration under the second branch of section 91(2).[75] In order for federal legislation to satisfy the fifth *General Motors* indicia, there must be a "constitutional gap" or a "regulatory vacuum"[76] caused by the inability of the provinces to legislate.

While the above passage may be taken to suggest that the *General Motors* factors are necessary criteria to support federal legislation under the second branch of section 91(2), the Court affirmed Dickson C.J.'s holding in *General Motors* that the criteria are not exhaustive and that it is not necessary that they be present in every case.[77] Applying the *General Motors* indicia to the proposed Act, the Court held that the legislation could not be upheld. The first two criteria were clearly met; the Act proposed a national regulatory regime for securities and there would have been oversight by a national regulatory agency. However, the Court held that the legislation failed the third, fourth, and fifth elements of the test.

With respect to the third element of the *General Motors* test, the Court acknowledged that "[a] long-standing exercise of power does not confer constitutional authority to legislate, nor does the historic presence of the provinces in securities regulation preclude a federal claim to regulatory jurisdiction."[78] However, it placed considerable emphasis on the fact that the provinces had regulated securities for many years, a theme that was repeated several times throughout the course of the judgment. For instance, the Court stated that "[t]he propriety of . . . a constitutional realignment cannot simply be assumed" and the "shift in regulatory authority . . . requires justification," noting that the day-to-day regulation of securities markets "have long been considered local

---

74 *Ibid*.

75 Some authors have argued that it was possible to read the fourth and fifth criteria in *General Motors* as requiring a consideration of the relative efficacy of federal and provincial legislation: see I.B. Lee, "Balancing and its Alternatives: Jurisprudential Choice, Federal Securities Legislation and the Trade and Commerce Power" (2011) 50 Can. Bus. L.J. 95 at 99–104.

76 The Court has used the language of "regulatory vacuums" in the context of interjurisdictional immunity jurisprudence: *British Columbia (Attorney General) v. Lafarge Canada Inc.*, 2007 SCC 23 at paras. 4 and 73.

77 *Securities Reference*, above note 69 at para. 81.

78 *Ibid*. at para. 116, citing *Ontario Hydro v. Ontario (Labour Relations Board)*, [1993] 3 S.C.R. 327 at 357, Lamer C.J.

concerns subject to provincial legislative competence."[79] In the end, the Court concluded that Canada had failed to discharge its burden of demonstrating that the legislation engaged "trade as a whole," citing a lack of evidentiary support for Canada's claim for federal jurisdiction. According to the Court, Canada had not shown that the regulation of securities "has evolved to become a matter of transcendent national concern that brings it within the s. 91(2) general trade and commerce power."[80]

The Court's reasoning on the fourth element of the *General Motors* test was rather short and perfunctory. The Court reiterated its earlier conclusion that the proposed legislation dealt with the day-to-day regulation of securities market participants. It noted that the "proposed Act reflects an attempt that goes well beyond . . . matters of undoubted national interest and concern and reaches down into the detailed regulation of all aspects of securities."[81] The Court then drew a rather curious distinction between the federal *Combines Investigation Act* upheld in *General Motors* and the proposed securities Act. Whereas competition law regulates "*only* anti-competitive contracts and conduct—a particular aspect of economic activity that falls squarely within the federal domain," the proposed Act was said to regulate "*all* aspects of contracts for securities within the provinces."[82]

With respect to the fifth element of the *General Motors* test, the Court held that the proposed Act would "not founder if a particular province declined to participate in the federal scheme," noting that the opt-in feature of the scheme contemplated the possibility that not all provinces would participate.[83]

As discussed above, the Court held that the issue of the relative efficacy of federal or provincial securities legislation was constitutionally irrelevant. On this basis, it declined to engage in any detailed analysis of the considerable evidence from experts that had been filed by the parties with respect for the need for federal intervention in securities

---

79 *Securities Reference*, above note 69 at paras. 5–6.

80 *Ibid*. at para. 114.

81 *Ibid*. at para. 122.

82 *Ibid*. This distinction appears rather superficial and amounts to little more than an assertion that securities regulation (as opposed to competition regulation) is by nature local, rather than international. It is arguable that the regulation of securities market participants is necessary to protect investors and ensure market fairness for *Canadian* capital markets. Furthermore, it is noteworthy that prior to the *Securities Reference*, commentators had suggested that there was a close parallel between the competition legislation considered in *General Motors* and the proposed *Securities Act* (see Lee, above note 75 at 116–18).

83 *Securities Reference*, above note 69 at para. 123.

markets. The Court only referred to the evidence in passing, stating that:

> A reasonable reading of the reports suggests that routine securities regulation is mainly concerned with the regulation of securities as an industry. It also confirms the local nature of much of Canada's securities industry.[84]

The Court went on to note that there was industry specialization across the country; for instance, many mining companies list their shares in British Columbia, Ontario's securities market was largely attributable to large financial services companies, Alberta dominated the market for oil and gas, and Quebec had a large number of technology listings.[85]

While the Court held that the Act, viewed as whole, could not be upheld under section 91(2), it did note that certain aspects of the Act could potentially be upheld under the general trade and commerce power. The Court stated that management of "systemic risk" (risks whereby the default by one market participant impacts the ability of others to fulfil their obligations) and "national data collection" addressed matters of genuine national importance. The provinces, acting alone or in concert, lacked the constitutional capacity to sustain a viable national regulatory scheme in relation to such matters.[86] Furthermore, although the Court held that the Act as a whole could not be upheld under section 91(2), it suggested that a cooperative federalism approach could be used to establish a national securities regime, alluding to the interlocking federal and provincial marketing schemes considered in the *Egg Reference*.[87]

The Supreme Court's decision in the *Securities Reference* has been criticized by some commentators as unduly formalistic.[88] While acknowledging that the history of provincial regulation in securities was not determinative of the constitutional issue, the Court placed considerable emphasis on the existence of provincial regulation in coming to the conclusion that the proposed Act was related to trade in a "particular industry" rather than "trade as a whole." As one commentator puts it, "[t]his decision essentially sends the message that this is

---

84 *Ibid*. at para. 127.

85 *Ibid*.

86 *Ibid*. at paras. 117–21 and 123.

87 *Ibid*. at paras. 58 and 132.

88 P. Puri, "The Supreme Court's Securities Act Reference Fails to Demonstrate an Understanding of the Canadian Capital Markets" (2012) 52 Can. Bus. L.J. 190. However, others have praised the decision: see E. Spink, "Reacting to the Status Quo in Securities Regulation" (2012) 52 Can. Bus. L.J. 182.

how we have always done it and therefore, we are going to continue in this way."[89] The Supreme Court's reasoning in the *Securities Reference* has been contrasted with its approach in previous reference cases such as the *Reference re Same Sex Marriage*,[90] in which the Court rejected "frozen concepts" reasoning in favour of a "living tree" approach to interpretation that examines the modern context underpinning the constitutional issue.[91]

Furthermore, the Court's decision has been criticized for failing to demonstrate an appropriate understanding of Canadian capital markets. The Court's passing reference to the expert evidence and the cryptic suggestion that the "reports" confirmed the "local" nature of the securities industry has been criticized as simplistic and anachronistic. As Professor Puri states:

> It is accurate to state that British Columbia and Ontario host a high proportion of mining issuers, Alberta hosts a high proportion of oil and gas issuers, and Ontario hosts a high number of financial services issuers. However, the province in which the issuer is headquartered determines who the primary regulator is . . . but not much else. The reality for many issuers is that their investors are located throughout Canada, with nationwide or international and gross domestic product impact. The location of the headquarters of an issuer does not determine where the market is and provides little explanatory benefit to understanding the scope of the capital markets.
>
> It is more telling that two-thirds of reporting issuers in Canada are reporting in more than one jurisdiction, meaning that they are raising capital in more than one jurisdiction.[92]

Whatever the merits of the Supreme Court's decision, as a result of the *Securities Reference*, it is now clear that the "day-to-day" regulation of securities market participants is a matter that falls within the exclusive jurisdiction of the provinces. However, as discussed above, the Court did suggest that there may be a role for federal regulation under the general trade and commerce power in relation to matters such as systemic risk and national data collection. In addition, the Court suggested the possibility of the introduction of a cooperative federalism scheme to achieve some form of national regulatory standard. This Court's decision has left the door open (albeit slightly) for future federal legislative intervention in securities markets.

89 Puri, above note 88 at 193.
90 [2004] 3 S.C.R. 698.
91 *Ibid.* at para. 22.
92 Puri, above note 88 at 192.

In September 2014, the federal government and the governments of British Columbia, New Brunswick, Ontario, Prince Edward Island, and Saskatchewan signed a memorandum of agreement to formalize a new scheme of interlocking federal and provincial legislation following the release of the Supreme Court's decision in the *Securities Reference*. The Yukon agreed to join the initiative in April 2015. Draft federal legislation,[93] a uniform draft enactment[94] to be passed by each of the participating provinces and territories, has been released for comment. The draft legislation contemplates a single pan-Canadian regulator called the Capital Markets Regulatory Authority. The Government of Quebec has challenged the constitutionality of the initiative through a reference to the Quebec Court of Appeal. Alberta has also declared its opposition to a single securities regulator and neither Manitoba nor Nova Scotia has chosen to join the initiative. As of the time of writing, it remains to be seen whether the scheme will progress further and whether the Courts will conclude that federal legislation, if enacted, falls within Parliament's authority under the general trade and commerce power.

D. IMPLEMENTATION OF INTERNATIONAL TRADE AGREEMENTS

A number of academic commentators[95] have suggested that the *General Motors* test would support federal legislation implementing such international trade agreements as the *Canada–U.S. Free Trade Agreement* (FTA) and the *North American Free Trade Agreement* (NAFTA).[96] This section considers the scope of Parliament's authority to implement international trade agreements, as well as its jurisdiction to enact legislation to strengthen the Canadian economic union and to reduce interprovincial barriers to trade.

Canada has entered into a number of important and far-reaching international trade agreements, including the Canada–U.S. and North

93 *Capital Markets Stability Act (Canada)*, online: http://ccmr-ocrmc.ca/publications/legislation.

94 *Capital Markets Act*, online: http://ccmr-ocrmc.ca/publications/legislation.

95 See, for example, R. Howse, "NAFTA and the Constitution: Does *Labour Conventions* Really Matter Any More?" (1994) 5 Const. Forum Const. 54; and M.A. Luz, "NAFTA, Investment and the Constitution of Canada: Will the Watertight Compartments Spring a Leak" (2000–2001) 32 Ottawa L. Rev. 35.

96 See the *Canada–United States Free Trade Agreement*, 22 December 1987, 27 I.L.M. 281 [FTA] and the *North American Free Trade Agreement*, 17 December 1992, 32 I.L.M. 289 [NAFTA].

American free trade agreements, as well as the Agreement Establishing the World Trade Organization. While these treaties deal with a number of matters that are clearly within federal jurisdiction, such as tariffs and border measures, they also deal with matters that might otherwise be regarded as falling within provincial jurisdiction. As a result, questions have been raised about the ability of Parliament to enact legislation implementing these agreements.

1) Treaty Execution versus Treaty Implementation

In analyzing the constitutional issues relating to international trade agreements, it is important to distinguish between the power to enter into the treaties as opposed to the power to implement treaties. The federal government has plenary authority to negotiate and enter into international agreements on Canada's behalf. This authority is not limited to matters that fall under federal jurisdiction according to the domestic division of powers. The federal executive's power to enter into international agreements derives from the Crown's delegation of prerogative powers over foreign affairs to the governor general of Canada.[97] Treaty implementation usually involves the enactment of legislation incorporating the provisions of a treaty into the domestic law of Canada. Although Canada is bound by a treaty as a matter of international law, the terms of a treaty are not automatically incorporated into the domestic law of Canada.[98] Therefore, to the extent that the domestic law of Canada is inconsistent with the terms of a treaty, it will be necessary to enact a statute that will bring domestic law into conformity with the terms of the treaty.[99]

---

97 The *Letters Patent Constituting the Office of Governor General and Commander-in-Chief of Canada*, C. Gaz., vol. LXXXI, No. 12 (1 October 1947) provides that the Governor General is authorized "to exercise all powers and authorities lawfully belonging to Us [the King] in respect of Canada." As Professor Hogg notes, "[t]his language undoubtedly delegates to the federal government of Canada the power to enter into treaties binding Canada" (Hogg, above note 24 at 11.2). See also: M. Pilkington, "Constitutional Jurisdiction Pertaining to Certain Aspects of the Free Trade Agreement" in *Fourteenth Report of the Standing Committee on Foreign Affairs* (Ottawa: Supply and Services Canada, 1988).

98 See *Francis v. Canada*, [1956] S.C.R. 618 at 625; *Capital Cities Communications Inc. v. Canadian Radio-Television Commission*, [1978] 2 S.C.R. 141 at 172–73; *Baker v. Canada (Minister of Citizenship and Immigration)*, [1999] 2 S.C.R. 817 at para. 69.

99 It will not always be necessary to pass a statute in order to "implement" a treaty. An "implementing" statute is required only in cases where domestic law is at variance with the international obligations assumed by Canada under a treaty. Where domestic law already meets all the obligations of the treaty, the treaty has already been "implemented" into domestic law. There are other cases

2) The *Labour Conventions* Case

Section 132 of the *Constitution Act, 1867* provides that the Parliament of Canada has exclusive authority to enact legislation necessary in order to implement treaties signed by Britain on Canada's behalf. However, the drafters of the *Constitution Act, 1867* did not anticipate that Canada would eventually acquire the status of a fully independent state and enter into treaties with foreign states on its own behalf. Accordingly, the *Constitution Act, 1867* does not expressly address the legislative authority of Parliament or the provinces to implement treaties. In the *Labour Conventions* case,[100] the Privy Council decided that the authority to implement treaties is divided between Parliament and the provincial legislatures in accordance with their respective legislative jurisdiction. In other words, if the subject matter of the treaty deals with a matter falling within provincial jurisdiction in accordance with section 92, only the provinces may enact legislation implementing that treaty into domestic law and *vice versa*.

The *Labour Conventions* case has proven extremely controversial, particularly among English-Canadian commentators. The decision has been criticized as effectively handcuffing Canada in its attempts to negotiate international treaties, since the federal government cannot guarantee that treaties dealing with matters under provincial jurisdiction will be implemented.[101] There have been calls over the years for the courts to overrule the decision.[102] On the other hand, experience has shown that the *Labour Conventions* case has not precluded Canada from negotiating comprehensive trade agreements, including WTO, FTA, and NAFTA.

3) Application of *Labour Conventions* to Trade Agreements

The question that arises is how the *Labour Conventions* rule applies in cases of comprehensive trade agreements such as WTO, the FTA, and NAFTA. To the extent that the agreements deal with matters falling within federal authority, such as tariffs and border measures, federal

---

where a treaty can be executed through executive or administrative action. For instance, in *R. v. Hape*, 2007 SCC 26, LeBel J. stated at para. 39 that "the doctrine of adoption operates in Canada such that prohibitive rules of customary international law should be incorporated into domestic law *in the absence of conflicting legislation*" [emphasis added]. See, generally, Hogg, above note 24 at 11.5.

100 *Can. (A.G.) v. Ont. (A.G.)*, [1937] A.C. 326 (P.C.) [*Labour Conventions*].

101 See the discussion in G.V. La Forest, "The *Labour Conventions* Case Revisited" (1974) Can. Y.B. Int'l Law 137.

102 See the sources cited by La Forest, *ibid*.

legislation implementing the agreements would fall under federal jurisdiction. Federal legislation implementing the FTA and NAFTA is primarily concerned with the amendment of federal laws that would otherwise have been inconsistent with these agreements.[103] However, these comprehensive agreements also deal with non-tariff or indirect barriers to trade, including laws and practices of the provincial governments. The fact that the agreements are intended to impose limitations on provincial powers is confirmed by the "Extent of Obligations" clauses in both the FTA and the NAFTA, in which the federal government undertakes to ensure the observance of the agreements by the provinces.[104]

In 2006, the Ontario Court of Appeal dismissed an application by a public interest group that challenged the investor state provisions of Chapter 11 of NAFTA.[105] Chapter 11 provides that signatory states may initiate claims to determine whether another NAFTA country has violated its obligations under the agreement through international arbitration. Arbitral tribunals are directed to apply international law and are empowered to award damages or restitution. Chapter 11 provides that arbitration awards must be enforced in each signatory state. The implementation of these provisions in Canada was achieved through section 50 of the *North American Free Trade Agreement Implementation Act*, which amended the *Commercial Arbitration Act* to ensure that its enforcement provisions applied to NAFTA arbitration awards. The Council of Canadians launched a constitutional challenge to the enforcement of awards to foreign investors for damages caused by government action in Canada. The challenge was based on the exclusive jurisdiction of superior courts to adjudicate under section 96 of the *Constitution Act, 1867*, the principles of judicial independence, the rule of law, and the *Charter*. The Ontario Court of Appeal rejected the interest group's argument that the NAFTA tribunal had been incorporated into Canadian law under the federal statute.

The *Council of Canadians* case did not consider the validity of the *North American Free Trade Agreement Implementation Act* under the trade and commerce power. However, there is a broad consensus among commentators that the legislation implementing the FTA and NAFTA is constitutionally valid, either on the basis of Parliament's power in relation

103 The *North American Free Trade Agreement Implementation Act*, S.C. 1993, c. 44 [NAFTA Implementing Legislation]; *Canada–United States Free Trade Agreement Implementation Act*, S.C. 1988, c. 65 [FTA Implementing Legislation].

104 See Article 103 of the FTA, above note 96, and Article 105 of the NAFTA, above note 96.

105 *Council of Canadians v. Canada (Attorney General)* (2006), 277 D.L.R. (4th) 527 (Ont. C.A.) [*Council of Canadians*].

to international trade or through its power to provide for the general regulation of trade.[106]

a) Parliament's Power over International Trade

The most powerful argument in favour of a federal power to implement international trade agreements is, quite simply, that international treaties are concerned with international trade. Although treaties may have an effect on matters falling within provincial jurisdiction, incidental effects do not detract from the validity of a statute whose main purpose, or pith and substance, is international trade.[107] For example, Professor Ivan Bernier of Laval University testified before the Standing Senate Committee on Foreign Affairs in 1988 on Parliament's ability to implement the FTA. In Professor Bernier's view there is compelling support for Parliament's jurisdiction to implement the treaty pursuant to its power in relation to international trade:

> What it really comes down to is this: "What is the true nature of the legislative measures adopted?" A free trade agreement such as the one proposed or currently under consideration seeks to impose restrictions or prohibit certain transactions. More specifically, I would say that the provisions concerning national treatment seek to eliminate all forms of discrimination against products, manufacturers or even Americans themselves. Thus it is an essentially negative approach designed to do away with discrimination. I believe that such an approach would be viewed broadly by the courts as flowing from international trade.[108]

As noted earlier, the federal legislation implementing both the FTA and NAFTA dealt mainly with amendments to federal statutes. In both instances, the main legislative changes that were immediately required by the treaties were to provisions in federal laws. The main exception was in relation to provincial regulations relating to the distribution of wine and distilled spirits. At the time the FTA was signed, certain provincial regulations dealing with wine and spirits were not in compliance with Canada's obligations under the FTA. Certain provinces indicated that they intended to make the necessary amendments so as to bring their regulations into line with the FTA. However, the FTA Implementing Legislation also granted the federal Cabinet the power to make regulations

106 See Hogg, above note 24 at 11.5(c); Pilkington, above note 97 (reviewing testimony of a number of constitutional experts, the majority of whom concluded that Parliament had authority to implement the FTA).

107 See Chapter 4, Section 6(a) for a discussion of the pith and substance doctrine.

108 See Pilkington, above note 97 at 18.

so as to ensure that provincial laws were in conformity with the treaty. The FTA Implementing Legislation authorized regulations "requiring or prohibiting the doing of anything in relation to which a regulation may be made under this subsection and prescribing penalties for the contravention of or non-compliance with any such regulation."[109]

Had the federal Cabinet ever been called on to exercise this regulation-making authority, it would obviously have had a significant impact on matters under provincial jurisdiction. Arguably, however, such a regulation would have been valid because its main purpose, or pith and substance, would have been to ensure that Canada was in conformity with its international treaty obligations. Countries will only enter into international trade agreements with Canada if they can be assured that Canada has the capacity to ensure compliance from provincial governments. In this sense, the ability to enforce compliance is a necessary and essential feature of these agreements. The impact on provincial jurisdiction is, in constitutional terms, necessarily incidental to the exercise of federal powers because it is a condition precedent to the very existence of the treaties themselves.

b) Parliament's Power over the General Regulation of Trade

It may also be argued that Parliament has the capacity to implement international trade agreements pursuant to the second branch of the trade and commerce power. Professor Fairley, for example, has argued that federal implementing legislation for the *Canada–U.S. Free Trade Agreement* meets the five-part test established by Justice Dickson in *General Motors*:[110] (1) the Treaty and the legislation form a unified and comprehensive whole and therefore qualify as a regulatory scheme; (2) there is ongoing supervision by various panels and commissions established under the agreements; (3) the focus of the agreement is said to be trade in general as opposed to particular trades or professions; (4) the provinces could not jointly or severally negotiate and implement these agreements; and (5) the failure of one or more provinces to comply would jeopardize the entire scheme.

The most significant difficulty with Fairley's analysis relates to the third criterion—the requirement that legislation deal with trade in general as opposed to individual trades and professions. The FTA and the NAFTA establish certain general obligations that are applicable to

---

109 FTA Implementing Legislation, above note 103, s. 9. An identical provision was included in the NAFTA Implementing Legislation, above note 103.

110 H.S. Fairley, "Implementing the Canada–United States Free Trade Agreement" in D.M. McRae & D.P. Steger, eds., *Understanding the Free Trade Agreement* (Halifax: Institute for Research on Public Policy, 1988).

all legislative and governmental measures affecting trade matters, such as the obligation to extend national treatment to foreign firms. However, the agreements also include a number of specific chapters setting out limitations on government measures in particular sectors of the economy, such as labour mobility, energy, and transportation. It could be argued that these specific chapters constitute an attempt to regulate particular trades and that legislation implementing the agreements cannot be justified on the basis that they regulate trade in general. On the other hand, it is important to bear in mind the distinction between the terms of the treaties themselves as opposed to the federal implementing legislation. While the treaties themselves might contain detailed codes of government conduct in particular sectors of the economy, the implementing legislation is more limited. Its main focus is on amending the federal statutes that would otherwise have been in violation of the requirements of the treaties. It seems highly unlikely that the courts would conclude that the implementing legislation constitutes an impermissible attempt by Parliament to regulate particular trades or professions.

E. THE CANADIAN ECONOMIC UNION AND THE CONSTITUTION

The issue of interprovincial barriers to trade within the Canadian economic union has been a recurring issue on the Canadian political agenda. In 1994, the government of Canada and the governments of the provinces and territories signed the *Agreement on Internal Trade*,[111] designed to reduce or eliminate these barriers. The agreement itself has been a mixed success.[112] It is not legally enforceable and has led to minimal changes in federal and provincial laws and regulations. Given its limited success, the question arises whether Parliament possesses sufficient authority to legislate directly so as to reduce or eliminate barriers to internal trade within Canada. This, in turn, raises the question of whether Parliament has the constitutional jurisdiction to legislate to enhance the proper and efficient functioning of the Canadian economic union.

For most of the first century after Confederation, the courts in Canada and in England evinced little concern over the effect that consti-

111 The agreement has undergone a number of amendments. See the 2015 Consolidation of the Agreement on Internal Trade, online: www.ait-aci.ca/index_en/ait.htm.

112 See, generally, M.J. Trebilcock & D. Schwanen, eds., *Getting There: An Assessment of the Agreement on Internal Trade* (Toronto: C.D. Howe Institute, 1995).

tutional jurisprudence might have on the proper functioning of the Canadian economic union. However, two important Supreme Court cases have recognized that maintaining and strengthening the Canadian economic union is a key principle underlying the Canadian constitutional framework. The cases have also expressly stated that Parliament has the legislative authority to enact legislation designed to enhance the functioning of the economic union.

1) The *Morguard* and *Hunt* Cases

We have already examined *Morguard Investments Ltd. v. De Savoye*[113] and *Hunt v. T & N plc*[114] in the context of Parliament's peace, order, and good government power in Chapter 8. The cases are also relevant in terms of the scope of the federal trade and commerce power. In *Morguard*, La Forest J. concluded that a regime of mutual recognition of judgments across the country "is inherent in a federation." He also stated that the "integrating character of our constitutional arrangements" may have important implications for the division of legislative authority between Parliament and the provincial legislatures. La Forest J. identified certain key elements of the Canadian constitutional framework that are directed to the creation of a single country:

> A common citizenship ensured the mobility of Canadians across provincial lines, a position reinforced today by s. 6 of the *Charter*. . . . In particular, significant steps were taken to foster economic integration. One of the central features of the constitutional arrangements incorporated in the *Constitution Act, 1867* was the creation of a common market. Barriers to interprovincial trade were removed by s. 121. Generally trade and commerce between the provinces was seen to be a matter of concern to the country as a whole; see *Constitution Act, 1867*, s. 91(2). The Peace, Order and Good Government clause gives the federal Parliament powers to deal with interprovincial activities. . . . And the combined effect of s. 91(29) and s. 92(10) does the same for interprovincial works and undertakings.[115]

In *Hunt*, La Forest J. expanded on *Morguard*. He held that a provincial "blocking" statute that prohibited the removal of documents relating to a business concern in Quebec was constitutionally inapplicable to other provinces. La Forest J. began by noting that legal systems and rules must respect the diversity of societies and differences in legal

113 [1990] 3 S.C.R. 1077 [*Morguard*].
114 [1993] 4 S.C.R. 289 [*Hunt*].
115 *Morguard*, above note 113 at 1099.

systems. But respect for diversity must be tempered by the need to coordinate diversity, since the failure to ensure coordination will mean that "the anarchic system's worst attributes emerge, and individual litigants will pay the inevitable price of unfairness." La Forest J. stated that the rules developed in the context of private international law may well be inappropriate in the context of a federal system. The legal rules applicable between the constituent units in Canada must take account of the "legal interdependence under the scheme of confederation established in 1867."[116] La Forest J. then explored the significance of the *Morguard* case. The main objective of the *Morguard* decision was to reform certain common law rules regarding recognition and enforcement of judgments, which were "rooted in an outmoded conception of the world that emphasized sovereignty and independence, often at the cost of unfairness." These rules were said to be unsuited to a modern era "when international transactions involve a constant flow of products, wealth and people across the globe."[117] Moreover, La Forest J. stated that these outmoded rules are particularly inappropriate within the context of the Canadian federation, referring to, among other things, "the common market created by the union":

> Among the factors I identified [in *Morguard*] that would also support a more cooperative spirit in recognition and enforcement were (1) common citizenship, (2) interprovincial mobility of citizens, (3) the common market created by the union as reflected in ss. 91(2), 91(10), 121 and the peace, order and good government clause, and (4) the essentially unitary structure of our judicial system with the Supreme Court of Canada at its apex.[118]

According to La Forest J., the implications of the "integrating character of our constitutional arrangements" are not limited to the issue of the recognition by courts of judgments from other provinces. They are "constitutional imperatives" that impose limits on the jurisdiction of the provinces and confer legislative authority on Parliament.

In terms of provincial jurisdiction, the provinces cannot override what La Forest J. terms "the minimum standards of order and fairness addressed in *Morguard*." The blocking statute at issue in *Hunt* was inapplicable to B.C. litigation since it offended the basic structure of the Canadian federation:

---

116 *Hunt*, above note 114 at para. 51.

117 *Ibid.*

118 *Ibid.*

> It is inconceivable that in devising a scheme of union comprising a common market stretching from sea to sea, the Fathers of Confederation would have contemplated a situation where citizens would be effectively deprived of access to the ordinary courts in their jurisdiction in respect of transactions flowing from the existence of that common market. The resultant higher transactional costs for interprovincial transactions constitute an infringement on the unity and efficiency of the Canadian marketplace . . . as well as unfairness to the citizen.[119]

In terms of federal jurisdiction, La Forest J. stated that the imperatives of the Canadian economic union confer authority on Parliament to enact legislation for the purpose of protecting and maintaining the union. La Forest J. also suggested that Parliament's authority in this regard is not limited to constitutionalizing the common law rules enunciated in *Morguard*. Rather, there might well be valid and overlapping legislation on the same matter enacted by Parliament and a provincial legislature. In such a circumstance, the provincial law would not be unconstitutional, but it would be subject to the overriding and paramount powers of Parliament.[120]

2) Parliament's Power to Enhance the Economic Union

Morguard and *Hunt* suggest that Parliament has jurisdiction to legislate to maintain and enhance the proper functioning of the Canadian economic union. As Robert Howse states:

> [E]ven in cases such as *Hunt*, where no federal statute has been at issue, the Supreme Court has emphasized the importance of federal jurisdiction to securing the economic union. In *Hunt*, the Court even went so far as to suggest that the federal government could set rules for the recognition and enforcement of private law judgments by provincial courts where necessary to ensure order and fairness within the Canadian economic union. I do not think one could ever expect a clearer statement by the Court on the link between the ex-

119 *Ibid*.

120 In *Club Resorts Ltd. v. Van Breda*, [2012] S.C.R. 572, the Supreme Court considered the common law rules for the assumption of jurisdiction by provincial courts in two appeals involving tort claims against out-of-province defendants for accidents that occurred in foreign countries. The Court noted that *Morguard* and *Hunt* established constitutional limits on the powers of the Superior Courts to assume jurisdiction. However, La Forest J.'s *dicta* regarding Parliament's ability to legislate in relation to the recognition and enforcement of judgments was not discussed by the Court.

> panded scope of the federal government's general powers and the need for harmonization of provincial laws to secure the Canadian economic union.[121]

The nature and extent of Parliament's jurisdiction to legislate to enhance the economic union have not been delineated by the Supreme Court.[122] However, assistance may be drawn from the trade law context.

The distinction between negative and positive integration is a familiar one to trade lawyers. Negative integration focuses on removing measures that discriminate against another party. As Trebilcock and Behboodi note, negative integration "tells parties *what they may not do*."[123] International trade agreements such as the General Agreement on Trade and Tariffs (GATT) have traditionally focused on negative integration. These agreements prohibit measures that are explicitly discriminatory against external trading partners or that, while neutral on their face, have a disparate impact on external parties and amount to disguised barriers to trade.[124] Positive integration, in contrast, is concerned with positive measures taken by parties to harmonize divergent laws or practices, or to provide for the mutual recognition of different standards. Positive integration measures reduce transaction costs and aid in the free movement of factors of production across jurisdictional borders. Positive integration requires the creation of political institutions that have the authority to provide for minimum standards, mutual recognition, and harmonization of divergent laws.[125]

Assuming that Parliament has a role to play in enhancing the economic union, one potential role for Parliament could be focused on the achievement of negative integration. Measures designed to achieve negative integration achieve the objective of enhancing the economic union, but do so in a way that is less intrusive to provincial jurisdiction.

---

121 Robert Howse, "Securing the Canadian Economic Union: Legal and Constitutional Options for the Federal Government," Canadian Union Papers Commentary Series (Toronto: C.D. Howe Institute, 1996) at 12.

122 The *Morguard* and *Hunt* cases were not considered by the Court in the *Securities Reference*, above note 69. As discussed above, the proponents of the Act relied solely on the second branch of the trade and commerce power.

123 See M.J. Trebilcock & R. Behboodi, "The Canadian Agreement on Internal Trade: Retrospect and Prospects" in Trebilcock & Schwanen, eds., above note 112, 20 at 36 [emphasis in original].

124 *Ibid.* at 33–34.

125 See P.M. Leslie, *The European Community: A Political Model for Canada?* (Ottawa: Supply and Services Canada, 1991); P. Monahan, *Political and Economic Integration: The European Experience and Lessons for Canada* (North York: York University Centre for Public Law and Public Policy, 1992).

Negative integration measures may include some or all of the following elements:

- Parliament could legislate so as to give effect to a "non-discrimination" principle (a principle underlying all international trade agreements as well as the *Agreement on Internal Trade*), such that one province would not be permitted to impose discriminatory standards on the goods, services, investments, or persons of another province. Imposition of such discriminatory measures strikes at the heart of the effective functioning of the economic union and the common rights of Canadian citizens, and is probably unconstitutional in any event.[126]
- Parliament could prevent restrictions on the free movement of persons, goods, services, or investments across provincial boundaries (a principle also reflected in international trade agreements as well as the *Agreement on Internal Trade*). The free movement of factors of production across provincial boundaries is essential to the effective conduct of interprovincial trade, the regulation of which has always been clearly a matter of federal jurisdiction.
- Parliament could legislate so as to prevent or eliminate obstacles to internal trade—measures that are more trade restrictive than necessary or are adopted as disguised restrictions on trade. In *Hunt*, La Forest J. stated that measures which are designed to discourage interprovincial commerce and the efficient allocation of resources (as opposed to the achievement of legitimate provincial objectives) offend the basic structure of the Canadian federation.
- Parliament could legislate so as to provide a common set of rules for the mutual recognition of standards or regulations by provinces. This approach is the corollary in the legislative context to the rule established by *Morguard* in the judicial context; that is, if Parliament can legislate so as to provide for common standards for the recognition of extra-provincial judgments by provincial courts (as *Morguard* states), it must similarly be able to legislate common standards for the recognition by provinces of the legislative or regulatory standards of sister provinces.
- Parliament could provide for the enforcement of these requirements by private individuals and persons, either through a specialized tribunal or through the ordinary courts. This proposition follows from the fact that, if Parliament has legislative authority to enact certain substantive standards or requirements, it must also possess the authority to provide for the effective enforcement of those standards. This result is made plain by the *Morguard* case itself which, of course,

126 See, for example, *Man. (A.G.) v. Manitoba Egg and Poultry Assoc.*, [1971] S.C.R. 689.

> concerned the right of a private party to seek enforcement of a court order. The precise enforcement mechanism selected—whether to rely on the courts or to employ a specialized tribunal—is a policy choice that should be left to Parliament, rather than mandated through the constitution.

The recognition of a federal power to eliminate trade barriers would not preclude the provinces from enacting legislation dealing with the same subject matter. Under the double aspect doctrine federal and provincial legislation may overlap. However, where there is a conflict between valid federal and provincial legislation, the provincial law is suspended or rendered inoperative to the extent of the inconsistency.[127] Therefore, to the extent that a federal law prohibiting barriers to internal trade was in conflict with a provincial law creating such barriers, the provincial law would be unenforceable. At the same time, the federal legislation could not in itself prescribe a single harmonized standard to replace any provincial legislation that was rendered inoperative. The harmonization, or positive integration, of provincial measures affecting internal trade would still require voluntary legislative or regulatory action on the part of the provinces.

The identification of those laws and regulations that constitute barriers to internal trade—as opposed to being measures enacted for the achievement of legitimate public policy objectives—is clearly not a simple or straightforward matter. Many commentators have argued that courts are unsuited to making these kinds of complicated assessments and that responsibility for determining measures that amount to barriers to internal trade should be reserved to an expert tribunal or agency. As noted above, once it has been determined that Parliament has the authority to enact binding standards in this area, the choice of an enforcement mechanism is a policy choice rather than a constitutional requirement. Parliament could select the enforcement mechanism that it believed would be most effective and appropriate in the circumstances. Moreover, if Parliament determined that these matters could best be dealt with through an expert agency or tribunal, it could create a new body whose exclusive mandate would be the enforcement of federal laws respecting internal trade; alternatively, it could opt to have this responsibility added to the mandate of an existing agency, such as the Competition Tribunal.

---

127 See the discussion in Chapter 4, Section C(6)(d).

FURTHER READINGS

BEAUDOIN, G.A., WITH P. THIBAULT, *La Constitution du Canada: institutions, partage des pouvoirs, Charte canadienne des droits et libertés*, 3d ed. (Montreal: Wilson & Lafleur, 2004) cc. 9 & 10

FAIRLEY, H.S., "Implementing the Canada–United States Free Trade Agreement" in D. McRae & D. Steger, eds., *Understanding the Free Trade Agreement* (Montreal: Institute for Research on Public Policy, 1988)

HOGG, P.W., *Constitutional Law of Canada*, 5th ed., loose-leaf (Toronto: Carswell, 2007) cc. 11, 20–21

MOULL, W., "Section 92A of the *Constitution Act, 1867*" (1983) 61 Can. Bar Rev. 715

SWINTON, K., "Law, Politics, and the Enforcement of the Agreement on Internal Trade" in M.J. Trebilcock & D. Schwanen, eds., *Getting There: An Assessment of the Agreement on Internal Trade* (Toronto: C.D. Howe Institute, 1995)

———, "Bora Laskin and Federalism" (1985) 35 U.T.L.J. 353

WEILER, P., *In the Last Resort* (Toronto: Carswell/Methuen, 1974)

WHYTE, J.D., *Constitutional Aspects of Economic Development Policy* (Toronto: University of Toronto Press, 1985)

CHAPTER 10

PROPERTY AND CIVIL RIGHTS IN THE PROVINCE

A. DEFINING PROPERTY AND CIVIL RIGHTS

The most important power assigned to the exclusive jurisdiction of the provincial legislatures in section 92 of the *Constitution Act, 1867*[1] is "property and civil rights in the province." Virtually all legislation affects civil rights in one manner or another. In a purely grammatical sense, the subject "property and civil rights" could be thought to encompass the entire field of law-making apart from criminal law.[2]

In fact, this was generally the manner in which the Privy Council interpreted the property and civil rights power. In the 1881 judgment in *Citizens' Insurance Company v. Parsons*,[3] the Board upheld an Ontario statute regulating the terms of insurance policies. Sir Montague Smith observed that section 94 of the *Constitution Act, 1867* provided that Parliament could enact uniform laws relating to property and civil rights

1 The *Constitution Act, 1867* (formerly the *British North America Act, 1867*) (U.K.), 30 & 31 Vict., c. 3.

2 Of course, the same could be said of certain classes of subjects assigned to the exclusive jurisdiction of Parliament under s. 91 of the *Constitution Act, 1867*, particularly "Peace, Order and good Government" and "Trade and Commerce." However, as discussed in Chapters 8 and 9, the Privy Council narrowed these federal classes of subjects in s. 91 and simultaneously interpreted the scope of provincial authority over "property and civil rights in the province" in an extremely broad manner.

3 (1881), 7 App. Cas. 96 [*Parsons*].

in the provinces of Ontario, New Brunswick, and Nova Scotia, but not in Quebec. In his view, the obvious intention underlying the exclusion of Quebec from section 94 was to ensure that matters regulated by the Quebec Civil Code would not be subject to uniform legislation enacted by the federal Parliament. Accordingly, it followed that the term "civil rights" in the *Constitution Act, 1867* (including section 92(13)) must be interpreted broadly in order to ensure that the wide range of matters dealt with by Quebec's Civil Code would be excluded from the operation of section 94. Sir Montague Smith also observed that the terms "property and civil rights" had been used in their "largest sense" in the *Quebec Act, 1774* to encompass all matters apart from the criminal law. This reinforced his conclusion that the drafters of the *Constitution Act, 1867* had intended that section 92(13) be interpreted in a broad and expansive manner.

In effect, the provincial authority over property and civil rights became a *de facto* residuary clause during the Privy Council era. The Privy Council held that any laws regulating or dealing with legal rights in a province—which, as a practical matter, encompassed all manner of laws apart from the criminal law—fell within the subject property and civil rights.[4] The specific enumerated categories in section 91 were treated as exceptions to the power of the provinces under section 92(13) to enact legislation dealing with legal rights. Federal legislation in relation to matters such as banking (section 91(15)), bills of exchange and promissory notes (section 91(18)), interest (section 91(19)), bankruptcy and insolvency (section 91(21)), patents (section 91(22)), and copyright (section 91(23)) were upheld despite their incidental impact on property or civil rights, since such matters were specifically assigned to the exclusive authority of Parliament. However, non-criminal enactments that fell outside of the specific enumerations in section 91 were generally regarded by the Privy Council as falling within provincial jurisdiction under section 92(13), rather than within Parliament's authority to enact laws for the peace, order, and good government (POGG) of Canada. Fields as the regulation of contractual rights,[5] labour relations,[6] busi-

---

4 It should also be noted that provincial laws that in pith and substance relate to "property and civil rights" may incidentally affect the federal power over criminal law. For example, in *Bedard v. Dawson*, [1923] S.C.R. 681, a provincial law which authorized the closing of "disorderly houses" (defined as houses where certain *Criminal Code* offences had been committed) was upheld as valid. For a discussion of the provincial authority to enact penal legislation dealing with matters of morality, see Chapter 11, Section C.

5 *Parsons*, above note 3.

6 *Toronto Electric Commissioners v. Snider*, [1925] A.C. 396.

ness activity generally in a province,[7] insurance,[8] unemployment relief,[9] securities regulation,[10] agricultural products,[11] price regulation,[12] and many other diverse matters were held to be subject to exclusive provincial jurisdiction.

The term "property and civil rights" was not only interpreted broadly to cover a wide range of subjects; it was interpreted so as to authorize provincial regulation over any transaction or activity that occurred within the province.[13] Provincial enactments that affected matters outside of the province were upheld even if they had a significant impact outside the province, particularly in the area of trade. For example, in *Shannon v. British Columbia (Lower Mainland Dairy Products Board)*,[14] the Privy Council upheld a B.C. statute providing for the creation of a B.C. marketing board, with powers to control the marketing of natural products in the province. The marketing board's powers extended to all-natural products sold in the province, whether locally produced or imported. But the Privy Council upheld the statute on the basis that it applied only to transactions that would be completed within the province: "[T]he Act is clearly confined to dealings with such products as are situate within the Province."[15]

The Privy Council's expansive approach to provincial jurisdiction over trade matters carried forward into the jurisprudence of the Supreme Court of Canada. For example, in *Carnation Co. v. Quebec (Agricultural Marketing Board)*,[16] a Quebec statute granted a provincially appointed board the power to fix the price paid by Carnation for raw milk purchased from local dairy farmers. Carnation argued that the statute was unlawful since, after processing the milk, it shipped and/or sold most of the product outside Quebec. But the Supreme Court held that the ultimate destination of the product could not affect the validity of the provincial statute because it was directed at a transaction—the sale of the milk from the farmers to Carnation—taking place wholly within the province. Fixing the price to be paid by Carnation for raw

7 *Can. (A.G.) v. Alta. (A.G.) (Insurance)*, [1916] 1 A.C. 588.
8 *Ibid.*
9 *Can. (A.G.) v. Ont. (A.G.) (Employment Insurance)*, [1937] A.C. 355.
10 *Lymburn v. Mayland*, [1932] A.C. 318. See the discussion and *Reference Re Securities Act*, [2011] 3 S.C.R. 837 in Chapter 9, Section C(3).
11 *Shannon v. B.C. (Lower Mainland Dairy Products Board)*, [1938] A.C. 708 [*Shannon*].
12 *Home Oil Distributors v. B.C. (A.G.)*, [1940] S.C.R. 444.
13 The "within the province" limitation has proven to be a significant constraint on provincial jurisdiction, as discussed below at Section C.
14 *Shannon*, above note 11.
15 *Ibid.* at 719, Lord Atkin.
16 [1968] S.C.R. 238.

milk would certainly have an impact on its export trade, in the sense that it would affect the company's cost of doing business in the province. However, the Court noted that labour costs also affect the cost of doing business in a province. There has never been any doubt as to the ability of the province to regulate wage rates in the province. Accordingly, while the provincial legislation might affect interprovincial or export trade, this was not its primary purpose. The main object, or pith and substance of the law, was the regulation of a local transaction.

One potential difficulty with this expansive interpretation of provincial trade powers is that it makes it possible for provinces to enact laws that, although directed at matters within a particular province, restrict the free flow of goods or services between provinces. By enacting an ostensibly non-discriminatory statute, provinces might impose conditions or restrictions that favour local producers and effectively bar the sale of cheaper or more desirable imported products. Indeed, provinces may have a political incentive to establish discriminatory schemes because local producers have significant lobbying power, whereas extra-provincial or foreign producers may be less organized and lack political clout in the province.

An illustration of this scenario was provided by the so-called chicken and egg war that gave rise to the *Manitoba Egg Reference* in 1971.[17] At the time, Ontario farmers produced an abundance of cheap eggs, and Quebec farmers produced an abundance of cheap chickens. The Ontario egg producers exported their surplus to Quebec, while Quebec chicken farmers did likewise into the Ontario market. Local producers in each province lobbied their respective provincial governments for protection against cheap imports, and each province was only too happy to oblige. Quebec established an egg marketing board with power to restrict egg imports in order to protect Quebec producers. Ontario created a similar board with similar powers with respect to chickens sold in the province. Both provinces, however, were careful to draft the legislation in such a manner as to disguise the discrimination and to make the marketing schemes appear neutral.[18] Chicken and egg farmers in other provinces found themselves being shut out of the two largest Canadian markets for their products. The other provinces had lobbied the federal government in an effort to have it refer the Ontario and Quebec statutes to the Supreme Court of Canada in order to test

---

17 *Man. (A.G.) v. Manitoba Egg and Poultry Assn.*, [1971] S.C.R. 689 [*Manitoba Egg*].

18 See the account of the background to the case set out in P. Weiler, *In the Last Resort: A Critical Study of the Supreme Court of Canada* (Toronto: Carswell/Methuen, 1974) at 156–57.

their constitutional validity.[19] When the federal government refused, the province of Manitoba came up with a novel scheme to bring the issue before the country's highest court. Manitoba drafted legislation and regulations that were virtually identical to the Quebec scheme and referred the proposed legislative package to the Manitoba Court of Appeal for a constitutional ruling. The Court of Appeal, in a decision written by Dickson J.A. (as he then was), ruled that the legislation was *ultra vires*. Manitoba was then able to appeal the loss as of right to the Supreme Court.[20]

Martland J. wrote the majority decision. He noted that the legislation "is to be operated by and for the benefit of the egg producers of Manitoba, to be carried out by a Board armed with the power to control the sale of eggs in Manitoba, brought in from outside Manitoba, by means of quotas, or even outright prohibition."[21] In Martland J.'s view, therefore, the legislation not only "affects" interprovincial trade but was aimed "at the regulation of such trade" and was therefore unconstitutional:

> It is an essential part of this scheme, the purpose of which is to obtain for Manitoba producers the most advantageous marketing conditions for eggs, specifically to control and regulate the sale in Manitoba of imported eggs. It is designed to restrict or limit the free flow of trade between provinces as such. Because of that, it constitutes an invasion of the exclusive legislative authority of the Parliament of Canada over the matter of the regulation of trade and commerce.[22]

Certain commentators were extremely critical of the Court's reasoning in *Manitoba Egg*, arguing that the case was indistinguishable from *Carnation*. It was also claimed that *Manitoba Egg* would prevent the provinces from enacting fairly administered schemes to control the marketing within their territory of imported goods.[23] Yet the Court's decision in *Manitoba Egg* was surely right. Otherwise, the provincial power over property and civil rights could be used by one province to erect protectionist and discriminatory barriers against goods produced

---

19 Under the *Supreme Court Act*, R.S.C. 1985, c. S-26, only the federal government can refer a matter directly to the Supreme Court.

20 Although provinces cannot refer a matter directly to the Supreme Court, the *Supreme Court Act*, *ibid.*, provides an appeal as of right from a reference to a provincial Court of Appeal.

21 *Manitoba Egg*, above note 17 at 701.

22 *Ibid.* at 703.

23 See Weiler, above note 18 at 41–47.

in other provinces, thereby potentially carving up the Canadian economic union into ten separate provincial economies.

One of the significant underlying objectives of the confederation bargain in 1867 was to create a properly functioning economic union in which the entire country would operate as a single market. This intention was reflected in the granting to Parliament of exclusive power over matters that are central to the achievement and maintenance of the economic union, including powers over trade and commerce, taxation, public debt and property, banking, and currency. But a properly functioning economic union does not simply require adequate powers being granted to Parliament; it also requires that there be some limits on provincial powers, so that the provinces are not permitted to impede the free flow of goods, services, labour, and capital across provincial borders.[24] The legislation considered in *Manitoba Egg* was designed with the clear intention of carving up the Canadian market for eggs into ten separate provincial markets. In our view, the Court was correct to hold that it was *ultra vires*.

While the Court in *Manitoba Egg* clearly established that the provinces could not unilaterally carve up the Canadian egg market along provincial lines, it said nothing about the possibility of achieving this objective through the joint action of Parliament and the provinces. In 1972, the federal government and the provinces agreed to establish the Canadian Egg Marketing Agency (CEMA) and to assign to each province a share of the national egg market. The agreement was implemented through dovetailing federal and provincial legislation, with the federal statute implementing the interprovincial elements of the plan and provincial statutes implementing the intraprovincial elements. The Supreme Court upheld the validity of the federal–provincial scheme.[25] More recently, the Court confirmed that a provincial board operating under this federal–provincial scheme could reduce a producer's quota to zero, even if that producer's output was destined largely for export

24 There is an imperfect recognition of this fact in s. 121 of the *Constitution Act, 1867*, which guarantees free entry of goods between provinces: "All Articles of the Growth, Produce, or Manufacture of any one of the Provinces shall . . . be admitted free into each of the other Provinces." Section 121 binds both the federal Parliament and the provincial legislatures. However, s. 121 has been interpreted narrowly as only prohibiting tariffs between provinces and as not reaching other kinds of discriminatory barriers such as the marketing scheme considered in *Manitoba Egg*: see *Atlantic Smoke Shops Ltd. v. Conlon*, [1943] A.C. 550 (P.C.).

25 *Reference Re Agricultural Products Marketing Act, 1970 (Canada)*, [1978] 2 S.C.R. 1198 [*Egg Reference*]. In fact, the Court did rule one particular provision to be unconstitutional, but this ruling did not threaten the viability of the scheme as a whole.

from the province.[26] The result was that through joint federal–provincial action, the two levels of government were able to establish a scheme that was beyond the powers of either level acting alone. This outcome is hardly remarkable, given the long-standing constitutional principle that the distribution of powers between Parliament and the provinces is exhaustive.[27] Because of the principle of exhaustiveness, it is usually open to Parliament and the provinces to overcome limitations on their powers in sections 91 and 92 through joint action. But this should not be a cause for concern since, assuming both the national and provincial authorities are in agreement on the desirability of a legislative scheme, any federalism concerns or objections associated with the scheme will presumably have been satisfied.[28]

B. PROVINCIAL JURISDICTION OVER NATURAL RESOURCES

1) The Natural Resource Decisions of the 1970s

In *Manitoba Egg*, the Supreme Court signalled a willingness to depart from the Privy Council's decisions assigning exclusive jurisdiction to the provinces over transactions or persons physically located within the province. *Manitoba Egg* seems to suggest that where the underlying purpose of provincial regulation is to impede the free flow of goods between provinces, the regulation will be struck down even if it extends only to persons or things physically within the province and appears on its face to be neutral. The Court carried forward and extended this new, more restrictive approach to provincial powers in two significant

26 *Fédération des producteurs de volailles du Québec v. Pelland*, [2005] 1 S.C.R. 292, discussed in Chapter 9.

27 The principle of exhaustiveness means that the totality of legislative power is distributed between Parliament and the legislatures: see *Ont. (A.G.) v. Can. (A.G.)*, [1912] A.C. 571 at 581 (P.C.).

28 The discussion in the text deals only with the interpretation of ss. 91 & 92 of the *Constitution Act, 1867*, and not with other provisions of the constitution that impose limits on both levels of government, such as s. 6 of the *Canadian Charter of Rights and Freedoms*, Part I of the *Constitution Act, 1982*, being Schedule B to the *Canada Act 1982* (U.K.), 1982, c. 11, or s. 121 of the *Constitution Act, 1867*. In the *Egg Reference*, above note 25, the federal-provincial legislation was challenged on the basis of s. 121, as well as on the basis of the division of powers in ss. 91 & 92. Laskin C.J. rejected the s. 121 challenge. In so doing, he seemed to rely on the fact that Parliament had endorsed the scheme before the Court: "[W]hat may amount to a tariff or customs duty under a provincial regulatory statute may not have that character at all under a federal regulatory statute" (at 1267).

decisions in the late 1970s involving provincial jurisdiction over natural resources.

The first case was *Canadian Industrial Gas & Oil Ltd. v. Saskatchewan*.[29] Following the sharp rise in the world oil price in the early 1970s, the province of Saskatchewan enacted legislation designed to capture the increased economic rent accruing to producers. The legislation imposed a royalty surcharge on oil produced in the province equal to the difference between the actual well-head price received and the basic well-head price. The basic well-head price was a statutory figure approximating the price-per-barrel received by producers prior to the energy crisis. The legislation also provided that where the minister was of the opinion that oil was being disposed of at less than its fair market value, he could determine what the well-head price should have been and calculate the tax payable on the basis of this determination. Canadian Industrial Gas and Oil Ltd. (CIGOL) was a producer of crude oil in Saskatchewan. It sold its entire production at the well site. Virtually all its product was then exported from the province for refining by others in eastern Canada or the United States. CIGOL argued that because the surcharge would affect the price of its product in the extra-provincial market, the legislation amounted to an unwarranted provincial intrusion into the field of trade and commerce.

On the surface, the parallel between the facts of *CIGOL* and *Carnation* is striking. In both cases, the province regulated the sale within the province of a good destined for export; in *Carnation*, the province was setting the price for the local sale of the product, while in *CIGOL*, the province was taxing the producer. Yet the Court came to opposite conclusions. Martland J., the author of the Court's judgment in *Carnation*, concluded in *CIGOL* that the tax was an invalid attempt to regulate trade and commerce.[30] Martland J. focused on the provisions in the legislation permitting the minister to fix the well-head price for purposes of calculating the tax payable where he or she was of the opinion that oil had been disposed of for less than fair market value. Martland J. argued that the effect of this provision was to compel the producer to sell the product at the price fixed by the minister, since the producer would otherwise be unable to recoup the full amount of the tax paid. The effect of the legislation, according to Martland J., is to "set a floor price

29 [1978] 2 S.C.R. 545 [*CIGOL*].

30 Martland J. also held that the tax was an indirect tax and was invalid on this ground. The discussion in the text is limited to Martland J.'s analysis on the trade and commerce issue.

for Saskatchewan oil purchased for export . . . or to ensure that the incremental value is not appropriated by persons outside the Province."[31]

As the dissenting judgment of Dickson J. (as he then was) pointed out, Martland J.'s emphasis on the power of the minister to fix the well-head price was misplaced; the ministerial price-fixing power was an anti-avoidance provision to prevent oil from being disposed of at less than fair-market value merely in order to avoid the tax liability.[32] On the other hand, Martland J. was surely right in concluding that the entire scheme was directed at appropriating for the Saskatchewan government the entire incremental value in the price of oil as a result of market developments and circumstances occurring outside Saskatchewan. In effect, there were no circumstances or matters existing within Saskatchewan that gave rise to or required this scheme of regulation. The entire scheme was driven by and structured around international market events, without reference to any needs or interests found within the province, apart from the desire to obtain more revenue for provincial coffers. In this sense, the facts in CIGOL were arguably distinguishable from those in *Carnation*, where the province was attempting to ensure the continued viability and profitability of the dairy industry and dairy farmers in Quebec.

While the Court came to opposite conclusions in the two cases, the findings in CIGOL reinforced the decision in *Manitoba Egg*; it was clearly no longer open to a province to assume that legislation that fastened on a transaction occurring within the province was automatically valid. It was necessary to inquire into the underlying purpose and context for such legislation in order to determine whether its ultimate aim was a matter outside of the province.

The Court adopted a similar approach in the 1978 *Central Canada Potash* decision.[33] The litigation arose out of attempts by the government of Saskatchewan in the late 1960s and early 1970s to stabilize the North American market for potash. Saskatchewan is one of the largest potash producers in the world. It exports the bulk of its production to the United States. In the late 1960s, there was a serious excess of supply and a drop in the world price of potash. The Saskatchewan government, in concert with the largest U.S. potash supplier, devised a plan to limit production and increase market prices. The scheme fixed production quotas for potash producers and established a floor price for potash free on board the mine as a condition for obtaining a licence. The legislation was challenged by Central Canada Potash, a Saskatchewan producer

31 *Ibid.* at 567.
32 *Ibid.* at 601–2, Dickson J.
33 *Central Canada Potash Co. v. Saskatchewan* (1978), [1979] 1 S.C.R. 42.

that had an assured market for production in excess of its production allocation. The province sought to uphold the legislation on the basis that it established production quotas rather than marketing quotas. Saskatchewan argued that the provincial power over property and civil rights included the power to impose controls on production of natural resources within the province. The problem with this argument was that the whole purpose of the legislation was to stabilize the market for potash in the U.S. The regulatory framework operated at the point of production, but its purpose was to ensure that Saskatchewan producers received a fair return on the sale of their resources outside the province.

Laskin C.J., who wrote for a unanimous Court on the constitutional issue, noted that the Court had to determine the true nature and character of the legislation. This issue could be resolved only by considering "the circumstances under which the Potash Conservation Regulations, came into being . . . [and] the market to which they were applied and in which they had their substantial operation."[34] Looking to those broader factors, the Chief Justice had little difficulty in concluding that the statute amounted to an attempt to regulate the export market in potash. The fact that the legislation took the form of quotas on production was irrelevant.

2) Section 92A

The decisions in CIGOL and *Central Canada Potash* raised an outcry in the western provinces. Some premiers even claimed that the Supreme Court was biased in favour of the federal government. These concerns led to the enactment in 1982 of section 92A of the *Constitution Act, 1867*, which was designed to confirm and extend provincial powers in relation to natural resources. Section 92A(1) states that the provinces have exclusive authority to enact laws in relation to the following matters:

(a) exploration for non-renewable natural resources in the province;
(b) development, conservation and management of non-renewable natural resources and forestry resources in the province, including laws in relation to the rate of primary production therefrom; and
(c) development, conservation and management of sites and facilities in the province for the generation and production of electrical energy.

Certain commentators have argued that section 92A did not expand, but merely declared provincial powers as determined in *Central*

34 *Ibid.* at 75.

Canada Potash.[35] This is said to follow from the fact that the provision makes no mention of those cases where the natural resources are destined for export, which was the fatal element of the potash prorationing scheme in *Central Canada Potash.*

In our view, this is an unduly restrictive reading of section 92A(1). The section explicitly grants provinces the power to enact laws in relation to the primary production of natural resources found within the province. There are no limiting words or qualifications on the scope of this power. Whether or not the product is destined for export should therefore be irrelevant. This interpretation is reinforced by the principle of statutory interpretation that legislation should not be interpreted in a manner such that its purpose is defeated or it is rendered pointless or futile.[36] The clear intention of section 92A was to reverse the decision in *Central Canada Potash* and to grant exclusive authority to the provinces to regulate their natural resources.

Section 92A(3) provides that nothing in subsection (2) derogates from federal legislative authority and that, in the event of a conflict between federal and provincial legislation, the federal law prevails. The omission in section 92A(3) of any reference to section 92A(1) may be read to suggest that section 92A(1) *is* intended to narrow or limit federal authority. In *Ontario Hydro v. Ontario (Labour Relations Board),*[37] a majority of the Supreme Court of Canada suggested that section 92A(1) may derogate from the federal government's exclusive jurisdiction over federal local works and undertakings. The issue in the case was whether labour relations over Ontario Hydro's nuclear electrical generating station fell within federal jurisdiction.[38] One of the issues considered by the Court was whether the enactment of section 92A(1)(c) in 1982 had affected the scope of the federal power over local works and undertakings declared by Parliament to be for the general advantage of Canada or the advantage of two or more of the provinces. The Court concluded that section 92A(1)(c) did not narrow the declaratory power. However, La Forest J., for the majority, suggested that section 92A may affect the scope of federal jurisdiction over interprovincial

35 See W.D. Moull, "Section 92A of the *Constitution Act, 1867*" (1983) 61 Can. Bar Rev. 715.

36 See *Rizzo & Rizzo Shoes Ltd. (Re)*, [1998] 1 S.C.R. 27 at para. 27.

37 [1993] 3 S.C.R. 327 [*Ontario Hydro*].

38 Ontario Hydro's works and undertakings in respect of atomic power had been declared to be a work for the general advantage of Canada under s. 92(10)(c) of the *Constitution Act, 1867*, and were clearly under federal jurisdiction. The issue in the case was whether the s. 92(10)(c) declaration had the effect of sweeping labour relations matters at those facilities under federal jurisdiction. Section 92(10)(c) is discussed in more detail in Chapter 12.

works and undertakings under section 92(10)(a).[39] The jurisprudence in respect of interprovincial works and undertakings has suggested that federal jurisdiction extends to facilities situated within a single province, if those facilities are integrated with or part of a work or undertaking that extends beyond the province. In the *Ontario Hydro* case, La Forest J. suggested that one purpose of section 92A was to remove the danger that this approach to section 92(10)(a) might be used to extend federal jurisdiction over the entire electricity industry. He noted that, in most provinces, the generation and distribution of electrical energy is done by the same undertaking, with an integrated and interconnected system beginning at the generating plant and extending to the ultimate destination. This interconnectedness raised the possibility that the whole undertaking, from production to export, could be viewed as falling under federal jurisdiction pursuant to section 92(10)(a). According to La Forest J., section 92A "ensures the province the management . . . of the sites and facilities for the generation and production of electrical energy that might otherwise be threatened by s. 92(10)(a)."[40]

In the subsequent *Westcoast Energy* case,[41] the Supreme Court narrowed La Forest J.'s comments in *Ontario Hydro*. The Supreme Court found that federal jurisdiction over a natural gas pipeline extended to facilities where the gas was processed, on the basis that the facilities were operated as a single integrated transportation undertaking. One argument considered by the Court was whether section 92A(1)(b), which recognizes exclusive provincial jurisdiction over the "development, conservation and management of non-renewable natural resources," had the effect of establishing provincial jurisdiction over the gas-processing facilities. The Supreme Court, by an eight to one majority,[42] found that section 92A does not derogate from Parliament's jurisdiction over works and undertakings under section 92(10)(a). The majority judgment of Iacobucci and Major JJ. stated that La Forest J.'s comments in *Ontario Hydro* on the relationship between section 92A and 92(10)(a) were *obiter*, since the *Ontario Hydro* case involved the federal declaratory power, rather than the power over interprovincial works and undertakings. *Westcoast Energy* therefore reaffirms that the enactment of section

39 As is explained in Chapter 12, federal jurisdiction over interprovincial works and undertakings arises because of s. 92(10)(a) of the *Constitution Act, 1867*.

40 *Ontario Hydro*, above note 37 at 378.

41 *Westcoast Energy Inc. v. Canada (National Energy Board)*, [1998] 1 S.C.R. 322 [*Westcoast Energy*].

42 Justice McLachlin, as she then was, dissented.

92A does not derogate from or impair federal jurisdiction over interprovincial works and undertakings pursuant to sections 92(10)(a) or (c).[43]

Section 92A(2) grants provinces the power to enact laws in relation to "the export from the province to another part of Canada of the primary production from non-renewable natural resources and forestry resources in the province." Section 92A(2) also states that provincial laws in relation to export cannot provide for discrimination in prices or in supplies exported to another part of Canada. It would appear that the power in section 92A(2) is separate from and in addition to the power in section 92A(1). That is, after having enacted laws dealing with the development, conservation, or management of a non-renewable natural resource, the province may then enact further limitations or controls on the export of the resulting production to other parts of Canada. However, the qualifications on the power in section 92A(2) suggest that it is more strictly confined and limited than the authority under section 92A(1). For example, if the province attempted to encourage local processing of natural resources by establishing a different, and more favourable, taxation regime for products processed locally as opposed to those processed elsewhere in Canada, such restrictions would appear to fall outside the power in section 92A(2).[44]

C. THE MEANING OF "WITHIN THE PROVINCE"

As discussed above, the term "property and civil rights" has been interpreted by the courts in its literal and grammatical sense as encompassing all legislation dealing with legal rights apart from criminal statutes. Despite this generous interpretation, section 92(13) is limited to legis-

---

43 The majority judgment also pointed out that s. 92A(1)(c) refers to provincial jurisdiction over "sites and facilities" involved in the generation of electrical energy, whereas s. 92A(1)(b) makes no reference to "sites and facilities" but simply affirms provincial jurisdiction over the "development, conservation and management" of non-renewable natural resources. Yet surely this difference in wording is not material since provincial jurisdiction under s. 92(1)(b) must include jurisdiction over sites and facilities involved in the development or management of natural resources. The point is simply that in neither s. 92A(1)(b) nor 1(c) does this recognition of provincial jurisdiction limit or derogate from federal jurisdiction pursuant to s. 92(10)(a) or (c).

44 This reading of s. 92A(2) is reinforced by s. 92A(4), which provides the province with power to levy indirect taxes on natural resources, but provides that any such taxes cannot discriminate on the basis of whether or not the production is exported from the province.

lation dealing with matters "in the province." While the courts have not been consistent in interpreting these limiting words, the territorial restriction in section 92(13) has nonetheless proven to be a significant substantive constraint on the property and civil rights power.

1) The Early and Restrictive Approach

In the early twentieth century, a series of cases struck down provincial laws, adopting a relatively restrictive approach to the territorial limitations on the property and civil rights power. The first such case was *Royal Bank v. R.*,[45] which arose following an attempt by the province of Alberta to appropriate the proceeds of a bond issue that had been raised in London in order to finance construction of a railway in Alberta. The funds raised from the bond issue had been paid to the Royal Bank in New York, and then credited to a special account at a Royal Bank branch in Alberta. When the railway company defaulted on its obligation to construct the railway, the province enacted legislation which provided that the whole of the proceeds of the bond issue should form part of the general revenue fund of the province free from all claims of the railway company. The statute also provided that the province would be liable to the bondholders for the appropriated proceeds. The Privy Council noted that the effect of the statute was to extinguish a contractual right of the bondholders to recover the proceeds of the bond issue, and that such a right existed outside of the province of Alberta.[46] As such, the legislation could not be said to be "confined to property and civil rights in the province nor directed solely to matters of merely local or private nature."[47]

The reasoning in *Royal Bank* was applied in a number of cases that arose in the 1930s, in which provinces sought to override certain contracts or reduce their debt obligations as a response to the financial difficulties created by the Depression. For example, in *Ottawa Valley*

---

45 [1913] A.C. 283 [*Royal Bank*].

46 The reasoning of Viscount Haldane on this point was extremely technical and turned on the particular facts of the case. He held that the enactment of the provincial legislation gave rise to a right in the bondholders to seek recovery of the money from the Royal Bank head office in Montreal, which had issued the direction to the New York branch to credit the special purpose account in Alberta. On these facts, the bondholders thus had a right of action in the province of Quebec. This suggests that had the bondholders paid the money directly to the account in Alberta, rather than paying it to New York, there would have been no purely extraprovincial right (since no direction from the Montreal head office would have been necessary) and the statute would have been upheld as valid.

47 *Ibid.* at 298.

Power Co. v. The Hydro Electric Power Commission,[48] an Ontario statute purported to nullify contracts between the Hydro-Electric Power Commission of Ontario and Ottawa Valley Power Company, a Quebec company distributing power in Quebec. The province of Ontario had passed orders in council authorizing the commission to enter into and perform the contracts with Ottawa Valley. Some years later, the province enacted a statute declaring the contracts to be "illegal, void and unenforceable" and barred recourse to the courts for their enforcement. The Ontario Court of Appeal held that the statute was invalid because it was directed at the extinguishment of contractual rights outside of the province.[49] Similar results were reached in a number of other cases in this period.[50]

2) The Pith and Substance Doctrine

In later cases, the Privy Council and the Supreme Court adopted a more flexible approach in determining the validity of provincial statutes having extraterritorial implications. The Privy Council, and subsequently the Supreme Court of Canada, applied the pith and substance doctrine, upholding provincial legislation with incidental extraprovincial effects.

In *Ladore v. Bennett*,[51] the Privy Council upheld provincial legislation under which certain municipalities in Ontario were amalgamated into the City of Windsor. In the process of amalgamation, the securities for the debts of the various component municipalities were replaced by new bonds issued by the City of Windsor, with modifications in interest rates and other terms of indebtedness. Certain securities were held by persons located outside the province, and a number of ratepayers and debenture holders who were unhappy with the proposed arrangement sought a declaration that the legislation was invalid on grounds that it

48 [1937] O.R. 265 (C.A.) [*Ottawa Valley*].

49 Two of the three justices in the majority also advanced a broader theory to the effect that the legislation was invalid because it barred access to the courts, which was said to be contrary to "implied guarantees" relating to the jurisdiction of provincial superior courts. See, in particular, the judgment of Fisher J.A. at 333, as well as the discussion of this aspect of the case in P.J. Monahan, "Is the Pearson Airport Legislation Unconstitutional? The Rule of Law as a Limit on Contract Repudiation by Government" (1995) 33 Osgoode Hall L.J. 411.

50 See, for example, *Credit Foncier Franco-Canadien v. Ross*, [1937] 3 D.L.R. 365 (Alta. C.A.), striking down Alberta legislation reducing interest on debts; *Beauharnois Light, Heat and Power Co. v. The Hydro-Electric Power Commission of Ontario*, [1937] O.R. 796 (C.A.), striking down the same legislation considered in the *Ottawa Valley* case, above note 48.

51 [1939] A.C. 468 [*Ladore*].

affected rights outside of the province. The Privy Council rejected the challenge, noting that the legislation in question was a law of general application dealing with the process of municipal restructuring in the province. There was no suggestion that the province was deliberately attempting to exceed its jurisdiction with a view to impairing the rights of persons outside the province. It simply happened that certain persons outside of the province were incidentally affected by a provincial statute directed at the regulation of municipal affairs in the province.[52] Since the purpose of the legislation was directed at a valid provincial purpose, the fact that it collaterally or incidentally affected rights outside of the province was immaterial.

The Supreme Court attempted to reconcile these conflicting lines of authority in *Reference Re Upper Churchill Water Rights Reversion Act*.[53] The *Churchill Falls* case concerned the validity of a Newfoundland statute that expropriated without compensation the assets of a company generating electricity at Churchill Falls in Labrador. The expropriation had the effect of ensuring that the company would not be able to perform under a sixty-five-year contract with Hydro-Quebec calling for the supply of power in Quebec at fixed prices. The Supreme Court found that the real purpose of the expropriating statute was to abrogate the contract with Hydro-Quebec. Since the contract provided for the delivery of power in Quebec, the pith and substance of the statute was the destruction of contractual rights outside of the province. McIntyre J., for the Court, stated that the Privy Council's reasoning in *Ladore* was to be preferred to the *Royal Bank* line of cases. McIntyre J. held that a provincial statute could not be found to be invalid merely on account of the fact that it incidentally or collaterally affected civil rights outside of the province. Only where the pith and substance or main purpose of a provincial enactment is to derogate rights outside the province will such an enactment be found to be beyond provincial powers:

> Where the pith and substance of the provincial enactment is in relation to matters which fall within the field of provincial legislative competence, incidental or consequential effects on extra-provincial rights will not render the enactment *ultra vires*. Where, however, the pith and substance of the provincial enactment is the derogation from or elimination of extra-provincial rights then, even if it is cloaked in the proper constitutional form, it will be *ultra vires*.[54]

---

52 See the judgment of Lord Atkin, *ibid*. at 482.

53 [1984] 1 S.C.R. 297 [*Churchill Falls*].

54 *Ibid*. at 332.

Applying this reasoning, McIntyre J. held that the Newfoundland statute was invalid since the true purpose of the legislation was to nullify the electricity contract with Hydro-Quebec, which was a contractual right situated outside of the province.

The pith and substance approach in *Churchill Falls* was reaffirmed by the Supreme Court of Canada in subsequent cases. In *Global Securities Corp. v. B.C. (Securities Commission)*,[55] the Court considered a provision in the B.C. *Securities Act* which permitted the provincial Securities Commission to order a registrant in British Columbia to produce records "to assist in the administration of the securities law of another jurisdiction." This provision was challenged on the basis that it purported to enforce the securities laws of other jurisdictions, a matter beyond the territorial competence of the B.C. legislature. But the Supreme Court unanimously upheld the validity of the impugned provision. Iacobucci J., who wrote the judgment of the Court, found that the true purpose of the provision was to ensure the effective enforcement of British Columbia's securities laws. The effective enforcement of British Columbia's securities laws would from time to time require access to records outside of the province. Access to these extraprovincial records would only be forthcoming if British Columbia was prepared to provide assistance to foreign regulators in respect of records located in British Columbia. Thus, by providing for such assistance on a reciprocal basis, British Columbia was in fact enhancing the effective administration of its own statute.[56] Having concluded that the pith and substance of the legislation was a matter within the province, the fact that the provision might incidentally affect matters outside of the province was constitutionally irrelevant.

Significantly, *Global Securities* also advanced a second, alternative basis upon which a provincial law with extraterritorial effects may be upheld: the ancillary or necessarily incidental doctrine.[57] Prior to *Global Securities*, the ancillary doctrine had been applied only in respect of the validity of *federal* legislation. In *Global Securities*, Iacobucci J. held that this doctrine is equally applicable to provincial legislation. Thus, a provision in a provincial law directed at a matter outside of the province may be upheld if it is a necessary incident of effective regulation of a local

55 [2000] 1 S.C.R. 494 [*Global Securities*]. See the discussion in Chapter 9, Section B(2)(c).

56 Iacobucci J. noted that the province also had a separate, distinct interest in facilitating the investigation of possible wrongdoing by a B.C. registrant that had occurred in a foreign jurisdiction, and that this was an alternative basis upon which the validity of the impugned measure could be upheld.

57 See *General Motors v. City National Leasing*, [1989] 1 S.C.R. 641.

matter.[58] In *Global Securities*, it was not necessary to invoke the ancillary doctrine, since the Court found that the true purpose of the impugned provision was the regulation of securities registrants in the province. Had this not been the case, however, Iacobucci J. stated that the measure could have been upheld on the basis that it was ancillary or necessarily incidental to a valid provincial regulatory scheme.[59]

3) Extraterritoriality and Applicability

In *Churchill Falls* and *Global Securities*, the Supreme Court held that the issue of the territorial limits on provincial powers is to be resolved by the application of the pith and substance doctrine. A provincial law having only incidental effects on persons or matters outside of the province will be upheld. However, in later cases, the Supreme Court of Canada departed from the pith and substance approach. The Court borrowed from conflict of laws jurisprudence on adjudicatory jurisdiction as developed in *Morguard Investments v. De Savoye*[60] and *Hunt v. T&N plc*,[61] and introduced a doctrine of constitutional "inapplicability" for determining the territorial limits on provincial legislation.

Traditionally, the issue of adjudicatory jurisdiction—the jurisdiction of the courts to decide a particular dispute—was analytically distinct from the issue of the extraterritorial limits on provincial legislative power.[62] In *Morguard*, a case concerning recognition and enforcement

58 As in the analysis of federal legislation, the impact of the measure on extraprovincial matters will be a relevant consideration; in cases where a provision has a more substantial impact on extraprovincial matters, it will be necessary for a province to demonstrate a closer functional integration within a broader scheme of regulation in order for the impugned measure to be upheld.

59 However, it is noteworthy that in *Committee for the Equal Treatment of Asbestos Minority Shareholders v. Ontario (Securities Commission)*, [2001] 2 S.C.R. 132, the Supreme Court upheld a decision of the Ontario Securities Commission declining to exercise its "public interest" jurisdiction in respect of a takeover bid in Quebec on the basis that there was an insufficient connection or nexus between the bid and Ontario. Similarly, in *Ewachniuk v. Law Society of British Columbia*, [1998] B.C.J. No. 372 (C.A.), the British Columbia Court of Appeal held that the provincial law society could not obtain testimony from a witness located in the U.S. The proposed hearing represented an extraterritorial application of the jurisdiction of a tribunal limited by its enabling statute to sitting in British Columbia. Moreover, it was beyond the jurisdiction of the province to confer such extraterritorial jurisdiction on a provincial tribunal.

60 [1990] 3 S.C.R. 1077 [*Morguard*].

61 [1993] 4 S.C.R. 289 [*Hunt*]. Both cases are discussed at length in Chapters 8 and 9.

62 See E. Edinger & V. Black, "A New Approach to Extraterritoriality: *Unifund Assurance Co. v. I.C.B.C.*" (2004) 40 Can. Bus. L.J. 161 at 166. The issue of adjudicatory jurisdiction may be said to concern three principal questions: (1) whether

of an Alberta judgment in British Columbia, La Forest J. held that the issue of whether a Canadian court should recognize and enforce judgments from sister provinces should be guided by the principles of "order and fairness." In order for the courts of one province to recognize and enforce a judgment emanating from another province, there had to be a "real and substantial connection."[63]

Morguard concerned adjudicative jurisdiction. However, in *Hunt*, La Forest J. held that the principles of "real and substantial connection" and "order and fairness" discussed in *Morguard* were "constitutional imperatives" and placed limits on the legislative jurisdiction of the provinces. He held that a Quebec statute that had the effect of prohibiting the removal of corporate records from Quebec for production in B.C. litigation was constitutionally *inapplicable* to the B.C. action. That is, although the statute was presumably valid writ large, it was not applicable to the B.C. litigation at issue. In La Forest J.'s view, the principles of "order and fairness" underlying the recognition of interprovincial judgments applied equally to "provincial legislatures as well as the courts."[64]

Hunt thus established the doctrine of constitutional applicability in the context of the territorial limitations on provincial powers. Not only could it be argued that a provincial statute was invalid because it had an extraprovincial aim or object as opposed to merely incidental extraprovincial effects (as in *Churchill Falls*), but it could be said that the statute was constitutionally inapplicable in the particular circum-

---

the court has jurisdiction over a particular dispute (jurisdiction *simpliciter*); (2) whether the court should, as a matter of discretion, decline to exercise its jurisdiction because there is a more convenient forum (*forum non conveniens*); and (3) whether a court should recognize and enforce a judgment emanating from another province (recognition and enforcement). In *Club Resorts Ltd. v. Van Breda*, [2012] 1 S.C.R. 572 [*Van Breda*], the Supreme Court reconsidered the "real and substantial connection" test in the context of tort claims brought in Ontario against out-of-province defendants arising from accidents in foreign countries. The Court held that the "real and substantial connection" test was both a common law rule and a constitutional principle. As a constitutional principle, the test imposes territorial limits on both provincial legislative competence and on the authority of the superior courts of the provinces (para. 31).

63 It was unclear from *Morguard* what the "real and substantial connection" test referred to. La Forest J. variously referred to a "real and substantial connection" "between the subject-matter of the action and the territory where the action is brought," "between the jurisdiction and the wrongdoing," "between the damages suffered and the jurisdiction," "between the defendant and the forum province," "with the transaction or the parties," and "with the action." See *Morguard*, above note 60 at paras. 45, 47, 50, 51, & 52. The test for jurisdiction was clarified in *Van Breda*, above note 62.

64 *Hunt*, above note 61 at para. 56.

stances of the case. *Hunt* suggested that the constitutional applicability of a provincial statute turned on the concept of a "real and substantial connection" discussed in *Morguard*, an imprecise term whose ambit La Forest J. expressly declined to define.[65]

In *Unifund Assurance Co. v. Insurance Corporation of British Columbia*,[66] the Court expanded on La Forest J.'s judgments in *Morguard* and *Hunt*. The case involved a motor vehicle accident in British Columbia in which two Ontario residents were seriously injured. The Ontario residents had successfully sued a B.C. driver and obtained judgment for $2.5 million, which was paid by the Insurance Corporation of British Columbia (ICBC). In addition, the Ontario residents also received statutory accident (no-fault) benefits of approximately $750,000 from their Ontario insurer. The accident benefits paid in Ontario were deducted from the damages award payable by the B.C. insurer in accordance with B.C. law. The Ontario insurer then sought indemnification from ICBC for the amounts it had paid in the form of accident benefits, relying on Ontario law. The Supreme Court of Canada held, in a four to three decision, that indemnification should not be permitted since the application of Ontario law to the B.C. insurer in the circumstances of the case would involve the extraterritorial application of Ontario law.

Binnie J. delivered the majority judgment. His judgment intermingled cases on adjudicatory jurisdiction with early federalism cases on extraterritoriality such as *Ladore* and *Royal Bank*. Binnie J. laid down a new test for the constitutional applicability of a provincial law to persons or matters outside of the province. Constitutional applicability was said to be "organized around" four propositions:

1. The territorial limits on the scope of provincial legislative authority prevent the application of the law of a province to matters not sufficiently connected to it;
2. What constitutes a "sufficient" connection depends on the relationship among the enacting jurisdiction, the subject matter of the legislation and the individual or entity sought to be regulated by it;
3. The applicability of an otherwise competent provincial legislation to out-of-province defendants is conditioned by the requirements of order and fairness that underlie our federal arrangements;

---

65 As La Forest J. stated in *Hunt*, *ibid.* at para. 58, "[t]he exact limits of what constitutes a reasonable assumption of jurisdiction were not defined [in *Morguard*], and I add that no test can perhaps ever be rigidly applied; no court has ever been able to anticipate all of these."

66 [2003] 2 S.C.R. 63 [*Unifund*].

4. The principles of order and fairness, being purposive, are applied flexibly according to the subject matter of the legislation.[67]

Binnie J. held that there was no meaningful connection between Ontario and the B.C. insurer, since the B.C. insurer was not authorized to sell insurance in Ontario, nor was it in fact doing so. The accident did not take place in Ontario, and the B.C. insurer received the benefit of the $750,000 deduction by virtue of B.C. rather than Ontario law. As such, there was no meaningful connection between the enacting province and either the person sought to be regulated or the subject matter of the legislation. Further, applying the Ontario law to a B.C. insurer in respect of a B.C. motor vehicle accident solely on the basis that it involved Ontario residents would offend the principles of "order and fairness," since it could lead to the application of conflicting rules to the same set of events.

It was not clear why the majority placed such significance on the issue of constitutional applicability. The case could have been resolved as a matter of ordinary statutory interpretation, by considering whether the Ontario legislature had intended the *Insurance Act* to apply to ICBC in the particular circumstances of the case. Alternatively, the Court could have considered which province's statute law applied to the dispute according to traditional common law rules on choice of law. Furthermore, the application of the "meaningful connection" test is difficult to understand. Binnie J. found it significant, if not determinative, that the accident had occurred in British Columbia. While the law of British Columbia determined liability and damages for the accident, under traditional choice of law rules, it is not clear that British Columbia law would have applied to the liability of the insurers as between themselves. As Black and Edinger have observed, the *Unifund* analysis breaks down when considering an accident in a third province, such as Saskatchewan. In that situation, ICBC would still have relied on British Columbia law to deduct the statutory accident benefits and Unifund, an Ontario insurer, would still have claimed reimbursement under the Ontario insurance legislation. However, it could be argued that neither insurer could rely on the provincial legislation in their respective provinces because the accident occurred in Saskatchewan, and there was no meaningful connection among the enacting province, the subject matter of the legislation, and the persons sought to be regulated.[68]

Furthermore, the implications of *Unifund* for the pith and substance doctrine were unclear. While Binnie J. laid down four propositions for

---

67 *Ibid.* at para. 56.

68 Edinger & Black, above note 62 at 184.

determining the *applicability* (as opposed to validity) of a provincial statute with extraterritorial implications, he treated cases on validity and applicability together in his judgment. After discussing a number of cases, he said that "in each case, the court assessed the relationship between the enacting jurisdiction and the out-of-province individual or entity sought to be regulated by it in light of the subject matter of the legislation to determine *if the relation was 'sufficient' to support the validity or the applicability of the legislation in* question."[69] It was unclear whether the "sufficient connection" test in *Unifund* was intended to displace the traditional pith and substance analysis for determining the territorial limits on provincial legislative jurisdiction. The issue was further obfuscated by the dissenting judgment of Bastarache J., who dealt with the constitutional issue in *Unifund* in one paragraph. Bastarache J. suggested that the pith and substance doctrine applied to *both* validity and applicability. He stated that the Court in *Churchill Falls* had "opined that valid provincial legislation can affect extra-provincial rights in an 'incidental' manner" and that the Ontario *Insurance Act* fell within provincial jurisdiction and was applicable to ICBC.[70]

In *British Columbia v. Imperial Tobacco Ltd.*,[71] the Supreme Court of Canada confirmed that the pith and substance doctrine remains the governing approach to determining the constitutional *validity* of a provincial enactment having extraterritorial effect. The case concerned the validity of a provincial statute that made extraprovincial manufacturers of tobacco products liable for health care costs incurred in British Columbia in respect of tobacco-related diseases. Liability was dependent on individuals having been exposed to tobacco products because of the manufacturer's breach of a duty owed to persons in British Columbia, and on the British Columbia government having incurred health care expenditures in treating disease caused by such exposure. Fourteen tobacco companies sued by the province under the statute challenged the validity of the legislation on several grounds, including that the legislation was *ultra vires* the provincial legislature by reason of extraterritoriality.

Major J. delivered the unanimous judgment of the Court. He held that the legislation was a valid exercise of the property and civil rights power and that the extraterritorial effects of the legislation were incidental. Major J. cited *Unifund* for the proposition that territorial limitations on provincial legislative competence reflect the requirements of order and fairness and "serve to ensure that provincial legislation both

69 *Unifund*, above note 66 at para. 65 [emphasis added].

70 *Ibid.* at para. 140.

71 [2005] 2 S.C.R. 473 [*Imperial Tobacco*].

has a meaningful connection to the province enacting it, and pays respect to 'the sovereignty of the other provinces within their respective legislative spheres.'"[72] However, he reaffirmed the pith and substance approach for determining the validity of a provincial statute having extraterritorial implications, citing *Churchill Falls* and *Global Securities*:

> Where the validity of provincial legislation is challenged on the basis that it violates territorial limitations on provincial legislative competence, the analysis centres on the pith and substance of the legislation. If its pith and substance is in relation to matters falling within the field of provincial legislative competence, the legislation is valid. Incidental or ancillary extra-provincial aspects of such legislation are irrelevant to its validity.[73]

Major J. drew a distinction between tangible matters and intangible matters. If the matter is tangible, then "the question of whether it respects the territorial limitations in s. 92 is easy to answer"; if the matter is located in the province, the legislation is valid. However, if the matter is intangible (as in *Churchill Falls*), then the issue is more difficult. Citing *Unifund*, Major J. held that in the case of an intangible matter, one must look to "the relationships among the enacting territory, the subject matter of the law, and the person[s] sought to be subjected to its regulation" in determining the validity of the legislation.[74]

In *Imperial Tobacco*, the pith and substance of the legislation was the creation of a civil cause of action, an intangible matter. The creation of civil causes of action were generally within the exclusive jurisdiction of the provinces under the property and civil rights power in section 92(13). There were said to be strong relationships among the enacting territory (British Columbia), the subject-matter of the law (compensation for the government of British Columbia's tobacco-related health care costs) and the persons made subject to it (the tobacco manufacturers ultimately responsible for those costs). Further, the Act respected the legislative sovereignty of other jurisdictions. The cause of action related to expenditures by the government of British Columbia for the health care of British Columbians. The Court held that no other jurisdiction could possibly assert a stronger connection to that cause of action than British Columbia. Thus, the Act could apply to tobacco manufacturers even though their corporate decision makers and manufacturing facilities might be located outside the province.

---

72 *Ibid.* at para. 27, citing *Unifund*, above note 66 at para. 51.
73 *Imperial Tobacco*, above note 71 at para. 28.
74 *Ibid.* at para. 36.

Imperial Tobacco provides confirmation that the constitutional validity of a provincial statute falls to be determined by the application of the traditional pith and substance doctrine. Furthermore, it proposes a framework for determining the validity of a provincial law dealing with intangible matters that focuses on contacts and connections among the subject matter of the legislation, the persons regulated, and the enacting province. This analysis is similar to the "real and substantial" connection approach to adjudicative jurisdiction laid down in *Morguard* and subsequent cases.[75] Unfortunately, however, *Imperial Tobacco* did not consider the doctrine of constitutional inapplicability developed in *Hunt* and *Unifund*. As a result, it remains unclear whether and to what extent the doctrine of applicability discussed in *Unifund* applies in cases concerning provincial legislation sought to be justified under the heading of "Property and Civil Rights in the Province" in section 92(13).

FURTHER READINGS

EDINGER, E., & V. Black, "A New Approach to Extraterritoriality: *Unifund Assurance Co. v. I.C.B.C.*" (2004) 40 Can. Bus. L.J. 161

HOGG, P.W., *Constitutional Law of Canada*, 5th ed., loose-leaf (Toronto: Carswell, 2007) cc. 13, 21

MAGNET, J., *Constitutional Law of Canada: Cases, Notes and Materials*, 9th ed. (Edmonton: Juriliber Limited, 2007) vol. 1

75 It has been suggested that the "meaningful connection" test for extraterritoriality is less stringent than the "real and substantial connection" test for adjudicative jurisdiction. See the judgment of Bastarache J., dissenting, in *Castillo v. Castillo*, [2005] 3 S.C.R. 870, suggesting that "meaningful" is different than "real and substantial." See also the discussion in E. Edinger, "*British Columbia v. Imperial Tobacco Canada Ltd.*: Extraterritoriality and Fundamental Principles" (2006) 43 Can. Bus. L.J. 301 at 306–10.

CHAPTER 11

CRIMINAL LAW

A. INTRODUCTION

The drafters of the *Constitution Act, 1867*[1] divided responsibility for criminal justice between the federal and provincial levels of government. Under section 91(27), Parliament was given the exclusive legislative authority over criminal law and procedure.[2] However, the enforcement of the criminal law was allocated to the provinces pursuant to section 92(14), which provides that the provinces have exclusive power in relation to the "Administration of Justice in the Province." The phrase "administration of justice in the province" has been interpreted as including the establishment and maintenance of police forces, the power to lay charges, and the right to prosecute offences. Criminal prosecutions are also conducted in courts established and maintained by the provinces. Thus, while Parliament defines the substantive criminal law, administration and enforcement is under provincial control, making for a balance between the federal and provincial levels of government in the criminal justice system.

---

1 The *Constitution Act, 1867* (U.K.), 30 & 31 Vict., c. 3.

2 The Canadian constitution differs from that of both Australia and the United States, where criminal law is the responsibility of the state governments.

B. FEDERAL CRIMINAL LAW POWER

As LeBel and Deschamps JJ. stated in *Reference re Assisted Human Reproduction Act*,[3] "[d]efining the limits of the federal criminal law power has always been a difficult task."[4] Early cases established a narrow and static test. In *Reference Re Board of Commerce Act, 1919 (Can.)*,[5] the Privy Council held that the subject matter of a federal law must by its very nature belong to the "domain of criminal jurisprudence." However, in *Reference Re The Combines Investigation Act (Can.) s. 36*,[6] the Privy Council rejected this static and formalistic test. Lord Atkin observed that "the domain of criminal jurisprudence can only be ascertained by examining what acts at any particular period are declared by the State to be crimes."[7] Lord Atkin held that in order for legislation to be valid under the criminal law power, there must be a prohibition coupled with a penalty.

In the *Margarine Reference*,[8] Rand J. for the Supreme Court added a third criterion for valid criminal law power: the law must be enacted for a criminal purpose. Rand J. held:

> [A]s prohibitions are not enacted in a vacuum, we can properly look for some evil or injurious or undesirable effect upon the public against which the law is directed. That effect may be in relation to social, economic or political interests; and the legislature has had in mind to suppress the evil or to safeguard the interest threatened.
>
> . . .
>
> Is the prohibition . . . enacted with a view to a public purpose which can support it as being in relation to criminal law? Public peace, order, security, health, morality: these are the ordinary though not exclusive ends served by that law.[9]

The *Margarine Reference* remains the starting point for the analysis of the federal criminal law power under section 91(27). For legislation to be upheld under section 91(27), it must contain three elements: (1) a

---

3 [2010] 3 S.C.R. 457 [*Human Reproduction Reference*].

4 *Ibid.*, LeBel and Deschamps JJ. at para. 230.

5 [1922] 1 A.C. 191 (P.C.).

6 [1931] A.C. 310 (P.C.).

7 *Ibid.* at para. 16.

8 *Reference Re Validity of s. 5(A) of Dairy Industry Act (Canada)*, [1949] S.C.R. 1 [*Margarine Reference*]. The matter was appealed to the Privy Council, which adopted the reasons of Rand J. See *Canadian Federation of Agriculture v. Qué. (A.G.)* (1950), [1951] A.C. 179 (P.C.).

9 *Margarine Reference*, above note 8 at 49–50.

prohibition; (2) backed by a penalty; (3) with a valid criminal law purpose.[10] The first two elements serve as formal constraints and the last criterion serves as a substantive limitation.

The substantive requirement that the law have a "criminal . . . public purpose" might be thought to constitute a fairly significant limitation on the scope of the criminal law power. Yet the practical effect of this "criminal purpose" requirement will depend on how broadly or narrowly the relevant purposes are framed. The catalogue of purposes identified by Rand J. in the *Margarine Reference*—particularly health and morality—is extremely broad and amorphous. Moreover, many cases have construed the "criminal law" purposes of federal legislation in liberal and flexible terms. As a result, the criminal law power has served as a plenary grant of authority, supporting federal regulation of matters that might otherwise fall within provincial jurisdiction as an aspect of property and civil rights, or matters of a merely local or private nature in the province. The approach taken in the criminal law jurisprudence can be contrasted with the approach taken with other federal powers, such as the POGG power and the trade and commerce power. In these areas, the courts have repeatedly held that federal legislation cannot be supported on the basis of broad or generalized purposes such as "inflation" or "protection of the environment."[11] No such limitation has been attached to the use of the criminal law power, with the list of traditional criminal public purposes including such amorphous subjects as health or the protection of the environment.

The instances in which the Supreme Court has struck down federal legislation enacted in reliance on the criminal law power have been relatively rare. In the *Margarine Reference*, the Supreme Court held that a provision of the *Dairy Industry Act* prohibiting importation, production, and consumption of margarine in Canada could not be upheld under the criminal law power. The legislation satisfied the first two requirements for a valid criminal law. However, Rand J. held that the law could not be supported under section 91(27) because it was not "enacted with a view to a public purpose which can support it as being in relation to criminal law." Had there been evidence indicating that margarine was unsafe or unhealthy, Parliament's authority to prohibit its sale would have been clear, since "health" was a valid criminal purpose. However, the federal government had conceded that margarine

---

10 *Reference Re Firearms Act (Can.)*, [2000] 1 S.C.R. 783 at para. 27 [*Firearms Reference*]; *Human Reproduction Reference*, above note 3 at para. 35, McLachlin C.J.

11 See, for example, the *R. v. Crown Zellerbach Canada Ltd.*, [1988] 1 S.C.R. 401 requirement that legislation under POGG's "national concern" branch deal with a discrete and narrowly defined subject matter, as discussed in Chapter 8.

was a perfectly healthy and safe product. The purpose of prohibiting dealings in margarine was to protect the dairy industry by banning products that would compete with butter. Rand J. held that this was an "economic" purpose designed to "give trade protection to the dairy industry in the production and sale of butter; to benefit one group of persons as against competitors in business in which, in the absence of the legislation, the latter would be free to engage in the provinces."[12] This was a "trade" purpose as opposed to a "criminal" purpose and, accordingly, the legislation could not be supported as criminal law.[13]

In *Labatt Breweries v. Canada*,[14] the Court struck down regulations promulgated under the *Food and Drugs Act* stipulating the alcohol content for beer marketed as "light beer." The majority decision, written by Estey J., recognized that the federal criminal law power could be used to regulate false, deceptive, or confusing labelling practices. However, Estey J. held that the regulations in question were not enacted with any of these purposes in mind but were, rather, an attempt to regulate the beer industry. Several commentators have criticized this decision on the basis that the regulations were designed to prevent consumer deception and therefore should have been upheld on the basis of the criminal law power.[15]

Another of the relatively rare cases that have struck down federal legislation as being beyond the criminal law power was *R. v. Boggs*.[16] In *Boggs*, the Court considered a provision of the *Criminal Code* mak-

12 *Margarine Reference*, above note 8 at 50.

13 Rand J. also held that the legislation could not be supported on the basis of the trade and commerce power because it applied to the local production and sale of margarine, matters subject to the exclusive control of the provinces pursuant to their authority over property and civil rights in the province. The law also banned the importation of margarine; Rand J. upheld this aspect of the law as being within the "first branch" of *Citizens' Insurance Co. v. Parsons* (1881), 7 App. Cas. 96 (P.C.), which provides that Parliament has exclusive authority over the regulation of international trade. Rand J. also held that the valid portion of the enactment (the ban on importation) could be "severed" from the invalid portion, on the theory that Parliament would have enacted the ban on importation alone if it had been aware of the fact that the ban on local production and sale was constitutionally invalid. This conclusion is open to serious question, since the ban on importation would be entirely ineffective if it was open to local producers to manufacture and sell margarine.

14 *Labatt Breweries of Canada Ltd. v. Can. (A.G.)*, [1980] 1 S.C.R. 914 [*Labatt*]. See the discussion of this case in Chapter 9.

15 See J.C. MacPherson, "Economic Regulation and the British North America Act: Labatt Breweries and Other Constitutional Imbroglios" (1980) 5 Can. Bus. L.J. 172; P.W. Hogg, *Constitutional Law of Canada*, loose-leaf, 5th ed. (Toronto: Carswell, 2007) at 18-9 to 18-10.

16 [1981] 1 S.C.R. 49 [*Boggs*].

ing it an offence to drive a motor vehicle while one's provincial driver's licence is suspended. The driver's licence of the accused had been suspended because he had been convicted of driving while impaired, a *Criminal Code* offence. Had the provincial licence suspension been triggered in this kind of circumstance only, the related *Criminal Code* offence of "driving while suspended" would have been valid, since it would have been related to the objective of promoting public safety, a valid criminal law purpose. However, Estey J. noted that provincial drivers' licences could also be suspended for breach of various provincial regulations and the failure to pay taxes, judgments, and other fees. Estey J. concluded that there was no relationship between these grounds for licence suspension and the criminal law purpose of public safety. Accordingly, the *Criminal Code* provision was unconstitutional. The ruling in *Boggs* suggests that the criminal law cannot be used as an adjunct to provincial regulatory and taxation regimes and must be linked to a valid and identifiable federal public purpose. This does not seem to be a particularly onerous or unfair hurdle for federal criminal legislation to surmount. For example, in 1985, Parliament amended the *Criminal Code* to limit the application of the offence of "driving while suspended" in the manner suggested by Estey J. in *Boggs*, and the amended provision is undoubtedly valid.[17]

In contrast to the handful of cases that have struck down federal legislation sought to be justified under section 91(27), Parliament's criminal law jurisdiction has been used to justify a wide range of federal enactments, including the regulation of the manufacture, sale, or use of a great variety of products that Parliament deems to be dangerous or harmful,[18] regulation of trade practices injurious to the public interest such as anti-competitive conduct,[19] price discrimination,[20] or resale price maintenance,[21] the advertising of tobacco products,[22] the prohibition of lotteries or gaming activities other than those authorized

---

17 See *Criminal Code*, R.S.C. 1985, c. C-46, ss. 259(4) & (5) which provide that the offence of "driving while suspended" becomes operative only in circumstances where the driver's licence was suspended by reason of a conviction for certain *Criminal Code* offences.

18 See, for example, the *Hazardous Products Act*, R.S.C. 1985, c. H-3 and the *Controlled Drugs and Substances Act*, S.C. 1996, c. 19.

19 See *Goodyear Tire and Rubber Co. of Canada v. R.*, [1956] S.C.R. 303, upholding the anti-merger provisions of what was then the *Combines Investigation Act*, R.S.C. 1985, c. C-34.

20 *B.C. (A.G.) v. Can. (A.G.)*, [1937] A.C. 368 (P.C.).

21 *R. v. Campbell* (1965), 58 D.L.R. (2d) 673 (S.C.C.).

22 *RJR-MacDonald Inc. v. Canada (Attorney General)*, [1995] 3 S.C.R. 199 [*RJR-MacDonald*].

or conducted by the provinces,[23] and the regulation of assisted human reproduction.[24] The Supreme Court has dramatically expanded federal jurisdiction under section 91(27), in some cases adopting reasoning that is rather strained and artificial.

For instance, in *RJR-MacDonald*,[25] a majority of the Court upheld the *Tobacco Products Control Act* under section 91(27). The Act broadly prohibited, with certain exceptions, the advertising and promotion of tobacco products and the sale of a tobacco product unless the package included prescribed health warnings. The prohibitions in the Act were not limited to interprovincial or international trade or to transactions that crossed provincial borders. The bans on advertising and promotion, as well as the requirements of health warnings, applied to all dealings in tobacco. However, the Act—except for a prohibition on the distribution of free samples of tobacco products—did not proscribe the sale, distribution, or use of tobacco products. Both the Quebec Superior Court and the Court of Appeal ruled that the legislation could not be supported on the basis of the criminal law power. Brossard J.A. found it significant that the Act did not prohibit tobacco consumption. He reasoned that Parliament cannot criminalize an ancillary activity (the advertising of a product) when the principal activity (the consumption of that product) remained legal.[26]

La Forest J., writing for seven members of the nine-member Supreme Court, disagreed and held that the legislation was supportable under Parliament's criminal law power.[27] La Forest J. began his discussion of this issue by noting that the criminal law power "is plenary in nature and this Court has always defined its scope broadly."[28] Accord-

---

23 *R. v. Furtney*, [1991] 3 S.C.R. 89 [*Furtney*].

24 *Human Reproduction Reference*, above note 3.

25 Above note 22.

26 See *RJR-MacDonald Inc. v. Canada (A.G.)* (1993), 102 D.L.R. (4th) 289 at 341–42 (Que. C.A.). However, although the Court of Appeal ruled that the legislation was not supportable as criminal law, the Court upheld the legislation on the basis of the federal peace, order, and good government power.

27 Above note 22. Although La Forest J. upheld the law on federalism grounds, he went on to conclude that the legislation violated s. 2(b) of the *Canadian Charter of Rights and Freedoms*, Part I of the *Constitution Act, 1982*, Schedule B to the *Canada Act 1982* (U.K.), 1982, c. 11. La Forest J. held that this violation could be upheld under s. 1. (However, the majority of the Court, in a judgment written by McLachlin J. (as she then was) found that the legislation violated section 2(b) and could not be upheld under s. 1.) Major J., with whom Sopinka J. concurred, dissented on the criminal law issue, but indicated, in *obiter*, that he would have upheld the legislation on the basis of Parliament's power over peace, order, and good government.

28 *Ibid.* at para. 28.

ing to La Forest J., section 91(27) of the *Constitution Act, 1867* must be read as assigning to Parliament exclusive jurisdiction over criminal law "in the widest sense of the term."[29] After noting that the *Tobacco Control Act* prohibited certain acts and that these prohibitions were accompanied by penal sanctions, La Forest J. held that these features of the law create "at least a *prima facie* indication that the Act is criminal law."[30] The fact that the Act contained broad exemptions from its prohibitions did not detract from the criminal nature of the legislation. La Forest J. pointed out that the Court had recently upheld *Criminal Code* provisions regulating gaming and lotteries even though the legislation contained extremely broad exemptions.[31] In addition, the former *Criminal Code* provisions regulating abortion had also contained broad exemptions that did not affect the Court's characterization of the legislation as criminal law.[32] In short, it was open to Parliament to criminalize certain activity and to provide broad exemptions from the relevant prohibitions, as long as the legislation did not "colourably" invade areas of exclusive provincial jurisdiction.[33]

The remaining question was whether the legislation had an underlying criminal public purpose. La Forest J. formulated the "criminal purpose" test in the broadest possible terms. He asked "whether the prohibition with penal consequences is directed at an 'evil' or injurious effect upon the public."[34] In effect, La Forest J. held that any law that takes the form of a prohibition accompanied by a penalty will be valid as criminal law as long as it is directed at an identifiable matter of legitimate public concern. La Forest J. had little trouble in concluding that the *Tobacco Control Act* satisfied the broad criminal purposes test that he had formulated. The evil targeted by Parliament was the detrimental health effects caused by tobacco consumption. This was a valid criminal law concern. Indeed, extensive and convincing evidence was introduced at trial demonstrating that tobacco consumption is widespread in Canadian society and that it poses serious health risks. La Forest J. noted that "health," like other amorphous subjects such as "the environment,"

---

29 *Ibid.*, citing Estey J. in *Scowby v. Glendinning*, [1986] 2 S.C.R. 226 at 238 [*Scowby*].

30 *Ibid.* at para. 29.

31 See *Furtney*, above note 23, upholding the gaming provisions in the *Criminal Code*. The relevant *Code* provisions prohibit lotteries and gaming, but then provide that such conduct is not unlawful if it occurs under provincial control or licence.

32 See *R. v. Morgentaler*, [1988] 1 S.C.R. 30.

33 In other words, Parliament cannot enact legislation dealing with matters within provincial jurisdiction by simply using the criminal law form of a prohibition with penal consequences: see *Scowby*, above note 29 at 237.

34 *RJR-MacDonald*, above note 22 at para. 29.

was not an enumerated power for purposes of the division of powers in the *Constitution Act, 1867*. Consequently, both the provinces and Parliament could legislate so as to protect public health. But the possibility of provincial health–related legislation did not diminish Parliament's plenary power to legislate to protect public health as part of its criminal law jurisdiction. La Forest J. noted that Rand J. in the *Margarine Reference* had made it clear that health is one of the "ordinary ends" of criminal law and that the criminal law power "may validly be used to safeguard the public from any 'injurious or undesirable effect.'"[35] Parliament therefore had a broad power to create criminal legislation with respect to health matters, "circumscribed only by the requirements that the legislation must contain a prohibition accompanied by a penal sanction and must be directed at a legitimate public health evil."[36]

The only remaining question was whether the legislation was a "colourable" attempt to regulate property and civil rights, on the theory that Parliament had criminalized the advertising and promotion of tobacco but not its sale and use. La Forest J. stated that it was clearly established that the criminal law power could be used to impose labelling and packaging requirements on dangerous products with a view to informing the public. He cited provisions in the *Food and Drugs Act* prohibiting the sale of drugs prepared under unsanitary conditions or the false or misleading advertisement of drugs, which had previously been upheld by the courts as valid criminal law.[37] La Forest J. reasoned that it must be open to Parliament to require cigarette manufacturers to include warnings about the health risks associated with smoking on their packages. La Forest J. was also not impressed with the argument that Parliament could not prohibit the advertising and/or promotion of tobacco products because it had not banned the sale and use of the products. Parliament had evidently concluded that it was not practical to ban the sale or use of cigarettes, given their widespread use in society, and had opted instead for the ban on advertising and promotion as a second-best alternative. Yet this was not a basis for impugning the constitutional validity of the legislation, since "the wisdom of Parliament's choice of method cannot be determinative with respect to

35 *Ibid.* at para. 32.

36 *Ibid.*

37 See *R. v. Wetmore*, [1983] 2 S.C.R. 284 [*Wetmore*], cited by La Forest J. in *RJR-MacDonald*, above note 22 at para. 40. La Forest J. quoted a passage from *Wetmore* in which Laskin C.J. stated that the criminal law power supports legislation aimed at protecting the "physical health and safety of the public" as well as the "moral health" of the public (*ibid.*).

Parliament's power to legislate."[38] As long as Parliament is legislating for a valid purpose, the courts ought not to be concerned with whether Parliament had acted wisely or whether there were alternative means of achieving the same objectives in a more effective manner.[39]

Similarly, in *R. v. Hydro-Quebec*,[40] a narrow majority of the Supreme Court of Canada upheld a comprehensive environmental scheme under section 91(27). The *Canadian Environmental Protection Act* permitted the federal minister of the environment to prescribe requirements concerning the release of "toxic substances" into the environment. The definition of toxic substances was extremely broad, and included substances that could pose a risk either to the environment or to human life and health. The federal minister (at that time, Lucien Bouchard) had issued an order restricting the release into the environment of polychlorinated biphenyls (PCBS). Hydro-Quebec, which had been charged with breaching the order, brought a motion to have the ministerial order and the statutory provisions on which it was based declared invalid. Two lower courts in Quebec as well as the Quebec Court of Appeal held the provisions to be *ultra vires* the federal government, ruling that the legislation was regulatory rather than prohibitory and therefore exceeded the domain of criminal law.[41] But the Supreme Court, by a five to four majority,[42] allowed the appeal and upheld the legislation as valid criminal law. All nine members of the Court agreed that the "protection of the environment" should be added to the list of criminal public

---

38 *RJR-MacDonald, ibid.* at para. 44.

39 *Ibid.*, Major and Sopinka JJ. dissenting on this point. Major J. would have upheld the requirement of health warnings on cigarette packages on the basis that "[i]t is undisputed that Parliament may legislate with respect to hazardous, unsanitary, adulterated and otherwise dangerous foods and drugs" (at para. 195), but he held that the ban on advertising of a product "which is both legal and licensed for sale throughout Canada lacks a typically criminal public purpose" (at para. 209). He reasoned that tobacco advertising "is in itself not sufficiently dangerous or harmful to justify criminal sanctions" (at para. 212). Major J. also relied on the fact that the legislation contained broad exemptions, which he interpreted as indicative of the fact that the proscribed conduct was not "truly criminal" (at para. 213).

40 [1997] 3 S.C.R. 213 [*Hydro-Quebec*].

41 In addition to relying on the criminal law power, the Attorney General of Canada had sought to support the provisions on the basis of the federal POGG power as well as the power to regulate trade and commerce. The lower courts likewise rejected these justifications.

42 La Forest J. wrote a decision concurred in by L'Heureux-Dubé, Gonthier, Cory, and McLachlin JJ. Lamer C.J. and Iacobucci J. wrote a dissenting opinion, with which Sopinka and Major JJ. concurred.

purposes identified by Rand J. in the *Margarine Reference* as capable of supporting the enactment of criminal legislation.[43]

The Court divided on the issue of the formal requirements of the legislation. Lamer C.J. and Iacobucci J., dissenting, pointed out that the legislation appeared to be regulatory rather than prohibitory in nature. The relevant provisions in the Act granted the government the authority to enact regulations "imposing requirements respecting . . . the quantity or concentration of a substance that may be released into the environment." While the statute did contain provisions stating that failure to comply with a regulation was an offence, these provisions were merely ancillary to the regulatory scheme as a whole, and such provisions were commonly included in virtually all regulatory schemes. Moreover, until the promulgation of an order by the minister or a regulation by the government, there were no regulatory requirements, and thus no prohibition, on the emission of PCBS. Lamer C.J. and Iacobucci J. pointed out that there was no precedent for a criminal enactment whose prohibitions were entirely dependent on an administrative decision by a delegated decision maker.

The majority judgment of La Forest J. did not directly answer these questions. La Forest J. described the relevant statutory provisions as defining "situations where the use of a substance in the List of Toxic Substances in Schedule 1 is prohibited."[44] In fact, as noted above, the relevant statutory provisions contain no requirements or prohibitions but merely authorize the enactment of regulations prescribing requirements respecting the release of toxic substances into the environment. In this sense, La Forest J.'s reference to the statute and the regulations as being concerned with the enactment of "prohibitions" is entirely at odds with the plain and obvious wording of the legislation.

In *Reference Re Firearms Act (Can.)*,[45] a decision handed down following La Forest J.'s retirement, the Court retreated slightly from the expansive approach to the criminal law power set out in *RJR-MacDonald* and *Hydro-Quebec*. The *Firearms Reference* arose from a reference by the government of Alberta to the Alberta Court of Appeal of a series of questions relating to the constitutional validity of the federal *Firearms Act*.[46] For many years, the *Criminal Code* had prohibited or restricted the use of certain firearms, mainly automatic weapons and handguns. In

43 In this sense, the fact that the relevant legislative provisions applied to emissions that, while harmful to the environment, may not have been harmful to human health, did not constitute a basis for overturning the legislation.

44 *Hydro-Quebec*, above note 40 at para. 150.

45 Above note 10.

46 S.C. 1995, c. 39, enacting amendments to the *Criminal Code*, above note 17.

1995, Parliament expanded the reach of these *Criminal Code* provisions by regulating the acquisition and possession of all firearms, including rifles and shotguns, through a licensing and registration system. The province of Alberta challenged the amendments on grounds that they dealt with matters that did not raise legitimate concerns relating to public safety and, therefore, were a colourable attempt to regulate the property rights of firearms owners. Alberta's argument was unsuccessful in the Alberta Court of Appeal, as that court upheld the legislation as criminal law by a narrow three to two margin, and the province appealed to the Supreme Court.

In a unanimous decision, the Supreme Court held that the legislation satisfied the three requirements of criminal legislation and was thus constitutionally justifiable on the basis of Parliament's jurisdiction over criminal law. In terms of the substantive requirement, the predominant purpose of the legislation was to combat the misuse of firearms and the threat this posed to public safety, which was a well-established criminal purpose. In terms of formal requirements, the legislation contained clear prohibitions backed by penalties, since the relevant provisions prohibited possession of a firearm where the licensing and registration requirements had not been complied with. The Court noted that the presence of prohibitions backed by penalties was sufficient to avoid the difficulty that had been identified by the dissenting judgment of Lamer C.J. and Iacobucci J. in *Hydro-Quebec*, namely, that the legislation in that case did not directly prohibit anything. While the licensing and regulatory scheme for firearms was certainly complicated and contemplated the exercise of administrative discretion by officials responsible for administering the scheme, such features were compatible with the enactment of criminal legislation. Finally, the fact that the scheme might incidentally affect the property rights of gun owners was no grounds for constitutional objection, provided that the legislation's purpose, or pith and substance, was directed at the matter of public safety. But, perhaps tellingly, the Court made no reference to the expansive reasoning employed by La Forest J. in *Hydro-Quebec* and, in fact, pointed out that the *Firearms Act* was clearly distinguishable from the legislation and regulations at issue in that case.

The extent to which Parliament may enact regulation through the exercise of its criminal law power was considered again in the *Human Reproduction Reference*.[47] Following a Royal Commission on New Reproductive Technologies (the Baird Commission), Parliament enacted the *Assisted Human Reproduction Act*. Sections 5 to 9 of the Act contained prohibitions on various activities including cloning, commercialization

47 Above note 3.

of reproductive material, reproductive functions, and non-consensual *in vitro* fertilization. Sections 10 to 13 prohibited various "controlled activities" unless carried out in accordance with regulations made under the Act, under licence, and in licensed premises. These controlled activities involve manipulation of human reproductive material or *in vitro* embryos, transgenic engineering, and reimbursement of expenditures of donors and surrogate mothers. The remainder of the Act set up a regulatory scheme for the administration and enforcement of the legislation. Sections 14 to 19 established an information management system; sections 20 to 39 created a federal Assisted Human Reproduction Agency; sections 40 to 59 set out the agency's administrative and enforcement powers, including the power to issue licences under the Act; sections 60 to 61 contained penalty provisions; and sections 65 to 67 authorized the promulgation of further regulations. Notably, section 68 of the Act permitted the Governor in Council to exempt provinces with equivalent legislation from the Act. Sections 5 to 9 of the Act were conceded to have been valid exercises of the criminal law power. However, the Attorney General of Quebec challenged the constitutionality of sections 8 to 19, 40 to 53, 60 to 61 and 68 by way of a reference to the Quebec Court of Appeal. The Court of Appeal held that the impugned provisions could not be upheld under section 91(27) and that they were in pith and substance related to the regulation of medical practice and research in the area of assisted reproduction.

The Supreme Court of Canada divided into three camps on appeal. McLachlin C.J. (with whom Binnie, Fish, and Charron JJ. concurred) would have upheld all of the impugned provisions as valid exercises of the criminal law power under section 91(27). LeBel and Deschamps JJ. (with whom Abella and Rothstein JJ. concurred) would have upheld the judgment of the Quebec Court of Appeal and struck down all of the impugned provisions. Cromwell J. delivered short reasons, disagreeing with the judgments of both McLachlin C.J. and LeBel and Deschamps JJ. Cromwell J. would have struck down the impugned provisions, with the exception of sections 8 to 12, 19, and 60, which, in his view, were valid exercises of the criminal law power. In the result, certain of the more patently regulatory provisions of the Act were struck down, while many of the provisions of the Act pertaining to prohibitions and enforcement were upheld.

The judgments in the *Human Reproduction Reference* (particularly the judgments of McLachlin C.J. and LeBel and Deschamps JJ.) were strongly worded. Each camp accused the other of misapplying constitutional principles and fundamentally misconstruing the criminal law power under section 91(27).

McLachlin C.J.'s judgment advocated a broad and expansive reading of the criminal law power consistent with La Forest J.'s judgments in *RJR-MacDonald* and *Hydro-Quebec*. In terms of form, the prohibition on "controlled activities" except in accordance with federal regulations was sufficient to satisfy the first two *Margarine Reference Requirements*, in her opinion. According to McLachlin C.J., such provisions were "carve-outs" from a general prohibition and constituted a prohibition backed by a penalty. In her view, it was open to Parliament to prohibit "reprehensible" conduct absolutely (as in the general prohibitions under sections 5 to 9 of the Act) as well as to prohibit "only the harmful aspects of the conduct at issue" through a general prohibition "subject to exceptions" set out by federal regulations.[48] In terms of the substantive requirement, she construed the "criminal" purposes of the Act in extremely broad terms. In her view, the Act as a whole and the impugned provisions in isolation were concerned with morality, public health, and security, purposes that properly fell within the purview of the criminal law.

McLachlin C.J. adopted an extremely deferential approach to Parliament in determining whether federal legislation sought to be upheld under section 91(27) has a valid criminal law purpose. With respect to morality, she held that "Parliament need only have a reasonable basis to expect that its legislation will address a moral concern of fundamental importance."[49] In other words, the role of the courts is limited to ensuring that the law "in pith and substance relates to conduct that Parliament views as contrary to our central moral precepts, and that there is a consensus in society that the regulated activity engages a moral concern of fundamental importance."[50] Similarly, Parliament may use the criminal law power to legislate in relation to "health" so as to target any conduct that elevates a *risk* of harm to individuals. McLachlin C.J. expressly affirmed La Forest J.'s broad interpretation of the substantive requirement for the invocation of the criminal law power in *RJR-MacDonald:* "[t]he scope of the federal power to create criminal legislation with respect to health matters is broad, and is circumscribed only by the requirements that the legislation must contain a prohibition accompanied by a penal sanction and must be directed at a legitimate public health evil."[51]

By contrast, LeBel and Deschamps JJ. held that the impugned provisions in pith and substance dealt with the regulation of assisted human reproduction. The dominant purpose of the provisions was to

48 *Ibid.* at para. 26.
49 *Ibid.* at para. 50.
50 *Ibid.* at para. 51.
51 *Ibid.* at para. 56, citing *RJR-MacDonald*, above note 22 at para. 32.

regulate a specific type of health service provided in health care institutions by professionals, to individuals who needed help with reproduction. The legislative history and the wording and structure of the Act established that there was a critical distinction between prohibited activities and controlled activities. The impugned provisions dealing with controlled activities were enacted in order to establish national standards for assisted human reproduction, not to prohibit "reprehensible conduct." Furthermore, LeBel and Deschamps JJ. noted that the impugned provisions interfered with several overlapping statutes in Quebec and thereby trenched on provincial jurisdiction. In other words, LeBel and Deschamps JJ. suggested (although they did not expressly state) that the provisions were a colourable intrusion on provincial jurisdiction over hospitals (section 92(17)), property and civil rights (section 92(13)), and matters of a merely local or private nature in the province (section 92(16)).

In contrast to McLachlin C.J.'s expansive interpretation of criminal law purposes, LeBel and Deschamps JJ. introduced a novel and significant change to the third element of the *Margarine Reference* test. LeBel and Deschamps JJ. cited the *Margarine Reference* for the proposition that a valid criminal law must be directed at "suppressing an evil" or "safeguarding a threatened interest." It is not sufficient that Parliament desires to establish national standards to regulate conduct that is considered to be beneficial. LeBel and Deschamps JJ. added that courts were not simply to defer to Parliament's judgment; rather, the court must ensure that the evil is "real" and there is a "reasoned apprehension of harm," a concept borrowed from jurisprudence under section 1 of the *Charter of Rights and Freedoms*. According to LeBel and Deschamps JJ., this threshold "helps give concrete form to the substantive component of the criminal law" and serves to ensure that the federal power under section 91(27) has rational limits.[52]

Cromwell J. did not expressly agree with LeBel and Deschamps JJ.'s "reasoned apprehension" test. However, he did agree that most of the impugned provisions were in pith and substance regulation of the research and clinical practice of assisted human reproduction. The challenged provisions were therefore best classified as relating to the establishment, maintenance, and management of hospitals, property and civil rights, and matters of a merely local or private nature in the province.

The lack of consensus in the *Assisted Human Reproduction* case is unfortunate. While there is consensus on the three-part test set out in the *Margarine Reference*, the extent to which federal regulatory schemes

---

52 *Human Reproduction Reference*, above note 3 at para. 236.

may be upheld under section 91(27) remains unsettled. The Court fundamentally disagreed not only on the characterization of the legislation at issue, but on the proper approach to the formal and substantive requirements for valid criminal legislation. McLachlin C.J.'s judgment suggests that Parliament may establish comprehensive schemes to regulate virtually any conduct, as long as the legislation is structured so that it contains a general prohibition with "carve-outs" for permissible conduct. In our view, McLachlin C.J.'s approach is too expansive. It will almost always be possible for Parliament to impose regulations on an activity by enacting a general ban subject to exemptions for compliance with prescribed standards. Moreover, McLachlin C.J.'s interpretation of the third *Margarine Reference* requirement establishes virtually no limit on the type of legislation that may be enacted by Parliament under section 91(27). It will almost always be possible for Parliament to establish that it has a "reasonable basis" to expect that the legislation addresses an important moral concern; the fact that legislation has been enacted may be taken as proof of an important moral objective. As LeBel and Deschamps JJ. argue, if McLachlin C.J.'s analysis were accepted, the "federal government would have the authority under the Constitution to make laws in respect of any matter, provided that it cited its criminal law power and that it gave part of its legislation the form of a prohibition with criminal sanctions."[53]

However, LeBel and Deschamps JJ.'s gloss on the third *Margarine Reference* requirement is problematic, in our opinion. As discussed above, the concept of a "reasoned apprehension" of harm is borrowed from the jurisprudence under section 1 of the *Charter*. LeBel and Deschamps JJ. assert without analysis that the inquiry under section 1 of the *Charter* is relevant to determining whether a federal law has a valid criminal law objective. In fact, the analysis is very different. As McLachlin C.J. noted, the validity of a law under sections 91 or 92 of the *Constitution Act, 1867* is a completely different inquiry than judicial review under the *Charter*:

> Whether a federal law falls within Parliament's criminal law power under s. 91(27) of the *Constitution Act, 1867*, is a question of *which level* of government has jurisdiction to enact this law. This question relates to the powers of one level of government *vis-à-vis* the other, and it is resolved by determining the law's pith and substance. The degree to which the Act may impact on individual liberties is not relevant to this inquiry.[54]

53 *Ibid.* at para. 240.

54 *Ibid.* at para. 44 [emphasis in original].

There are good reasons to keep the federalism and *Charter* analysis distinct, as McLachlin C.J. suggests. As a matter of logic, jurisdiction on federalism grounds should precede *Charter* analysis. A *Charter* challenge presumes that the law in question may be enacted by the applicable level of government; if the law is *ultra vires* the enacting government, the *Charter* cannot apply. Furthermore, there are practical benefits of keeping the division of powers and *Charter* analysis separate. If a law is upheld as valid on federalism grounds, but struck down on *Charter* grounds, it may be re-enacted so as to cure the interference with individual rights and liberties identified by the Court at first instance. However, if *Charter* considerations inform the jurisdictional issue as advocated by LeBel and Deschamps JJ., the ability of the government to legislate in relation to the entire subject matter of the legislation may be jeopardized.[55]

In our view, the appropriate limits on the criminal law power should not be defined by introducing *Charter* considerations such as the "reasoned apprehension" of harm test. Rather, the issue of whether federal legislation can be upheld under section 91(27) falls to be determined by a purposive analysis of the true nature of the enactment. As in almost all areas of constitutional analysis, there are no bright-line rules. In terms of the substantive requirement, the criminal law purpose cannot be defined so broadly so as to intrude into areas of provincial jurisdiction. The overarching question is whether the law was intended to suppress a public evil or safeguard a public interest, as opposed to regulate matters or conduct. In terms of the formal requirements, it may be appropriate in some cases for Parliament to exercise its criminal law jurisdiction through something other than an absolute prohibition. However, the case for federal jurisdiction weakens "when the criminal regulation of beneficial conduct for the purpose of checking its potential harms takes the form of regulating through a public agency and adopts the regulatory instruments of investigation, standard setting through regulations, granting licences and administrative approvals."[56] As Professor Whyte argues:

> Criminal law is usually a general prohibition. Its coercive effects are thought to be most legitimately imposed when they have a degree of constancy and are created through generally available public statutes.

---

55 See M. Carter, "Federalism Analysis and the *Charter*" (2011) 74 Sask L. Rev. 5. See also: P. Hogg & A. Bushell, "The *Charter* Dialogue Between Courts and Legislatures" (1997) 35 Osgoode Hall L.J. 75.

56 J.D. Whyte, "Federalism and Moral Regulation: A Comment on *Reference Re Assisted Human Reproduction Act*" (2011) 74 Sask. L. Rev. 45 at 52.

> If the conduct that is criminal is evident only after an administrative determination, this represents an attenuated form of criminal proscription and is possibly unfair to those who are not part of the administrative process. . . . Second, it will often be the case that the conduct being regulated falls within provincial jurisdiction, such as driving, health care, market activity, or environmental protection. When there is simple proscription of some acts in these areas, it is reasonable to consider that the primary aspect of the federal law is its criminal law power. The constitution has recognized a specific instrument as suitable for federal use notwithstanding that its use will often affect matters within provincial jurisdiction. Insofar as there are limits—both formal and substantive—on this jurisdiction, its use should not dramatically alter the basic constitutional balance between the federal and provincial legislative capacities.[57]

C. PROVINCIAL POWER TO ENACT PENAL LAWS

While section 91(27) of the *Constitution Act, 1867* grants Parliament exclusive authority to enact criminal law, section 92(15) grants the provinces the power to impose "Punishment by Fine, Penalty or Imprisonment" for the purpose of enforcing otherwise valid provincial legislation. Thus, a province can enact "quasi-criminal legislation" that resembles, in form at least, criminal laws enacted by the federal Parliament. Provinces commonly rely on this power by including in statutes provisions making it an offence to violate provisions in a statute and setting out penalties, including imprisonment, for breach of the provisions in question. Given the existence of section 92(15), the vast majority of such quasi-criminal provisions are constitutionally valid. Some difficulty has arisen in instances where the provinces have enacted legislation that regulates conduct that is also subject to criminal prohibitions found in the *Criminal Code*. The question in such cases is whether the legislation is sufficiently anchored in a head of power in section 92 that the province can argue that it is not a colourable attempt to enact criminal legislation. Unfortunately, the results in the cases considering these near-criminal provisions have been confusing and contradictory, and it is extremely difficult to distinguish the cases on the basis of any discernible principle.

57 *Ibid.*

In *Bedard v. Dawson*,[58] the Supreme Court of Canada upheld a provincial law authorizing the closing of "disorderly houses," which were primarily defined as houses where there had been *Criminal Code* convictions for gambling or prostitution. Despite the close similarity between the provincial legislation and the related *Criminal Code* provisions, the Supreme Court upheld the law on the basis that it did not purport to create a criminal offence but rather provided a civil remedy (i.e., an order to close the disorderly house) where a continuing offence under the *Criminal Code* was being committed. As such, the Court characterized it as a regulation of the use of property as well as a law directed at suppressing the conditions that would cause crime, rather than as a criminal law. Other cases extended the reasoning in *Bedard* and upheld provincial laws that created quasi-criminal offences in terms that were virtually identical to prohibitions included in the *Criminal Code*. For example, a series of cases dealing with provincial driving offences, including *Egan*[59] and *O'Grady*,[60] held that the relevant provincial legislation was distinguishable in some way from similar *Criminal Code* provisions and could be upheld as valid.

At the same time, however, a contrary and inconsistent line of cases struck down a variety of provincial penal provisions on grounds that they regulated matters that were properly within Parliament's exclusive criminal law domain. In *Reference Re Alberta Legislation*,[61] the Supreme Court considered an Alberta statute that required newspapers to publish statements clarifying "the true and exact objects of the policy of the Government and as to the hindrances to or difficulties in achieving such objects to the end that the people may be informed with respect thereto."[62] The case is most often cited for Duff C.J.'s holding that it was beyond the power of the provinces to enact legislation restricting the right of "free public discussion of affairs." However, Cannon J. relied on more conventional division of powers grounds to find that the provincial law was unconstitutional. Cannon J. reasoned that the bill was an attempt to revive the old English crime of seditious libel, under which it had been a crime to criticize government policy. Seditious libel had

58 [1923] S.C.R. 681 [*Bedard*].

59 *P.E.I. (Provincial Secretary) v. Egan*, [1941] S.C.R. 396 [*Egan*] (upholding provincial law automatically suspending the driver's licence of anyone convicted of the *Criminal Code*'s impaired driving offences).

60 *O'Grady v. Sparling*, [1960] S.C.R. 804 [*O'Grady*] (upholding provincial law making it an offence to drive carelessly, which was virtually identical to a *Criminal Code* offence of dangerous driving).

61 [1938] S.C.R. 100.

62 See the preamble to the *Act to ensure the Publication of Accurate News and Information*, quoted in the judgment of Cannon J., *ibid.* at 142.

been abolished in England and in Canada in 1792. Cannon J. held that Alberta was in effect attempting to amend the *Criminal Code* to recreate the crime of seditious libel and was on that basis invalid.

Cannon J.'s reasoning was followed and developed in a series of cases in the 1950s dealing with provincial laws attempting to restrict civil liberties. In *Henry Birks & Sons (Montreal) Ltd. v. Montreal (City)*,[63] the Supreme Court unanimously struck down a city by-law that compelled observance of certain Catholic religious holidays. The majority held that the by-law was, in pith and substance, legislation in relation to criminal law and beyond provincial competence. In *Switzman v. Elbling*,[64] the Supreme Court struck down a provincial statute providing for the closing of any house used to propagate communism or bolshevism and made it unlawful to print or publish material directed toward the same end. This "padlock law" was obviously modelled on the provision that had been upheld as valid in the *Bedard* case. Nevertheless, the Supreme Court distinguished *Bedard* on the basis that it had been concerned with the effect of certain activity on the use and enjoyment of neighbouring properties, whereas the legislation before the Court in *Switzman* was designed to prevent the propagation of communism within the province. There was no evidence that this activity constituted a local nuisance in the same manner as the disorderly houses in *Bedard,* and the province was in reality attempting to enact criminal legislation.[65]

These cases seemed to suggest that a province could prohibit conduct that was also prohibited under the criminal law as long as the province was acting for a purpose that was somehow distinguishable or separate from the purpose being pursued by Parliament. However, the 1978 *McNeil* case[66] significantly relaxed this relatively modest limitation on provincial jurisdiction. *McNeil* considered the constitutional validity of provincial legislation establishing a board of censors with power to regulate or prohibit the public exhibition of films. The majority opinion of Ritchie J. upheld the legislation on the basis that it was enacted for the purpose of regulating the film business in the province. Ritchie J.

---

63 [1955] S.C.R. 799.

64 [1957] S.C.R. 285 [*Switzman*].

65 See also *Johnson v. Alta. (A.G.)*, [1954] S.C.R. 127 [*Johnson*], in which the Supreme Court struck down an Alberta statute providing for the seizure and forfeiture of slot machines. Like the legislation in *Bedard*, above note 58, the provincial law in this case did not create an offence with respect to the use or possession of slot machines, but purported to deal only with the property right in the machines. The Court divided evenly on the question of whether the legislation was a colourable attempt to enact a criminal law. The tie was broken by Rand J., who held the law inoperative on grounds that it conflicted with the federal criminal provisions.

66 *McNeil v. N.S. (Board of Censors)*, [1978] 2 S.C.R. 662 [*McNeil*].

characterized the legislation as concerned with dealings in and the use of property (films) rather than criminal legislation. He acknowledged that the board of censors would make its decision whether to permit the exhibition of a film based on moral grounds—whether the film was considered unsuitable for viewing based on local standards of morality. He relied on the fact that the legislation did not create a criminal offence or provide for punishment but was directed at the establishment of a regulatory regime for theatres and film distributors. Ritchie J.'s conclusion seems primarily founded on the form of the legislation, emphasizing the fact that it was not framed in traditional criminal law terms of a prohibition coupled with a penalty. This concern was reflected in his further conclusion that a particular provincial regulation prohibiting an "indecent performance" was unconstitutional as an invasion of Parliament's criminal law jurisdiction. Ritchie J. pointed out that the wording of the provincial regulation was virtually identical to a *Criminal Code* provision making it an offence to exhibit an "indecent show" publicly, citing the *Johnson* case as authority for the proposition that this regulation was beyond the authority of the province.[67]

Having seemingly loosened the restrictions on provincial power to regulate morality through penal legislation in *McNeil*, the Court abruptly reversed course in *Westendorp v. R.*[68] At issue in *Westendorp* was a Calgary by-law regulating the use of city streets, including provisions controlling soliciting or carrying on business on any street. Calgary had amended the by-law in 1981 to prohibit persons from being present or approaching another person on a street for the purpose of prostitution. The recitals to the by-law stated that prostitutes tended to gather in groups and attract crowds on city streets, thereby creating a local nuisance. The Alberta Court of Appeal had upheld the by-law on the basis that it was an attempt to deal with a public nuisance, since its prohibitions were limited to activities occurring on public streets and did not purport to regulate prostitution as such. However, Laskin C.J., writing for a unanimous Supreme Court, held that "[i]t is specious to regard . . . [the by-law] as relating to control of the streets."[69] Had this been the concern of the city, it would have directed its regulation at congregation of persons on the streets generally, regardless of the

67 Significantly, the provincial legislation in *Johnson*, above note 65, did not create an offence but merely purported to regulate property rights in slot machines. On the reasoning employed in *McNeil*, above note 66, one might have thought that the legislation considered in *Johnson* might have been valid, since it was not enacted in the form of a prohibition coupled with a penalty.

68 *Westendorp v. R.*, [1983] 1 S.C.R. 43 [*Westendorp*].

69 *Ibid.* at 51.

reason for their presence there. The fact that the by-law was triggered only by communication for the purpose of prostitution indicated that the city was attempting to control or punish prostitution directly. It is extremely difficult to reconcile *Westendorp* with the more expansive approach to provincial jurisdiction adopted in cases such as *McNeil*, *Bedard*, or the provincial "driving offences" cases.[70]

The Supreme Court's decision in *Rio Hotel Ltd. v. New Brunswick (Liquor Licensing Board)*[71] further confused the issue. In *Rio Hotel*, the Court upheld provincial legislation prohibiting nude performances in licensed drinking establishments. There were various provisions in the *Criminal Code* regulating public nudity, and a hotel owner argued that the provincial regulation was invalid because it was in purpose and effect criminal legislation. The Supreme Court disagreed, holding that the provincial regulation was unobjectionable because it merely imposed conditions on the owner of licensed premises. The plurality opinion of Dickson C.J. emphasized that there was no conflict between the provincial regulations and the relevant *Criminal Code* prohibitions on public nudity, since "[i]t is perfectly possible to comply with both the provincial and the federal legislation."[72] In an analysis that was broadly similar to that of Ritchie J. in *McNeil*, Dickson C.J. emphasized that the form of the provincial law was entirely different from the analogous *Criminal Code* provisions; the penalty for breach of the provincial regulation was cancellation of the liquor licence rather than a fine or imprisonment. Dickson C.J. argued that the *Westendorp* case was clearly distinguishable; in *Westendorp*, the impugned provision was not part of a "regulatory scheme," whereas the licence conditions in *Rio Hotel* were "part of a comprehensive scheme regulating the sale of liquor in New Brunswick."[73] Significantly, Dickson C.J. did not claim that the provincial regulations upheld in *Rio Hotel* had a different purpose from the comparable *Criminal Code* provisions: in both instances, the underlying concern was to control nudity for reasons of public morality. What the Chief Justice seemed to have been saying is that provincial regulation of public morality is acceptable as long as it is drafted in the form of a licence condition (as opposed to a prohibition coupled with a penalty), is part of a broader regulatory scheme, and does not conflict in any way with comparable *Criminal Code* provisions.

---

70 See *Egan*, above note 59, and *O'Grady*, above note 60.

71 [1987] 2 S.C.R. 59 [*Rio Hotel*].

72 *Ibid.* at 66. Dickson C.J. wrote an opinion concurred in by McIntyre, Wilson, and Le Dain JJ.; Estey J. wrote a concurring opinion with which Lamer J. (as he then was) agreed; and Beetz J. wrote a separate concurring opinion.

73 *Ibid.*

This emphasis on the form of legislation, as opposed to its underlying purpose or function, also featured prominently in the subsequent case of *R. v. Morgentaler.*[74] Following the Supreme Court's 1988 decision striking down the *Criminal Code* provisions regulating abortion on grounds that they violated the *Charter*, the province of Nova Scotia enacted the *Medical Services Act.* The legislation prohibited the performance of designated medical services other than in a hospital, denied those violating the Act reimbursement under the provincial *Health Services and Insurance Act*, and made contravention of the Act a summary conviction offence. Abortion was one of nine medical services designated for purposes of the Act. When Dr. Henry Morgentaler opened a free-standing abortion clinic in Halifax and began performing abortions, he was charged with fourteen counts of violating the *Medical Services Act.* The Supreme Court unanimously struck down the provisions making it an offence to perform abortions outside a hospital and upheld a lower court's acquittal of Dr. Morgentaler. Sopinka J., writing for a unanimous Supreme Court, emphasized that the provisions de-insuring designated services performed outside hospitals were not before the Court; he limited his analysis to the "offence-creating" provisions in the legislation. Sopinka J. advanced a variety of considerations which led him to conclude that the offence-creating provisions were unconstitutional. First, he noted that the provisions dealt with a matter that had historically been considered to be part of the criminal law—the prohibition of the performance of abortions with penal consequences—and was thus "suspect on its face." Further, its legal effect was to "partially . . . [reproduce] that of the now defunct section 251 of the *Criminal Code*, in so far as both precluded the establishment and operation of free-standing abortion clinics." A province, according to Sopinka J., cannot "invade the criminal field by attempting to stiffen, supplement or replace the criminal law."[75] Finally, the legislative history of the enactment, including debates in the legislature, revealed that the purpose of the legislation was to suppress the perceived harm of abortion clinics. Sopinka J. could find no evidence of any other motivation, such as concern over the cost and quality of medical services or a desire to prevent the growth of private health clinics. The legislation was invalid because it "involves the regulation of the place where an abortion may be obtained, not from the viewpoint of health care policy, but from the viewpoint of public wrongs or crimes."[76]

The difficulty with Sopinka J.'s analysis in *Morgentaler* is that much of his reasoning is flatly inconsistent with the Court's prior jurispru-

---

74 [1993] 3 S.C.R. 463.

75 *Ibid.* at 498.

76 *Ibid.* at 513.

dence on the power of a province to enact penal laws. For example, the suggestion that the province cannot regulate conduct from the viewpoint of "public wrongs" or morality is directly contradicted by both *McNeil* and *Rio Hotel*, in which provincial laws motivated by concerns over public morality were upheld. Nor does Sopinka J.'s statement that the provinces cannot regulate a subject that has been historically regarded as part of the criminal law find any support in prior cases. It has been clearly established that the provinces may regulate the same conduct that is the subject of long-standing criminal prohibitions, as long as they do so for purposes that are somehow distinct from those underlying the criminal law. Likewise, the decision that the provinces cannot "stiffen" or "supplement" criminal prohibitions is directly contrary to numerous cases such as *Bedard, McNeil*, and *Rio Hotel*, in which provincial legislation dovetailed with analogous *Criminal Code* prohibitions; the main concern of the courts in these cases was to ensure that there was no conflict between the applicable federal and provincial laws. The only remaining argument advanced by Sopinka J. is that provinces cannot enact legislation that takes the form of a prohibition coupled with a penalty. This distinction is obviously entirely unsatisfactory, since the province can achieve precisely the same legal and practical effect as would have resulted from a prohibition and penalty simply by altering the form of the enactment. Moreover, the form of an enactment is not always determinative. The courts have struck down provincial legislation in cases where the law did not take the form of a prohibition coupled with a penalty.[77] Conversely, many provincial statutes which prohibit conduct in terms that are virtually identical to analogous *Criminal Code* provisions have been upheld.[78] Nevertheless, the form of the provincial enactment is evidently a significant consideration from the perspective of the Supreme Court, with the Court being more likely to strike down provincial laws that are framed as prohibitions coupled with penalties.

An Ontario Court of Appeal decision dealing with the provincial regulation of the practice of lap dancing sought to discern a set of identifiable indicia from this confusing line of cases.[79] The municipality of Metropolitan Toronto had over the years passed a variety of

77 See, for example, *Switzman*, above note 64.

78 See, for example, the provincial "driving offence" cases, cited above at notes 59 and 60.

79 See *Ontario Adult Entertainment Bar Assn. v. Metropolitan Toronto (Municipality)* (1997), 35 O.R. (3d) 161 (C.A.), leave to appeal to S.C.C. refused, [1997] S.C.C.A. No. 594 [*Ontario Adult Entertainment Bar Assn.*].

by-laws regulating "adult entertainment parlours."[80] However, before 1994, these by-laws did not regulate or prohibit physical contact between attendants and customers in adult entertainment parlours.[81] In early 1994, a provincial court judge determined that the practice of lap dancing, in which an attendant would perform a dance for a customer involving physical contact or touching, was not "indecent" for purposes of the *Criminal Code*.[82] This decision had a profound effect on activities in adult entertainment parlours, which began to permit lap dancing and create "VIP booths" (that is, rooms in which patrons could be afforded a private show). In response to public concern over these practices, in August 1995, Toronto amended its by-law governing adult entertainment parlours to prohibit physical contact or touching between attendants and customers. The amendment was challenged by an association of the owners of such establishments on a number of grounds, including the claim that it represented a colourable attempt to regulate morality and, as such, infringed the exclusive criminal law power of Parliament. The bar owners pointed out that the solicitor for Metropolitan Toronto had warned the members of council before the enactment of the amendment that there was insufficient evidence of health or safety concerns to justify the prohibition of close-contact dancing. The Court of Appeal unanimously dismissed the challenge to the by-law. Finlayson J.A. relied in particular on the concurring judgment of Estey J. in *Rio Hotel*, which suggested that a province had broader scope for regulating conduct that occurs in premises or establishments that are licensed by the province.[83] In *Rio Hotel*, Estey J. had stated that where a province is regulating conduct in a licensed establishment, "it is much easier to determine provincial validity because the reference to conduct is only in relation to the operation of an activity which properly falls within provincial competence."[84] Finlayson J.A. found this

---

80 For example, City of Toronto, By-law No. 20-85, required owners and "attendants" in adult entertainment parlours to be licensed; it also regulated a variety of matters relating to the manner in which services are to be provided in such premises.

81 Such physical contact was regarded as prohibited under provisions in the *Criminal Code*, making it an offence to engage in performances that were "indecent."

82 See *R. v. Mara*, [1994] O.J. No. 264 (Ont. Prov. Div.). This decision was subsequently overturned on appeal: (1996), 27 O.R. (3d) 643 (C.A.), aff'd [1997] 2 S.C.R. 630.

83 *Ontario Adult Entertainment Bar Assn.*, above note 79. Finlayson J.A. pointed out that Estey J.'s reasons in *Rio Hotel* were concurred in by Lamer J., that Beetz J., in his separate concurring opinion, had agreed with Estey J., and that the majority opinion of Dickson C.J. agreed with Estey "in the result."

84 *Rio Hotel*, above note 71 at 80, Estey J.

reasoning to be determinative since the impugned by-law was directed at conduct occurring entirely in licensed establishments, where the provinces have the right "to enact regulations in the nature of police or municipal regulation of a merely local character to preserve in the municipality, peace and public decency, and to repress drunkenness and disorderly or riotous conduct."[85] The Court of Appeal also relied on the fact that there were legitimate health and safety concerns raised by the practice of lap dancing and that these concerns could support the enactment of provincial legislation.

The *Ontario Adult Entertainment* case goes further in the direction of recognizing provincial jurisdiction than *Rio Hotel*. *Rio Hotel* did not involve prohibitions coupled with a penalty. The by-laws in *Rio Hotel* set out licensing conditions and provided for revocation of the licence in the event of breach of the conditions. In *Ontario Adult Entertainment*, the Court was prepared to uphold by-laws that were framed as prohibitions coupled with a penalty, primarily on the basis that the by-laws were directed at conduct occurring in licensed establishments, as well as the fact that they were motivated by health and safety concerns. The Supreme Court denied leave to appeal, and subsequent courts in Ontario have followed this decision, interpreting it as authorizing municipal by-laws provided that the "dominant purpose" is not a moral one.[86]

The Supreme Court has upheld provincial legislation prescribing civil consequences for criminal conduct. In *Chatterjee v. Ontario (Attorney General)*,[87] the Court dismissed a constitutional challenge to the Ontario *Civil Remedies Act, 2001*.[88] The Act authorized the Attorney General of the province to apply to the Court for an order forfeiting property determined to be the proceeds of "unlawful activity." A criminal conviction was not required and the standard of proof was the civil standard of a balance of probabilities. Furthermore, unlawful activity was broadly defined as any act or omission that is an offence in Canada or Ontario (or any act or omission that would be an offence in another jurisdiction if a similar act or omission would be an offence in Canada or Ontario). The Court held that the purpose of the Act was to make crime unprofitable, to capture resources tainted by crime and to help compensate individuals for costs of past crime. In the Court's view, these were valid provincial

85 *Ontario Adult Entertainment Bar Assn.*, above note 79 at 167.

86 See, for example, *1515545 Ontario Ltd. v. Niagara Falls (City)* (2006), 78 O.R. (3d) 783 (C.A.); and *Adult Entertainment Association of Canada v. Ottawa (City)*, 2007 ONCA 389.

87 [2009] 1 S.C.R. 624.

88 *Remedies for Organized Crime and Other Unlawful Activities Act, 2001*, S.O. 2001, c. 28, re-enacted as the *Civil Remedies Act, 2001*, S.O. 2001, c. 28.

objectives under the property and civil rights power. Although the Act incidentally affected criminal law and procedure, it was, in pith and substance, in relation to property and civil rights in the province. Significantly, the Court reached this conclusion despite the fact that it had earlier upheld the *Criminal Code* forfeiture provisions as a valid exercise of the criminal law power.[89] The Court held that the forfeiture and compensation provisions in the *Criminal Code* were part of the sentencing process, and that the provincial legislation was independent of that process and fell within provincial competence.

D. ADMINISTRATION OF JUSTICE IN THE PROVINCE

Provincial jurisdiction over the administration of justice in the province includes the power to establish and maintain police forces.[90] Police forces maintained or controlled by the provinces have the authority to enforce both the *Criminal Code* and all provincial and municipal legislation. The policing function includes investigation and prevention of crime as well as the laying of charges where there are reasonable and probable grounds to believe an offence has been committed. Ontario and Quebec have chosen to establish their own provincial police forces for these purposes in addition to municipal police forces. In the other eight provinces, provincial policing is provided by the RCMP pursuant to contracts entered into between the provincial government and the federal force. In performing services under those contracts, the RCMP is subject to the control and direction of the province. However, the courts have also held that the investigation of complaints made in respect of RCMP conduct, as well as the disciplining of RCMP officers, is an exclusive federal responsibility, regardless of whether the officers are acting pursuant to contracts with the provinces.[91]

The provincial policing power flowing from section 92(14) extends only to federal legislation enacted pursuant to the criminal law jurisdiction of Parliament.[92] Enforcement of laws enacted by Parliament

89 *R. v. Zelensky*, [1978] 2 S.C.R. 940.

90 See, for example, *O'Hara v. B.C.*, [1987] 2 S.C.R. 591.

91 See *Alberta (Attorney General) v. Putnam*, [1981] 2 S.C.R. 267.

92 This power has been interpreted in practice as extending only to the enforcement of the *Criminal Code*. Other federal laws that depend in part on Parliament's criminal law jurisdiction, such as the *Food and Drugs Act*, R.S.C. 1985, c. F-27, are not seen as falling within provincial enforcement responsibility and are enforced in all provinces by the RCMP.

pursuant to heads of authority in section 91 other than section 91(27) are a federal rather than a provincial responsibility. Thus, in all provinces, the enforcement of non-criminal federal statutes[93] is performed by the RCMP, not pursuant to contract with the province but directly through authority contained in the *Royal Canadian Mounted Police Act*.[94]

Once criminal charges have been laid, the prosecution of those charges is also a provincial responsibility pursuant to section 92(14). Section 2 of the *Criminal Code* defines the term "Attorney General" for purposes of the *Criminal Code* as being the Attorney General of the province in which the proceeding is taken. A series of cases in the late 1970s and early 1980s decided that Parliament had the power to provide for federal prosecution of criminal laws.[95] Thus, it would appear that Parliament could amend the definition of "Attorney General" in the *Criminal Code* so as to restrict or limit the role of the provincial Attorney General in relation to the prosecution of criminal offences.

FURTHER READINGS

Beaudoin, G.A., with P. Thibault, *La Constitution du Canada: institutions, partage des pouvoirs, Charte canadienne des droits et libertés*, 3d ed. (Montreal: Wilson & Lafleur, 2004) c. 16

Hogg, P.W., *Constitutional Law of Canada*, 5th ed., loose-leaf (Toronto: Carswell, 2007) cc. 17–18

93 See, for example, the *Income Tax Act*, R.S.C. 1985 (5th Supp.), c. 1.

94 R.S.C. 1985, c. R-10.

95 See, in particular, *Wetmore*, above note 37, holding that federal prosecution of offences under the *Food and Drugs Act* was valid.

CHAPTER 12

THE CONSTITUTION AND TRANSPORTATION

A. INTRODUCTION

"Transportation" is not an enumerated head of power assigned exclusively to Parliament or the provincial legislatures. Rather, transportation is regulated by federal and provincial governments pursuant to various provisions of the *Constitution Act, 1867*.[1] This chapter examines the relevant provisions in the Canadian constitution that allocate jurisdiction over the field of transportation. It considers the extent to which the courts have modified or supplemented the original division of powers of transportation contemplated by the *Constitution Act, 1867*. It also examines the extent to which the division of powers has constrained the ability of governments to respond to changing circumstances in transportation. Finally, it considers how legislative jurisdiction has been exercised in practice by the federal and provincial governments in certain key areas of transportation.

1 The *Constitution Act, 1867* (formerly, the *British North America Act, 1867*) (U.K.), 30 & 31 Vict., c. 3.

B. BASIC DIVISION OF RESPONSIBILITIES OVER TRANSPORTATION

In general terms, the *Constitution Act, 1867* allocates jurisdiction over interprovincial and international transportation to the federal government, while reserving responsibility for intraprovincial transportation to the provinces. This territorial approach to transportation is reflected most clearly in section 92(10) of the *Constitution Act, 1867.* Section 92(10) provides that the provinces have exclusive jurisdiction over "Local Works and Undertakings" except "Works and Undertakings connecting the Province with any other or others of the Provinces, or extending beyond the Limits of the Province."

Other provisions in the *Constitution Act, 1867* which allocate jurisdiction to the federal Parliament include: "Beacons, Buoys, Lighthouses, and Sable Island" (section 91(1)); "Navigation and Shipping" (section 91(10)); "Ferries between a Province and any British or Foreign Country or between Two Provinces" (section 91(13)); power to declare local works for the "general Advantage of Canada" (section 92(10)(c)); and where certain public works and property in each province were transferred to Canada, including canals, public harbours, railways, and military roads (section 108).[2]

On its face, the federal power over trade and commerce in section 91(2) would appear to be relevant to the field of transportation. However, as discussed in Chapters 9 and 10, the courts have construed this provision narrowly, and it has never been interpreted as adding significantly to federal authority in the area of transportation.[3] Federal authority over criminal law in section 91(27) has also permitted the

---

2 See the Third Schedule to the *Constitution Act, 1867*, which sets out the classes of provincial property that passed to the dominion at the time of Confederation. The transfer of title to the dominion was effective at the moment of each province's entry into Confederation. As transportation was in a stage of infancy at the relevant dates, dominion proprietary rights acquired in this way have not proven to be significant factors in the regulation of transportation. See C.H. McNairn, "Transportation, Communication and the Constitution: The Scope of Federal Jurisdiction" (1969) 47 Can. Bar Rev. 355 at 366.

3 It should be noted, however, that the trade and commerce power has been used to regulate the safety of new cars and components. The *Motor Vehicle Safety Act*, R.S.C. 1985, c. M-10, requires all motor vehicles imported into Canada to comply with federal safety and environmental regulations. In addition, vehicles manufactured in Canada must have a National Safety Mark indicating that they meet the relevant safety and environmental standards.

federal government to establish a set of criminal prohibitions and sanctions relating to the operation of motor vehicles, vessels, and aircraft.[4]

Provincial authority in relation to transportation matters flows from section 92(10) ("Local Works and Undertakings"); section 92(13) ("Property and Civil Rights in the Province"); and section 92(16) ("Matters of a merely local or private Nature in the Province").

In addition to the enumerated heads of power dealing with transportation, the courts have also been called on to supplement the division of powers as new modes or methods of transportation have arisen. Of greatest significance in this regard is air travel, which was unknown in 1867 and was therefore not mentioned in the original division of powers. As discussed below, the courts have interpreted the federal Parliament's power to make laws for the peace, order, and good government (POGG) of Canada as including the exclusive authority to regulate all aspects of air travel.

C. JURISDICTION OVER WORKS AND UNDERTAKINGS

Section 92(10) has been the greatest single source of constitutional litigation in the field of transportation. The principles the courts have developed in their interpretation of this provision make up the bulk of the constitutional jurisprudence in the area of transportation.

Section 92(10) of the *Constitution Act, 1867* provides that the provincial legislatures have exclusive power to make laws in relation to local works and undertakings other than those in the following classes:

> (*a*) Lines of Steam or Other Ships, Railways, Canals, Telegraphs, and other Works and Undertakings connecting the Province with any other or others of the Provinces, or extending beyond the Limits of the Province;
>
> (*b*) Lines of Steam Ships between the Province and any British or Foreign Country;
>
> (*c*) Such Works as, although wholly situate within the Province, are before or after their Execution declared by the Parliament of Canada to be for the general Advantage of Canada or for the Advantage of Two or more of the Provinces.

Although section 92(10) is framed as a grant of legislative power to the provinces, the "exceptions" in subsections (a), (b), and (c) provide a

4 See the *Criminal Code*, R.S.C. 1985, c. C-46, ss. 249–61.

source of exclusive federal jurisdiction over interprovincial and international works and undertakings.

The relationship between federal and provincial authority under section 92(10) was discussed by the Supreme Court of Canada in the 2009 decision of *Consolidated Fastfrate Inc. v. Western Canada Council of Teamsters*.[5] Rothstein J., for the majority, advocated a narrow scope of federal jurisdiction:

> Section 92(10) provides that "Works and Undertakings" are subject to local regulation. A work or undertaking is subject to federal jurisdiction only where an exception is made out. Local regulation is the rule; federal regulation, the exception.[6]

Rothstein J.'s comments in this regard are somewhat surprising. Rothstein J. himself noted that section 92(10)(a) was "originally conceived as a primary grant of authority to the federal government."[7] He noted that resolutions passed at the Quebec Conference in October 1864 provided that the federal government would have primary legislative authority over "Lines of Steam or Other Ships, Railways, Canals and other works, connecting any two or more of the Provinces together or extending beyond the limits of any Province" and that the provincial governments would have authority over "Local Works." However, Rothstein J. asserted that ultimately, a "preference for provincial regulation" had been expressed by the British Parliament in the text of section 92(10), apparently because federal authority was framed as an exception from provincial jurisdiction.

However, it is far from clear that a narrow interpretation of federal authority over transportation was intended by the text of section 92(10). As Binnie J. stated for the minority in *Fastfrate*:

> The manner in which the *Constitution Act, 1867* is structured does not mean that federal jurisdiction over interprovincial undertakings should receive a cramped interpretation.
>
> . . .
>
> The Constitution nowhere gives the provinces general jurisdiction in relation to "Works and Undertakings." Section 92(10), as stated, gives the provinces jurisdiction only over *local* works and undertakings, and even this grant is qualified to the extent such *local* works and undertakings connect the province "with any other or others of

---

5 [2009] 3 S.C.R. 407 [*Fastfrate*].
6 *Ibid*. at para. 31.
7 *Ibid*. at para. 34.

the Provinces, or extending beyond the Limits of the Province", in which case they are regulated federally pursuant to s. 91(29).[8]

Furthermore, prior to *Fastfrate*, both the Privy Council and the Supreme Court had interpreted federal authority over local works and undertakings relatively broadly.[9] In any event, regardless of the breadth of federal jurisdiction under section 92(10), it is clear that the "exceptions" in subsections (a), (b), and (c) are an important source of federal jurisdiction.

1) Works and Undertakings Defined

Section 92(10) draws a distinction between "works" and "undertakings." The courts have interpreted an "undertaking" as involving both a physical and an organizational element. Viscount Dunedin in the 1932 *Radio Reference* referred to an undertaking as "not a physical thing, but . . . an arrangement under which . . . physical things are used."[10] In the 1954 *Winner* case,[11] the Privy Council held that Parliament possessed jurisdiction not only over the buses that provided the interprovincial transportation but also over the bus company itself. This functional approach means that federal authority over interprovincial undertakings extends to all aspects of the organization or enterprise that provides the service in question.

2) Undivided Jurisdiction over Particular Undertakings

The Courts have held that jurisdiction over a work or undertaking must be allocated to a single level of government. The courts have consistently rejected the idea of dividing jurisdiction between the federal and the provincial governments over a single undertaking. This principle was first established in the *Bell Telephone* case of 1905.[12] The Privy Council held that a telephone company's long-distance business and its local business could not be separated for the purpose of allocating legislative jurisdiction. The Board held that the telephone company was engaged in an interprovincial undertaking and thereby the whole of the com-

8 *Ibid.* at para. 96 [emphasis in original].

9 See, for example, *Northern Telecom Ltd. v. Communications Workers of Canada*, [1980] 1 S.C.R. 115 and *Alberta Government Telephones v. Canada (Canadian Radio-television and Telecommunications Commission)*, [1989] 2 S.C.R. 225 [*AGT*].

10 *Reference Re Regulation & Control of Radio Communication in Canada*, [1932] A.C. 304 at 315 (P.C.) [*Radio Reference*].

11 *Ont. (A.G.) v. Winner*, [1954] A.C. 541 (P.C.) [*Winner*].

12 See *Toronto (City) v. Bell Telephone Co.*, [1905] A.C. 52 (P.C.).

pany's business, including its strictly local activity, fell under federal jurisdiction.[13]

This "undivided" approach is quite different from the Privy Council's interpretation of the federal trade and commerce power. As discussed in Chapter 9, the Privy Council restricted federal authority over trade and commerce to the interprovincial or international aspects of trade; the local aspects of trade remained subject to exclusive provincial jurisdiction.[14] By contrast, once an undertaking is classified as interprovincial, federal jurisdiction extends to all aspects of the enterprise, including features that are strictly local. This has meant that federal authority to regulate transportation undertakings has been much more extensive and more effective than in other areas of federal jurisdiction such as trade and commerce.

The courts' resistance to dual jurisdiction in the transportation field has had important implications in terms of the central issues that have emerged in litigation surrounding section 92(10). The allocation of jurisdiction has been treated by the courts as "an all or nothing affair";[15] a transportation undertaking is subject either to federal jurisdiction or to provincial jurisdiction but not simultaneously to both. As a result, the key question for purposes of section 92(10) is one of characterization: is the undertaking interprovincial or merely local? This has led, in turn, to two recurring questions that continue to dominate the jurisprudence in this area:

1) What extent of interprovincial activity or connection is necessary to qualify as an interprovincial as opposed to a merely local undertaking?
2) To what extent can federal jurisdiction be extended to an otherwise local undertaking by virtue of its integration or connection with an interprovincial undertaking?

---

13 At the same time, however, separate undertakings under common ownership may be subject to regulation by different levels of government. For instance, in *Canadian Pacific Railway Co. v. British Columbia (Attorney General)*, [1950] A.C. 122, the Privy Council held that the Empress Hotel in Victoria, which was owned by the Canadian Pacific Railway, was a separate undertaking such that employment in the hotel was regulated by provincial, rather than federal, law.

14 As discussed in Chapter 9, the Supreme Court of Canada has expanded the trade and commerce power and recognized federal authority to regulate "general trade and commerce": see *General Motors of Canada Ltd. v. City National Leasing*, [1989] 1 S.C.R. 641.

15 *AGT*, above note 9 at 257, Dickson C.J.

3) Interprovincial Works and Undertakings

The bar for interprovincial activity required for an undertaking to qualify as interprovincial has been set fairly low. The courts have consistently held that an undertaking falls within federal regulatory authority even if only a small percentage of its business activity is interprovincial or international. The primary test is whether the interprovincial or international services are a "continuous and regular" part of the undertaking's operations. If this requirement is met, then the undertaking is subject to exclusive federal regulation.

In *Re Tank Truck Transport*,[16] the Ontario High Court of Justice held that the *Ontario Labour Relations Act* did not apply to an Ontario trucking company whose operations were predominantly confined to the province of Ontario. In 1959, the trucking firm had completed 94 percent of its trips within the province, with just 6 percent extending beyond provincial borders. However, the court held that the interprovincial activity was a "continuous and regular" aspect of the trucking firm's operations and, as a result, the whole of the undertaking, including the local operations within Ontario, was subject to the exclusive authority of Parliament.[17] A similar ruling was made in the *Liquid Cargo* case,[18] where only 1.6 percent of a trucking firm's trips extended beyond provincial boundaries.

In *Alberta Government Telephones* (*AGT*),[19] the Supreme Court held that AGT, a provincial Crown corporation operating a telephone system in Alberta, fell under federal authority. AGT's physical facilities were located entirely within the province of Alberta, and the system could carry telephone messages only within the province. However, the AGT system was connected with other telephone companies outside the province to enable local subscribers to make telephone connections outside the province. AGT argued that it fell under provincial regulatory authority because its activities were totally confined to the province of Alberta. The Supreme Court unanimously rejected this argument and held that AGT was subject to exclusive federal authority.[20] In reaching this conclusion, the Court articulated a number of general principles that should guide the section 92(10)(a) analysis:

---

16 *Re Tank Truck Transport Ltd.*, [1960] O.R. 497 (H.C.J.).

17 This result was affirmed by the Court of Appeal without written reasons: see [1963] O.R. 272 (C.A.).

18 *R. v. Cooksville Magistrate's Court*, [1965] 1 O.R. 84 (H.C.J.) [*Liquid Cargo*].

19 *AGT*, above note 9.

20 *Ibid.* All the members of the Court agreed on the issue of jurisdiction; Wilson J. dissented on the issue of whether AGT was entitled to assert a claim of Crown immunity.

1) The location of the physical apparatus of an undertaking in a single province and the fact that all the recipients of a service are within a single province will not preclude a finding that an undertaking is interprovincial in scope. The primary concern is "not the physical structures or their geographical location, but rather the service which is provided by the undertaking through the use of its physical equipment."[21]
2) In considering the nature of the service or operation, one must look to the "normal or habitual activities of the business as those of 'a going concern,' without regard for exceptional or casual factors."[22]
3) It is impossible to formulate in the abstract a single comprehensive test which will be useful in all cases; instead, the court must be guided by the "particular facts in each situation."[23]

Applying these principles to AGT, the Court found that the operations of the Crown corporation were interprovincial and international in scope. The primary basis for this conclusion seemed to be that AGT provided a service that enabled residents of Alberta to communicate beyond the borders of the province. Dickson C.J. stated that "AGT is, through various commercial arrangements of a bilateral and multilateral nature, organized in a manner which enables it to play a crucial role in the national telecommunications system."[24] It was the capacity to provide this extraprovincial service that supported the finding that AGT was subject to exclusive federal authority.[25]

---

21 *Ibid.* at 259.

22 *Ibid.* at 257.

23 *Ibid.* at 258.

24 *Ibid.* at 262.

25 Historically, federal regulatory authority had included telephone companies operating in Ontario, Quebec, British Columbia, the Yukon Territory, the Northwest Territories (including the area that is now Nunavut), and parts of Newfoundland. Federal authority over Bell Canada (formerly, the Bell Telephone Company, serving Ontario and Quebec) and BC Tel was based on provisions in their respective special Acts. (See *An Act to incorporate The Bell Telephone Company of Canada*, S.C. 1880, c. 67; *An Act to incorporate the Western Canada Telephone Company*, S.C. 1916, c. 66.) The companies were declared to be works "for the general advantage of Canada"; telephone service in the Yukon, NWT, and Newfoundland had historically been provided by subsidiaries of CN Railway, which was subject to federal authority by virtue of provisions in its enabling legislation. However, telephone companies in other provinces had traditionally been subject to provincial or local control. In this sense, *AGT* opened the door for federal regulatory authority in an area that had traditionally been regarded as subject to exclusive control of the provinces. Parliament has now assumed jurisdiction over all telephone companies, including provincially owned companies such as AGT under the *Telecommunications Act*, S.C. 1993, c. 38. For a summary

The *AGT* decision represents a more expansive reading of federal authority over works and undertakings than had previously been adopted.[26] The fact that a local undertaking is capable of providing a service beyond the borders of a single province had previously been regarded as an insufficient basis for federal regulatory jurisdiction under section 92(10). For example, in *Cannet Freight Cartage*,[27] a freight-forwarding company provided local customers with the opportunity to ship goods beyond the borders of the province. The company took delivery of goods in one province and made all the arrangements necessary to ship the goods to another province by rail. The Federal Court of Appeal held that the freight forwarder was subject to exclusive provincial jurisdiction because its own operations were limited to a single province. The Court reasoned that the freight forwarder did not become an interprovincial undertaking by virtue of shipping goods on an interprovincial railway.

Similarly, in *Re The Queen and Cottrell Forwarding Co.*,[28] the Ontario Divisional Court held that the provincial *Commercial Vehicles Act* was applicable to Cottrell, which was charged with operating as an unlicensed freight forwarder under the Act. Cottrell assumed responsibility for shipment of goods from Ontario to Western Canada and was the only entity that appeared on customers' bills of lading. Steele J. acknowledged that Cottrell's business allowed customers to benefit from economies of scale in order to "reduce the otherwise applicable rate for shipment." However, he held that since the company was not *physically* involved in the transportation of goods or persons across provincial boundaries, Cottrell was not an interprovincial undertaking. Steele J. stated that "[t]he railway company is the only body carrying on the interprovincial undertaking. . . . The mere fact that by contract Cottrell agrees with that individual customer to enter into the contract with the railway company and become the shipper itself, does not make Cottrell anything other than a shipper."[29]

---

and discussion of the regulatory situation prior to the *AGT* case, see C.M. Dalfen & L.J.E. Dunbar, "Transportation and Communications: The Constitution and the Canadian Economic Union" in M. Krasnick, ed., *Case Studies in the Division of Powers* (Toronto: University of Toronto Press, 1986) at 156–60.

26 See P.W. Hogg, "Comment: Jurisdiction over Telecommunication: *Alberta Government Telephones v. CRTC*" (1990) 35 McGill L.J. 480.

27 *I.B. of T.C.W. & H. of A., Local 419 v. Cannet Freight Cartage Ltd.*, [1976] 1 F.C. 174 (C.A.) [*Cannet*] (approved by the Supreme Court of Canada in *U.T.U. v. Central Western Railway*, [1990] 3 S.C.R. 1112 at 1145–47 [*Central Western Railway*].

28 (1981), 124 D.L.R. (3d) 674 (Div. Ct.) [*Cottrell*].

29 *Ibid.* at 679.

Cannet and *Cottrell* were affirmed by a majority of the Supreme Court in the 2009 decision in *Fastfrate*.[30] Fastfrate was a freight-forwarding company that had branches in Toronto, Montreal, Winnipeg, Regina, Saskatoon, Edmonton, Calgary, and Vancouver, as well as smaller facilities elsewhere. Although Fastfrate did not transport its freight interprovincially using its own property or employees, it had a network of relationships with freight transporters, with which it contracted to deliver freight to its customers. Furthermore, in addition to collecting goods in the province of origin, Fastfrate de-consolidated shipment and delivered to consignees in the province of destination. As in *Cottrell*, customers saw Fastfrate on the bill of lading and would not know which freight transporter physically shipped the goods.

The majority held that Fastfrate was a local, rather than interprovincial undertaking and that it was therefore subject to provincial jurisdiction over its labour relations. As in *Cannet* and *Cottrell*, the fact that Fastfrate did not itself carry the goods over provincial boundaries was considered to be determinative. According to Rothstein J., "an undertaking that performs consolidation and deconsolidation and local pickup and delivery services does not become an interprovincial undertaking simply because it has an integrated national corporate structure and contracts with third-party interprovincial carriers."[31] Rothstein J. distinguished *AGT* on the basis that "communication" and "transportation" undertakings are different. He stated that communications undertakings can operate and provide international and interprovincial communication services from a *fixed* point. However, in the transportation context, it was said to be impossible for an undertaking to operate an interprovincial transportation service where it does not itself perform the interprovincial carriage.[32]

Rothstein J.'s judgment in *Fastfrate* is difficult, if not impossible, to reconcile with the Supreme Court's previous decision in *AGT*. As Binnie J. stated for the minority in *Fastfrate*:

> It was said in *AGT* that "one could not separate the local from the non-local without emasculating AGT's enterprise as it presently exists" (p. 255). The same is true of Fastfrate.
>
> If *AGT* is subject to federal regulation by reason of its provision of interprovincial and international *services*, which can only be performed by relying on contractual arrangements with other facilities providers,

30 Above note 5. Rothstein J. delivered the majority judgment on behalf of himself and LeBel, Deschamps, Abella, Charron, and Cromwell JJ. Binnie J. delivered the minority judgment on behalf of himself, McLachlin C.J., and Fish J.

31 *Ibid*. at para. 3.

32 *Ibid*. at paras. 60–61.

> Fastfrate should receive similar treatment, especially as its facilities (unlike those of AGT) are engaged at both pickup and delivery.[33]

Furthermore, Rothstein J.'s distinction between transportation and communications undertakings finds little support in prior jurisprudence or constitutional principle. As Binnie J. stated, the cases have never drawn a distinction between the legal test under section 92(10) depending on whether the undertaking in question is engaged in "communications" or "transportation." Rather, the legal test under section 92(10) in all cases has focused on "the nature or character of the undertaking that is in fact being carried on."[34] As a matter of constitutional principle, there is no meaningful distinction between communications undertakings and transportation undertakings. The division of authority between the federal and provincial orders of government in both cases is derived from the same provision of the *Constitution Act, 1867.* There is no indication in either the text of section 92(10)(a) or the jurisprudence to suggest that the test should depend on whether the undertaking is in the communications or transportation industry. As Binnie J. stated:

> the relevant distinction in the s. 92(10)(a) jurisprudence is not between undertakings engaged in transportation and those engaged in communications, but between local undertakings within the province and undertakings whose service (whether transportation or communication) extends beyond the province.[35]

Moreover, the analysis of Rothstein J. in *Fastfrate* (and the lower court rulings in *Cannet* and *Cottrell,* which he followed) seems to place undue significance on the physical movement of goods across interprovincial boundaries. As Binnie J. noted in *Fastfrate*, technology has resulted in changes to the methods of transportation and communications undertakings well beyond what had been envisaged in 1867. In an economy where the contracting-out of services is commonplace, a test focusing on physical shipment seems inappropriate and could lead to anomalous results. The majority's reasoning would result in either federal or provincial jurisdiction depending on whether the physical transportation services are delivered by the undertaking directly, on its own account, or through contract with other entities.[36] While Fastfrate

33 *Ibid.* at paras. 100–1 [emphasis in original].

34 *AGT*, above note 9 at 257–58.

35 *Fastfrate*, above note 5 at para. 88.

36 Thus in *Fastfrate*, Binnie J. stated that outcome under s. 92(10) should "not depend on whether, in carrying out its interprovincial freight contracts," the entity "does or does not contract with another corporate entity to move the goods across an interprovincial or international boundary" (para. 86).

did not physically ship goods across provincial boundaries itself, it is difficult to quarrel with Binnie J.'s conclusion that it was in substance an interprovincial undertaking engaged in the provision of interprovincial transportation. As Binnie J. stated, "[w]hat Fastfrate does—the service it provides, its 'undertaking'—is to move freight from the hands of a customer in one part of the country to the hands of a customer in another part of the country."[37]

In our view, the minority judgment in *Fastfrate* has much to commend it and the majority judgment is problematic. The inquiry under section 92(10)(a) in each case should focus on the true nature of the undertaking in question; that is, whether the undertaking is in substance an interprovincial or international concern, as opposed to an entity confined to the provision of services solely within the province.

4) Integration of Local and Interprovincial Undertakings

A transportation undertaking can be classified as federal if the undertaking itself is regarded as interprovincial (as in the *AGT* case), or if a purely local undertaking is integrated or connected with another undertaking that is itself interprovincial. The precise degree of the connection or integration required has been the subject of extensive litigation over the years.

A 1912 Privy Council case determined that mere physical connection between a local railway and an interprovincial railway was insufficient to bring the local railway under federal authority.[38] Integration in an operational or functional sense is required before local undertakings fall within federal authority. For example, in 1927, a local railway line that was operated under a formal management agreement by the Canadian National Railway was held to fall within federal authority.[39] Similarly, a company supplying stevedore services in Toronto to seven shipping companies involved in international shipping was held to be subject to federal labour legislation.[40] Although the stevedore company was independent of the shipping companies, the services it provided were integral to the successful operation of the shipping enterprises. The same reasoning was applied in the 1975 *Letter Carriers* case,[41] in which a trucking company that had contracted with the post office to

37 *Ibid.* at para. 118.

38 See *Montreal (City) v. Montreal Street Railway*, [1912] A.C. 333 (P.C.).

39 *Luscar Collieries Ltd. v. McDonald*, [1927] A.C. 925 (P.C.).

40 *Reference Re Validity of Industrial Relations and Disputes Investigation Act (Canada)*, [1955] S.C.R. 529.

41 *L.C.U.C. v. C.U.P.W.* (1974), [1975] 1 S.C.R. 178 [*Letter Carriers*].

deliver and collect mail was found to be within federal authority. The Court found that the trucking operation was integral and necessary to the operation of the post office itself. By contrast, in *Tessier Ltée v. Quebec (Commission de la santé et de la sécurité du travail)*,[42] the Supreme Court held that a heavy equipment rental company that rented cranes used for stevedoring was subject to provincial jurisdiction with respect to its labour relations. The crane rental activity represented 14 percent of the company's overall revenue and 20 percent of the salaries paid to its employees. The stevedoring services were not performed by a discrete business unit and the employees were fully integrated into the company's workforce. The Court held the company devoted most of its work to provincially regulated activities and that its essential operation was in nature local. The stevedoring activities, which were integrated into its overall operations, formed only a relatively minor part of the overall operation. As a result, the company's employees were subject to provincial occupational health and safety legislation.

In the *Central Western Railway* case,[43] the issue was whether Central Western Railway, a small railway located entirely within the province of Alberta, fell within federal or provincial jurisdiction. Central Western used its 170 kilometres (105 miles) of track in central Alberta to transport grain from nine elevators to the CNR's interprovincial rail line. The grain cars were then transported by CNR to Vancouver for export. Central Western's tracks were separated from those of CNR by a ten-centimetre (four-inch) gap, and CNR controlled the device that regulated entry onto its line. The issue was whether the degree of connection and integration between Central Western and CNR was sufficient to subject the local railway to federal jurisdiction. Dickson C.J., writing for a majority of the Court,[44] rejected the argument that Central Western could be regarded itself as an interprovincial railway, noting that mere physical connection between a local and an interprovincial rail line was an insufficient basis for establishing federal jurisdiction. He cited the *AGT* case, arguing that "[t]he linchpin in the *A.G.T. v. C.R.T.C.* decision was this court's finding that A.G.T., by virtue of its role in Telecom Canada and its bilateral contracts with other telephone companies, was able to provide its clients with an interprovincial and, indeed, international telecommunications service."[45] Dickson C.J. regarded Central Western's operation as quite different from that of AGT.

---

42 2012 SCC 23.

43 Above note 27.

44 Dickson C.J. spoke for eight members of the Court on the constitutional issue. Wilson J. dissented.

45 *Ibid.* at 1135.

He noted that Central Western simply moved grain within Alberta, and that the interprovincial transportation of grain was handled entirely by CNR. On this basis, he concluded that Central Western was a local railway and not itself part of an interprovincial undertaking.

Dickson C.J. then turned to the second possible basis for finding in favour of federal authority. Even though Central Western was a local railway, it would fall under federal authority if it could be characterized as an integral part of a federal work or undertaking. Dickson C.J. indicated that this integration might be found in two different ways.[46] First, the management and operation of Central Western might be coordinated or undertaken in common with that of an interprovincial undertaking. Second, the effective operation of a federal undertaking might be dependent on the services of Central Western. Dickson C.J. concluded that Central Western was not functionally integrated with any interprovincial undertaking and therefore not subject to federal authority. He reasoned that Central Western and CNR were operated as separate undertakings rather than in common; further, CNR was not dependent on the services of Central Western for its own operations—nor was Central Western integrated in a functional sense within a so-called Western Grain Transportation Network.[47]

Despite the result in this case, Dickson C.J.'s judgment illustrates the broad reach of federal regulatory authority under section 92(10). Even where there is in form two separate undertakings, the courts will inquire into the degree of practical or operational integration between them. Federal regulatory authority will extend to any operations that are regarded as essential or are conducted in common with a core interprovincial undertaking. The practical effect of this approach is to ensure an expansive interpretation to federal authority under sections 92(10)(a) and (b) of the *Constitution Act, 1867*. Thus, in *Westcoast Energy Inc. v. Canada (National Energy Board)*,[48] the Supreme Court held that Parliament had exclusive jurisdiction over natural gas processing facilities located entirely within a single province, on the basis that the facilities were functionally integrated and managed in common as part of an interprovincial pipeline undertaking.

---

46 *Ibid*. at 1140–43.

47 It was argued that there was an integrated network for the transportation of grain within western Canada and that Central Western formed part of this network. However, Dickson C.J. concluded that "I do not agree that a Western Grain Transportation Network exists for the purposes of the jurisdictional designation of the Central Western . . . . [T]he fact that several entities involved in the transport of grain fall under federal jurisdiction cannot on its own serve to bring everything connected with that industry under federal jurisdiction" (*ibid*. at 1143–44).

48 [1998] 1 S.C.R. 322 [*Westcoast Energy*].

A similarly expansive approach to federal jurisdiction was taken in *Téléphone Guèvremont Inc. v. Quebec (Régie des télécommunications)*.[49] Téléphone Guèvremont was a small local telephone company operating in Quebec. It was not a part of the Stentor Network but it was connected with Bell Canada and its subscribers could make calls anywhere in the world using their local telephone equipment. The Supreme Court, in a short judgment, essentially affirmed the result and the reasoning in the Court of Appeal, which had held that the company was subject to exclusive federal jurisdiction. The Court of Appeal had come to this conclusion on the basis that the company was "the medium by which its local subscribers receive interprovincial and international communications."[50] Téléphone Guèvremont was "merely one of the links in a chain that reaches its subscribers or that links its subscribers to other provinces and to the rest of the world."[51] As a practical matter, all telephone companies must offer the kinds of services that were available from Téléphone Guèvremont in order to remain competitive. The practical implication of *Téléphone Guèvremont* is that telephone companies are subject to exclusive federal jurisdiction.

As discussed in Chapter 10,[52] in *Ontario Hydro v. Ontario (Labour Relations Board)*,[53] La Forest J. suggested that the broad approach that the Court has developed generally in respect of section 92(10)(a) may not be applicable in the context of the natural resource sector, by virtue of the enactment of section 92A in 1982. La Forest J. stated that even where there is an interconnection and integration of physical facilities as part of an interprovincial network, section 92A indicates that jurisdiction over production, processing, and development of natural resources remains with the provinces. However, in the subsequent *Westcoast Energy* case,[54] a majority of the Supreme Court rejected this view, and held that the enactment of section 92A was not intended to narrow or alter the application of section 92(10)(a) to (c) of the *Constitution Act, 1867*.

5) Jurisdiction over Internet-Related Undertakings

The Internet has been described as a "huge communications facility which consists of a worldwide network of computer networks deployed

49 [1994] 1 S.C.R. 878 [*Téléphone Guèvremont*].
50 (1992), 99 D.L.R. (4th) 241 at 256 (Que. C.A.), Rousseau-Houle J.A.
51 *Ibid.*
52 See Chapter 10, Section B(2).
53 [1993] 3 S.C.R. 327.
54 Above note 48.

to communicate information."[55] A wide variety of federal and provincial laws apply to persons or entities engaged in activities on the Internet, including criminal laws, copyright and trademark legislation, privacy legislation, defamation laws, laws regulating contractual rights, securities laws, and laws relating to consumer protection.[56] Moreover, given the global nature of the Internet, it will often be difficult to determine the precise law or legal forum that will apply to or govern a particular factual dispute.[57] However, for domestic constitutional purposes, it would appear that undertakings providing Canadian residents with access to the Internet would fall within the definition of interprovincial undertakings in section 92(10)(a) of the *Constitution Act, 1867*. For example, Internet service providers, the so-called gatekeepers to the Internet, allow computers connected through networks to communicate, transmit, and receive information across the world.[58] Since Internet service providers are integral to the transmission of telecommunications from one province to another and around the world, they must be regarded as federal undertakings subject to exclusive federal jurisdiction pursuant to section 92(10)(a).[59] Moreover, any other undertakings that participate in or facilitate the transmission of communications or information via the Internet as a regular or continuous part of

---

55 *Society of Composers, Authors and Music Publishers of Canada v. Canadian Assn. of Internet Providers*, [2004] 2 S.C.R. 427 at para. 8 [*SOCAN*]. For a similar definition see *Re City TV*, [1999] C.I.R.B. No. 22 at para. 65 (Canada Industrial Relations Board) [*City TV*], in which the Internet is described as "a network of computer networks interconnected by means of telecommunication transmission facilities using common protocol and standards that allow for the exchange of information between each interconnected computer." The C.I.R.B. further describes the Internet as "the world's largest computer network, linking mainframes, minicomputers, personal computers, and networks around the world."

56 See, generally, G.S. Takach, *Computer Law*, 2d ed. (Toronto: Irwin Law, 2003); B.B. Sookman, *Computer, Internet and Electronic Commerce Law*, loose-leaf (Toronto: Carswell, 2001).

57 See *Braintech Inc. v. Kostiuk* (1999), 171 D.L.R. (4th) 46 (B.C.C.A.), leave to appeal to S.C.C. refused, [1999] S.C.C.A. No. 236, holding that a defamation judgment obtained in a Texas court against a resident of B.C. involving material on a website maintained in B.C. did not have a "real and substantial connection" to Texas and thus was not enforceable in B.C. See also: *Tucows.com Co. v. Lojas Renner S.A.*, 2011 ONCA 548 [*Tucows*], holding that Ontario courts had jurisdiction over a dispute between a Nova Scotia company with a head office in Toronto and a Brazilian company over the domain name renner.com.

58 *Re Island Telecom*, [2000] C.I.R.B. No. 12 at para. 53 (Canada Industrial Relations Board) [*Re Island Telecom*].

59 See *ibid.*, holding that an Internet service provider is subject to exclusive federal jurisdiction and, on this basis, its employees were subject to the *Canada Labour Code*.

their business must also be regarded as falling within exclusive federal jurisdiction.

In the *City TV* case,[60] the Canada Industrial Relations Board considered whether CityInteractive, a business whose primary activity was the design and marketing of Internet websites, was subject to the jurisdiction of the federal board. Approximately 10 percent of City-Interactive's employee time was devoted to interactive services, such as live on-line chats. Because these interactive services were a regular and continuous part of CityInteractive's business, the entity was found to be a federal undertaking and its employees were therefore subject to the *Canada Labour Code*, notwithstanding the fact that the significant majority of its business was directed at matters that would appear to be *prima facie* within provincial jurisdiction.[61] Further, undertakings that are essential, vital, or integral to businesses that provide access to the Internet, will also fall under exclusive federal jurisdiction in accordance with the criteria identified in the *Central Western Railway* case.[62] Of course, federally regulated undertakings are still subject to provincial laws of general application but only to the extent that such laws do not affect a vital or essential aspect of the management or operation of the undertaking. Thus, those entities whose involvement with the Internet is such that they must be regarded as falling within exclusive federal authority would be immune from the application of provincial legislation that would have such an impact on the undertaking.

In *SOCAN*, the Supreme Court considered whether Canadian copyright law should extend so as to protect musical composers and artists for their Canadian copyright in music downloaded in Canada from a foreign country via the Internet. Although the legal issue in the case revolved around the interpretation of a specific provision in the *Copyright Act*, Binnie J.'s majority judgment included a detailed discussion of

---

60 Above note 55.

61 The board noted that the design of websites and material for use on the Internet would *prima facie* appear to be subject to provincial jurisdiction. Note, however, that the *Central Western Railway* case, above note 27, has determined that if a federally regulated entity is dependent on another entity for its normal operation, that other entity must also be subject to federal jurisdiction. Thus, to the extent that a federal work or undertaking is dependent on another entity that provides services, such as the design of websites or material for use on the Internet, that other business may be found to be subject to exclusive federal jurisdiction.

62 In *City TV*, above note 55, the C.I.R.B. also found that CityInteractive was operated in common with a broadcast undertaking and was subject to federal jurisdiction on this basis (as well as on the basis that a regular and continuous part of CityInteractive's business consisted of services that linked consumers to the Internet).

jurisdictional issues relating to the Internet. Binnie J. indicated that the federal *Copyright Act* should be extended to communications that have international participants in cases where there is a "real and substantial connection" with Canada. Although this test has previously been applied by the Court mainly in the context of issues revolving around the jurisdiction of provincial courts,[63] Binnie J. held that the "real and substantial connection" test has generally been viewed as an appropriate way to "prevent overreaching . . . and [to restrict] the exercise of jurisdiction over extraterritorial and transnational transactions."[64] The test reflects the reality of the "territorial limits of law under the international legal order" and "respect for the legitimate actions of other states inherent in the principle of international comity."[65] In the context of Internet communications, relevant connecting factors would include the *situs* of the content provider, the host server, the intermediaries, and the end user, with "the weight to be given to any particular factor [varying] with the circumstances."[66] However, in Binnie J.'s view, there will be a sufficient connection for Canada to take jurisdiction if Canada is the country of transmission *or* the country of reception.[67] The Ontario Court of Appeal has held that a similar approach applies to determining whether a court has jurisdiction over disputes regarding Internet domain names. The relevant connecting factors include the location of the registrant, the location of the registrar, and intermediary servers.[68]

It would seem likely that the "real and substantial connection" test will be applied as a basis for resolving jurisdictional disputes involving provincial regulation of Internet-related activities. As discussed by Binnie J. in *SOCAN*, the test would support provincial jurisdiction in cases where a communication originated in, or was received in, a province. At the same time, federal jurisdiction would be subject to the caveat that provinces cannot regulate a "vital or essential aspect" of an interprovincial work or undertaking, regardless of whether there is a substantial connection with the province in question.

---

63 See the discussion of the "real and substantial connection" test in Chapter 10, Section C.

64 *SOCAN*, above note 55 at para. 60, citing the Court's earlier decision in *Tolofson v. Jensen*, [1994] 3 S.C.R. 1022.

65 *SOCAN*, above note 55.

66 *Ibid.* at para. 61.

67 *Ibid.* at para. 62.

68 *Tucows*, above note 57 at para. 71.

6) Works Declared for the General Advantage of Canada

Paragraph 92(10)(c) of the *Constitution Act, 1867* provides an exception to the principle that local works and undertakings are subject to exclusive provincial jurisdiction. This subsection provides that the Parliament of Canada may declare that a local work is "for the general Advantage of Canada or for the Advantage of Two or more of the Provinces." Such a declaration is sufficient to bring an otherwise local work within federal regulatory authority. This power has been used close to five hundred times, mostly in the late nineteenth and early twentieth centuries and in most cases in relation to railways. It can be used in relation to a specific work or to a broad class of works.[69] Moreover, the works in question need not be limited to the field of transportation or communication but can involve any sort of physical or tangible thing.[70] Once the declaration is issued, the courts will not inquire into whether the work is in fact for the general advantage of Canada. The declaration by Parliament will be regarded by the courts as dispositive.[71]

Various commentators have suggested that the declaratory power is inconsistent with classical principles of federalism because it permits the federal government to increase its jurisdiction unilaterally at the expense of the provinces.[72] The power has fallen into relative disuse and has been used very infrequently.[73] In 1991, the federal government proposed that the power be abolished.[74]

The criticisms of the declaratory power must be balanced against the recognition of the important role this power has played in the past. For example, shortly after the Second World War, the federal government used the declaratory power to establish federal jurisdiction over atomic energy. The existence of the declaratory power was important in this context because it permitted swift and effective action on the part of the federal government—a necessary response because of the implications of atomic energy for national security. It is arguable that the courts would have eventually recognized that atomic energy fell under federal authority as a matter of national concern under the POGG power.

---

69 See *Jorgenson v. Can. (A.G.)*, [1971] S.C.R. 725.

70 *Ibid.*

71 See N. Finkelstein, ed., *Laskin's Canadian Constitutional Law*, 5th ed. (Toronto: Carswell, 1986) at 627–31.

72 See A. Lajoie, *Le pouvoir déclaratoire du Parlement* (Montreal: Université de Montréal, 1969) at 70–72.

73 See *Cape Breton Development Corporation Act*, S.C. 1967, c. 6, s. 35(1); *Teleglobe Canada Reorganization and Divestiture Act*, S.C. 1987, c. 12, s. 9 [*Teleglobe Act*].

74 See *Shaping Canada's Future Together: Proposals* (Ottawa: Supply and Services Canada, 1991), Proposal 23.

But even so, there would have been a period of uncertainty regarding the status of federal regulation. The existence of the declaratory power provided a means of eliminating this uncertainty and ensuring effective and timely federal intervention.

Some commentators have suggested that since the declaratory power has fallen into disuse, its abolition would have little practical effect. In fact, while it has been used sparingly in recent years, it was relied on by Parliament as recently as 2014.[75] Since it is impossible to predict the kinds of situations or problems that may emerge in the future, the existence of the declaratory power preserves the flexibility needed to ensure that the federal government is able to respond effectively to changing circumstances. Despite these considerations in favour of retaining the declaratory power, it would seem preferable to impose some kind of limitation on its use by the federal government. The existence of such a unilateral and unconstrained power is inconsistent with the fundamental equality of the two orders of government. The compromise position adopted in the *Charlottetown Accord*, whereby any future utilization of the declaratory power would require a legislative resolution by the province(s) in which the work in question is situated, seems an appropriate protection for provincial interests, while preserving some limited scope for the continued use of the declaratory power.

D. PEACE, ORDER, AND GOOD GOVERNMENT

The opening words of section 91 of the *Constitution Act, 1867* grant the Parliament of Canada power "to make Laws for the Peace, Order and Good Government of Canada, in relation to all Matters not coming within the Classes of Subjects by this Act assigned exclusively to the Legislatures of the Provinces." Although this source of federal authority has generally been interpreted relatively narrowly by the courts, as discussed in Chapter 8, one important exception has been in the field of transportation. The POGG power has been held to support exclusive federal jurisdiction over air transportation.[76] The Supreme Court has decided that aeronautics is a distinct subject matter beyond local concern and "must from its inherent nature be the concern of the Dominion as a whole."[77] The effect of the 1951 *Johannesson* case is to subject

75 *New Bridge for the St. Lawrence Act*, S.C. 2014, c. 20, s. 375.

76 See *Johannesson v. West St. Paul (Rural Municipality)* (1951), [1952] 1 S.C.R. 292 [*Johannesson*].

77 *Ibid.* at 309.

all aspects of aeronautics to exclusive federal authority, including purely local aeronautics undertakings. Therefore, the distinction between interprovincial and local undertakings, which has been critical in the judicial interpretation of section 92(10), has no application to the field of aeronautics. Even purely local airline operations fall under exclusive federal regulatory authority, regardless of whether they are connected to or integrated with an interprovincial undertaking.[78]

Given the relatively settled nature of federal jurisdiction over aeronautics, the litigation in this field has tended to focus on a variety of subsidiary issues such as the extent to which provincial laws of general application apply to airports. Under the doctrine of interjurisdictional immunity, the courts have held that airports and aeronautics undertakings are exempt from the application of any provincial legislation that affects a vital part of the federal undertaking. For example, it has been determined that airports are exempt from municipal zoning bylaws of general application,[79] as well as from height restrictions imposed by a province on land adjacent to an airport.[80] Further, airports are exempt from provincial building code regimes, which regulate the physical structure of buildings, such that airport authorities need not obtain building permits or pay development charges prior to undertaking construction projects.[81] In *Quebec (Attorney General) v. Canadian Owners and Pilots Association*,[82] the Supreme Court applied the doctrine of interjurisdictional immunity and held that provincial legislation prohibiting the use of lots in a designated agricultural region for a purpose other than agriculture was constitutionally inapplicable to an aerodrome registered under the federal *Aeronautics Act*. The provincial legislation at issue limited the location of aerodromes and thereby trenched on the core of the exclusive federal power.

However, provincial laws of general application will apply where they do not trench on the core of the aeronautics undertaking or the federal aeronautics power. For instance:

- a provincial minimum wage law was held to apply to a construction firm engaged in building a runway at Mirabel airport in Montreal;[83]

---

78 See *Jorgenson v. North Vancouver Magistrates* (1959), 28 W.W.R. 265 (B.C.C.A.).

79 See *Orangeville Airport Ltd. v. Caledon (Town)* (1975), 11 O.R. (2d) 546 (C.A.).

80 See *Walker v. Chatham (City)* (1983), 41 O.R. (2d) 9 (C.A.).

81 *Mississauga v. Greater Toronto Airports Authority* (2000), 50 O.R. (3d) 641 (C.A.); leave to appeal to S.C.C. refused, [2001] S.C.C.A. No. 83.

82 2010 SCC 39 [*Canadian Owners*].

83 *Quebec (Minimum Wage Commission) v. Construction Montcalm Inc.*, [1979] 1 S.C.R. 754.

- occupational health and safety legislation was held to apply to contractors and employees working on an expansion project at Pearson Airport in Toronto;[84]
- companies offering porter services or limousine service to and from the airport were subject to provincial legislation in Ontario;[85] and
- an Ontario levy on liquor loaded onto aircraft from an airport in the province for passenger consumption in the air was held to apply to Air Canada since it did not affect the operation of the aircraft.[86]

E. OTHER SOURCES OF FEDERAL AUTHORITY

Three other enumerated classes of subjects assigned to Parliament in section 91 of the *Constitution Act, 1867* deal explicitly with matters related to the field of transportation. These classes are:

- beacons, buoys, lighthouses, and Sable Island (section 91(9));
- navigation and shipping (section 91(10)); and
- ferries between a province and any British or foreign country or between two provinces (section 91(13)).

Federal authority over transportation matters is also supplemented by section 108, which provides for federal ownership of public works and property set out in the Third Schedule of the *Constitution Act, 1867*.[87] Although the Third Schedule transfers to the federal government all improvements or public works associated with rivers and waterways, the ownership of the rivers themselves remains with the provinces.[88] The provinces may legislate with respect to the use of these waters, as long as their legislation does not interfere with federal legislation in relation to navigation and shipping.

The most important source of federal authority from the above catalogue of powers is section 91(10), "Navigation and Shipping." The language in the section is unqualified, suggesting that federal authority

84 *R. v. EllisDon Corporation Ltd.*, 2008 ONCA 789, Sharpe J.A.

85 See *Colonial Coach Lines Ltd. v. Ontario (Highway Transport Board)*, [1967] 2 O.R. 25 (H.C.J.), aff'd [1967] 2 O.R. 243 (C.A.); *Murray Hill Limousine Service v. Batson*, [1965] B.R. 778 (Que. C.A.).

86 *Air Canada v. Ontario (Liquor Control Board)*, [1997] 2 S.C.R. 581.

87 The Third Schedule includes the following classes of provincial public works and property: 1. Canals, with Lands and Water Power connected therewith. 2. Public Harbours. 3. Lighthouses and Piers, and Sable Island. 4. Steamboats, Dredges, and Public Vessels. 5. Rivers and Lake Improvements. 6. Railways and Railway Stocks, Mortgages, and other debts due by the Railway Companies. 7. Military Roads.

88 See *Reference Re Provincial Fisheries*, [1898] A.C. 700 (P.C.).

could be extended to all aspects of the subject. However, for many years, the courts have interpreted section 91(10) as being subject to the same limits that had been developed with respect to federal undertakings under section 92(10)(a).[89] For example, in *Agence Maritime v. Canada (Labour Relations Board)*,[90] the Supreme Court held that local shipping was subject to provincial labour relations legislation.[91] Similarly, ferries that operated largely within the waters of British Columbia were held to be within provincial jurisdiction for purposes of labour legislation.[92] The courts interpreted federal authority over navigation and shipping as extending primarily to interprovincial and international undertakings.

A more recent decision of the Supreme Court may be taken to suggest a somewhat broader reading of federal authority over navigation and shipping. In *Whitbread v. Walley*,[93] the issue was whether certain limitations of civil liability contained in the *Canada Shipping Act* applied to a pleasure boat operated within provincial waters. The Supreme Court unanimously held that the provisions in the *Canada Shipping Act* applied uniformly to all shipping, including local shipping as well as pleasure boats. La Forest J., writing for the Court, distinguished the federal power over navigation and shipping in section 91(10) from the federal authority over works and undertakings in section 92(10)(a). Whereas federal jurisdiction over works and undertakings was limited to interprovincial and international transportation, there was no such limitation with respect to navigation and shipping. La Forest J. stated that Parliament's jurisdiction over maritime law should be viewed as territorially coextensive with its jurisdiction in respect of navigable waterways. He rejected a distinction between local shipping and interprovincial shipping. Instead, he took the view that all navigable waterways within Canada are part of a single navigational network that must be subject to a uniform legal regime. La Forest J. drew an analogy between navigation and shipping and the field of aeronautics, which, as discussed above, has been regarded as a single subject matter within the exclusive authority of Parliament. This is so, La Forest J. suggested,

---

89 This view, for example, was expressed by Dalfen and Dunbar in their study for the Macdonald Commission in 1985; see Dalfen and Dunbar, above note 25 at 150.

90 [1969] S.C.R. 851.

91 See also: *R. v. Mersey Seafoods Ltd.*, 2008 NSCA 67 (seagoing fishing vessels in Nova Scotia subject to Nova Scotia *Occupational Health and Safety Act*); and *Jim Pattison Enterprises Ltd. v. British Columbia (Workers' Compensation Board)*, 2011 BCCA 35 (*Occupational Health and Safety Regulation* under British Columbia legislation applying to commercial fishing vessels).

92 *Singbeil v. Hansen* (1985), 19 D.L.R. (4th) 48 (B.C.C.A.).

93 [1990] 3 S.C.R. 1273 [*Whitbread*].

because it is functionally impossible to make a distinction between local and interprovincial or international air travel. The same situation holds true, according to La Forest J., with respect to navigation and shipping. Therefore, there is a need for a uniform regulatory and legal regime for navigation and shipping and for "a broad reading of the relevant head of federal jurisdiction."[94]

The analogy drawn between navigation and shipping and aeronautics in *Whitbread* is significant. The federal power over navigation and shipping has never been regarded as being as extensive as the power over aeronautics.[95] This result is somewhat ironic, given the fact that the area of navigation and shipping is an enumerated head of federal authority, while aeronautics has simply been added through judicial interpretation of the federal residual power. The reasoning in *Whitbread* indicates that the Supreme Court may be willing to expand the limits of federal authority over navigation and shipping.[96]

As in the case of aeronautics, the Supreme Court has also applied the doctrine of interjurisdictional immunity to protect an "unassailable core" of federal legislative jurisdiction over navigation and shipping. In *Ordon Estate v. Grail*,[97] the Court held that Ontario legislation permitting negligence claims to be brought by family members of deceased persons was constitutionally inapplicable to maritime negligence actions arising from accidents in navigable waters. The Court held that the statutes must be read down to exclude maritime negligence cases, since application of the provincial statutes would result in "an intrusion upon the unassailable core of federal maritime law" reserved to the federal Parliament under section 91(10).[98] However, the Court went on to reverse years of federal maritime law so as to permit causes of action

94 *Ibid.* at para. 31.

95 For example, labour relations matters in all aeronautics undertakings are subject to exclusive federal authority; in the field of navigation and shipping, federal authority has been limited to undertakings engaged in interprovincial and international activity.

96 However, in *Isen v. Simms*, [2006] 2 S.C.R. 349, the Court held that a tort claim for injury on a pleasure craft was not governed by federal maritime law, but rather provincial law. Rothstein J., for the Court, stated that "Parliament does not have jurisdiction over pleasure craft *per se*" and "[t]he mere involvement of a pleasure craft in an incident is not sufficient to ground Parliament's jurisdiction." Rather, "a court must look at the allegedly negligent acts and determine whether that activity is integrally connected to the act of navigating the pleasure craft on Canadian waterways such that it is practically necessary for Parliament to have jurisdiction over the matter" (para. 24).

97 See *Ordon Estate v. Grail*, [1998] 3 S.C.R. 437.

98 *Ibid.* at para. 85.

to be brought by family members of the deceased and bring the federal common law in line with provincial legislation.

Similarly, in *British Columbia (Attorney General) v. LaFarge Canada Inc.*,[99] the Court considered the applicability of a municipal land use by-law in relation to a proposal to build a concrete batch plant in the port of Vancouver. While the marine facility came within federal authority over navigation and shipping, the municipal land use by-law did not trench on the "core" of the federal authority under section 91(10). As a result, the doctrine of interjurisdictional immunity did not apply. However, the majority held that the by-law was constitutionally inoperative because it was inconsistent with the *Canada Marine Act*.

In 2013, a unanimous Supreme Court took a more cooperative view of the interaction between provincial liability statutes and federal maritime law. In *Ryan Estate*,[100] the Court held that Newfoundland and Labrador's workers' compensation statute, which prohibited recovery in tort for workplace accidents as part of its no-fault insurance scheme, applied to a maritime action by the estates of deceased fishermen against their employer. Although the provincial statute trenched on the core of federal power of navigation and shipping, as identified in *Ordon Estate*, it did not rise to the level of "impairment," as required by the modern doctrine of interjurisdictional immunity for the provincial law to be inapplicable. The Court's comment that *Ordon Estate* was not decided under the higher threshold for interjurisdictional immunity set in *Canadian Western Bank* (discussed in Chapter 4) confirms that the contemporary standard will be applied going forward.

F. REGULATORY FRAMEWORK

It is evident that the courts have taken a much more expansive approach to federal authority over transportation matters than in other fields, such as trade and commerce. To what extent does the federal and provincial legislation enacted in the transportation field reflect the centralized scheme contemplated by the formal constitution? The short answer to this question is that the regulatory framework does recognize a leading role for the federal government over transportation matters. However, in certain instances, the federal government has chosen not to exercise the full range of authority it has been allocated under the constitution. What follows is a brief overview of the regulatory

---

99 [2007] 2 S.C.R. 86.

100 *Marine Services International Ltd. v. Ryan Estate*, [2013] 3 S.C.R. 53 [*Ryan Estate*].

framework that has been put in place in the four principal modes of public passenger transportation: air, water, rail, and motor vehicle. The focus of this analysis is on particular modes of transportation or forms of regulation that have been an important source of litigation or court decisions in the past. As such, we do not attempt to provide a comprehensive outline of federal or provincial legislation relating to transportation matters.[101] The main purpose of including this overview is to allow for a more complete understanding of how governments have actually used their formal powers set out in the constitution.

1) Air Transportation

The federal government currently dominates the regulation of all air passenger transportation in Canada. Under the *Canada Transportation Act*,[102] Parliament has exclusive responsibility for regulating the provision of all air services in Canada; and under the *Aeronautics Act*,[103] it regulates the safety and security of passengers, aircraft, and airport and aviation facilities. All air carriers in Canada are subject to exclusive federal regulation under these statutes, including carriers engaged in purely local transportation. The provincial role in the transportation field is currently limited to establishing and directly operating certain airports as well as subsidizing some air passenger services. Almost all the airports and airstrips owned and operated by provincial governments are located in remote, northern areas of the provinces. Moreover, all provincially operated airports as well as all air passenger services must be federally licensed and must meet relevant federal regulatory requirements. In short, the regulatory framework governing aeronautics reflects the centralized interpretation developed by the Supreme Court in this area.

2) Marine Transportation

The primary public mode of marine passenger transportation is provided by passenger and automobile ferries. The Parliament of Canada has established safety requirements under the *Canada Shipping Act, 2001*[104] which apply to all ferry services, including ferries operating within

---

101 For example, the regulatory framework with respect to the road system or to private passenger automobiles is not included in this discussion.

102 S.C. 1996, c. 10. This legislation repealed the *National Transportation Act, 1987*, S.C. 1987, c. 34.

103 R.S.C. 1985, c. A-2.

104 S.C. 2001, c. 26.

a province. This statute represents a codification of the rules of the "road" for all navigation and shipping within Canadian navigable waters. The federal government also assumes responsibility for the provision of ferry services between provinces,[105] as well as for certain ferry services that are intraprovincial in nature.[106] Many of the provinces also provide local ferry services, the most important being provided by British Columbia, Ontario, Newfoundland, and Quebec. However, even these provincially operated services are subject to the safety and operational requirements of the *Canada Shipping Act, 2001*, thus ensuring a uniform regulatory framework across the country. The provinces have not imposed any additional ferry safety requirements on services they operate or subsidize but would be free to do so as long as their regulations did not conflict with the paramount provisions in federal law.

3) Rail Transportation

Parliament regulates the vast majority of passenger rail services in Canada. It has responsibility for all interprovincial and international railways, as well as for any other railways that have been declared to be for the general advantage of Canada. This group includes the vast majority of all passenger rail operations in the country. These rail services are regulated by the *Canada Transportation Act*.[107] The *Canada Transportation Act* generally provides for a more commercially oriented process for railway companies to sell or lease surplus rail lines to new operators, rather than discontinue service. It provides for an adminis-

---

105 Certain of these ferry services are a constitutional obligation of the federal government, including ferries in Newfoundland and B.C. and, until recently, P.E.I. These obligations are contained in the respective Terms of Union admitting these provinces to Canada. Each of the obligations is thus part of the Constitution of Canada and takes precedence over all federal and provincial legislation. Further, the obligations may only be amended in accordance with the procedures set down in Part V of the *Constitution Act, 1982*. For a discussion of the precise nature and implications of these various obligations, see P.J. Monahan, "Transportation Obligations and the Canadian Constitution," in *Directions: The Final Report of the Royal Commission on National Passenger Transportation* (Ottawa: Supply and Services Canada, 1992) vol. 3 at 883.

106 The federal government has, in recent years, sought to devolve responsibility for the provision of intraprovincial ferry services to the provinces. The usual arrangement has the province agreeing to assume responsibility for a service in exchange for payment of a fixed sum from the federal government. For a discussion, see IBI Group, *Intercity Passenger Transportation Policy Framework: Federal Legislation Review* (Working Paper prepared for the Royal Commission on National Passenger Transportation), June 1990 [IBI Group] at 14–16.

107 S.C. 1996, c. 10.

trative agency, the Canadian Transportation Agency, which has regulatory powers in relation to federally regulated passenger rail services. Certain decisions of the agency can be varied or rescinded by the federal Cabinet. Provincial regulation of passenger rail services is extremely limited. In British Columbia, Ontario, and Quebec, various provincially operated or subsidized local rail services are subject to provincial regulation, but they are confined mainly to commuter rail networks or to remote, northern regions. The vast majority of all passenger rail activity is subject to exclusive federal regulation.

4) Motor Vehicle Transportation

The primary public mode of motor vehicle transportation is provided by the bus industry. As noted above, the Privy Council decision in the *Winner* case established that bus undertakings engaged in regular interprovincial service fell under exclusive federal authority.[108] However, the bus industry had traditionally been regulated at the provincial level, and the federal government had no regulatory structure in place to assume control over the industry. Accordingly, within months of the Privy Council decision in *Winner*, the federal government delegated the regulation of interprovincial undertakings to the provinces. The *Motor Vehicle Transport Act*[109] transferred regulatory authority over interprovincial motor vehicle undertakings to provincially appointed boards. The provincial boards are granted the authority to license the undertakings and to determine the terms and conditions under which they will operate.

It is an established principle of Canadian constitutional law that one level of government cannot directly delegate legislative powers to another level of government.[110] Thus, it was inevitable that questions would be raised regarding the validity of the delegation to provincial boards under the *Motor Vehicle Transport Act*. However, the Supreme Court of Canada upheld the validity of the delegation in *Coughlin v. Ontario (Highway Transport Board)*,[111] ruling that a provincial board, validly constituted under provincial law to regulate local undertakings, could be vested with the authority to regulate extraprovincial undertakings. Regulation of the bus industry was left to the provinces, re-

108 Above note 11.

109 R.S.C. 1985, c.29 (3d Supp.).

110 This principle was established by the Supreme Court in *N.S. (A.G.) v. Can. (A.G.)* (1950), [1951] S.C.R. 31.

111 [1968] S.C.R. 569.

sulting in significant variations in the applicable regimes governing bus operations across the country.[112]

However, there do appear to be some limits to the capacity of the federal government to delegate regulatory authority in this area to the provinces. In *Coughlin*, the provincial board that was granted regulatory authority was already validly established under provincial law. The decision therefore suggests an implicit requirement that the provincial legislation establishing the provincial board is valid, independent of any federal law. This would mean that the province could not establish a board or agency whose sole purpose was to regulate interprovincial undertakings. The provincial legislation establishing such an agency would be beyond the constitutional capacity of the provinces, since there would be no valid provincial purpose that the agency was fulfilling.

G. TRANSPORTATION OBLIGATIONS

One of the distinctive features of the Canadian constitution is the inclusion of a significant number of transportation-related obligations imposed on the federal government. For example, under section 145 of the *Constitution Act, 1867*, the federal government was required to commence construction of the Intercolonial Railway (linking the maritime provinces with Quebec) within six months of confederation; Term 11 of the *British Columbia Terms of Union* required the construction of a transcontinental railway; the *Prince Edward Island Terms of Union* required the Canadian government to maintain a ferry service linking the island with the mainland; and the *Newfoundland Terms of Union* provide a guarantee of ferry service between the province and the Canadian mainland. Students of Canadian history have long remarked on the number and specificity of these constitutional obligations.

The instruments setting out these constitutional obligations are all included within the definition of the Constitution of Canada in section 52 of the *Constitution Act, 1982*.[113] Thus, any federal laws that are inconsistent with the relevant obligations would be of no force and effect. However, most of the constitutional obligations require Canada to construct transportation undertakings, as opposed to operate those undertakings on their completion. Thus, to a large extent, Canada's

---

112 For a discussion of these provincial variations, see IBI Group, above note 106 at 20–33.

113 The *Constitution Act, 1982*, being Schedule B to the *Canada Act 1982* (U.K.), 1982, c. 11.

obligations in this regard were fulfilled in the latter half of the nineteenth century. The termination or reduction of passenger rail service in Canada in the past few decades has prompted two provinces, Prince Edward Island and British Columbia, to argue that these reductions in service are unconstitutional, since they violate constitutional guarantees relating to transportation. However, both of these challenges proved unsuccessful. In Prince Edward Island, the shutdown of all rail lines on the island was challenged on the basis that the rail lines were inextricably bound up with and necessary to the operation of the ferry service. But this argument was rejected by the Federal Court of Appeal on the basis that the constitutional obligation to operate a ferry service did not extend to the operation of an associated railway.[114] In British Columbia, the province challenged the shutdown of a small railway on Vancouver Island on the basis that it violated the requirement in Term 11 of the *British Columbia Terms of Union* that Canada construct a transcontinental railway. A majority of the Supreme Court rejected this argument on the basis that Canada was obliged to construct but not to operate the railway.[115] It was thus lawful for Canada to terminate the island railway service.

Canada has assumed certain limited constitutional obligations to provide or operate transportation services. For example, the *Prince Edward Island Terms of Union* guaranteed an "[e]fficient Steam Service for the conveyance of mails and passengers, to be established and maintained between the Island and the mainland." However, in 1993, the terms of union were amended so as to permit the substitution of a fixed crossing joining the island to the mainland in place of the ferry service.[116] The fixed link (Confederation Bridge) was constructed and opened to the public in 1997. Presumably, the fixed link must be maintained and operated in an efficient manner, since the guarantee in respect of the ferry service, which the fixed link has now replaced, described the obligation in this manner.

---

114 See *P.E.I. (Min. Transportation and Public Works) v. Canadian National Railway Co.* (1990), [1991] 1 F.C. 129 (C.A.), Iacobucci J.A. (as he then was).

115 *B.C. (A.G.) v. Can. (A.G.)*, [1994] 2 S.C.R. 41, Iacobucci J.

116 See the *Constitution Amendment Proclamation, 1993 (Prince Edward Island)*, SI/94–50, C. Gaz. 1994. II. 2021.

FURTHER READINGS

DALFEN, C., & L. DUNBAR, "Transportation and Communications: The Constitution and the Canadian Economic Union" in M. Krasnick, ed., *Case Studies in the Division of Powers* (Toronto: University of Toronto Press, 1985)

MCNAIRN, C., "Aeronautics and the Constitution" (1971) 49 Can. Bar Rev. 411

———, "Transportation, Communication and the Constitution" (1969) 47 Can. Bar Rev. 355

MONAHAN, P.J., "Constitutional Jurisdiction over Transportation: Recent Developments and Proposals for Change" in *Directions: The Final Report of the Royal Commission on National Passenger Transportation* (Ottawa: Royal Commission on National Passenger Transportation, 1991) vol. 3

———, "Transportation Obligations and the Canadian Constitution" in *Directions: The Final Report of the Royal Commission on National Passenger Transportation* (Ottawa: Royal Commission on National Passenger Transportation, 1991) vol. 3

TAKACH, G.S., *Computer Law*, 2d ed. (Toronto: Irwin Law, 2003) cc. 4 and 7

PART FIVE

THE *CHARTER* AND ABORIGINAL RIGHTS

CHAPTER 13

THE *CANADIAN CHARTER OF RIGHTS AND FREEDOMS*: STRUCTURE AND APPLICATION

A. THE ENACTMENT OF THE *CHARTER*

Following the end of the Second World War, there was growing international support for the concept of constitutionally protecting human rights. In 1948, the United Nations adopted the *Universal Declaration of Human Rights*[1] and, over the next few decades, human rights protection was incorporated in a number of international covenants and conventions,[2] as well as in the domestic constitutions of many states. In Canada, this international trend was reflected in the enactment of the *Canadian Bill of Rights* in 1960,[3] as well as the adoption of human rights codes at the provincial and federal level.[4] However, the *Canadian Bill of*

---

1 1948 G.A. Res. 217A (III), U.N. Doc. A/810, at 71.

2 See, for example, the *International Covenant on Civil and Political Rights*, 999 U.N.T.S. 171 and the *International Covenant on Economic, Social and Cultural Rights*, 999 U.N.T.S. 3.

3 S.C. 1960, c. 44; R.S.C. 1985, App. III.

4 The first human rights code was enacted in Saskatchewan in 1947: see the *Saskatchewan Bill of Rights, 1947*, S.S. 1947, c. 35. This was followed by similar codes enacted by the other provinces and, in 1978, the *Canadian Human Rights Act* (S.C. 1976–77, c. 33; R.S.C. 1985, c. H-6) was enacted by Parliament. Human rights codes are primarily concerned with prohibiting unlawful discrimination in the provision of certain goods, services, facilities, or employment; as such, they have a much more restricted scope than fundamental rights documents, such as the *Canadian Charter of Rights and Freedoms*, Part 1 of the *Constitution Act, 1982*, being Schedule B to the *Canada Act 1982* (U.K.), 1982, c. 11 [*Charter*].

Rights and the provincial and federal human rights codes were not constitutionally entrenched. Furthermore, the *Canadian Bill of Rights* was a federal statute and could not be applied to matters within provincial jurisdiction. Moreover, the Bill was interpreted in an extremely narrow fashion by the judiciary. From 1960 to 1982, claimants invoking the *Canadian Bill of Rights* were successful in just five of the thirty-five cases that reached the Supreme Court of Canada. The Supreme Court found that a provision in a federal statute was inoperative in just one instance.[5]

Following his election as prime minister in 1968, Pierre Trudeau attempted to obtain the support of the provinces for the enactment of an entrenched charter of rights that would be constitutionally binding on both levels of government. Trudeau initiated a three-year process of constitutional negotiations with the provinces that culminated in May 1971 with the drafting of a "Canadian Constitutional Charter," commonly referred to as the *Victoria Charter*. The *Victoria Charter*, which included guarantees for political rights and language rights, was approved in principle by the premiers of all ten provinces at a meeting in Victoria on 16 June 1971. All eleven governments were to indicate by 28 June 1971 whether they approved the draft *Charter* without further amendments and whether they would submit it to their respective legislatures for approval. While eight of the ten provinces subsequently approved the draft *Charter*, Quebec and Saskatchewan were unwilling to proceed without amendments, which put a temporary end to the constitutional discussions.

Despite the failure of the *Victoria Charter*, Trudeau remained committed to the constitutional entrenchment of a charter of rights. In the May 1980 Quebec referendum, Trudeau had promised "renewed federalism" in return for a vote against the Quebec government's proposals for sovereignty association. When federal-provincial negotiations over the summer and early fall of 1980 failed to produce a consensus on constitutional reform, Trudeau introduced a parliamentary resolution in October 1980, which included a proposal for a charter of rights.[6]

Human rights codes apply to private as well as public bodies, whereas the *Charter* applies only to legislatures and governments.

5 *R. v. Drybones*, [1970] S.C.R. 282 [*Drybones*]. Although not constitutionally entrenched, the *Canadian Bill of Rights* contained a provision stating that federal laws were to be "construed and applied as not to abrogate, abridge or infringe . . . any of the rights or freedoms herein recognized and declared." In *Drybones*, the Supreme Court relied on this language to hold that, in cases where provisions in a federal statute were necessarily in conflict with rights protected by the Bill, the offending statutory provisions were rendered inoperative.

6 These negotiations are discussed in Chapter 5, Section C(4).

The proposed charter of rights sparked a fierce political debate over the 1980–82 period. On one side of the debate were those who argued that a charter of rights would transfer undue power from elected politicians and into the hands of unelected and unaccountable judges. Premier Allan Blakeney of Saskatchewan was perhaps the most articulate critic of an entrenched charter. Blakeney's concerns over the charter stemmed from his social democratic principles and the belief that the state was a positive instrument for achieving social justice and equality.[7] For Blakeney, a charter of rights would expand the authority of unaccountable and socially conservative judges, who would thwart the redistributive goals of the state. Blakeney was particularly troubled by the American experience with the Bill of Rights during the "Lochner era" in the early twentieth century, in which the U.S. Supreme Court rolled back a wide variety of socially progressive statutes.[8] For Blakeney, the legislature was the appropriate body to balance individual and collective interests. Blakeney believed that rights are best protected by Parliament and not by a constitution that is interpreted by the courts.[9] In the end, Blakeney was prepared to accept an entrenched charter of rights only if it included a "notwithstanding" clause, which he believed would permit legislatures to ensure that the courts did not unduly limit the choices made by elected politicians.[10]

Blakeney was not the only premier to express concerns about the increased judicial power associated with an entrenched charter. Manitoba

7 See, generally, D. Greunding, *Promises to Keep: A Political Biography of Allan Blakeney* (Saskatoon: Western Producer Prairie Books, 1990) at 192–96.

8 The Lochner era refers to the period from 1905–37, in which the U.S. Supreme Court held that the guarantee of "due process of law" in the fourteenth amendment required courts to assess the substantive fairness of legislation. This era of substantive due process began with *Lochner v. New York*, 198 U.S. 45 (1905), in which the U.S. Supreme Court struck down a New York statute imposing maximum hours of work in bakeries, on the basis that the statute interfered with freedom of contract. When the U.S. Supreme Court struck down a number of New Deal statutes on a similar basis in the mid-1930s, President Franklin Delano Roosevelt threatened to "pack the Court" with additional appointees more favourable to the government's position. In *West Coast Hotel v. Parrish*, 300 U.S. 379 (1937), *Lochner* and the other substantive due process cases of that era were overruled. Since 1937, the U.S. Supreme Court has applied minimal scrutiny to social and economic legislation limiting liberty of contract.

9 R. Sheppard & M. Valpy, *The National Deal: The Fight for a Canadian Constitution* (Toronto: Fleet Books, 1982) at 145.

10 R.J. Romanow, J.D. Whyte, & H.A. Leeson, *Canada—Notwithstanding: The Making of the Constitution, 1976–1982* (Toronto: Carswell/Methuen, 1984) at 197–214. The notwithstanding clause was incorporated in s. 33 of the *Charter*. The role and significance of the notwithstanding clause is discussed in Section C(4), below in this chapter.

Premier Sterling Lyon was ideologically opposed to the *Charter*, fearing that it would undermine the doctrine of parliamentary sovereignty and the role of the monarchy in Canada, while Alberta's Premier Peter Lougheed feared it would undermine the autonomy of the provinces.[11] Even Prime Minister Trudeau, the ultimate champion of the *Charter*, seemed extremely sensitive to the dangers associated with judicial limits on parliamentary sovereignty. The federal government's original draft of the *Charter*, tabled in the House of Commons on 2 October 1980, appeared to offer relatively limited protection for individual rights.[12] For example, the limitation clause in the original federal version stated that rights under the draft *Charter* were subject to such "reasonable limits as are generally accepted in a free and democratic society with a parliamentary system of government."[13] This language appeared to be an attempt to continue jurisprudence built up under the *Canadian Bill of Rights* tolerating established or accepted limits on individual rights.[14]

Despite concern by governments and first ministers, the idea of an entrenched charter was supported by a wide variety of interest groups and legal activists. For these groups, the primary concern was to strengthen and expand the guarantees of rights found in the draft proposed by Trudeau. A campaign was mounted in the parliamentary committee hearings held over the winter of 1980–81 designed to remedy what was described as a "seriously flawed" document.[15] Women's groups, civil liberties organizations, ethnic and racial minorities, the disabled community, and even Canada's human rights commissioner all urged the federal government to go back to the drawing-board and produce a charter that would have real teeth. This grassroots campaign proved to be remarkably effective, and led to a variety of amendments, designed to strengthen the rights guarantees.[16]

---

11 Sheppard & Valpy, above note 9 at 268.

12 Romanow, Whyte, & Leeson, above note 10 at 248–50.

13 *Ibid.*

14 *Ibid.* at 243. The reference to a "parliamentary system of government" seemed to reinforce this tendency, by suggesting that particular attention be paid to the experience in the U.K. which, unlike the U.S., had no constitutional guarantees of individual rights.

15 Sheppard & Valpy, above note 9 at 135.

16 The campaign was particularly effective in strengthening ss. 1 to 15 of the draft *Charter*. For example, s. 1 was amended such that measures limiting rights under the *Charter* could be upheld only if the limit could be "demonstrably justified" in a free and democratic society. The original draft of s. 1 provided that rights were subject to "reasonable limits as are generally accepted in a free and democratic society with a parliamentary system of government." The equality provision in s. 15 was amended in a variety of ways. For example, the guarantee of "equality before the law" was amended to provide for "equality before *and under* the law,"

Interest groups and activists supporting the *Charter* did not particularly voice concerns over the potential increase in judicial power. To the extent that judicial discretion was regarded as a problem at all, it was apparently seen as a matter that could be dealt with through appropriate drafting. The primary focus was on strengthening the rights guarantees so that the courts would give real meaning and substance to constitutionally entrenched rights and freedoms.

These contrasting political agendas—one associated with governments and first ministers, the other with interest groups and activists—dominated the debates over the *Charter* in the 1980–82 period. At the same time, it was understood that there were larger, more general political considerations and purposes at play in the debate. Many believed that the importance of the *Charter* lay not so much in the details of particular clauses as much as the broader political effects the *Charter* would have on Canadian society as a whole.[17] The *Charter* was seen as an instrument of nation-building. It emphasized common values of citizenship, entrenching rights enjoyed equally by all Canadians.[18] In this sense, the *Charter* was viewed as a bridge between regional and provincial particularism that had historically dominated Canadian politics. The *Charter* provided a common reference point for all Canadians and gave symbolic expression to the idea that Canadians enjoy a collective political identity.[19]

---

while the guarantee of "equal protection of the law" was amended to provide for the "equal protection *and equal benefit* of the law" [emphasis added]. These amendments were a direct response to a number of Supreme Court cases decided under the *Canadian Bill of Rights*, which had dismissed equality claims on the basis that the Bill did not guarantee "equality under the law" or the "equal benefit" of the law: see, for example, *Bliss v. A.G. Canada*, [1979] 1 S.C.R. 183 (dismissing a claim to maternity benefits on the basis that the Bill did not provide for the "equal benefit" of the law). The drafters of s. 15 were attempting to signal expressly to the courts that the equality jurisprudence developed under the Bill was not to be followed in the interpretation of the *Charter*, a signal that was understood and accepted by the Supreme Court in its *Charter* equality rights jurisprudence. Equality rights are discussed in further detail in Chapter 14.

17 See, generally, D. Milne, *The Canadian Constitution: The Players and the Issues in the Process That Has Led from Patriation to Meech Lake to an Uncertain Future*, 2d rev ed. (Toronto: James Lorimer, 1991).

18 It should be noted that the rights and freedoms in the *Charter* are not necessarily universal. For instance, the "fundamental freedoms" set out in s. 2 and the legal rights in ss. 7–14 apply to "everyone." The democratic rights in ss. 3 to 5, mobility rights in s. 6 and minority language educational rights in s. 23 apply only to Canadian "citizens." The equality rights in s. 15 apply to "every individual."

19 See P. Russell, "The Political Purposes of the *Canadian Charter of Rights and Freedoms*" (1983) 61 Can. Bar Rev. 30.

These broader political purposes were central to Prime Minister Trudeau's desire for an entrenched *Charter*. Reviewing the patriation experience in later years, Trudeau claimed that the goal of the *Charter* was to strengthen national unity by "basing the sovereignty of the Canadian people on a set of values common to all, and in particular on the notion of equality among all Canadians."[20] Trudeau believed that the adoption of the *Charter* was a reflection of the "purest liberalism" in which each individual is regarded as a "human personality" who has absolute dignity and infinite value. It follows that "only the individual is the possessor of rights" and that certain inalienable rights can never be interfered with by any collectivity, whether the collectivity be a state, nation, or another group.[21] The *Charter* would serve as an important instrument for Canadians to transcend provincial and regional particularism and focus on a set of common values.

Canada's experience with the *Charter* suggests that, on balance, it has made a significant positive contribution to the Canadian legal and political landscape. Courts have adopted a much more robust interpretation of the *Charter* than was applied to the *Canadian Bill of Rights*.[22] The success rate for *Charter* claims in cases decided by the Supreme Court has been approximately one in three.[23] In this way, the courts have ensured that the *Charter* operates as a meaningful and substantive limitation on the authority of governments and legislatures. At the same time, the courts have avoided many of the potential pitfalls that were

---

20 P. Trudeau, "The Values of a Just Society" in P. Trudeau & T. Axworthy, eds., *Towards a Just Society: The Trudeau Years* (Markham, ON: Viking Books, 1990) 357 at 363.

21 *Ibid.*

22 The Supreme Court decided almost immediately that interpretations adopted under the *Canadian Bill of Rights* would not be binding in cases under the *Charter* even in relation to constitutional provisions with similar wording. As Le Dain J. stated in *R. v. Therens*, [1985] 1 S.C.R. 613 at para. 44, "[a]lthough it is clear that in several instances . . . the framers of the *Charter* adopted the wording of the *Canadian Bill of Rights*, it is also clear that the *Charter* must be regarded, because of its constitutional character, as a new affirmation of rights and freedoms and of judicial power and responsibility in relation to their protection." See also: *R. v. Big M Drug Mart*, [1985] 1 S.C.R. 295 (striking down the federal *Lord's Day Act*, a statute that had been upheld under the *Canadian Bill of Rights*).

23 In the first two years of *Charter* adjudication (1984–86), the Supreme Court favoured the *Charter* claimant in over half of decided cases. Moreover, this early wave of cases included some of the most important and enduring decisions of the Court, including *R. v. Oakes*, [1986] 1 S.C.R. 103 [*Oakes*], which established the framework for analysis under s. 1 of the *Charter*. However, after this initial wave of activism, the Court settled into a pattern in which approximately one in three *Charter* claims were decided in favour of the claimant.

identified by the *Charter*'s critics during the debates that preceded its enactment. For example, the courts have generally steered clear of debates over social and economic policy, in most cases deferring to the legislature's assessments of the best balance between competing claims for scarce resources.[24] The courts have in most cases adopted a balanced and measured approach to the interpretation of the *Charter*'s guarantees of minority language and educational rights, so as to avoid the criticism that it is stifling provincial variation and autonomy.[25]

The courts have been most active and vigilant in enforcing *Charter* rights in the areas of criminal law and procedure. These matters are subject to exclusive federal jurisdiction under section 91(27) of the *Constitution Act, 1867*,[26] and are areas where the judiciary's expertise and legitimacy is high. The courts have also tended to favour interpretations of the *Charter* that permit governments to substitute alternative legislation or policy in cases where a statute is ruled invalid. For example, in cases where the Supreme Court has found that a statute is inconsistent with the *Charter* and cannot be justified under section 1, the Court has in most cases concluded that there are alternative legislative means that could have been utilized to achieve the same objective which would have a lesser impact on fundamental rights and freedoms.

The *Charter* is certainly popular with Canadians. Strong majorities in all regions of the country, including the province of Quebec, regard the enactment of the *Charter* as a "good thing for Canada."[27] A strong

24 There have, however, been some exceptions to this generalization, most notably *Chaoulli v. Quebec*, [2005] 1 S.C.R. 791 [*Chaoulli*], in which the Court ruled that provisions in Quebec law prohibiting the sale of private insurance for medically necessary services violated s. 7 of the *Charter* due to excessive waiting times for many services in the public system. *Chaoulli* is discussed in Chapter 14.

25 Note, however, that in *Ford v. Quebec (A.G.)*, [1988] 2 S.C.R. 712 [*Ford*], the Supreme Court struck down Quebec's prohibition of English-language commercial signs. It should be noted that most of the Court's controversial decisions involving language and educational rights came in the early years of the *Charter*. Since the early 1990s, the courts have adopted a narrower and more cautious approach to issues of language and culture. For example, several comprehensive provincial reform initiatives affecting minority language or religious education rights have been upheld in recent years: see, for example, *Ontario English Catholic Teachers Association v. Ontario (Attorney General)*, [2001] 1 S.C.R. 470; *Public School Boards' Assn of Alberta v. Alberta (Attorney General)*, [2000] 2 S.C.R. 409; and *Solski (Tutor of) v. Quebec (Attorney General)*, [2005] S.C.R. 201.

26 The *Constitution Act, 1867* (formerly, the *British North America Act, 1867*) (U.K.), 30 & 31 Vict., c. 3.

27 See J. Fletcher & P. Howe, "Public Opinion and the Courts" (May 2000) 6 *Choices* 3 at 6, reporting that in surveys conducted in 1987 and 1999, approximately 80 percent of Canadians who have heard of the *Charter* say it is a "good thing for Canada." In Quebec, where politicians have been critical of the

majority of Canadians also believe that the *Charter* has strengthened Canadian national identity and that the document has not weakened the power of the provinces.[28] In a country as divided by regional and linguistic discord as Canada is reputed to be, the continuing political popularity of this constitutional document among ordinary Canadian citizens is testament to the success of the courts in striking the appropriate balance between individual rights and the advancement of collective welfare.

B. COURTS AND LEGISLATURES

One of the major concerns raised by early critics of the *Charter* was that it would be used to thwart governments from redistributing property rights or economic entitlements, as had occurred in the U.S. in the early years of the twentieth century.[29] Critics charged that individual rights and freedoms guaranteed in the *Charter* were based on a laissez-faire theory of state and market, designed to protect individuals from state interference as opposed to guaranteeing positive rights to social services or health care. In the words of one prominent *Charter* skeptic, the *Charter* was a "nineteenth century liberal document set loose on a twentieth-century welfare state."[30] But the possibility that the *Charter* would be used to dismantle or roll back the modern welfare state was quickly scotched by Dickson C.J., who noted in an early *Charter* case that: "courts must be cautious to ensure that [the *Charter*] does not

---

Charter on the basis that it was enacted without the consent of the Quebec National Assembly, support for the *Charter* is as high as it is elsewhere in Canada. In the 1999 survey, 70.4 percent of Quebec respondents said that the *Charter* is a "good thing" while only 6.7 percent stated that the *Charter* is a "bad thing." The remainder either had no opinion or had not heard of the *Charter*.

28 Fletcher & Howe, *ibid*. at 9–10, reporting that in 1999, 58.6 percent of respondents stated that the *Charter* strengthened national identity, while 28.6 percent disagreed with this view; a similar majority agreed that the *Charter* has not weakened the powers of the provinces.

29 For academic commentary that develops this line of criticism see, for example, M. Mandel, *The Charter of Rights and the Legalization of Politics in Canada*, rev. ed. (Toronto: Thompson Educational Publishing, 1994); A.C. Hutchinson, *Waiting for CORAF: A Critique of Law and Rights* (Toronto: University of Toronto Press, 1995); J. Bakan, *Just Words: Constitutional Rights and Social Wrongs* (Toronto: University of Toronto Press, 1997). For a critique of this literature, see R. Penner, "The Canadian Experience with the *Charter of Rights*: Are there Lessons for the United Kingdom?" (1996) P.L. 104.

30 A. Petter, "Immaculate Deception: The *Charter*'s Hidden Agenda" (1987) 45 Advocate 857.

simply become an instrument of better situated individuals to roll back legislation which has as its object the improvement of conditions of less advantaged persons."[31] The Supreme Court subsequently ruled that economic rights are generally not protected by the *Charter.*[32] The Court extrapolated from the fact that the drafters of the *Charter* had deliberately omitted protection for property rights in section 7,[33] holding that other purely economic rights such as rights of contract or the right to engage in collective bargaining were not protected under the *Charter.*[34] The result has been that governments and legislatures have generally been free to design economic and social welfare policies with relatively little fear that their choices will be overturned by the judiciary.[35] Even in cases where certain social or economic policy measures have been

31 *R. v. Edwards Books and Art Ltd.*, [1986] 2 S.C.R. 713 at 779 [*Edwards Books*].

32 See *Irwin Toy v. Quebec*, [1989] 1 S.C.R. 927 at 1003–004 [*Irwin Toy*].

33 Both the U.S. *Bill of Rights* and the 1960 *Canadian Bill of Rights* had included protection for property rights. A proposal to include a similar guarantee in s. 7 was ultimately abandoned by the Trudeau government. In the 1980s, the House of Commons and the New Brunswick and Ontario legislative assemblies supported the addition of property rights to the *Charter*. The federal government proposed to add protection for property rights to the *Charter* as part of a package of comprehensive proposals to amend the Constitution. See Government of Canada, *Shaping Canada's Future Together: Proposals* (Ottawa: Supply and Services Canada, 1991) at 3 [*Shaping Canada's Future*]. However, the parliamentary committee that held hearings and sponsored a series of conferences on the government proposal heard a great deal of opposition to the proposal: see *A Renewed Canada: The Report of the Special Joint Committee of the Senate and House of Commons* (G. Beaudoin & D. Dobbie, co-chairs) (28 February 1992) at 34–35 [Beaudoin-Dobbie]. Ultimately, the proposal to include property rights in the *Charter* did not find its way into the *Charlottetown Accord*.

34 See, for example, *Professional Institute v. NWT*, [1990] 2 S.C.R. 367 [*Professional Institute*] (holding that freedom of association does not protect the right to bargain collectively); *Retail, Wholesale and Department Store Union v. Saskatchewan*, [1987] 1 S.C.R. 460 [*R.W.D.S.U.*] (holding that freedom of association does not protect the right to strike). But see *Health Services and Support—Facilities Subsector Bargaining Assn. v. British Columbia*, [2007] 2 S.C.R. 391 [*Health Services Bargaining*] (overruling the earlier jurisprudence and holding that s. 2(d) of the *Charter* protects the rights of union members to bargain collectively). These cases are discussed in more detail in section C(5)(a) below.

35 Note, however, that some commentators have criticized decisions such as *R.W.D.S.U.*, above note 34, on the basis that they demonstrate that the courts are unsympathetic to the arguments of organized labour. Yet the effect of decisions such as *R.W.D.S.U.* is simply to leave the regulation of the right to strike or to bargain collectively to the legislature through ordinary statute. This would have been the result had the *Charter* never been enacted in the first place. Thus, the enactment of the *Charter* has neither prejudiced nor advanced the position of trade unions and organized labour in terms of the right to bargain collectively or to strike.

held to violate *Charter* rights,[36] the courts have often been prepared to uphold violations as a reasonable limit under section 1.[37] Furthermore, the *Charter* has been effectively utilized by such public interest groups as LEAF (the Women's Legal Education and Action Fund), the Canadian Civil Liberties Association, and other public interest organizations representing traditionally disadvantaged groups, to force reforms of discriminatory laws or practices.[38]

In fact, public interest organizations representing traditionally disadvantaged groups have been so successful in *Charter* cases that they have given rise to criticism that the Supreme Court has been captured by a "Court Party."[39] Morton and Knopff identify the "Court Party" as a cluster of liberal or progressive interest groups such as feminist, gay and lesbian, ethnic, and other identity-based groups that have successfully invoked the *Charter* to force changes in government policy. Morton and Knopff argue that this "*Charter* revolution" is undemocratic in that proposals and arguments that have been accepted by the courts had previously been rebuffed by Parliament and legislatures.[40]

36 Government welfare and benefit programs are subject to potential *Charter* attack through s. 15, on the basis that they deny the "equal benefit" of the law to recipients. However, the courts have generally been willing to defer to legislature choices in the design of welfare and benefit plans, absent a compelling justification for judicial intervention: see, for example, *McKinney v. University of Guelph*, [1990] 3 S.C.R. 229 [*McKinney*] (upholding mandatory retirement from s. 15 attack); *Law v. Canada (Minister of Employment and Immigration)*, [1999] 1 S.C.R. 497 [*Law*] (upholding Canada Pension Plan provisions imposing age requirements on recipients of survivor's pension); *Gosselin c. Québec (Procureur général)*, [2002] 4 S.C.R. 429 (upholding reductions in social assistance benefits for younger recipients). But see, *M. v. H.*, [1999] 2 S.C.R. 3 (striking down the definition of "spouse" in the Ontario *Family Law Act* on the basis that it excluded same-sex spouses).

37 Under s. 1, laws that violate a *Charter* right are nevertheless to be upheld, if they impose reasonable limits that can be demonstrably justified in a free and democratic society. As explained below, the courts have recognized a margin of appreciation in favour of the legislature in cases where a law involves the allocation of scarce resources or entitlements between competing groups; in these cases, the law will be upheld as long as it limits the *Charter* right "as little as reasonably possible": see *Edwards Books*, above note 31, upholding Ontario Sunday closing law.

38 See, for example, *Vriend v. Alberta*, [1998] 1 S.C.R. 493 [*Vriend*] (adding sexual orientation as a prohibited ground of discrimination in Alberta's human rights legislation); *M. v. H.*, note 36 above (striking down the definition of spouse in Ontario legislation on the basis that it excluded same-sex spouses).

39 See F.L. Morton & R. Knopff, *The Charter Revolution and the Court Party* (Peterborough, ON: Broadview Press, 2000).

40 For example, the Ontario legislature had previously defeated legislature proposals designed to extend the definition of "spouse" to include same-sex

However, it is important to place these claims of undemocratic judicial activism in context. First, the *Charter* was itself the product of a democratic process, in which it was clearly contemplated and understood that the judiciary would be assigned a much more prominent role in reviewing the substance of legislation.[41] The *Charter* was drafted with the express purpose of avoiding a deferential and restrained interpretation that had been given to the *Canadian Bill of Rights*.[42] Thus, in giving a robust interpretation to the *Charter*, the judiciary has responded to the conscious political choices that were made in 1980–82 rather than engaging in an unauthorized and illegitimate exercise in judicial law making. As Lamer J. noted in an early landmark *Charter* case:

> It ought not to be forgotten that the historic decision to entrench the *Charter* in our Constitution was taken not by the courts but by the elected representatives of the people of Canada. It was those representatives who extended the scope of constitutional adjudication and entrusted the courts with this new and onerous responsibility. Adjudication under the *Charter* must be approached free of any lingering doubts as to its legitimacy.[43]

It should also be noted that *Charter* adjudication and democratic values are not necessarily inconsistent. Democracy implies something more than simply majoritarian or popular rule. It requires a broadening of the opportunities for, and the scope of, collective deliberation and debate in a political community. Judicial review can reinforce democratic values by protecting existing opportunities and opening new avenues for democratic debate and dialogue.[44] As Iacobucci J. stated in *Vriend*, democracy requires that legislators

---

couples, prior to the Supreme Court decision in *M. v. H.*, above note 36, to the effect that a statutory definition that was limited to opposite-sex couples violated s. 15 of the *Charter*.

41 See, generally, P.W. Hogg, "The Charter Revolution: Is It Undemocratic?" McDonald Lecture in Constitutional Studies, University of Alberta, 22 March 2001.

42 See above note 22.

43 *Re Motor Vehicle Act (B.C.)*, [1985] 2 S.C.R. 486 at para. 15. Justice Lamer's claim is supported by the legislative history of the *Charter* which indicates that ss. 1 and 52 of the *Charter* were intended to give the judiciary a "mandate to review the substance of legislation for its conformity to human rights standards and to render legislation inconsistent with those standards of no force and effect": see A.F. Bayefsky, "The Judicial Function under the *Canadian Charter of Rights and Freedoms*" (1987) 32 McGill L.J. 791.

44 See, generally, P.J. Monahan, *Politics and the Constitution: The Charter, Federalism and the Supreme Court of Canada* (Toronto: Carswell, 1987) c. 6.

> take into account the interests of majorities and minorities alike, all of whom will be affected by the decisions they make. [Accordingly], [w]here the interests of a minority have been denied consideration, especially where that group has historically been the target of prejudice and discrimination . . . judicial intervention is warranted.[45]

A strong case can be made that judicial review under the *Charter* has enhanced, rather than undermined, democratic principles. The majority of *Charter* litigation involves a challenge to executive or police action, as opposed to the validity of a statute.[46] If the courts rule that a search of a suspect's home was carried out improperly, or that an individual who was arrested was denied his/her right to counsel, there has been no threat to the proper functioning of our democratically elected legislative institutions for the simple and obvious reason that the legislature did not authorize or carry out the particular activity that was the subject of constitutional challenge. Moreover, in cases where the courts find that government or police officials have engaged in activities that have violated an individual's rights, they have typically done so on the basis that the proper procedure was not followed. In such cases, the legislature can generally cure the procedural defect through the enactment of remedial legislation.[47]

Even in cases where statutory provisions have been struck down, Parliament and the legislatures have often enacted remedial legislation addressing procedural defects or unnecessarily broad intrusions on rights and freedoms that have been identified by the courts. For example:

- In *Hunter v. Southam*,[48] the Supreme Court struck down the search and seizure provisions in the *Combines Investigation Act* on grounds that there was no provision for prior independent review by a judicial officer

---

45 *Vriend*, above note 38 at 577, Iacobucci J.

46 See P.J. Monahan, "The Supreme Court of Canada's 1998 Constitutional Cases: The Debate over Judicial Activism Heats Up" (October 1999) 7 *Canada Watch* 69; J.B. Kelly, "The *Charter of Rights and Freedoms* and the Rebalancing of Liberal Constitutionalism in Canada, 1982–1997" (1997) 37 Osgoode Hall L.J. 625 at 654.

47 See, for example, *R. v. Feeney*, [1997] 2 S.C.R. 13, in which the Court held that a search warrant is required before police can enter a private residence to make an arrest. Within six months of the decision, Parliament amended the *Criminal Code* to establish a procedure for obtaining search warrants to enter residences and make arrests and in some cases to undertake a warrantless search. See *Criminal Code Amendment Act*, S.C. 1997, c. 39, s. 2 (adding ss. 529–529.5 to the *Criminal Code*). It should also be noted that Feeney himself was tried a second time following the Supreme Court decision overturning his first conviction. Even though the police were prevented from introducing the illegally obtained evidence, he was convicted at the second trial.

48 [1984] 2 S.C.R. 145.

of the appropriateness of the search. Parliament subsequently amended the legislation to provide that searches could not be conducted without the prior issuance of a search warrant approved by a judge.[49]

- In *R. v. Swain*,[50] the Supreme Court struck down provisions in the *Criminal Code* providing for automatic committal of persons acquitted for insanity. Soon after the decision, Parliament amended the *Criminal Code* to provide a procedure involving review boards and disposition hearings in such cases.[51]
- In *RJR-MacDonald v. Canada*,[52] the Supreme Court struck down the federal *Tobacco Products Control Act*, which contained a broad prohibition on advertising of cigarettes and other tobacco products. In response to the decision, the federal government enacted new legislation banning advertising of tobacco products but with more limited exceptions for certain types of advertising. In the 2007 decision of *Canada v. JTI-Macdonald Corp.*,[53] the Supreme Court upheld the new legislation, describing the Act as "more restrained and nuanced than its predecessor," which "represented a genuine attempt by Parliament to craft controls on advertising and promotion that would meet its objectives as well as the concerns expressed by the majority of this Court in *RJR*."[54]
- In *Charkaoui v. Canada (Citizenship and Immigration)*,[55] the Supreme Court struck down certain provisions of the *Immigration and Refugee Protection Act* that allowed federal ministers to issue certificates declaring foreign nationals and permanent residents inadmissible to Canada on grounds of security. A declaration led to a detention of the person named in the certificate. The scheme provided for a review of the certificate and detention by a judge of the Federal Court, but the person named on the certificate could be denied access to some or all of the information forming the basis for its issuance. The Court held that there were other less intrusive means to achieve the federal government's objective of protecting national security and related intelligence sources, including the use of special counsel to act on behalf

---

49 See *Competition Act*, S.C. 1986, c. 26, s. 124.

50 [1991] 1 S.C.R. 933.

51 See *Criminal Code*, S.C. 1991, c. 43, s. 672.12. For a helpful discussion of Parliament's response to this and other cases of judicial invalidation of search powers, see K. Roach, "Constitutional and Common Law Dialogues Between the Supreme Court and Canadian Legislatures" (2000) 80 Can. Bar Rev. 481.

52 [1995] 3 S.C.R. 199 [*RJR-Macdonald*].

53 *Canada (Attorney General) v. JTI-Macdonald Corp.*, [2007] 2 S.C.R. 610 [*JTI-Macdonald Corp*].

54 *Ibid.* at para. 7.

55 [2007] 1 S.C.R. 350 [*Charkaoui*].

of named persons. Following the decision, the federal government enacted Bill C-3,[56] which introduced a scheme for security-cleared special advocates modelled on the British system.[57] The new scheme was ultimately upheld as constitutional.[58]

- In *Dunmore v. Ontario*,[59] the Supreme Court struck down the exclusion of agricultural workers from the province's *Labour Relations Act*, which provides collective bargaining rights to employees. The Legislature responded with the *Agricultural Employees Protection Act*, which provided the particular bargaining rights identified in *Dunmore*, but declined to incorporate agricultural workers wholesale into the *Labour Relations Act*. A majority of the Court upheld the validity of the new scheme.[60]

Dean Peter Hogg and Allison Bushell, in their important and widely cited 1997 article on *Charter* dialogue,[61] argue that the potential anti-majoritarian character of judicial review under the *Charter* is mitigated by conceiving of judicial review as part of a dialogue between the courts and legislatures. Hogg and Bushell point out that judicial decisions striking down a law on *Charter* grounds have nearly always left room for an alternative or substitute law to be re-enacted in a form that accomplishes the objectives of the original invalid law.[62] After reviewing sixty-five

---

56 *An Act to amend the Immigration and Refugee Protection Act (certificate and special advocate) and to make a consequential amendment to another Act*, S.C. 2008, c. 3.

57 For criticisms of the federal government's legislative response, see: C. Forcese & L. Waldman, "A Bismarckian Moment: *Charkaoui* and Bill C-3" (2008) 42 Sup. Ct. L. Rev. (2d) 355; and K. Roach, "*Charkaoui* and Bill C-3: Some Implications for Anti-Terrorism Policy and Dialogue between Courts and Legislatures" (2008) 42 Sup. Ct. L. Rev. (2d) 281.

58 *Canada (Citizenship and Immigration) v. Harkat*, [2014] 2 S.C.R. 33.

59 [2001] 3 S.C.R. 1016.

60 *Ontario (Attorney General) v. Fraser*, [2011] 2 S.C.R. 3.

61 P.W. Hogg & A. Bushell, "The *Charter* Dialogue Between Courts and Legislatures" (1997) 35 Osgoode Hall L.J. 75.

62 The authors point to four features of judicial review under the *Charter* which in their view facilitate such a dialogue:

(i) s. 33 of the *Charter*, which permits legislative bodies to override the effect of a court decision in certain cases by inserting a notwithstanding clause in the impugned legislation;

(ii) the test in *Oakes*, above note 23, under s. 1 of the *Charter*, which requires the Court to evaluate possible alternatives to the impugned legislation (and which usually results in the Court suggesting a less restrictive measure which would satisfy the *Charter* concerns);

(iii) certain *Charter* rights, such as the guarantee against unreasonable search and seizure in s. 8, which are framed in qualified terms and which therefore usually admit of a corrective legislative response; and

different instances in which courts ruled legislation to be invalid due to conflict with the *Charter*, Hogg and Bushell found that subsequent legislative action of some kind occurred in fifty-three or 80 percent of the cases examined. This analysis has been updated by Hogg, Bushell Thornton, and Wright, who find that of twenty-three cases from the 1997–2006 period in which the Supreme Court of Canada had held a law to be invalid for breach of the *Charter*, the judicial decision had provoked a legislative response in fourteen or 61 percent of the cases.[63]

An indication of the influential nature of the Hogg and Bushell article is the fact that this dialogue theory was almost immediately adopted by the Supreme Court.[64] In *Vriend*, Iacobucci J., writing on behalf of eight of the nine members of the Court, referred with approval to the Hogg and Bushell article, stating that the "dynamic interaction among the branches of governance . . . has been aptly described as a 'dialogue.'"[65] Iacobucci J. pointed out that the *Charter* dialogue between courts and legislatures promotes accountability and enhances democratic values, since "[t]he work of the legislature is reviewed by the courts and the work of the court in its decisions can be reacted to by the legislature in

---

(iv) equality rights claims which, while requiring the legislature to accommodate an excluded individual or group, usually do not prevent the legislature from achieving its original goal provided it is prepared to extend the benefits of the law to the previously excluded class.

63 P.W. Hogg, A.A. Bushell Thornton, & W.K. Wright, "*Charter* Dialogue Revisited—'Or Much Ado about Metaphors'" (2007) 45 Osgoode Hall L.J. 1.

64 The Hogg & Bushell article, above note 61, has also provoked a vast body of academic commentary. Some of the more significant discussions include: C. Manfredi & J. Kelly, "Six Degrees of Dialogue: A Response to Hogg and Bushell" (1999) 37 Osgoode Hall L.J. 513; P.W. Hogg & A.A. Thornton, "Reply to 'Six Degrees of Dialogue'" (1999) 37 Osgoode Hall L.J. 529; K. Roach, *The Supreme Court on Trial: Judicial Activism or Democratic Dialogue*, rev ed (Toronto: Irwin Law, 2016); A. Petter, "Twenty Years of *Charter* Justification: Liberal Legalism to Dubious Dialogue" (2003) 52 U.N.B.L.J. 187; J. Waldron, "Some Models of Dialogue Between Judges and Legislators" (2004) 23 Sup. Ct. L. Rev. (2d) 7; K. Roach, "Dialogic Judicial Review and its Critics" (2004) 23 Sup. Ct. L. Rev. (2d) 49; C.P. Manfredi, "The Life of a Metaphor: Dialogue in the Supreme Court, 1998–2003" (2004) 23 Sup. Ct. L. Rev. (2d) 105; P.W. Hogg, A.A. Bushell Thornton, & W.K. Wright, *ibid.*, above note 63, and related commentary and reply at 67–91 and 193–202; K. Roach, "A Dialogue About Principle and a Principled Dialogue: Justice Iacobucci's Substantive Approach to Dialogue" (2007) 57 U.T.L.J. 449; and R. Dixon, "The Supreme Court of Canada, *Charter* Dialogue and Deference" (2009) 47 Osgoode Hall L.J. 235.

65 *Vriend*, above note 38 at para. 138.

the passing of new legislation (or even overarching laws under s. 33 of the *Charter*)."[66]

The Hogg and Bushell thesis reflects the reality that a court decision on a constitutional issue is rarely the final word on the matter. Nor should this conclusion come as a surprise, since it is entirely consistent with findings that have become widely accepted amongst scholars studying other fields of law. Indeed, the proposition that judicial decisions rarely determine the distribution of social, political, and economic entitlements in society was the key insight of Ronald Coase in his classic 1961 article "The Problem of Social Cost."[67] Coase demonstrated that individuals will seek to bargain around legal rules in order to achieve more efficient results. In the absence of transaction costs, parties will bargain to the efficient result regardless of the liability rule announced by the court.[68] What was radical about this thesis was the idea that a judicial determination of liability might not conclusively dictate the allocation of resources between parties.

The concept of governments, as opposed to private parties, bargaining around adverse court decisions may seem somewhat more applicable in the federalism context than in the context of *Charter* litigation. In federalism cases, a judicial finding of invalidity merely involves a determination that the wrong level of government has enacted a law, leaving the field open for a substitute law enacted by another government.[69] In *Charter* cases, a finding of invalidity precludes the enactment of a particular law by either level of government. However, what is common to both federalism and *Charter* cases is the phenomenon of substitution of alternative legislative and regulatory instruments for those ruled invalid by the courts. This substitution process occurs because governments, through control of the legislature, can enact a law that pursues the same objective but in a slightly different fashion.[70]

---

66 *Ibid*. at para. 139. As of the spring of 2016, Hogg & Bushell, above note 61, have been cited by the Supreme Court of Canada on eight occasions.

67 R. Coase, "The Problem of Social Cost" (1961) 3 J.L. & Econ. 1.

68 Of course, Coase also recognized that in the real world, transaction costs are always greater than zero, which means that parties will often fail to bargain to the efficient result.

69 Elsewhere, we have explored these questions in the context of federalism litigation. See P.J. Monahan, above note 44 at c. 10.

70 In this sense governments are in a better position than private parties who generally cannot cause the enactment of remedial legislation. Thus, private parties are generally forced to accept the law as declared by the courts. It is for this reason that they must resort to bargaining in order to achieve an efficient result, notwithstanding the liability rule announced by the court.

How is such substitution legally feasible in the face of a court ruling that a legislative measure offends the *Charter* and cannot be justified under section 1? In addition to the factors identified by Hogg and Bushell, common law decision making, including constitutional decision making, is particularistic rather than universal. Common law courts will generally only adjudicate in relation to a specific factual dispute, as opposed to offering generalized advice as to the scope of governmental regulatory authority.[71] What is legally binding on future courts and legislatures is the court-announced rule that was necessary in order to resolve the concrete factual dispute before the court.[72] In a constitutional case, the decision focuses on the validity and application of a particular statutory provision to a specific set of facts and parties. As such, the validity of alternative legislative mechanisms not before the court is generally not authoritatively determined.[73]

Further evidence of the force of the democratic-dialogue thesis is provided by the manner in which governments have restructured the policy process in order to take *Charter* rights into account. All of the federal and provincial governments now routinely subject policy proposals to a rigorous advance review to ensure consistency with the *Charter*. For example, the federal government initiated a process in 1991 requiring legal services staff in individual departments to review policy proposals at the earliest stage of policy development to identify and deal with potential *Charter* issues.[74] The policy proposal can then be tailored or fine-tuned to address *Charter* issues that may arise. Prior to a mat-

71 The exception, of course, is the Court's advisory function on a reference. However, only the Governor in Council has jurisdiction to order a reference and the Court retains the discretion to refuse to answer a question with an insufficient factual record or foundation, or where providing an answer would be inappropriate for other reasons. See *Reference Re Same-Sex Marriage*, [2004] 3 S.C.R. 698 at paras. 61–71; *Reference Re Secession of Quebec*, [1998] 2 S.C.R. 217 at paras. 25–26 and 105; *Reference Re Canada Assistance Plan*, [1991] 2 S.C.R. 525 at 545.

72 This is what is known as the *ratio decidendi* of the case: see *R. v. Henry*, [2005] 3 S.C.R. 609 at paras. 52–57; and *Quinn v. Leathem*, [1901] A.C. 495 at 506 (H.L.).

73 However, a decision may be relevant to the validity of alternative provisions, and, in some cases, courts may identify alternative and less intrusive legislative means to achieve the governmental objective. See, for example, *Charkaoui*, above note 55.

74 See P.J. Monahan & M. Finkelstein, eds., *The Impact of the* Charter *on the Public Policy Process* (Toronto: York University, 1993); J. Kelly, "Bureaucratic Activism and the *Charter of Rights and Freedoms*: The Department of Justice and its Entry into the Centre of Government" (1999) 42 Can. Pub. Admin. 476; M. Dawson, "Governing in a Rights Culture" (2001) 14 Sup. Ct. L. Rev. (2d) 251; L.R. Sterling, "The *Charter*'s Impact on the Legislative Process: Where the Real 'Dialogue' Takes Place" (2007 2008) 23 N.J.C.L. 139.

ter proceeding to Cabinet, the attorney general is required to certify that the proposal is consistent with the *Charter*. Far from frustrating or thwarting the policy development process, the early involvement of legal staff and attention to *Charter* analysis broadens and deepens the process. The legislative and executive branches, rather than the courts, remain in the policy driver's seat. The end result is that legislation is much more carefully tailored and balanced in order to take account of *Charter* values, and is also much more likely to survive *Charter* scrutiny in the courts. Kent Roach has rightly observed: "[T]he *Charter* has not taken away the ability of strongly committed elected governments to determine matters of public policy, albeit in a manner that recognizes limits on and derogations from rights."[75]

In summary, while the Supreme Court's performance under the *Charter* has certainly not been free of criticism, on balance it has been a significant success. The Court has given real meaning and substance to *Charter* rights. Governments contemplating legislation that limits individual rights and freedoms must now carefully consider whether those limits are consistent with the *Charter*.[76] Although courts have ensured that the *Charter* operates as a meaningful constraint on government policy-making, they have generally avoided usurping or eliminating the primary role of politicians in shaping Canada's political choices. The courts have been particularly active in the application of the *Charter* in relation to criminal law and procedure. Moreover, where statutes have been struck down, this has arguably enhanced the democratic process, by forcing governments to more carefully tailor their proposals to protect individual rights and freedoms. As Sharpe and Roach conclude, "[a]s interpreted by the courts to date, the *Charter* neither precludes nor entrenches particular socio-economic outcomes but rather enriches the democratic process."[77]

---

75 See Kelly, above note 74 at 505–6, who notes that the statutes that have been ruled invalid by the Supreme Court have tended to be laws that were enacted prior to the more rigorous screening process put in place in 1991.

76 Under the federal *Department of Justice Act*, R.S.C. 1985, c. J-2, s. 4.1, the Minister of Justice has an obligation to review draft regulations and statutes for compliance with the *Charter*, and report to Parliament of any non-compliance. There has never been such a report. In *Schmidt v. Canada (Attorney General)*, 2016 FC 269, the Federal Court interpreted the statute as requiring the Minister to report where "no credible argument could be advanced in support of the consistency with guaranteed rights of the proposed legislation" (para. 245).

77 See R.J. Sharpe & K. Roach, *The Charter of Rights and Freedoms*, 5th ed. (Toronto: Irwin Law, 2013) at 45.

C. THE *CHARTER*: AN OVERVIEW

1) The *Charter* Defined

The *Canadian Charter of Rights and Freedoms*, Part I of the *Constitution Act, 1982*, consists of sections 1 to 34. The *Charter* is included within the definition of the "Constitution of Canada" set out in section 52 of the 1982 Act. Therefore, it is part of the supreme law of Canada, and takes precedence over inconsistent federal or provincial laws. However, the *Charter* is separate and distinct from the guarantees of Indigenous rights set out in section 35 of the *Constitution Act*, *1982*. While there are certain similarities between the *Charter* and the guarantees of Indigenous rights in section 35, there are also important distinctions between the two categories of rights. Some of the key differences are highlighted below and in Chapter 14.

2) Application of the *Charter*

Section 32 of the *Charter* provides that the *Charter* applies to the "Parliament and government of Canada" and to the "legislatures and governments of the provinces." The reference to Parliament and the provincial legislatures means that the *Charter* applies to laws enacted by these bodies.[78] The references to "government" also indicate that the *Charter* applies to the executive or administrative branches of government.[79]

While the *Charter* applies to Parliament, the legislatures, and the executive or administrative branches, it does not apply to purely private activity. The effect of this rule is that *Charter* claims cannot be brought against private persons, unconnected with government, on the basis that they have violated the *Charter*.[80] In *Dolphin Delivery*,[81] McIntyre J. for a unanimous Supreme Court quoted with approval the following passage from Peter Hogg's text explaining the limits on the *Charter* in the following terms:

---

78 In addition to statutes, this would include legal enactments having the force of law, such as regulations, directives, or orders in council, which are created through statute. See *Eldridge v. B.C.*, [1997] 3 S.C.R. 624 [*Eldridge*].

79 *Retail, Wholesale and Department Store Union, Local 580 [R.W.D.S.U.] v. Dolphin Delivery Ltd.*, [1986] 2 S.C.R. 573 at para. 33 [*Dolphin Delivery*].

80 Note, however, that where government itself engages in commercial or private activity (for example, by the creation of Crown corporations that compete with privately owned entities), the activities of the Crown agent are subject to the *Charter*. See *Lavigne v. Ontario Public Service Employees Union*, [1991] 2 S.C.R. 211 at 314 [*Lavigne*].

81 Above note 79.

> The rights guaranteed by the *Charter* take effect only as restrictions on the power of government over the persons entitled to the rights. The *Charter* regulates the relations between government and private persons, but it does not regulate the relations between private persons and private persons. Private action is therefore excluded from the application of the *Charter*. Such actions as an employer restricting an employee's freedom of speech or assembly, a parent restricting the mobility of a child, or a landlord discriminating on the basis of race in his selection of tenants, cannot be breaches of the *Charter*, because in no case is there any action by the Parliament or government of Canada or by the Legislature or government of a province. In cases where private action results in a restriction of a civil liberty, there may be a remedy for the aggrieved person under a human rights code, under labour law, family law, tort law, contract law or property law, or under some other branch of the law governing relations between private persons; but there will be no breach of the *Charter*.[82]

Some commentators have criticized the decision to exclude purely private activity from *Charter* scrutiny.[83] It has been argued that the courts are a part of government such that the *Charter* should apply to disputes between private parties. However, the rule in *Dolphin Delivery* is consistent with the underlying purpose of section 32, which was designed to limit the impact of the *Charter* to the relationship between the state and individuals. The point was well-expressed by McIntyre J. in *Dolphin Delivery*, in which he agreed with the view of commentators that

> the *Charter*, like most written constitutions, was set up to regulate the relationship between the individual and the Government. It was intended to restrain government action and to protect the individual.

---

82 *Dolphin Delivery*, *ibid.* at para. 28, citing P.W. Hogg, *Constitutional Law of Canada*, 2d ed. (Toronto: Carswell, 1985) at 674–75. However, while the *Charter* does not apply to common law disputes between private individuals, the Supreme Court has repeatedly developed common law rules in a manner consistent with *Charter* values: see *Dolphin Delivery*; *R. v. Salituro*, [1991] 3 S.C.R. 654 at 666 and 675; *Hill v. Church of Scientology of Toronto*, [1995] 2 S.C.R. 1130 at 1169; *Retail, Wholesale and Department Store Union, Local 558 v. Pepsi-Cola Canada Beverages (West) Ltd.*, [2002] 1 S.C.R. 156; and *Grant v. Torstar Corp.*, [2009] 3 S.C.R. 640.

83 See A.C. Hutchinson & A. Petter, "Private Rights/Public Wrongs: The Liberal Lie of the *Charter*" (1988) 38 U.T.L.J. 278; D.M. Beatty, "Constitutional Conceits: The Coercive Authority of Courts" (1987) 37 U.T.L.J. 183; B. Slattery, "The *Charter*'s Relevance to Private Litigation: Does *Dolphin* Deliver?" (1987) 32 McGill L.J. 905.

> It was not intended in the absence of some governmental action to be applied in private litigation.[84]

Furthermore, the application of the *Charter* to purely private activity would vastly increase the role and power of the judiciary, since courts would be required to create a set of judge-made rules to ensure that private dealings between individuals were consistent with the requirements of the *Charter*.[85] It would also significantly constrain the jurisdiction of legislatures, since judicial codes of constitutional conduct would take precedence over ordinary statutes. If the *Charter* applied to private disputes, the only manner in which judge-made rules could be amended by government would be through the cumbersome device of constitutional amendment.[86] Therefore, there are compelling practical considerations supporting the Supreme Court's decision in *Dolphin Delivery*.

While the rule in *Dolphin Delivery* is analytically sound, it is often difficult to determine whether there is sufficient government involvement to trigger *Charter* scrutiny in a particular case. As discussed above, section 32 refers to Parliament, legislatures, and government. It is clear that government, for the purposes of section 32, includes the entire executive branch, including ministers, civil servants, and regulatory agencies appointed by government. Section 32 also refers to "all matters within the authority of" Parliament, the legislatures, and government. For this reason, the *Charter* extends to entities which are constituted through statute and exercise governmental power.[87] As Lamer J. explained in

---

84 *Dolphin Delivery*, above note 79 at para. 26.

85 See A.A. McLellan & B.P. Elman, "To Whom Does the *Charter* Apply? Some Recent Cases on Section 32" (1986) 24 Alta. L. Rev. 361.

86 In contrast, common law rules, which are also judge-made, are generally subject to amendment by ordinary statute. Common law rules are subject to being declared of no force and effect due to inconsistency with the *Charter* but only to the extent that such rules are applied in the context of litigation that involves government. The result is that if the common law is invoked in the context of purely private litigation, the relevant common law rule remains subject to amendment through ordinary statute.

87 On this basis municipalities have been held to be subject to *Charter* review. See *Ramsden v. Peterborough (City)*, [1993] 2 S.C.R. 1084; *Godbout v. Longueuil (City)*, [1997] 3 S.C.R. 844 [*Godbout*]; *Montréal (City) v. 2952-1366 Québec Inc.*, [2005] 3 S.C.R. 141; and *Greater Vancouver Transportation Authority v. Canadian Federation of Students—British Columbia Component*, [2009] 2 S.C.R. 295 at paras. 18–19 [*Greater Vancouver*]. A governmental power is a statutory power that involves a power of compulsion or regulation that is not available to natural persons. See *Blencoe v. B.C. (Human Rights Commission)*, [2000] 2 S.C.R. 307 at para. 36 [*Blencoe*] (adopting an argument advanced by Peter Hogg on this point). In *Eldridge*, above note 78, La Forest J. stated that the mere fact that an entity performed a public function does not mean it is part of government for

Godbout, were it otherwise, "the federal government and the provinces could easily shirk their *Charter* obligations by conferring certain of their powers on other entities and having those entities carry out what are, in reality, governmental activities or policies."[88]

The Supreme Court has established two distinct tests under section 32 for determining whether the *Charter* applies to a particular entity. The two tests were summarized by Deschamps J. in *Greater Vancouver* as follows:

> Thus, there are two ways to determine whether the *Charter* applies to an entity's activities: by enquiring into the nature of the entity or by enquiring into the nature of its activities. If the entity is found to be "government", either because of its very nature or because the government exercises substantial control over it, all its activities will be subject to the *Charter*. If an entity is not itself a government entity but nevertheless performs governmental activities, only those activities which can be said to be governmental in nature will be subject to the *Charter*.[89]

On the basis of the "control test," community colleges, which are subject to significant ministerial or governmental control, have been considered part of government for purposes of *Charter* review, even though they are not formally part of the executive branch of government.[90] Similarly, the Vancouver transit authority was held to be sufficiently controlled by the provincial government so as to attract *Charter* scrutiny.[91] By contrast, universities[92] and hospitals,[93] which have been said to enjoy a greater measure of institutional autonomy, were held not to constitute government for purposes of section 32 of the *Charter*.

The "governmental activities" test has its genesis in the Supreme Court of Canada's decision in *Eldridge*. In *Eldridge*, the Court held that if an act

---

purposes of this analysis. In addition, La Forest J. said at para. 43, the body in question must be implementing a "specific governmental policy or program." See further discussion of this point below in this section.

88 *Godbout*, above note 87 at para. 48.

89 *Greater Vancouver*, above note 87 at para. 16.

90 *Douglas/Kwantlen Faculty Assn. v. Douglas College*, [1990] 3 S.C.R. 570; and *Lavigne*, above note 80.

91 *Greater Vancouver*, above note 87.

92 *McKinney v. University of Guelph*, [1990] 3 S.C.R. 229; *Harrison v. University of British Columbia*, [1990] 3 S.C.R. 451.

93 *Stoffman v. Vancouver General Hospital*, [1990] 3 S.C.R. 483 [*Stoffman*]; and *Eldridge*, above note 78.

> is truly "governmental" in nature — for example, the implementation of a specific statutory scheme or a government program — the entity performing it will be subject to review under the *Charter* only in respect of that act, and not its other, private activities.[94]

In *Eldridge*, hospitals delivering medical services in accordance with a provincial statutory scheme failed to provide sign language interpretation for deaf persons. The relevant statutes were silent on the question of funding for sign language interpretation, and it would have been possible for hospitals to have funded the services out of their global budgets received from the provincial government.[95] The provincial government argued that the decision not to fund sign language interpretation was a decision of the hospitals rather than the government, and that the *Charter* did not apply.[96] However La Forest J., for a unanimous Court, rejected this argument. La Forest J. concluded that hospitals operated within the context of a "comprehensive social program" for the delivery of medically necessary services, with hospitals being the "vehicles the legislature has chosen to deliver this program."[97] There was, therefore, a "direct and . . . precisely-defined connection" between the failure to provide sign language interpretation and the medical service delivery system instituted by the legislation. The decision not to provide sign language interpretation was not a matter of "internal hospital management" but was, instead, an expression of government policy.[98]

In coming to this conclusion, La Forest J. distinguished the Supreme Court's earlier decision in *Stoffman*.[99] In *Stoffman*, the Supreme Court held that the imposition of a mandatory retirement scheme was made by a hospital board and was not a reflection of government policy. In *Eldridge*,[100] La Forest J. did not expressly overrule the conclusion in *Stoffman* that hospitals are autonomous from government. Nor did he

---

94 *Eldridge*, *ibid.* at para. 44.

95 Under the relevant statutes, hospitals were provided with a global budget, and were accorded significant discretion in determining how to allocate that budget, provided that they offered all services that were "medically required." The Medical Services Commission, a statutory body, determined which services were medically required but the commission had not designated sign language interpretation for the deaf as medically required, which meant that hospitals were not required (but were permitted) to provide such services.

96 This argument had been accepted by a majority of the B.C. Court of Appeal, which had dismissed the *Charter* challenge on this basis. See: (1995), 7 B.C.L.R. (3d) 156 (C.A.).

97 *Eldridge*, above note 78 at para. 50.

98 *Ibid.* at para. 51.

99 Above note 93.

100 Above note 78.

find that the specific decision with respect to funding of sign language interpretation was one made by the government itself.[101] Rather, La Forest J.'s conclusion in *Eldridge* was based on the fact that the delivery of medically necessary services was part of a comprehensive program that is *generally* defined and controlled by government. Therefore, decisions as to the specific services to be provided were necessarily subject to *Charter* review, even in cases where a particular decision might have been made by a non-government body, such as hospitals.[102]

The "governmental activities" test from the *Eldridge* case was invoked by a group of highly ranked female ski jumpers who brought a constitutional challenge against the Vancouver Organizing Committee for the 2010 Olympic Games (VANOC).[103] VANOC was an organizing committee responsible for planning, organizing, financing, and staging the 2010 Olympic Games. The applicants claimed that VANOC's failure to plan, organize, finance, and stage a ski-jumping event for women violated their equality rights under section 15(1) of the *Charter*. On appeal, the applicants conceded that VANOC was not part of government within the meaning of the "control test." However, they argued that the activity of selecting and staging male ski-jumping to the exclusion of female ski-jumping was a matter that came within the authority of government under section 32 of the *Charter*. In support of their claim, the applicants pointed to a multiparty agreement, the goal of which was to have Vancouver chosen as the host city for the 2010 Olympic Games.

---

101 The record indicated that sign language interpretation had previously been provided by a private, not-for-profit institute. This institute decided that it could no longer afford to continue providing this service. Prior to terminating the program, it applied to the government for funding, but the application was turned down. However, La Forest J. did not rely on this specific refusal as evidence that the decision not to fund sign language interpretation was made by government, and held that the delivery of medically necessary services in general is a government program that is subject to the *Charter*. Although the government had not required the service to be provided, it had not determined that the service was medically unnecessary.

102 The Medical Services Commission, a statutory body exercising a governmental function (defining "medically required services"), was a body whose decisions were subject to the *Charter* in accordance with existing jurisprudence. La Forest J. concluded, therefore, that the decision by the commission not to include sign language interpretation as a medically necessary service was subject to *Charter* review. However, he also held that, apart from the role of the commission, the *Charter* applied to decisions or actions of hospitals in the delivery of medical services. It is this aspect of his decision that is novel and of potential significance in future cases.

103 *Sagen v. Vancouver Organizing Committee for the 2010 Olympic and Paralympic Winter Games*, 2009 BCCA 522, leave to appeal to S.C.C. refused, [2009] S.C.C.A. No. 459 [*Sagen*].

The federal, provincial, and two levels of local government (Vancouver and Whistler) were party to the agreement. In a unanimous decision, the British Columbia Court of Appeal held that the *Charter* did not apply to VANOC's decision. While the government was party to the multiparty agreement, nothing in the agreement suggested that it was a governmental obligation or function to determine the slate of events for the Olympic Games. In fact, the evidence was clear that the decision regarding which games to host rested with the International Olympic Committee (IOC), an international body independent of all orders of Canadian government. Therefore, the decision not to add women's ski-jumping was not a "policy" choice that was made by a Canadian government and VANOC's staging of men's ski-jumping could not "reasonably be viewed as furthering any Canadian government policy or program."[104]

As discussed above, the *Charter* extends to entities that are constituted through statute and exercise governmental power.[105] The *Charter* may apply to executive or administrative bodies created by statute in one of two ways. First, the statute that created the statutory body (called the "enabling statute") may contain a provision that violates the *Charter*. Since the *Charter* applies to legislation, any such provision in the enabling statute, and any decisions that depend for their validity on the existence of the provision, will be invalid and of no force and effect in accordance with section 52 of the 1982 Act. Second, the *Charter* may apply where the enabling statute merely provides for a statutory discretion. While the statute itself may not offend the *Charter*, decisions of the statutory body may be subject to *Charter* scrutiny, either because the statutory body is exercising a governmental power,[106] or because it is implementing a specific government policy. In the event that the *Charter* applies, the courts will

---

104 *Ibid*. at para. 49.

105 A governmental power is a statutory power that involves a power of compulsion or regulation that is not available to natural persons. See *Blencoe*, above note 87 at para. 36 (adopting an argument advanced by Peter Hogg on this point). In *Eldridge*, above note 78, La Forest J. stated that the mere fact that an entity performed a public function does not mean it is part of government for purposes of this analysis. In addition, La Forest J. said at para. 43, the body in question must be implementing a "specific governmental policy or program."

106 See *Slaight Communications Inc. v. Davidson*, [1989] 1 S.C.R. 1038 [*Slaight*], in which the decisions of an arbitrator appointed pursuant to statute were held to be subject to the *Charter*. In *Slaight* itself, Lamer J. (as he then was), who wrote for the majority of the Court on this point, seemed to suggest that the decisions of the arbitrator were subject to *Charter* review merely because the arbitrator was appointed pursuant to statute. However, in *Eldridge*, above note 78, the Supreme Court clarified this point, and stated that the arbitrator in *Slaight* was subject to the *Charter* because he had been exercising governmental or coercive power.

require that the statutorily created body exercise its discretion in a manner consistent with the *Charter*. As a corollary rule, the mere fact that a body is constituted under a statute will not in itself make the decisions of that body subject to the *Charter*. For example, business corporations are constituted pursuant to statute, and such statutes define the nature and extent of their powers. However, since the decisions and actions of business corporations are generally controlled by private parties rather than the government, they are not subject to *Charter* scrutiny.[107]

3) Guarantee of and Limitations on Rights: Section 1

The drafters of the *Charter* wanted to ensure that courts would understand that rights are not absolute and that it is sometimes necessary to limit rights in order to advance or protect collective interests. The *Charter* therefore contains a general limitation clause providing that the rights and freedoms protected by the *Charter* can be limited in appropriate circumstances.[108] The primacy of the drafters' concern is reflected in the fact that the limitations clause actually precedes the enumeration of individual rights.[109]

Section 1 provides that the rights contained in the *Charter* are guaranteed "subject only to such reasonable limits prescribed by law as can be demonstrably justified in a free and democratic society."[110] As a result, *Charter* analysis proceeds in two distinct stages: first, the claimant must demonstrate that the impugned law or government action limits or violates a right protected by the *Charter*; second, the government must demonstrate that the limitation or violation can be justified under section 1. In each case, the standard of proof is the civil standard of a

---

107 See the discussion of this point in *Eldridge*, above note 78 at para. 35.

108 The use of a *general* limitations clause was innovative. The U.S. *Bill of Rights* does not contain any express limitations clause, while the *European Convention on Human Rights* (U.K.T.S. 1953, No. 71, 1 E.T.S. No. 5, 4 November 1950) includes specific limitations in the actual description of the enumerated rights and freedoms.

109 See, generally, J. Hiebert, "The Evolution of the Limitation Clause" (1990) 28 Osgoode Hall L.J. 103. As Hiebert explains, the concept of including a general limitation clause had first been introduced by the federal government in the *Victoria Charter* in 1971, in an attempt to allay provincial government concerns that constitutionally protecting individual rights would hobble provincial legislative jurisdiction.

110 The final version of s. 1 narrowed the scope of permissible limitations on rights, largely in response to trenchant criticism of the October 1980 version of s. 1. One of the most influential critics in terms of prompting changes to the wording of the limitations clause was Walter Tarnopolsky, then president of the Canadian Civil Liberties Association and later a justice of the Ontario Court of Appeal. See Hiebert, *ibid.* at 123–24.

balance of probabilities. However, the Supreme Court has held that the "preponderance of probability test must be applied rigorously."[111]

The legal framework for analysis under section 1 of the *Charter* is found in the historic decision of Dickson C.J. in *R. v. Oakes*.[112] In Dickson C.J.'s view, the text of section 1 indicated that limits on rights are exceptions to their general guarantee and that "the presumption is that the rights and freedoms are guaranteed unless the party invoking s. 1 can bring itself within the exceptional criteria which justify their being limited."[113] That is why government must prove that the limitation or violation of the right is justified under section 1 at the second stage of analysis. Dickson C.J. identified a normative standard to assess whether particular violations of rights could be justified under section 1. This normative standard was provided by the inclusion of the words "free and democratic society," which was the underlying purpose of the *Charter* as a whole. Accordingly, the courts should be guided by the underlying values and principles essential to a free and democratic society in determining whether limitations on rights are permissible under section 1. These essential underlying values include "respect for the inherent dignity of the human person, commitment to social justice and equality, accommodation of a wide variety of beliefs, respect for cultural and group identity, and faith in social and political institutions which enhance the participation of individuals and groups in society."[114] Dickson C.J. described these values as the "ultimate standard" for identifying permissible limitations on protected rights.

Dickson C.J. set out a four-part test for applying this ultimate standard in particular cases. This test can be summarized as follows:

1) Pressing and Substantial Objective — the objective of the law must be of "sufficient importance" to justify overriding a *Charter* right. Only an objective that is "pressing and substantial in a free and democratic society" qualifies as being of sufficient importance.

---

111 *Oakes*, above note 23 at para. 67.

112 Above note 23. Note that *Oakes* deals only with the "demonstrable justification" requirement of s. 1, which requires that a limit be "prescribed by law." This means that the limit must be provided for (either expressly or by implication) in a statute or a rule of common law: see *R. v. Therens*, [1985] 1 S.C.R. 613; *R. v. Thomsen*, [1988] 1 S.C.R. 640. For a discussion see R.J. Sharpe & K. Roach, *The Charter of Rights and Freedoms*, 3d ed. (Toronto: Irwin Law, 2005) c. 4.

113 *Oakes*, above note 23 at 137. In contrast, in federalism cases, there is sometimes said to be a "presumption of constitutionality" under which it is presumed that the legislature intended to enact laws that are *intra vires*: see J. Magnet, "The Presumption of Constitutionality" (1980) 18 Osgoode Hall L.J. 87.

114 *Oakes*, above note 23 at 136.

2) Rational Connection—the measures adopted must be "carefully designed" or "rationally connected" to the pressing and substantial objective.
3) Minimal Impairment—the law must impair the right as little as possible. This step involves a comparison of the impugned measure with other available alternatives, in order to assess whether the government could have achieved its objectives with a less significant impact on rights and freedoms.
4) Proportionality—there must be proportionality between the "salutary" and "deleterious" effects of the law. This step involves a consideration of whether the benefits achieved from the law outweigh its negative impact on rights.

The *Oakes* test has become the touchstone of judicial analysis under section 1 of the *Charter*. However, courts have generally ignored the ultimate standard principle which Dickson C.J. espoused in the first part of the decision.[115] The reason for this tendency is that the ultimate standard portion of the *Oakes* test is explicitly normative, referring to values essential to a free and democratic society, such as the inherent dignity of the human person and a commitment to social justice and equality. While powerful, these concepts are also extremely general and politically contested. They provide relatively weak guidance for courts, especially in close cases on the margins. Moreover, the promotion of values, such as democracy or social justice, is generally thought to be a matter for the legislature, rather than the courts. If the courts relied on these kinds of political concepts as the basis for upholding or striking down laws under section 1, the judiciary would be subject to criticism that it was substituting its judgment for that of the legislature.

As a result of these concerns, courts have largely ignored Dickson C.J.'s ultimate standard analysis and focused, instead, on the four-part test set out above. In fact, in cases where it has struck down a law or government action, the Supreme Court has traditionally relied on one particular element of that framework—minimal impairment. The reliance on the minimal impairment component of the *Oakes* test is not surprising. Minimal impairment is primarily concerned with the degree of fit between the objective and the means chosen to implement the objective. It asks whether the same objective could have been achieved through reliance on a more carefully tailored measure with less adverse impact on rights. In this way, it calls into question only the means chosen to

---

115 For an excellent analysis and overview of the use of the *Oakes* test, which makes this point among others, see L. Trakman, W. Cole-Hamilton, & S. Gatien, "*R. v. Oakes* 1986–1997: Back to the Drawing Board" (1998) 36 Osgoode Hall L.J. 83.

achieve a particular legislative objective, without impugning the validity of the underlying objective itself. In cases where legislation is ruled invalid on the basis of failure to satisfy the minimum impairment test, it is usually open to the legislature to pursue the same objective with different means. This ensures that legislatures and executives rather than courts retain the primary role in the public policy process, and reduces the potential for conflict between the various branches of government.[116]

While framed in rigorous terms, the elements of the *Oakes* test (and in particular, minimal impairment) were relaxed in subsequent cases. Just a few months after *Oakes* was released, the Supreme Court upheld Ontario's Sunday-closing legislation in *Edwards Books*.[117] Dickson C.J. noted that in *Oakes*, the Court had been careful to avoid "rigid and inflexible standards" under section 1 and stated that a limit on rights was permissible as long as it impaired the right "as little as is *reasonably* possible."[118] In *Irwin Toy*,[119] the Supreme Court in a decision written once again by Dickson C.J., suggested that a more deferential standard of review under section 1 should apply in cases where the legislature was "mediating between the competing claims of different groups."[120] Where the state was acting as a mediator between groups, it will inevitably be called upon to draw lines between competing claims without access to complete knowledge. Therefore, as long as the legislature has made a "reasonable assessment as to where the line is most properly drawn . . . it is not for the court to second guess."[121] In Dickson C.J.'s view, the legislature must be accorded a "margin of appreciation to form legitimate objectives based on somewhat inconclusive social science evidence."[122]

---

116 See the discussion in Hogg & Bushell, above note 61.

117 Above note 31.

118 *Ibid.* at 772 [emphasis added]. The adjective "reasonably" had been absent in the original formulation in *Oakes*, above note 23.

119 Above note 32.

120 *Ibid.* at para. 79. The Court distinguished such instances from those in which the state was the singular antagonist of an individual, in which case a rigorous s. 1 standard would continue to apply. But later cases indicated that the line between the mediating and the singular antagonist cases was not easy to draw, and that criminal statutes often involved a mediating role for the state. See, for example, *R. v. Butler*, [1992] 1 S.C.R. 452 [*Butler*], applying a deferential standard of review to the *Criminal Code* obscenity provisions.

121 *Irwin Toy*, above note 32 at para. 74.

122 *Ibid.* On the basis of this margin of appreciation, the Supreme Court in *Irwin Toy* upheld a provincial law banning most forms of commercial advertising aimed at children, defined as persons under thirteen years of age. The attorney general had filed a number of studies suggesting that at some point between the age of seven and adolescence children become as capable as adults in understanding and responding to advertising. However, these studies were inconclusive as to the exact age at which this occurs.

Moreover, courts were instructed to be mindful of the "legislature's representative function" and of the fact that "[d]emocratic institutions are meant to let us all share in the responsibility for these difficult choices."[123]

While the Supreme Court has continued to adhere to the four-part *Oakes* methodology, it has not always applied the framework in a uniform manner. In some cases, the Court appeared to adopt a very relaxed approach to the type of proof required of the government in order to justify a rights violation under section 1,[124] while in others it applied a much more exacting standard.[125] The inconsistency in the application of section 1 is due in part to the text of the enumerated rights and the way they have been interpreted by the Supreme Court. For instance, some rights are framed in relatively unqualified terms, while others have limiting language. For instance, fundamental rights and freedoms such as freedom of expression are framed very broadly. Furthermore, as discussed in Chapter 14, the Supreme Court has placed almost no limit on the definition of what constitutes "expression" for the purposes of section 2(b). As a result, it is typically an easy matter for claimants to demonstrate that section 2(b) has been infringed and in almost all cases the government must defend the limitation of freedom of expression under section 1. Other rights, such as the equality provisions in section 15, have been interpreted more narrowly, with the result that claims under section 15 are more likely to be dismissed at the first stage of analysis. Furthermore, some rights have internal limits that render the section 1 analysis wholly or partially redundant. For example, section 7 provides that everyone has the right to "life, liberty and security of the person and the right not to be deprived thereof except in accordance with the principles of fundamental justice." Similarly, section 8 protects everyone against the right to an "unreasonable" search and seizure and section 9 guarantees everyone the right not to be "arbitrarily" detained or imprisoned. Normative concepts such as the "principles of fundamental justice" and arbitrariness require courts to inquire into the same types of considerations mandated under section 1. For instance, the Supreme Court has held that it is a principle of fundamental justice that laws shall not be arbitrary. A law that de-

123 *Ibid.* at para. 79.

124 See *Alberta v. Hutterian Brethren of Wilson Colony*, [2009] 2 S.C.R. 567 [*Hutterian Brethren*] (photographs needed for driver's licences to avoid identity theft); *JTI-Macdonald Corp*, above note 53 (tobacco health warnings justified as compelled expression); *Harper v. Canada (Attorney General)*, [2004] 1 S.C.R. 827 (third party spending limits in elections).

125 See for example *R v. Nur*, [2015] 1 S.C.R. 773 (mandatory minimum for firearm offence not minimally impairing); *Canada (Attorney General) v. Bedford*, [2013] 3 S.C.R. 1101 [*Bedford*] (sex work provisions not minimally impairing); *R. v. Appulonappa*, [2015] 3 S.C.R. 754 (broad smuggling human prohibition not necessary).

prives people of the right to life, liberty, and security of the person in an arbitrary way will breach section 7. According to the Supreme Court, "[a] law is arbitrary 'where it bears no relation to, or is inconsistent with, the objective that lies behind [it].'"[126] It is difficult to see how such an arbitrary law could possibly pass the rational connection test under section 1. At one point, in *Chaoulli*, the Court questioned "whether an arbitrary provision, which . . . cannot further its stated objective, will ever meet the rational connection test under *R. v. Oakes*."[127] More recently, however, the Court has mused that sections 1 and 7 "ask different questions" and suggested that a section 7 "qualitative" rights violation may be justified by the "quantitative" logic of section 1.[128]

As discussed above, most section 1 cases have turned on the third stage of the *Oakes* test—minimal impairment. It has been suggested that the final stage of the *Oakes* test—proportionality between the salutary and deleterious effects—is redundant. Professor Hogg has argued that a finding that the law's objective is "pressing and substantial" will always produce a conclusion that its effects are proportionate. According to Hogg, the proportionality test "has no work to do, and can safely be ignored."[129] While Hogg's argument was carefully considered by the Supreme Court, it was ultimately rejected in *Alberta v. Hutterian Brethren of Wilson Colony*,[130] which placed newfound emphasis on the fourth and final branch of the *Oakes* test.

Since 1974, the province of Alberta required photographs on driver's licences, subject to discretionary exemptions for religious objectors. In 2003, the province instituted a universal photo requirement so that the photos could be included in a facial recognition data bank. The data bank was established in order to reduce the risk of identity theft in the province. In addition, the system was adopted to harmonize with national and international standards for photo identification and to assist with roadside identification and safety. In *Hutterian Brethren*, the Wilson Colony of the Hutterian Brethren challenged the universal photo requirement on the grounds that it violated their religious beliefs. The Hutterian Brethren believe that having their photos taken violates the Second Commandment, which prohibits idolatry. The Court unanimously held that the elimination of the photo exemption infringed the Colony's right

126 *Chaoulli*, above note 24 at para. 130.
127 *Ibid.* at para. 155.
128 *Bedford*, above note 125 at paras. 124–29.
129 P.W. Hogg, *Constitutional Law of Canada*, 5th ed., loose-leaf, vol. 2 (Toronto: Carswell, 2007) at s. 38.12.
130 *Hutterian Brethren*, above note 124.

to freedom of religion under section 2(a) of the *Charter*. A majority of the Court upheld the elimination of the exemption under section 1.

McLachlin C.J., for the majority, held that the legislative objective of preventing identity theft was pressing and substantial. In addition, the regulation satisfied the minimal impairment branch of the *Oakes* test. McLachlin C.J.'s reasoning on minimal impairment represented a significant departure from the Court's previous jurisprudence. Citing an article by the former President of the Israeli Supreme Court, she stated that both the rational connection test and the minimal impairment test are "essentially determined against the background of the proper objective, and are derived from the need to realize it."[131] Accordingly, the minimal impairment test requires "only that the government choose the least drastic means of *achieving its objective*" and "[l]ess drastic means which do not actually achieve the government's objective are not considered at this stage."[132] In previous cases, the Court had been willing to consider legislative alternatives that may have compromised achievement of the government's objective. However, in *Hutterian Brethren*, McLachlin C.J. held that only measures that "substantially satisfy the government's objective" should be analyzed.[133] She held that the universal photo requirement was the only way to reduce the risk of identity theft "as much as possible" and that the alternative of religious exemptions is "not appropriate for consideration at the minimal impairment stage."[134]

McLachlin C.J. rejected Hogg's argument that the proportionality test is redundant. She adopted President Barak's view that unlike rational connection and minimal impairment, "the test of proportionality . . . examines whether the realization" of the legislative objective "is commensurate with the deleterious effect upon the human right" and "requires placing colliding values and interests side by side and balancing them according to their weight."[135] According to McLachlin C.J.,

> [w]here no alternative means are reasonably capable of satisfying the government's objective, the real issue is whether the impact of the rights infringement is disproportionate to the likely benefits of the impugned law. Rather than reading down the government's objective

---

131 *Ibid.* at para. 54, citing A. Barak, "Proportional Effect: The Israeli Experience" (2007) 57 U.T.L.J. 369 at 374. For a careful critique of the Supreme Court of Canada's interpretation of President Barak's approach to proportionality, see S. Weinrib, "The Emergence of the Third Step of the *Oakes* Test in *Alberta v. Hutterian Brethren of Wilson Colony*" (2010) 68 U.T. Fac. L. Rev. 77.

132 *Hutterian Brethren*, above note 124 [emphasis in original].

133 *Ibid.* at paras. 59–61.

134 *Ibid.* at paras. 59–60.

135 *Ibid.* at para. 76, citing Barak, above note 131 at 374.

> within the minimal impairment analysis, the court should acknowledge that no less drastic means are available and proceed to the final stage of *Oakes*.[136]

McLachlin C.J. concluded that the salutary effects of the regulation outweighed the deleterious effects. Salutary effects of the photo requirement included enhancing the security of the driver's licensing scheme, as well as ensuring roadside safety and identification and harmonizing Alberta's licensing system with other jurisdictions. While the photo requirement would impose additional costs and inconvenience on the Hutterian Brethren, in McLachlin C.J.'s view, it would not deprive them of a meaningful choice regarding their religious practices. McLachlin C.J. suggested that the Hutterian Brethren could hire people with drivers' licences, or otherwise arrange third-party transportation.

Three judges wrote dissenting reasons.[137] Abella J. held that the province had failed to discharge its onus under section 1. With respect to minimal impairment, she held that there was insufficient evidence that the claimants' proposal of non-photo licences would significantly compromise the legislative objective. Like McLachlin C.J., Abella J. focused largely on the proportionality test. According to Abella J.:

> The minimal impairment stage should not . . . be seen to routinely end the s. 1 analysis. It is possible, for example, to have a law, which is not minimally impairing but may, on balance, given the importance of the government objective, be proportional. In my view, most of the heavy conceptual lifting and balancing ought to be done at the final step—proportionality. Proportionality is, after all, what s. 1 is about.[138]

In Abella J.'s view, the government had failed to demonstrate that the salutary effects of the universal photo requirement outweighed the deleterious effects. She found the salutary effects to be speculative, observing that there was no evidence that the long-standing photo exemption threatened the government's objective of preventing identity theft. In particular, adding 250 un-photographed Hutterites to the database would have had a marginal impact on preventing identity fraud given that there were 700,000 unlicensed Albertans in the province. On the other hand, the photo requirement was said to cause significant harm to the religious rights of the Hutterites.

---

136 *Ibid*.

137 Fish J. agreed with the reasons of LeBel J. and the disposition of the appeal proposed by Abella and LeBel JJ.

138 *Ibid*. at para. 149.

LeBel J. agreed with Abella J. that the photo requirement could not be justified under section 1. LeBel J. challenged the notion that the government's objective is "unassailable" and held that alternative means that do not fully achieve the legislative objective may be considered at the minimal impairment stage. LeBel J. stated that there was "more than a kernel of truth" to Professor Hogg's sentiment that section 1 litigation really revolves around minimal impairment.[139] However, LeBel J. cautioned against drawing "sharp analytical distinctions between the minimal impairment and balancing of effects parts of the *Oakes* test" and treated the final two stages of analysis together in his reasons.[140] According to LeBel J., "the overall objective of the s. 1 analysis remains constant: to preserve constitutional rights, by looking for a solution that will reach a better balance, even if it demands a more restricted understanding of the scope and efficacy of the objectives of the measure."[141] In the end, LeBel J. agreed with Abella J. that the government had failed to justify the regulation under section 1, either because it failed the minimal impairment branch, because it was disproportionate, or both:

> Other approaches to identity fraud might be devised that would fall within a reasonable range of options and that could establish a proper balance between the social and constitutional interests at stake. This balance cannot be obtained by belittling the impact of the measures on the beliefs and religious practices of the Hutterites and by asking them to rely on taxi drivers and truck rental services to operate their farms and to preserve their way of life. Absolute safety is probably impossible in a democratic society. A limited restriction on the Province's objective of minimizing identity theft would not unduly compromise this aspect of the security of Alberta residents and might lie within the range of reasonable and constitutional alternatives. Indeed, the Province's stated purpose is not set in stone and does not need to be achieved at all costs. The infringing measure was implemented in order to reach a hypothetical objective of minimizing identity theft, by requiring driver's licences with photos. But a small number of people carrying a driver's licence without a photo will not significantly compromise the safety of the residents of Alberta. On the other hand, under the impugned regulation, a small group of people is being made to carry a heavy burden. The photo requirement was not a proportionate limitation of the religious rights at stake.[142]

139 *Ibid.* at para. 191.
140 *Ibid.* at para. 192.
141 *Ibid.* at para. 195.
142 *Ibid.* at para. 201.

In our view, the shift in emphasis from means-based analysis to proportionality in *Hutterian Brethren* poses challenges for the courts. The proportionality test requires a "delicate balancing of competing societal interests" and "reflects the same kinds of broad policy questions more typically faced by lawmakers" than by courts.[143] As discussed above, it is for this very reason that the courts have previously focused on minimal impairment, which requires the court to consider the degree of fit between the legislative objective and the means chosen to achieve it. The proportionality test, by contrast, requires unelected judges to directly engage in value judgments regarding the relative importance of governmental objectives and the rights of particular individuals and groups. As Monahan and Yap argue:

> under the final, proportionality analysis of *Oakes*, the issue is essentially whether the legislature made a wise (or, conversely, an ill-informed) choice in enacting the impugned measure. There seems little reason to prefer the views of judges on such essentially political questions to those of legislators, since the judiciary can claim no special expertise in assessing the wisdom of political choices by legislatures and governments. It will thus be interesting to observe whether the emphasis placed on the final branch of the proportionality test in *Hutterian Brethren* is taken up in future cases, or whether the Court reverts to its traditional focus on minimal impairment as the linchpin of section 1 analysis.[144]

Furthermore, as the division of opinion in *Hutterian Brethren* makes clear, emphasis on the proportionality part of the *Oakes* test is likely to lead to considerable uncertainty.[145] While it may be argued that section 1 analysis is never completely predictable, the result in *Hutterian Brethren* illustrates the uncertainty engendered by resolving *Charter* claims by outright weighing of the salutary and deleterious effects of a particular law. The four majority judges and three dissenting judges reached diametrically opposed conclusions based on the relative importance they ascribed to the legislative objective of preventing identity fraud and the religious freedom of the Hutterites.

Some critics have argued that the Court's section 1 jurisprudence has become so unpredictable that the *Oakes* test should be abandoned

---

143 P.J. Monahan & J. Yap, "Constitutional Cases 2009: An Overview" (2010) 51 Sup. Ct. L. Rev. (2d) 3 at 13.

144 *Ibid*. at 14.

145 See D.M. McAllister, "Supreme Court *Charter* Decisions: 2008–2009 Highlights" (2009) 27 N.J.C.L. 13 at 42–43.

entirely.[146] However, in our view, *Charter* analysis in general and section 1 analysis in particular requires the courts to engage in difficult assessments of complicated legislation. As the Supreme Court noted in *Thomson Newspapers*,[147] section 1 requires the courts to consider such matters as the vulnerability of the group that the legislator seeks to protect, whether a particular public harm can be measured scientifically, and the nature of the activity which is limited by the legislative measure.[148] This reflects a contextual approach to *Charter* interpretation, which proceeds on the theory that "a particular right or freedom may have a different value depending on the context" and that it is necessary to "bring into sharp relief the aspect of the right or freedom which is truly at stake in the case as well as the relevant aspect of any values in competition with it."[149] Given the complex and multidimensional nature of the balancing required in *Charter* cases, it is impossible to safely predict the results in future cases. In this sense, the *Oakes* framework is less of a test than it is a methodology which lends a degree of structure and coherence to the courts' inquiry, without eliminating the need for the application of judgment. However, in our view, courts would be wise to focus on the means analysis rather than proportionality. As discussed above, means analysis reduces the likelihood of courts usurping

---

146 See C.D. Bredt & A.M. Dodek, "The Increasing Irrelevance of Section 1 of the *Charter*" (2001) 14 Sup. Ct. L. Rev. 175, who argue that the *Oakes* test has been so diluted by the Supreme Court that it should be abandoned entirely. Trakman *et al.*, above note 115, do not suggest that *Oakes* should be abandoned but argue for the development of a normative standard that will lend greater coherence to the decisions of the courts.

147 *Thomson Newspapers v. Can.* (A.G.), [1998] 1 S.C.R. 877 [*Thomson Newspapers*].

148 The Court suggested that these were contextual factors that supported deference to the legislature. Conversely, the absence of such factors militated in favour of a more exacting standard of review. In *Thomson Newspapers* itself, the majority found that legislation prohibiting the publication of poll results immediately prior to a federal election should be subject to a fairly rigorous scrutiny (since none of the contextual factors arguing in favour of deference was present) and struck down the prohibition on this basis.

149 See *Edmonton Journal v. Alta. (A.G.)*, [1989] 2 S.C.R. 1326 at 1355–56, Wilson J., concurring [*Edmonton Journal*]. *Edmonton Journal* is generally seen as providing the origins for the contextual approach, which the Supreme Court has now embraced in *Charter* interpretation generally. Under the contextual approach, there is a recognition that rights may have variable meanings depending on the socio-political context in which they are raised, and that it is necessary to consider the impact of various legal interpretations on the actual litigants before the court. For a helpful discussion, see S.M. Sugunasiri, "Contextualism: The Supreme Court's New Standard of Judicial Analysis and Accountability" (1999) 22 Dal. L.J. 126.

the role of elected legislatures by substituting judicial opinions on the wisdom of legislation for those of legislators.

4) The Override

A key compromise that secured the consent of most provinces for the enactment of the *Charter* at the constitutional conference held in November 1981 was inclusion of a provision permitting legislatures to override certain *Charter* rights through the enactment of ordinary legislation.[150] Section 33 of the *Charter* permits either Parliament or the provincial legislatures to declare that a statute shall operate notwithstanding sections 2 or 7 to 15 of the *Charter*. The inclusion of a notwithstanding clause immunizes the statute in question from a *Charter* challenge founded on any of those particular *Charter* provisions for a period of five years.[151] Moreover, there is no need for the legislature to specify which particular *Charter* right is being overridden, nor is the use of the override subject to judicial review on grounds that it is unreasonable or illegitimate in the circumstances.[152] However, section 33 cannot be utilized retroactively.[153]

The override has been used very rarely. The federal government has never used the override, and the only provinces that have done so are

150 Previous drafts of the *Charter* had not included an override, with the federal government arguing that the inclusion of a general limitations clause eliminated the need for an override. However, the federal government agreed to an override applicable to certain of the rights in the *Charter* at the constitutional conference in November 1981 to secure provincial agreement to the constitutional amendment package. The override was based on a provision in the *Canadian Bill of Rights*, above note 3, which had permitted Parliament to declare that a statute would operate notwithstanding the Bill.

151 The use of the override may be renewed for successive five-year periods by the legislature. Note, however, that the override cannot be used to override *Charter* rights other than those protected in ss. 2 and 7 to 15. Further, one of the purposes of including s. 28 in the *Charter* was to prevent use of the override in relation to gender equality rights under s. 15; this is thought to be the effect of the use of the phrase "notwithstanding anything in this *Charter*" in s. 28. However, this particular theory of the relationship between ss. 15, 28, and 33 has never been tested in the courts.

152 See *Ford*, above note 25. Note, however, that the use of the override must be express, rather than implied, and it must be set out in a statute.

153 *Ibid.*, striking down a provision in a Quebec statute that purported to give retroactive effect to a blanket override of the *Charter* in respect of all Quebec legislation. However, although the retroactive effect of the override was ruled invalid, the blanket use of the override was found to be permissible.

Saskatchewan,[154] Quebec,[155] and Alberta.[156] Moreover, when the Alberta government proposed in 1998 to use the override to shield legislation providing compensation to the victims of sterilization from *Charter* attack, it provoked a national outcry and the government was forced to withdraw the proposal.[157] The public response in this case illustrates the potential that the override has to provide for a useful and constructive debate over the protection of individual rights.

There is reason to believe that such debates will lead to a deeper and more mature appreciation of the need to balance individual rights against

154 In 1986, the Saskatchewan legislature used s. 33 to foreclose a constitutional challenge to legislation ending a government employees' strike. The override turned out to be unnecessary when the Supreme Court later ruled that the right to strike was not protected by the *Charter*: see *R.W.D.S.U.*, above note 34.

155 In June 1982, the Quebec National Assembly repealed and re-enacted all existing statutes, inserting into all of its laws a blanket s. 33 override. It also automatically inserted an override into all new statutes. This use of the override was approved by the Supreme Court in *Ford*, above note 25. With the defeat of the Parti Québécois government by the Liberals under Robert Bourassa in 1985, the government ceased the practice of automatically inserting an override into new statutes, and the blanket use of the override was permitted to lapse at the end of its five-year term in 1987. However, following the Supreme Court decision in *Ford*—which also found that a total ban on the use of English on commercial signs was inconsistent with the *Charter*—the National Assembly enacted a new signs law and protected that legislation with a new five-year override. This was a key factor in the unpopularity of the *Meech Lake Accord* outside of Quebec and its eventual defeat. See P.J. Monahan, *Meech Lake: The Inside Story* (Toronto: University of Toronto Press, 1991).

156 In 2000, Alberta amended the *Marriage Act*, R.S.A. 1980, c. M-6 to define "marriage" as a marriage between a man and a woman, and provided that the statute was to operate notwithstanding ss. 2 and 7 to 15 of the *Charter*: see S.A. 2000, c. 3. This amendment was enacted following the Supreme Court's decision in *M v. H.*, above note 36, ruling that Ontario legislation which defined "spouse" by reference to persons of the opposite sex was inconsistent with s. 15 of the *Charter*. Note, however, that "Marriage and Divorce" is a matter of exclusive federal jurisdiction under s. 91(26) of the *Constitution Act, 1867*. On 26 July 2005, the federal *Civil Marriage Act*, S.C. 2005, c. 33 received Royal Assent. The *Civil Marriage Act* defines marriage for civil purposes as the "lawful union of two persons to the exclusion of all others," thereby permitting same-sex marriages. The Supreme Court of Canada held that the draft version of the Act was constitutionally valid and consistent with the *Charter*: see *Reference Re Same-Sex Marriage*, [2004] 3 S.C.R. 698.

157 Note also that when the Supreme Court in *Vriend*, above note 38, struck down provisions of Alberta's *Individual Rights Protection Act* on grounds that it failed to include a prohibition on discrimination on the ground of sexual orientation, there was a vigorous debate in the province on whether the decision should be overturned through use of s. 33. Premier Ralph Klein decided not to use the override and to accept the Supreme Court ruling.

collective concerns within society more generally. As Peter Russell has observed, there is value in subjecting fundamental questions to a wide public discussion, so that "the politically active citizenry participate in and share responsibility for the outcome."[158] Critics of the override argue that it is most likely to be used in an oppressive manner to impose very serious burdens on unpopular minorities.[159] Far from imposing a political cost on the government, the use of the override may well produce political gains, at least in the short term, it is argued. Such critics argue that this is precisely the kind of oppression of minorities by majorities that the enactment of the *Charter* was designed to prevent.

From time to time there have been proposals to restrict the use of the override. In 1991, the federal government proposed that section 33 should be available only if at least 60 percent of all members of a legislature voted in favour of it.[160] However, the Special Joint Committee of the Senate and House of Commons, which held extensive hearings on the government's 1991 constitutional proposals, reported that there was no consensus on the desirability of this change, and recommended further study.[161] In the result, the *Charlottetown Accord*, which was agreed to unanimously by federal, provincial, and territorial governments as well as Indigenous leaders in August 1992, did not include any proposed amendment to section 33. During the televised leaders' debate in the January 2006 federal election campaign, then Prime Minister Paul Martin proposed the enactment of legislation providing that section 33 would never be utilized by the federal Parliament. Since this would have been an ordinary federal statute passed pursuant to section 44 of the *Constitution Act, 1982* and not a direct amendment of section 33 itself,[162] it would have been subject to repeal by a subsequent Parliament. However, it would have increased the political cost associated with the use of the notwithstanding clause. Martin's proposal was criticized by the other party leaders and following the defeat of the Martin government in the election of 23 January 2006, it was abandoned.

---

158 See P. Russell, "Standing up for Notwithstanding" (1991) 29 Alta. L. Rev. 293.

159 See, for example, J. Whyte, "On Not Standing for Notwithstanding" (1990) 28 Alta. L. Rev. 347.

160 See *Shaping Canada's Future*, above note 33 at 4.

161 See Beaudoin-Dobbie, above note 33, and the discussion in Chapter 5.

162 A direct amendment to s. 33 would require a constitutional amendment supported by the federal houses as well as by seven provinces representing at least 50 percent of the provincial populations, under s. 38 of the *Constitution Act, 1982*. Mr. Martin was proposing unilateral action by Parliament through legislation; on this basis he could not have amended s. 33 directly even with respect to Parliament's powers in relation to the notwithstanding clause.

While the override is likely to continue to prove controversial, experience with the notwithstanding clause thus far indicates that the fears of the critics may have been overstated. The drafters of the *Charter* assumed that the override should be utilized rarely, if at all. This assumption has been reflected in practice; the federal government and over two-thirds of the provinces have never used the override. Moreover, in the relatively few cases where governments have contemplated invoking the override, this has provoked heated and principled debates in the legislature as well as the broader political community. In some of these cases, the political controversy was sufficient to persuade the government concerned to refrain from using the override. These kinds of debates positively reinforce and strengthen the Canadian commitment to the protection of rights and freedoms.

Another advantage of the override is that it serves as a check on judicial power, ensuring that the legislature has a mechanism to trump an exceptional judicial decision that imposes unacceptably high and inappropriate costs on the Canadian community. This reflects a belief in the fallibility of judicial institutions, and provides for a check and balance on decisions of the courts. The existence of such checks and balances is generally wise in the design of governmental institutions, since it protects a society against making large mistakes. On balance, therefore, there is evidence to suggest that the override has made a positive contribution to the *Charter* and that it should be retained.

D. CONCLUSION

It is clear that the enactment of the *Charter* represents one of the most significant political developments in Canada in the twentieth century. The courts now routinely review a wide variety of legislative enactments which, prior to 1982, would have been regarded as wholly outside the province of the judiciary. This new and expanded judicial role is not surprising. The drafters of the *Charter* envisaged and intended that the *Charter* operate as a constraint on the ability of legislatures to interfere with individual rights and freedoms. These constitutional constraints can only be given real meaning if the courts are prepared to review the complex and value-laden decisions of legislatures and governments, so as to ensure that concerns about individual rights are taken seriously. In exercising these new responsibilities, Canadian courts have, for the most part, escaped the kinds of controversies that have surrounded the constitutional role of the U.S. Supreme Court. In part, this has been a result of the fact that the Supreme Court of Canada has carefully balanced competing interests in difficult cases, so as to arrive at compromise results which seem broadly acceptable to most elements of the public as well as to most governments.

FURTHER READINGS

BAKAN, J., *Just Words: Constitutional Rights and Social Wrongs* (Toronto: University of Toronto Press, 1997)

HOGG, P.W., *Constitutional Law of Canada*, loose-leaf (Toronto: Carswell, 2007) cc. 34–39, 42–57

HOGG, P.W., & A. BUSHELL, "The *Charter* Dialogue Between Courts and Legislatures" (1997) 35 Osgoode Hall L.J. 75

HOGG, P.W., A. BUSHELL THORNTON, & W. WRIGHT, "*Charter* Dialogue Revisited—'Or Much Ado About Metaphors'" (2007) 45 Osgoode Hall L.J. 1

HUTCHINSON, A.C., *Waiting for CORAF: A Critique of Law and Rights* (Toronto: University of Toronto Press, 1995)

KELLY, J.B., "The *Charter of Rights and Freedoms* and the Rebalancing of Liberal Constitutionalism in Canada" (1997) 37 Osgoode Hall L.J. 625

MAGNET, J., "The Presumption of Constitutionality" (1980) 18 Osgoode Hall L.J. 87

MANDEL, M., *The* Charter of Rights *and the Legalization of Politics in Canada*, rev. ed. (Toronto: Thompson Educational Publishing, 1994)

MORTON, F.L., & R. KNOPFF, *The* Charter *Revolution and the Court Party* (Peterborough, ON: Broadview Press, 2000)

PENNER, R., "The Canadian Experience with the *Charter of Rights*: Are There Lessons for the United Kingdom?" (1996) P.L. 104

ROACH, K., *The Supreme Court on Trial: Judicial Activism or Democratic Dialogue*, rev ed (Toronto: Irwin Law, 2016)

SHARPE, R.J., & K. Roach, *The Charter of Rights and Freedoms*, 5th ed. (Toronto: Irwin Law, 2013)

TRAKMAN, L., W. COLE-HAMILTON, & S. GATIEN, "*R. v. Oakes* 1986–1997: Back to the Drawing Board" (1998) 36 Osgoode Hall L.J. 83

CHAPTER 14

RIGHTS AND FREEDOMS OF THE *CHARTER*

The rights protected by the *Charter* are grouped into six categories: fundamental freedoms, democratic rights, mobility rights, equality rights, and language rights. This chapter provides an overview of how the Supreme Court has interpreted each category since the enactment of the *Charter*. This period has seen relative consistency in some areas, such as freedom of religion, and continual jurisprudential tweaking in others, such as equality rights.

A. FUNDAMENTAL FREEDOMS

The fundamental freedoms portion of the *Charter* is contained in section 2, which protects freedom of conscience and religion (section 2(a)), freedom of expression and the press (section 2(b)), freedom of peaceful assembly (section 2(c)), and freedom of association (section 2(d)).

1) Freedom of Religion

The starting point and leading case on freedom of religion is *R. v. Big M Drug Mart*.[1] In *Big M*, the Supreme Court struck down the federal *Lord's Day Act* as a violation of freedom of conscience and religion. Dickson C.J.'s decision in *Big M* is one of the most frequently cited by later courts

1 *R. v. Big M Drug Mart*, [1985] 1 S.C.R. 295 [*Big M*].

for its holding that *Charter* rights should receive a purposive interpretation. The purposive approach requires that the underlying purpose of a *Charter* right be ascertained by reference to the larger objects of the *Charter* as a whole, to the language chosen to articulate the specific right or freedom, and to the historical origins of the concepts enshrined. According to Dickson C.J., this purposive method will be "generous rather than . . . legalistic," and it will be aimed at "securing for individuals the full benefit of the *Charter*'s protection."[2] Dickson C.J. identified the purpose of section 2(a) as being to ensure that any individual is "free to hold and manifest whatever beliefs and opinions his or her conscience dictates, provided *inter alia* only that such manifestations do not injure his or her neighbours or their parallel rights to hold and manifest beliefs and opinions of their own."[3] Dickson C.J. concluded that the purpose of the *Lord's Day Act* was to compel observance with the Christian Sabbath, and that the legislation was therefore unconstitutional.

In *Edwards Books*,[4] the Court held that the Ontario *Retail Business Holidays Act* violated the right to freedom of religion. The purpose of the Act was secular; the legislation was intended to provide a common day of rest for retail workers. However, the Court held that the *effect* of the legislation imposed a burden on retailers who observed Sabbath on a day other than Sunday, which thereby infringed freedom of religion under section 2(a). The legislation was upheld under section 1 of the *Charter* on the basis that a common day of rest for retail workers justified the limitation on freedom of religion.

Section 2(a) has been held to protect a wide variety of religious beliefs and practices. The Supreme Court has endorsed a broad and subjective view of freedom of religion, which looks to the genuine religious beliefs and practices of an individual, without regard to whether a particular practice or belief is required by official religious dogma or is in conformity with the position of religious officials. For instance, in *Syndicat Northcrest v. Amselem*,[5] the Court held that Orthodox Jews could construct a succah (a temporary structure on their apartment balconies) in order to observe a religious festival, even though they had signed contracts prohibiting construction on their balconies and had been offered an alternative communal succah on a common site. There was expert evidence before the Court that Orthodox Jews were under no obligation to build their own succahs. However, the majority held that the claimants were required to show only that their practice was part of a sincere belief that

2 *Ibid.* at para. 117.
3 *Ibid.* at para. 123.
4 *R. v. Edwards Books and Art Ltd.*, [1986] 2 S.C.R. 713 [*Edwards Books*].
5 [2004] 2 S.C.R. 551.

was "of religious significance" *to them*, regardless of whether it was part of an established belief system that was shared by others. Similarly, in *Multani v. Commission scolaire Marguerite-Bourgeoys*,[6] the Supreme Court held that a thirteen-year-old Sikh boy was permitted to wear a kirpan (a metal dagger in a sheath) to school and that the school's statutorily authorized code of conduct prohibiting weapons violated his right to freedom of religion.[7] In order to prove that the school's code of conduct infringed his rights under section 2(a), the boy was required to show only "that his personal and subjective belief in the religious significance of the kirpan is sincere."[8] As discussed in Chapter 13, in *Hutterian Brethren*,[9] the Supreme Court held that a colony of the Hutterian Brethren had demonstrated a sincere religious belief that prohibited them being photographed for the purpose of obtaining driver's licences in Alberta.[10]

2) Freedom of Expression

Section 2(b) of the *Charter* guarantees everyone "freedom of thought, belief, opinion and expression, including freedom of the press and other media of communication." The Supreme Court has identified three broad purposes underlying the right to freedom of expression: (1) democratic discourse; (2) truth-finding; and (3) individual self-fulfilment.[11] The Supreme Court has defined freedom of expression in the broadest possible terms. The word "expression" has been held to cover any activity that "attempts to convey meaning,"[12] except violence.[13] The Court has refrained from scrutinizing the content of expression under section 2(b), preferring instead to recognize all limitations on expression as *prima facie* violations of section 2(b). As a result of the expansive definition of "expression" and the inclusion of "individual self-fulfilment" as a purpose worthy of *Charter* protection, almost all claims under section

---

6 [2006] 1 S.C.R. 256.

7 The majority held that the school was required to permit the student to wear the kirpan but that it be kept in a wooden sheath and sewn into the student's clothing so that it could not be easily removed.

8 *Ibid.* at para. 37.

9 *Alberta v. Hutterian Brethren of Wilson Colony*, [2009] 2 S.C.R. 567 [*Hutterian Brethren*].

10 However, the law was upheld under s. 1.

11 *Irwin Toy Ltd. v. Quebec (Attorney General)*, [1989] 1 S.C.R. 927 at 976 [*Irwin Toy*]; *Montreal (City) v. 2952-1366 Que.*, [2005] 3 S.C.R. 141 at para. 74.

12 *Reference Re ss. 193 and 195.1(1)(c) of Criminal Code (Man.)*, [1990] 1 S.C.R. 1123 at 1187 [*Prostitution Reference*].

13 *Irwin Toy*, above note 11 at 927 and 970; *R. v. Keegstra*, [1990] 3 S.C.R. 697 at 731 [*Keegstra*].

2(b) will be made out at the first stage of the analysis, and it will fall to the government to justify the limitation under section 1. For instance, the right to freedom of expression has been held to encompass possession of child pornography,[14] dissemination of hate propaganda,[15] communication for the purpose of prostitution,[16] and publication of defamatory libel.[17] However, in each of these cases, *Criminal Code* provisions prohibiting such activities were upheld (in whole or in part) under section 1.

The Supreme Court's "content-neutral" approach to section 2(b) has been criticized as overly expansive. The Court has held that many forms of expression are worthy of constitutional protection that seem to have a tenuous connection with the purpose of section 2(b). This catch-all approach to section 2(b) is arguably inconsistent with Dickson C.J.'s admonition in *Big M* that "[t]he meaning of a right or freedom guaranteed by the *Charter* [is] to be ascertained by an analysis of the *purpose* of such a guarantee" and is to be "understood, in other words, in the light of the interests it was meant to protect."[18] As Dickson C.J. stated, it is important to interpret rights generously, but "not to overshoot the actual purpose of the right or freedom in question."[19] It is arguable that certain forms of expression such as the promotion of racial hatred, or the possession of child pornography were not meant to be protected under section 2(b). While laws limiting such forms of expression may nonetheless be upheld under section 1, the expansive scope of section 2(b) has tended to lead to a more relaxed and subjective section 1 analysis in freedom of expression cases. Both courts and commentators have expressed the concern that the broad scope of section 2(b) has led to a concomitant relaxation of the standard of justification under section 1.[20] Indeed, the Supreme Court has acknowledged that "low value of the expression" will be "more easily outweighed by the government objective" of the infringing legislation.[21]

3) Freedom of Association

Section 2(d) guarantees everyone the fundamental freedom of association. Freedom of association cases under section 2(d) have arisen relatively infrequently before the Supreme Court of Canada. During the first

---

14 *R. v. Sharpe*, [2001] 1 S.C.R. 45.

15 *Keegstra*, above note 13.

16 *Prostitution Reference*, above note 12.

17 *R. v. Lucas*, [1998] 1 S.C.R. 439 [*Lucas*].

18 *Big M*, above note 1 at para. 116 [emphasis added].

19 *Ibid.* at para. 117.

20 *Lucas*, above note 17 at para. 115, McLachlin J., dissenting.

21 *Thomson Newspapers Co. v. Canada (Attorney General)*, [1998] 1 S.C.R. 877 at para. 91 [*Thomson Newspapers*].

two decades of the *Charter*, the Court was largely unreceptive to such claims. The Court initially held that freedom of association does not include the right to bargain collectively or to go on strike,[22] nor does it protect a non-unionized employee from being required to contribute dues to a union and have those dues applied for political purposes.[23] The Supreme Court has also upheld a Quebec scheme that requires construction workers to join a union in order to obtain work on construction projects in the province.[24]

Early cases excluded activities such as collective bargaining and the right to strike from the ambit of section 2(d) on the basis that freedom of association was an individual, rather than a collective right. However, the Court has slowly reversed this position, starting with *Dunmore v. Ontario (Attorney General)*.[25] In *Dunmore*, the Court relied on section 2(d) to strike down legislation that excluded agricultural workers from Ontario's statutory regime governing collective bargaining. The Court took a more robust view of the guarantee in section 2(d), holding that it imposed a positive duty on the legislature to extend statutory protection to a group of workers that lacked the means to form an association to protect its interests. Bastarache J., for the majority, stated that some collective activities should be protected by section 2(d), because they were "central to freedom of association even though they are inconceivable on the individual level."[26]

After *Dunmore*, the Supreme Court continued the reversion of its prior jurisprudence and held that collective bargaining by unions is protected by section 2(d). In *Health Services Bargaining*,[27] the Court held that section 2(d) "protects the capacity of members of labour unions to engage, in association, in collective bargaining on fundamental workplace issues"; in other words, to join together to pursue common goals of negotiating workplace conditions and terms of employment with their employer.[28] The Court struck down provisions of B.C.'s *Health and Social Services*

---

22 *Reference Re Public Service Employee Relations Act (Alta.)*, [1987] 1 S.C.R. 313; *PSAC v. Canada*, [1987] 1 S.C.R. 424; *Retail, Wholesale and Department Store Union v. Saskatchewan*, [1987] 1 S.C.R. 460 [*R.W.D.S.U.*]; *Professional Institute of the Public Service of Canada v. Northwest Territories (Commissioner)*, [1997] 2 S.C.R. 367.

23 *Lavigne v. Ontario Public Service Employees Union*, [1991] 2 S.C.R. 211 [*Lavigne*].

24 *R. v. Advance Cutting & Coring Ltd*, [2001] 3 S.C.R. 209 [*Advance Cutting*]. Note, however, that a majority of the Court in *Advance Cutting* affirmed that s. 2(d) of the *Charter* includes a right not to associate and that the legislative scheme violated that right.

25 [2001] 3 S.C.R. 1016 [*Dunmore*].

26 *Ibid*. at para. 17.

27 *Health Services and Support – Facilities Subsector Bargaining Assn. v. British Columbia*, [2007] 2 S.C.R. 391 [*Health Services Bargaining*].

28 *Ibid*. at paras. 2, 38, and 92.

Delivery Improvement Act, which provided for, among other things, the contracting out of health services, laying off of employees, and the restriction of bumping options of laid-off employees. The Act conflicted with and expressly stated that it was to take precedence over existing collective agreements. However, the Court held that the statute interfered with the rights of union members to bargain collectively. While the Court characterized the right to collective bargaining as a "procedural right," the effect of the Court's decision was that the "fruits of" the collective bargaining process—the provisions of existing collective agreements—took precedence over the legislation. While recognizing the right to collective bargaining, the majority did not recognize the right to strike, stating only that "the present case does not concern the right to strike, which was considered in earlier litigation."[29]

The Court then retreated in part from its position in *Health Services Bargaining* in a decision released just four years later. In *Ontario (Attorney General) v. Fraser*,[30] a majority of the Court upheld the Ontario *Agricultural Employees Protection Act, 2002*.[31] The legislation was enacted in response to *Dunmore*, which had held that the previous legislative scheme was invalid. The *AEPA* legislation granted farm workers the right to form and join an employees' association, to participate in its activities, to assemble, to make representations to their employers on terms and conditions of employment, and the right to be protected against interference, coercion, and discrimination in the exercise of their rights. The statute required that the employer must give an association the opportunity to make representations regarding the terms and conditions of employment. The employer must listen to the representations or read them. In addition, the statute provided for a tribunal to hear and decide disputes under the Act. The legislation was challenged on the basis that it infringed farm workers' rights under sections 2(d) and 15 of the *Charter* by failing to provide for the right to organize and bargain collectively under the full terms of Ontario's labour relations statute.

The constitutional challenge to *AEPA* was dismissed by eight of nine judges of a divided Court, which issued a total of four different sets of reasons.[32] The majority, led by McLachlin C.J. and LeBel J., re-

---

29 *Ibid*. at para. 19.

30 [2011] 2 S.C.R. 3 [*Fraser*].

31 S.O. 2002, c. 16 [*AEPA*].

32 McLachlin C.J. and LeBel J. wrote reasons that were concurred in by Binnie, Fish, and Cromwell JJ. Rothstein J. (with whom Charron J. concurred) concurred in the result but for different reasons. Deschamps J. wrote separate reasons concurring in the result. Finally, Abella J. dissented and would have struck down the legislation.

fused to overrule *Health Services Bargaining*. According to the majority, *Health Services Bargaining* remained good law and the legislature was required to protect the rights of farm workers to bargain collectively. While affirming *Health Services Bargaining*, the majority afforded considerable latitude to governments to satisfy this right. The majority stressed that section 2(d) does not impose a particular process, a particular model of labour relations, or a specific bargaining method. All that is required is a "meaningful process" for employer and employees to meet and bargain in good faith in the pursuit of peaceful and productive accommodation. The *AEPA* satisfied the constitutional right of farm workers under section 2(d). While the Act did not expressly require employers to consider employee representations in good faith, the majority held that it included this requirement "by implication." In essence, the majority "read in" a requirement that employers consider employee representations in good faith. Rothstein J. (who was joined by Charron J.) concurred in the result, but would have expressly overruled the *Health Services Bargaining* case.

Despite the retreat of *Fraser*, four years later the Court pushed further into the subject of collective bargaining, again over the objections of Justice Rothstein. In the 2015 labour "trilogy" (a moniker reminiscent of the 1987 trilogy with the opposite holding), a 5:2 majority of the Court expanded again the scope of section 2(d) to include the right to strike, or to a binding dispute resolution process in the absence of such ability.[33] In another case, a 6:1 majority held that the inability of Royal Canadian Mounted Police officers to form a union and collectively bargain infringed section 2(d).[34] However, in the third case, the Court held that a one-time cancellation of a collectively bargained wage increase in the face of fiscal crisis did not run afoul of freedom of association.[35]

The five post-*Dunmore* decisions, issued over the course of seven years, suggest that the constitutionalization of labour law in Canada is now the status quo. Where a statute or executive action "substantially interferes with the right to a meaningful process of collective bargaining," the Court will intervene.[36] Despite the Court's insistence that section 2(d) does not enshrine a particular process, the result is that labour relations policy, a complex social and economic area which past Supreme Court judges declined to enter into, is now subject to judicial supervision. In our view, it is questionable whether courts have the institutional

---

33 *Saskatchewan Federation of Labour v. Saskatchewan*, [2015] 1 S.C.R. 245.

34 *Mounted Police Association of Ontario v. Canada (Attorney General)*, [2015] 1 S.C.R. 3 [*Mounted Police*].

35 *Meredith v. Canada (Attorney General)*, [2015] 1 S.C.R. 125.

36 *Mounted Police*, above note 34 at paras. 67–68.

expertise required to effectively carry out this role. It remains to be seen whether the Court will further clarify its jurisprudence in this area.

B. DEMOCRATIC RIGHTS

The second category of *Charter* rights is democratic rights, comprised of sections 3 to 5 of the *Charter*. These provisions guarantee citizens of Canada the right to vote in federal and provincial elections (section 3), require elections every five years (section 4), and require that Parliament and the provincial legislatures sit at least once each year (section 5). There has been relatively little litigation surrounding these provisions that has reached the Supreme Court. In *Sauvé v. Canada (Attorney General)*,[37] the Supreme Court held that a provision of the *Canada Elections Act* denying prison inmates the right to vote violated section 3 of the *Charter*.[38] Lower courts have ruled that similar provisions prohibiting the mentally incompetent,[39] federally appointed judges,[40] and citizens absent from Canada[41] are unconstitutional. The Ontario Court of Appeal (by a 2:1 majority, with a powerful dissent by Laskin J.A.) upheld provisions of the *Canada Elections Act*[42] denying the right to vote to citizens residing outside of Canada for more than five years as a reasonable and justifiable limit of section 3.[43]

The Supreme Court has held that section 3 is intended to guarantee every citizen effective representation in the House of Commons. On this basis, the Court struck down a requirement in federal legislation that had the effect of providing advantages to larger political parties.[44] However, the Court has rejected constitutional challenges to legislative provisions that permit wide disparities in the numbers of electors in each

---

37 [1993] 2 S.C.R. 438.

38 Parliament subsequently amended the federal elections legislation so that only persons serving sentences of two years or more are disqualified from voting. This amended two-year rule was subsequently challenged, with the Supreme Court ruling that it, too, was unconstitutional. See *Sauvé v. Canada (Chief Electoral Officer)*, [2002] 3 S.C.R. 519. In the result, all prison inmates have the right to vote.

39 *Canada Disability Rights Council v. Canada*, [1988] 3 F.C. 622 (T.D.).

40 *Muldoon v. Canada*, [1988] 3 F.C. 628 (T.D.).

41 *Hoogbruin v. British Columbia (Attorney General)* (1985), 24 D.L.R. (4th) 718 (B.C.C.A.).

42 S.C. 2000, c. 9.

43 *Frank v. Canada (Attorney General)*, 2015 ONCA 536, leave to appeal to S.C.C. granted, [2015] S.C.C.A. 396.

44 *Figueroa v. Canada (Attorney General)*, [2003] 1 S.C.R. 912.

electoral constituency on the basis that such disparities provide more "effective representation" for sparsely populated regions of the country.[45]

C. MOBILITY RIGHTS

The third category of *Charter* rights is mobility rights in section 6. Every "citizen" of Canada has the right to enter, remain in, and leave Canada (section 6(1)). Citizens and permanent residents also have the right to move to and take up residence in any province and pursue the gaining of a livelihood there (section 6(2)); however, the latter rights are subject to a number of limitations, including laws or practices of general application in a province that do not discriminate primarily on the basis of present or previous residence (section 6(3)). Provincial restrictions on interprovincial law firms have been ruled unconstitutional as a violation of mobility rights, leading to the emergence of national law firms.[46] The Supreme Court has also held that the protection of section 6 extends beyond mere physical movement from one province to another and protects attempts by an individual to create wealth in another province, such as through the sale of goods, or the offering of services in a province by a resident of another province. Furthermore, the process of extraditing a Canadian citizen to stand trial in another country engages section 6, although such infringements have been justified under section 1.[47]

The Supreme Court has limited the scope of section 6(2) by ruling that only provincial laws whose primary purpose or pith and substance is to discriminate against out of province residents will be found to be contrary to section 6(2).[48] Further, section 6 does not grant citizens or permanent residents a freestanding right to work in a province; it only applies in circumstances where a law restricts interprovincial mobility, such as when a provincial law prevents a non-resident from moving to a province and being employed there.[49] In general terms, section 6 has

45 See *Reference Re Provincial Electoral Boundaries (Sask.)*, [1991] 2 S.C.R. 158 (upholding disparities of up to 25 percent in the riding populations in a province). In contrast, the U.S. Supreme Court has embraced a rule of one person/one vote under which the voting power of each person's vote must carry roughly equal weight, which rules out the wide disparities that have been permitted in Canada.

46 See *Black v. Law Society of Alberta*, [1989] 1 S.C.R. 591. The law firm at issue in *Black* was McCarthy & McCarthy (now McCarthy Tétrault LLP).

47 *United States of America v. Cotroni*, [1989] 1 S.C.R. 1469; *United States v. Burns*, [2001] 1 S.C.R. 283; *Lake v. Canada (Minister of Justice)*, [2008] 1 S.C.R. 761.

48 See *Canadian Egg Marketing Agency v. Richardson*, [1998] 3 S.C.R. 157.

49 See *Law Society of Upper Canada v. Skapinker*, [1984] 1 S.C.R. 357.

had very limited impact on the extent to which provincial laws impose barriers to the interprovincial movement of people, goods, or services.[50]

D. LEGAL RIGHTS

The fourth category of *Charter* rights is legal rights protected by sections 7 to 14. Section 7 protects the right to "life, liberty and security of the person" and the right not to be deprived thereof, except in accordance with the principles of fundamental justice, while sections 8 to 14 are primarily focused on rights in the criminal law process, including the right against unreasonable search and seizure (section 8), the right to counsel upon an arrest or detention (section 10(b)), the right to be tried within a reasonable time (section 11(b)), and the right to be presumed innocent until proven guilty in a fair and public hearing (section 11(d)). These legal rights provisions have been the most frequently litigated *Charter* provisions before the Supreme Court, but typically in the context of police conduct instead of legislation.

The structure of section 7 claims mirrors the provision's text: first, the applicant must establish that the impugned law deprives her of her life, liberty, or security of the person, and second, that this deprivation is contrary to the principles of fundamental justice. The Supreme Court has recognized relatively few principles of fundamental justice under this section, which is appropriate given that any law that may result in imprisonment will be measured against the entire collection of such principles. To be recognized, a principle must be (1) a legal principle; (2) there must be societal consensus that it is fundamental to the way in which a legal system should operate; and (3) it must be identified with sufficient precision to yield a manageable standard against which to measure deprivations.[51]

Many of the recognized principles relate to traditional fair trial rights in the criminal process, such as the right to make full answer and defence and the right to silence.[52] However, the Supreme Court held only three years into the *Charter* era that despite ample evidence that the drafters intended to provide only procedural protections, fundamental justice also includes substantive principles, such as the

---

50 It should be noted that in 1994, the governments of Canada, the ten provinces, and two territories signed an Agreement on Internal Trade, designed to enhance the free movement of goods, services, and investment. See the discussion in Chapter 9.

51 *R. v. Malmo-Levine*, [2003] 3 S.C.R. 571.

52 *R. v. Stinchcombe*, [1991] 3 S.C.R. 326; *R. v. Hebert*, [1990] 2 S.C.R. 15.

requirement of *mens rea* for criminal offences.[53] Later substantive principles recognized in the criminal law realm included the presumption of diminished moral culpability for young offenders, and the principle that one cannot be convicted for a "morally involuntary" act.[54]

The most interest in recent years has been in the "instrumentalist" principles prohibiting arbitrariness, overbreadth, and gross disproportionality in those laws that engage the first step of section 7. These principles are similar to principles engaged by the *Oakes* analysis under section 1, in that they examine the relationship between the impugned provisions and the legislative objective. As with the analysis under section 1, there is a considerable degree of judgment involved.

Section 7 has a history of being the source of some of the most significant and controversial *Charter* decisions to date.[55] For example, in 1988, Dr. Henry Morgentaler relied on section 7 to persuade the Court to strike down *Criminal Code* provisions restricting a woman's right to obtain an abortion.[56] Section 7 was successfully invoked to require that an oral hearing be provided to all refugee claimants.[57] In the landmark 2005 *Chaoulli* case, the Supreme Court struck down prohibitions on the sale of private medical insurance on the basis that they created excessive wait times in the public health system, leading to a violation of the rights protected by section 7.[58] In *Canada (Attorney General) v. PHS Community Services Society*,[59] the Court held that the Minister of Health's refusal to provide an exemption from the drug possession provisions under the *Controlled Drugs and Substances Act* violated the section 7 rights of clients of a safe injection site in Vancouver. In *Carter v. Canada (Attorney General)*,[60] the Supreme Court overruled its prior decision in *Rodriguez v. British Columbia*,[61] striking down provisions of the *Criminal Code* that have the effect of prohibiting physician-assisted suicide. The Court held

53 *Re B.C. Motor Vehicle Act*, [1985] 2 S.C.R. 486.

54 *R. v. D.B.*, [2008] 2 S.C.R. 3; *R. v. Ruzic*, [2001] 1 S.C.R. 687.

55 For a detailed consideration of the s. 7 jurisprudence, see H. Stewart, *Fundamental Justice: Section 7 of the Canadian Charter of Rights and Freedoms* (Toronto: Irwin Law, 2012).

56 *R. v. Morgentaler*, [1988] 1 S.C.R. 30 [*Morgentaler*]. An attempt by the federal government to enact a substitute law that would have re-criminalized abortion in certain circumstances was defeated in the Senate in 1991 on a tie vote. No further attempt has been made to enact criminal prohibitions, with the result that the *Criminal Code* does not currently impose any restrictions on the availability of abortion.

57 *Singh v. Canada (Minister of Employment and Immigration)*, [1985] 1 S.C.R. 177.

58 *Chaoulli v. Quebec (Attorney General)*, [2005] 1 S.C.R. 791 [*Chaoulli*].

59 [2011] 3 S.C.R. 134.

60 [2015] 1 S.C.R. 331 [*Carter*].

61 [1993] 3 S.C.R. 519.

that physician-assisted death is permissible for competent adults who: (1) clearly consent to the termination of life; and (2) have a grievous and irremediable medical condition that causes enduring suffering that is intolerable to the individual in the circumstances of their condition.[62]

By contrast, section 7 arguments failed in challenges brought by Joseph Borowski on behalf of unborn foetuses,[63] a former provincial Cabinet minister to a human rights proceeding on grounds of excessive delay,[64] parents of a Jehovah's Witness child to refuse medically necessary blood transfusions,[65] and a poverty lawyer who contested a tax on legal services.[66] The Supreme Court has also ruled that "liberty" in section 7 does not include purely economic rights such as freedom of contract.[67]

Section 7 also played an important role in the constitutional debates concerning national security legislation that took centre stage in the decade after the September 11, 2001, terrorist attacks. Anti-terrorism laws are often seen as distinct from the traditional criminal process and therefore not subject to the same protections. For example, in *Charkaoui v. Canada (Citizenship and Immigration)*,[68] the federal government argued that the section 7 liberty interest was not engaged by "administrative" detention under provisions of the *Immigration and Refugee Protection Act*,[69] as compared to detention for criminal offences. The Supreme Court disagreed and held that detention pursuant to the provisions at issue required a minimum standard of due process.

---

62 Following the decision, the federal government introduced legislation to amend the *Criminal Code* and other enactments to comply with the Supreme Court's decision in *Carter*: *An Act to amend the Criminal Code and to make related amendments to other Acts (medical assistance in dying)*, S.C. 2016, c. 3. The Act received royal assent on 17 June 2016.

63 *Borowski v. Canada (Attorney General)*, [1989] 1 S.C.R. 342. The Court ruled that the case was moot, since Borowski was challenging the same provisions of the *Criminal Code* that had already been ruled unconstitutional in *Morgentaler*, above note 56.

64 *Blencoe v. B.C. (Human Rights Commission)*, [2000] 2 S.C.R. 307.

65 *A.C. v. Manitoba (Director of Child and Family Services)*, [2009] 2 S.C.R. 181.

66 *British Columbia (Attorney General) v. Christie*, [2007] 1 S.C.R. 873.

67 *Irwin Toy*, above note 11; *A & L Investments Ltd. v. Ontario (Ministry of Housing)* (1997), 36 O.R. (3d) 127 (C.A.), (holding that retroactive rent control legislation did not infringe landlords' s. 7 rights); *Clitheroe v. Hydro One Inc.*, 2010 ONCA 458 (holding that retroactive reduction in a pension does not engage s. 7); *Gosselin c. Québec (Procureur général)*, [2002] 4 S.C.R. 429 (holding that s. 7 does not guarantee welfare rights.) However in *Gosselin*, the Supreme Court left open the possibility that a right to basic subsistence rights might at some point in the future be incorporated in s. 7.

68 [2007] 1 S.C.R. 350 [*Charkaoui*].

69 S.C. 2001, c. 27.

In *Canada (Justice) v. Khadr*,[70] the Supreme Court held that the federal government was required to disclose transcripts of interviews of Omar Khadr taken by CSIS and the Department of Foreign Affairs and International Trade during his detention in Guantanamo Bay. Subsequently, the Supreme Court held that the Canadian government's refusal to repatriate Mr. Khadr to Canada violated his rights to liberty and security of the person.[71] Both cases attracted significant media attention.

As discussed above, in *Charkaoui*,[72] the Supreme Court struck down provisions of the certificate scheme in the *Immigration and Refugee Protection Act*. The certificate scheme was found to be inconsistent with the principles of fundamental justice since it denied persons the right to a fair hearing, including the "opportunity to know the case to meet, and an opportunity to meet the case."[73] After an unprecedented closed hearing pursuant to the Act, which was held at a secret location, the Supreme Court upheld a modified regime, which provided for the adversarial process of "special advocates" (security-cleared lawyers not permitted to disclose confidential information to their clients) arguing in closed hearings against the issuance of such certificates.[74]

Similarly, in *R. v. Ahmad*,[75] the Supreme Court upheld provisions of the *Canada Evidence Act* that provide federal attorneys general and judges of the Federal Court with the authority to restrict disclosure to the accused in a criminal trial before provincial Superior Courts on the basis that the disclosure contains potentially injurious or sensitive government information. The accused in *Ahmad* were charged with offences relating to a suspected plot to commit terrorist acts in Toronto.

E. EQUALITY RIGHTS

The fifth category of *Charter* rights is equality rights, protected by sections 15 and 28. Section 15 was carefully drafted so as to signal to the courts that narrow interpretations of equality that had been applied in relation to the *Canadian Bill of Rights* were not to be followed under the *Charter*.[76] Section 15 also includes language stating that the guarantee of equality does not prevent governments from enacting so-called affirma-

70 [2008] 2 S.C.R. 125.
71 *Canada (Prime Minister) v. Khadr*, [2010] 1 S.C.R. 44.
72 Above note 68.
73 *Ibid.* at para. 61.
74 *Canada (Citizenship and Immigration) v. Harkat*, [2014] 2 S.C.R. 33.
75 [2011] 1 S.C.R. 110 [*Ahmad*].
76 See discussion in Chapter 13, Section A.

tive action laws designed to ameliorate the conditions of traditionally disadvantaged individuals or groups (section 15(2)), and a separate provision was also included with a view to preventing the use of the section 33 override to shield laws that are discriminatory on grounds of sex.[77]

Equality is a comparative concept. In a legal context, it involves a consideration of legislative distinctions that impose burdens or disadvantages on various categories or groups of persons.[78] Equality cases concern whether such distinctions can be justified, by reference to differences in the needs, circumstances, or abilities of the persons affected by legislation. Moreover, the differences in needs, circumstances, or abilities must be *relevant*, in the sense that they are regarded as justifying the imposition of differential treatment in law. For example, in determining whether to impose a harsher sentence on one of two individuals convicted of the identical crime of assault, the fact that two accused committed the assaults on a different day of the week would not be regarded as a relevant difference, since it does not tell us anything about the relative blameworthiness of the conduct, which is the relevant criteria for imposing penalties under the criminal law. Therefore, were a law to impose a different penalty for the crime of assault based on the day of the week that the offence was committed, the differential treatment would be inconsistent with the principle of equality. In other words, there must be a fit or congruence between the distinctions or categories established by a law, and some relevant differences in the needs, circumstances or abilities of persons that are subject to that law. The essence of the idea of equality is captured by Aristotle's formulation to the effect that "things that are alike should be treated alike, while things that are unalike should be treated unalike in proportion to their unalikeness."[79]

---

77 See s. 28, which provides that "notwithstanding anything in this *Charter*, the rights and freedoms referred to in it are guaranteed equally to male and female persons."

78 It is not just the making of legislative distinctions, but also the failure to make appropriate or relevant distinctions, that can give rise to an equality rights claim. That is, where a law treats two individuals identically, but where the needs and circumstances of those individuals are materially different such that differential treatment is more appropriate, it is possible to challenge a law on the basis that it fails to accord that differential treatment. This point has been emphasized repeatedly not only in academic commentaries but by the Supreme Court itself: see *Andrews v. Law Society of British Columbia*, [1989] 1 S.C.R. 143 at 164–65 [*Andrews*].

79 Aristotle, *Ethica Nichomacea*, trans. W. Ross, Book V3 at 1131a-6, cited by McIntyre J. in *Andrews*, above note 78 at para. 27. As discussed below, the Supreme Court in *Andrews* expressly rejected this similarly situated test on the grounds that it ostensibly prevented any consideration of the substance of laws. However, McIntyre J.'s discussion of the Aristotelian view of equality seemed to proceed on a mistaken understanding of the nature of the analysis, since Aristotle clearly

A potential difficulty arising from the inclusion of section 15(1) in the *Charter* was the possibility that virtually all laws would be subject to challenge on the basis of violation of equality rights. This is because virtually all laws make distinctions between categories or groups of individuals.[80] Thus, in a broad sense, any legislative distinction could give rise to a violation of equality on the basis that the distinction was not sufficiently linked to relevant differences between the persons affected by it. The Supreme Court made it clear that this methodology was not to be applied in relation to section 15 in its first equality rights decision in *Andrews v. Law Society of British Columbia*.[81] In *Andrews*, McIntyre J. held that section 15(1) required a consideration of substantive equality, as opposed to the purely formal question of whether a law is applied equally.[82] Furthermore, he held that only particular types of distinctions in legislation could be subject to constitutional challenge on the basis of section 15(1). McIntyre J. held that only laws that imposed burdens or disadvantages based on grounds that were expressly enumerated in section 15(1),[83] or on grounds analogous to those enumerated,[84] could

contemplated the necessity of examining the substance of laws. See, generally, D. Gibson, *The Law of the Charter: Equality Rights* (Toronto: Carswell, 1990) at 70–81.

80 For example, a law making it an offence to commit a robbery distinguishes between those who commit robberies and those who do not.

81 Above note 78.

82 A test of formal equality, under which the courts merely inquired as to whether a law was being administered in accordance with its terms, had dominated the equality jurisprudence under the *Canadian Bill of Rights*. McIntyre J. was right to reject this test of formal equality, since it fails to take account of whether the substance of the law itself is consistent with equal treatment. However, McIntyre J. also argued that a test of formal equality was somehow a product or result of the similarly situated test, which is generally associated with the writings of Aristotle. According to McIntyre J., the similarly situated test was deficient because it could be used to uphold the Nuremberg laws of Hitler, since similar treatment was contemplated for all Jews. With respect, this misunderstands the nature of Aristotle's writing or of the similarly situated test; a proper application of Aristotle's framework would have led to the condemnation of the Nuremberg laws, since the differential treatment contemplated for Jews as distinct from non-Jews could not be justified by reference to any relevant differences between them: see J. Tussman & J. tenBroek, "The Equal Protection of Laws" (1949) 37 Cal. L. Rev. 341.

83 The enumerated grounds in s. 15 are race, national or ethnic origin, colour, religion, sex, age, and mental or physical disability.

84 McIntyre J. did not give a definition of those grounds that were to be regarded as analogous to the expressly enumerated grounds in s. 15. However, he found that citizenship was an analogous ground based on the claim that non-citizens were a "discrete and insular minority," citing the famous "footnote 4" in the 1938 decision of the U.S. Supreme Court in *United States v. Carolene Products*, 304 U.S. 144 (1938). In this footnote, Justice Stone had argued that "prejudice

give rise to a section 15(1) claim. Finally, he held that merely imposing differential treatment on enumerated or analogous grounds will not necessarily result in a violation of section 15(1); in addition, the law must be discriminatory.

A corollary of the focus on substantive equality and discrimination—as opposed to mere formal equality—is that section 15(1) may be infringed where a law is seemingly neutral on its face. For instance, in *British Columbia (Public Service Employee Relations Commission) v. British Columbia Government and Service Employees Union (B.C.G.S.E.U.) (Meiorin Grievance)*,[85] the Supreme Court held that uniform minimum aerobic standards for firefighters unfairly discriminated against female employees. The standards were seemingly neutral on their face in that they were common to both men and women. However, the standards had a disproportionate and discriminatory impact on women, who had a lower aerobic capacity than most men. The evidence fell short of establishing that the claimant, a female firefighter who failed the aerobic threshold, posed a risk to herself, her colleagues, or the public. While the case was decided on the basis of human rights legislation, the Court relied on section 15(1) for the proposition that the principal concern in equality cases is the *effect* of the impugned law on the claimant.

In *Andrews*, McIntyre J. did not provide a clear and comprehensive definition of the term "discrimination." The Supreme Court has struggled with the definition of this elusive concept ever since.[86] In the 1999 decision in *Law v. Canada*,[87] a unanimous Supreme Court attempted to find common ground between the approaches that had been proposed by various members of the Court. Iacobucci J., who wrote for the unanimous Court, stated that equality analysis is comparative in nature; it examines whether differential treatment accorded to an individual or

---

against discrete and insular minorities" could have the effect of distorting the political process, by excluding those minorities or making it more difficult for them to obtain effective political representation. This has led to arguments that judicial review of measures that impose burdens or disadvantages on such minorities is justified, as a means of correcting these flaws in the political process: see J.H. Ely, *Democracy and Distrust: A Theory of Judicial Review* (Cambridge: Harvard University Press, 1980). Subsequent cases have held that sexual orientation, marital status, and the residency status of status "Indians" are analogous grounds for purposes of s. 15.

85 [1999] 3 S.C.R. 3.

86 See, in particular, the so-called 1995 trilogy of equality decisions, *Egan v. Canada*, [1995] 2 S.C.R. 513; *Miron v. Trudel*, [1995] 2 S.C.R. 418; and *Thibaudeau v. Canada*, [1995] 2 S.C.R. 627 [*Thibaudeau*], in which there were three distinct theories advanced by various members of the Court as to the meaning of the term "discrimination" in s. 15.

87 [1999] 1 S.C.R. 497 [*Law*].

group can be justified.[88] Further, in accordance with *Andrews*, it is necessary to establish that the legislation accords differential treatment on the basis of grounds that are either enumerated in section 15, or are analogous to those grounds. Iacobucci J. stated that a law is discriminatory when it demeans an individual's "essential human dignity [through the] stereotypical application of presumed group or personal characteristics, or otherwise has the effect of perpetuating or promoting the view that the individual is less capable, or less worthy of recognition or value as a human being or as a member of Canadian society."[89] Conversely, laws are not discriminatory when they are "sensitive to the needs, capacities, and merits of different individuals, taking into account the context underlying their differences."[90] Iacobucci J. did not define "human dignity" exhaustively, but set out four factors relevant to the inquiry: (1) the existence of pre-existing disadvantage, stereotyping, prejudice, or vulnerability; (2) the correspondence between the distinction and the claimant's characteristics or circumstances; (3) the existence of ameliorative purposes or effects on other groups; and (4) the nature of the interest affected.

Applying this framework, Iacobucci J. held that an age qualification for receipt of a survivor's pension under the Canada Pension Plan was not discriminatory. Even though the provision differentiated on the grounds of age (an enumerated ground under section 15), the age requirement was based on the assumption that younger survivors of pension contributors would be better able to find employment after the death of a spouse. In Iacobucci J.'s view, this assumption corresponded to the "actual situation of individuals it affects."[91] Excluding or eliminating pensions for younger survivors did not proceed on the basis of stereotypes, nor did it presume that younger persons were less capable or less deserving of respect or dignity. Rather, it proceeded on the basis of relevant and appropriate differences between younger and older claimants.

Just nine years after *Law* was decided, in the 2008 case of *R. v. Kapp*,[92] the Supreme Court reversed its decision and substituted the "human

88 McIntyre J. in *Andrews*, above note 78, had also noted that equality rights analysis is comparative in nature. However, confusion had arisen in later cases as a result of McIntyre J.'s insistence that the similarly situated test was inappropriate for purposes of s. 15 analysis; this had led some lower courts to conclude that s. 15 analysis could somehow avoid a consideration of whether differential treatment in legislation was justified by reference to differences between the persons falling within the legislative classification and those falling outside of it.

89 *Law*, above note 87 at para. 51.

90 *Ibid.* at para.53.

91 *Ibid.* at para. 102.

92 [2008] 2 S.C.R. 483 [*Kapp*].

dignity" test with a "discrimination" test, a concept that the Court since *Andrews* had been unable to define. In rejecting "human dignity" as a "legal test,"[93] the Court cited academic criticism that the concept was abstract and overly burdensome for equality claimants.[94] The Court attempted to simplify the *Law* framework, collapsing the analysis into two questions: (1) Does the law create a distinction based on an enumerated or analogous ground? (2) Does the distinction create a disadvantage by perpetuating prejudice or stereotyping? Interestingly, the Court in *Kapp* expressly maintained the four *Law* factors identified by Iacobucci J. for the purposes of determining whether a law interfered with human dignity.

Cases since *Kapp* have turned on the second part of the test. For instance, in *Ermineskin Indian Band and Nation v. Canada*,[95] the Court dismissed a claim by Indian bands that the *Indian Act* precluded the government from investing royalty revenues in external investments rather than keeping them in the consolidated revenue fund. The bands claimed that the Act discriminated against them on the basis of race. The Supreme Court dismissed the claim. Assuming that the law created a distinction based on race, it did not perpetuate a disadvantage through prejudicing or stereotyping. Similarly, in *Hutterian Brethren*,[96] the Court held that a universal photograph requirement for obtaining a driver's licence in Alberta infringed the right to freedom of religion (which was saved under section 1), but that it did not violate section 15, since the law did not arise from any "demeaning stereotype but from a neutral and rationally defensible policy choice."[97] In *Withler v. Canada (Attorney General)*,[98] the Court dismissed a section 15(1) claim by widows of federal supplementary death benefits whose benefits had been reduced because of the age of their husbands at the time of death. The age-based reduction provisions in the legislation at issue constituted an "obvious . . . distinction based on an enumerated ground."[99] However, the rules were part of a broader pension benefit scheme "designed to benefit a number of groups in different circumstances and with different interests" and did not perpetuate prejudice or stereotype.

93 The Court nonetheless stated at para. 21 that "human dignity is an essential value underlying the s. 15 guarantee."

94 The academic criticism of the *Law* framework is extensive. Many of the relevant articles are collected at fns. 1 and 2 in *Kapp*, above note 92.

95 [2009] 1 S.C.R. 222.

96 Above note 9.

97 *Ibid.* at para. 108.

98 [2011] 1 S.C.R. 396 [*Withler*].

99 *Ibid.* at para. 69.

Although the Court's consensus on the basic structure of the *Kapp* test has prevailed, there was serious disagreement as to its application in *Quebec (Attorney General) v. A*, which concerned the lack of common law marriage and associated support obligations under Quebec law.[100] Four judges concluded that the lack of support obligations for long-term cohabiting partners under Quebec law was not discrimination on the basis of marital status. Four judges concluded at least some of the relevant provisions were discriminatory contrary to section 15(1), and that such discrimination could not be justified under section 1. Chief Justice McLachlin cast the deciding vote, holding that while parts of the law did violate section 15(1), this violation was justified under section 1 in pursuit of the government objective of promoting choice and autonomy. The result is continued disagreement over the meaning, in practice, of "substantive discrimination," but with governments taking solace in their ability to rely on section 1 in the face of such uncertainty. The Court did return to unanimity in 2015, citing Abella J.'s characterization of the test for substantive discrimination in *Quebec (Attorney General) v. A*.[101]

Ultimately, the Supreme Court has provided little definitive guidance for determining whether a law is "discriminatory" or creates a "disadvantage." Largely for this reason, some critics have recommended that the current framework be abandoned and that an infringement of section 15 be automatically established if the claimant can demonstrate that the law creates a distinction based on an enumerated or analogous ground. The burden would then shift to the government to justify the law under section 1.[102] This approach has certain attractions. It would make the section 15 analysis far more straightforward and predictable. However, such a broad reading of section 15 would leave virtually all claims to be decided under section 1, as has occurred with the expansive definition of "expression" that the Supreme Court of Canada has given to section 2(b). It would almost always fall to the government to justify its legislation or conduct pursuant to section 1.

Furthermore, it is arguable that this approach would risk overshooting the purpose of the equality guarantee. In our view, section 15 was not intended to encompass all laws that create a distinction based on an enumerated or analogous ground. Section 15(1) cannot have been intended to encompass claims based on all laws that draw a distinction on grounds of race, national or ethnic origin, colour, religion, sex, age, mental or physical disability, or analogous grounds. As the Supreme Court

100 *Quebec (Attorney General) v. A*, [2013] 1 S.C.R. 61.

101 *Kahkewistahaw First Nation v. Taypotat*, [2015] 2 S.C.R. 548 at para. 16.

102 Professor Hogg favours this view. See: P.W. Hogg, *Constitutional Law of Canada*, 5th ed., loose-leaf, vol. 2 (Toronto: Carswell, 2007) at s. 55.9(d).

stated in *Withler*, section 15(1) "does not protect a right to identical treatment" but rather "every person's equal right to be free from discrimination."[103] A proper understanding of the concept of equality requires a contextual consideration of whether differential treatment is appropriate in the particular circumstances of the case. This contextual approach requires courts to examine relevant differences or similarities between the claimant and others. In short, it is true that the Supreme Court has struggled to provide clear guidance to litigants and courts on the meaning of concepts such as "discrimination" or "disadvantage" in section 15(1) cases. However, this uncertainty is unavoidable in light of the nature and purpose of the equality guarantee and the interests it was meant to protect. In our view, section 15(1) claims can only be decided with a careful attention to context, including a consideration of the needs and circumstances of the persons who are alleging unequal treatment, and a consideration of the actual impact of the legislation upon them.

F. LANGUAGE RIGHTS

The sixth category of *Charter* rights is language rights, protected by sections 16 to 23. Section 16 provides that French and English are the official languages of Canada and of the province of New Brunswick, and both languages have equality of status in legislative and governmental institutions. Section 16.1, added by a constitutional amendment in 1993, guarantees the equal status, rights, and privileges of the English and French linguistic communities in New Brunswick, including the right to distinct educational and cultural institutions as are necessary to preserve and promote those communities. Any member of the public has a right to communicate and receive available services from the governments of Canada and New Brunswick in either official language (section 20). The right to use English and French in Parliament and the New Brunswick legislature (section 18), and in court proceedings (section 19) is also guaranteed.

In addition to these rights guaranteeing the use of English and French in relation to government and courts, the *Charter* also provides important minority language educational rights. Section 23(1) guarantees citizens of Canada who received their primary school instruction in the language of the official language minority in the province in which they reside with the right to have their children educated in that same

---

103 *Withler*, above note 98 at para. 31.

language. This so-called Canada clause[104] was enacted with a view to overriding Quebec's language legislation, which provided that only those who had been educated in English in Quebec had the right to send their children to English-language schools there. In 1984, the Supreme Court ruled that the Quebec legislation could not be characterized as a mere limit on rights for purposes of section 1, since it was in direct contradiction with the relevant *Charter* guarantee; accordingly, the Quebec legislation was struck down and Canadian citizens who had received primary school instruction in English anywhere in Canada—as opposed to only in the province of Quebec—were recognized as having the right to send their children to English schools in Quebec.[105] These rights build on those protected by sections 133 and 93 of the *Constitution Act, 1867*.[106] Section 133 guaranteed the use of English or French in the Parliament of Canada and the legislature of Quebec, as well as in Quebec and federally established courts. Section 93 provided educational guarantees for the Catholic minority in Ontario and the Protestant minority in Quebec, guarantees that were replicated for religious minorities in a number of other provinces that joined confederation after 1867.[107] Although section 93 and its counterparts in the other provinces were framed in terms of religion rather than language, the Catholic community in Ontario and the Protestant community in Quebec were significantly defined in terms of language as well as religion.[108] These protections for minority rights

---

104 See s. 23(1)(b), so named because it extends minority language education rights to persons who attended primary school *in Canada* in the official language minority of the province in which they reside. Note that there is a broader right contained in s. 23(1)(a), which extends minority education rights to any citizen whose language first learned and still understood is that of the minority language minority of the province in which they reside. The difference between s. 23(1)(a) and (b) is that paragraph (a) does not require citizens to have received minority language education *in Canada*. However, s. 23(1)(a) does not apply in the province of Quebec (although it does apply elsewhere in Canada): see s. 59(1) of the *Constitution Act, 1982*.

105 See *Quebec (Attorney General) v. Quebec Association of Protestant School Boards*, [1984] 2 S.C.R. 66. Note that the rights in s. 23 are qualified by the requirement that there must be sufficient numbers of children with minority education rights to warrant the provision of minority language instruction out of public funds.

106 See the *Constitution Act, 1867*, 30 & 31 Vict., c. 3 and the discussion in Chapters 4 and 5.

107 See, for example, s. 22 of the *Constitution Act, 1871* (Manitoba); s. 17 of the *Alberta Act*; s. 17 of the *Saskatchewan Act*; and Term 17 of the *Newfoundland Act*.

108 Note, however, that in a controversial decision early in the twentieth century, the Privy Council ruled that s. 93 did not include minority language protection. See *Ottawa Roman Catholic Separate School Trustees v. Mackell*, [1917] A.C. 62 (P.C.).

have been described as a central concern of the confederation bargain,[109] and protection for minority rights has been declared to be one of four "fundamental and organizing principles of the Constitution."[110]

The language rights guarantees in the *Charter* have received very limited consideration by the Supreme Court. Most of the litigation that has reached the Supreme Court has revolved around the interpretation of the minority language education rights in section 23. The right to minority language education may be triggered even where there are less than a hundred students entitled to section 23 rights.[111] The Court has ruled that section 23 protects not just the right to the provision of school facilities, but also the right to management and control of those facilities by the official language minority.[112] Where there are sufficient numbers of students, the right of management and control may even include the right to the establishment of a separate minority language school board.[113] It also protects not only the existence of minority language schools, but guarantees that the educational experience they offer to be of "substantial equivalence" to majority language schools.[114] Furthermore, the Supreme Court has paid considerable deference to legislative attempts, particularly in Quebec, designed to promote and maintain the French language. For example, in *Solski (Tutor of) v. Quebec (Attorney General)*,[115] the Court upheld a provision in the Quebec *Charter of the French Language* which restricted admission to Quebec English-language schools to children who had received the "major part" of their schooling in Canada in English. The Court held that a qualitative restriction

---

109 See *Reference Re Legislative Authority of Parliament of Canada in Relation to the Upper House*, [1980] 1 S.C.R. 54 at 71.

110 *Reference Re Secession of Quebec*, [1998] 2 S.C.R. 217 at 261.

111 See *Arsenault-Cameron v. P.E.I.*, [2000] 1 S.C.R. 3, holding that s. 23 mandated a French-language school in Summerside, P.E.I., where there were fewer than a hundred students prepared to enrol in the school. French-language instruction was available in another community 28 kilometres away but the Supreme Court held that requiring the students to travel to that community would not have been consistent with the requirements of s. 23.

112 See *Mahé v. Alberta*, [1990] 1 S.C.R. 342.

113 See *Reference Re Public Schools Act (Man.) s. 79(3), (4) and (7)*, [1993] 1 S.C.R. 839, where there were at least 5600 potential French-language students in the province, thereby justifying the establishment of an independent French-language school board under control of the minority.

114 *Association des parents de l'école Rose-des-vents v. British Columbia (Education)*, [2015] 2 S.C.R. 139.

115 [2005] 1 S.C.R. 201.

requiring a "significant part" of the child's schooling to have been in English did not violate section 23(2).[116]

FURTHER READINGS

HOGG, P.W., *Constitutional Law of Canada*, loose-leaf (Toronto: Carswell, 2007) cc. 34–36, 42–57

SHARPE, R.J., & K. ROACH, *The Charter of Rights and Freedoms*, 5th ed. (Toronto: Irwin Law, 2013)

STEWART, H., *Fundamental Justice: Section 7 of the Canadian Charter of Rights and Freedoms* (Toronto: Irwin Law, 2012)

---

116 However, in the later case of *Quebec (Education, Recreation and Sports) v. Nguyen*, [2009] 3 S.C.R. 208, the Court concluded that provisions of the *Charter of the French Language* designed to discourage temporary enrolment in unsubsidized "bridging schools" to ensure subsequent eligibility in publicly funded English schools was unconstitutional.

CHAPTER 15

INDIGENOUS PEOPLES AND THE CANADIAN CONSTITUTION

A. THE NATURE OF INDIGENOUS RIGHTS

1) Rights Existing at Common Law

Prior to the arrival of Europeans in North America, many diverse Indigenous peoples had occupied the lands that now comprise Canada. The arrival of European settlers and the defeat of French forces by the British in 1760 established British laws and the ultimate sovereignty of the British Crown over British North America.[1] Despite the ultimate sovereignty of the Crown, British law recognized the right of Indigenous peoples to continue occupying their traditional lands and hunting grounds. The *Royal Proclamation of 1763*[2] was issued by George III in order to establish the form of civil government applicable to the British colonies in British North America. The *Royal Proclamation* expressly reserved to Indigenous peoples "such Parts of Our Dominions and Territories as, not having been ceded to or purchased by Us, are reserved to them, or any of them, as their Hunting Grounds."[3] The *Royal Proclamation* also recognized that Indigenous interest in lands appropriated for settlement could only be purchased through agreements concluded with the Crown following a public meeting involving the Indigenous

---

1 *Guerin v. R.*, [1984] 2 S.C.R. 335 [*Guerin*]. See also the discussion in Chapter 2, Section B(1).

2 (U.K.), reprinted in R.S.C. 1985, App. II, No. 1.

3 *Ibid.*

community. Further, it provided that no private person could directly acquire Indigenous interest in land.

Until relatively recently, the precise origins, nature, and status of Indigenous rights at common law was somewhat unclear.[4] In 1888, the Privy Council, in the *St. Catherine's Milling* case,[5] stated that on the successful assertion of British sovereignty, the Crown acquired a "substantial and paramount estate" over all territories subject to such sovereignty. However, the Privy Council also held that Indigenous peoples continued to have a possessory right, or a right of continued occupancy, in their traditional lands. Lord Watson described the Indigenous possessory interest as a "personal and usufructuary right." It was said to be a "qualification" or a "mere burden" on the underlying and paramount Crown estate.[6] Lord Watson also stated that the Indigenous interest in land had been created through its express recognition in the *Royal Proclamation*.[7]

It was not until 1973, in the historic and celebrated decision in *Calder v. British Columbia (Attorney-General)*,[8] that the Supreme Court expressed a different view as to the origins of Indigenous rights. Although the ultimate result in the case was inconclusive, six of the seven members of the Court agreed that Indigenous title was a legal right derived from Indigenous peoples' historic occupation and possession of their tribal

---

4 However, pre-Confederation governments did enact legislation relating to Indigenous peoples in various statutes. See for example, *An Act respecting the Assessment of Property in Upper Canada*, C.S.U.C. 1859, c. 55, ss. 20–22 defining "Indians" as "Indians or persons of Indian blood or intermarried with Indians, acknowledged as members of Indian Tribes or Bands residing upon lands which have never been surrendered to the Crown (or which having been so surrendered have been set apart or are then reserved for the use of any Tribe or Band of Indians in common)." See also the discussion below at Section B(2).

5 *St. Catherine's Milling and Lumber Co. v. R.* (1888), 14 A.C. 46 [*St. Catherine's Milling*].

6 According to the Privy Council, on surrender or extinguishment of the Indigenous interest, the Crown's estate became a *plenum dominium*, which was no longer burdened by the Indigenous interest. Further, the Privy Council decided in *St. Catherine's Milling* that on surrender, the entire estate in land reverted to the provincial Crown rather than the federal Crown, even if the surrender had been negotiated by the federal Crown, through the operation of s. 109 of the *Constitution Act, 1867*. Section 109 granted the provinces ownership of all public lands, subject to any "interest other than that of the Province."

7 According to Lord Watson: "[t]heir possession, such as it was, can only be ascribed to the general provisions made by the Royal proclamation in favour of all Indian tribes then living under the sovereignty and protection of the British Crown" (*ibid.* at 54).

8 [1973] S.C.R. 313 [*Calder*].

lands, rather than as a result of the *Royal Proclamation*.[9] As such, the Indigenous interest arose through the operation of the common law and did not depend on "treaty, executive order, or legislative enactment."[10] A few months after the release of *Calder*, the government of Canada reversed a long-standing policy and announced its willingness to negotiate land claims based on outstanding or unsurrendered Indigenous title.

In *Guerin v. R.*,[11] the Supreme Court affirmed and expanded on the reasoning in *Calder*. According to Dickson J., who wrote the reasons of the majority,[12] Indigenous title is a legal right to occupy and possess certain lands and the ultimate title rests with the Crown. There are two characteristics of Indigenous title, which makes the interest *sui generis* or unique. First, Indigenous title is inalienable except to the Crown and cannot be transferred to a third party. The basis for this limitation was that the Crown should be interposed between Indigenous peoples and prospective purchasers so as to prevent exploitation, a principle that was recognized in the *Royal Proclamation*.[13] Second, a surrender to the Crown

---

9 Judson J., with whom Martland and Ritchie JJ. concurred, found that whatever rights the Indigenous peoples in British Columbia possessed had been extinguished through general land enactments in the province, while Hall J., with whom Spence and Laskin JJ. concurred, held that Indigenous peoples' rights had not been extinguished through the enactments. However, both Judson and Hall JJ. agreed that the *Royal Proclamation* was not the exclusive source of Indigenous interests in land in the province. The seventh member of the Court, Pigeon J., dismissed the claim on technical grounds and did not express a view as to the nature of Indigenous rights.

10 *Ibid.* at 390 (per Hall J., Spence and Laskin JJ. concurring). This holding allowed the Court to avoid having to determine the precise territorial application of the *Royal Proclamation*. Judson J. did express the view that the *Royal Proclamation* did not extend throughout British Columbia, while Hall J. was of the view that the Proclamation did apply to all of British Columbia. Because Indigenous rights arise through the operation of common law, they apply throughout Canada without regard to whether the territory in question was subject to the *Royal Proclamation*. See B. Slattery, "Making Sense of Indigenous and Treaty Rights" (2000) 79 Can. Bar Rev. 196.

11 Above note 1. Note that, although decided in 1984, this litigation was commenced prior to 1982 and thus made no reference to the enactment of s. 35(1) of the *Constitution Act, 1982*.

12 Dickson J. (as he then was) wrote reasons with which Beetz, Chouinard, and Lamer JJ. concurred. Estey J., with whom Wilson J. concurred, wrote separate reasons, concurring in the result.

13 Justice Dickson did not explain why the rule of inalienability except to the Crown arises from the common law. As discussed above, the principle was set out in the *Royal Proclamation*. Furthermore, as Dickson J. pointed out, successive versions of the *Indian Act* carried forward this policy and permitted alienation of Indigenous interests in land only to the Crown. Therefore, it is unclear why Dickson J. held that the source of the limitation of inalienability arises

gives rise to a fiduciary obligation, such that the Crown is obliged to deal with surrendered land in the best interests of the Indigenous peoples concerned. This fiduciary relationship demands "utmost loyalty" on the part of the Crown to the Indigenous interest.[14] Dickson J. cautioned that it was "unnecessary and potentially misleading" to attempt to describe Indigenous rights more precisely, beyond the above two key features. Applying these principles, Dickson J. found that the Crown had failed to discharge its fiduciary duty adequately, since it had leased surrendered land to a third party on terms less favourable than those that had been promised orally to the Indigenous people at the time of the surrender.[15]

Certain members of the Supreme Court have departed from Dickson J.'s caution in *Guerin* and attempted to elaborate the specific content of Indigenous land rights in far greater detail. In *R. v. Van der Peet*,[16] Lamer C.J. set out a general theory regarding the legal sources and nature of Indigenous rights.[17] Lamer C.J. affirmed the basic principle established in *Calder* and *Guerin* that Indigenous rights arise at common law by virtue of the fact that "when Europeans arrived in North America, Aboriginal peoples *were already here*, living in communities on the land, and participating in distinctive cultures, as they had done for centuries."[18] Lamer C.J. noted that this view found support in the early nineteenth-century opinions of Marshall C.J. of the U.S. Supreme Court,[19] as well as the 1992

---

from historic use and occupation of land by Indigenous peoples as opposed to imperial or federal statutes.

14 *Guerin*, above note 1 at 389.

15 Similarly, in *Blueberry River Indian Band v. Canada (Department of Indian Affairs and Northern Development)*, [1995] 4 S.C.R. 344, the Court held that a sale of mineral rights by the Crown was not in the best interest of an Indian band.

16 [1996] 2 S.C.R. 507 [*Van der Peet*]. Lamer C.J. wrote the majority opinion, in which La Forest, Sopinka, Gonthier, Cory, Iacobucci, and Major JJ. concurred. L'Heureux-Dubé and McLachlin JJ. wrote separate dissenting opinions.

17 The term "Indigenous rights" includes both Indigenous title to land, and the rights to those activities protected under the test in *Van der Peet*, as described in this section. In some usages, the phrase is used to refer only to the second category. In our usage, it refers to both categories.

18 *Ibid.* at 538 [emphasis in original].

19 See, in particular, the opinions of Marshall C.J. in *Johnson and Graham's Lessee v. McIntosh*, 21 U.S. (8 Wheat.) 543 (1823) [*Johnson*] and *Worcester v. Georgia*, 31 U.S. (6 Pet.) 515 (1832) [*Worcester*]. Marshall C.J. had advanced the theory that the effect of European discovery was to give title to the discovering European government *as against other European governments*. The exclusion of other Europeans therefore gave to the discovering government "the sole right of acquiring the soil from the natives"; however, the rights of the original inhabitants were "in no instance entirely disregarded . . . . They were admitted to be the rightful occupants of the soil, with a legal as well as a just claim to retain possession of it, and to use it according to their own discretion": see *Johnson*, cited in *Van der*

decision of the Australian High Court in *Mabo v. Queensland (No. 2)*.[20] Lamer C.J. then set out a test for identifying Indigenous rights based on identifying the "practices, traditions and customs central to the Aboriginal societies that existed in North America prior to contact with the Europeans."[21] In order to be an Indigenous right, an activity must be "an element of a practice, custom, or tradition integral to the distinctive culture of the Aboriginal group claiming the right."[22] Lamer C.J. set out a number of indicia for applying this "integral to a distinctive culture test," including the fact that the practice, custom, or tradition must have been "one of the things that truly *made the society what it was*"; that the relevant period for making this determination is prior to contact between European and Indigenous societies; and that claims to Indigenous rights must be adjudicated on a specific rather than a general basis.[23]

Lamer C.J. also distinguished between Indigenous rights and Indigenous title. Indigenous title, which is the exclusive right to occupy and use land, is a subcategory of Indigenous rights. Although Indigenous rights arise from the occupation of land, they can also arise from the prior social organization and distinctive cultures of Indigenous peoples on their land. Thus, even in a case where an Indigenous people cannot

---

Peet, above note 16 at 541. Lamer C.J. considered these decisions to be "as relevant to Canada as they are to the United States," a comment that is noteworthy given the Canadian Supreme Court's general tendency not to follow American precedents in its interpretation of the *Charter*.

20 (1992), 175 C.L.R. 1 [*Mabo*]. In *Mabo*, the High Court of Australia found that native title (as it is called in Australia) existed as a burden on the Crown's ultimate title and that the content of native title was based on traditional laws and customs of the Indigenous inhabitants of a territory. In *Van der Peet*, above note 16, Lamer C.J., at 544, described *Mabo* as "persuasive in the Canadian context."

21 *Van der Peet*, *ibid.* at 548. Lamer C.J. was discussing Indigenous rights in the specific context of s. 35(1) of the *Constitution Act, 1982*. However, the analysis attempted to elaborate on the legal implications of the fact that Indigenous peoples occupied North America in distinctive societies prior to the arrival of Europeans, which had been recognized in *Guerin* and confirmed in *Van der Peet* as the legal foundation for Indigenous rights at common law. For these reasons, the test for the identification of Indigenous rights proposed in *Van der Peet* is also relevant to identifying the legal content of Indigenous rights at common law.

22 *Van der Peet*, *ibid.* at 549.

23 *Ibid.* at 550–62 [emphasis added]. In *R. v. Powley*, [2003] 2 S.C.R. 207 [*Powley*], the Court modified the relevant time frame in respect of the determination of Métis rights under s. 35 of the *Constitution Act, 1982*. Since the Métis peoples arose as a result of the contact between Indigenous peoples and Europeans, it was evident that a "pre-contact" time frame for the identification of Métis rights would not be appropriate, since it would effectively deny the Métis the protection of s. 35. The Court held that Métis rights were to be determined by reference to the date of "effective control" by Europeans.

prove a right to exclusive occupancy and use of particular lands (which would ground a claim to Indigenous title), they may be able to demonstrate that they engaged in a practice or activity that was integral to their distinctive culture that rises to the level of a protected Indigenous right.

Lamer C.J. elaborated on the distinction between Indigenous rights and Indigenous title in *Delgamuukw v. British Columbia*.[24] According to Lamer C.J., Indigenous title is "simply one manifestation of a broader-based conception of Indigenous rights."[25] Indigenous title arises where the connection of an Indigenous people with a piece of land was "of central significance to their distinctive culture." An Indigenous right is a distinctive practice, custom, or tradition that may or may not be connected to a specific location or piece of land.[26] Lamer C.J. then set out a list of characteristics or features of Indigenous title at common law:

- it is held communally, and cannot be held by individual Indigenous persons;[27]
- it is subject to an "inherent limit," in that lands subject to Indigenous title "cannot be used in a manner that is irreconcilable with the nature of the attachment to the land which forms the basis of the group's claim to [Indigenous] title";[28]

---

24 [1997] 3 S.C.R. 1010 [*Delgamuukw*]. Lamer C.J. wrote a decision concurred in by Cory, McLachlin, and Major JJ. La Forest J., with whom L'Heureux-Dubé J. concurred, concurred in the result but for different reasons. McLachlin J., although concurring with Lamer C.J., also expressed "substantial agreement with the comments of Justice La Forest." Sopinka J., a member of the panel that heard the case, took no part in the judgment of the Court. In the result, the decision of Lamer C.J. enjoyed the support of a plurality of four members of the Supreme Court. It should be noted that the Court in *Delgamuukw* did not actually resolve the dispute that gave rise to the litigation. The Court held that a new trial should be ordered because the trial judge had not given sufficient weight to oral histories of the Indigenous claimants. Thus, the entire discussion of the content of Indigenous rights and title in the case is, strictly speaking, *obiter dicta*.

25 *Ibid*. at 1094, citing *R. v. Adams*, [1996] 3 S.C.R. 101 at para. 25 [*Adams*].

26 Lamer C.J. held that even though an Indigenous practice or activity may not have involved exclusive possession of land—and thus may not be sufficient to ground a claim of title—it may be linked or tied to a particular tract of land, in which case it will be site-specific. On the other hand, an Indigenous right need not be connected to any particular tract of land in order to qualify as a legally protected right: see *Delgamuukw*, above note 24 at 1093–95. La Forest J., in his concurring decision, seemed to accept this methodology for distinguishing between Indigenous rights and Indigenous title: see *ibid*. at 1126–27.

27 *Ibid*. at 1082.

28 *Ibid*. at 1088. For example, Lamer C.J. stated that if occupation is established with reference to use of land as a hunting ground, then the people that successfully claim Indigenous title may not use it in such a fashion as to destroy its value for hunting (for example, by strip mining it). With respect, this seems

- however, subject to this inherent limitation, Indigenous peoples are free to utilize lands subject to Indigenous title in any manner of their own choosing and are not restricted to activities they engaged in prior to contact with Europeans;
- the relevant time period for the establishment of Indigenous title is the time at which the Crown asserts sovereignty over the land subject to title;[29]
- the occupation of land must have been exclusive in order to establish a claim of title; and
- where such exclusive occupation can be established, this is sufficient in itself to demonstrate that title to the land is "of central significance to the culture of the claimants" in accordance with the *Van der Peet* test.

In contrast to Lamer C.J.'s expansive definition of Indigenous rights and title, La Forest J.'s concurring reasons in *Delgamuukw* stressed Dickson J.'s admonition in *Guerin* that it is unnecessary and potentially misleading to attempt to precisely define the content of Indigenous rights. La Forest J.'s reiteration of Dickson J.'s caution was particularly timely, since (as explained in more detail below), section 35(1) of the *Constitution Act, 1982,* "recognized and affirmed" existing Indigenous and treaty rights.[30] The enactment of a constitutional provision highlights the danger in specific and universal definitions of Indigenous rights at common law: judge-made rules may be indirectly constitutionalized

---

like a puzzling limitation. Consider, for example, a situation where Indigenous lands were originally used as hunting grounds but are no longer suitable for such use as a result of settlement patterns and the disappearance of wildlife. It is difficult to understand how or why the inherent limitation proposed by Lamer C.J. would apply in such circumstances.

29 This differs from the relevant time for the establishment of an Indigenous right to engage in specific activities, which is the time prior to contact with Europeans. This inconsistency seems at odds with Lamer C.J.'s statement that Indigenous title is a subcategory of Indigenous rights, since the relevant time frame for the subcategory (title) differs from the relevant time for the general category (rights). Moreover, as Slattery has pointed out, the distinction could lead to anomalous and inconsistent results in which a claim for an Indigenous right to engage in a specific activity may fail and yet a claim for title could succeed. This could occur where there is insufficient evidence to establish that the activity is "integral to the distinctive culture" of the Indigenous people. The result would be that the Indigenous people would have the right to engage in the particular activity, since title gives the right to engage in any activities of the Indigenous peoples' choosing regardless of whether they are "integral to a distinctive culture," provided only that the activity does not violate the inherent limit proposed by Lamer C.J., as described in the preceding footnote. See Slattery, above note 10.

30 See Chapter 5 for a discussion of the enactment of this provision.

through the operation of section 35(1), thereby inhibiting the development of Indigenous rights that will better advance the interests of Indigenous Canadians.[31] The attempt to precisely describe the characteristics of Indigenous rights or Indigenous title in the absence of a concrete factual dispute before the courts[32] may frustrate the natural and incremental evolution of the law pertaining to Indigenous peoples.[33]

In 2014, the Supreme Court applied the principles from *Delgamuukw* to grant its first declaration of Indigenous title to the Tsilhqot'in Nation, a group of six bands who had semi-nomadically inhabited a remote valley in British Columbia for centuries.[34] The Court held that in determining whether historic occupation by an Indigenous group was "exclusive," one looks to the Indigenous culture and practices, and compares them in a culturally sensitive way with what was required at common law to establish title on the basis of occupation. The Court rejected the Province of British Columbia's argument that only specific, intensively occupied areas can qualify for Indigenous title, and found

---

31 It is useful to distinguish between rules for proving the existence of Indigenous title, which are an appropriate and necessary element of judicial decision making, as opposed to attempts to spell out in detail the characteristics of Indigenous title, which seem entirely unnecessary and, as Dickson J. cautioned in *Guerin*, potentially misleading. It is difficult to see what is achieved, for example, by Lamer C.J.'s declaration in *Delgamuukw* that Indigenous rights cannot be held by individual Indigenous persons, or that they are subject to an inherent limit such that any use of Indigenous lands cannot be incompatible with the original use of such lands.

32 In *R. v. Powley* (2001), 53 O.R. (3d) 35 (C.A.), Sharpe J.A. stated at para. 75, that courts should "guard against the temptation to pronounce broadly upon all possible aspects of the rights of the Métis people and should instead confine ourselves to what is necessary for the resolution of the case before us . . . . A full articulation of the shape and subtle contours of constitutionally protected Métis rights will undoubtedly unfold over time in the usual incremental fashion of the common law." The Court of Appeal's decision was subsequently upheld by the Supreme Court of Canada: see *Powley*, above note 23.

33 The irresistible tendency will be for the courts to look to the existing terms of the *Indian Act*, R.S.C. 1985, c. I-5, as well as to previous government policy in relation to Indigenous peoples, and declare that certain elements of existing laws or policies are an inherent feature of Indigenous rights or title at common law. Indeed, this has been the approach of Canadian courts in their approach to the definition of Indigenous rights at common law dating back to *Guerin*. As discussed above at note 13, *Guerin* held that a general rule of inalienability except to the Crown, which was introduced by the *Royal Proclamation* and carried forward through successive versions of the *Indian Act*, was an "inherent feature" of Indigenous rights at common law.

34 *Tsilhqot'in Nation v. British Columbia*, [2014] 2 S.C.R. 257 [*Tsilhqot'in*].

that the Tsilhqot'in Nation, having regularly used the territory in question and repelled others from entry, had met this test.

2) Treaty Rights

Indigenous rights and the treaty rights of Indigenous peoples differ in both origins and structure. Whereas Indigenous rights flow from the historic use and occupation of land by Indigenous peoples and the distinctive culture they practised, treaty rights find their source in official agreements between the Crown and Indigenous peoples. Treaties thus create enforceable obligations based primarily on the mutual consent of the parties.

Historic treaties between the Crown and Indigenous peoples date back to the early eighteenth century. During the period when the British and the French were competing for control of lands in North America, the two colonial powers formed strategic alliances with some Indigenous peoples. For example, in what are now New Brunswick and Nova Scotia, the British made a series of "Peace and Friendship" treaties with the Mi'kmaq and Maliset Nations between 1725 and 1779. Following the issuance of the *Royal Proclamation of 1763* but prior to Confederation in 1867, a series of treaties were signed with Indigenous peoples, including the Upper Canada Treaties (1764 to 1862) and the Vancouver Island Treaties (1850 to 1854). Under these treaties, Indigenous peoples surrendered interests in lands in areas of what are now Ontario and British Columbia in exchange for certain benefits including reserves,[35] annuities, or other types of payment, and certain rights to hunt and fish.

Following Confederation, eleven "numbered treaties" were entered into with various Indigenous nations between 1871 and 1921. These treaties enabled the Canadian government to pursue settlement and development of the Canadian west and north. The lands subject to the eleven treaties cover Northern Ontario, Manitoba, Saskatchewan, Alberta, and portions of the Yukon, Northwest Territories, and British Columbia. Under these treaties, Indigenous Nations ceded vast tracts of land to the Crown in exchange for reserve lands and other benefits like agricultural implements and livestock, annuities, ammunition, clothing, and rights to hunt and fish.

As discussed above, following the *Calder* decision in 1973, the federal government announced a willingness to negotiate and settle outstanding land claims with Indigenous peoples. Two types of claims were

---

35 A "reserve" is land set aside by the Crown for the use and occupancy of an "Indian" Band, under s. 18(1) of the *Indian Act*, above note 33.

recognized: comprehensive and specific. A comprehensive claim deals with areas of Canada where Indigenous peoples' claims have not previously been dealt with by treaty or other legal means. The first of these modern-day treaties was the *James Bay and Northern Quebec Agreement*, signed in 1975.[36] As of June 2016, twenty-six comprehensive claims have been negotiated with Indigenous peoples, dealing with such matters as land title, self-government rights, fishing and trapping, financial compensation, and other social and economic benefits.[37]

Specific claims deal with specific grievances of First Nations regarding the fulfillment of treaties, or relating to the administration of First Nations lands under the *Indian Act*. As of June 2016, 1,235 specific claims have been concluded across the country and approximately 350 specific claims are under negotiation.[38]

As discussed above, treaties find their source in historic agreements between Indigenous peoples and the Crown. A treaty is characterized by the intention to create legal relations, the presence of mutually binding obligations, and a certain measure of solemnity.[39] The Supreme Court has held that, in determining whether a particular document constitutes a "treaty," it is necessary to take a "generous and liberal" approach, based on whether the Indigenous peoples would have believed that the document was intended to create legally binding relations with the Crown. On this basis, a short one-paragraph document in which a British general had "certified" that certain Indigenous persons were entitled to protection and the free exercise of religious, customary, and trade rights, but that had not been signed by the Indigenous peoples themselves, was found to constitute a treaty.[40]

Indigenous treaties constitute a unique type of agreement and attract special principles of interpretation.[41] Treaties are to be liberally construed and any ambiguities in the terms of the document are construed in favour of the Indigenous peoples concerned.[42] This rule has been imposed since the treaties were drafted in English by representa-

---

36 *James Bay and Northern Québec Agreement*, 1975. For a recent decision concerning environmental assessment provisions in this treaty, see *Quebec (Attorney General) v. Moses*, [2010] 1 S.C.R. 557 [*Moses*].

37 Indigenous Affairs and Northern Development Canada, *Comprehensive Claims*, online: www.aadnc-aandc.gc.ca/eng/1100100030577/1100100030578.

38 Indigenous Affairs and Northern Development Canada, *National Summary on Specific Claims*, online: http://services.aadnc-aandc.gc.ca/SCBRI_E/Main/ReportingCentre/PreviewReport.aspx?output=HTML.

39 See *R. v. Sioui*, [1990] 1 S.C.R. 1025 [*Sioui*].

40 *Ibid.*

41 *R. v. Sundown*, [1999] 1 S.C.R. 393 at para. 24 [*Sundown*].

42 *Sioui*, above note 39; *Simon v. R.*, [1985] 2 S.C.R. 387 [*Simon*].

tives of the Crown and were never translated into the various Indigenous languages. Moreover, Indigenous peoples "made their agreements orally and recorded their history orally."[43] Because treaties are treated as a sacred exchange of promises in which the honour of the Crown is engaged, no sharp practice will be tolerated and any verbal promises made by the Crown's representatives at the time they were concluded "are of great significance in their interpretation."[44] For instance, in *Ermineskin Indian Band and Nation v. Canada*,[45] the Supreme Court held that it would be unconscionable for the Crown to ignore oral terms and rely simply on the written words of a treaty.[46] On the other hand, it has been said that while the courts are to construe treaties generously, the terms of the treaty cannot be altered.[47]

The rule that a treaty is defined by the terms of the written document was materially qualified by the Supreme Court in *Marshall (No. 1)*.[48] In *Marshall (No. 1)*, a Mi'kmaq had been charged with fishing for eels out of season and with an illegal net, and for selling eels without a licence. In defence, he asserted that he had engaged in activity that was protected by a 1760 treaty. The treaty did not say anything specifically about fishing. However, it did include a clause about a "truck house" (that is, a type of trading post). The treaty stated that the Indians agreed that they would engage in trade only with the managers of "such Truck houses as shall be appointed or established by His Majesty's Governor." The evidence in the case established that the truck houses had disappeared by 1764 and, by 1780, a replacement regime of government-licensed traders had also fallen into disuse.

Binnie J., who wrote for the majority, acknowledged that the written terms of the truck house clause merely set out a restrictive covenant and said nothing about a positive right to trade, hunt, or fish. Nevertheless, in Binnie J.'s view, the written treaty was not limited to the terms of the document executed on 10 March 1760. Binnie J. held that the written

---

43 *R. v. Badger*, [1996] 1 S.C.R. 771 at para. 55 [*Badger*].

44 *Ibid.*

45 [2009] 1 S.C.R. 222.

46 The oral terms of the applicable treaty included a promise by the Lieutenant Governor of Manitoba and the Northwest Territories that if any part of reserves lands were sold, the proceeds of sale would be "put away to increase" for the benefit of Indian bands. The Court noted that representatives of the bands hearing this representation would have considered this a promise that proceeds of sale of reserve lands would be kept by the Crown safely and securely and would increase over time. The Court held that the Crown had discharged its obligation to the bands in this regard (see *ibid.* at paras. 53–64).

47 See *Badger*, above note 43 at para. 76.

48 *R. v. Marshall*, [1999] 3 S.C.R. 456 [*Marshall (No. 1)*].

document did not reflect all the terms that had been agreed to by the parties. In support of this conclusion, he relied on documents setting out an account of a meeting that had taken place some weeks prior to the execution of the 1760 treaty involving certain other Indigenous peoples, one of whom lived in what is now New Brunswick.[49] The documents indicated that at earlier meetings with the other Indigenous peoples, the British had agreed to establish a truck house at a particular location "for the furnishing them with necessaries, in Exchange for their Peltry." The 1760 treaty with the Mi'kmaq made no reference to this promise to establish a truck house, and merely contained a one-sided restrictive covenant requiring the Indigenous peoples to trade at truck houses. In Binnie J.'s view, this demonstrated the "inadequacy and incompleteness of the written memorial of the treaty terms by selectively isolating the restrictive trade covenant."[50] It was therefore appropriate to determine the actual treaty terms, "not only by reference to the fragmentary historical record . . . but also in light of the stated objectives of the British and Mi'kmaq in 1760 and the political and economic context in which those objectives were reconciled."[51] Looking to this broader context, Binnie J. found it appropriate to read into the treaty an "implied term" granting the Mi'kmaq the right to hunt and fish, so that they would have something to bring to the truck houses.[52] However, this implied term only

49 Binnie J. stated, *ibid.* at para. 26, that it was appropriate to rely on the record of the meeting with these other groups, since the trial judge had found that the "key negotiations took place not with the Mi'kmaq people directly, but with the St. John River Indians, part of the Maliseet First Nation, and the Passamaquody First Nation, who lived in present-day New Brunswick."

50 *Ibid.* at para. 35.

51 *Ibid.* at para. 41.

52 Ironically, however, Binnie J. found that there was no obligation to maintain the system of truck houses itself. This seems at odds with Binnie J.'s earlier finding that the British had promised to establish a truck house in the negotiations preceding the signing of the treaty; moreover, the existence of the promise to establish a truck house was a critical element in his reasoning, since it was the absence of any reference to this promise in the wording of the treaty which had led Binnie J. to conclude that the written treaty was an incomplete record of what had been agreed to. Yet Binnie J. rejected the argument that the treaty imposed an obligation to maintain one or more truck houses stating that this argument "suffers from the same quality of unreasonableness as does the Crown's argument that the Treaty left the Mi'kmaq with nothing more than a restrictive covenant" (*ibid.* at para. 53). He concluded, at para. 54, that the promise to establish the truck houses was the mere "mechanism created to facilitate the exercise of the right," which was access to "necessaries" through trade in wildlife. Thus, the closure of the system of truck houses did not in itself amount to a breach of the treaty; but the denial of the right to hunt, fish, or gather for the purpose of bringing goods to a truck house did.

gave the right to hunt and gather "necessaries," since the minutes of the meeting with the other Indigenous peoples had made reference to trading "necessaries" in return for "peltry" as the reason or purpose for establishing the truck houses.

As Binnie J. pointed out in *Marshall (No. 1)*, courts have historically interpreted treaty rights so as to make their exercise effective and meaningful.[53] What was novel about the approach of the majority in *Marshall (No. 1)*, however, was the Court's willingness to imply a new term into a treaty to recognize a right that was not a part of the written treaty. The approach in *Marshall (No. 1)* invites litigants to argue that the "real treaty" is the understanding of the parties, as reflected in the context underlying the negotiations, as opposed to what is stated in the terms of the treaty document. On this theory, the written document merely becomes a piece of evidence of the understanding of the parties.

Following *Marshall (No. 1)*, the Supreme Court issued additional reasons in response to an application for a rehearing of the case. In *Marshall (No. 2)*,[54] Binnie J., who authored a unanimous judgment of the Court, stated that treaty rights pertaining to activities other than fishing, such as logging, would have to be decided based on the circumstances and facts of future cases.

Subsequently, groups of Mi'kmaq Indians in Nova Scotia and New Brunswick commenced logging activities on Crown lands in Nova Scotia and New Brunswick contrary to provincial legislation. They were arrested and charged. In defence to the charges, the accused relied upon the 1760 treaties considered in *Marshall (No. 1)* and *Marshall (No. 2)*. They argued that at the time of the treaties, their ancestors used forest products for a variety of purposes, from housing and heat to sleds and snowshoes, and "indeed occasionally traded products made of wood, all to sustain themselves."[55] In their submission, logging was simply a modern extension of their historical rights that was protected by treaty. McLachlin C.J., for a majority of the Court (who dissented in *Marshall (No. 1)*), rejected this argument. Unlike eel fishing considered in *Marshall (No. 1)*, logging was not a traditional Mi'kmaq activity, but was "a European activity, in which the Mi'kmaq began to participate only decades after the treaties of 1760–61."[56]

---

53 See, for example, *Sundown*, above note 41, holding that a treaty right to hunt included the right to build shelters required to carry out the hunt.

54 *R. v. Marshall*, [1999] 3 S.C.R. 533 [*Marshall (No. 2)*].

55 *R. v. Marshall; R. v. Bernard*, [2005] 2 S.C.R. 220 at para. 14 [*Marshall (No. 3)*].

56 *Ibid.* at para. 34. By contrast, in *R. v. Sappier; R. v. Gray*, [2006] 2 S.C.R. 686, the Court upheld acquittals entered against a Maliseet individual and a Mi'kmaq individual for unlawful possession or cutting of Crown timber from Crown lands

While *Marshall (No. 3)* made clear that *Marshall (No. 1)* does not protect commercial logging by the Mi'kmaq peoples on Crown lands, the Supreme Court has continued to imply unwritten rights and obligations between parties to written treaties. For instance, in *Mikisew Cree First Nation v. Canada (Minister of Canadian Heritage)*,[57] Binnie J., for a unanimous Court, found that the Crown was under a duty to consult the Mikisew Cree First Nation before building a road on surrendered lands over which the Mikisew held hunting and trapping rights, even though the treaty document clearly provided that the Crown could take up lands for settlement, mining, lumbering, trading, or other purposes. As discussed below, the duty of consultation has been implied in the context of the performance of all treaties, including sophisticated modern comprehensive treaties entered into between well-resourced and -represented Indigenous groups after extensive negotiations with federal, provincial, and territorial governments. The result of this approach is no matter how specific and detailed a written treaty may be, unwritten rights and obligations may be implied by the courts.

It should be noted that treaty rights need not be identical to, or limited by, the extent of Indigenous rights that exist apart from agreement. For example, in *Sioui*,[58] it was argued that a treaty conferring certain rights on the Huron Nation was ineffective because the Huron could not establish historical occupation or possession of the lands in question. The Supreme Court rejected this argument, stating that "[t]here is no basis for excluding agreements in which the Crown may have chosen to create, for the benefit of a tribe, rights over territory other than its traditional territory."[59] Thus, there is no need to establish identity between rights recognized through treaty and those existing at common law.

---

under the New Brunswick *Crown Lands and Forests Act*. The accused harvested logs from lands traditionally used by their respective First Nations. One of the accused used the logs to construct a house and for community firewood. The other accused used the logs to fashion furniture. Unlike in *Marshall (No. 3)*, the accused were not engaged in commercial logging activity and had no intention of selling the logs or any product made from them. The Court held that the accused had proved their claim to an Indigenous right to harvest wood for domestic use. The accused also relied on their treaty rights, but the Court found that it was not necessary to consider this issue.

57 [2005] 3 S.C.R. 388 [*Mikisew*].

58 Above note 39.

59 *Ibid*. at para. 40. See also *Badger*, above note 43, where Cory J., at para. 76, described treaties as "analogous to contracts" which "create enforceable obligations based on the mutual consent of the parties." The scope of treaty rights is to be derived from the wording of the agreement, rather than on the pre-existing rights of the parties.

B. CONSTITUTIONAL STATUS OF INDIGENOUS RIGHTS PRIOR TO 1982

1) Introduction

Prior to 1982, the doctrine of parliamentary sovereignty applied to Indigenous rights, which meant that Indigenous rights could be limited or extinguished through legislation enacted by the appropriate legislative body. However, although there was no constitutional protection for Indigenous rights *per se*, there was a variety of constitutional rules governing how the limitation or extinguishment of Indigenous rights could occur.

2) Federal Legislative Power

Section 91(24) of the *Constitution Act, 1867* confers on the Parliament of Canada the authority to enact laws in relation to "Indians and Lands reserved for Indians." The original version of the *Indian Act*, enacted in 1876, defined an "Indian" generally as any "*male* person of Indian blood reputed to belong to a particular band," any of his children, and his legal wife.[60] This definition proved controversial since it meant that an Indian woman who married a non-Indian man would lose her status for the purposes of the *Indian Act*. Conversely, a non-Indian woman who married an Indian man would automatically acquire status.[61] Successive versions of the *Indian Act* also identified a number of other ways that "Indians" could lose status under the *Indian Act*.[62] In 1985, Parliament

60 S.C. 1876, c. 18, s. 3 [emphasis added].

61 This discriminatory impact on "Indian" women was nevertheless upheld against a challenge based on the *Canadian Bill of Rights*, S.C. 1960, c. 44; R.S.C. 1985, App. III, by the Supreme Court in *Canada (A.G.) v. Lavell*, [1974] S.C.R. 1349. As explained below, this discriminatory rule was repealed on the coming into force of s. 15 of the *Charter* and many of those who had been disenfranchised on the basis of previous versions of the statute were given an opportunity to be registered.

62 For example, colonial statutes dating back to the 1850s provided for a process of enfranchisement, whereby an "Indian" over the age of twenty-one who had attained a certain degree of education, was free of debt, and "of good moral character" could be declared to be enfranchised. Enfranchisement meant that the person was no longer considered to be an "Indian" and there was no legal distinction between an enfranchised "Indian" and a non-"Indian." See *An Act to encourage the Gradual Civilization of Indian Tribes*, S. Prov. C. 1857, c. 26. Provisions for enfranchisement were carried forward into the *Indian Act*, above note 33. In fact, a 1933 amendment to the *Indian Act* permitted the government to order the enfranchisement of Band members who met the qualifications set out in the Act even when they had not requested it.

repealed these discriminatory provisions and restored status to many Indigenous persons who had voluntarily or involuntarily lost their status in the past.[63] The contemporary statutory definition of the term "Indian" is based on those persons who were entitled to be registered as "Indians" immediately prior to 17 April 1985.[64]

The meaning of the term "Indian" for purposes of section 91(24) of the *Constitution Act, 1867* is not limited to the definition in the *Indian Act*. For example, in 1939, the Supreme Court held that Inuit were subject to federal jurisdiction and fell within the definition of "Indians" for purposes of section 91(24).[65] The case did not address the definition of "Indian" under the *Indian Act* and, in fact, the statute was subsequently amended to expressly exclude the Inuit from its application.[66] The Supreme Court of Canada has held that the federal legislative jurisdiction under section 91(24) includes the Métis people and non-status Indians.[67] The Métis are a distinctive people of Indian and European heritage who "in addition to their mixed ancestry, developed their own customs, way of life, and recognizable group identity separate from their Indian or Inuit and European forebears."[68] A "non-status Indian" is generally a person of Indigenous ancestry who either chose not to register or could not register as a status Indian under the *Indian Act*.

Section 91(24) authorizes Parliament to enact laws dealing with "Indians" and "lands reserved for Indians" that would not be permissible in relation to non-Indians. For example, the *Indian Act* contains provisions regulating such matters as the validity of wills, the distribution of property on intestacy, guardianship in relation to minors, and the management of Indian lands, all of which would normally be regarded as falling within provincial jurisdiction in relation to property and civil rights. However, because these provisions deal with the status or rights

---

63 S.C. 1985, c. 27 [Bill C-31].

64 The *Indian Act*, above note 33, provides for maintenance of a register of "status Indians." All those who were registered as status Indians immediately prior to 17 April 1985 are deemed to be entitled to be registered. Other persons who were deregistered by virtue of various limiting provisions in earlier versions of the Act are entitled to apply to be registered. See the definition of "Indian" in s. 2(1) and the identification of persons entitled to be registered under s. 6(1).

65 See *Reference Re British North America Act, 1867 (U.K.) s. 91*, [1939] S.C.R. 104.

66 Section 4(1) of the *Indian Act*, above note 33, provides that "[a] reference in this Act to an Indian does not include any person of the race of aborigines commonly referred to as Inuit."

67 *Daniels v. Canada (Indian Affairs and Northern Development)*, 2016 SCC 12.

68 *Powley* above note 23 at para. 10.

of Indigenous persons only, they are validly enacted by Parliament pursuant to its jurisdiction under section 91(24).[69]

Prior to 1982, Parliament could regulate, limit, or even extinguish Indigenous rights, existing at common law or by treaty through the enactment of legislation.[70] However, any legislation purporting to extinguish Indigenous rights had to evince a "clear and plain intention." Extensive and detailed regulation of a right would not meet the clear and plain intention test. For example, in *Sparrow*,[71] the Supreme Court considered regulations enacted under the *Fisheries Act* dating to 1878, which had subjected the Indigenous right to fish to increasingly restrictive and detailed regulatory control. Pursuant to these regulations, Indigenous persons wishing to fish for food required a special licence issued to individual Indians at the discretion of the minister and subject to terms and conditions which, if breached, could result in the cancellation of the licence. The Supreme Court, in a judgment written by Dickson C.J. and La Forest J., held that such detailed regulation did not demonstrate the requisite clear and plain intention to extinguish the Indigenous right to fish. According to Dickson C.J. and La Forest J., there is a distinction between regulation and extinguishment, and even detailed and restrictive control over a right does not amount to a clear and plain intention to extinguish that right. Subsequently, in *Gladstone*,[72] the Supreme Court held that an Indigenous right to fish for commercial purposes survived despite a regulation which permitted Indigenous fishing for food purposes only. Clearly, the trend in the modern cases is to apply a very strict test in determining whether legislation manifests a clear and plain intention to extinguish an Indigenous right.

As discussed above, section 35(1) of the *Constitution Act, 1982* provides that Indigenous and treaty rights are recognized and affirmed. As a result, since 1982, it is no longer open to Parliament to extinguish Indigenous or treaty rights. Indigenous or treaty rights can only be extinguished by voluntary surrender of rights by Indigenous peoples to

---

69 See *Canada (A.G.) v. Canard*, [1976] 1 S.C.R. 170, upholding succession provisions in the *Indian Act*.

70 See, for example, *R. v. Sikyea*, [1964] S.C.R. 642; *R. v. George*, [1966] S.C.R. 267. Indigenous rights could also be extinguished through express provision in a regulation: see *R. v. Sparrow*, [1990] 1 S.C.R. 1075 [*Sparrow*]. Note that only federal legislation could extinguish Indigenous rights prior to 1982. See the discussion below at Section B(3).

71 *Ibid*.

72 *R. v. Gladstone*, [1996] 2 S.C.R. 723 [*Gladstone*].

the Crown[73] or by the process of constitutional amendment, discussed in further detail below.

3) Provincial Legislative Power

a) Provincial Laws of General Application

Although provinces cannot enact laws in relation to "Indians"—a matter expressly reserved to Parliament under section 91(24)—provincial laws of general application may apply to "Indians" or "Indian" lands.[74] This is a straightforward application of the pith and substance doctrine; laws validly enacted by one level of government may incidentally affect matters otherwise subject to the jurisdiction of the other level. Thus, provincial traffic laws or labour relations laws can validly apply to "Indians," even in respect of activities occurring on an "Indian" reserve.[75] Since the pith and substance or main purpose of such legislation is to ensure traffic safety or to regulate employer–union relations rather than to regulate Indigenous peoples *per se*, the legislation may be validly applied throughout the province, including in respect of Indigenous peoples. On the other hand, if a province enacted legislation specifically aimed at derogating from the rights of Indigenous peoples, the legislation would be *ultra vires*, since it would represent an impermissible intrusion into an area of exclusive federal jurisdiction.[76] Such a law is sometimes said to be invalid on the basis that it has singled out Indigenous peoples for special or differential treatment.

A provincial law may be primarily intended to apply to Indigenous peoples, and still be validly enacted by a province. In *Lovelace v. Ontario*,[77] the province of Ontario had entered into an agreement with First

---

73 See *Ontario (Attorney General) v. Bear Island Foundation*, [1991] 2 S.C.R. 570 and *R. v. Howard*, [1994] 2 S.C.R. 299.

74 See, for example, *Paul v. British Columbia (Forest Appeals Commission)*, [2003] 2 S.C.R. 585 at para. 12, Bastarache J., holding that the British Columbia *Forest Practices Code* is "a law of general application" which "applies *ex proprio vigour* to Indians, to the extent that it does not touch on the 'core of Indianness' and is not unjustifiably inconsistent with s. 35 of the *Constitution Act, 1982*." See also: *Kitkatla Band v. British Columbia (Minister of Small Business, Tourism and Culture)*, [2002] 2 S.C.R. 146 at para. 66 [*Kitkatla*]; and *R. v. Morris*, [2006] 2 S.C.R. 915 at para. 84 [*Morris*].

75 *R. v. Francis*, [1988] 1 S.C.R. 1025; *Four B Manufacturing v. United Garment Workers*, [1980] 1 S.C.R. 1031.

76 See *R. v. Sutherland*, [1980] 2 S.C.R. 451, holding a provision in provincial wildlife legislation to be invalid on the basis that the sole purpose was to derogate from "Indian" rights to hunt on unoccupied Crown lands as guaranteed by the *Manitoba Natural Resources Transfer Agreement*.

77 [2000] 1 S.C.R. 950 [*Lovelace*].

Nations in the province for the development of a commercial casino on an Indian reserve. The proceeds from the casino were to be allocated largely for the benefit of Ontario Bands registered under the *Indian Act*. The casino development was attacked by a number of non-status Indian and Métis communities in the province on the basis that it was an *ultra vires* attempt to regulate a matter reserved to Parliament under section 91(24).[78] The Supreme Court rejected this argument, holding that section 91(24) does not preclude the development of provincial programs aimed specifically at Indigenous people or communities. According to the Court, section 91(24) operates to protect matters touching on the "core of Indianness" from provincial regulation. The courts have defined this "core of Indianness" through reference to the test in *Van der Peet*,[79] as encompassing those activities that "are integral to the distinctive culture" of the Indigenous group claiming a protected right. In this case, the provincial decision to establish a commercial casino on a reserve had done nothing to impair the status or capacity of Métis or non-status Indians. Further, the Supreme Court had already determined that the regulation of gaming is not a protected Indigenous right.[80] Therefore, the province was acting within its constitutional jurisdiction in providing for a First Nation casino and regulating the use of its proceeds.[81]

Similarly, in *NIL/TU,O Child and Family Services Society v. B.C. Government and Service Employees' Union*,[82] the Supreme Court held that a society that provides child welfare services to children and families of British Columbia First Nations was a provincial rather than a federal undertaking and that its labour relations were subject to provincial jurisdiction. The majority characterized the essential nature of the society

---

78 The casino development was also challenged on the basis of s. 15 of the *Charter*. See the discussion at Section C(2).

79 Above note 16.

80 See *R. v. Pamajewon*, [1996] 2 S.C.R. 821 [*Pamajewon*].

81 In this case, the casino development had not required the enactment of legislation referring specifically to Indigenous peoples. Rather, the development of the casino was undertaken pursuant to a provincial law of general application dealing with the conduct, management, and operation of commercial casinos in the province: see the *Ontario Casino Corporation Act, 1993*, S.O. 1993, c. 25 (since repealed and replaced by the *Ontario Lottery and Gaming Corporation Act, 1999*, S.O. 1999, c. 12, Sch. L). However, given the reasoning of Iacobucci J. on this point in *Lovelace*, above note 77, there seems no reason in principle why the province could not have made express statutory provision for the operation of a First Nation casino.

82 [2010] 2 S.C.R. 696 [*NIL/TU,O*]. See also the companion case of *Communications, Energy and Paperworkers Union of Canada v. Native Child and Family Services of Toronto*, [2010] 2 S.C.R. 737, dealing with the Native Child and Family Services of Toronto.

as the provision of child and family services, a matter that fell within provincial jurisdiction. The society was regulated by the province and its employees exercised delegated provincial authority. The fact that the beneficiaries of the society were Indigenous did not fundamentally change the nature of the undertaking.

According to the reasoning in *Lovelace* and *NIL/TU,O*, it would appear that provinces may make special provision for the needs and circumstances of Indigenous peoples through provincial programs without having those laws declared invalid as being laws in relation to "Indians or lands reserved for Indians" under section 91(24).[83] Such laws are necessarily incidental to the exercise of valid provincial powers and, as such, do not involve a derogation from exclusive federal jurisdiction under section 91(24). However, as discussed below, this rule is subject to the limit that provincial laws cannot affect the "core" or "integral part" of federal jurisdiction over Indians and lands reserved for Indians.

b) Provincial Laws Affecting "Indianness" and Section 88 of the *Indian Act*

Federal works, undertakings, and heads of legislative power may be immune from the application of provincial laws in certain circumstances.[84] As discussed in Chapter 4, the doctrine of "interjurisdictional immunity" extends to provincial laws of general application. Although such laws remain valid, the federally regulated person or undertaking is exempted from the law's application. The interjurisdictional immunity doctrine has been applied in respect of the exclusive federal power over "Indians and lands reserved for Indians" under section 91(24).

The core of federal jurisdiction under section 91(24) prevents application of provincial laws to matters affecting "Indianness." The precise scope of the protected core of "Indianness" has not been comprehensively defined. Provincial laws that affect the status, capacities,

83 Many other provincial laws make express provision for the special needs and circumstances of Indigenous peoples: see, for example, the *Tobacco Control Act*, S.O. 1994, c. 10, s. 13, suspending the application of certain prohibitions if an activity is carried out "for traditional Indigenous cultural or spiritual purposes" in order to "acknowledge the traditional use of tobacco that forms part of Indigenous culture and spirituality"; *Heritage Conservation Act*, R.S.B.C. 1996, c. 187, s. 13(2)(c), prohibiting the alteration without a permit of an "Indigenous rock painting or Indigenous rock carving that has historical or archaeological value." The latter provision was considered by the B.C. Court of Appeal to be part of a valid law of provincial application, dealing with all heritage sites in the province, that could validly be applied to Indigenous heritage sites and this was upheld by the Supreme Court of Canada. See *Kitkatla*, above note 74.

84 See the discussion of interjurisdictional immunity in Chapter 4, Section C(6)(c).

or rights of "Indians" *qua* "Indians,"[85] the possession or use of Indian lands,[86] or treaty rights[87] have all been held to touch on matters that are within the core of "Indianness" and beyond the reach of otherwise valid provincial laws. However, the doctrine of interjurisdictional immunity does not preclude valid provincial legislation that justifiably infringes Indigenous and treaty rights pursuant to the test in *Sparrow*.[88]

In *Kitkatla*,[89] the Supreme Court considered the validity of a provision in B.C. legislation which permitted a provincial minister to license the destruction of heritage property. Heritage property was defined in such a way that it included "culturally modified trees," which were trees that had been altered in some fashion by Indigenous people, thereby acquiring cultural significance for the Indigenous peoples concerned. It was argued that licensing the destruction of property that had cultural significance for Indigenous peoples impaired the status or capacity of Indigenous people and affected their "Indianness." This argument was rejected by the Supreme Court, which upheld the validity of the legislation. The Court pointed out that the main purpose of the legislative scheme was to protect heritage property, including property of cultural significance to Indigenous peoples. Destruction of the property was an exception, in cases where there were countervailing values at stake. The Court also noted that the legislation did not apply to any Indigenous object or site which is the subject of an established Indigenous right or title. It was thus tailored so as to not affect the established rights of Indigenous peoples, and could not be said to impair their essential or core status or condition.

Similarly, in *Lovelace*,[90] the Court rejected the contention that the exclusion of non-status Indians from the provincial casino program touched on the protected core of federal jurisdiction over "Indianness." The provincial program did not impair the status or capacity of non-status Indians and the doctrine of interjurisdictional immunity therefore

85 *Natural Parents v. Superintendent of Child Welfare*, [1976] 2 S.C.R. 751, holding that a provincial adoption law providing for adoption of an "Indian" child by non-Indigenous parents cannot deprive the child of "Indian" status under the *Indian Act*, above note 33.

86 *Paul v. Paul*, [1986] 1 S.C.R. 306, holding that a provincial law dealing with the occupancy of a family residence upon marriage breakdown is inapplicable on an "Indian" reserve.

87 *Simon*, above note 42.

88 *Tsilhqot'in*, above note 34 at paras. 128–52; *Grassy Narrows First Nation v. Ontario (Natural Resources)*, [2014] 2 S.C.R. 447 at para. 53.

89 Above note 74.

90 Above note 77.

did not apply. And in *NIL/TU,O*,[91] McLachlin C.J., Binnie, and Fish JJ., concurring in the result, held that the child welfare society did not affect the "protected core of Indianness" under section 91(24), since the society did touch on issues of Indian status or rights.

It should be noted that the operation of the doctrine of interjurisdictional immunity in the context of section 91(24) is tempered by section 88 of the *Indian Act*. Section 88 provides as follows:

> Subject to the terms of any Treaty and any other Act of the Parliament of Canada, all laws of general application from time to time in force in any province are applicable to and in respect of Indians in the province, except to the extent that such laws are inconsistent with this Act or any other order, rule, regulation or by-law made thereunder, and except to the extent that such laws make provision for any matter for which provision is made by or under this Act.

Section 88 extends the effect of provincial laws of general application which cannot apply to Indians and Indian lands *ex proprio vigore* because they touch on the "Indianness" at the core of section 91(24). Such laws are incorporated by reference through section 88, subject to the enumerated exceptions. However, section 88 only incorporates provincial laws that are of "general application," which has been defined as laws that apply uniformly throughout the province and are not intended to single out Indigenous peoples for differential treatment.[92] The corollary is that section 88 cannot be used to reinvigorate provincial laws that are invalid or *ultra vires* because they are in pith and substance in relation to Indians or lands reserved for Indians. Moreover, section 88 does not extend the application of provincial laws that are inconsistent with the terms of a treaty, or with any other federal law, including the *Indian Act* itself.

On the other hand, section 88 does give federal force to those provincial laws of general application that *impair* or *limit* Indigenous rights that are not protected by treaty or federal statute.[93] On this basis, a provincial wildlife statute was held to be applicable to an "Indian" through the operation of section 88, even though the statute affected his status *qua* "Indian."[94] However, section 88 does not authorize the

---

91 Above note 82.

92 *R. v. Dick*, [1985] 2 S.C.R. 309 [*Dick*].

93 With the enactment of s. 35(1) of the *Constitution Act, 1982*, any provincial or federal law affecting a right protected under s. 35(1) must satisfy the justification test set out in *Sparrow*, above note 70.

94 *Dick*, above note 92.

extinguishment of an Indigenous right, since it fails to evince the clear and plain intent required to extinguish Indigenous rights.[95]

C. CONSTITUTIONAL STATUS OF INDIGENOUS RIGHTS SINCE 1982

1) Section 35

The constitutional status and rights of Indigenous peoples in Canada were fundamentally altered by the enactment of section 35 of the *Constitution Act, 1982*. As discussed above, section 35(1) provides that "[t]he existing Indigenous and treaty rights of the Indigenous peoples of Canada are hereby recognized and affirmed." Section 35 defines the "Aboriginal peoples of Canada" as including the Indian, Inuit, and Métis peoples of Canada and provides that "treaty rights" include rights acquired under land claim agreements entered into after section 35 came into force.[96] Section 35 also provides that it guarantees rights equally to male and female persons.[97]

Section 35 is included in Part II of the *Constitution Act, 1982*. It is not part of the *Charter of Rights and Freedoms*. This means that the rights protected pursuant to section 35 are not subject to limitation under section 1 nor are they subject to legislative override through the use of a notwithstanding clause enacted under section 33. Further, the rights guaranteed by section 35 are binding on private parties and not just legislatures or governments, since section 32—the clause limiting the application of the *Charter* to legislatures and government—does not apply to section 35.

Section 35 means that Indigenous rights are no longer subject to the doctrine of parliamentary supremacy which, prior to 1982, permitted Parliament to abrogate or derogate from Indigenous rights through statutes that evinced a clear and plain intention to achieve this result. On the other hand, section 35 does not provide absolute protection for Indigenous rights from the application of inconsistent federal or provincial laws. Instead, the Supreme Court has developed a framework for the interpretation of section 35 which requires a careful balancing of interests between Indigenous rights on the one hand and the role

---

95 *Delgamuukw*, above note 24 at 1122.

96 See ss. 35(2) & (3), respectively, of the *Constitution Act, 1982*.

97 See s. 35(4). This provision, which was added in an amendment enacted in 1983, is similar in wording to s. 28 of the *Charter*.

of Parliament and the provincial legislatures to advance the collective interests of the community as a whole on the other.

a) Section 35 Framework: The *Sparrow* Test

In *Sparrow*,[98] the Supreme Court developed a four-part test for the application of section 35(1) of the *Constitution Act, 1982*. First, a claimant must demonstrate that he or she was acting pursuant to a right protected by section 35. Second, the right in question must be an "existing" right,[99] which the Court in *Sparrow* defined as a right that had not been extinguished by Parliament prior to 1982. Third, there must be an infringement of the protected Indigenous right. Fourth, if there has been an infringement, it must be determined whether the infringement can be justified.[100]

The first step in the *Sparrow* test—proof of a protected Indigenous right—is governed either by the terms of a treaty or in accordance with the test elaborated in *Van der Peet*.[101] *Van der Peet* decided that the determination of whether there is a protected Indigenous right involves two elements. The first is to "identify precisely the nature of the claim being made." The court will look to the nature of the particular activities that

---

98 *Sparrow*, above note 70; *Gladstone*, above note 72 at 723 (identifying four stages of the *Sparrow* test).

99 Note that s. 35(1) of the *Constitution Act, 1982* recognizes and affirms "existing" Indigenous and treaty rights. The word "existing" was incorporated into s. 35 following the conference of 5 November 1981 that had resulted in an agreement between the federal government and nine provinces on a constitutional reform package. The 5 November 1981 agreement had deleted a clause that had been included in the earlier versions of the federal proposals that would have provided express protection for Indigenous and treaty rights. This omission proved controversial, with the result that it was subsequently agreed to reinsert a clause protecting Indigenous and treaty rights; however, the clause in question (which became s. 35) introduced the modifier "existing" in relation to Indigenous and treaty rights, in response to concerns raised by a number of provincial premiers as to the potential scope and impact of the clause. Representatives of the Indigenous peoples objected to the inclusion of the word "existing," and even initiated litigation in the U.K. designed to block the enactment of the *Constitution Act, 1982*, by the Westminster Parliament, but these attempts failed: see *R. v. Secretary of State for Foreign and Commonwealth Affairs, ex parte Indian Association of Alberta and Others*, [1982] 2 All E.R. 118 (C.A.), leave to appeal to the House of Lords dismissed 11 March 1982.

100 Note that, although there are four stages to this framework, certain stages are themselves subdivided into a number of criteria or elements, as explained below.

101 *Van der Peet*, above note 16, which applies in the context of Indigenous rights at common law. Where the right claimed is pursuant to treaty, the existence of a protected Indigenous right is determined by reference to the terms of the treaty rather than on the basis of the *Van der Peet* test.

were being engaged in by the Indigenous claimant, as well as the nature of the impugned government regulation, and the nature of the custom or tradition that is being relied on to establish an Indigenous right. It is also essential to take into account the perspective of the Indigenous people claiming the right. The activities in question will be considered at a general rather than a specific level. For example, in *Van der Peet*, the Indigenous claimant had been charged with selling fish caught under the authority of an Indigenous food fishing licence. The Court of Appeal held that the right being claimed was the right to sell fish "on a commercial basis." However, the Supreme Court held that this characterization was in error and that the right in question should be characterized more generally as simply the practice of "selling fish."[102] Other cases have generally described the right in question as involving the right to engage in specific activities such as hunting or fishing for specific purposes in relation to particular lands or territories.[103]

The second element in the determination of whether the claim qualifies as a protected Indigenous right is whether it is based on a "practice, custom, or tradition integral to the distinctive culture of the aboriginal group claiming the right."[104] Such rights will be specific rather than universal, and must be determined on a case-by-case basis. The relevant period of time for determining whether the activity or practice in question was "integral to the distinctive culture" is generally prior to contact with Europeans;[105] moreover, there must be continuity between the contemporary activity or practice for which constitutional protection is claimed and the pre-contact activity or practice.[106] On the

102 See the discussion in *Van der Peet*, *ibid*. at 551–53.

103 See, for example, *Sparrow*, above note 70 at 1101, where the right was "the Aboriginal right to fish for food and social and ceremonial purposes"; *Adams*, above note 25 at 122, where the right was to "fish for food in Lake St. Francis"; *R. v. Côté*, [1996] 3 S.C.R. 139 at 176 [*Côté*], where the right was to "fish for food within the lakes and rivers" of the relevant territory.

104 *Van der Peet*, above note 16 at 553.

105 Note, however, that this test does not work for Métis peoples, who resulted from the intermarriage between Indigenous and European peoples; a "pre-contact" time frame would effectively deny them access to the protection of s. 35. Accordingly, the Supreme Court in *Powley*, above note 23, decided that the relevant time frame for the identification of Métis rights was the date of effective control by Europeans. In *Powley*, this turned out to be 1850, which was the date of effective European control in the Sault Ste. Marie area (where the relevant Métis community had been established).

106 For example, in *Lax Kw'alaams Indian Band v. Canada (Attorney General)*, [2011] 3 S.C.R. 535, the Court dismissed an action by the Lax Kw'alaams and other First Nations who claimed that they had an Indigenous right in respect of the commercial harvesting and sale of all species of fish within their traditional

other hand, Indigenous rights must be interpreted flexibly, so as to recognize that customs and traditions will evolve over time.[107] Moreover, courts should apply evidentiary rules flexibly, taking into account the difficulty of proving a right that originated in times when there were no written records of the practices, customs, or traditions engaged in. This means, for example, attempting to take appropriate account of oral histories in establishing the existence of Indigenous claims.[108]

If the existence of a protected Indigenous right is established, either because the *Van der Peet* test is satisfied or because the activity in question is protected through a treaty, the court moves to the second stage of the *Sparrow* test—the determination of whether the right was an "existing" right at the time of the enactment of section 35(1) of the *Constitution Act, 1982*. An "existing" right is a right that was not previously extinguished through the enactment of valid *federal* legislation or regulation. Provincial laws can limit but cannot extinguish Indigenous rights.[109] Only federal enactments that evince a clear and plain intention to extinguish an Indigenous right can have this effect. As discussed above, the test for determining whether this intention is present is a

---

waters. The evidence established that prior to European contact, the Lax Kw'alaams harvested fish primarily for consumption and that trade in most fish products was not integral to its distinctive culture. The only fish product that was traded was eulachon grease, which was used as a preservative for perishable food stuffs and was primarily traded among kin. Trade in other fish was "low volume, opportunistic, irregular . . . and incidental to fundamental pre-contact . . . kinship relations" (para. 6).

107 For instance, in *Morris*, above note 74, the Court considered an 1852 treaty between the Governor of Vancouver Island and the Saanich Nation. The treaty provided that in exchange for surrendering their lands, the Saanich Indians were "at liberty to hunt over the unoccupied lands . . . as formerly." Two members of a band of the Saanich Nation were caught driving a truck along a road, using a spotlight to identify game and rifles to shoot them. They were charged with several offences under the British Columbia *Wildlife Act*, including hunting at night and hunting wildlife with the aid of a light or illuminating device. A majority of the Supreme Court, held at para. 32, that the accused's right to hunt at night with the aid of illuminating devices was protected by the treaty and that the use of guns, spotlights, and cars reflected the "evolution of the Tsartlip's historic hunting practices."

108 The importance of oral histories was developed further in *Delgamuukw*, above note 24, in which the Supreme Court ordered a new trial on the basis that the trial judge had failed to take adequate account of oral histories. The Supreme Court held that oral histories must be placed on an "equal footing" with documentary historical records. In this case, the trial judge had given oral histories "no independent weight at all," which the Supreme Court held to be in error (see discussion at 1064–79).

109 See *Delgamuukw, ibid.* at 1120–21.

demanding one. Even detailed regulation and prohibition of certain activities have been interpreted in recent cases as being consistent with the continued existence of an Indigenous right.

If the right in question was not extinguished prior to 1982, the third stage of the *Sparrow* test involves a consideration of whether there has been a *prima facie* infringement of the right. A *prima facie* infringement will generally be found where the regulation in question significantly burdens the preferred mode or manner of exercise of a protected right. Thus, regulatory schemes that provide for broad or unstructured administrative discretion, where the exercise of such discretion may carry significant consequences for the exercise of an Indigenous right, will generally constitute a *prima facie* infringement.[110] However, not all forms of regulation will amount to a *prima facie* infringement of a protected right. In *Côté*,[111] the Supreme Court distinguished between a licensing scheme that did not prescribe any criteria for the exercise of discretion—which was found to infringe an Indigenous right—and a regulation requiring the payment of a fee in order to exercise an Indigenous right—which was found not to infringe the right. Chief Justice Lamer, who wrote reasons concurred in by seven of the nine members of the Court, emphasized the fact that the fee requirement was not a pure revenue-raising measure but was, instead, a carefully tailored user fee directed at the repair and improvement of a modern transportation network on the relevant lands. Although it imposed a financial burden on the exercise of a protected right, this burden did not amount to a *prima facie* infringement of the relevant Indigenous right.

The fourth stage of the *Sparrow* test asks whether the infringement can be justified. Although section 35 is not subject to limitation under section 1 of the *Charter*, *Sparrow* established that Indigenous and treaty rights are not absolute, and may be limited in appropriate circumstances by federal or provincial legislation.[112] The justification analysis is itself broken down into two distinct stages. First, the impugned law must be enacted for a "compelling and substantial objective," which the Supreme Court has described as objectives directed at the reconciliation of the prior occupation of North America by Indigenous peoples with the assertion of the sovereignty of the Crown.[113] The objective of achieving reconciliation of Indigenous societies with the broader community justifies laws enacted for conservation purposes, since such laws are

---

110 See *Sparrow*, above note 70 and *Adams*, above note 25.

111 Above note 103.

112 Both federal and provincial laws are subject to the same test of justification: see *Côté*, *ibid*.

113 *Gladstone*, above note 72 at para. 72.

designed to ensure that there are sufficient natural resources available for the entire community, including Indigenous peoples. Other compelling and substantial objectives include the pursuit of "economic and regional fairness" and "the recognition of the historical reliance upon, and participation in the fishery" by non-Indigenous groups, since these objectives also further the goal of reconciling Indigenous rights with the interests of the broader community.[114] On the other hand, the objective of promoting sports fishing without a significant economic component would fail this aspect of the test of justification.[115]

In *Sparrow*, the Court held that the use of the phrase "recognized and affirmed" in section 35 incorporated the fiduciary obligations owed by the Crown to Indigenous peoples. Thus, the second stage of the justification test involves consideration of whether an infringement unduly restricts the Indigenous right in question, and whether the restriction can be accommodated with the Crown's special fiduciary relationship with Indigenous peoples. The fiduciary duty requires that some form of priority be given to Indigenous claims as compared with claims advanced by other groups. The extent of this priority will vary with the nature of the claim that is being advanced. For example, a right to fish for food is inherently self-limiting, since it is defined by the food requirements of the Indigenous peoples involved. The doctrine of priority in this context would justify granting Indigenous rights holders priority in the fishery, subject only to the limits of conservation, since granting such priority will still permit other users to participate in the fishery. However, where the Indigenous right is not self-limiting, such as a right to hunt or fish for commercial purposes, the doctrine of priority merely requires that "the government demonstrate that, in allocating the resource, it has taken account of the existence of aboriginal rights and allocated the resource in a manner respectful of the fact that those rights have priority over the exploitation of the resource by other users."[116] Factors such as whether there has been consultation and compensation to Indigenous peoples, whether the government has taken measures to accommodate Indigenous users (such as through reduced licence fees), and the extent of the participation in the fishery of Indigenous rights holders relative to their percentage of the population, are all relevant in determining whether government has conducted itself in accordance with its fiduciary obligations to Indigenous peoples.

---

114 *Ibid.* at para. 75.

115 *Adams*, above note 25.

116 *Gladstone*, above note 72 at para. 62.

b) Rights to Self-Government

The 1992 *Charlottetown Accord* proposed to amend the Constitution of Canada to recognize the existence of an "inherent right of self government." The right was inherent in the sense that it was said to arise from the historic use and occupation of lands in North America by Indigenous peoples, as opposed to through legislative enactment or the agreement of Canada.[117] The inherent right of self-government was defined as including the authority of "duly constituted legislative bodies of the Aboriginal peoples . . . to safeguard and develop their languages, cultures, economies, identities, institutions and traditions." However, with the defeat of the *Charlottetown Accord* and the absence of any subsequent negotiations directed at a constitutional amendment, attention has focused on the question of whether section 35(1) of the *Constitution Act, 1982* already includes some form of protection for inherent rights of self-government. Certain commentators have taken the position that self-government rights are already included within section 35(1), and the government of Canada has recognized the inherent right to self-government as an existing right under section 35(1).[118]

The Supreme Court has thus far refused to indicate whether section 35(1) includes an inherent right of self-government. While claims to self-government have been raised in argument before the Court, the Court has been able to dispose of the issues before it without expressing a definitive view on Indigenous self-government. However, the framework that the Court has now elaborated for the identification of Indigenous rights makes it likely that some form of self-government right will be recognized as an "Aboriginal right." The more difficult question is whether such a common law right to self-government will meet the four-part *Sparrow* test for Indigenous rights under section 35(1).

---

117 At a First Ministers Conference held in March 1987, the Government of Canada had proposed to entrench a constitutional provision granting constitutional protection to self-government rights set out in agreements reached with Indigenous peoples. Such recognition was described as a "contingent" right to self-government, since it depended on agreement with the federal or provincial governments. However, this proposal was rejected by the Indigenous organizations participating in the Conference, who maintained that their right to self-government was inherent, and no such amendment was enacted.

118 See Royal Commission on Indigenous Peoples, *Final Report* (Ottawa: Supply and Services Canada, 1996) vol. 5 at 158; P.W. Hogg, *Constitutional Law of Canada*, 5th ed., loose-leaf (Toronto: Carswell, 2007) at 28.25 to 28.28; Canada, *Indigenous Self-Government: The Government of Canada's Approach to Implementation of the Inherent Right and Negotiation of Indigenous Self-Government* (Ottawa: Department of Indian Affairs and Northern Development, 1995). The Government of Canada continues to state that it recognizes the inherent right of self-government as an existing Indigenous right under s. 35 of the *Constitution Act, 1982*.

With respect to the existence of a right to self-government, both *Van der Peet* and *Delgamuukw* strongly imply that the historic use and occupation of land by Indigenous peoples must include some form of legal protection for self-government.[119] In *Van der Peet*, Lamer C.J. referred with approval to Marshall C.J.'s observation in *Worcester v. Georgia* that prior to the arrival of Europeans, Indigenous peoples had "institutions of their own . . . governing themselves by their own laws."[120] *Van der Peet* also referred with approval to the statement by the Australian High Court in *Mabo* that native title has its origins in the "traditional laws acknowledged by and the traditional customs observed by the aboriginal inhabitants of a territory."[121] The Supreme Court then set out a test for identifying protected Indigenous rights that focused on whether a practice, custom, or tradition was of central significance to the Indigenous society in which it existed. If, as the Supreme Court decided, Indigenous rights arise from the "social organization and distinctive culture" of Indigenous peoples, it would seem to follow that Indigenous rights must include some form of right to self-government. Self-government is the very embodiment of the social organization and cultural identity of Indigenous peoples, providing the context and the foundation for a social order in which certain practices, customs, and traditions can develop and flourish. What *Van der Peet* implies is that Indigenous rights do not merely consist of the right to perform certain activities; they also encompass the right to regulate and govern the manner in which those activities are carried out. Similarly, in *Delgamuukw*, Lamer C.J. noted that a source of Indigenous title is the "relationship between the common law and pre-existing systems of Aboriginal law."[122] Lamer C.J. also described Indigenous title as being held communally and stated that decisions with respect to that land are made by the community.[123] These comments reinforce the suggestion that Indigenous rights to self-government are capable of being recognized at common law.

The Supreme Court has held that to the extent that rights to self-government exist, they cannot be framed in broad or generalized terms. For example, in *Pamajewon*,[124] it was argued that the right to self-government was protected under section 35(1), and that this right included the right to regulate gaming activities on a reserve. The Supreme

119 *Van der Peet*, above note 16; *Delgamuukw*, above note 24.

120 *Van der Peet*, above note 16 at para. 107; *Worcester*, above note 19.

121 *Van der Peet*, above note 16 at para. 40; *Mabo*, above note 20.

122 Above note 24 at 1082. See also *ibid*. at 1088 for a further reference to "systems of Aboriginal law."

123 *Ibid*. at 1082–83.

124 Above note 80.

Court, in a unanimous judgment written by Lamer C.J., assumed for the sake of the analysis that a right to self-government existed. However, he noted that any such right would be subject to the test for the identification of Indigenous rights set out in *Van der Peet*. Lamer C.J. noted that the appellants in *Pamajewon* had characterized their claim as a "broad right to manage the use of their reserve lands."[125] However, he rejected this characterization on the basis that this would "cast the Court's inquiry at a level of excessive generality" and reformulated the right as being the right "to participate in, and to regulate, gambling activities on their respective reserve lands." Lamer C.J. then turned to the second part of the *Van der Peet* test, considering whether this activity was an "integral part of the distinctive cultures of the Shawanaga or Eagle Lake First Nations." Upon examining the evidentiary record, Lamer C.J. concluded that the appellants had failed to demonstrate that the activities in question satisfied this test.

A similar analysis was adopted by Lamer C.J. in *Delgamuukw*. He noted that the right to self-government that was advanced before the Court in that case was framed in broad terms. However, since "rights to self-government, if they existed, cannot be framed in excessively general terms," the type of claim to self-government advanced in this case was "not cognizable under s. 35(1)."[126] At the same time, Lamer C.J. indicated that this conclusion was without prejudice to the parties to advance more specific claims to self-government at the new trial that was ordered.

More recently, the Court has commented on several statutes and treaties that provide for institutions of self-government for Indigenous peoples. In *Alberta (Aboriginal Affairs and Northern Development) v. Cunningham*,[127] the Court upheld an Alberta statute allowing Métis to maintain their separate identity as Métis, as distinct from Indians, and rejected a claim that the Act infringed the equality provisions in section 15 of the *Charter*. The Court held that the legislation was an ameliorative program designed to enhance and preserve the "identity, culture and self-governance of the Métis."[128] In *R. v. Kapp*,[129] Bastarache J., in concurring reasons, stated that section 25 of the *Charter* (discussed below), would encompass "statutory rights which seek to protect interests associated with aboriginal culture, territory, *self-government*

125 *Ibid.* at 834.
126 See *Delgamuukw*, above note 24 at 1114–15.
127 [2011] 2 S.C.R. 670 [*Cunningham*].
128 *Ibid.* at para. 54.
129 [2008] 2 S.C.R. 483 [*Kapp*].

. . . and settlement agreements that are a replacement for treaty and aboriginal rights."[130]

It has been argued that the recognition of an inherent right of self-government is somehow incompatible or inconsistent with the *Constitution Act, 1867*. A number of Privy Council decisions in the early part of the twentieth century stated that sections 91 and 92 of the *BNA Act* exhaustively distributed all legislative power between the federal and provincial orders of government.[131] On this basis, it has been suggested that any right of self-government for Indigenous peoples must have been extinguished by the *Constitution Act, 1867*. This view was accepted by Macfarlane J.A. in the British Columbia Court of Appeal decision in *Delgamuukw*.[132] According to Macfarlane J.A., sections 91 and 92 of the 1867 Act cover "the whole area of self-government in Canada."[133] It has also been suggested that the Privy Council's decision in *Reference Re Initiative and Referendum Act (Man.)*,[134] which holds that legislative powers conferred on Parliament or the provincial legislatures cannot be exercised by any other body, is inconsistent with the recognition of a "third order of government" in Canada.

The difficulty with this theory is that the *Constitution Act, 1867* was not intended to extinguish or limit the rights of Indigenous peoples. Instead, its object was to establish a new form of political organization in place of the previous colonial governments that had existed in British North America. The *Constitution Act, 1867* does not evince any intention to extinguish any pre-existing right of self-government. Statements made in Privy Council cases that the Act involved an exhaustive distribution of powers between Canada and the provinces were made in a different context and for a different purpose. The theory of the exhaustive distribution of powers was intended to clarify that, as between Parliament and the provincial legislatures, all the power that had previously been exercised by the colonial administrations had been exhaustively distributed.[135]

---

130 *Ibid.* at para. 105 [emphasis added].

131 *Ontario (A.G.) v. Canada (A.G.)* (1912), 3 D.L.R. 509. See also *Reference Re Initiative and Referendum Act (Man.)*, [1919] A.C. 935.

132 *Delgamuukw v. B.C.* (1993), 104 D.L.R. (4th) 470 at 515–20 (B.C.C.A.), var'd, above note 24.

133 *Ibid.* at 519 (citing the Privy Council decision in *Ontario (A.G.) v. Canada (A.G.)*, above note 131 at 511).

134 Above note 131.

135 See, for example, *Campbell v. British Columbia (Attorney General)*, [2000] B.C.J. No. 1524 (S.C.), dismissing a challenge to the self-government provisions in the *Nisga'a Final Agreement Act*, S.C. 2000, c. 7. See also: *House of Sga'nisim v. Canada (Attorney General)*, 2011 BCSC 1394.

On the basis of the above analysis, it would appear highly likely that Indigenous rights at common law must include some form of protection for self-government. The more difficult question is the extent to which such rights will satisfy the four-part framework for the application of section 35(1) of the *Constitution Act, 1867* set out in *Sparrow*. As discussed above, the Supreme Court has already stated that the first stage of the *Sparrow* test will apply to claims for self-government rights. This will limit self-government claims to the right to regulate or govern those activities, practices, or customs that were an integral part of the distinctive culture of the Indigenous people claiming the right. Further, any self-government right must be shown to be an existing right at the time of the enactment of section 35(1) in 1982. While the courts have held that extensive regulation of an Indigenous right is consistent with the continued existence of that right, it would seem difficult to sustain this conclusion in respect of a right to self-government. A right to self-government is premised on the notion that Indigenous peoples have the collective right to *govern* or *regulate* particular activities, practices, or traditions.[136] Yet it is evident that for over a century prior to 1982, dating at least to the enactment of the first *Indian Act* in 1876, Indigenous affairs were subject to regulation and control by Parliament and by the Department of Indian and Northern Affairs rather than by Indigenous peoples. While it may be that this extensive regulation did not extinguish the right to engage in specific activities—such as the right to hunt or fish in the manner engaged in historically by Indigenous peoples, or to engage in other activities integral to the distinctive culture of a people claiming a right—it seems less plausible to maintain that the right to *regulate* or *govern* such activities survived such regulation.[137] Of course, any such determination will necessarily have to be made on a case-by-case basis, and with a proper evidentiary foundation, in accordance with *Van der Peet*. It is therefore possible that certain limited forms of self-government could be found to have continued in existence as of 1982. Moreover, regardless of the extent to which a right of self-government continues to exist for purposes of section 35, it is open to federal and provincial governments to negotiate agreements

136 In *Pamajewon*, above note 80, Lamer C.J. referred to the right of self-government as involving the right to *regulate* gaming.

137 In 1995, the government of Canada recognized the inherent right of self-government as an existing right for purposes of s. 35(1) (see note 118 above). However, there was no explanation provided as to how such a right could have survived the regulatory regime established for Indigenous peoples prior to 1982.

providing for self-government rights. Indeed, a number of such agreements have been successfully concluded and implemented.[138]

c) Duty to Consult and Accommodate Indigenous Rights

In a landmark 2005 decision, the Supreme Court set out the obligations of the Crown in disputed areas before a final judicial determination as to the existence and scope of an Indigenous right has been made. In *Haida Nation*,[139] the Council of the Haida Nation brought an application for judicial review of decisions of British Columbia's Minister of Forests to allow logging in parts of the Queen Charlotte Islands. The Haida people had claimed title to these lands for more than one hundred years, and also claimed that red cedar trees from the Island's old growth forests were an integral part of the Haida culture. The Supreme Court of Canada unanimously held that the Crown was obliged under section 35 to consult with the Haida people and, if necessary, accommodate their concerns pending final resolution of the legal claims. This duty arose from the concept of the honour of the Crown, which, the Court said, means that the Crown "cannot cavalierly run roughshod over Aboriginal interests where claims affecting these interests are being seriously pursued in the process of treaty negotiation and proof."[140] To do otherwise, suggests the Court, may render the rights (in this case, land claims) devoid of meaningful content, since if and when the right is finally established in court, the Indigenous interest may have been significantly impaired.

The extent of the duty to accommodate will turn on a preliminary assessment of the strength of the particular Indigenous claim, as well as on the potential effect of the government's planned actions on the right. Furthermore, the duty affects the conduct of both sides—while the Crown must provide for a meaningful process of consultation, the Indigenous group must not take unreasonable positions to thwart government action.[141] The actual onus on the Crown may range from a mere duty to give notice, provide information, and discuss any issues raised in response (in the case where a very weak claim to title has

---

138 For an overview of concluded self-government agreements and ongoing negotiations toward self-governance, see Indigenous and Northern Affairs Canada, *General Briefing Note on Canada's Self-Government and Land Claims Policies and the Status of Negotiations*, online: www.aadnc-aandc.gc.ca/eng/1373385502190/1373385561540.

139 *Haida Nation v. British Columbia (Minister of Forests)*, [2004] 3 S.C.R. 511 [*Haida Nation*].

140 *Ibid.* at para. 27.

141 The duty applies to both the federal and provincial governments, but not to private parties (*ibid.* at para. 55). On this basis, the claim against the logging company was dismissed.

been raised) to a duty of deep consultation with formal participation of Indigenous groups in the decision-making process (in the case where a strong *prima facie* claim to title has been established). The main question is always whether reasonable efforts have been made to effect reconciliation between the parties regarding the interests at stake.

In a companion case, *Taku River Tlingit First Nation v. British Columbia*,[142] the Court made it clear that it will be willing in appropriate cases to accept that governments acting in good faith have satisfied the requirement of the duty to consult. In *Taku River*, the First Nation had claimed lands that included a mine that had recently been reopened over their objections. However, the decision to reopen the mine had been made after an environmental assessment that took over three years to complete. The First Nation had been included in the environmental assessment process. The ultimate approval had included measures designed to take account of the Indigenous concerns. In these circumstances, the Court held that the duty to consult and accommodate had been satisfied.

In *Rio Tinto Alcan Inc. v. Carrier Sekani Tribal Council*,[143] the Supreme Court elaborated on the *Haida Nation* test. The Court held that the duty of consultation would be triggered if the following three conditions were met:

- The Crown must have real or constructive knowledge of a potential Indigenous claim or right. Proof that the claim will succeed is not required.
- There must be Crown conduct or a Crown decision. Crown conduct or Crown decisions are not confined to the exercise of statutory powers or decisions that have an immediate impact on lands and resources. The duty to consult extends to "strategic, higher level decisions" that may have an impact on Indigenous claims and rights.
- There must be a possibility that the Crown conduct may affect the Indigenous claim or right. Past wrongs, speculative impacts, and adverse effects on negotiating positions will not suffice.

In *Rio Tinto*, the Court held that a decision of the British Columbia Utilities Commission to approve a 2007 agreement for the purchase and sale of electricity from Alcan to BC Hydro did not trigger the duty of consultation with First Nations. The electricity sold under the agreement was generated by a dam built in the 1950s and Alcan had sold excess power (power not used for aluminum smelting) to BC Hydro

142 *Taku River Tlingit First Nation v. British Columbia (Project Assessment Director)*, [2004] 3 S.C.R. 550 [*Taku River*].

143 [2010] 2 S.C.R. 650 [*Rio Tinto*].

since 1961. Although the Carrier Sekani Tribal Council First Nations had long used the Nechako River for fishing and sustenance, the evidence before the Commission was that the 2007 agreement would not have any physical impacts on water levels or fishing. The Crown had failed to consult the First Nations when originally building the dam. However, that was an underlying infringement, which may give rise to a claim for compensation, but did not trigger a "fresh duty" to consult. Thus, *Rio Tinto* makes clear that claimants cannot rely on past breaches of the duty to consult to found an obligation of consultation based on the honour of the Crown. As the third element of the test makes clear, there must be a nexus between the impugned conduct or decision and the Indigenous claim or right being asserted.

The Supreme Court has held that the obligation to consult applies not only in the case of unresolved or pending claims to Indigenous right or title, but also in the context of the performance of written treaties. In *Mikisew*,[144] Treaty 8 granted the Mikisew Cree First Nation rights to hunt, trap, and fish throughout territories that they had surrendered to the Crown, with the exception of tracts "as may be required or taken up from time to time for settlement, mining, lumbering, trading or other purposes." Binnie J., for a unanimous Court, held that the federal government had breached its duty to consult the Mikisew in approving a winter road within the Treaty 8 lands. Binnie J. rejected the argument, which had been accepted by Rothstein J.A. (as he then was) for the majority in the Federal Court of Appeal, that approval of the winter road was simply an exercise of the Crown's right to "take up" land under the express terms of the treaty. Furthermore, he rejected the Crown's contention that any duty to consult or accommodate had been discharged during the process of the extensive consultations with the First Nations in 1899 at the time the treaty was negotiated. Binnie J. held that determining the terms of the written treaty was only a "stage" in "the long process of reconciliation" between Indigenous peoples and non-Indigenous peoples.[145] The treaty was said not to be "the complete discharge of the duty arising from the honour of the Crown, but a rededication of it."[146] Since the proposed road could have an adverse impact on the hunting and trapping rights of the Mikisew, the principle of the honour of the Crown imposed a duty on the government to consult prior to approving the road. Relying on *Haida Nation*, Binnie J. stated that the scope of the duty to consult was "governed by context." In this case, Binnie J. found the required scope of consultation fell "at the

144 Above note 57.
145 *Ibid.* at para. 54.
146 *Ibid.*

lower end of the spectrum." The Crown was required to provide notice to the Mikisew about the road project, to engage directly with them by providing information, to solicit and listen carefully to their concerns, and to attempt to minimize adverse impacts on hunting, fishing, and trapping rights. Binnie J. held that the process followed by the minister was insufficient to discharge the duty to consult.

Furthermore, the Supreme Court has found that the duty to consult may be implied even in the case of modern comprehensive treaties that contain express terms regarding consultation between governments and Indigenous peoples. In *Beckman v. Little Salmon/Carmacks First Nation*,[147] the Supreme Court considered a 1997 land claims agreement (the LSCFN Treaty) among the governments of Canada and the Yukon and the Little Salmon/Carmacks First Nation. Binnie J., for the Court, noted that "[t]he increased detail and sophistication of modern treaties represents a quantum leap beyond the pre-Confederation historical treaties such as . . . Treaty No. 8 [considered in] *Mikisew*."[148] While such early treaties were "typically expressed in lofty terms of high generality and were often ambiguous," modern land claims such as the LSCFN Treaty were "intended to create some precision around property and governance rights and obligations."[149] Binnie J. went on to characterize the LSCFN Treaty as "a comprehensive lawyerly document," which was the product of twenty years of negotiations among "adequately resourced and professionally represented parties."[150] He stated that the Court should strive to respect the product of the attempts of the parties to "order their own affairs."[151]

Despite this emphasis on giving effect to the parties' intentions as set out in their written agreement, Binnie J. held that the Crown had an implied duty to consult the LSCFN prior to taking up settlement lands for the purposes of agriculture, even though the LSCFN treaty permitted such "taking up." Furthermore, Binnie J. arrived at this conclusion despite the fact that the LSCFN Treaty set out elaborate consultation procedures—the treaty referred to consultation in more than sixty different places but did not expressly provide a consultation process for land grant approvals. Binnie J. nonetheless held that the territorial gov-

---

147 [2010] 3 S.C.R. 103 [*Beckman*].

148 *Ibid*. at para. 12.

149 *Ibid*.

150 *Ibid*. at paras. 54 and 58.

151 *Ibid*. at para. 54. See also *Moses*, above note 36 at para. 7, in which Binnie J. for the majority, stated that the "contract analogy" with treaties "is even more apt in relation to a modern comprehensive treaty whose terms . . . are not constituted by an exchange of verbal promises reduced to writing in a language many of the Aboriginal signatories did not understand."

ernment was required to consult the LSCFN prior to approving a land grant to a Yukon resident. Relying on *Haida Nation*, Binnie J. stated that the Crown cannot "contract out of its duty of honourable dealing with Aboriginal people," which is "a doctrine that applies independently of the expressed or implied intention of the parties."[152] Binnie J. did hold open the possibility that the duty to consult could be excluded by the terms of a treaty, provided that the parties negotiated "a different mechanism which . . . upholds the honour of the Crown."[153] In the case of the LSCFN Treaty, however, the duty of consultation had not been excluded by the lack of reference to consultation procedures in the case of land grant approvals for surrendered land.

In terms of the scope of the duty to consult, Binnie J. stated that the adequacy of "what passed (or failed to pass) between the parties must be assessed in light of the role and function to be served by consultation on the facts of the case and whether that purpose was, on the facts, satisfied."[154] Although there was no express duty to consult with respect to land grant approvals, the consultation procedures set out in other parts of the LSCFN Treaty were said to be relevant to the scope of the implied duty to consult. As in *Mikisew*, Binnie J. found that the duty to consult in *Beckman* was "at the lower end of the spectrum." Curiously, he noted that this standard was "consistent with the LSCFN Treaty itself which sets out the elements [of consultation] the parties themselves regarded as appropriate."[155]

By contrast, in concurring reasons, which we find quite compelling, LeBel and Deschamps JJ. emphasized the need to give effect to the terms of comprehensive written treaties. They held that the Court should not superimpose further rights and obligations relating to matters already provided for in a comprehensive land claims agreement. An implied duty to consult would only apply if the parties had failed to address the issue of consultation in their treaty document. The content of the duty of consultation should be defined by the measures set out in the treaty. If no such measures are specified, resort must be had to the principles set out in *Haida Nation* and its progeny. Unlike Binnie J., LeBel and Deschamps JJ. held that the parties had in fact incorporated consultation provisions in the treaty with respect to the Crown's right

152 *Beckman*, above note 147 at para. 61.

153 *Ibid.* at para. 71.

154 *Ibid.* at para. 72.

155 *Ibid.* at para. 74. This reasoning is difficult to understand. If the parties regarded it appropriate to set out specific consultation procedures in certain circumstances (land grant approvals not being one of them), then it is unclear why those procedures should be relevant to the other circumstances (i.e., land grant approvals).

to transfer land. The minority relied on a Final Agreement, which provided for development assessment procedures requiring consultation with concerned First Nations and participation in the assessment of a project such as the land grant to the Yukon resident. On the facts, LeBel and Deschamps JJ. held that the LSCFN received more than what they were entitled to under the treaty and there was no basis for finding that the Crown had breached its duty to consult.

It is clear from the above decisions that the Crown will in all cases have an overarching duty to act honourably towards Indigenous peoples, both in respect of unsettled claims and the performance of treaties. The ambit of the duty to act honourably is unclear. It would appear from the decisions that consultation will generally be required to fulfil the duty of honourable dealing and that the duty of consultation could only be excluded in a very clear case.[156] Furthermore, assuming consultation is required, the scope of that consultation will be extremely difficult to predict in any given situation. The Supreme Court has provided very little guidance and the test appears to be totally context-dependent and results-driven. Whether there has been adequate consultation in any given case will likely depend significantly on value judgments regarding the conduct and behaviour of the Crown towards the Indigenous peoples concerned. This seems an uncertain and unsatisfactory basis for constitutional decision making.

2) The *Charter* and Indigenous Peoples

When the *Charter* was enacted, there was a concern that the constitutional entrenchment of individual rights might give rise to a challenge to legislative provisions granting or recognizing differential treatment for Indigenous peoples. In order to avoid this result, section 25 of the *Charter* was included:

> The guarantee in this Charter of certain rights and freedoms shall not be construed so as to abrogate or derogate from any Aboriginal, Treaty or other rights or freedoms that pertain to the Aboriginal peoples of Canada including
> (a) any rights or freedoms that have been recognized by the *Royal Proclamation* of October 7, 1763; and
> (b) any rights or freedoms that now exist by way of land claims agreements or may be so acquired.

---

156 Even if the duty to consult were excluded, according to Binnie J.'s decision in *Beckman*, some other "mechanism" would have to apply in order to ensure that the honour of the Crown is fulfilled. See *Beckman*, *ibid.* at para. 71.

There are certain obvious differences between sections 25 and 35. First, unlike section 35, section 25 does not purport to guarantee rights, but merely provides that the guarantee of rights elsewhere in the *Charter* should not be construed as derogating from Indigenous or treaty rights. Section 25 appears to have been intended to prevent other sections of the *Charter* from being used to invalidate Indigenous rights and freedoms. Section 25 also seems to apply to a broader class of entitlements than section 35. Section 25 refers to Indigenous and Treaty rights but also refers to "other rights or freedoms that pertain to the Aboriginal peoples of Canada." Moreover, section 25 does not utilize the word "existing" when referring to Indigenous rights. It is arguable that this language suggests that section 25 shields rights or freedoms acquired or recognized pursuant to statute or government action, regardless of whether they are constitutionally protected under section 35.

The Supreme Court has yet to provide an authoritative framework for the interpretation of section 25. In *Corbiere v. Canada*,[157] a provision in the *Indian Act* restricting the right to vote in Band elections to "Indian" residents off a reserve was challenged on the basis that it infringed the equality provisions in section 15 of the *Charter*. The Court held that the *Indian Act* drew a distinction between Indians who lived on the reserve and Indians who lived off the reserve, which was a breach of section 15 that could not be justified under section 1. L'Heureux-Dubé J., in an opinion concurred in by three other members of the Court, commented on the wording of section 25, particularly its reference to "other rights and freedoms." In her view, section 25 seemed to suggest that Indigenous rights or freedoms protected by statute were shielded from Charter attack through the operation of section 25, even though such rights may not be protected under section 35. However, L'Heureux-Dubé J. concluded that it was not necessary on the facts of the case to determine the scope of section 25. She noted that there had been no evidence presented to demonstrate that the relevant statutory provisions violated an Indigenous or treaty right. She also observed that section 25 could not be invoked merely because a statutory provision made reference to Indigenous peoples. She proceeded to rule that the statutory provision violated equality rights of status Indians residing off reserve and that this infringement could not be justified under section 1 of the *Charter*.

In *R. v. Kapp*,[158] the Supreme Court unanimously dismissed a claim by commercial fishermen who alleged that a federal Indigenous fish-

---

157 [1999] 2 S.C.R. 203 [*Corbiere*].

158 Above note 129.

eries strategy breached the right to equality under section 15(1) of the *Charter.* Bastarache J., concurring in the result, held that section 25 was a complete answer to the appellants' claim. Bastarache J. held that section 25 was not merely an interpretative provision, but included "statutory rights which seek to protect interests associated with Aboriginal culture, territory, self-government . . . and settlement agreements that are a replacement for treaty and Aboriginal rights." By contrast, "private rights of individual Indians held in a private capacity as ordinary Canadian citizens would not be protected."[159] The majority in *Kapp* held that the federal fisheries strategy was an ameliorative program that fell within the ambit of section 15(2) of the *Charter* and expressly declined to comment on section 25. However, the majority did signal its "concerns with aspects of the reasoning of Bastarache J."[160] In their view, "only rights of a constitutional character are likely to benefit from s. 25."[161] The majority's comments are in direct conflict with L'Heureux-Dubé J.'s judgment in *Corbiere.* As a result of *Corbiere* and the division of opinion in *Kapp*, the proper approach to section 25 of the *Charter* remains unclear.

As *Kapp* indicates, programs aimed at enhancing the position of particular Indigenous groups or communities have been upheld as ameliorative programs under section 15(2) of the *Charter.* In *Cunningham*,[162] the Court set out a two-part test for the application of section 15(2). The first question is whether the law makes an adverse distinction against the claimant group on an enumerated or analogous ground. If so, the second question is whether the distinction is saved by section 15(2). At the second stage, the government must demonstrate on the evidence that the program is a "genuinely ameliorative program" directed at improving the situation of a group in need of ameliorative assistance in order to enhance substantive equality, that there is a correlation between the program and the disadvantage suffered by the target group, and that rational means are used to pursue the ameliorative goal.[163] In *Cunningham*, Métis claimants in Alberta opted to register as status Indians in order to obtain medical benefits under the *Indian Act*. Under the Alberta *Métis Settlements Act*, their membership in the Métis settlement was automatically revoked. The claimants sought a declaration that the denial of their Métis status was unconstitutional, relying on section 15(1). The Court dismissed the claim, holding that

159 *Ibid.* at para. 105.
160 *Ibid.* at para. 62.
161 *Ibid.* at para. 63.
162 Above note 127.
163 *Ibid.* at para. 44.

the legislation was an ameliorative program protected by section 15(2). Assuming that the distinction between the Métis and status Indians under the Act was based on an enumerated or analogous ground, the program was genuinely ameliorative. The object of the legislation was to enhance and preserve the identity, culture, and self-governance of the Métis through the establishment of a Métis land base. Excluding Métis who were also status Indians from membership was permissible, since the Métis had a distinctive culture and defined themselves as a people (although some people identified as both Indian and Métis).

3) Constitutional Change and Indigenous Peoples

It would appear that amendments to the constitutional provisions that make specific reference to Indigenous peoples can be effected through the general amending formula in section 38(1) of the *Constitution Act, 1982*.[164] Section 38(1) requires authorizing resolutions of both Houses of Parliament and the legislative assemblies of seven provinces representing at least 50 percent of the total population of the ten provinces.

Section 35.1 of the *Constitution Act, 1982* requires that, prior to an amendment to section 91(24) of the *Constitution Act, 1867* or sections 25 and 35 of the *Constitution Act, 1982*, a First Ministers Conference must be convened to consider the proposed amendment, and representatives of the Indigenous peoples of Canada must be invited to participate in the discussions. This requires effective and meaningful consultation of Indigenous peoples prior to the enactment of constitutional amendments directly affecting them. Further, it is likely that the obligation of effective and meaningful consultation would apply irrespective of section 35.1, as a result of the fiduciary obligation of the federal and provincial governments towards Indigenous peoples. As described above, the fiduciary obligations of the Crown require that governments consult with Indigenous peoples and take their perspectives, needs, and circumstances into account prior to exercising a discretion that may

---

164 In 1983, s. 35 of the *Constitution Act, 1982* was amended so as to add ss. (3) & (4) pursuant to the amending procedure set out in s. 38. Further, this same amendment added s. 35.1, which requires that a constitutional conference involving representatives of Indigenous peoples be convened prior to a future amendment to certain constitutional provisions of particular significance to Indigenous peoples. (Quebec, which was boycotting constitutional negotiations at the time, refused to participate in the constitutional conference at which the amendment had been agreed to, or to pass an authorizing resolution. Thus, although the amendment received the consents necessary for an amendment under s. 38, it did not meet the thresholds required under ss. 41 or 43.)

limit or impair constitutionally protected Indigenous or treaty rights.[165] Such a fiduciary obligation would certainly apply to discretionary decisions of the federal government in the negotiation of a constitutional amendment limiting or impairing constitutionally protected rights of the Indigenous peoples of Canada, regardless of whether the proposed amendment directly amended the specific provisions mentioned in section 35.1. For example, an amendment permitting the secession of a province from Canada would clearly and significantly impact the legal and constitutional rights of Indigenous peoples residing in the province that was attempting to secede.[166] Thus, prior to proceeding with an amendment authorizing secession, the government of Canada would be legally obliged to consult with Indigenous peoples, particularly in the relevant province, and to ensure that their constitutionally protected rights and interests were adequately taken into account in the proposed amendment.[167]

FURTHER READINGS

Burrows, T., *Canada's Indigenous Constitution* (Toronto: University of Toronto Press, 2010)

Canada, *Aboriginal Self-Government: The Government of Canada's Approach to Implementation of the Inherent Right and Negotiation of Aboriginal Self-Government* (Ottawa: Department of Indian Affairs and Northern Development, 1995)

Flanagan, T., *First Nations?: Second Thoughts* (Montreal: McGill-Queen's University Press, 2000)

Hogg, P.W., *Constitutional Law of Canada*, 5th ed., loose-leaf (Toronto: Carswell, 2007) c. 28

---

165 See, for example, *Haida Nation*, above note 139.

166 For example, the continued existence of a fiduciary relationship between the Crown and Indigenous peoples in the seceding province would be precluded following secession.

167 As described in Chapter 6, the so-called *Clarity Act* (*An Act to give effect to the requirement for clarity as set out in the opinion of the Supreme Court of Canada in the Quebec Secession Reference*), S.C. 2000, c. 26 requires the House of Commons to take into account the views of the Indigenous peoples of Canada in determining the clarity of a referendum question and the clarity of the result in a referendum on secession. Section 3(2) requires that the "rights, interest and territorial claims of the Indigenous peoples of Canada" be addressed in negotiations. These statutory obligations reinforce the general fiduciary obligation of the Crown.

LAW COMMISSION OF CANADA, *In Whom We Trust: A Forum on Crown–Aboriginal Fiduciary Relationships* (Toronto: Irwin Law, 2002)

MACKLEM, P., *Indigenous Difference and the Constitution of Canada* (Toronto: University of Toronto Press, 2001)

———, & D. SAUNDERSON, eds., *From Recognition to Reconciliation: Essays on the Constitutional Entrenchment of Indigenous and Treaty Rights* (Toronto: University of Toronto Press, 2015)

MCNEIL, K., *Emerging Justice?: Essays on Indigenous Rights in Canada and Australia* (Saskatoon: Native Law Centre, University of Saskatchewan, 2001)

SLATTERY, B., "Making Sense of Aboriginal and Treaty Rights" (2000) 79 Can. Bar Rev. 196

PART SIX

CONCLUSION

CHAPTER 16

THE CANADIAN CONSTITUTION IN THE TWENTY-FIRST CENTURY

A. ALL QUIET ON THE CONSTITUTIONAL FRONT?

In February 2012, a group of retired politicians and scholars gathered at the University of Toronto to debate the "Quebec question for the next generation." The conference was prompted by the remarkable fact that for more than a decade, the issue of Quebec's place in Canada had largely disappeared from public view. The result was that an entire generation of political leaders and scholars outside Quebec had developed without any sustained immersion in issues relating to the "Quebec question." What was unclear was whether this silence on the constitutional front, which had persisted for more than a full decade, was permanent (a "new normal") or whether it was merely transitory and the country was destined to revert to a discussion of the same constitutional questions and debates that had dominated Canadian political discourse throughout the 1980s and 1990s.

Although there was no consensus on this issue amongst the participants at the February 2012 Toronto gathering, few believed that the constitutional question would re-emerge to take centre stage in Canadian politics anytime soon. The subsequent four years have proven this prediction to be accurate, at least in the short term. Despite a major reconfiguration of the federal political landscape in the 2015 general election, there was no re-emergence of the Bloc Québécois. A short-lived

Parti Québécois government in Quebec made no plans for a referendum, and in 2014 voters returned the Liberal Party of Quebec to power.

In retrospect, the constitutional policy pursued by Jean Chrétien in the late 1990s, in the aftermath of the 1995 sovereignty referendum, has proven to be remarkably successful. Chrétien's success was all the more noteworthy given the disarray in the federalist ranks in the latter stages of the 1995 referendum campaign itself and the extremely close referendum result. It seemed, then, to be only a matter of time before a third sovereignty referendum would be held. Faced with this continued threat to the survival of the country, many federalists, particularly those in Quebec, advocated continued pursuit of "Plan A," focused on securing incremental changes and adjustments to the federation so as to respond to Quebecers' apparent desire for greater constitutional autonomy. But Chrétien eschewed this advice and avoided all discussion of constitutional change. He pursued, instead, a "Plan B" aimed at clarifying the ground rules for any future referendum and stressing the costs and uncertainties associated with secession.

The Chrétien government opted decisively for the Plan B strategy in 1996 with the *Secession Reference*,[1] followed by the enactment of the *Clarity Act* in June 2000.[2] These initiatives significantly reformulated the ground rules that would apply in any future sovereignty referendum, particularly in terms of the wording of the question and the majority necessary to effect secession.[3] Moreover, while these initiatives did provoke an immediate outcry among the sovereignist political leadership in Quebec (which claimed that Quebec alone would determine the ground rules for a referendum and possible secession), public support for sovereignty among ordinary Quebec residents eventually began to decline during the early 2000s. The election of a majority Liberal government headed by Jean Charest in 2003 eliminated the possibility of a third sovereignty referendum for the mandate of the government. By the fall of 2005, a group of respected Quebec public figures headed by former PQ premier Lucien Bouchard called for a new political agenda focused on reducing public debt and investing in education and training, mentioning sovereignty only in passing.[4]

---

1 *Reference Re Secession of Quebec*, [1998] 2 S.C.R. 217. Although the case was not argued until 1998, the Reference questions were referred to the Court in the fall of 1996.

2 *Clarity Act* (*An Act to give effect to the requirement for clarity as set out in the opinion of the Supreme Court of Canada in the Quebec Secession Reference*), S.C. 2000, c. 26.

3 See Chapter 6 for a detailed discussion of these matters.

4 See L. Bouchard *et al.*, *For a Clear-Eyed Vision of Quebec* (Quebec, QC: pourunquebeclucide.com, 2005).

As of this writing in 2016, there continues to be no appetite among federalist politicians for undertaking another round of formal constitutional negotiations aimed at securing the Quebec government's formal adherence to the *Constitution Act, 1982*. That road was tried, unsuccessfully, at Meech Lake in the late 1980s and again at Charlottetown in 1992. The prospects for a successful resolution to such negotiations seem even lower today than they were then. The basic, continuing problem is that any constitutional changes designed to address Quebec's "traditional demands" are likely to be seen within Quebec as offering too little and, outside Quebec, as offering too much. More fundamentally, the Meech and Charlottetown experiences seem to reflect the lack of consensus on constitutional fundamentals in Canada. It is unclear whether Canadians are capable of agreeing on a single organizing vision of what the country is about or what it should aspire to become. Without such an underlying consensus, any future package proposing amendments to the Canadian constitution would likely meet the same unhappy fate dealt to both the *Meech Lake* and the *Charlottetown Accords*.

The precedent set during the ratification process for the *Charlettown Accord* has made future constitutional bargaining particularly unlikely to be successful. For the first time, Canadians were given an opportunity to approve constitutional change in a national referendum. Having consulted the people once, it will be virtually impossible to avoid consulting them in the future. It would take a brave politician to come forward now with significant constitutional changes without promising to submit them to the people for ratification. It should also be remembered, as discussed in Chapter 6, that several provinces now legally require a referendum before formal approval of a constitutional amendment. This requirement solidifies the political necessity of submitting significant constitutional changes to a pan-Canadian referendum.

Although this referendum commitment is an important and welcome advance for democratic legitimacy, it significantly limits the prospect of constitutional change. International experience suggests that it is extremely difficult to secure popular ratification for a complicated package of constitutional amendments through a referendum. When voters are presented with complicated packages, they tend to focus on those parts of the package they dislike rather than on the parts they support. The possibility of success in a referendum seems to be maximized when voters are presented with a narrow and specific "stand-alone" amendment with effects that can be clearly stated and defended, rather than with a complicated package that will necessarily include some items that are unclear or unpopular.

The problem for Canada is that any future set of formal amendment proposals designed to obtain Quebec's political consent to the constitution is likely to be in the form of a complex constitutional package rather than as a limited number of stand-alone amendments. Moreover, any complex constitutional package would be correctly perceived as an attempt to achieve long-term closure on the agenda of formal constitutional change. This would fuel the insistence of groups and constituencies with agendas that their concerns be dealt with simultaneously, rather than being postponed to a future round of constitutional change.

As a result, it is unlikely that Quebec will be reconciled with the Canadian constitution through amendment of the formal terms of the constitution. This is a sobering realization and means that Quebec residents have essentially two main political options. The first is to work within the existing Canadian constitution to increase the powers of the province to the extent permitted within the constitution as it now stands. The second possibility is to opt for an entirely new set of constitutional arrangements by choosing political sovereignty.

Many Canadian federalists have tended to avoid making this choice explicit for fear that it would drive many undecided Quebec residents into the sovereignist camp. But since the election of the Charest government in 2003, the political agenda in Quebec has focused on economic issues rather than changes to the formal constitution. This reflects the reality that, under the existing Canadian constitution, the provinces wield significant power over social, political, and economic matters. While the Supreme Court has in recent years broadened the authority of Parliament, it has continued to favour an expansive interpretation of provincial powers. This reality is underlined by the main complaint that has been made by successive Quebec governments. Political leaders in Quebec have not been able to point to any significant policy areas—apart from the conduct of international relations—where the province lacks constitutional jurisdiction. Rather, the continuing complaint in Quebec City and a number of other provincial capitals is that the federal government should withdraw from areas that are said to belong exclusively to the provinces under the *Constitution Act, 1867*. For example, the main thrust of the changes in the division of powers contained in the ill-fated *Charlottetown Accord* was to require the federal government to withdraw from certain areas under exclusive provincial jurisdiction. No new powers or jurisdiction would have been conferred on the provinces, for the simple but often overlooked reason that the provinces already have all the constitutional jurisdiction they could exercise responsibly in a federation.

The fact that provinces already possess ample constitutional jurisdiction decreases the likelihood of formal constitutional amendment. Assuming it would be desirable to reduce the federal government's presence in areas formally designated as provincial under the constitution, it is not necessary to amend the constitution. The federal government can voluntarily withdraw from areas of provincial jurisdiction through administrative and legislative change without a formal constitutional amendment. In this sense, the existing constitution permits adjustments to the roles of the federal and provincial governments.

Of course, it must be acknowledged that the Meech Lake and Charlottetown proposals to constitutionally entrench the recognition of Quebec's distinct society constitutionally could not be achieved through mere intergovernmental agreement. However, the reality of Quebec's distinctiveness is already a central feature of the judicial interpretation of the constitution. For example, in interpreting the *Charter*, the Supreme Court has held that the objective of protecting and promoting the French language in Quebec is sufficiently important to justify imposing limits on *Charter* rights.[5] In this sense, while entrenchment of a distinct society clause would be symbolically important, it would have little practical effect on the daily lives of Quebec residents or Canadians elsewhere in the country.

The decline in political support for sovereignty in Quebec and the decade-long season of constitutional peace that has ensued seems to have been welcomed in all regions of the country. Moreover, if the national unity question did resurface, the Supreme Court's decision in the *Secession Reference*, as well as the enactment of the *Clarity Act*, will prove of some assistance to sovereignists as well as federalists. The *Secession Reference* and the *Clarity Act*[6] have conferred legitimacy on the sovereignty agenda by stating that a clear mandate for secession would give rise to a constitutional duty to negotiate the terms of Canada's break up. Some commentators have insisted that the recognition of a duty to negotiate secession is harmless since the duty was already a political reality. Yet prior to the *Secession Reference*, federalists in Ottawa and the provinces had never stated clearly how they would react to a majority "Yes" vote in a sovereignty referendum. Even if political realities would have forced the federal government to respond to such a referendum outcome, the commencement of secession negotiations would have been only one of a number of possible options. Other possibilities would have included holding a second referendum, in Quebec or nationwide, and establishing some form of independent national commission or other body with a mandate to develop proposals for a renewed federation. The recognition of a constitutional duty to commence secession negotiations

---

5 See *Ford v. Quebec (A.G.)*, [1988] 2 S.C.R. 712. The *Canadian Charter of Rights and Freedoms* is Part I of the *Constitution Act, 1982*, being Schedule B to the *Canada Act 1982* (U.K.), 1982, c. 11.

6 See above notes 1 and 2.

following a clear referendum mandate has materially reduced the federal government's flexibility in this regard. This reduced flexibility makes it more difficult for the federal government to extract concessions in return for its agreement to commence secession negotiations. Even if the result of any positive mandate for secession would have been political negotiation, the advance recognition of a constitutional duty to negotiate has likely altered the scope, nature, and timing of those discussions.

The recognition of a constitutional duty to negotiate secession will not only affect the conduct of negotiations, but it will also colour any future referendum campaign. A key element of the federalist strategy in the referendum campaigns of 1980 and 1995 was to emphasize the uncertainties associated with voting "Yes." The existence of a constitutional duty to negotiate reduces the element of uncertainty somewhat. Sovereignist political leaders will be able to rebut claims that a "Yes" vote would plunge Quebec into a legal black hole with the Supreme Court decision and the *Clarity Act*. Instead, voting "Yes" may be portrayed as a way to force the federal government to commence negotiations to address Quebec's demands. Indeed, it is likely that in any future referendum, sovereignists will argue that Quebec will have everything to gain and relatively little to lose from voting for secession negotiations. If negotiations are successful, Quebec would gain new powers, either as part of an agreement whereby it becomes sovereign or through a profound decentralization of the federation. If the negotiations failed, however, the sovereignists could claim that this was proof positive that Canadian federalism itself is a failure and that the time has come for Quebec to strike out on its own.

To be sure, we believe that the best option for all Canadians, including all Quebec residents, is to avoid the necessity of engaging in such an exercise in the first place. But in the event that political support for sovereignty increases and a third referendum is initiated, it cannot be assumed that the *Secession Reference* or the *Clarity Act* have assured a positive outcome for federalists. To the contrary, these developments have altered the dynamic of any future sovereignty referendum in profound ways for both federalists as well as sovereignists.

B. REFORM TO CENTRAL INSTITUTIONS: THE EXCESSIVE POWER OF THE EXECUTIVE BRANCH

The area with the greatest need for constitutional change is not part of Quebec's agenda. In our view, the greatest shortcoming of the existing Canadian constitution continues to be the excessive power that the executive branch wields over the legislature. As has been made clear in this book, there are few institutional checks and balances on a majority government in Canada at either the federal or the provincial level. The opposition parties and ordinary MPs (even those from the government party) typically lack any meaningful role or input into the policy process, which is dominated by the prime minister, senior officials in the bureaucracy, and a limited number of Cabinet ministers. We recognize that it is important that majority governments have the tools necessary to implement their agenda. However, the problem with the current Canadian parliamentary system is that it seems to have swung too far in the direction of protecting the prerogatives of the executive, while often reducing ordinary Members of Parliament to the role of mere bystanders.

There are no clear or easy remedies for the imbalance between the roles of the executive and the legislature. One proposal that achieved a degree of popularity in certain parts of the country in the 1990s is the so-called Triple-E Senate.[7] Depending on how it was configured, a Triple-E Senate might impose some limits on the power of the executive, since it could increase the ability of the Senate to block proposals from the House of Commons. But this outcome is by no means assured, since the primary purpose of the Triple-E Senate is to equalize provincial representation in the Upper House rather than to achieve a balance between the powers of the government and Parliament. The difficulties created by this single-minded pursuit of equal provincial representation in the Senate were made manifest in the *Charlottetown Accord*. In order to offset the fact that the eight smaller provinces would dominate representation in the Senate, representation from Ontario and Quebec in the House of Commons was increased and a complicated and untested "joint sitting" procedure was proposed to resolve deadlocks between the House of Commons and the Senate. The practical impact of these changes was simply unknown.[8] Canadians were asked to endorse a radically redesigned Parliament without any real idea of how it would function. It was hardly surprising that the strongest support for the accord was in British Columbia and Alberta, where support for the Triple-E Senate was strongest.

---

7 The three "*E*'s" refer to an elected Senate, with effective powers, and with equal representation from each province.

8 See, for example, the thoughtful critique of the institutional reform proposals in D. Elton, "The *Charlottetown Accord* Senate: Effective or Emasculated?" in K. McRoberts & P.J. Monahan, *The Charlottetown Accord, the Referendum and the Future of Canada* (Toronto: University of Toronto Press, 1993) at 37.

Debate over the merits of proposals for constitutional change to federal institutions is unlikely to occur in the near future. As noted above, there are considerable obstacles standing in the way of formal constitutional amendment. Furthermore, the Supreme Court has recently confirmed the necessity of formal constitutional amendment for changes to significant Canadian institutions in *Reference re Senate Reform*[9] and *Reference re Supreme Court Act, ss. 5 and 6*.[10] However, in 2016, federal actors appear to now be turning their focus to what might be called informal constitutional amendment—that is, changing the day-to-day practices of institutions without modifying the underlying binding law. In the case of the Supreme Court, Prime Minister Trudeau has instructed his Attorney General, via the non-binding instrument of a mandate letter, to consider only bilingual candidates. Elsewhere, those members of the Senate formerly part of the Liberal caucus now sit as "independent Liberals" who are formally de-coupled from the Government, and Trudeau's own Senate appointees have, to date, sat exclusively as independents. This change, which results in an upper chamber whose members may feel less of an obligation to support the Prime Minister's legislation, has the potential to be significant to the workings of Parliament.

C. CANADA IN THE TWENTY-FIRST CENTURY

A century ago, Prime Minister Wilfrid Laurier was bold enough to predict that the twentieth century would belong to Canada. Few would offer a similar prediction for Canada's prospects in the twenty-first. The challenge today seems focused on maintaining our position amongst an increasingly competitive and globalized community of nations, as opposed to assuming a position of dominance or even clear leadership. Yet, one welcome and positive development is that the political agenda through the first decade of the twenty-first century has shifted away from the national unity questions that dominated through much of the 1980s and 1990s. Canadians in all parts of the country seem unwilling to continue living on a constitutional knife-edge, uncertain of whether they will be living in one country or two this time next year. The turbulent events that unfolded following September 11, 2001, followed by the financial crisis later in the decade, highlighted the benefits of political stability and the interdependence of a united Canada in the North American continent. This shift in political emphasis away from

9 [2014] 1 S.C.R. 704.
10 [2014] 1 S.C.R. 433.

the constitution and in favour of broader economic, social, and political concerns suggests that Canadians will be in a better position to grapple with the large challenges facing us in the years ahead.

FURTHER READINGS

BAYEFSKY, A., ed., *Self-Determination in International Law: Quebec and Lessons Learned: Legal Opinions* (Boston: Kluwer, 2000)

CAMERON, D., *The Referendum Papers: Essays on Secession and National Unity* (Toronto: University of Toronto Press, 1999)

MONAHAN, P., *Doing the Rules: An Assessment of the Federal Clarity Act in Light of the Quebec Secession Reference* (Toronto: C.D. Howe Institute, 2000)

NEWMAN, W., *The Quebec Secession Reference, the Rule of Law and the Position of the Attorney General of Canada* (Toronto: York University Centre for Public Law and Public Policy, 1999)

RUSSELL, P.H., *Constitutional Odyssey: Can Canadians Become a Sovereign People?* (Toronto: University of Toronto Press, 1992) c. 10 and Conclusion

GLOSSARY

Aboriginal peoples The original inhabitants of North America prior to the arrival of European settlers. Section 35 of the *Constitution Act, 1982* defines the "Aboriginal peoples of Canada" as including the Indian, Inuit, and Metis peoples of Canada.

Act A bill that has been approved or "read" three times by the Parliament or legislature and signed into law by the queen's representative (the governor general or lieutenant governor). Also known as a statute.

Administrative (non-constitutional) judicial review A legal proceeding in which a decision or action of a public body is challenged on the basis that the decision or action exceeded the body's legal powers.

British North America Act, 1867 The British statute creating Canada in 1867 out of the colonies of Canada, New Brunswick, and Nova Scotia. In 1982 it was renamed the *Constitution Act, 1867*.

Cabinet The group of ministers of state named by the prime minister whose function is to advise the prime minister and governor general on measures for the administration of public affairs.

Canadian Bill of Rights A federal statute, enacted in 1960, which provided that all federal legislation should be interpreted so as not to infringe on certain fundamental individual rights.

Charlottetown Accord The agreement reached in August 1992 between the prime minister, premiers, territorial leaders, and Aboriginal leaders providing for comprehensive changes to the Canadian constitution.

The accord was rejected in a national referendum on October 26, 1992, with 54 percent of those casting ballots voting against it.

Canadian Charter of Rights and Freedoms Sections 1–34 of the *Canada Act, 1982*, which protects a wide variety of individual and collective rights of Canadians, and which binds both the federal and provincial levels of government.

Common law In contrast to statute law, common law is law that relies for its authority on the decisions of the courts and is recorded in the law reports as decisions of judges, along with the reasons for their decisions.

Confederation Strictly defined as a loose association of states in which the state governments take precedence over the central government. Although the term "confederation" is used to describe the Canadian union of provinces, the Canadian central government is not, and has never been, the delegate of the provinces. It is independent of the provinces and coordinates with them.

Constitution of Canada The supreme law of Canada. Laws inconsistent with the Constitution of Canada are of no force or effect. Section 52(2) of the *Constitution Act, 1982* defines it as including the *Constitution Acts, 1867–1982*, the *Canada Act 1982*, and thirty Acts and orders in the schedule to the *Constitution Act, 1982*.

Constitutional amending formula The procedures set out in Part V of the *Constitution Act, 1982* which, for the first time, enable all parts of the Constitution of Canada to be domestically amended without recourse to the United Kingdom Parliament. In general, consent of the Parliament of Canada, some or all of the provincial legislatures, and the governor general is required for an amendment.

Constitutional conventions Non-legal rules that limit political powers and ensure that such powers are used in accordance with democratic principles. These rules of the constitution are occasionally recognized, but are not enforced, by the courts, and are regarded as politically binding by the governmental actors.

Constitutional judicial review A court proceeding in which a statute, or a decision or action of a public body, is challenged on the basis of inconsistency with a provision of the Constitution of Canada. If such inconsistency is found, the statute, decision, or action is invalid and of no legal force or effect.

Constitutional law The system of principles and fundamental law, written and unwritten, which defines the powers of government, allocates powers between different political institutions, protects individual and group rights, and recognizes certain fundamental political values. In Canada, examples of constitutional law include the Constitution of Canada, constitutional conventions, and many statutes, orders in council, proclamations, and court decisions of a constitutional nature.

Crown The sovereign power as head of the state or monarchy. In all Commonwealth countries, including Canada, which acknowledge the queen of England as the formal head of state, the government (or state) is commonly referred to as "the Crown."

Disallowance The power of the federal Cabinet, acting through the governor general, to disallow any provincial law within two years of its enactment. This power has not been used for many years and current constitutional convention dictates that it remain dormant.

Entrenched Alterable solely through the use of the constitutional amending formula.

Executive branch The branch of government, consisting of the queen (as represented by the governor general), the Cabinet, and the ministries of the government, vested with the responsibility of administering and enforcing laws.

Federal constitution A constitution, such as Canada's, which prescribes a government based on the federal principle; that is, sovereignty is divided between two orders of government (central and regional), with each level of government restricted to the areas of jurisdiction assigned to it, and neither able to control or direct the activities of the other.

Federalism The governmental power of a state is distributed between a central (or federal) government and several regional (provincial) governments. Individuals are subject to the laws of both authorities, and the central and regional authorities' powers must be independent from each other and not subject to being taken away, altered, or controlled by the other level.

First reading The vote that takes place on the introduction of a bill into Parliament or the legislature. First reading is passed without amendment or debate, and is coupled with an order to print the bill.

Government bill A bill approved by Cabinet and introduced into a legislature by a minister.

Government of Canada The framework of political institutions by means of which the state carries on its executive, judicial, legislative, and administrative functions. In Canada, the term "government" includes the governor general, Cabinet, individual ministers, and the thousands of public servants within all departments of government. Also included are certain Crown corporations and agencies that are not within the formal governmental structure but are subject to a high degree of ministerial control, and thus are deemed to be "agents" of the Crown.

Governor general The queen's representative in Canada. Although the governor general retains extensive formal legal powers, constitutional convention dictates that the governor general's authority must only be exercised on the advice of the prime minister, who, in turn, must enjoy the confidence of the elected House of Commons.

House of Commons The lower house of the Canadian Parliament, currently composed of 308 members of Parliament, elected in single-member constituencies representing the entire country. The House of Commons is elected based on the principle of a universal adult right to vote. The government in power must enjoy the confidence of the House of Commons in order to remain in office.

Indigenous *See Aboriginal*

Interjurisdictional immunity A doctrine that precludes the application of an otherwise valid law to the extent that it impairs a vital or essential part of a constitutional head of power.

Judicial branch The branch of government, consisting of the system of courts and all judges, vested with the responsibility to interpret, construe, and apply the law.

Judicial Committee of the Privy Council (JCPC) A tribunal of senior English judges, established in 1833 by the British Crown, which heard appeals from English colonies, including those in British North America. From 1867 to 1949 the JCPC was the highest court of appeal for matters of Canadian law. However, in 1949 appeals to the JCPC were abolished and the Supreme Court of Canada became the highest Canadian court.

Judicial review The review by the courts of the legal validity of actions taken by the state.

Legislative branch The branch of government vested with the responsibility of making laws. At the federal level it consists of the queen (as represented by the governor general), the House of Commons (elected), and the Senate (appointed by the governor general). At the provincial level it consists of the lieutenant governor and the Legislative Assembly.

Lieutenant governor The representative of the queen within the province, appointed by the governor general, who acts as the head of the executive branch of that province.

Meech Lake Accord The 1987 agreement between the prime minister and the ten provincial premiers reached at Meech Lake, Quebec, proposing a series of constitutional changes designed to secure the consent of the government of Quebec to the *Constitution Act, 1982*. The most controversial of the proposed changes was the constitutional entrenchment of the recognition of Quebec as a distinct society. By 22 June 1990 the accord had been ratified by resolutions of the Senate, House of Commons, and eight provincial legislatures. However, because it required the approval of all ten provinces within a three-year period, it failed to become law in Canada.

Minister A minister is selected by the prime minister and appointed by the governor general to manage a particular portfolio (department) of government and advise the governor general in accordance with the principle of responsible government. All ministers must be either members of the House of Commons or the Senate. Collectively, the ministers constitute the Cabinet.

Money bill A bill to impose, alter, or regulate taxation, to pay debt, to supply government requirements, or for other financial purposes. A money bill can only be introduced into the House of Commons by a minister, and must first be recommended by the governor general.

Order in council An order made by the lieutenant governor or the governor general by and with the advice of the executive or the privy council. In accordance with the principles of responsible government, all orders in council are drafted and approved by the Cabinet.

Paramountcy The principle of judicial review stating that a valid federal law will prevail over a valid but inconsistent provincial law. The provincial law is rendered inoperative to the extent of the inconsistency.

Parliament The federal lawmaking body composed of the Senate, House of Commons, and the queen.

Parliamentary sovereignty or supremacy The doctrine that states that the Parliament or a legislature, acting within its jurisdiction, may enact or repeal any law it chooses. This doctrine lies at the heart of the United Kingdom constitutional tradition, but, in Canada, parliamentary supremacy has always been limited by the terms of the *Constitution Act, 1867*. The principle of parliamentary supremacy has been further limited by the enactment of the *Constitution Act, 1982*, which placed certain entrenched individual and group rights beyond the power of either level of government.

Patriation The termination of the United Kingdom Parliament's authority over Canada, achieved in 1982 with the passage of the *Canada Act 1982*.

Prerogative power An inherent power or legal privilege of the Crown, defined in accordance with principles of common law. The prerogative is subject to statute, and today there are very few remaining areas in which the Crown prerogative survives; the vast majority of Crown powers are defined through statute.

Prime minister/premier The chief minister of the Crown who is asked by the governor general to form a government or Cabinet. The prime minister is selected by the governor general, and he or she must be the leader of the political party that is able to control a majority in the House of Commons. Among the most important powers of the prime minister is the right to advise the governor general as to whom to summon or dismiss as ministers, and the right to advise the governor general to call a general election.

Private bill A bill relating to matters of particular interest or benefit to a specific individual or group. Private bills are often introduced by a private member, and they are enacted by a different and simpler procedure that does not require government sponsorship.

Private member's bill A bill, either public or private, introduced by a member of Parliament who is not a member of the government (i.e., who is not a minister or a parliamentary assistant to a minister).

Public bill A bill which relates to public policy matters.

Queen's Privy Council for Canada A group of more than one hundred persons, including all current and former Cabinet ministers and certain other notable Canadians such as former provincial premiers or the leaders of opposition parties, with the legal right to advise the governor general as to the exercise of the powers of the Crown. In practice, the Privy Council does not meet and has no role or function. The Cabinet, which is technically a "committee of the Privy Council" made up of ministers appointed on the advice of the prime minister, exercises the powers of the Privy Council on a day-to-day basis.

Report stage A stage in the legislative process, usually directly after second reading, when amendments agreed to by the committee that examined the bill are considered, and any members of the House of Commons may propose amendments of their own to the bill.

Representative government A government that is elected by, and therefore representative of, the people. The term "representative government" refers to the requirement that laws must only be made by a legislature that has been elected by the people (as opposed to by the Crown legislating through the use of the royal prerogative).

Reservation The power of the governor general to withhold the royal assent from a bill that has been passed by both Houses of Parliament.

Residual power The power conferred on the federal Parliament by section 91 of the *Constitution Act, 1867* to make laws for the "Peace, Order, and good Government of Canada." It is residual in relation to provincial governments as it is specifically limited to matters not assigned to the provincial legislatures. The provincial residual power is conferred on provincial parliaments by section 92(16) of the *Constitution Act, 1867*, which gives provincial legislatures power over "all Matters of a merely local or private Nature in the Province."

Resolution A motion approved by the legislature that does not have the force of law, but merely expresses the legislature's views or opinion on a matter of public concern.

Responsible government The constitutional conventions which require that the prime minister and Cabinet may hold office only for so long as they can control a majority in the House of Commons or legislature, and which dictates that the formal head of state (governor general, lieutenant governor) must always act under the direction of the Cabinet.

Royal assent Approval of a bill by the governor general or lieutenant governor after the bill has been agreed to by both the Senate and the House of Commons or the legislature. This approval makes the bill a statute and gives it the force of law. In accordance with the principles of responsible government, the governor general always grants royal assent on the advice of the Cabinet.

Rule of law The doctrine stating that all state power must be exercised in accordance with law as recognized by the courts, originally recognized in the *Magna Carta* in England in 1215. The rule of law is also sometimes said to require that laws be known to the citizen, be understandable, and control the exercise of discretion by state officials.

Second reading A motion proposing approval in principle of a bill and referral to a committee for detailed examination. No amendments are allowed at this stage, although extensive debate on the merits of the bill does occur.

Senate The appointed federal legislative body. Senate approval is required for all ordinary bills and for most constitutional amendments.

Separation of powers The division of the functions of government into executive, legislative, and judicial branches.

Third reading A vote to give final approval of a bill by a legislative body. No amendments are permitted on third reading of a bill.

Ultra vires A finding by a court that a statute or public decision is beyond the powers conferred by the Constitution of Canada on the body purporting to make it. The consequence of a finding of *ultra vires* is invalidity.

Unitary state A state in which undivided sovereignty is conferred on the national (central) government, as distinguished from a federal or confederal system. While local governments may be established within a unitary system, their powers are defined by the national government, which is the only constitutionally recognized order of government.

CONSTITUTION ACTS 1867 TO 1982*

THE CONSTITUTION ACT, 1867

* Source: Department of Justice Canada, online: http://laws.justice.gc.ca/en/const.

30 & 31 Victoria, c. 3. (U.K.)

(Consolidated with amendments)

An Act for the Union of Canada, Nova Scotia, and New Brunswick, and the Government thereof; and for Purposes connected therewith

[*29th March 1867.*]

Whereas the Provinces of Canada, Nova Scotia, and New Brunswick have expressed their Desire to be federally united into One Dominion under the Crown of the United Kingdom of Great Britain and Ireland, with a Constitution similar in Principle to that of the United Kingdom:

And whereas such a Union would conduce to the Welfare of the Provinces and promote the Interests of the British Empire:

And whereas on the Establishment of the Union by Authority of Parliament it is expedient, not only that the Constitution of the Legislative Authority in the Dominion be provided for, but also that the Nature of the Executive Government therein be declared:

And whereas it is expedient that Provision be made for the eventual Admission into the Union of other Parts of British North America:[1]

I. PRELIMINARY

Short title

1. This Act may be cited as the *Constitution Act, 1867.*[2]

[*Repealed*]

2. Repealed.[3]

II. UNION

Declaration of Union

3. It shall be lawful for the Queen, by and with the Advice of Her Majesty's Most Honourable Privy Council, to declare by Proclamation that, on and after a Day therein appointed, not being more than Six Months after the passing of this Act, the Provinces of Canada, Nova Scotia, and New Brunswick shall form and be One Dominion under the Name of Canada; and on and after that Day those Three Provinces shall form and be One Dominion under that Name accordingly.[4]

Construction of subsequent Provisions of Act

4. Unless it is otherwise expressed or implied, the Name Canada shall be taken to mean Canada as constituted under this Act.[5]

Four Provinces

5. Canada shall be divided into Four Provinces, named Ontario, Quebec, Nova Scotia, and New Brunswick.[6]

Provinces of Ontario and Quebec

6. The Parts of the Province of Canada (as it exists at the passing of this Act) which formerly constituted respectively the Provinces of Upper Canada and Lower Canada shall be deemed to be severed, and shall form Two separate Provinces. The Part which formerly constituted the Province of Upper Canada shall constitute the Province of Ontario; and the Part which formerly constituted the Province of Lower Canada shall constitute the Province of Quebec.

Provinces of Nova Scotia and New Brunswick

7. The Provinces of Nova Scotia and New Brunswick shall have the same Limits as at the passing of this Act.

Decennial Census

8. In the general Census of the Population of Canada which is hereby required to be taken in the Year One thousand eight hundred and seventy-one, and in every Tenth Year thereafter, the respective Populations of the Four Provinces shall be distinguished.

III. EXECUTIVE POWER

Declaration of Executive Power in the Queen

9. The Executive Government and Authority of and over Canada is hereby declared to continue and be vested in the Queen.

Application of Provisions referring to Governor General

10. The Provisions of this Act referring to the Governor General extend and apply to the Governor General for the Time being of Canada, or other the Chief Executive Officer or Administrator for the Time being carrying on the Government of Canada on behalf and in the Name of the Queen, by whatever Title he is designated.

Constitution of Privy Council for Canada

11. There shall be a Council to aid and advise in the Government of Canada, to be styled the Queen's Privy Council for Canada; and the Persons who are to be Members of that Council shall be from Time to Time chosen and summoned by the Governor General and sworn in as Privy Councillors, and Members thereof may be from Time to Time removed by the Governor General.

All Powers under Acts to be exercised by Governor General with Advice of Privy Council, or alone

12. All Powers, Authorities, and Functions which under any Act of the Parliament of Great Britain, or of the Parliament of the United Kingdom of Great Britain and Ireland, or of the Legislature of Upper Canada, Lower Canada, Canada, Nova Scotia, or New Brunswick, are at the Union vested in or exerciseable by the respective Governors or Lieutenant Governors of those Provinces, with the Advice, or with the Advice and Consent, of the respective Executive Councils thereof, or in conjunction with those Councils, or with any Number of Members thereof, or by those Governors or Lieutenant Governors individually, shall, as far as the same continue in existence and capable of being exercised after the Union in relation to the Government of Canada, be vested in and exerciseable by the Governor General, with the Advice or with the Advice and Consent of or in conjunction with the Queen's Privy Council for Canada, or any Members thereof, or by the Governor General individually, as the Case requires, subject nevertheless (except with respect to such as exist under Acts of the Parliament of Great Britain or of the Parliament of the United Kingdom of Great Britain and Ireland) to be abolished or altered by the Parliament of Canada.[7]

Application of Provisions referring to Governor General in Council

13. The Provisions of this Act referring to the Governor General in Council shall be construed as referring to the Governor General acting by and with the Advice of the Queen's Privy Council for Canada.

Power to Her Majesty to authorize Governor General to appoint Deputies

14. It shall be lawful for the Queen, if Her Majesty thinks fit, to authorize the Governor General from Time to Time to appoint any Person or any Persons jointly or severally to be his Deputy or Deputies within any Part or Parts of Canada, and in that Capacity to exercise during the Pleasure of the Governor General such of the Powers, Authorities, and Functions of the Governor General as the Governor General deems it necessary or expedient to assign to him or them, subject to any Limitations or Directions expressed or given by the Queen; but the Appointment of such a Deputy or Deputies shall not affect the Exercise by the Governor General himself of any Power, Authority, or Function.

Command of Armed Forces to continue to be vested in the Queen

15. The Command-in-Chief of the Land and Naval Militia, and of all Naval and Military Forces, of and in Canada, is hereby declared to continue and be vested in the Queen.

Seat of Government of Canada

16. Until the Queen otherwise directs, the Seat of Government of Canada shall be Ottawa.

IV. LEGISLATIVE POWER

Constitution of Parliament of Canada

17. There shall be One Parliament for Canada, consisting of the Queen, an Upper House styled the Senate, and the House of Commons.

Privileges, etc., of Houses

18. The privileges, immunities, and powers to be held, enjoyed, and exercised by the Senate and by the House of Commons, and by the members thereof respectively, shall be such as are from time to time defined by Act of the Parliament of Canada, but so that any Act of the Parliament of Canada defining such privileges, immunities, and powers shall not confer any privileges, immunities, or powers exceeding those at the passing of such Act held, enjoyed, and exercised by the Commons House of Parliament of the United Kingdom of Great Britain and Ireland, and by the members thereof.[8]

First Session of the Parliament of Canada

19. The Parliament of Canada shall be called together not later than Six Months after the Union.[9]

[Repealed]

20. Repealed.[10]

THE SENATE

Number of Senators

21. The Senate shall, subject to the Provisions of this Act, consist of One Hundred and five Members, who shall be styled Senators.[11]

Representation of Provinces in Senate

22. In relation to the Constitution of the Senate Canada shall be deemed to consist of *Four* Divisions:

1. Ontario;
2. Quebec;
3. The Maritime Provinces, Nova Scotia and New Brunswick, and Prince Edward Island;
4. The Western Provinces of Manitoba, British Columbia, Saskatchewan, and Alberta;

which Four Divisions shall (subject to the Provisions of this Act) be equally represented in the Senate as follows: Ontario by twenty-four senators; Quebec by twenty-four senators; the Maritime Provinces and Prince Edward Island by twenty-four senators, ten thereof representing Nova Scotia, ten thereof representing New Brunswick, and four thereof representing Prince Edward Island; the Western Provinces by twenty-four senators, six thereof representing Manitoba, six thereof representing British Columbia, six thereof representing Saskatchewan, and six thereof representing Alberta; Newfoundland shall be entitled to be represented in the Senate by six members; the Yukon Territory and the Northwest Territories shall be entitled to be represented in the Senate by one member each.

In the Case of Quebec each of the Twenty-four Senators representing that Province shall be appointed for One of the Twenty-four Electoral Divisions of Lower Canada specified in Schedule A. to Chapter One of the Consolidated Statutes of Canada.[12]

Qualifications of Senator

23. The Qualifications of a Senator shall be as follows:

(1) He shall be of the full age of Thirty Years:
(2) He shall be either a natural-born Subject of the Queen, or a Subject of the Queen naturalized by an Act of the Parliament of Great Britain, or of the Parliament of the United Kingdom of Great Britain and Ireland, or of the Legislature of One of the Provinces of Upper Canada, Lower Canada, Canada, Nova Scotia, or New Brunswick, before the Union, or of the Parliament of Canada after the Union:
(3) He shall be legally or equitably seised as of Freehold for his own Use and Benefit of Lands or Tenements held in Free and Common Socage, or seised or possessed for his own Use and Benefit of Lands or Tenements held in Franc-alleu or in Roture, within the Province for which he is appointed, of the Value of Four thousand Dollars, over and above all Rents, Dues, Debts, Charges, Mortgages, and Incumbrances due or payable out of or charged on or affecting the same:
(4) His Real and Personal Property shall be together worth Four thousand Dollars over and above his Debts and Liabilities:
(5) He shall be resident in the Province for which he is appointed:
(6) In the Case of Quebec he shall have his Real Property Qualification in the Electoral Division for which he is appointed, or shall be resident in that Division.[13]

Summons of Senator

24. The Governor General shall from Time to Time, in the Queen's Name, by Instrument under the Great Seal of Canada, summon qualified Persons to the Senate; and, subject to the Provisions of this Act, every Person so summoned shall become and be a Member of the Senate and a Senator.

[Repealed]

25. Repealed.[14]

Addition of Senators in certain cases

26. If at any Time on the Recommendation of the Governor General the Queen thinks fit to direct that Four or Eight Members be added to the Senate, the Governor General may by Summons to Four or Eight qualified Persons (as the Case may be), representing equally the Four Divisions of Canada, add to the Senate accordingly.[15]

Reduction of Senate to normal Number

27. In case of such Addition being at any Time made, the Governor General shall not summon any Person to the Senate, except on a further like Direction by the Queen on the like Recommendation, to represent one of the Four Divisions until such Division is represented by Twenty-four Senators and no more.[16]

Maximum Number of Senators

28. The Number of Senators shall not at any Time exceed One Hundred and thirteen.[17]

Tenure of Place in Senate

29. (1) Subject to subsection (2), a Senator shall, subject to the provisions of this Act, hold his place in the Senate for life.

Retirement upon attaining age of seventy-five years

(2) A Senator who is summoned to the Senate after the coming into force of this subsection shall, subject to this Act, hold his place in the Senate until he attains the age of seventy-five years.[18]

Resignation of Place in Senate

30. A Senator may by Writing under his Hand addressed to the Governor General resign his Place in the Senate, and thereupon the same shall be vacant.

Disqualification of Senators

31. The Place of a Senator shall become vacant in any of the following Cases:

(1) If for Two consecutive Sessions of the Parliament he fails to give his Attendance in the Senate:
(2) If he takes an Oath or makes a Declaration or Acknowledgment of Allegiance, Obedience, or Adherence to a Foreign Power, or does

an Act whereby he becomes a Subject or Citizen, or entitled to the Rights or Privileges of a Subject or Citizen, of a Foreign Power:

(3) If he is adjudged Bankrupt or Insolvent, or applies for the Benefit of any Law relating to Insolvent Debtors, or becomes a public Defaulter:

(4) If he is attainted of Treason or convicted of Felony or of any infamous Crime:

(5) If he ceases to be qualified in respect of Property or of Residence; provided, that a Senator shall not be deemed to have ceased to be qualified in respect of Residence by reason only of his residing at the Seat of the Government of Canada while holding an Office under that Government requiring his Presence there.

Summons on Vacancy in Senate

32. When a Vacancy happens in the Senate by Resignation, Death, or otherwise, the Governor General shall by Summons to a fit and qualified Person fill the Vacancy.

Questions as to Qualifications and Vacancies in Senate

33. If any Question arises respecting the Qualification of a Senator or a Vacancy in the Senate the same shall be heard and determined by the Senate.

Appointment of Speaker of Senate

34. The Governor General may from Time to Time, by Instrument under the Great Seal of Canada, appoint a Senator to be Speaker of the Senate, and may remove him and appoint another in his Stead.[19]

Quorum of Senate

35. Until the Parliament of Canada otherwise provides, the Presence of at least Fifteen Senators, including the Speaker, shall be necessary to constitute a Meeting of the Senate for the Exercise of its Powers.

Voting in Senate

36. Questions arising in the Senate shall be decided by a Majority of Voices, and the Speaker shall in all Cases have a Vote, and when the Voices are equal the Decision shall be deemed to be in the Negative.

THE HOUSE OF COMMONS

Constitution of House of Commons in Canada

37. The House of Commons shall, subject to the Provisions of this Act, consist of two hundred and ninety-five members of whom ninety-nine shall be elected for Ontario, seventy-five for Quebec, eleven for Nova Scotia, ten for New Brunswick, fourteen for Manitoba, thirty-two for British Columbia, four for Prince Edward Island, twenty-six for Alberta, fourteen for Saskatchewan, seven for Newfoundland, one for the Yukon Territory and two for the Northwest Territories.[20]

Summoning of House of Commons

38. The Governor General shall from Time to Time, in the Queen's Name, by Instrument under the Great Seal of Canada, summon and call together the House of Commons.

Senators not to sit in House of Commons

39. A Senator shall not be capable of being elected or of sitting or voting as a Member of the House of Commons.

Electoral districts of the four Provinces

40. Until the Parliament of Canada otherwise provides, Ontario, Quebec, Nova Scotia, and New Brunswick shall, for the Purposes of the Election of Members to serve in the House of Commons, be divided into Electoral Districts as follows:

1. **Ontario**
Ontario shall be divided into the Counties, Ridings of Counties, Cities, Parts of Cities, and Towns enumerated in the First Schedule to this Act, each whereof shall be an Electoral District, each such District as numbered in that Schedule being entitled to return One Member.

2. Quebec
Quebec shall be divided into Sixty-five Electoral Districts, composed of the Sixty-five Electoral Divisions into which Lower Canada is at the passing of this Act divided under Chapter Two of the Consolidated Statutes of Canada, Chapter Seventy-five of the Consolidated Statutes for Lower Canada, and the Act of the Province of Canada of the Twenty-third Year of the Queen, Chapter One, or any other Act amending the same in force at the Union, so that each such Electoral Division shall be for the Purposes of this Act an Electoral District entitled to return One Member.

3. Nova Scotia
Each of the Eighteen Counties of Nova Scotia shall be an Electoral District. The County of Halifax shall be entitled to return Two Members, and each of the other Counties One Member.

4. New Brunswick
Each of the Fourteen Counties into which New Brunswick is divided, including the City and County of St. John, shall be an Electoral District. The City of St. John shall also be a separate Electoral District.

Each of those Fifteen Electoral Districts shall be entitled to return One Member.[21]

Continuance of existing Election Laws until Parliament of Canada otherwise provides

41. Until the Parliament of Canada otherwise provides, all Laws in force in the several Provinces at the Union relative to the following Matters or any of them, namely,—the Qualifications and Disqualifications of Persons to be elected or to sit or vote as Members of the House of Assembly or Legislative Assembly in the several Provinces, the Voters at Elections of such Members, the Oaths to be taken by Voters, the Returning Officers, their Powers and Duties, the Proceedings at Elections, the Periods during which Elections may be continued, the Trial of controverted Elections, and Proceedings incident thereto, the vacating of Seats of Members, and the Execution of new Writs in case of Seats vacated otherwise than by Dissolution,—shall respectively apply to Elections of Members to serve in the House of Commons for the same several Provinces.

Provided that, until the Parliament of Canada otherwise provides, at any Election for a Member of the House of Commons for the District of Algoma, in addition to Persons qualified by the Law of the Province of Canada to vote, every Male British Subject, aged Twenty-one Years or upwards, being a Householder, shall have a Vote.[22]

[*Repealed*]

42. Repealed.[23]

[*Repealed*]

43. Repealed.[24]

As to Election of Speaker of House of Commons

44. The House of Commons on its first assembling after a General Election shall proceed with all practicable Speed to elect One of its Members to be Speaker.

As to filling up Vacancy in Office of Speaker

45. In case of a Vacancy happening in the Office of Speaker by Death, Resignation, or otherwise, the House of Commons shall with all practicable Speed proceed to elect another of its Members to be Speaker.

Speaker to preside

46. The Speaker shall preside at all Meetings of the House of Commons.

Provision in case of Absence of Speaker

47. Until the Parliament of Canada otherwise provides, in case of the Absence for any Reason of the Speaker from the Chair of the House of Commons for a Period of Forty-eight consecutive Hours, the House may elect another of its Members to act as Speaker, and the Member so elected shall during the Continuance of such Absence of the Speaker have and execute all the Powers, Privileges, and Duties of Speaker.[25]

Quorum of House of Commons

48. The Presence of at least Twenty Members of the House of Commons shall be necessary to constitute a Meeting of the House for the Exercise of its Powers, and for that Purpose the Speaker shall be reckoned as a Member.

Voting in House of Commons

49. Questions arising in the House of Commons shall be decided by a Majority of Voices other than that of the Speaker, and when the Voices are equal, but not otherwise, the Speaker shall have a Vote.

Duration of House of Commons

50. Every House of Commons shall continue for Five Years from the Day of the Return of the Writs for choosing the House (subject to be sooner dissolved by the Governor General), and no longer.[26]

Readjustment of representation in Commons

51. (1) The number of members of the House of Commons and the representation of the provinces therein shall, on the completion of each decennial census, be readjusted by such authority, in such manner, and from such time as the Parliament of Canada provides from time to time, subject and according to the following rules:

Rules

1. There shall be assigned to each of the provinces a number of members equal to the number obtained by dividing the population of the province by the electoral quotient and rounding up any fractional remainder to one.
2. If the number of members assigned to a province by the application of rule 1 and section 51A is less than the total number assigned to that province on the date of the coming into force of the *Constitution Act, 1985 (Representation)*, there shall be added to the number of members so assigned such number of members as will result in the province having the same number of members as were assigned on that date.
3. After the application of rules 1 and 2 and section 51A, there shall, in respect of each province that meets the condition set out in rule 4, be added, if necessary, a number of members such that, on the completion of the readjustment, the number obtained by dividing the number of members assigned to that province by

the total number of members assigned to all the provinces is as close as possible to, without being below, the number obtained by dividing the population of that province by the total population of all the provinces.

4. Rule 3 applies to a province if, on the completion of the preceding readjustment, the number obtained by dividing the number of members assigned to that province by the total number of members assigned to all the provinces was equal to or greater than the number obtained by dividing the population of that province by the total population of all the provinces, the population of each province being its population as at July 1 of the year of the decennial census that preceded that readjustment according to the estimates prepared for the purpose of that readjustment.
5. Unless the context indicates otherwise, in these rules, the population of a province is the estimate of its population as at July 1 of the year of the most recent decennial census.
6. In these rules, "*electoral quotient*" means
   (*a*) 111,166, in relation to the readjustment following the completion of the 2011 decennial census, and
   (*b*) in relation to the readjustment following the completion of any subsequent decennial census, the number obtained by multiplying the electoral quotient that was applied in the preceding readjustment by the number that is the average of the numbers obtained by dividing the population of each province by the population of the province as at July 1 of the year of the preceding decennial census according to the estimates prepared for the purpose of the preceding readjustment, and rounding up any fractional remainder of that multiplication to one.

Population estimates

(1) For the purpose of the rules in subsection (1), there is required to be prepared an estimate of the population of Canada and of each province as at July 1, 2001 and July 1, 2011 — and, in each year following the 2011 decennial census in which a decennial census is taken, as at July 1 of that year — by such authority, in such manner, and from such time as the Parliament of Canada provides from time to time.[27]

Marginal note: Yukon Territory, Northwest Territories and Nunavut

(2) The Yukon Territory as bounded and described in the schedule to chapter Y-2 of the Revised Statutes of Canada, 1985, shall be entitled to one member, the Northwest Territories as bounded and de-

scribed in section 2 of chapter N-27 of the Revised Statutes of Canada, 1985, as amended by section 77 of chapter 28 of the Statutes of Canada, 1993, shall be entitled to one member, and Nunavut as bounded and described in section 3 of chapter 28 of the Statutes of Canada, 1993, shall be entitled to one member.[28]

Constitution of House of Commons

51A. Notwithstanding anything in this Act a province shall always be entitled to a number of members in the House of Commons not less than the number of senators representing such province. [29]

Increase of Number of House of Commons

52. The Number of Members of the House of Commons may be from Time to Time increased by the Parliament of Canada, provided the proportionate Representation of the Provinces prescribed by this Act is not thereby disturbed.

MONEY VOTES; ROYAL ASSENT

Appropriation and Tax Bills

53. Bills for appropriating any Part of the Public Revenue, or for imposing any Tax or Impost, shall originate in the House of Commons.

Recommendation of Money Votes

54. It shall not be lawful for the House of Commons to adopt or pass any Vote, Resolution, Address, or Bill for the Appropriation of any Part of the Public Revenue, or of any Tax or Impost, to any Purpose that has not been first recommended to that House by Message of the Governor General in the Session in which such Vote, Resolution, Address, or Bill is proposed.

Royal Assent to Bills, etc.

55. Where a Bill passed by the Houses of the Parliament is presented to the Governor General for the Queen's Assent, he shall declare, according to his Discretion, but subject to the Provisions of this Act and to Her Majesty's Instructions, either that he assents thereto in the Queen's Name, or that he withholds the Queen's Assent, or that he reserves the Bill for the Signification of the Queen's Pleasure.

Disallowance by Order in Council of Act assented to by Governor General

56. Where the Governor General assents to a Bill in the Queen's Name, he shall by the first convenient Opportunity send an authentic Copy of the Act to One of Her Majesty's Principal Secretaries of State, and if the Queen in Council within Two Years after Receipt thereof by the Secretary of State thinks fit to disallow the Act, such Disallowance

(with a Certificate of the Secretary of State of the Day on which the Act was received by him) being signified by the Governor General, by Speech or Message to each of the Houses of the Parliament or by Proclamation, shall annul the Act from and after the Day of such Signification.

Signification of Queen's Pleasure on Bill reserved

57. A Bill reserved for the Signification of the Queen's Pleasure shall not have any Force unless and until, within Two Years from the Day on which it was presented to the Governor General for the Queen's Assent, the Governor General signifies, by Speech or Message to each of the Houses of the Parliament or by Proclamation, that it has received the Assent of the Queen in Council.

An Entry of every such Speech, Message, or Proclamation shall be made in the Journal of each House, and a Duplicate thereof duly attested shall be delivered to the proper Officer to be kept among the Records of Canada.

V. PROVINCIAL CONSTITUTIONS

Executive Power

Appointment of Lieutenant Governors of Provinces

58. For each Province there shall be an Officer, styled the Lieutenant Governor, appointed by the Governor General in Council by Instrument under the Great Seal of Canada.

Tenure of Office of Lieutenant Governor

59. A Lieutenant Governor shall hold Office during the Pleasure of the Governor General; but any Lieutenant Governor appointed after the Commencement of the First Session of the Parliament of Canada shall not be removeable within Five Years from his Appointment, except for Cause assigned, which shall be communicated to him in Writing within One Month after the Order for his Removal is made, and shall be communicated by Message to the Senate and to the House of Commons within One Week thereafter if the Parliament is then sitting, and if not then within One Week after the Commencement of the next Session of the Parliament.

Salaries of Lieutenant Governors

60. The Salaries of the Lieutenant Governors shall be fixed and provided by the Parliament of Canada.[30]

Oaths, etc., of Lieutenant Governor

61. Every Lieutenant Governor shall, before assuming the Duties of his Office, make and subscribe before the Governor General or some

Person authorized by him Oaths of Allegiance and Office similar to those taken by the Governor General.

Application of Provisions referring to Lieutenant Governor

62. The Provisions of this Act referring to the Lieutenant Governor extend and apply to the Lieutenant Governor for the Time being of each Province, or other the Chief Executive Officer or Administrator for the Time being carrying on the Government of the Province, by whatever Title he is designated.

Appointment of Executive Officers for Ontario and Quebec

63. The Executive Council of Ontario and of Quebec shall be composed of such Persons as the Lieutenant Governor from Time to Time thinks fit, and in the first instance of the following Officers, namely,—the Attorney General, the Secretary and Registrar of the Province, the Treasurer of the Province, the Commissioner of Crown Lands, and the Commissioner of Agriculture and Public Works, with in Quebec the Speaker of the Legislative Council and the Solicitor General.[31]

Executive Government of Nova Scotia and New Brunswick

64. The Constitution of the Executive Authority in each of the Provinces of Nova Scotia and New Brunswick shall, subject to the Provisions of this Act, continue as it exists at the Union until altered under the Authority of this Act.[32]

Powers to be exercised by Lieutenant Governor of Ontario or Quebec with Advice, or alone

65. All Powers, Authorities, and Functions which under any Act of the Parliament of Great Britain, or of the Parliament of the United Kingdom of Great Britain and Ireland, or of the Legislature of Upper Canada, Lower Canada, or Canada, were or are before or at the Union vested in or exerciseable by the respective Governors or Lieutenant Governors of those Provinces, with the Advice or with the Advice and Consent of the respective Executive Councils thereof, or in conjunction with those Councils, or with any Number of Members thereof, or by those Governors or Lieutenant Governors individually, shall, as far as the same are capable of being exercised after the Union in relation to the Government of Ontario and Quebec respectively, be vested in and shall or may be exercised by the Lieutenant Governor of Ontario and Quebec respectively, with the Advice or with the Advice and Consent of or in conjunction with the respective Executive Councils, or any Members thereof, or by the Lieutenant Governor individually, as the Case requires, subject nevertheless (except with respect to such as exist under Acts of the Parliament of Great Britain, or of the Parliament of the United Kingdom of Great Britain and Ireland,) to be abolished or altered by the respective Legislatures of Ontario and Quebec.[33]

Application of Provisions referring to Lieutenant Governor in Council

66. The Provisions of this Act referring to the Lieutenant Governor in Council shall be construed as referring to the Lieutenant Governor of the Province acting by and with the Advice of the Executive Council thereof.

Administration in Absence, etc., of Lieutenant Governor

67. The Governor General in Council may from Time to Time appoint an Administrator to execute the Office and Functions of Lieutenant Governor during his Absence, Illness, or other Inability.

Seats of Provincial Governments

68. Unless and until the Executive Government of any Province otherwise directs with respect to that Province, the Seats of Government of the Provinces shall be as follows, namely,—of Ontario, the City of Toronto; of Quebec, the City of Quebec; of Nova Scotia, the City of Halifax; and of New Brunswick, the City of Fredericton.

LEGISLATIVE POWER

1. Ontario

Legislature for Ontario

69. There shall be a Legislature for Ontario consisting of the Lieutenant Governor and of One House, styled the Legislative Assembly of Ontario.

Electoral districts

70. The Legislative Assembly of Ontario shall be composed of Eighty-two Members, to be elected to represent the Eighty-two Electoral Districts set forth in the First Schedule to this Act.[34]

2. Quebec

Legislature for Quebec

71. There shall be a Legislature for Quebec consisting of the Lieutenant Governor and of Two Houses, styled the Legislative Council of Quebec and the Legislative Assembly of Quebec.[35]

Constitution of Legislative Council

72. The Legislative Council of Quebec shall be composed of Twenty-four Members, to be appointed by the Lieutenant Governor, in the Queen's Name, by Instrument under the Great Seal of Quebec, one being appointed to represent each of the Twenty-four Electoral Divisions of Lower Canada in this Act referred to, and each holding Office for the Term of his Life, unless the Legislature of Quebec otherwise provides under the Provisions of this Act.

Qualification of Legislative Councillors

73. The Qualifications of the Legislative Councillors of Quebec shall be the same as those of the Senators for Quebec.

Resignation, Disqualification, etc.

74. The Place of a Legislative Councillor of Quebec shall become vacant in the Cases, *mutatis mutandis*, in which the Place of Senator becomes vacant.

Vacancies

75. When a Vacancy happens in the Legislative Council of Quebec by Resignation, Death, or otherwise, the Lieutenant Governor, in the Queen's Name, by Instrument under the Great Seal of Quebec, shall appoint a fit and qualified Person to fill the Vacancy.

Questions as to Vacancies, etc.

76. If any Question arises respecting the Qualification of a Legislative Councillor of Quebec, or a Vacancy in the Legislative Council of Quebec, the same shall be heard and determined by the Legislative Council.

Speaker of Legislative Council

77. The Lieutenant Governor may from Time to Time, by Instrument under the Great Seal of Quebec, appoint a Member of the Legislative Council of Quebec to be Speaker thereof, and may remove him and appoint another in his Stead.

Quorum of Legislative Council

78. Until the Legislature of Quebec otherwise provides, the Presence of at least Ten Members of the Legislative Council, including the Speaker, shall be necessary to constitute a Meeting for the Exercise of its Powers.

Voting in Legislative Council

79. Questions arising in the Legislative Council of Quebec shall be decided by a Majority of Voices, and the Speaker shall in all Cases have a Vote, and when the Voices are equal the Decision shall be deemed to be in the Negative.

Constitution of Legislative Assembly of Quebec

80. The Legislative Assembly of Quebec shall be composed of Sixty-five Members, to be elected to represent the Sixty-five Electoral Divisions

or Districts of Lower Canada in this Act referred to, subject to Alteration thereof by the Legislature of Quebec: Provided that it shall not be lawful to present to the Lieutenant Governor of Quebec for Assent any Bill for altering the Limits of any of the Electoral Divisions or Districts mentioned in the Second Schedule to this Act, unless the Second and Third Readings of such Bill have been passed in the Legislative Assembly with the Concurrence of the Majority of the Members representing all those Electoral Divisions or Districts, and the Assent shall not be given to such Bill unless an Address has been presented by the Legislative Assembly to the Lieutenant Governor stating that it has been so passed.[36]

3. Ontario and Quebec

[Repealed]
81. Repealed.[37]

Summoning of Legislative Assemblies
82. The Lieutenant Governor of Ontario and of Quebec shall from Time to Time, in the Queen's Name, by Instrument under the Great Seal of the Province, summon and call together the Legislative Assembly of the Province.

Restriction on election of Holders of offices
83. Until the Legislature of Ontario or of Quebec otherwise provides, a Person accepting or holding in Ontario or in Quebec any Office, Commission, or Employment, permanent or temporary, at the Nomination of the Lieutenant Governor, to which an annual Salary, or any Fee, Allowance, Emolument, or Profit of any Kind or Amount whatever from the Province is attached, shall not be eligible as a Member of the Legislative Assembly of the respective Province, nor shall he sit or vote as such; but nothing in this Section shall make ineligible any Person being a Member of the Executive Council of the respective Province, or holding any of the following Offices, that is to say, the Offices of Attorney General, Secretary and Registrar of the Province, Treasurer of the Province, Commissioner of Crown Lands, and Commissioner of Agriculture and Public Works, and in Quebec Solicitor General, or shall disqualify him to sit or vote in the House for which he is elected, provided he is elected while holding such Office.[38]

Continuance of existing Election Laws
84. Until the legislatures of Ontario and Quebec respectively otherwise provide, all Laws which at the Union are in force in those Provinces respectively, relative to the following Matters, or any of them, namely,—the Qualifications and Disqualifications of Persons to be

elected or to sit or vote as Members of the Assembly of Canada, the Qualifications or Disqualifications of Voters, the Oaths to be taken by Voters, the Returning Officers, their Powers and Duties, the Proceedings at Elections, the Periods during which such Elections may be continued, and the Trial of controverted Elections and the Proceedings incident thereto, the vacating of the Seats of Members and the issuing and execution of new Writs in case of Seats vacated otherwise than by Dissolution,—shall respectively apply to Elections of Members to serve in the respective Legislative Assemblies of Ontario and Quebec.

Provided that, until the Legislature of Ontario otherwise provides, at any Election for a Member of the Legislative Assembly of Ontario for the District of Algoma, in addition to Persons qualified by the Law of the Province of Canada to vote, every Male British Subject, aged Twenty-one Years or upwards, being a Householder, shall have a Vote.[39]

Duration of Legislative Assemblies

85. Every Legislative Assembly of Ontario and every Legislative Assembly of Quebec shall continue for Four Years from the Day of the Return of the Writs for choosing the same (subject nevertheless to either the Legislative Assembly of Ontario or the Legislative Assembly of Quebec being sooner dissolved by the Lieutenant Governor of the Province), and no longer.[40]

Yearly Session of Legislature

86. There shall be a Session of the Legislature of Ontario and of that of Quebec once at least in every Year, so that Twelve Months shall not intervene between the last Sitting of the Legislature in each Province in one Session and its first Sitting in the next Session.[41]

Speaker, Quorum, etc.

87. The following Provisions of this Act respecting the House of Commons of Canada shall extend and apply to the Legislative Assemblies of Ontario and Quebec, that is to say,—the Provisions relating to the Election of a Speaker originally and on Vacancies, the Duties of the Speaker, the Absence of the Speaker, the Quorum, and the Mode of voting, as if those Provisions were here re-enacted and made applicable in Terms to each such Legislative Assembly.

4. Nova Scotia and New Brunswick

Constitutions of Legislatures of Nova Scotia and New Brunswick

88. The Constitution of the Legislature of each of the Provinces of Nova Scotia and New Brunswick shall, subject to the Provisions of this Act, continue as it exists at the Union until altered under the Authority of this Act.[42]

5. ONTARIO, QUEBEC, AND NOVA SCOTIA

[*Repealed*]

89. Repealed.[43]

6. THE FOUR PROVINCES

Application to Legislatures of Provisions respecting Money Votes, etc.

90. The following Provisions of this Act respecting the Parliament of Canada, namely,—the Provisions relating to Appropriation and Tax Bills, the Recommendation of Money Votes, the Assent to Bills, the Disallowance of Acts, and the Signification of Pleasure on Bills reserved,—shall extend and apply to the Legislatures of the several Provinces as if those Provisions were here re-enacted and made applicable in Terms to the respective Provinces and the Legislatures thereof, with the Substitution of the Lieutenant Governor of the Province for the Governor General, of the Governor General for the Queen and for a Secretary of State, of One Year for Two Years, and of the Province for Canada.

VI. DISTRIBUTION OF LEGISLATIVE POWERS

Powers of the Parliament

Legislative Authority of Parliament of Canada

91. It shall be lawful for the Queen, by and with the Advice and Consent of the Senate and House of Commons, to make Laws for the Peace, Order, and good Government of Canada, in relation to all Matters not coming within the Classes of Subjects by this Act assigned exclusively to the Legislatures of the Provinces; and for greater Certainty, but not so as to restrict the Generality of the foregoing Terms of this Section, it is hereby declared that (notwithstanding anything in this Act) the exclusive Legislative Authority of the Parliament of Canada extends to all Matters coming within the Classes of Subjects next hereinafter enumerated; that is to say,

1. Repealed.[44]
1A. The Public Debt and Property.[45]
2. The Regulation of Trade and Commerce.
2A. Unemployment insurance.[46]
3. The raising of Money by any Mode or System of Taxation.
4. The borrowing of Money on the Public Credit.
5. Postal Service.
6. The Census and Statistics.
7. Militia, Military and Naval Service, and Defence.

8. The fixing of and providing for the Salaries and Allowances of Civil and other Officers of the Government of Canada.
9. Beacons, Buoys, Lighthouses, and Sable Island.
10. Navigation and Shipping.
11. Quarantine and the Establishment and Maintenance of Marine Hospitals.
12. Sea Coast and Inland Fisheries.
13. Ferries between a Province and any British or Foreign Country or between Two Provinces.
14. Currency and Coinage.
15. Banking, Incorporation of Banks, and the Issue of Paper Money.
16. Savings Banks.
17. Weights and Measures.
18. Bills of Exchange and Promissory Notes.
19. Interest.
20. Legal Tender.
21. Bankruptcy and Insolvency.
22. Patents of Invention and Discovery.
23. Copyrights.
24. Indians, and Lands reserved for the Indians.
25. Naturalization and Aliens.
26. Marriage and Divorce.
27. The Criminal Law, except the Constitution of Courts of Criminal Jurisdiction, but including the Procedure in Criminal Matters.
28. The Establishment, Maintenance, and Management of Penitentiaries.
29. Such Classes of Subjects as are expressly excepted in the Enumeration of the Classes of Subjects by this Act assigned exclusively to the Legislatures of the Provinces.

And any Matter coming within any of the Classes of Subjects enumerated in this Section shall not be deemed to come within the Class of Matters of a local or private Nature comprised in the Enumeration of the Classes of Subjects by this Act assigned exclusively to the Legislatures of the Provinces.[47]

Exclusive Powers of Provincial Legislatures

Subjects of exclusive Provincial Legislation

92. In each Province the Legislature may exclusively make Laws in relation to Matters coming within the Classes of Subjects next hereinafter enumerated; that is to say,

1. Repealed.[48]
2. Direct Taxation within the Province in order to the raising of a Revenue for Provincial Purposes.
3. The borrowing of Money on the sole Credit of the Province
4. The Establishment and Tenure of Provincial Offices and the Appointment and Payment of Provincial Officers.
5. The Management and Sale of the Public Lands belonging to the Province and of the Timber and Wood thereon.
6. The Establishment, Maintenance, and Management of Public and Reformatory Prisons in and for the Province.
7. The Establishment, Maintenance, and Management of Hospitals, Asylums, Charities, and Eleemosynary Institutions in and for the Province, other than Marine Hospitals.
8. Municipal Institutions in the Province.
9. Shop, Saloon, Tavern, Auctioneer, and other Licences in order to the raising of a Revenue for Provincial, Local, or Municipal Purposes.
10. Local Works and Undertakings other than such as are of the following Classes:
    (*a*) Lines of Steam or other Ships, Railways, Canals, Telegraphs, and other Works and Undertakings connecting the Province with any other or others of the Provinces, or extending beyond the Limits of the Province:
    (*b*) Lines of Steam Ships between the Province and any British or Foreign Country:
    (*c*) Such Works as, although wholly situate within the Province, are before or after their Execution declared by the Parliament of Canada to be for the general Advantage of Canada or for the Advantage of Two or more of the Provinces.
11. The Incorporation of Companies with Provincial Objects.
12. The Solemnization of Marriage in the Province.
13. Property and Civil Rights in the Province.
14. The Administration of Justice in the Province, including the Constitution, Maintenance, and Organization of Provincial Courts, both of Civil and of Criminal Jurisdiction, and including Procedure in Civil Matters in those Courts.
15. The Imposition of Punishment by Fine, Penalty, or Imprisonment for enforcing any Law of the Province made in relation to any Matter coming within any of the Classes of Subjects enumerated in this Section.
16. Generally all Matters of a merely local or private Nature in the Province.

Non-Renewable Natural Resources, Forestry Resources and Electrical Energy

Laws respecting non-renewable natural resources, forestry resources and electrical energy

92A. (1) In each province, the legislature may exclusively make laws in relation to

(*a*) exploration for non-renewable natural resources in the province;

(*b*) development, conservation and management of non-renewable natural resources and forestry resources in the province, including laws in relation to the rate of primary production therefrom; and

(*c*) development, conservation and management of sites and facilities in the province for the generation and production of electrical energy.

Export from provinces of resources

(2) In each province, the legislature may make laws in relation to the export from the province to another part of Canada of the primary production from non-renewable natural resources and forestry resources in the province and the production from facilities in the province for the generation of electrical energy, but such laws may not authorize or provide for discrimination in prices or in supplies exported to another part of Canada.

Authority of Parliament

(3) Nothing in subsection (2) derogates from the authority of Parliament to enact laws in relation to the matters referred to in that subsection and, where such a law of Parliament and a law of a province conflict, the law of Parliament prevails to the extent of the conflict.

Taxation of resources

(4) In each province, the legislature may make laws in relation to the raising of money by any mode or system of taxation in respect of

(*a*) non-renewable natural resources and forestry resources in the province and the primary production therefrom, and

(*b*) sites and facilities in the province for the generation of electrical energy and the production therefrom,

whether or not such production is exported in whole or in part from the province, but such laws may not authorize or provide for taxation that differentiates between production exported to another part of Canada and production not exported from the province.

"Primary production"

(5) The expression "primary production" has the meaning assigned by the Sixth Schedule.

Existing powers or rights

(6) Nothing in subsections (1) to (5) derogates from any powers or rights that a legislature or government of a province had immediately before the coming into force of this section.[49]

Education

Legislation respecting Education

93. In and for each Province the Legislature may exclusively make Laws in relation to Education, subject and according to the following Provisions:

(1) Nothing in any such Law shall prejudicially affect any Right or Privilege with respect to Denominational Schools which any Class of Persons have by Law in the Province at the Union:
(2) All the Powers, Privileges, and Duties at the Union by Law conferred and imposed in Upper Canada on the Separate Schools and School Trustees of the Queen's Roman Catholic Subjects shall be and the same are hereby extended to the Dissentient Schools of the Queen's Protestant and Roman Catholic Subjects in Quebec:
(3) Where in any Province a System of Separate or Dissentient Schools exists by Law at the Union or is thereafter established by the Legislature of the Province, an Appeal shall lie to the Governor General in Council from any Act or Decision of any Provincial Authority affecting any Right or Privilege of the Protestant or Roman Catholic Minority of the Queen's Subjects in relation to Education:
(4) In case any such Provincial Law as from Time to Time seems to the Governor General in Council requisite for the due Execution of the Provisions of this Section is not made, or in case any Decision of the Governor General in Council on any Appeal under this Section is not duly executed by the proper Provincial Authority in that Behalf, then and in every such Case, and as far only as the Circumstances of each Case require, the Parliament of Canada may make remedial Laws for the due Execution of the Provisions of this Section and of any Decision of the Governor General in Council under this Section.[50]

Quebec

93A. Paragraphs (1) to (4) of section 93 do not apply to Quebec.[51]

Uniformity of Laws in Ontario, Nova Scotia, and New Brunswick

Legislation for Uniformity of Laws in Three Provinces

94. Notwithstanding anything in this Act, the Parliament of Canada may make Provision for the Uniformity of all or any of the Laws relative to Property and Civil Rights in Ontario, Nova Scotia, and New Brunswick, and of the Procedure of all or any of the Courts in those Three Provinces, and from and after the passing of any Act in that Behalf the Power of the Parliament of Canada to make Laws in relation to any Matter comprised in any such Act shall, notwithstanding anything in this Act, be unrestricted; but any Act of the Parliament of Canada making Provision for such Uniformity shall not have effect in any Province unless and until it is adopted and enacted as Law by the Legislature thereof.

Old Age Pensions

Legislation respecting old age pensions and supplementary benefits

94A. The Parliament of Canada may make laws in relation to old age pensions and supplementary benefits, including survivors' and disability benefits irrespective of age, but no such law shall affect the operation of any law present or future of a provincial legislature in relation to any such matter.[52]

Agriculture and Immigration

Concurrent Powers of Legislation respecting Agriculture, etc.

95. In each Province the Legislature may make Laws in relation to Agriculture in the Province, and to Immigration into the Province; and it is hereby declared that the Parliament of Canada may from Time to Time make Laws in relation to Agriculture in all or any of the Provinces, and to Immigration into all or any of the Provinces; and any Law of the Legislature of a Province relative to Agriculture or to Immigration shall have effect in and for the Province as long and as far only as it is not repugnant to any Act of the Parliament of Canada.

VII. JUDICATURE

Appointment of Judges

96. The Governor General shall appoint the Judges of the Superior, District, and County Courts in each Province, except those of the Courts of Probate in Nova Scotia and New Brunswick.

Selection of Judges in Ontario, etc.

97. Until the Laws relative to Property and Civil Rights in Ontario, Nova Scotia, and New Brunswick, and the Procedure of the Courts in those Provinces, are made uniform, the Judges of the Courts of those Provinces appointed by the Governor General shall be selected from the respective Bars of those Provinces.

Selection of Judges in Quebec

98. The Judges of the Courts of Quebec shall be selected from the Bar of that Province.

Tenure of office of Judges

99. (1) Subject to subsection two of this section, the Judges of the Superior Courts shall hold office during good behaviour, but shall be removable by the Governor General on Address of the Senate and House of Commons.

Termination at age 75

(2) A Judge of a Superior Court, whether appointed before or after the coming into force of this section, shall cease to hold office upon attaining the age of seventy-five years, or upon the coming into force of this section if at that time he has already attained that age.[53]

Salaries, etc., of Judges

100. The Salaries, Allowances, and Pensions of the Judges of the Superior, District, and County Courts (except the Courts of Probate in Nova Scotia and New Brunswick), and of the Admiralty Courts in Cases where the Judges thereof are for the Time being paid by Salary, shall be fixed and provided by the Parliament of Canada.[54]

General Court of Appeal, etc.

101. The Parliament of Canada may, notwithstanding anything in this Act, from Time to Time provide for the Constitution, Maintenance, and Organization of a General Court of Appeal for Canada, and for the Establishment of any additional Courts for the better Administration of the Laws of Canada.[55]

VIII. REVENUES; DEBTS; ASSETS; TAXATION

Creation of Consolidated Revenue Fund

102. All Duties and Revenues over which the respective Legislatures of Canada, Nova Scotia, and New Brunswick before and at the Union had and have Power of Appropriation, except such Portions thereof as are by this Act reserved to the respective Legislatures of the Provinces, or are raised by them in accordance with the special Powers conferred on them by this Act, shall form One Consolidated Revenue Fund, to be appropriated for the Public Service of Canada in the Manner and subject to the Charges in this Act provided.

Expenses of Collection, etc.

103. The Consolidated Revenue Fund of Canada shall be permanently charged with the Costs, Charges, and Expenses incident to the Collection, Management, and Receipt thereof, and the same shall form the First Charge thereon, subject to be reviewed and audited in such Manner as shall be ordered by the Governor General in Council until the Parliament otherwise provides.

Interest of Provincial Public Debts

104. The annual Interest of the Public Debts of the several Provinces of Canada, Nova Scotia, and New Brunswick at the Union shall form the Second Charge on the Consolidated Revenue Fund of Canada.

Salary of Governor General

105. Unless altered by the Parliament of Canada, the Salary of the Governor General shall be Ten thousand Pounds Sterling Money of the United Kingdom of Great Britain and Ireland, payable out of the Consolidated Revenue Fund of Canada, and the same shall form the Third Charge thereon.[56]

Appropriation from Time to Time

106. Subject to the several Payments by this Act charged on the Consolidated Revenue Fund of Canada, the same shall be appropriated by the Parliament of Canada for the Public Service.

Transfer of Stocks, etc.

107. All Stocks, Cash, Banker's Balances, and Securities for Money belonging to each Province at the Time of the Union, except as in this Act mentioned, shall be the Property of Canada, and shall be taken in Reduction of the Amount of the respective Debts of the Provinces at the Union.

Transfer of Property in Schedule

108. The Public Works and Property of each Province, enumerated in the Third Schedule to this Act, shall be the Property of Canada.

Property in Lands, Mines, etc.

109. All Lands, Mines, Minerals, and Royalties belonging to the several Provinces of Canada, Nova Scotia, and New Brunswick at the Union, and all Sums then due or payable for such Lands, Mines, Minerals, or Royalties, shall belong to the several Provinces of Ontario, Quebec, Nova Scotia, and New Brunswick in which the same are situate or arise, subject to any Trusts existing in respect thereof, and to any Interest other than that of the Province in the same.[57]

Assets connected with Provincial Debts

110. All Assets connected with such Portions of the Public Debt of each Province as are assumed by that Province shall belong to that Province.

Canada to be liable for Provincial Debts

111. Canada shall be liable for the Debts and Liabilities of each Province existing at the Union.

Debts of Ontario and Quebec

112. Ontario and Quebec conjointly shall be liable to Canada for the Amount (if any) by which the Debt of the Province of Canada exceeds at the Union Sixty-two million five hundred thousand Dollars, and shall be charged with Interest at the Rate of Five per Centum per Annum thereon.

Assets of Ontario and Quebec

113. The Assets enumerated in the Fourth Schedule to this Act belonging at the Union to the Province of Canada shall be the Property of Ontario and Quebec conjointly.

Debt of Nova Scotia

114. Nova Scotia shall be liable to Canada for the Amount (if any) by which its Public Debt exceeds at the Union Eight million Dollars, and shall be charged with Interest at the Rate of Five per Centum per Annum thereon.[58]

Debt of New Brunswick

115. New Brunswick shall be liable to Canada for the Amount (if any) by which its Public Debt exceeds at the Union Seven million Dollars, and shall be charged with Interest at the Rate of Five per Centum per Annum thereon.

Payment of interest to Nova Scotia and New Brunswick

116. In case the Public Debts of Nova Scotia and New Brunswick do not at the Union amount to Eight million and Seven million Dollars respectively, they shall respectively receive by half-yearly Payments in advance from the Government of Canada Interest at Five per Centum per Annum on the Difference between the actual Amounts of their respective Debts and such stipulated Amounts.

Provincial Public Property

117. The several Provinces shall retain all their respective Public Property not otherwise disposed of in this Act, subject to the Right of Canada to assume any Lands or Public Property required for Fortifications or for the Defence of the Country.

[Repealed]

118. Repealed.[59]

Further Grant to New Brunswick

119. New Brunswick shall receive by half-yearly Payments in advance from Canada for the Period of Ten Years from the Union an additional Allowance of Sixty-three thousand Dollars per Annum; but as long as the Public Debt of that Province remains under Seven million Dollars, a Deduction equal to the Interest at Five per Centum per Annum on such Deficiency shall be made from that Allowance of Sixty-three thousand Dollars.[60]

Form of Payments

120. All Payments to be made under this Act, or in discharge of Liabilities created under any Act of the Provinces of Canada, Nova Scotia, and New Brunswick respectively, and assumed by Canada, shall, until the Parliament of Canada otherwise directs, be made in such Form and Manner as may from Time to Time be ordered by the Governor General in Council.

Canadian Manufactures, etc.

121. All Articles of the Growth, Produce, or Manufacture of any one of the Provinces shall, from and after the Union, be admitted free into each of the other Provinces.

Continuance of Customs and Excise Laws

122. The Customs and Excise Laws of each Province shall, subject to the Provisions of this Act, continue in force until altered by the Parliament of Canada.[61]

Exportation and Importation as between Two Provinces

123. Where Customs Duties are, at the Union, leviable on any Goods, Wares, or Merchandises in any Two Provinces, those Goods, Wares, and Merchandises may, from and after the Union, be imported from one of those Provinces into the other of them on Proof of Payment of the Customs Duty leviable thereon in the Province of Exportation, and on Payment of such further Amount (if any) of Customs Duty as is leviable thereon in the Province of Importation.[62]

Lumber Dues in New Brunswick

124. Nothing in this Act shall affect the Right of New Brunswick to levy the Lumber Dues provided in Chapter Fifteen of Title Three of the Revised Statutes of New Brunswick, or in any Act amending that Act before or after the Union, and not increasing the Amount of such Dues; but the Lumber of any of the Provinces other than New Brunswick shall not be subject to such Dues.[63]

Exemption of Public Lands, etc.

125. No Lands or Property belonging to Canada or any Province shall be liable to Taxation.

Provincial Consolidated Revenue Fund

126. Such Portions of the Duties and Revenues over which the respective Legislatures of Canada, Nova Scotia, and New Brunswick had before the Union Power of Appropriation as are by this Act reserved to the respective Governments or Legislatures of the Provinces, and all Duties and Revenues raised by them in accordance with the special Powers conferred upon them by this Act, shall in each Province form One Consolidated Revenue Fund to be appropriated for the Public Service of the Province.

IX. MISCELLANEOUS PROVISIONS

General

[*Repealed*]

127. Repealed.[64]

Oath of Allegiance, etc.

128. Every Member of the Senate or House of Commons of Canada shall before taking his Seat therein take and subscribe before the Governor General or some Person authorized by him, and every Member of a Legislative Council or Legislative Assembly of any Province shall before taking his Seat therein take and subscribe before the Lieutenant Governor of the Province or some Person authorized by him, the Oath of Allegiance contained in the Fifth Schedule to this Act; and every Member of the Senate of Canada and every Member of the Legislative Council of Quebec shall also, before taking his Seat therein, take and subscribe before the Governor General, or some Person authorized by him, the Declaration of Qualification contained in the same Schedule.

Continuance of existing Laws, Courts, Officers, etc.

129. Except as otherwise provided by this Act, all Laws in force in Canada, Nova Scotia, or New Brunswick at the Union, and all Courts of Civil and Criminal Jurisdiction, and all legal Commissions, Powers, and Authorities, and all Officers, Judicial, Administrative, and Ministerial, existing therein at the Union, shall continue in Ontario, Quebec, Nova Scotia, and New Brunswick respectively, as if the Union had not been made; subject nevertheless (except with respect to such as are enacted by or exist under Acts of the Parliament of Great Britain or of the Parliament of the United Kingdom of Great Britain and Ireland), to be repealed, abolished, or altered by the Parliament of Canada, or by the Legislature of the respective Province, according to the Authority of the Parliament or of that Legislature under this Act.[65]

Transfer of Officers to Canada

130. Until the Parliament of Canada otherwise provides, all Officers of the several Provinces having Duties to discharge in relation to Matters other than those coming within the Classes of Subjects by this Act assigned exclusively to the Legislatures of the Provinces shall be Officers of Canada, and shall continue to discharge the Duties of their respective Offices under the same Liabilities, Responsibilities, and Penalties as if the Union had not been made.[66]

Appointment of new Officers

131. Until the Parliament of Canada otherwise provides, the Governor General in Council may from Time to Time appoint such Officers as the Governor General in Council deems necessary or proper for the effectual Execution of this Act.

Treaty Obligations

132. The Parliament and Government of Canada shall have all Powers necessary or proper for performing the Obligations of Canada or of any Province thereof, as Part of the British Empire, towards Foreign Countries, arising under Treaties between the Empire and such Foreign Countries.

Use of English and French Languages

133. Either the English or the French Language may be used by any Person in the Debates of the Houses of the Parliament of Canada and of the Houses of the Legislature of Quebec; and both those Languages shall be used in the respective Records and Journals of those Houses; and either of those Languages may be used by any Person or in any Pleading or Process in or issuing from any Court of Canada established under this Act, and in or from all or any of the Courts of Quebec.

The Acts of the Parliament of Canada and of the Legislature of Quebec shall be printed and published in both those Languages.[67]

Ontario and Quebec

Appointment of Executive Officers for Ontario and Quebec

134. Until the Legislature of Ontario or of Quebec otherwise provides, the Lieutenant Governors of Ontario and Quebec may each appoint under the Great Seal of the Province the following Officers, to hold Office during Pleasure, that is to say,—the Attorney General, the Secretary and Registrar of the Province, the Treasurer of the Province, the Commissioner of Crown Lands, and the Commissioner of Agriculture and Public Works, and in the Case of Quebec the Solicitor General, and may, by Order of the Lieutenant Governor in Council, from Time to Time prescribe the Duties of those Officers, and of the several Departments over which they shall preside or to which they shall belong, and of the Officers and Clerks thereof, and may also appoint other and additional Officers to hold Office during Pleasure, and may from Time to Time prescribe the Duties of those Officers, and of the several Departments over which they shall preside or to which they shall belong, and of the Officers and Clerks thereof.[68]

Powers, Duties, etc. of Executive Officers

135. Until the Legislature of Ontario or Quebec otherwise provides, all Rights, Powers, Duties, Functions, Responsibilities, or Authorities at the passing of this Act vested in or imposed on the Attorney General, Solicitor General, Secretary and Registrar of the Province of Canada, Minister of Finance, Commissioner of Crown Lands, Commissioner of Public Works, and Minister of Agriculture and Receiver General, by any Law, Statute, or Ordinance of Upper Canada, Lower Canada, or Canada, and not repugnant to this Act, shall be vested in or imposed on any Officer to be appointed by the Lieutenant Governor for the Discharge of the same or any of them; and the Commissioner of Agriculture and Public Works shall perform the Duties and Functions of the Office of Minister of Agriculture at the passing of this Act imposed by the Law of the Province of Canada, as well as those of the Commissioner of Public Works.[69]

Great Seals

136. Until altered by the Lieutenant Governor in Council, the Great Seals of Ontario and Quebec respectively shall be the same, or of the same Design, as those used in the Provinces of Upper Canada and Lower Canada respectively before their Union as the Province of Canada.

Construction of temporary Acts

137. The words "and from thence to the End of the then next ensuing Session of the Legislature," or Words to the same Effect, used in any temporary Act of the Province of Canada not expired before the Union, shall be construed to extend and apply to the next Session of the Parliament of Canada if the Subject Matter of the Act is within the Powers of the same as defined by this Act, or to the next Sessions of the Legislatures of Ontario and Quebec respectively if the Subject Matter of the Act is within the Powers of the same as defined by this Act.

As to Errors in Names

138. From and after the Union the Use of the Words "Upper Canada" instead of "Ontario," or "Lower Canada" instead of "Quebec," in any Deed, Writ, Process, Pleading, Document, Matter, or Thing shall not invalidate the same.

As to issue of Proclamations before Union, to commence after Union

139. Any Proclamation under the Great Seal of the Province of Canada issued before the Union to take effect at a Time which is subsequent to the Union, whether relating to that Province, or to Upper Canada, or to Lower Canada, and the several Matters and Things therein proclaimed, shall be and continue of like Force and Effect as if the Union had not been made.[70]

As to issue of Proclamations after Union

140. Any Proclamation which is authorized by any Act of the Legislature of the Province of Canada to be issued under the Great Seal of the Province of Canada, whether relating to that Province, or to Upper Canada, or to Lower Canada, and which is not issued before the Union, may be issued by the Lieutenant Governor of Ontario or of Quebec, as its Subject Matter requires, under the Great Seal thereof; and from and after the Issue of such Proclamation the same and the several Matters and Things therein proclaimed shall be and continue of the like Force and Effect in Ontario or Quebec as if the Union had not been made.[71]

Penitentiary

141. The Penitentiary of the Province of Canada shall, until the Parliament of Canada otherwise provides, be and continue the Penitentiary of Ontario and of Quebec.[72]

Arbitration respecting Debts, etc.

142. The Division and Adjustment of the Debts, Credits, Liabilities, Properties, and Assets of Upper Canada and Lower Canada shall be referred to the Arbitrament of Three Arbitrators, One chosen by the Government of Ontario, One by the Government of Quebec, and One by the Government of Canada; and the Selection of the Arbitrators shall not be made until the Parliament of Canada and the Legislatures of Ontario and Quebec have met; and the Arbitrator chosen by the Government of Canada shall not be a Resident either in Ontario or in Quebec.[73]

Division of Records

143. The Governor General in Council may from Time to Time order that such and so many of the Records, Books, and Documents of the Province of Canada as he thinks fit shall be appropriated and delivered either to Ontario or to Quebec, and the same shall thenceforth be the Property of that Province; and any Copy thereof or Extract therefrom, duly certified by the Officer having charge of the Original thereof, shall be admitted as Evidence.[74]

Constitution of Townships in Quebec

144. The Lieutenant Governor of Quebec may from Time to Time, by Proclamation under the Great Seal of the Province, to take effect from a Day to be appointed therein, constitute Townships in those Parts of the Province of Quebec in which Townships are not then already constituted, and fix the Metes and Bounds thereof.

X. INTERCOLONIAL RAILWAY

[Repealed]

145. Repealed.[75]

XI. ADMISSION OF OTHER COLONIES

Power to admit Newfoundland, etc., into the Union

146. It shall be lawful for the Queen, by and with the Advice of Her Majesty's Most Honourable Privy Council, on Addresses from the Houses of the Parliament of Canada, and from the Houses of the respective Legislatures of the Colonies or Provinces of Newfoundland, Prince Edward Island, and British Columbia, to admit those Colonies or Provinces, or any of them, into the Union, and on Address from the Houses of the Parliament of Canada to admit Rupert's Land and the North-western Territory, or either of them, into the Union, on such Terms and Conditions in each Case as are in the Addresses expressed and as the Queen thinks fit to approve, subject to the Provisions of this Act; and the Provisions of any Order in Council in that Behalf shall have effect as if they had been enacted by the Parliament of the United Kingdom of Great Britain and Ireland.[78]

As to Representation of Newfoundland and Prince Edward Island in Senate

147. In case of the Admission of Newfoundland and Prince Edward Island, or either of them, each shall be entitled to a Representation in the Senate of Canada of Four Members, and (notwithstanding anything in this Act) in case of the Admission of Newfoundland the normal Number of Senators shall be Seventy-six and their maximum Number shall be Eighty-two; but Prince Edward Island when admitted shall be deemed to be comprised in the third of the Three Divisions into which Canada is, in relation to the Constitution of the Senate, divided by this Act, and accordingly, after the Admission of Prince Edward Island, whether Newfoundland is admitted or not, the Representation of Nova Scotia and New Brunswick in the Senate shall, as Vacancies occur, be reduced from Twelve to Ten Members respectively, and the Representation of each of those Provinces shall not be increased at any Time beyond Ten, except under the Provisions of this Act for the Appointment of Three or Six additional Senators under the Direction of the Queen.[78]

SCHEDULES

. . .

THE THIRD SCHEDULE

Provincial Public Works and Property to be the Property of Canada

1. Canals, with Lands and Water Power connected therewith.
2. Public Harbours.
3. Lighthouses and Piers, and Sable Island.
4. Steamboats, Dredges, and public Vessels.
5. Rivers and Lake Improvements.
6. Railways and Railway Stocks, Mortgages, and other Debts due by Railway Companies.
7. Military Roads.
8. Custom Houses, Post Offices, and all other Public Buildings, except such as the Government of Canada appropriate for the Use of the Provincial Legislatures and Governments.
9. Property transferred by the Imperial Government, and known as Ordnance Property.
10. Armouries, Drill Sheds, Military Clothing, and Munitions of War, and Lands set apart for general Public Purposes.

THE FIFTH SCHEDULE

Oath of Allegiance

I *A.B.* do swear, That I will be faithful and bear true Allegiance to Her Majesty Queen Victoria.

Note. The Name of the King or Queen of the United Kingdom of Great Britain and Ireland for the Time being is to be substituted from Time to Time, with proper Terms of Reference thereto.

Declaration of Qualification

I *A.B.* do declare and testify, That I am by Law duly qualified to be appointed a Member of the Senate of Canada [*or as the Case may be*], and that I am legally or equitably seised as of Freehold for my own Use and Benefit of Lands or Tenements held in Free and Common Socage [*or* seised or possessed for my own Use and Benefit of Lands or Tenements held in Franc-alleu or in Roture (*as the Case may be*),] in the Province of Nova Scotia [*or as the Case may be*] of the Value of Four thousand Dollars over and above all Rents, Dues, Debts, Mortgages, Charges, and Incumbrances due or payable out of or charged on or affecting the same, and that I have not collusively or colourably obtained a Title to or become possessed of the said Lands and Tenements or any Part thereof for the Purpose of enabling me to become a Member of the Senate of Canada [*or as the Case may be*], and that my Real and Personal Property are together worth Four thousand Dollars over and above my Debts and Liabilities.

THE SIXTH SCHEDULE[79]

Primary Production from Non-Renewable Natural Resources and Forestry Resources

1. For the purposes of section 92A of this Act,
   (*a*) production from a non-renewable natural resource is primary production therefrom if
      (i) it is in the form in which it exists upon its recovery or severance from its natural state, or
      (ii) it is a product resulting from processing or refining the resource, and is not a manufactured product or a product resulting from refining crude oil, refining upgraded heavy crude oil, refining gases or liquids derived from coal or refining a synthetic equivalent of crude oil; and
   (*b*) production from a forestry resource is primary production therefrom if it consists of sawlogs, poles, lumber, wood chips, sawdust or any other primary wood product, or wood pulp, and is not a product manufactured from wood.

THE CONSTITUTION ACT, 1982

SCHEDULE B

CONSTITUTION ACT, 1982[80]

PART I
CANADIAN CHARTER OF RIGHTS AND FREEDOMS

Whereas Canada is founded upon principles that recognize the supremacy of God and the rule of law:

Guarantee of Rights and Freedoms

Rights and freedoms in Canada

1. The *Canadian Charter of Rights and Freedoms* guarantees the rights and freedoms set out in it subject only to such reasonable limits prescribed by law as can be demonstrably justified in a free and democratic society.

Fundamental Freedoms

Fundamental freedoms

2. Everyone has the following fundamental freedoms:

(*a*) freedom of conscience and religion;

(*b*) freedom of thought, belief, opinion and expression, including freedom of the press and other media of communication;

(*c*) freedom of peaceful assembly; and

(*d*) freedom of association.

Democratic Rights

Democratic rights of citizens

3. Every citizen of Canada has the right to vote in an election of members of the House of Commons or of a legislative assembly and to be qualified for membership therein.

Maximum duration of legislative bodies

4. (1) No House of Commons and no legislative assembly shall continue for longer than five years from the date fixed for the return of the writs of a general election of its members.[80]

Continuation in special circumstances

(2) In time of real or apprehended war, invasion or insurrection, a House of Commons may be continued by Parliament and a legislative assembly may be continued by the legislature beyond five years if such continuation is not opposed by the votes of more than one-third of the members of the House of Commons or the legislative assembly, as the case may be.[82]

Annual sitting of legislative bodies

5. There shall be a sitting of Parliament and of each legislature at least once every twelve months.[83]

Mobility Rights

Mobility of citizens

6. (1) Every citizen of Canada has the right to enter, remain in and leave Canada.

Rights to move and gain livelihood

(2) Every citizen of Canada and every person who has the status of a permanent resident of Canada has the right

(*a*) to move to and take up residence in any province; and

(*b*) to pursue the gaining of a livelihood in any province.

Limitation

(3) The rights specified in subsection (2) are subject to

(*a*) any laws or practices of general application in force in a province other than those that discriminate among persons primarily on the basis of province of present or previous residence; and

(*b*) any laws providing for reasonable residency requirements as a qualification for the receipt of publicly provided social services.

Affirmative action programs

(4) Subsections (2) and (3) do not preclude any law, program or activity that has as its object the amelioration in a province of conditions of individuals in that province who are socially or economically disadvantaged if the rate of employment in that province is below the rate of employment in Canada.

Legal Rights

Life, liberty and security of person

7. Everyone has the right to life, liberty and security of the person and the right not to be deprived thereof except in accordance with the principles of fundamental justice.

Search or seizure

8. Everyone has the right to be secure against unreasonable search or seizure.

Detention or imprisonment

9. Everyone has the right not to be arbitrarily detained or imprisoned.

Arrest or detention

10. Everyone has the right on arrest or detention

(*a*) to be informed promptly of the reasons therefor;

(*b*) to retain and instruct counsel without delay and to be informed of that right; and

(*c*) to have the validity of the detention determined by way of *habeas corpus* and to be released if the detention is not lawful.

Proceedings in criminal and penal matters

11. Any person charged with an offence has the right

(*a*) to be informed without unreasonable delay of the specific offence;

(*b*) to be tried within a reasonable time;

(*c*) not to be compelled to be a witness in proceedings against that person in respect of the offence;

(*d*) to be presumed innocent until proven guilty according to law in a fair and public hearing by an independent and impartial tribunal;

(*e*) not to be denied reasonable bail without just cause;
(*f*) except in the case of an offence under military law tried before a military tribunal, to the benefit of trial by jury where the maximum punishment for the offence is imprisonment for five years or a more severe punishment;
(*g*) not to be found guilty on account of any act or omission unless, at the time of the act or omission, it constituted an offence under Canadian or international law or was criminal according to the general principles of law recognized by the community of nations;
(*h*) if finally acquitted of the offence, not to be tried for it again and, if finally found guilty and punished for the offence, not to be tried or punished for it again; and
(*i*) if found guilty of the offence and if the punishment for the offence has been varied between the time of commission and the time of sentencing, to the benefit of the lesser punishment.

Treatment or punishment
12. Everyone has the right not to be subjected to any cruel and unusual treatment or punishment.

Self-crimination
13. A witness who testifies in any proceedings has the right not to have any incriminating evidence so given used to incriminate that witness in any other proceedings, except in a prosecution for perjury or for the giving of contradictory evidence.

Interpreter
14. A party or witness in any proceedings who does not understand or speak the language in which the proceedings are conducted or who is deaf has the right to the assistance of an interpreter.

Equality Rights

Equality before and under law and equal protection and benefit of law
15. (1) Every individual is equal before and under the law and has the right to the equal protection and equal benefit of the law without discrimination and, in particular, without discrimination based on race, national or ethnic origin, colour, religion, sex, age or mental or physical disability.

Affirmative action programs
(2) Subsection (1) does not preclude any law, program or activity that has as its object the amelioration of conditions of disadvantaged

individuals or groups including those that are disadvantaged because of race, national or ethnic origin, colour, religion, sex, age or mental or physical disability.[84]

Official Languages of Canada

Official languages of Canada

16. (1) English and French are the official languages of Canada and have equality of status and equal rights and privileges as to their use in all institutions of the Parliament and government of Canada.

Official languages of New Brunswick

(2) English and French are the official languages of New Brunswick and have equality of status and equal rights and privileges as to their use in all institutions of the legislature and government of New Brunswick.

Advancement of status and use

(3) Nothing in this Charter limits the authority of Parliament or a legislature to advance the equality of status or use of English and French.

English and French linguistic communities in New Brunswick

16.1 (1) The English linguistic community and the French linguistic community in New Brunswick have equality of status and equal rights and privileges, including the right to distinct educational institutions and such distinct cultural institutions as are necessary for the preservation and promotion of those communities.

Role of the legislature and government of New Brunswick

(2) The role of the legislature and government of New Brunswick to preserve and promote the status, rights and privileges referred to in subsection (1) is affirmed.[85]

Proceedings of Parliament

17. (1) Everyone has the right to use English or French in any debates and other proceedings of Parliament.[86]

Proceedings of New Brunswick legislature

(2) Everyone has the right to use English or French in any debates and other proceedings of the legislature of New Brunswick.[87]

Parliamentary statutes and records

18. (1) The statutes, records and journals of Parliament shall be printed and published in English and French and both language versions are equally authoritative.[88]

New Brunswick statutes and records

(2) The statutes, records and journals of the legislature of New Brunswick shall be printed and published in English and French and both language versions are equally authoritative.[89]

Proceedings in courts established by Parliament

19. (1) Either English or French may be used by any person in, or in any pleading in or process issuing from, any court established by Parliament.[90]

Proceedings in New Brunswick courts

(2) Either English or French may be used by any person in, or in any pleading in or process issuing from, any court of New Brunswick.[91]

Communications by public with federal institutions

20. (1) Any member of the public in Canada has the right to communicate with, and to receive available services from, any head or central office of an institution of the Parliament or government of Canada in English or French, and has the same right with respect to any other office of any such institution where

(*a*) there is a significant demand for communications with and services from that office in such language; or

(*b*) due to the nature of the office, it is reasonable that communications with and services from that office be available in both English and French.

Communications by public with New Brunswick institutions

(2) Any member of the public in New Brunswick has the right to communicate with, and to receive available services from, any office of an institution of the legislature or government of New Brunswick in English or French.

Continuation of existing constitutional provisions

21. Nothing in sections 16 to 20 abrogates or derogates from any right, privilege or obligation with respect to the English and French languages, or either of them, that exists or is continued by virtue of any other provision of the Constitution of Canada.[92]

Rights and privileges preserved

22. Nothing in sections 16 to 20 abrogates or derogates from any legal or customary right or privilege acquired or enjoyed either before or after the coming into force of this Charter with respect to any language that is not English or French.

Minority Language Educational Rights

Language of instruction

23. (1) Citizens of Canada

(*a*) whose first language learned and still understood is that of the English or French linguistic minority population of the province in which they reside, or

(*b*) who have received their primary school instruction in Canada in English or French and reside in a province where the language in which they received that instruction is the language of the English or French linguistic minority population of the province,

have the right to have their children receive primary and secondary school instruction in that language in that province.[93]

Continuity of language instruction

(2) Citizens of Canada of whom any child has received or is receiving primary or secondary school instruction in English or French in Canada, have the right to have all their children receive primary and secondary school instruction in the same language.

Application where numbers warrant

(3) The right of citizens of Canada under subsections (1) and (2) to have their children receive primary and secondary school instruction in the language of the English or French linguistic minority population of a province

(*a*) applies wherever in the province the number of children of citizens who have such a right is sufficient to warrant the provision to them out of public funds of minority language instruction; and

(*b*) includes, where the number of those children so warrants, the right to have them receive that instruction in minority language educational facilities provided out of public funds.

Enforcement

Enforcement of guaranteed rignts and freedoms

24. (1) Anyone whose rights or freedoms, as guaranteed by this Charter, have been infringed or denied may apply to a court of competent jurisdiction to obtain such remedy as the court considers appropriate and just in the circumstances.

Exclusion of evidence bringing administration of justice into disrepute

(2) Where, in proceedings under subsection (1), a court concludes that evidence was obtained in a manner that infringed or denied any

rights or freedoms guaranteed by this Charter, the evidence shall be excluded if it is established that, having regard to all the circumstances, the admission of it in the proceedings would bring the administration of justice into disrepute.

General

Aboriginal rights and freedoms not affected by Charter

25. The guarantee in this Charter of certain rights and freedoms shall not be construed so as to abrogate or derogate from any aboriginal, treaty or other rights or freedoms that pertain to the aboriginal peoples of Canada including

(*a*) any rights or freedoms that have been recognized by the Royal Proclamation of October 7, 1763; and

(*b*) any rights or freedoms that now exist by way of land claims agreements or may be so acquired.[94]

Other rights and freedoms not affected by Charter

26. The guarantee in this Charter of certain rights and freedoms shall not be construed as denying the existence of any other rights or freedoms that exist in Canada.

Multicultural heritage

27. This Charter shall be interpreted in a manner consistent with the preservation and enhancement of the multicultural heritage of Canadians.

Rights guaranteed equally to both sexes

28. Notwithstanding anything in this Charter, the rights and freedoms referred to in it are guaranteed equally to male and female persons.

Rights respecting certain schools preserved

29. Nothing in this Charter abrogates or derogates from any rights or privileges guaranteed by or under the Constitution of Canada in respect of denominational, separate or dissentient schools.[95]

Application to territories and territorial authorities

30. A reference in this Charter to a Province or to the legislative assembly or legislature of a province shall be deemed to include a reference to the Yukon Territory and the Northwest Territories, or to the appropriate legislative authority thereof, as the case may be.

Legislative powers not extended

31. Nothing in this Charter extends the legislative powers of any body or authority.

Application of Charter

Application of Charter

32. (1) This Charter applies

(*a*) to the Parliament and government of Canada in respect of all matters within the authority of Parliament including all matters relating to the Yukon Territory and Northwest Territories; and

(*b*) to the legislature and government of each province in respect of all matters within the authority of the legislature of each province.

Exception

(2) Notwithstanding subsection (1), section 15 shall not have effect until three years after this section comes into force.

Exception where express declaration

33. (1) Parliament or the legislature of a province may expressly declare in an Act of Parliament or of the legislature, as the case may be, that the Act or a provision thereof shall operate notwithstanding a provision included in section 2 or sections 7 to 15 of this Charter.

Operation of exception

(2) An Act or a provision of an Act in respect of which a declaration made under this section is in effect shall have such operation as it would have but for the provision of this Charter referred to in the declaration.

Five year limitation

(3) A declaration made under subsection (1) shall cease to have effect five years after it comes into force or on such earlier date as may be specified in the declaration.

Re-enactment

(4) Parliament or the legislature of a province may re-enact a declaration made under subsection (1).

Five year limitation

(5) Subsection (3) applies in respect of a re-enactment made under subsection (4).

Citation

Citation

34. This Part may be cited as the *Canadian Charter of Rights and Freedoms*.

PART II
RIGHTS OF THE ABORIGINAL PEOPLES OF CANADA

Recognition of existing aboriginal and treaty rights

35. (1) The existing aboriginal and treaty rights of the aboriginal peoples of Canada are hereby recognized and affirmed.

Definition of "aboriginal peoples of Canada"

(2) In this Act, "aboriginal peoples of Canada" includes the Indian, Inuit and Métis peoples of Canada.

Land claims agreements

(3) For greater certainty, in subsection (1) "treaty rights" includes rights that now exist by way of land claims agreements or may be so acquired.

Aboriginal and treaty rights are guaranteed equally to both sexes

(4) Notwithstanding any other provision of this Act, the aboriginal and treaty rights referred to in subsection (1) are guaranteed equally to male and female persons.[96]

Commitment to participation in constitutional conference

35.1 The government of Canada and the provincial governments are committed to the principal that, before any amendment is made to Class 24 of section 91 of the "*Constitution Act, 1867*", to section 25 of this Act or to this Part,

(*a*) a constitutional conference that includes in its agenda an item relating to the proposed amendment, composed of the Prime Minister of Canada and the first ministers of the provinces, will be convened by the Prime Minister of Canada; and

(*b*) the Prime Minister of Canada will invite representatives of the aboriginal peoples of Canada to participate in the discussions on that item.[97]

PART III
EQUALIZATION AND REGIONAL DISPARITIES

Commitment to promote equal opportunities

36. (1) Without altering the legislative authority of Parliament or of the provincial legislatures, or the rights of any of them with respect to the exercise of their legislative authority, Parliament and the legislatures, together with the government of Canada and the provincial governments, are committed to

(*a*) promoting equal opportunities for the well-being of Canadians;

(*b*) furthering economic development to reduce disparity in opportunities; and
(*c*) providing essential public services of reasonable quality to all Canadians.

Commitment respecting public services

(2) Parliament and the government of Canada are committed to the principle of making equalization payments to ensure that provincial governments have sufficient revenues to provide reasonably comparable levels of public services at reasonably comparable levels of taxation.[98]

PART IV
CONSTITUTIONAL CONFERENCE

37. [99]

PART IV.I
CONSTITUTIONAL CONFERENCES

37.1 [100]

PART V
PROCEDURE FOR AMENDING CONSTITUTION OF CANADA[101]

General procedure for amending Constitution of Canada

38. (1) An amendment to the Constitution of Canada may be made by proclamation issued by the Governor General under the Great Seal of Canada where so authorized by

(*a*) resolutions of the Senate and House of Commons; and
(*b*) resolutions of the legislative assemblies of at least two-thirds of the provinces that have, in the aggregate, according to the then latest general census, at least fifty per cent of the population of all the provinces.

Majority of members

(2) An amendment made under subsection (1) that derogates from the legislative powers, the proprietary rights or any other rights or privileges of the legislature or government of a province shall require a resolution supported by a majority of the members of each of the Senate, the House of Commons and the legislative assemblies required under subsection (1).

Expression of dissent

(3) An amendment referred to in subsection (2) shall not have effect in a province the legislative assembly of which has expressed its dissent thereto by resolution supported by a majority of its members

prior to the issue of the proclamation to which the amendment relates unless that legislative assembly, subsequently, by resolution supported by a majority of its members, revokes its dissent and authorizes the amendment.

Revocation of dissent

(4) A resolution of dissent made for the purposes of subsection (3) may be revoked at any time before or after the issue of the proclamation to which it relates.

Restriction on proclamation

39. (1) A proclamation shall not be issued under subsection 38(1) before the expiration of one year from the adoption of the resolution initiating the amendment procedure thereunder, unless the legislative assembly of each province has previously adopted a resolution of assent or dissent.

Idem

(2) A proclamation shall not be issued under subsection 38(1) after the expiration of three years from the adoption of the resolution initiating the amendment procedure thereunder.

Compensation

40. Where an amendment is made under subsection 38(1) that transfers provincial legislative powers relating to education or other cultural matters from provincial legislatures to Parliament, Canada shall provide reasonable compensation to any province to which the amendment does not apply.

Amendment by unanimous consent

41. An amendment to the Constitution of Canada in relation to the following matters may be made by proclamation issued by the Governor General under the Great Seal of Canada only where authorized by resolutions of the Senate and House of Commons and of the legislative assembly of each province:

(*a*) the office of the Queen, the Governor General and the Lieutenant Governor of a province;

(*b*) the right of a province to a number of members in the House of Commons not less than the number of Senators by which the province is entitled to be represented at the time this Part comes into force;

(*c*) subject to section 43, the use of the English or the French language;

(*d*) the composition of the Supreme Court of Canada; and

(*e*) an amendment to this Part.

Amendment by general procedure

42. (1) An amendment to the Constitution of Canada in relation to the following matters may be made only in accordance with subsection 38(1):

(*a*) the principle of proportionate representation of the provinces in the House of Commons prescribed by the Constitution of Canada;

(*b*) the powers of the Senate and the method of selecting Senators;

(*c*) the number of members by which a province is entitled to be represented in the Senate and the residence qualifications of Senators;

(*d*) subject to paragraph 41(*d*), the Supreme Court of Canada;

(*e*) the extension of existing provinces into the territories; and

(*f*) notwithstanding any other law or practice, the establishment of new provinces.

Exception

(2) Subsections 38(2) to (4) do not apply in respect of amendments in relation to matters referred to in subsection (1).

Amendment of provisions relating to some but not all provinces

43. An amendment to the Constitution of Canada in relation to any provision that applies to one or more, but not all, provinces, including

(*a*) any alteration to boundaries between provinces, and

(*b*) any amendment to any provision that relates to the use of the English or the French language within a province,

may be made by proclamation issued by the Governor General under the Great Seal of Canada only where so authorized by resolutions of the Senate and House of Commons and of the legislative assembly of each province to which the amendment applies.

Amendments by Parliament

44. Subject to sections 41 and 42, Parliament may exclusively make laws amending the Constitution of Canada in relation to the executive government of Canada or the Senate and House of Commons.

Amendments by provincial legislatures

45. Subject to section 41, the legislature of each province may exclusively make laws amending the constitution of the province.

Initiation of amendment procedures

46. (1) The procedures for amendment under sections 38, 41, 42 and 43 may be initiated either by the Senate or the House of Commons or by the legislative assembly of a province.

Revocation of authorization

(2) A resolution of assent made for the purposes of this Part may be revoked at any time before the issue of a proclamation authorized by it.

Amendments without Senate resolution

47. (1) An amendment to the Constitution of Canada made by proclamation under section 38, 41, 42 or 43 may be made without a resolution of the Senate authorizing the issue of the proclamation if, within one hundred and eighty days after the adoption by the House of Commons of a resolution authorizing its issue, the Senate has not adopted such a resolution and if, at any time after the expiration of that period, the House of Commons again adopts the resolution.

Computation of period

(2) Any period when Parliament is prorogued or dissolved shall not be counted in computing the one hundred and eighty day period referred to in subsection (1).

Advice to issue proclamation

48. The Queen's Privy Council for Canada shall advise the Governor General to issue a proclamation under this Part forthwith on the adoption of the resolutions required for an amendment made by proclamation under this Part.

Constitutional conference

49. A constitutional conference composed of the Prime Minister of Canada and the first ministers of the provinces shall be convened by the Prime Minister of Canada within fifteen years after this Part comes into force to review the provisions of this Part.

PART VI
AMENDMENT TO THE CONSTITUTION ACT, 1867

50. [102]

51. [103]

PART VII
GENERAL

Primacy of Constitution of Canada

52. (1) The Constitution of Canada is the supreme law of Canada, and any law that is inconsistent with the provisions of the Constitution is, to the extent of the inconsistency, of no force or effect.

Constitution of Canada

(2) The Constitution of Canada includes

(*a*) the *Canada Act 1982*, including this Act;
(*b*) the Acts and orders referred to in the schedule; and
(*c*) any amendment to any Act or order referred to in paragraph (*a*) or (*b*).

Amendments to Constitution of Canada

(3) Amendments to the Constitution of Canada shall be made only in accordance with the authority contained in the Constitution of Canada.

Repeals and new names

53. (1) The enactments referred to in Column I of the schedule are hereby repealed or amended to the extent indicated in Column II thereof and, unless repealed, shall continue as law in Canada under the names set out in Column III thereof.

Consequential amendments

(2) Every enactment, except the *Canada Act 1982*, that refers to an enactment referred to in the schedule by the name in Column I thereof is hereby amended by substituting for that name the corresponding name in Column III thereof, and any British North America Act not referred to in the schedule may be cited as the *Constitution Act*followed by the year and number, if any, of its enactment.

Repeal and consequential amendments

54. Part IV is repealed on the day that is one year after this Part comes into force and this section may be repealed and this Act renumbered, consequentially upon the repeal of Part IV and this section, by proclamation issued by the Governor General under the Great Seal of Canada.[104]

[*Repealed*]

54.1 [105]

French version of Constitution of Canada

55. A French version of the portions of the Constitution of Canada referred to in the schedule shall be prepared by the Minister of Justice of Canada as expeditiously as possible and, when any portion thereof sufficient to warrant action being taken has been so prepared, it shall be put forward for enactment by proclamation issued by the Governor General under the Great Seal of Canada pursuant to the procedure then applicable to an amendment of the same provisions of the Constitution of Canada.

English and French versions of certain constitutional texts

56. Where any portion of the Constitution of Canada has been or is enacted in English and French or where a French version of any portion of the Constitution is enacted pursuant to section 55, the English

and French versions of that portion of the Constitution are equally authoritative.

English and French versions of this Act

57. The English and French versions of this Act are equally authoritative.

Commencement

58. Subject to section 59, this Act shall come into force on a day to be fixed by proclamation issued by the Queen or the Governor General under the Great Seal of Canada.[106]

Commencement of paragraph 23(1)(a) in respect of Quebec

59. (1) Paragraph 23(1)(*a*) shall come into force in respect of Quebec on a day to be fixed by proclamation issued by the Queen or the Governor General under the Great Seal of Canada.

Authorization of Quebec

(2) A proclamation under subsection (1) shall be issued only where authorized by the legislative assembly or government of Quebec.[107]

Repeal of this section

(3) This section may be repealed on the day paragraph 23(1)(*a*) comes into force in respect of Quebec and this Act amended and renumbered, consequentially upon the repeal of this section, by proclamation issued by the Queen or the Governor General under the Great Seal of Canada.

Short title and citations

60. This Act may be cited as the *Constitution Act, 1982*, and the Constitution Acts 1867 to 1975 (No. 2) and this Act may be cited together as the *Constitution Acts, 1867 to 1982*.

References

61. A reference to the "*Constitution Acts, 1867 to 1982*" shall be deemed to include a reference to the "*Constitution Amendment Proclamation, 1983*".[108]

SCHEDULE TO THE CONSTITUTION ACT, 1982

MODERNIZATION OF THE CONSTITUTION

Item	Column I Act Affected	Column II Amendment	Column III New Name
1.	British North America Act, 1867, 30–31 Vict., c. 3 (U.K.)	(1) Section 1 is repealed and the following substituted therefor: "1. This Act may be cited as the *Constitution Act, 1867.*" (2) Section 20 is repealed. (3) Class 1 of section 91 is repealed. (4) Class 1 of section 92 is repealed.	Constitution Act, 1867
2.	An Act to amend and continue the Act 32–33 Victoria chapter 3; and to establish and provide for the Government of the Province of Manitoba, 1870, 33 Vict., c. 3 (Can.)	(1) The long title is repealed and the following substituted therefor: "*Manitoba Act, 1870.*" (2) Section 20 is repealed.	Manitoba Act, 1870
3.	Order of Her Majesty in Council admitting Rupert's Land and the North-Western Territory into the union, dated the 23rd day of June, 1870		Rupert's Land and North-Western Territory Order
4.	Order of Her Majesty in Council admitting British Columbia into the Union, dated the 16th day of May, 1871		British Columbia Terms of Union
5.	British North America Act, 1871, 34–35 Vict., c. 28 (U.K.)	Section 1 is repealed and the following substituted therefor: "1. This Act may be cited as the *Constitution Act, 1871.*"	Constitution Act, 1871
6.	Order of Her Majesty in Council admitting Prince Edward Island into the Union, dated the 26th day of June, 1873.		Prince Edward Island Terms of Union

Item	Column I Act Affected	Column II Amendment	Column III New Name
7.	Parliament of Canada Act, 1875, 38–39 Vict., c. 38 (U.K.)		Parliament of Canada Act, 1875
8.	Order of Her Majesty in Council admitting all British possessions and Territories in North America and islands adjacent thereto into the Union, dated the 31st day of July, 1880.		Adjacent Territories Order
9.	British North America Act, 1886, 49–50 Vict., c. 35 (U.K.)	Section 3 is repealed and the following substituted therefor: "3. This Act may be cited as the *Constitution Act, 1886.*"	Section 3 is repealed and the following substituted therefor: "3. This Act may be cited as the Constitution Act, 1886."
10.	Canada (Ontario Boundary) Act, 1889, 52-53 Vict., c. 28 (U.K.)		Canada (Ontario Boundary) Act, 1889
11.	Canadian Speaker (Appointment of Deputy) Act, 1895, 2nd Sess., 59 Vict., c. 3 (U.K.)	The Act is repealed.	
12.	The Alberta Act, 1905, 4–5 Edw. VII, c. 3 (Can.)		Alberta Act
13.	The Saskatchewan Act, 1905, 4–5 Edw. VII, c. 42 (Can.)		Saskatchewan Act
14.	British North America Act, 1907, 7 Edw. VII, c. 11 (U.K.)	Section 2 is repealed and the following substituted therefor: "2. This Act may be cited as the *Constitution Act, 1907.*"	Constitution Act, 1907
15.	British North America Act, 1915, 5–6 Geo. V, c. 45 (U.K.)	Section 3 is repealed and the following substituted therefor: "3. This Act may be cited as the *Constitution Act, 1915.*"	Constitution Act, 1915
16.	British North America Act, 1930, 20–21, Geo. V, c. 26 (U.K.)	Section 3 is repealed and the following substituted therefor: "3. This Act may be cited as the *Constitution Act, 1930.*"	Constitution Act, 1930

Item	Column I Act Affected	Column II Amendment	Column III New Name
17.	Statute of Westminster, 1931, 22 Geo. V, c. 4 (U.K.)	In so far as they apply to Canada, (*a*) section 4 is repealed; and (*b*) subsection 7(1) is repealed.	Statute of Westminster, 1931
18.	British North America Act, 1940, 3–4 Geo. VI, c. 36 (U.K.)	Section 2 is repealed and the following substituted therefor: "2. This Act may be cited as the *Constitution Act, 1940*."	Constitution Act, 1940
19.	British North America Act, 1943, 6–7 Geo. VI, c. 30 (U.K.)	The Act is repealed.	
20.	British North America Act, 1946, 9–10 Geo. VI, c. 63 (U.K.)	The Act is repealed.	
21.	British North America Act, 1949, 12–13 Geo. VI, c. 22 (U.K.)	Section 3 is repealed and the following substituted therefor: "3. This Act may be cited as the *Newfoundland Act*."	Newfoundland Act
22.	British North America (No.2) Act, 1949, 13 Geo. VI, c. 81 (U.K.)	The Act is repealed.	
23.	British North America Act, 1951, 14–15 Geo. VI, c. 32 (U.K.)	The Act is repealed.	
24.	British North America Act, 1952, 1 Eliz. II, c. 15 (Can.)	The Act is repealed.	
25.	British North America Act, 1960, 9 Eliz. II, c. 2 (U.K.)	Section 2 is repealed and the following substituted therefor: "2. This Act may be cited as the *Constitution Act, 1960*."	Constitution Act, 1960
26.	British North America Act, 1964, 12–13 Eliz. II, c. 73 (U.K.)	Section 2 is repealed and the following substituted therefor: "2. This Act may be cited as the *Constitution Act, 1964*."	Constitution Act, 1964

Item	Column I Act Affected	Column II Amendment	Column III New Name
27.	British North America Act, 1965, 14 Eliz. II, c. 4, Part I (Can.)	Section 2 is repealed and the following substituted therefor: "2. This Part may be cited as the *Constitution Act, 1965*."	Constitution Act, 1965
28.	British North America Act, 1974, 23 Eliz. II, c. 13, Part I (Can.)	Section 3, as amended by 25-26 Eliz. II, c. 28, s. 38(1) (Can.), is repealed and the following substituted therefor: "3. This Part may be cited as the *Constitution Act, 1974*."	Constitution Act, 1974
29.	British North America Act, 1975, 23–24 Eliz. II, c. 28, Part I (Can.)	Section 3, as amended by 25-26 Eliz. II, c. 28, s. 31 (Can.), is repealed and the following substituted therefor: "3. This Part may be cited as the *Constitution Act (No. 1), 1975*."	Constitution Act (No. 1), 1975
30.	British North America Act (No. 2), 1975, 23-24 Eliz. II, c. 53 (Can.)	Section 3 is repealed and the following substituted therefor: "3. This Act may be cited as the *Constitution Act (No. 2), 1975*."	Constitution Act (No. 2), 1975

NOTES

1. The enacting clause was repealed by the *Statute Law Revision Act, 1893*, 56–57 Vict., c. 14 (U.K.). It read as follows:

   Be it therefore enacted and declared by the Queen's most Excellent Majesty, by and with the Advice and Consent of the Lords Spiritual and Temporal, and Commons, in this present Parliament assembled, and by the Authority of the same, as follows:

2. As enacted by the *Constitution Act, 1982*, which came into force on April 17, 1982. The section originally read as follows:

   1. This Act may be cited as *The British North America Act, 1867*.

3. Section 2, repealed by the *Statute Law Revision Act, 1893*, 56–57 Vict., c. 14 (U.K.), read as follows:

   2. The Provisions of this Act referring to Her Majesty the Queen extend also to the Heirs and Successors of Her Majesty, Kings and Queens of the United Kingdom of Great Britain and Ireland.

4. The first day of July, 1867, was fixed by proclamation dated May 22, 1867.

5. Partially repealed by the *Statute Law Revision Act, 1893*, 56–57 Vict., c. 14 (U.K.). The section originally read as follows:

   4. The subsequent Provisions of this Act shall, unless it is otherwise expressed or implied, commence and have effect on and after the Union, that is to say, on and after the Day appointed for the Union taking effect in the Queen's Proclamation; and in the same Provisions, unless it is otherwise expressed or implied, the Name Canada shall be taken to mean Canada as constituted under this Act.

6. Canada now consists of ten provinces (Ontario, Quebec, Nova Scotia, New Brunswick, Manitoba, British Columbia, Prince Edward Island, Alberta, Saskatchewan and Newfoundland) and three territories (Yukon, the Northwest Territories and Nunavut).

   The first territories added to the Union were Rupert's Land and the North-Western Territory (subsequently designated the Northwest Territories), which were admitted pursuant to section 146 of the *Constitution Act, 1867* and the *Rupert's Land Act, 1868*, 31–32 Vict., c. 105 (U.K.), by the *Rupert's Land and North-Western Territory Order* of June 23, 1870, effective July 15, 1870. Prior to the admission of those territories the Parliament of Canada enacted *An Act for the temporary Government of Rupert's Land and the North-Western Territory when united with Canada* (32–33 Vict., c. 3), and the *Manitoba Act, 1870* (33 Vict., c. 3), which provided for the formation of the Province of Manitoba.

   British Columbia was admitted into the Union pursuant to section 146 of the *Constitution Act, 1867*, by the *British Columbia Terms of Union*, being Order in Council of May 16, 1871, effective July 20, 1871.

   Prince Edward Island was admitted pursuant to section 146 of the *Constitution Act, 1867*, by the *Prince Edward Island Terms of Union*, being Order in Council of June 26, 1873, effective July 1, 1873.

   On June 29, 1871, the United Kingdom Parliament enacted the *Constitution Act, 1871* (34–35 Vict., c. 28) authorizing the creation of additional provinces out of territories not included in any province. Pursuant to this statute, the Parliament of Canada enacted the *Alberta Act* (July 20, 1905, 4–5 Edw. VII, c. 3) and the *Saskatchewan Act* (July 20, 1905, 4–5 Edw. VII, c. 42), providing for the creation of the provinces of Alberta and Saskatchewan, respectively. Both of these Acts came into force on September 1, 1905.

   Meanwhile, all remaining British possessions and territories in North America and the islands adjacent thereto, except the colony of Newfoundland and its dependencies, were admitted into the Canadian Confederation by the *Adjacent Territories Order*, dated July 31, 1880.

   The Parliament of Canada added portions of the Northwest Territories to the adjoining provinces in 1912 by *The Ontario Boundaries Extension Act*, S.C. 1912, 2 Geo. V, c. 40, *The Quebec Boundaries Extension Act, 1912*, 2 Geo. V, c. 45 and *The Manitoba Boundaries Extension Act, 1912*, 2 Geo. V, c. 32, and further additions were made to Manitoba by *The Manitoba Boundaries Extension Act, 1930*, 20–21 Geo. V, c. 28.

   The Yukon Territory was created out of the Northwest Territories in 1898 by *The Yukon Territory Act*, 61 Vict., c. 6.

   Newfoundland was added on March 31, 1949, by the *Newfoundland Act*, 12–13 Geo. VI, c. 22 (U.K.), which ratified the Terms of Union of Newfoundland with Canada.

Nunavut was created out of the Northwest Territories in 1999 by the *Nunavut Act*, S.C. 1993, c. 28.

7. See note (65) to section 129, infra.
8. Repealed and re-enacted by the *Parliament of Canada Act, 1875*, 38–39 Vict., c. 38 (U.K.). The original section read as follows:

> 18. The Privileges, Immunities, and Powers to be held, enjoyed, and exercised by the Senate and by the House of Commons and by the Members thereof respectively shall be such as are from Time to Time defined by Act of the Parliament of Canada, but so that the same shall never exceed those at the passing of this Act held, enjoyed, and exercised by the Commons House of Parliament of the United Kingdom of Great Britain and Ireland and by the Members thereof.

9. Spent. The first session of the first Parliament began on November 6, 1867.
10. Section 20, repealed by the *Constitution Act, 1982*, read as follows:

> 20. There shall be a Session of the Parliament of Canada once at least in every Year, so that Twelve Months shall not intervene between the last Sitting of the Parliament in one Session and its first sitting in the next Session.

Section 20 has been replaced by section 5 of the *Constitution Act, 1982*, which provides that there shall be a sitting of Parliament at least once every twelve months.

11. As amended by the *Constitution Act, 1915*, 5-6 Geo. V, c. 45 (U.K.) and modified by the *Newfoundland Act*, 12-13 Geo. VI, c. 22 (U.K.), the *Constitution Act (No. 2), 1975*, S.C. 1974-75-76, c. 53, and the *Constitution Act, 1999 (Nunavut)*, S.C. 1998, c. 15, Part 2. The original section read as follows:

> 21. The Senate shall, subject to the Provisions of this Act, consist of Seventy-two Members, who shall be styled Senators.

The *Manitoba Act, 1870*, added two for Manitoba; the *British Columbia Terms of Union* added three; upon admission of Prince Edward Island four more were provided by section 147 of the *Constitution Act, 1867*; the *Alberta Act* and the *Saskatchewan Act* each added four. The Senate was reconstituted at 96 by the *Constitution Act, 1915*. Six more Senators were added upon union with Newfoundland, and one Senator each was added for the Yukon Territory and the Northwest Territories by the *Constitution Act (No. 2), 1975*. One Senator was added for Nunavut by the *Constitution Act, 1999 (Nunavut)*.

12. As amended by the *Constitution Act, 1915*, 5-6 Geo. V, c. 45 (U.K.), the *Newfoundland Act*, 12-13 Geo. VI, c. 22 (U.K.), and the *Constitution Act (No. 2), 1975*, S.C. 1974-75-76, c. 53 and the *Constitution Act, 1999 (Nunavut)*, S.C. 1998, c. 15, Part 2. The original section read as follows:

> 22. In relation to the Constitution of the Senate, Canada shall be deemed to consist of Three Divisions:
>
> 1. Ontario;
> 2. Quebec;
> 3. The Maritime Provinces, Nova Scotia and New Brunswick;
>
> which Three Divisions shall (subject to the Provisions of this Act) be equally represented in the Senate as follows: Ontario by Twenty-four Senators; Quebec by Twenty-four Senators; and the Maritime Provinces by Twenty-

four Senators, Twelve thereof representing Nova Scotia, and Twelve thereof representing New Brunswick.

In the case of Quebec each of the Twenty-four Senators representing that Province shall be appointed for One of the Twenty-four Electoral Divisions of Lower Canada specified in Schedule A. to Chapter One of the Consolidated Statutes of Canada.

13. Section 44 of the *Constitution Act, 1999 (Nunavut)*, S.C. 1998, c. 15, Part 2, provided that, for the purposes of that Part (which added one Senator for Nunavut), the word "Province" in section 23 of the *Constitution Act, 1867* has the same meaning as is assigned to the word "province" by section 35 of the *Interpretation Act*, R.S.C. 1985, c. I-21, as amended, which provides that the term "province" means "a province of Canada, and includes Yukon, the Northwest Territories and Nunavut".

    Section 2 of the *Constitution Act (No. 2), 1975*, S.C. 1974-75-76, c. 53, provided that for the purposes of that Act (which added one Senator each for the Yukon Territory and the Northwest Territories) the term "Province" in section 23 of the *Constitution Act, 1867* has the same meaning as is assigned to the term "province" by section 28 of the *Interpretation Act*, R.S.C. 1970, c. I-23, which provides that the term "province" means "a province of Canada, and includes the Yukon Territory and the Northwest Territories".

14. Repealed by the *Statute Law Revision Act, 1893*, 56-57 Vict., c. 14 (U.K.). The section read as follows:

    25. Such Persons shall be first summoned to the Senate as the Queen by Warrant under Her Majesty's Royal Sign Manual thinks fit to approve, and their Names shall be inserted in the Queen's Proclamation of Union.

15. As amended by the *Constitution Act, 1915*, 5-6 Geo. V, c. 45 (U.K.). The original section read as follows:

    26. If at any Time on the Recommendation of the Governor General the Queen thinks fit to direct that Three or Six Members be added to the Senate, the Governor General may by Summons to Three or Six qualified Persons (as the Case may be), representing equally the Three Divisions of Canada, add to the Senate accordingly.

16. As amended by the *Constitution Act, 1915*, 5-6 Geo. V, c. 45 (U.K.). The original section read as follows:

    27. In case of such Addition being at any Time made the Governor General shall not summon any Person to the Senate except on a further like Direction by the Queen on the like Recommendation, until each of the Three Divisions of Canada is represented by Twenty-four Senators and no more.

17. As amended by the *Constitution Act, 1915*, 5-6 Geo. V, c. 45 (U.K.), the *Constitution Act (No. 2), 1975*, S.C. 1974-75-76, c. 53, and the *Constitution Act, 1999 (Nunavut)*, S.C. 1998, c. 15, Part 2. The original section read as follows:

    28. The Number of Senators shall not at any Time exceed Seventy-eight.

18. As enacted by the *Constitution Act, 1965*, S.C. 1965, c. 4, which came into force on June 2, 1965. The original section read as follows:

    29. A Senator shall, subject to the Provisions of this Act, hold his Place in the Senate for Life.

19. Provision for exercising the functions of Speaker during his absence is made by Part II of the *Parliament of Canada Act*, R.S.C. 1985, c. P-1 (formerly the *Speaker*

of the Senate Act, R.S.C. 1970, c. S-14). Doubts as to the power of Parliament to enact the *Speaker of the Senate Act* were removed by the *Canadian Speaker (Appointment of Deputy) Act, 1895*, 2nd Sess., 59 Vict., c. 3 (U.K.), which was repealed by the *Constitution Act, 1982*.

20. The figures given here result from the application of section 51, as enacted by the *Constitution Act, 1985 (Representation)*, S.C. 1986, c. 8, Part I, and amended by the *Constitution Act, 1999 (Nunavut)*, S.C. 1998, c. 15, Part 2 and readjusted pursuant to the *Electoral Boundaries Readjustment Act*, R.S.C. 1985, c. E-3. The original section (which was altered from time to time as the result of the addition of new provinces and changes in population) read as follows:

    37. The House of Commons shall, subject to the Provisions of this Act, consist of one hundred and eighty-one members, of whom Eighty-two shall be elected for Ontario, Sixty-five for Quebec, Nineteen for Nova Scotia, and Fifteen for New Brunswick.

21. Spent. The electoral districts are now established by proclamations issued from time to time under the *Electoral Boundaries Readjustment Act*, R.S.C. 1985, c. E-3, as amended for particular districts by Acts of Parliament (see the most recent *Table of Public Statutes and Responsible Ministers*).
22. Spent. Elections are now provided for by the *Canada Elections Act*, S.C. 2000, c. 9; qualifications and disqualifications of members by the *Parliament of Canada Act*, R.S.C. 1985, c. P-1. The right of citizens to vote and hold office is provided for in section 3 of the *Constitution Act, 1982*.
23. Repealed by the *Statute Law Revision Act, 1893*, 56–57 Vict., c. 14 (U.K.). The section read as follows:

    42. For the First Election of Members to serve in the House of Commons the Governor General shall cause Writs to be issued by such Person, in such Form, and addressed to such Returning Officers as he thinks fit.

    The Person issuing Writs under this Section shall have the like Powers as are possessed at the Union by the Officers charged with the issuing of Writs for the Election of Members to serve in the respective House of Assembly or Legislative Assembly of the Province of Canada, Nova Scotia, or New Brunswick; and the Returning Officers to whom Writs are directed under this Section shall have the like Powers as are possessed at the Union by the Officers charged with the returning of Writs for the Election of Members to serve in the same respective House of Assembly or Legislative Assembly.

24. Repealed by the *Statute Law Revision Act, 1893*, 56–57 Vict., c. 14 (U.K.). The section read as follows:

    43. In case a Vacancy in the Representation in the House of Commons of any Electoral District happens before the Meeting of the Parliament, or after the Meeting of the Parliament before Provision is made by the Parliament in this Behalf, the Provisions of the last foregoing Section of this Act shall extend and apply to the issuing and returning of a Writ in respect of such Vacant District.

25. Provision for exercising the functions of Speaker during his absence is now made by Part III of the *Parliament of Canada Act*, R.S.C. 1985, c. P-1.
26. The term of the twelfth Parliament was extended by the *British North America Act, 1916*, 6–7 Geo. V., c. 19 (U.K.), which Act was repealed by the *Statute Law Revision Act, 1927*, 17–18 Geo. V, c. 42 (U.K.). See also subsection 4(1) of the

Constitution Act, 1982, which provides that no House of Commons shall continue for longer than five years from the date fixed for the return of the writs at a general election of its members, and subsection 4(2) thereof, which provides for continuation of the House of Commons in special circumstances.

27. As enacted by the *Fair Representation Act*, S.C. 2011, c. 26, s. 2, which came into force on royal assent on December 16, 2011.

The section, as originally enacted, read as follows:

> 51. On the Completion of the Census in the Year One Thousand eight hundred and seventy-one, and of each subsequent decennial Census, the Representation of the Four Provinces shall be readjusted by such Authority, in such Manner, and from such Time, as the Parliament of Canada from Time to Time provides, subject and according to the following Rules:
>
> (1) Quebec shall have the fixed Number of Sixty-five Members:
>
> (2) There shall be assigned to each of the other Provinces such a Number of Members as will bear the same Proportion to the Number of its Population (ascertained at such Census) as the Number Sixty-five bears to the Number of the Population of Quebec (so ascertained):
>
> (3) In the Computation of the Number of Members for a Province a fractional Part not exceeding One Half of the whole Number requisite for entitling the Province to a Member shall be disregarded; but a fractional Part exceeding One Half of that Number shall be equivalent to the whole Number:
>
> (4) On any such Re-adjustment the Number of Members for a Province shall not be reduced unless the Proportion which the Number of the Population of the Province bore to the Number of the aggregate Population of Canada at the then last preceding Re-adjustment of the Number of Members for the Province is ascertained at the then latest Census to be diminished by One Twentieth Part or upwards:
>
> (5) Such Re-adjustment shall not take effect until the Termination of the then existing Parliament.

The section was amended by the *Statute Law Revision Act, 1893*, 56–57 Vict., c. 14 (U.K.) by repealing the words after "of the census" to "seventy-one and" and the word "subsequent".

By the *British North America Act, 1943*, 6–7 Geo. VI, c. 30 (U.K.), which Act was repealed by the *Constitution Act, 1982*, redistribution of seats following the 1941 census was postponed until the first session of Parliament after the war. The section was re-enacted by the *British North America Act, 1946*, 9–10 Geo. VI, c. 63 (U.K.), which Act was also repealed by the *Constitution Act, 1982*, to read as follows:

> 51. (1) The number of members of the House of Commons shall be two hundred and fifty-five and the representation of the provinces therein shall forthwith upon the coming into force of this section and thereafter on the completion of each decennial census be readjusted by such authority, in such manner, and from such time as the Parliament of Canada from time to time provides, subject and according to the following rules:
>
> 1. Subject as hereinafter provided, there shall be assigned to each of the provinces a number of members computed by dividing the total population of the provinces by two hundred and fifty-four and by dividing the population of each province by the quotient so obtained, disregarding,

except as hereinafter in this section provided, the remainder, if any, after the said process of division.

2. If the total number of members assigned to all the provinces pursuant to rule one is less than two hundred and fifty-four, additional members shall be assigned to the provinces (one to a province) having remainders in the computation under rule one commencing with the province having the largest remainder and continuing with the other provinces in the order of the magnitude of their respective remainders until the total number of members assigned is two hundred and fifty-four.
3. Notwithstanding anything in this section, if upon completion of a computation under rules one and two, the number of members to be assigned to a province is less than the number of senators representing the said province, rules one and two shall cease to apply in respect of the said province, and there shall be assigned to the said province a number of members equal to the said number of senators.
4. In the event that rules one and two cease to apply in respect of a province then, for the purpose of computing the number of members to be assigned to the provinces in respect of which rules one and two continue to apply, the total population of the provinces shall be reduced by the number of the population of the province in respect of which rules one and two have ceased to apply and the number two hundred and fifty-four shall be reduced by the number of members assigned to such province pursuant to rule three.
5. Such readjustment shall not take effect until the termination of the then existing Parliament.

(2) The Yukon Territory as constituted by Chapter forty-one of the Statutes of Canada, 1901, together with any Part of Canada not comprised within a province which may from time to time be included therein by the Parliament of Canada for the purposes of representation in Parliament, shall be entitled to one member.

The section was re-enacted as follows by the *British North America Act, 1952*, S.C. 1952, c. 15 (which Act was also repealed by the *Constitution Act, 1982*):

51. (1) Subject as hereinafter provided, the number of members of the House of Commons shall be two hundred and sixty-three and the representation of the provinces therein shall forthwith upon the coming into force of this section and thereafter on the completion of each decennial census be readjusted by such authority, in such manner, and from such time as the Parliament of Canada from time to time provides, subject and according to the following rules:

1. There shall be assigned to each of the provinces a number of members computed by dividing the total population of the provinces by two hundred and sixty-one and by dividing the population of each province by the quotient so obtained, disregarding, except as hereinafter in this section provided, the remainder, if any, after the said process of division.
2. If the total number of members assigned to all the provinces pursuant to rule one is less than two hundred and sixty-one, additional members shall be assigned to the provinces (one to a province) having remainders in the computation under rule one commencing with the province

having the largest remainder and continuing with the other provinces in the order of the magnitude of their respective remainders until the total number of members assigned is two hundred and sixty-one.

3. Notwithstanding anything in this section, if upon completion of a computation under rules one and two the number of members to be assigned to a province is less than the number of senators representing the said province, rules one and two shall cease to apply in respect of the said province, and there shall be assigned to the said province a number of members equal to the said number of senators.
4. In the event that rules one and two cease to apply in respect of a province then, for the purposes of computing the number of members to be assigned to the provinces in respect of which rules one and two continue to apply, the total population of the provinces shall be reduced by the number of the population of the province in respect of which rules one and two have ceased to apply and the number two hundred and sixty-one shall be reduced by the number of members assigned to such province pursuant to rule three.
5. On any such readjustment the number of members for any province shall not be reduced by more than fifteen per cent below the representation to which such province was entitled under rules one to four of this subsection at the last preceding readjustment of the representation of that province, and there shall be no reduction in the representation of any province as a result of which that province would have a smaller number of members than any other province that according to the results of the then last decennial census did not have a larger population; but for the purposes of any subsequent readjustment of representation under this section any increase in the number of members of the House of Commons resulting from the application of this rule shall not be included in the divisor mentioned in rules one to four of this subsection.
6. Such readjustment shall not take effect until the termination of the then existing Parliament.

(2) The Yukon Territory as constituted by chapter forty-one of the statutes of Canada, 1901, shall be entitled to one member, and such other part of Canada not comprised within a province as may from time to time be defined by the Parliament of Canada shall be entitled to one member.

Subsection 51(1) was re-enacted by the *Constitution Act, 1974*, S.C. 1974-75-76, c. 13, to read as follows:

51. (1) The number of members of the House of Commons and the representation of the provinces therein shall upon the coming into force of this subsection and thereafter on the completion of each decennial census be readjusted by such authority, in such manner, and from such time as the Parliament of Canada from time to time provides, subject and according to the following Rules:

1. There shall be assigned to Quebec seventy-five members in the readjustment following the completion of the decennial census taken in the year 1971, and thereafter four additional members in each subsequent readjustment.

2. Subject to Rules 5(2) and (3), there shall be assigned to a large province a number of members equal to the number obtained by dividing the population of the large province by the electoral quotient of Quebec.
3. Subject to Rules 5(2) and (3), there shall be assigned to a small province a number of members equal to the number obtained by dividing
   (*a*) the sum of the populations, determined according to the results of the penultimate decennial census, of the provinces (other than Quebec) having populations of less than one and a half million, determined according to the results of that census, by the sum of the numbers of members assigned to those provinces in the readjustment following the completion of that census; and
   (*b*) the population of the small province by the quotient obtained under paragraph (*a*).
4. Subject to Rules 5(1)(*a*), (2) and (3), there shall be assigned to an intermediate province a number of members equal to the number obtained
   (*a*) by dividing the sum of the populations of the provinces (other than Quebec) having populations of less than one and a half million by the sum of the number of members assigned to those provinces under any of Rules 3, 5(1)(b), (2) and (3);
   (b) by dividing the population of the intermediate province by the quotient obtained under paragraph (a); and
   (c) by adding to the number of members assigned to the intermediate province in the readjustment following the completion of the penultimate decennial census one-half of the difference resulting from the subtraction of that number from the quotient obtained under paragraph (*b*).

5. (1) On any readjustment,
   (*a*) if no province (other than Quebec) has a population of less than one and a half million, Rule 4 shall not be applied and, subject to Rules 5(2) and (3), there shall be assigned to an intermediate province a number of members equal to the number obtained by dividing
      (i) the sum of the populations, determined according to the results of the penultimate decennial census, of the provinces, (other than Quebec) having populations of not less than one and a half million and not more than two and a half million, determined according to the results of that census, by the sum of the numbers of members assigned to those provinces in the readjustment following the completion of that census, and
      (ii) the population of the intermediate province by the quotient obtained under subparagraph (i);
   (*b*) if a province (other than Quebec) having a population of
      (i) less than one and a half million, or
      (ii) not less than one and a half million and not more than two and a half million

   does not have a population greater than its population determined according to the results of the penultimate decennial census, it shall, subject to Rules 5(2) and (3), be assigned the number of members assigned to it in the readjustment following the completion of that census.

(2) On any readjustment,

(*a*) if, under any of Rules 2 to 5(1), the number of members to be assigned to a province (in this paragraph referred to as "the first province") is smaller than the number of members to be assigned to any other province not having a population greater than that of the first province, those Rules shall not be applied to the first province and it shall be assigned a number of members equal to the largest number of members to be assigned to any other province not having a population greater than that of the first province;

(*b*) if, under any of Rules 2 to 5(1)(a), the number of members to be assigned to a province is smaller than the number of members assigned to it in the readjustment following the completion of the penultimate decennial census, those Rules shall not be applied to it and it shall be assigned the latter number of members;

(*c*) if both paragraphs (a) and (b) apply to a province, it shall be assigned a number of members equal to the greater of the numbers produced under those paragraphs.

(3) On any readjustment,

(*a*) if the electoral quotient of a province (in this paragraph referred to as "the first province") obtained by dividing its population by the number of members to be assigned to it under any of Rules 2 to 5(2) is greater than the electoral quotient of Quebec, those Rules shall not be applied to the first province and it shall be assigned a number of members equal to the number obtained by dividing its population by the electoral quotient of Quebec;

(*b*) if, as a result of the application of Rule 6(2)(a), the number of members assigned to a province under paragraph (a) equals the number of members to be assigned to it under any of Rules 2 to 5(2), it shall be assigned that number of members and paragraph (*a*) shall cease to apply to that province.

6. (1) In these Rules,

"*electoral quotient*" means, in respect of a province, the quotient obtained by dividing its population, determined according to the results of the then most recent decennial census, by the number of members to be assigned to it under any of Rules 1 to 5(3) in the readjustment following the completion of that census;

"*intermediate province*" means a province (other than Quebec) having a population greater than its population determined according to the results of the penultimate decennial census but not more than two and a half million and not less than one and a half million;

"*large province*" means a province (other than Quebec) having a population greater than two and a half million;

"*penultimate decennial census*" means the decennial census that preceded the then most recent decennial census;

"*population*" means, except where otherwise specified, the population determined according to the results of the then most recent decennial census;

"small province" means a province (other than Quebec) having a population greater than its population determined according to the results of the penultimate decennial census and less than one and half million.

(2) For the purposes of these Rules,

(*a*) if any fraction less than one remains upon completion of the final calculation that produces the number of members to be assigned to a province, that number of members shall equal the number so produced disregarding the fraction;

(*b*) if more than one readjustment follows the completion of a decennial census, the most recent of those readjustments shall, upon taking effect, be deemed to be the only readjustment following the completion of that census;

(*c*) a readjustment shall not take effect until the termination of the then existing Parliament.

Subsection 51(1) was re-enacted by the *Constitution Act, 1985 (Representation)*, S.C. 1986, c. 8, Part I, as follows:

51. (1) The number of members of the House of Commons and the representation of the provinces therein shall, on the coming into force of this subsection and thereafter on the completion of each decennial census, be readjusted by such authority, in such manner, and from such time as the Parliament of Canada from time to time provides, subject and according to the following rules:

Rules

1. There shall be assigned to each of the provinces a number of members equal to the number obtained by dividing the total population of the provinces by two hundred and seventy-nine and by dividing the population of each province by the quotient so obtained, counting any remainder in excess of 0.50 as one after the said process of division.
2. If the total number of members that would be assigned to a province by the application of rule 1 is less than the total number assigned to that province on the date of coming into force of this subsection, there shall be added to the number of members so assigned such number of members as will result in the province having the same number of members as were assigned on that date.

28. As enacted by the *Constitution Act, 1999 (Nunavut)*, S.C. 1998, c. 15, Part 2. Note that the description of the territory of Yukon is now set out in Schedule 1 to the *Yukon Act*, S.C. 2002, c. 7, which replaced R.S.C. 1985, c. Y-2. Subsection 51(2) was previously amended by the *Constitution Act (No. 1), 1975*, S.C. 1974-75-76, c. 28, and read as follows:

(2) The Yukon Territory as bounded and described in the schedule to chapter Y-2 of the Revised Statutes of Canada, 1970, shall be entitled to one member, and the Northwest Territories as bounded and described in section 2 of chapter N-22 of the Revised Statutes of Canada, 1970, shall be entitled to two members.

29. As enacted by the *Constitution Act, 1915*, 5-6 Geo. V, c. 45 (U.K.).
30. Provided for by the *Salaries Act*, R.S.C. 1985, c. S-3.
31. Now provided for in Ontario by the *Executive Council Act*, R.S.O. 1990, c. E.25, and in Quebec by the *Executive Power Act*, R.S.Q., c. E-18.

32. A similar provision was included in each of the instruments admitting British Columbia, Prince Edward Island, and Newfoundland. The Executive Authorities for Manitoba, Alberta and Saskatchewan were established by the statutes creating those provinces. See note (6) to section 5, supra.
33. See note (65) to section 129, infra.
34. Spent. Now covered by the *Representation Act, 2005*, S.O. 2005, c. 35, Schedule 1.
35. *An Act respecting the Legislative Council of Quebec*, S.Q. 1968, c. 9, provided that the Legislature for Quebec shall consist of the Lieutenant Governor and the National Assembly of Quebec, and repealed the provisions of the *Legislature Act*, R.S.Q. 1964, c. 6, relating to the Legislative Council of Quebec. Now covered by the *National Assembly Act*, R.S.Q. c. A-23.1. Sections 72 to 79 following are therefore completely spent.
36. *An Act respecting the electoral districts*, S.Q. 1970, c. 7, provides that this section no longer has effect.
37. Repealed by the *Statute Law Revision Act, 1893*, 56-57 Vict., c. 14 (U.K.). The section read as follows:

    > 81. The Legislatures of Ontario and Quebec respectively shall be called together not later than Six Months after the Union.

38. Probably spent. The subject-matter of this section is now covered in Ontario by the *Legislative Assembly Act*, R.S.O. 1990, c. L.10, and in Quebec by the *National Assembly Act*, R.S.Q. c. A-23.1.
39. Probably spent. The subject-matter of this section is now covered in Ontario by the *Election Act*, R.S.O. 1990, c. E.6, and the *Legislative Assembly Act*, R.S.O. 1990, c. L.10, and in Quebec by the *Election Act*, R.S.Q. c. E-3.3 and the *National Assembly Act*, R.S.Q. c. A-23.1.
40. The maximum duration of the Legislative Assemblies of Ontario and Quebec has been changed to five years. See the *Legislative Assembly Act*, R.S.O. 1990, c. L.10, and the *National Assembly Act*, R.S.Q. c. A-23.1, respectively. See also section 4 of the *Constitution Act, 1982*, which provides a maximum duration for a legislative assembly of five years but also authorizes continuation in special circumstances.
41. See also section 5 of the *Constitution Act, 1982*, which provides that there shall be a sitting of each legislature at least once every twelve months.
42. Partially repealed by the *Statute Law Revision Act, 1893*, 56-57 Vict., c. 14 (U.K.), which deleted the following concluding words of the original enactment:

    > and the House of Assembly of New Brunswick existing at the passing of this Act shall, unless sooner dissolved, continue for the Period for which it was elected.

    A similar provision was included in each of the instruments admitting British Columbia, Prince Edward Island and Newfoundland. The Legislatures of Manitoba, Alberta and Saskatchewan were established by the statutes creating those provinces. See note (6) to section 5, supra.

    See also sections 3 to 5 of the *Constitution Act, 1982*, which prescribe democratic rights applicable to all provinces, and subitem 2(2) of the Schedule to that Act, which sets out the repeal of section 20 of the *Manitoba Act, 1870*. Section 20 of the *Manitoba Act, 1870* has been replaced by section 5 of the *Constitution Act, 1982*. Section 20 read as follows:

20. There shall be a Session of the Legislature once at least in every year, so that twelve months shall not intervene between the last sitting of the Legislature in one Session and its first sitting in the next Session.

43. Repealed by the *Statute Law Revision Act, 1893*, 56-57 Vict., c. 14 (U.K.). The section read as follows:

89. Each of the Lieutenant Governors of Ontario, Quebec and Nova Scotia shall cause Writs to be issued for the First Election of Members of the Legislative Assembly thereof in such Form and by such Person as he thinks fit, and at such Time and addressed to such Returning Officer as the Governor General directs, and so that the First Election of Member of Assembly for any Electoral District or any Subdivision thereof shall be held at the same Time and at the same Places as the Election for a Member to serve in the House of Commons of Canada for that Electoral District.

44. A new class 1 was added by the *British North America (No. 2) Act, 1949*, 13 Geo. VI, c. 81 (U.K.). That Act and class 1 were repealed by the *Constitution Act, 1982*. The matters referred to in class 1 are provided for in subsection 4(2) and Part V of the *Constitution Act, 1982*. As enacted, class 1 read as follows:

1. The amendment from time to time of the Constitution of Canada, except as regards matters coming within the classes of subjects by this Act assigned exclusively to the Legislatures of the provinces, or as regards rights or privileges by this or any other Constitutional Act granted or secured to the Legislature or the Government of a province, or to any class of persons with respect to schools or as regards the use of the English or the French language or as regards the requirements that there shall be a session of the Parliament of Canada at least once each year, and that no House of Commons shall continue for more than five years from the day of the return of the Writs for choosing the House: provided, however, that a House of Commons may in time of real or apprehended war, invasion or insurrection be continued by the Parliament of Canada if such continuation is not opposed by the votes of more than one-third of the members of such House.

45. The original class 1 was re-numbered by the *British North America (No. 2) Act, 1949*, 13 Geo. VI, c. 81 (U.K.), as class 1A.
46. Added by the *Constitution Act, 1940*, 3-4 Geo. VI, c. 36 (U.K.).
47. Legislative authority has been conferred on Parliament by other Acts as follows:
    1. The *Constitution Act, 1871*, 34-35 Vict., c. 28 (U.K.):

       2. The Parliament of Canada may from time to time establish new Provinces in any territories forming for the time being part of the Dominion of Canada, but not included in any Province thereof, and may, at the time of such establishment, make provision for the constitution and administration of any such Province, and for the passing of laws for the peace, order, and good government of such Province, and for its representation in the said Parliament.
       3. The Parliament of Canada may from time to time, with the consent of the Legislature of any province of the said Dominion, increase, diminish, or otherwise alter the limits of such Province, upon such terms and conditions as may be agreed to by the said Legislature, and may, with the like consent, make provision respecting the effect

and operation of any such increase or diminution or alteration of territory in relation to any Province affected thereby.

4. The Parliament of Canada may from time to time make provision for the administration, peace, order, and good government of any territory not for the time being included in any Province.
5. The following Acts passed by the said Parliament of Canada, and intituled respectively,—"An Act for the temporary government of Rupert's Land and the North Western Territory when united with Canada"; and "An Act to amend and continue the Act thirty-two and thirty-three Victoria, chapter three, and to establish and provide for the government of "the Province of Manitoba", shall be and be deemed to have been valid and effectual for all purposes whatsoever from the date at which they respectively received the assent, in the Queen's name, of the Governor General of the said Dominion of Canada.
6. Except as provided by the third section of this Act, it shall not be competent for the Parliament of Canada to alter the provisions of the last-mentioned Act of the said Parliament in so far as it relates to the Province of Manitoba, or of any other Act hereafter establishing new Provinces in the said Dominion, subject always to the right of the Legislature of the Province of Manitoba to alter from time to time the provisions of any law respecting the qualification of electors and members of the Legislative Assembly, and to make laws respecting elections in the said Province.

The *Rupert's Land Act, 1868*, 31-32 Vict., c. 105 (U.K.) (repealed by the *Statute Law Revision Act, 1893*, 56-57 Vict., c. 14 (U.K.)), had previously conferred similar authority in relation to Rupert's Land and the North-Western Territory upon admission of those areas.

2. The *Constitution Act, 1886*, 49-50 Vict., c. 35 (U.K.):

1. The Parliament of Canada may from time to time make provision for the representation in the Senate and House of Commons of Canada, or in either of them, of any territories which for the time being form part of the Dominion of Canada, but are not included in any province thereof.

3. The *Statute of Westminster, 1931*, 22 Geo. V, c. 4 (U.K.):

3. It is hereby declared and enacted that the Parliament of a Dominion has full power to make laws having extra-territorial operation.

4. Under section 44 of the *Constitution Act, 1982*, Parliament has exclusive authority to amend the Constitution of Canada in relation to the executive government of Canada or the Senate and House of Commons. Sections 38, 41, 42 and 43 of that Act authorize the Senate and House of Commons to give their approval to certain other constitutional amendments by resolution.

48. Class 1 was repealed by the *Constitution Act, 1982*. As enacted, it read as follows:

1. The Amendment from Time to Time, notwithstanding anything in this Act, of the Constitution of the Province, except as regards the Office of Lieutenant Governor.

Section 45 of the *Constitution Act, 1982* now authorizes legislatures to make laws amending the constitution of the province. Sections 38, 41, 42 and 43 of that Act authorize legislative assemblies to give their approval by resolution to certain other amendments to the Constitution of Canada.

49. Added by section 50 of the *Constitution Act, 1982*.
50. An alternative was provided for Manitoba by section 22 of the *Manitoba Act, 1870*, 33 Vict., c. 3 (confirmed by the *Constitution Act, 1871*, 34-35 Vict., c. 28 (U.K.)), which section reads as follows:

> 22. In and for the Province, the said Legislature may exclusively make Laws in relation to Education, subject and according to the following provisions:
>
> (1) Nothing in any such Law shall prejudicially affect any right or privilege with respect to Denominational Schools which any class of persons have by Law or practice in the Province at the Union:
>
> (2) An appeal shall lie to the Governor General in Council from any Act or decision of the Legislature of the Province, or of any Provincial Authority, affecting any right or privilege, of the Protestant or Roman Catholic minority of the Queen's subjects in relation to Education:
>
> (3) In case any such Provincial Law, as from time to time seems to the Governor General in Council requisite for the due execution of the provisions of this section, is not made, or in case any decision of the Governor General in Council on any appeal under this section is not duly executed by the proper Provincial Authority in that behalf, then, and in every such case, and as far only as the circumstances of each case require, the Parliament of Canada may make remedial Laws for the due execution of the provisions of this section, and of any decision of the Governor General in Council under this section.

An alternative was provided for Alberta by section 17 of the *Alberta Act*, 1905, 4-5 Edw. VII, c. 3, which section reads as follows:

> 17. Section 93 of the *Constitution Act, 1867*, shall apply to the said province, with the substitution for paragraph (1) of the said section 93 of the following paragraph:
>
> (1) Nothing in any such law shall prejudicially affect any right or privilege with respect to separate schools which any class of persons have at the date of the passing of this Act, under the terms of chapters 29 and 30 of the Ordinances of the Northwest Territories, passed in the year 1901, or with respect to religious instruction in any public or separate school as provided for in the said ordinances.
>
> 2. In the appropriation by the Legislature or distribution by the Government of the province of any moneys for the support of schools organized and carried on in accordance with the said chapter 29 or any Act passed in amendment thereof, or in substitution therefor, there shall be no discrimination against schools of any class described in the said chapter 29.
>
> 3. Where the expression "by law" is employed in paragraph 3 of the said section 93, it shall be held to mean the law as set out in the said chapters 29 and 30, and where the expression "at the Union" is employed, in the said paragraph 3, it shall be held to mean the date at which this Act comes into force.

An alternative was provided for Saskatchewan by section 17 of the *Saskatchewan Act*, 1905, 4-5 Edw. VII, c. 42, which section reads as follows:

> 17. Section 93 of the *Constitution Act, 1867*, shall apply to the said province, with the substitution for paragraph (1) of the said section 93, of the following paragraph:
>
> (1) Nothing in any such law shall prejudicially affect any right or privilege with respect to separate schools which any class of persons have at the

date of the passing of this Act, under the terms of chapters 29 and 30 of the Ordinances of the Northwest Territories, passed in the year 1901, or with respect to religious instruction in any public or separate school as provided for in the said ordinances.

2. In the appropriation by the Legislature or distribution by the Government of the province of any moneys for the support of schools organized and carried on in accordance with the said chapter 29, or any Act passed in amendment thereof or in substitution therefor, there shall be no discrimination against schools of any class described in the said chapter 29.

3. Where the expression "by law" is employed in paragraph (3) of the said section 93, it shall be held to mean the law as set out in the said chapters 29 and 30; and where the expression "at the Union" is employed in the said paragraph (3), it shall be held to mean the date at which this Act comes into force.

An alternative was provided for Newfoundland by Term 17 of the Terms of Union of Newfoundland with Canada (confirmed by the *Newfoundland Act*, 12-13 Geo. VI, c. 22 (U.K.)). Term 17 of the Terms of Union of Newfoundland with Canada, set out in the penultimate paragraph of this note, was amended by the *Constitution Amendment, 1998 (Newfoundland Act)* (*see* SI/98-25) and the *Constitution Amendment, 2001 (Newfoundland and Labrador)* (*see* SI/2001-117), and now reads as follows:

17. (1) In lieu of section ninety-three of the *Constitution Act, 1867*, this term shall apply in respect of the Province of Newfoundland and Labrador.

(2) In and for the Province of Newfoundland and Labrador, the Legislature shall have exclusive authority to make laws in relation to education, but shall provide for courses in religion that are not specific to a religious denomination.

(3) Religious observances shall be permitted in a school where requested by parents.

Prior to the *Constitution Amendment, 1998 (Newfoundland Act)*, Term 17 of the Terms of Union of Newfoundland with Canada had been amended by the *Constitution Amendment, 1997 (Newfoundland Act)* (*see* SI/97-55) to read as follows:

17. In lieu of section ninety-three of the *Constitution Act, 1867*, the following shall apply in respect of the Province of Newfoundland:

In and for the Province of Newfoundland, the Legislature shall have exclusive authority to make laws in relation to education but

(*a*) except as provided in paragraphs (*b*) and (*c*), schools established, maintained and operated with public funds shall be denominational schools, and any class of persons having rights under this Term as it read on January 1, 1995 shall continue to have the right to provide for religious education, activities and observances for the children of that class in those schools, and the group of classes that formed one integrated school system by agreement in 1969 may exercise the same rights under this Term as a single class of persons;

(*b*) subject to provincial legislation that is uniformly applicable to all schools specifying conditions for the establishment or continued operation of schools,

(i) any class of persons referred to in paragraph (*a*) shall have the right to have a publicly funded denominational school established, maintained and operated especially for that class, and

(ii) the Legislature may approve the establishment, maintenance and operation of a publicly funded school, whether denominational or non-denominational;

(*c*) where a school is established, maintained and operated pursuant to subparagraph (*b*)(i), the class of persons referred to in that subparagraph shall continue to have the right to provide for religious education, activities and observances and to direct the teaching of aspects of curriculum affecting religious beliefs, student admission policy and the assignment and dismissal of teachers in that school;

(*d*) all schools referred to in paragraphs (*a*) and (*b*) shall receive their share of public funds in accordance with scales determined on a non-discriminatory basis from time to time by the Legislature; and

(*e*) if the classes of persons having rights under this Term so desire, they shall have the right to elect in total not less than two thirds of the members of a school board, and any class so desiring shall have the right to elect the portion of that total that is proportionate to the population of that class in the area under the board's jurisdiction.

Prior to the *Constitution Amendment, 1997 (Newfoundland Act)*, Term 17 of the Terms of Union of Newfoundland with Canada had been amended by the *Constitution Amendment, 1987 (Newfoundland Act)* (*see* SI/88-11) to read as follows:

17. (1) In lieu of section ninety-three of the *Constitution Act, 1867*, the following term shall apply in respect of the Province of Newfoundland:

In and for the Province of Newfoundland the Legislature shall have exclusive authority to make laws in relation to education, but the Legislature will not have authority to make laws prejudicially affecting any right or privilege with respect to denominational schools, common (amalgamated) schools, or denominational colleges, that any class or classes of persons have by law in Newfoundland at the date of Union, and out of public funds of the Province of Newfoundland, provided for education,

(*a*) all such schools shall receive their share of such funds in accordance with scales determined on a non-discriminatory basis from time to time by the Legislature for all schools then being conducted under authority of the Legislature; and

(*b*) all such colleges shall receive their share of any grant from time to time voted for all colleges then being conducted under authority of the Legislature, such grant being distributed on a non-discriminatory basis.

(2) For the purposes of paragraph one of this Term, the Pentecostal Assemblies of Newfoundland have in Newfoundland all the same rights and privileges with respect to denominational schools and denominational colleges as any other class or classes of persons had by law in Newfoundland at the date of Union, and the words "all such schools" in paragraph (*a*) of paragraph one of this Term and the words "all such colleges" in paragraph (*b*) of paragraph one of this Term include, respectively, the schools and the colleges of the Pentecostal Assemblies of Newfoundland.

Term 17 of the Terms of Union of Newfoundland with Canada (confirmed by the *Newfoundland Act*, 12-13 Geo. VI, c. 22 (U.K.)), which Term provided an alternative for Newfoundland, originally read as follows:

17. In lieu of section ninety-three of the *Constitution Act, 1867*, the following term shall apply in respect of the Province of Newfoundland:

In and for the Province of Newfoundland the Legislature shall have exclusive authority to make laws in relation to education, but the Legislature will not have authority to make laws prejudicially affecting any right or privilege with respect to denominational schools, common (amalgamated) schools, or denominational colleges, that any class or classes of persons have by law in Newfoundland at the date of Union, and out of public funds of the Province of Newfoundland, provided for education,

(*a*) all such schools shall receive their share of such funds in accordance with scales determined on a non-discriminatory basis from time to time by the Legislature for all schools then being conducted under authority of the Legislature; and

(*b*) all such colleges shall receive their share of any grant from time to time voted for all colleges then being conducted under authority of the Legislature, such grant being distributed on a non-discriminatory basis.

See also sections 23, 29 and 59 of the *Constitution Act, 1982*. Section 23 provides for new minority language educational rights and section 59 permits a delay in respect of the coming into force in Quebec of one aspect of those rights. Section 29 provides that nothing in the *Canadian Charter of Rights and Freedoms* abrogates or derogates from any rights or privileges guaranteed by or under the Constitution of Canada in respect of denominational, separate or dissentient schools.

51. Added by the *Constitution Amendment, 1997 (Quebec) (see* SI/97-141).

52. Amended by the *Constitution Act, 1964*, 12-13 Eliz. II, c. 73 (U.K.). As originally enacted by the *British North America Act, 1951*, 14-15 Geo. VI, c. 32 (U.K.), which was repealed by the *Constitution Act, 1982*, section 94A read as follows:

94A. It is hereby declared that the Parliament of Canada may from time to time make laws in relation to old age pensions in Canada, but no law made by the Parliament of Canada in relation to old age pensions shall affect the operation of any law present or future of a Provincial Legislature in relation to old age pensions.

53. Amended by the *Constitution Act, 1960*, 9 Eliz. II, c. 2 (U.K.), which came into force on March 1, 1961. The original section read as follows:

99. The Judges of the Superior Courts shall hold Office during good Behaviour, but shall be removable by the Governor General on Address of the Senate and House of Commons.

54. Now provided for in the *Judges Act*, R.S.C. 1985, c. J-1.

55. See the *Supreme Court Act*, R.S.C. 1985, c. S-26, the *Federal Courts Act*, R.S.C. 1985, c. F-7 and the *Tax Court of Canada Act*, R.S.C. 1985, c. T-2.

56. Now covered by the *Governor General's Act*, R.S.C. 1985, c. G-9.

57. Manitoba, Alberta and Saskatchewan were placed in the same position as the original provinces by the *Constitution Act, 1930*, 20-21 Geo. V, c. 26 (U.K.).

These matters were dealt with in respect of British Columbia by the *British Columbia Terms of Union* and also in part by the *Constitution Act, 1930*.

Newfoundland was also placed in the same position by the *Newfoundland Act*, 12-13 Geo. V1, c. 22 (U.K.).

With respect to Prince Edward Island, see the Schedule to the *Prince Edward Island Terms of Union*.

58. The obligations imposed sections 114, 115 and 116, and similar obligations under the instruments creating or admitting other provinces, have been carried into legislation of the Parliament of Canada and are now to be found in the *Provincial Subsidies Act*, R.S.C. 1985, c. P-26.

59. Repealed by the *Statute Law Revision Act, 1950*, 14 Geo. VI, c. 6 (U.K.). The section originally read as follows:

118. The following Sums shall be paid yearly by Canada to the several Provinces for the Support of their Governments and Legislatures:

	Dollars.
Ontario	Eighty thousand.
Quebec	Seventy thousand.
Nova Scotia	Sixty thousand.
New Brunswick	Fifty thousand.
Total	Two hundred and sixty thousand;

and an annual Grant in aid of each Province shall be made, equal to Eighty Cents per Head of the Population as ascertained by the Census of One thousand eight hundred and sixty-one, and in the Case of Nova Scotia and New Brunswick, by each subsequent Decennial Census until the Population of each of those two Provinces amounts to Four hundred thousand Souls, at which Rate such Grant shall thereafter remain. Such Grants shall be in full Settlement of all future Demands on Canada, and shall be paid half-yearly in advance to each Province; but the Government of Canada shall deduct from such Grants, as against any Province, all Sums chargeable as Interest on the Public Debt of that Province in excess of the several Amounts stipulated in this Act.

The section was made obsolete by the *Constitution Act, 1907*, 7 Edw. VII, c. 11 (U.K.), which provided:

1. (1) The following grants shall be made yearly by Canada to every province, which at the commencement of this Act is a province of the Dominion, for its local purposes and the support of its Government and Legislature:

(*a*) A fixed grant

where the population of the province is under one hundred and fifty thousand, of one hundred thousand dollars;

where the population of the province is one hundred and fifty thousand, but does not exceed two hundred thousand, of one hundred and fifty thousand dollars;

where the population of the province is two hundred thousand, but does not exceed four hundred thousand, of one hundred and eighty thousand dollars;

where the population of the province is four hundred thousand, but does not exceed eight hundred thousand, of one hundred and ninety thousand dollars;

where the population of the province is eight hundred thousand, but does not exceed one million five hundred thousand, of two hundred and twenty thousand dollars;

where the population of the province exceeds one million five hundred thousand, of two hundred and forty thousand dollars; and

(*b*) Subject to the special provisions of this Act as to the provinces of British Columbia and Prince Edward Island, a grant at the rate of eighty cents per head of the population of the province up to the number of two million five hundred thousand, and at the rate of sixty cents per head of so much of the population as exceeds that number.

(2) An additional grant of one hundred thousand dollars shall be made yearly to the province of British Columbia for a period of ten years from the commencement of this Act.

(3) The population of a province shall be ascertained from time to time in the case of the provinces of Manitoba, Saskatchewan, and Alberta respectively by the last quinquennial census or statutory estimate of population made under the Acts establishing those provinces or any other Act of the Parliament of Canada making provision for the purpose, and in the case of any other province by the last decennial census for the time being.

(4) The grants payable under this Act shall be paid half-yearly in advance to each province.

(5) The grants payable under this Act shall be substituted for the grants or subsidies (in this Act referred to as existing grants) payable for the like purposes at the commencement of this Act to the several provinces of the Dominion under the provisions of section one hundred and eighteen of the Constitution Act, 1867, or of any Order in Council establishing a province, or of any Act of the Parliament of Canada containing directions for the payment of any such grant or subsidy, and those provisions shall cease to have effect.

(6) The Government of Canada shall have the same power of deducting sums charged against a province on account of the interest on public debt in the case of the grant payable under this Act to the province as they have in the case of the existing grant.

(7) Nothing in this Act shall affect the obligation of the Government of Canada to pay to any province any grant which is payable to that province, other than the existing grant for which the grant under this Act is substituted.

(8) In the case of the provinces of British Columbia and Prince Edward Island, the amount paid on account of the grant payable per head of the population to the provinces under this Act shall not at any time be less than the amount of the corresponding grant payable at the commencement of this Act, and if it is found on any decennial census that the population of the province has decreased since the last decennial census, the amount paid on account of the grant shall not be decreased below the amount then payable, notwithstanding the decrease of the population.

See the *Provincial Subsidies Act*, R.S.C. 1985, c. P-26, and the *Federal-Provincial Fiscal Arrangements Act*, R.S.C. 1985, c. F-8.

See also Part III of the *Constitution Act, 1982*, which sets out commitments by Parliament and the provincial legislatures respecting equal opportunities, economic development and the provision of essential public services and a commitment by Parliament and the government of Canada to the principle of making equalization payments.

60. Spent.
61. Spent. Now covered by the *Customs Act*, R.S.C. 1985, c. 1 (2nd Supp.), the *Customs Tariff*, S.C. 1997, c. 36, the *Excise Act*, R.S.C. 1985, c. E-14, the *Excise Act, 2001*, S.C. 2002, c. 22 and the *Excise Tax Act*, R.S.C. 1985, c. E-15.
62. Spent.
63. These dues were repealed in 1873 by 36 Vict., c. 16 (N.B.). Also, see *An Act respecting the Export Duties imposed on Lumber*, etc. (1873) 36 Vict., c. 41 (Canada), and section 2 of the *Provincial Subsidies Act*, R.S.C. 1985, c. P-26.
64. Repealed by the *Statute Law Revision Act, 1893*, 56-57 Vict., c. 14 (U.K.). The section read as follows:

    > 127. If any Person being at the passing of this Act a Member of the Legislative Council of Canada, Nova Scotia, or New Brunswick, to whom a Place in the Senate is offered, does not within Thirty Days thereafter, by Writing under his Hand addressed to the Governor General of the Province of Canada or to the Lieutenant Governor of Nova Scotia or New Brunswick (as the Case may be), accept the same, he shall be deemed to have declined the same; and any Person who, being at the passing of this Act a Member of the Legislative Council of Nova Scotia or New Brunswick, accepts a Place in the Senate shall thereby vacate his Seat in such Legislative Council.

65. The restriction against altering or repealing laws enacted by or existing under statutes of the United Kingdom was removed by the *Statute of Westminster, 1931*, 22 Geo. V, c. 4 (U.K.), except in respect of certain constitutional documents. Comprehensive procedures for amending enactments forming part of the Constitution of Canada were provided by Part V of the *Constitution Act, 1982*.
66. Spent.
67. A similar provision was enacted for Manitoba by section 23 of the *Manitoba Act, 1870*, 33 Vict., c. 3, (confirmed by the *Constitution Act, 1871*, 34-35 Vict., c. 28 (U.K.)). Section 23 read as follows:

    > 23. Either the English or the French language may be used by any person in the debates of the Houses of the Legislature, and both these languages shall be used in the respective Records and Journals of those Houses; and either of those languages may be used by any person, or in any Pleading or Process, in or issuing from any Court of Canada established under the British North America Act, 1867, or in or from all or any of the Courts of the Province. The Acts of the Legislature shall be printed and published in both those languages.

    Sections 17 to 19 of the *Constitution Act, 1982* restate the language rights set out in section 133 in respect of Parliament and the courts established under the *Constitution Act, 1867*, and also guarantees those rights in respect of the legislature of New Brunswick and the courts of that province.

    Sections 16, 20, 21 and 23 of the *Constitution Act, 1982* recognize additional language rights in respect of the English and French languages. Section 22 preserves language rights and privileges of languages other than English and French.

68. Spent. Now covered in Ontario by the *Executive Council Act*, R.S.O. 1990, c. E.25 and in Quebec by the *Executive Power Act*, R.S.Q. c. E-18.
69. Probably spent.

70. Probably spent.
71. Probably spent.
72. Spent. Penitentiaries are now provided for by the *Corrections and Conditional Release Act*, S.C. 1992, c. 20.
73. Spent.
74. Probably spent. Two orders were made under this section on January 24, 1868.
75. Repealed by the *Statute Law Revision Act, 1893*, 56-57 Vict., c. 14 (U.K.). The section read as follows:

    145. Inasmuch as the Provinces of Canada, Nova Scotia, and New Brunswick have joined in a Declaration that the Construction of the Intercolonial Railway is essential to the Consolidation of the Union of British North America, and to the Assent thereto of Nova Scotia and New Brunswick, and have consequently agreed that Provision should be made for its immediate Construction by the Government of Canada; Therefore, in order to give effect to that Agreement, it shall be the Duty of the Government and Parliament of Canada to provide for the Commencement, within Six Months after the Union, of a Railway connecting the River St. Lawrence with the City of Halifax in Nova Scotia, and for the Construction thereof without Intermission, and the Completion thereof with all practicable Speed.

76. All territories mentioned in section 146 are now part of Canada. See note (6) to section 5, supra.
77. Spent. See notes [(11), (12), (15), (16) and (17)] to sections 21, 22, 26, 27 and 28, supra.
78. Spent. See *Representation Act*, R.S.O. 1990, c. R.26.
79. As enacted by section 51 of the *Constitution Act, 1982*.
80. Enacted as Schedule B to the *Canada Act 1982*, 1982, c. 11 (U.K.), which came into force on April 17, 1982. The *Canada Act 1982*, other than Schedules A and B thereto, reads as follows:

    An Act to give effect to a request by the Senate and House of Commons of Canada

    Whereas Canada has requested and consented to the enactment of an Act of the Parliament of the United Kingdom to give effect to the provisions hereinafter set forth and the Senate and the House of Commons of Canada in Parliament assembled have submitted an address to Her Majesty requesting that Her Majesty may graciously be pleased to cause a Bill to be laid before the Parliament of the United Kingdom for that purpose.

    Be it therefore enacted by the Queen's Most Excellent Majesty, by and with the advice and consent of the Lords Spiritual and Temporal, and Commons, in this present Parliament assembled, and by the authority of the same, as follows:

    1. The *Constitution Act, 1982* set out in Schedule B to this Act is hereby enacted for and shall have the force of law in Canada and shall come into force as provided in that Act.
    2. No Act of the Parliament of the United Kingdom passed after the *Constitution Act, 1982* comes into force shall extend to Canada as part of its law.
    3. So far as it is not contained in Schedule B, the French version of this Act is set out in Schedule A to this Act and has the same authority in Canada as the English version thereof.

4. This Act may be cited as the *Canada Act 1982*.

81. See section 50, and notes (40) and (42) to sections 85 and 88, of the *Constitution Act, 1867.*
82. Replaces part of Class 1 of section 91 of the *Constitution Act, 1867*, which was repealed as set out in subitem 1(3) of the Schedule the *Constitution Act, 1982*.
83. See notes (10), (41) and (42) to sections 20, 86 and 88 of the *Constitution Act, 1867.*
84. Subsection 32(2) provides that section 15 shall not have effect until three years after section 32 comes into force. Section 32 came into force on April 17, 1982; therefore, section 15 had effect on April 17, 1985.
85. Section 16.1 was added by the *Constitution Amendment, 1993 (New Brunswick)* (*see* SI/93-54).
86. See section 133 of the *Constitution Act, 1867* and note (67).
87. Ibid.
88. Ibid.
89. Ibid.
90. Ibid.
91. Ibid.
92. See, for example, section 133 of the *Constitution Act, 1867* and the reference to the *Manitoba Act, 1870* in note (67) to that section.
93. Paragraph 23(1)(*a*) is not in force in respect of Quebec. See section 59, infra.
94. Paragraph 25(*b*) was repealed and re-enacted by the *Constitution Amendment Proclamation, 1983* (*see* SI/84-102). Paragraph 25(*b*) as originally enacted read as follows:

    (*b*) any rights or freedoms that may be acquired by the aboriginal peoples of Canada by way of land claims settlement.

95. See section 93 of the *Constitution Act, 1867* and note (50).
96. Subsections 35(3) and (4) were added by the *Constitution Amendment Proclamation, 1983* (*see* SI/84-102).
97. Section 35.1 was added by the *Constitution Amendment Proclamation, 1983* (*see* SI/84-102).
98. See notes (58) and (59) to sections 114 and 118 of the *Constitution Act, 1867.*
99. Section 54 of the *Constitution Act, 1982* provided for the repeal of Part IV one year after Part VII came into force. Part VII came into force on April 17, 1982 thereby repealing Part IV on April 17, 1983. Section 37 read as follows:

    37. (1) A constitutional conference composed of the Prime Minister of Canada and the first ministers of the provinces shall be convened by the Prime Minister of Canada within one year after this Part comes into force.

    (2) The conference convened under subsection (1) shall have included in its agenda an item respecting constitutional matters that directly affect the aboriginal peoples of Canada, including the identification and definition of the rights of those peoples to be included in the Constitution of Canada, and the Prime Minister of Canada shall invite representatives of those peoples to participate in the discussions on that item.

    (3) The Prime Minister of Canada shall invite elected representatives of the governments of the Yukon Territory and the Northwest Territories to participate in the discussions on any item on the agenda of the conference

convened under subsection (1) that, in the opinion of the Prime Minister, directly affects the Yukon Territory and the Northwest Territories.

100. Part IV.1 (section 37.1), which was added by the *Constitution Amendment Proclamation, 1983* (*see* SI/84-102), was repealed on April 18, 1987 by section 54.1 of the *Constitution Act, 1982*. Section 37.1 read as follows:

> 37.1 (1) In addition to the conference convened in March 1983, at least two constitutional conferences composed of the Prime Minister of Canada and the first ministers of the provinces shall be convened by the Prime Minister of Canada, the first within three years after April 17, 1982 and the second within five years after that date.
>
> (2) Each conference convened under subsection (1) shall have included in its agenda constitutional matters that directly affect the aboriginal peoples of Canada, and the Prime Minister of Canada shall invite representatives of those peoples to participate in the discussions on those matters.
>
> (3) The Prime Minister of Canada shall invite elected representatives of the governments of the Yukon Territory and the Northwest Territories to participate in the discussions on any item on the agenda of a conference convened under subsection (1) that, in the opinion of the Prime Minister, directly affects the Yukon Territory and the Northwest Territories.
>
> (4) Nothing in this section shall be construed so as to derogate from subsection 35(1).

101. Prior to the enactment of Part V, certain provisions of the Constitution of Canada and the provincial constitutions could be amended pursuant to the *Constitution Act, 1867*. See notes (44) and (48) to section 91, Class 1 and section 92, Class 1 of that Act, respectively. Other amendments to the Constitution could only be made by enactment of the Parliament of the United Kingdom.
102. The text of this amendment is set out in the *Constitution Act, 1867*, as section 92A.
103. The text of this amendment is set out in the *Constitution Act, 1867*, as the Sixth Schedule.
104. Part VII came into force on April 17, 1982 (*see* SI/82-97).
105. Section 54.1, which was added by the *Constitution Amendment Proclamation, 1983* (*see* SI/84-102), provided for the repeal of Part IV.1 and section 54.1 on April 18, 1987. Section 54.1 read as follows:

> 54.1 Part IV.1 and this section are repealed on April 18, 1987.

106. The Act, with the exception of paragraph 23(1)(*a*) in respect of Quebec, came into force on April 17, 1982 by proclamation issued by the Queen (*see* SI/82-97).
107. No proclamation has been issued under section 59.
108. Section 61 was added by the *Constitution Amendment Proclamation, 1983* (*see* SI/84-102). See also section 3 of the *Constitution Act, 1985 (Representation)*, S.C. 1986, c. 8, Part I and the *Constitution Amendment, 1987 (Newfoundland Act)* (*see* SI/88-11).

TABLE OF CASES

INDEX